PORTFOLIO MANAGEMENT

For MBA (Finance), M.Com., MFA, MFC, PGDBA, PGDBM, PGDFM and CFA

By the Same Author

- Financial Services in India
- Financial Markets and Institutions

About the Author

Dr. G. Ramesh Babu, Lecturer in Commerce, S.S.R. Jyothi College, Khammam, has vast teaching experience of 18 years at U.G. and P.G. levels. Academically, he is Ph.D. in Industrial Finance. He has published many papers in various management and commerce journals of repute and has also presented papers in various conferences. He is an active member of the All India Management Association, New Delhi; Associate Member of Society for Capital Market and Research, New Delhi; and Associate Member of Indian Institute of Public Administration, New Delhi. His areas of interest include Financial Systems and Capital Market.

PORTFOLIO MANAGEMENT

(Including Security Analysis)

For MBA (Finance), M.Com., MFA, MFC, PGDBA, PGDBM, PGDFM and CFA

Dr. G. Ramesh Babu
M.Com., Ph.D, MIAM
Department of Commerce
S.S.R. Jyothi College
Khammam - 507 003, A.P.

CONCEPT PUBLISHING COMPANY, NEW DELHI-110059

Cataloging in Publication Data—DK
Courtesy: D.K. Agencies (P) Ltd. <docinfo@dkagencies.com>

Ramesh Babu, G. (Gunda), 1963-
Portfolio management : including security analysis/ G. Ramesh Babu.
p. cm.
In Indian context.
Includes index.
ISBN 818069416X

1. Stock exchanges—India—Textbooks.2. Investment analysis—Text books. 3. Portfolio management—India—Textbooks. 4. Corporations—India—Finance—Case studies. I. Title.

DDC 332.609 54 22

ISBN -10: 81-8069-416-X (HB)

First Published 2007

Published and Printed by
Ashok Kumar Mittal
Concept Publishing Company
A/15-16, Commercial Block, Mohan Garden
New Delhi-110059 (INDIA)

Phones : 25351460, 25351794
Fax : 091-11-25357103
Email : publishing@conceptpub.com

Dedicated to

LORD "SHIVA"

FOREWORD

S.S.R. Jyothi Arts and Science College

Jyothi Education Society

(Affiliated to **Kakatiya** University)

Principal: *Dr. D.R. Bose,* M.A., Ph.D.

Jammibanda Road,
Khammam–507 001
Ph: 232639, 248433

Date : 22/3/2006

Senate Member
Kakatiya University

- Concentration + Commitment = Confidence
- Confidence + Knowledge = Skills
- Skills + Abilities = Success
- Success – Ego + Hard work = Perfection

Portfolio Management is a subject to of growing interest. In recent times we hear widely popular words like "Liberalisation, Privatisation and Globalisaton" as policies of several governments in the digital world. There will be a misbelief that liberalisation will exploit the common man. Privatisation do harm to the society. Globalisation may help to capture the wealth by capitalists. However, poverty is the main hurdle to the developing nations. The creation of wealth by a nation could be done through powerful weapons such as "Capital, Scientific Technology and Skilled man power". All these weapons can be applied to fight poverty with the help of said policies.

The globe is rotating on the flow of money. Money is always travelling for profit as a destination within a stipulated period of time. Profit is always chased by the corporate sector. "Risk" is a threat component of the corporate sector. The efficient of growth of the economy stimulates the higher levels of the stock market. "Stock Market" is a very delicate instrument, which should be handled with utmost care to counter the poverty. India is a country with a large amount of small savings, which can be utilised for construction of "Modern India". Stock markets can be utilised as a weapon to start mega project of "Linking of Rivers" which helps the crores of farmers' lives. The mega project requires Rs. 6,00,000 crores over a period of 10 years, is an easy task to the financial markets. Sensex crossed 10,700 points is a milestone in the history of Indian Stock Market.

Hence, the efforts made by **Dr. G. Ramesh Babu** are a little task in the world of stock markets in the aspect of ***Portfolio Management***. This book is more useful to Finance Professionals, Stock Market Analysts, Fund Managers, Mutual Funds and MBA (Finance) students. I hope that this book will open a new dimension with a new analysis in the field of study. I wish him all success in his pursuit.

Dr. D. Ramachandra Bose

PREFACE

The New Economic Policy 1991 transformed successively towards a market oriented economy. The entire globe is rotating on the flow of money. After 1991 reforms, the financial sector has grown tremendously. The liberalisation and deregulations have provided a new era for the capital market. India's liberalisation policy has gained importance in the context of global business scenario. Modern economics is influenced by expansion and diversification. The revolution in the information technology has explored many avenues for invention of new financial products and services. Introduction of Automated Teller Machines, Internet banking, Internet trading, online services, online utility payments have changed the billions of peoples lifestyles. In the digital economy, everything is possible at a click of mouse. Internet has been changed the literate lifestyle. But it should become a common lifestyle.

In this book, an attempt is made to give a comprehensive coverage of Portfolio Management aspects. Portfolio means, a blend of mix of different kinds of financial assets. The aim of Portfolio Management is minimising risk and maximising return. Stock market is a game of risk and return factors. The return is always chased by risk. Sometimes risk dominates return. An intelligent investor escapes from risk factors and captures return. Escaping from risk and capturing return requires higher skills and talent. A common investor cannot play these games more effectively.

This book is divided into 4 units. All the parts are organised into related chapters. They are fairly independent of each other. Each unit consists of several chapters.

Since the book is synthesis, I am thankful to all authors who have contributed to the world of finance. I hope that I have interpreted their views accurately. I have made acknowledgements of every idea whose sources have been identified. It is my response to pay homage to Late Sri K. Ram Mohan, Jyothi Education Society who was always inspired towards achieving the goal. It is my pleasure to express grateful thanks to Sri P. Raghu Rama Rao who encourages every assignment taken up by me. I am thankful to Dr. D. Ramachandra Bose, who always inspires the talent and provides more useful information for completion of every project. I am also thankful to my professors Prof. P. Madhusudana Rao, Prof. A. Shankaraiah, Prof. V. Gangadhar, Prof. Narsimha Murthy, Prof. R. Sudarshan, Prof. Krishna Reddy, Prof. S. Ravi Prakash, Prof. Rajeswar Rao whose elderly advice has been of immense use to me. I must also place on record my sincere thanks to my teachers Sri K. V. Kameshwar Rao, Sri P.V. Anjaneyule, Sri G. Satyanarayana and Dr. K. Srinivasa Rao. I also record my gratitude to Dr. J.S. Gilani, Deputy Secretary Ministry of Education, Government of India. I am specially thankful to Dr. Venkateshwarlu, Sri Subramanya Sastry who provided me excellent cooperation in preparation of manuscript.

I owe my gratitude to Sri Ashok Kumar Mittal and Sri S.P. Sinha of Concept Publishing Company for giving their personal attention in expediting printing of this book.

Dr. G. Ramesh Babu
E-Mail: ramesh-238712@rediff.mail.com
Mobile: 9849623310

CONTENTS

Unit - I

- Nature and Type of Investment
  - (a) Nature
  - (b) Objectives
  - (c) Investment process
  - (d) Invest media
  - (e) Speculation
  - (f) Securities types, nature
  - (g) Securities market
  - (h) Secondary market
  - (i) Stock exchanges – BSE, NSE, OTC

1

INDIAN FINANCIAL SYSTEM

Introduction

"You can have brilliant ideas, but if you can't get them across, your ideas won't get you anywhere".

—Lee Lacocca

Incredible but true, way back in 1700, India was actually the world's largest economy accounting for **22.6** per cent of world income, second only to **China**. Three hundred years on, it is among the handful at the bottom and just chips in with just around **5** per cent of world's income.

Two centuries of colonial rule have taken their toll on the economy. After independence, India adopted **"Nehruvian Model"** of economic development and preferred import substitution in place of export motivation for industrialisation of Indian economy. The winds of change were blowing across the globe and transformed many economies from planned economy to market economy. Mr. Rajiv Gandhi took over as the Prime Minister in 1985 and gave the dream of launching the country into the **21st** century. The long-term fiscal policy measures to augment all-round productivity of the economy, rationalisation and simplification of the plethora of controls were the major thrust areas to accelerate the growth momentum of the economy.

The post-liberalisation era has marked with various economic stabilisation measures and structural reforms particularly in industrial and trade policies with the broad objective of stronger export performance through liberalised exports and turning domestic industrial sector global.

De-regulation and the delicencing initiatives have been undertaken in India with a view to increase production, improve quality and get access to market for products and services abroad to competition with other multi-national companies. There is a growing realisation on the part of the government that instead of itself doing business, it should concentrate on creating an environment in which business prospers and entrepreneurial instincts are aroused, so that the investors may get maximum output and returns from the efforts. The radical liberalisation has been ushered to make the Indian economy progressively market oriented and integrate it with the emerging global economic structure in a more meaningful way. The term **economic liberalisation** means and includes mainly:

(a) Dismantling of industrial licensing system built over past four decades,
(b) Reduction in physical restrictions on imports reduction also in the rate of import duties,
(c) Reduction in controls on foreign exchange, both current and capital account,
(d) Reform of financial system,
(e) Reduction in levels of personal and corporate taxation,
(f) Reduction in restrictions on foreign investments (direct and portfolio),
(g) Opening up of areas hitherto reserved for public sector **(basic industries, power, transport, banking, etc.)**,
(h) Partial privatisation of public sector units (with or without passing on majority control to the private shareholders),
(i) Change in approach towards industrial sickness,
(j) Softening of MRTP regulations, and
(k) Finally to make various sectors of Indian economy competitive on a global scale, by making them produce quality goods in a cost effective manner.

The Government of India had set up a panel of experts headed by Shri **M. Narasimhan** to suggest refers in the financial system of the country. The Committee submitted its report in **November, 1991**. The report contains a number of reforms giving a new dimension for the Indian financial system. The recent features of the report are as follows:

1. The Committee suggested to ensure financial sector reforms with a view to enhancing efficiency, productivity and profitability. The integrity and autonomy of operations of banks and development financial institutions have to be ensured for the reforms purpose.
2. The proliferation of financial institutions and instruments provides a wider choice for the financial investments to the saving class people.

3. The establishment of the **Discount and Finance House of India** and the **Securities and Exchange Board** have their import on the growth of money and capital markets in India.
4. Banks are to be computerised.
5. The existing cash reserve ratio should be reduced.
6. The RBI should be given authority to determine the level and structure of interest rates.
7. Branch licensing system should be abolished.
8. The structure of the banking system should be reshaped which consists 3 or 4 large banks **8 to 10** national banks, local banks and rural banks.
9. The government must assure that there would be no further nationalisation of banks.
10. Joint ventures between foreign banks and Indian banks should be permitted.
11. The bank rate should be the anchor rate of the money market.
12. The Indian banks at present is over-regulated and over-administered. Excessive controls on the working of the banks should be removed.
13. The supervision of the banks should be based on prudential norms.
14. The government should not interfere in the matter of internal organisation of the banks.
15. The banks are permitted to make their own recruitment of the required staff.
16. A regulatory framework for the merchant banks, mutual funds, leasing companies, venture capital and manufacturing companies have to be developed in **prudential norms**.
17. The foreign banks will be permitted to extend their branches on consideration of national advantage.

After liberalisation, the growth of corporate sector increased tremendously. The following data reveal the growth of business in India.

Table 1: The Following Statement Shows the Growth of Corporate Sector in India During 1956-2002

Year	*Government Companies*		*Non-Govt.Companies*		*Total Companies*	
(31-3-)	*Number*	*Paid up Capital (Rs. in crore)*	*Number*	*Paid up Capital (Rs. in crore)*	*Number*	*Paid up Capital (Rs. in crore)*
1957	74	73	29283	1005	29357	107
1958	91	257	28189	1050	28280	130
1959	104	429	27299	1087	27403	151

(Contd.)

Table 1 (*Contd.*)

Year	*Government Companies*		*Non-Govt.Companies*		*Total Companies*	
(31-3-)	*Number*	*Paid up Capital* ***(Rs. in crore)***	*Number*	*Paid up Capital* ***(Rs. in crore)***	*Number*	*Paid up Capital* ***(Rs. in crore)***
1960	125	477	26772	1142	26897	16
1961	142	547	26007	1272	26149	18
1962	154	630	24821	1389	24975	201
1963	160	786	25462	1470	25622	225
1964	176	961	25756	1640	25932	260
1965	183	1115	26038	1728	26621	284
1966	214	1248	26551	1878	26765	312
1967	232	1392	26795	2010	27027	340
1968	241	1559	27103	2115	27344	367
1969	259	1715	27765	2259	28024	397
1970	282	1791	28727	2300	29009	409
1971	314	2064	30008	2439	30322	450
1972	352	2369	31915	2572	32267	494
1973	390	2998	33966	2750	34356	574
1974	450	4645	37035	2986	37485	7631
1975	573	4966	40007	3235	40580	8201
1976	651	6122	42755	3497	43406	9620
1977	701	7175	45165	3705	45866	10880
1978	745	8528	47549	4070	48294	10880
1979	782	8315	50736	4260	51518	12575
1980	825	10070	55668	4536	56493	14607
1981	851	11443	61863	4914	62714	16357
1982	894	13309	71508	5626	72402	18936
1983	943	16735	81960	6321	82903	23056
1984	973	19511	93291	6990	94264	26500
1985	980	22447	108329	8150	109309	30597
1986	1020	27088	123359	9507	124379	36595
1987	1053	32873	139617	11095	140670	43968
1988	1104	37169	157220	12955	158324	50124
1989	1134	42572	179194	15131	180328	57704
1990	1160	47451	200968	17193	202128	64643
1991	1167	54485	223285	20313	224452	74798
1992	1180	57911	249181	26731	250361	84642
1993	1190	61163	275664	32892	276854	94055
1994	1203	67381	304422	46441	305625	113822
1995	1199	73300	352093	62719	353292	136019
1996	1216	76963	407926	87126	409142	164088
1997	1220	84318	449730	106201	450950	190519
1998	1223	88959	483277	128690	484500	217649
1999	1229	95918	510761	167441	511990	263359,
2000	1245	102850	541189	215960	542434	318810
2001	1266	109746	567834	247501	569100	357247
2002	1261	109916	587985	277108	589246	387020

1. *Economic and Political Weekly*, January 31, 2004, p. 397.

Table 2: Statement Shows Distribution of Companies by Industrial Activity as on 31-3-2002

Industrial Classification	*Public Ltd.*		*Private Ltd.*		*Total Companies*	
	Number	*Paid up Capital (Rs. in crore)*	*Number*	*Paid up Capital (Rs. in crore)*	*Number*	*Paid up Capital (Rs. in crore)*
1. Agriculture and allied activities	5241	3573	17254	1549	22495	512
2. Mining and quarrying	742	7405	5583	15781	6325	23186
3. Manufacturing						
(a) Food stuff, wood products and leather products	10213	26170	61847	11932	72060	3810
(b) Metals, chemicals, machinery and equipment	19096	96889	140028	37976	159124	13486
(c) Electricity, gas and power	893	29831	1854	6446	2747	3627
(d) Construction	2572	9730	30997	4509	33569	14239
4. Wholesale and retail trade and hotels	7908	19377	81673	16917	89851	3629
5. Transport, storage & communication	1462	7915	19095	4828	20557	1274
6. Finance, insurance, real estate	25848	52028	135665	23267	161513	7529
7. Community, social and personal services	2304	5797	18971	5104	21275	10901

Table 3: Statement shows the Distribution of Companies by Government Companies by Industrial Activity as on 31-3-2002

Industrial Classification	*No. of Companies*	*Paid up Capital (Rs. in Crore)*
1. Agriculture and allied activities	113	415
2. Mining and quarrying	50	20757
3. Manufacturing		
(a) Food stuff, wood products and leather products	201	4122
(b) Metals, chemicals, machinery and equipment	375	32844
(c) Electricity, gas and power	60	28862
(d) Construction	78	6702
4. Wholesale and retail trade restaurants and hotels	71	2188
5. Transport, storage & communication	56	3201
6. Finance, insurance, real estate	189	7704
7. Community, social and personal services	68	3121

The banking sector and the financial system are undergoing metamorphic changes following the process of liberalisation and reforms. The underlying principle behind every reform measuring re-orientation of monetary policy techniques, introduction of new money market instruments and institutions, adoption of stricter prudential norms, inducing structural changes in the financial system and strengthening regulatory arrangements has been to make the system more competitive efficient and profitable. Every performance indicator seems to reflect the impact of these reform measures, profitability of the banking industry was witnessed a steady improvement mainly as a result of these measures, but also due to mobilisation of equity and tier II capital by a few banks, capital adequacy ratio have crossed the norms prescribed for almost all banks. The banks have begun to focus on minimising their asset liability mismatches and on risk management.

The most intractable problem has been one of addressing the question of non-performing loan assets of banks. Loan write-offs rather than quicker recovery have helped to reduce the ratios of non-performing loans to gross advances from near **20** per cent in the first half of the 1990s to **10.4** per cent as of 2001-02 in respect of the public sector banks. The balance of the NPAs is still high and the cumulative provisions forming about **42.5** per cent of the bank's gross NPAs as on 31-3-2002 appear low (compared with about 100 per cent as per international standards). Hence the logic of the **Securitisation and Reconstruction of Financial Assets and Enforcement of Security Interest Act, 2002** which has stirred up the defaulting corporate world as the law frees the credit institutions from cumbersome litigation, even as it offers settlement opportunities to the defaulters. As part of the process of cleaning up of the bank's balance sheet, an asset reconstruction fund, the first of its kind, has been proposed under the above law. The Asset Reconstruction Corporation of India has been floated by a few banks and development financial institutions; it is expected to buy sticky assets of banks and create a market for them. A more radical change has been the acceptance of the principle of universal banking and the consequential shutting of major all India long-term financial institutions and independent DFIs. Apart from this mergers and acquisitions in the near future may change the face of the banking industry.

The reform of the formal financial sector, imperative as it has been, has nevertheless spawned a situation of neglect of practically every aspect of broaden societal goals embedded in the financial sector policies of the 1970s and 1980s promoting financial institutions, expanding their geographical spread, mobilising larger savings' from rural and far-flung areas and bringing about better regional sectoral and functional reach of institutional credit in India. A glaring fall out has been the neglect of credit needs of rural as well as informal sectors. Even as scheduled commercial banks have tended to give less attention to these sectors under the impulse of reform measure no attempt has made to strengthen the existing rural credit institutions and to promote new ones to serve the credit needs of the above sectors except for the self-help group based micro-credit programme which cannot touch even the fringe of the problem. Theoretically, it was not necessary that reform of the formal financial sector should result in a neglect of the rural and informal sectors. There could have been countervailing efforts to simultaneously serve the credit needs of these neglected areas. The reform process was inspired by the needs of broad based economic development and not by the objective of making banks competitive in the globalised environment a general refrain noticed in all public statements and policy documents. The following tables will reveal the growth and performance of the Indian economy.

Table 4: Statement shows the overall ranking position of Commercial Banks in India for the year 2003

Rank 2002	*Rank 2003*	*Bank*	*Productivity Rank*	*Safety Rank*	*Profitability*	*Growth Rank*	*Efficiency Rank*
11	1	Andhra Bank	05	12	02	03	32
04	2	State Bank of Indore	16	16	01	18	25
03	3	Jammu & Kashmir Bank	37	06	04	32	13
01	4	Catholic Syrian Bank	29	48	03	34	53
42	5	Union Bank of India	08	27	21	06	01
29	6	Indian Overseas Bank	09	34	05	16	33
06	7	Karur Vyshya Bank	25	07	12	25	18
23	8	Deutsche Bank	17	05	19	42	21
09	9	State Bank of Hyderabad	22	08	07	24	22
32	10	State Bank of Mysore	10	33	06	13	42
15	11	State Bank of Patiala	13	11	14	15	16
28	12	Vijaya Bank	07	18	10	07	40
31	13	Oriental Bank of Commerce	28	10	17	30	12
13	14	Canara Bank	14	21	08	31	28
24	15	Bank of Maharashtra	18	28	13	21	27
38	16	Bank of Rajasthan	04	37	11	09	34
17	17	Corporation Bank	21	03	30	22	14
39	18	Bank of India	12	35	09	10	38
14	19	State Bank of Bikaner & Rajasthan	32	17	18	39	36
27	20	State Bank of Travancore	14	32	15	20	31
08	21	UTI Bank	48	29	16	17	11
10	22	Bharath Overseas Bank	34	13	24	43	15
19	23	Bank of America	47	02	41	52	07
–	24	Kotak Mahindra Bank	53	01	47	26	09
25	25	City Union Bank	35	24	23	37	19
18	26	South Indian Bank	27	43	20	36	39
52	27	Syndicate Bank	15	36	22	14	37
22	28	Citi Bank	44	25	28	44	06
16	29	Karnataka Bank	38	23	25	41	47
34	30	IDBI Bank	40	40	26	12	10
12	31	HDFC Bank	43	22	33	08	05
40	32	Federal Bank	26	38	37	33	20
35	33	State Bank of India	30	15	32	27	35
10	34	Lord Krishna Bank	42	30	29	45	50
51	35	United Bank of India	03	09	36	04	45
30	36	ABN AMRO Bank	50	19	35	40	08
44	37	Bank of Baroda	33	26	34	28	30
33	38	State Bank of Saurashtra	31	14	39	38	24
26	39	Bank of Punjab	51	20	37	48	04
37	40	Lakshmi Vilas Bank	59	47	31	46	44

(Contd.)

Table 4. *(Contd.)*

Rank 2002	*Rank 2003*	*Bank*	*Productivity Rank*	*Safety Rank*	*Profitability*	*Growth Rank*	*Efficiency Rank*
48	**41**	Indus Ind Bank	46	31	38	11	03
45	**42**	HSBC	45	04	50	50	17
56	**43**	Allahabad Bank	06	42	40	05	23
64	**44**	Dena Bank	01	53	46	01	41
55	**45**	Central Bank of India	11	46	43	19	29
53	**46**	Dhanalakshmi Bank	23	51	42	23	51
49	**47**	Ing Vyshya Bank	19	45	44	29	49
54	**48**	UCO Bank	20	44	48	35	46
60	**49**	Development Credit Bank	49	50	45	49	26
41	**50**	Bank of Novascotia	52	41	51	53	02

Sources: *Business Standard*, Banking Annual, October, 2003.

Table 5: Statement shows the Profitability of the Public Sector Banks for the Period 2002 and 2003

Sl.No.	*Bank*	*Return on Assets*		*Return on Equity*		*Net Profit Margin*		*Net Profit Spread*	
		2002	***2003***	***2002***	***2003***	***2002***	***2003***	***2002***	***2003***
1.	Allahabad Bank	0.34	0.63	8.45	15.43	3.02	5.36	0.35	0.69
2.	Andhra Bank	0.98	1.77	24.66	40.31	8.67	14.40	1.09	1.91
3.	Bank of Baroda	0.81	1.05	15.20	18.81	7.86	10.50	0.88	1.16
4.	Bank of India	0.79	1.16	18.40	26.65	7.58	11.24	0.85	1.32
5.	Bank of Maharashtra	0.72	0.96	22.80	26.46	6.31	9.09	0.76	1.00
6.	Canara Bank	1.07	1.32	23.59	26.74	9.51	12.47	1.16	1.41
7.	Central Bank of India	0.33	0.56	7.20	13.82	3.11	5.43	0.35	0.6
8.	Corporation Bank	1.42	1.67	18.16	18.84	13.24	15.79	1.63	1.9
9.	Dena Bank	0.06	0.59	1.29	11.56	0.55	5.17	0.07	0.6
10	Indian Bank	0.12	0.58	0.94	4.05	1.19	6.18	0.14	0.7
11.	Indian Overseas Bank	0.70	1.09	22.29	32.10	6.22	10.39	0.72	1.13
12.	Oriental Bank of Commerce	1.98	1.38	20.23	24.51	9.12	11.91	1.13	1.5
13.	Punjab and Sindh Bank	0.17	0.63	5.27	0.98	1.54	0.28	0.18	0.0
14.	Punjab National Bank	0.82	1.06	19.11	23.24	7.38	9.64	0.88	1.11
15.	State Bank of Bikaner and Jaipur	1.12	1.21	24.17	24.56	9.92	11.43	1.41	1.54
16.	State Bank of Hyderabad	1.12	1.25	25.74	26.80	9.92	11.92	1.30	1.46
17.	State Bank of Indore	1.38	1.89	34.58	40.21	10.76	15.55	1.58	2.17
18.	State Bank of Mysore	0.67	1.07	20.49	29.63	5.47	8.71	0.77	1.29
19.	State Bank of Patiala	1.47	1.67	22.48	25.22	13.17	15.27	1.67	1.80
20.	State Bank of Saurashtra	0.91	0.91	15.16	15.51	0.07	8.27	1.08	1.0

(Contd.)

Table 5 (*Contd.*)

Sl.No.	*Bank*	*Return on Assets*		*Return on Equity*		*Net Profit Margin*		*Net Profit Spread*	
		2002	**2003**	**2002**	**2003**	**2002**	**2003**	**2002**	**2003**
21.	State Bank of Travancore	0.78	0.96	21.50	25.66	7.18	9.08	0.90	1.07
22.	State Bank of India	0.73	0.86	16.95	19.15	0.16	8.43	0.90	1.05
23.	Syndicate Bank	0.84	1.04	19.06	23.02	7.93	10.21	0.88	1.12
24.	UCO Bank	0.56	0.63	6.11	10.46	5.27	6.10	0.61	0.66
25.	Union Bank of India	0.75	1.16	15.88	23.65	6.96	10.77	0.79	1.24
26.	United Bank of India	0.57	1.36	16.41	28.54	4.90	11.98	0.61	1.45
27.	Vijaya Bank	0.86	1.12	20.74	26.66	7.58	9.75	0.89	1.15

Sources: *Business Standard*, Banking Annual, October, 2003.

Table 6: Ownership of Bank Deposits in India

(*Rs. in crores*)

Sl. No.	*Sector*	*1998*	*1999*	*2000*	*2001*	*2002*
1.	Government Sector	60,132	75,489	86,481	97,192	1,18,716
2.	Private Sector	24,711	30,262	32,670	45,255	63,975
3.	Financial Sector	44,753	65,057	65,499	71,110	77,126
4.	Household Sector	4,02,758	4,81,530	5,76,487	6,55,873	7,50,402
5.	Foreign Sector	72,457	84,664	91,696	1,07,031	1,14,154
		6,04,811	**7,37,002**	**8,52,814**	**9,76,460**	**11,24,372**

Table 7: The Following Statement Shows the Distribution of Outstanding Credit of Scheduled Commercial Banks According to Occupation (As on 31-3-2002)

(*Rs. in crores*)

Sl. No.	*Occupation*	*Number of Accounts*	*Credit Limit Amount*	*Outstanding Amount*
1.	Agriculture	1,98,43,289	61,974	51,730
2.	Industry	47,12,767	318,917	2,36,430
3.	Transport	6,43,494	10,962	8,701
4.	Personal Loans	1,62,72,488	81,315	65,940
5.	Trade	53,88,515	1,03,502	89,534
6.	Financial Institutions	36,668	37,121	26,456
7.	Miscellaneous	37,35,874	48,644	40,410
	Total Bank Credit	**5,23,64,395**	**6,86,951**	**5,38,434**

Source: EPW, August 9, 2003, p. 3335.

Savings

Saving is the most important factor for any kind of economy. A strong financial infrastructure will bè laid down only with the help of the saving formation. The saving habits in the community definitely will occupy a influential role in capital formation of the country. The capital formation is the most important factor in building a strong economy. The capital formation will influence the national income. The saving level of community is determined by national income and its distribution. Asset creation is only possible with the help of a high level saving amount of money. The high rate of saving level will also curb the present level of consumption. The basic foundation of the economy is only possible with the help of a higher level of saving amount. Saving is the sacrifice for the better future. The future is always depends upon the past. The past resources are only useful for the future and upcoming projects. The creation of strong financial resources are necessary for the developing economy. Savings are rewarded by the profit or interest element. Savings will be put in the form of financial instruments. The level of saving pattern in the community will show an impact as the general price level. For the proper development of the economy the savings ratio should be increased to a desired level. The saving rate in India has doubted in 46 years from 1951 to 1997. Savings are excess of income over expenditure. They are coming from households, corporate sector and government sector. The saving form for the specific objectives, like interest income, future needs, contingencies, precautionary purposes. All savings may lose in value due to inflation or rise in prices leading to depreciation of the rupee. All objective of income, capital appreciation, safety can be secured only by proper investment in corporate securities. The savings from household sector occupies a dominant role in the economy. The savings that flow into financial assets create wealth. Wealth creation is the most important element for enhancing the prosperity of the nation. The savings from the household sector may take in the form of currency, deposits with banks and companies, provident fund, insurance, corporate shares and bonds. The following data reveals the trend and progress of the different segments of the savings.

Table 8: Statement shows New Capital Issues by Non-Government Public Limited Companies

(Rs. in crores)

Year	*Equity*	*Preference*	*Debenture*	*Total*
1984-85	363	–	693	1056

(Contd.)

Table 8 (*Contd.*)

Year	*Equity*	*Preference*	*Debenture*	*Total*
1985-86	898	1	846	1745
1986-87	1007	1	1573	2581
1987-88	1105	7	675	1787
1988-89	1034	3	2187	3224
1989-90	1220	8	5282	6510
1990-91	1284	13	3015	4312
1991-92	1916	2	4275	6193
1992-93	9952	1	9850	19803
1993-94	9960	0	9370	19330
1994-95	17414	132	8871	26417
1995-96	12052	150	3970	16172
1996-97	6116	75	4233	10424
1997-98	1162	04	1972	3138
1998-99	2563	60	2390	5013
1999-2000	2753	–	2400	5153
2000-01	2608	142	3140	4890
2001-02	860	–	4832	5692
2002-03 (April to October)	395	–	218	613

Source: EPW, February 2, 2003, p. 499.

Table 9: The Following Statement Shows the Statistical Profile of Small Savings During the Period 1980-2002

(*Rs. in crores*)

Year	*Total Deposits*	*Total Certificates*	*PPF Total*	*Small Savings*
1980-81	6632	–	–	6632
1981-82	7470	2022	282	9936
1982-83	8296	2945	393	11667
1983-84	9112	4562	–	14449
1984-85	10824	7061	–	18069
1985-86	11772	8881	–	20653
1986-87	11518	13431	871	25819
1987-88	11812	6802	1228	29612
1988-89	11942	21359	1653	34954
1989-90	14515	27407	2255	44279
1990-91	17022	33257	–	50279
1991-92	20255	35744	2596	58697
1992-93	21694	38788	466	60948
1993-94	23208	43383	660	67696
1994-95	28066	54244	1027	8337
1995-96	29465	62131	1028	92624
1996-97	31800	72839	1472	106111
1997-98	38274	86065	2416	126755
1998-99	47124	104833	3339	155296

(*Contd.*)

Table 9 (*Contd.*)

Year	*Total Deposits*	*Total Certificates*	*PPF Total*	*Small Savings*
1999-2000	60639	122247	4624	187510
2000-01	80654	138041	6392	225087
2001-02	105078	149667	8111	262856

Total includes PPF from 1993-94 onwards.

Sources: *EPW*, February 1, 2003, p. 419.

Table 10: The Following Statement Shows the Investments of Scheduled Commercial Banks in India During the Period 1993-02

(Rs. in crores)

Category	*I. Investment by Offices in India*	*II. Investment by Foreign Offices of Indian Banks*	*Total*
1993	119742	1079	**120821**
1994	155812	1102	**156914**
1995	174146	2185	**176331**
1996	190233	2936	**193169**
1997	232970	5809	**238779**
1998	271218	8213	**279431**
1999	325970	6537	**332507**
2000	395869	7121	**402990**
2001	470102	10385	**480487**
2002	554667	13678	**568345**

Sources: *EPW*, March 15, 2003, p. 1003.

Table 12: The Following Statement shows the Profile of Foreign Investment Approvals and Actuals During the period August 1991 to March 2003

(Rs. in crores)

Name of the Industry	*Amount of FDI Approved*	*Percent to Total Amount*
I. Basic goods industries	108418	38
II. Capital goods industries	26184	9
III. Intermediate goods industries	5329	2
IV. Consumer non-durable industries	29848	10
V. Consumer durable goods industries	9436	3
VI. Services	106310	38
	285525	**100**

Source: *EPW*, October 25, 2003, p. 4499.

Table 13: The Following Statement shows the Country-wise Sources of Foreign Direct Investments During August, 1991 to March, 2003

(Rs. in crores)

	Country-wise Position	*Investment*	*Per cent to Total*
1.	U.S.	57434	20
2.	Mauritius	34350	12
3.	U.K.	23324	8
4.	Japan	11424	4
5.	South Korea	9827	3
6.	Germany	9242	3
7.	Netherlands	8951	3
8.	Australia	6781	2
9.	France	6558	2
10.	Malaysia	6057	2
11.	Singapore	5274	2
12.	Italy	4805	1
13.	Belgium	4511	1
14.	Israel	4245	1
15.	Cayman Island	3887	1
16.	Switzerland	3129	1
17.	Canada	2876	1
18.	Thailand	2461	1
19.	Hong Kong	2302	1
20.	Sweden	2060	1
21.	NRIs	10651	4
22.	ADRs/GDRs	48471	17
23.	Miscellaneous	17100	9
		285620	**100**

Source: *EPW*, October 25, 2003, p. 4499.

Table 14: The Following Statement shows State-wise Flow of Foreign Domestic Approvals During August, 1991 to March, 2003

(Rs. in crores)

State-wise Position	*Amount*	*Per cent to Total Amount*
I. Northern Region:		
Delhi	34087	11.9
Haryana	3622	1.3
Himachal Pradesh	1174	0.4
Punjab	1968	0.7
II. Western Region:		
Gujarat	18679	6.5
Maharashtra	49587	17.4
Rajasthan	3005	1.1

(Contd.)

Table 14 (*Contd.*)

State-wise Position	Amount	Per cent to Total Amount
III. Eastern Region:		
Bihar	739	0.3
Orissa	8229	2.9
West Bengal	9014	3.2
IV. North Eastern Region:	74	0
V. Central Region:		
Madhya Pradesh	9271	3.2
Uttar Pradesh	4815	1.7
VI. Southern Region:		
Andhra Pradesh	13218	4.6
Karnataka	23689	8.3
Kerala	1530	0.5
Tamil Nadu	23657	8.3
All Others	79166	27.7

Table 15: The Following Statement Shows the Growth in Estimated Corporate Investment During the Period 1999-2003

(*Rs. in crores*)

Industry	*1999–2000*		*2000–2001*		*2001–2002*		*2002–2003*	
	Amount	***%***	***Amount***	***%***	***Amount***	***%***	***Amount***	***%***
1. Infrastructure	20178	42.9	43373	62.5	10590	43	10360	55.3
2. Engineering	8508	18.1	7579	10.9	6387	25.9	550	2.9
3. Chemicals	4940	10.5	6770	9.8	961	3.9	1086	5.8
4. Cement	1627	3.5	1883	2.7	519	2.1	415	2.2
5. Textiles	3335	7.1	2252	3.2	999	4.1	1133	6.0
6. Sugar	998	2.1	339	0.5	248	1.0	255	1.4
7. Paper	457	1.0	638	0.9	388	1.6	291	1.6
8. Electronics	490	1.0	1312	1.9	368	1.5	–	–
9. Hotels	1603	3.4	1619	2.3	970	3.9	502	2.7
10. Construction	1461	3.1	710	1.0	555	2.3	781	4.2
11. Services	–	–	–	–	953	3.9	1406	7.5
12. Food Production	–	–	–	–	172	0.7	466	2.5
13. Information Technology	–	–	–	–	486	2.0	534	2.9
14. Others	2617	5.6	2926	4.2	1060	4.3	957	5.1

The prosperity of a nation is reflected in the growth of Income or Gross Domestic Product. The rate of growth and the distribution of income are the two important factors which influences the savings. The growth of an economy will be reflected in the standard of living of the people. Inflation is another important factor for the growth of the economy. The rate of rise in prices such as wholesale prices or consumers prices is known as inflation. A rise in price levels reduced the value of money and its purchasing power. These consequences leads to the lowering of

Table 16: The Following Statement shows the State-wise Distribution of Projects and Their Cost During the Period 1999-2003

(Rs. in crores)

States	*1999–2000*		*2000–2001*		*2001–2002*		*2002–2003*	
	Amount	*%*	*Amount*	*%*	*Amount*	*%*	*Amount*	*%*
1. Andhra Pradesh	5147	10.9	9088	13.1	3015	12.2	1937	10.3
2. Delhi	971	2.1	1374	2	602	2.4	4736	25.3
3. Gujarat	6707	14.3	14052	20.2	1552	6.3	1360.	7.3
4. Karnataka	2021	4.3	2647	3.8	1303	5.3	1523	8.1
5. Kerala	581	1.2	177	0.3	401	1.6	107	0.6
6. Madhya Pradesh	1289	2.7	988	1.4	302	1.2	744	4.0
7. Maharashtra	10987	23.4	12061	17.4	4665	18.9	2742	14.6
8. Punjab	2123	4.5	3955	5.7	178	0.7	251	1.3
9. Rajasthan	–	–	–	–	1305	5.3	879	4.7
10. Tamil Nadu	7571	16.1	11419	16.5	2289	9.3	1037	5.5
11. Uttar Pradesh	1946	4.1	5401	7.8	1221	5	855	4.6
12. West Bengal	2146	4.6	651	0.9	773	3.1	1457	7.8
13. Haryana	466	1	887	1.3	–	–	–	–
14. Orissa	3926	8.4	3591	5.2	–	–	135	0.7
15. Others	1127	2.4	3110	4.5	7051	28.6	972	5.2
	47009	**100**	**69400**	**100**	**24656**	**100**	**18736**	**100**

consumption of goods, which in turn leading to lower standard of living of the people. Savings are also influenced by poverty ratio. The lower poverty ratio may enhance the rising standard of living of the people. The peace of savings depends on the structure of the economy. Agriculture dominate the Indian economy and generates 80 per cent of employment opportunities are provided. There is a strong need to concentrate on agriculture sector rather than other segments. The agriculture sector in India is depended upon the availability of $\mathbf{H_2O}$. The cultivation of agriculture became as speculation activity. A boost in agriculture sector necessarily enhances the prosperity of India. The agriculture sector problems will only be solved with **linking of rivers.** The linking of rivers will be the mega project of this country. This project requires **Rs. 6,00,000 crores** in a span of 10 years. It is the dream project of Indian farmers to counter the poverty. This project is a weapon to change the entire agricultural scenario in India. The agriculturisation process in India will definitely attack the poverty. The farmers attitude should also be changed in tune with the changes in the agri-market. They should change their cultivating techniques, crop methods and seasonal problems. The productivity in agriculture sector is very low. The government is also take some steps to boost the agriculture sector. This sector should be mechanised, offer low rate of interest loans, training to the farmers, fixing more accountability to the agriculture staff in the government. The government should provide technical facilities such as soil testing, mobile labs, crop changing methods, usage of fertilisers and insecticides. The migration from agriculture sector to other sectors should be halted by providing all the above facilities. In addition to traditional cultivation, the agriculture sector should also be corporatised. The agri-business is becoming as a **sunrise industry**. The government should bring reforms in agriculture sector to become as a self-sufficient nation.

The development process involves a large amount of resources pooling for the purpose of capital formation. Capital formation creates wonderful events in the economy of a nation. The savings in financial form include savings in currency, bank deposits, non-bank deposits, life insurance funds, provident fund, pension fund, claims on government, shares, debentures units and trade debt. Currency and deposits are voluntary savings. These savings are motivated by income motive and precautionary motive. The savings in life insurance provident and pension funds are contractual. The savings in physical form include gold, silver, consumer durables, tractors and agricultural machinery. Household saving includes real estate, buildings, durable goods etc. The physical form of savings are less productive and depends upon the efficiency of their use.

2

INDIAN STOCK MARKET

"Plan your work and work your plan"

—Napolean Hill

Introduction

Investment: Investment is an economic activity. It stimulates the value of wealth. It creates the asset formation in the country. It is a part of the savings of individuals, corporates and business organisations of the country. The surplus amount of money which is diverted towards the economic activity of the nation is also called as "Investment". It increases the productivity of a nation. Investment is a person's commitment of funds towards his future. A person's future will be based on his investment strategy. Every individual has to make his investment decisions according to his financial position. It refers to the acquisition of assets which generates income. It means parking of one's idle funds in income generating assets. The use of money to earn more money by way of interest, dividend or capital appreciation. It provides either revenue income or capital appreciation. Investment is the allocation of monetary resources to various segments of the economy. Investment means the diversification of money from surplus place to sacrifice environment. The flow of money should be done on the basis of demand for it. The wealth of a nation can be increased only on the smooth flow of money to the required areas from surplus available sectors. It is an adjustment of supply and demand of money. It is the net addition to nation's capital stock. It is the sacrification of present consumption of a person. Investment reflects the curb of present consumption. Investors are postponing their desires for a future period of time. Savings of individual, business enterprises and corporate sector make more investment activities in the economy. **Savings** occupy an important element in deploying of resources in the economy. Savings are excess of income over present expenditure for any individual or a business concern. Higher earning capacity of the individuals, corporate sector, firms may stimulate the investment pattern. The quantum of savings will depend upon the savings habit of the people. The financial discipline of a community will encourage the motive of making investment habits. Hence the economy will get sufficient funds to start the **Mega Projects** which will influence the prosperity of a nation. The government should also make some measures to the large amount of fund savers. These benefits may be like in the form of tax incentives and other privileges.

Definition of Investment

> *"Commitment of funds made in the expectation of some positive rate of return. If the investment is properly undertaken, the return will commensurate with the risk the investor assumes".*
>
> **—Fisher and Jordan**

> *"Investment may be defined as the purchase by an individual or institutional investor of a financial or real asset that produces a return proportional to the risk assumed over some future investment period".*
>
> **—F. Amling**

Generally the investor who is having surplus money could invest in any form of kind like gold, real estate, securities or in simply deposit in bank account. The corporate sector's surplus money may like to invest in the extension of the existing firm or undertake new business ventures. All of these activities may make investment in the economy. Investment in any form indicates the risk factor. But a well-planned investment alone can ensure regular income or capital appreciation. The dynamics of economic system provide various opportunities for investors to invest their funds in different types of securities. The investment word can be analysed in two ways i.e., **Financial and Economic** aspects. As per the financial aspect, investment is a part of the savings of individuals, which flow into the capital market. The surplus amount of money may reach through primary or secondary market. The investment in primary market can stimulate the growth of **Gross Domestic Product** of a nation. The investment in secondary market cannot influence the growth of capital formation, but it will create inspiration to the primary market. The primary and secondary markets are interrelated aspects in the capital market. The development of secondary market will create a good financial environment in the primary market. Investment is the allocation of monetary resources to assets that are deployed to yield some return over a given period of time. The investor make his investment with a desire of future income in the form of **"Interest dividends, dividends, premium, pension benefits"** or the appreciation of the value of investment. As per the economic perception of the investment means, "the net additions to the capital stock of the society". The investment can boost the nation's **Gross Domestic Product, Net Domestic Product, Per Capita Income, Purchasing Power, Standard of Living and Inflation**. A net additions to the capital stock enhances the values of the buildings equipments or inventories. The speed of mass industrialisation in a country depends upon the flow of money to the corporate sector. A well-dignified and better living standards of the people will depend upon the level of investment made by that community of a nation.

Speculation

Speculation is a dynamic activity. It is a short-term phenomenon. It involves higher level of risk. Speculation means purchasing of marketable assets which are not meant for very long period of time. It is involved with the expectation of getting profit from the price fluctuations. Capturing of profit is the main intention of the speculator, within a short period of time. The speculator is interested in getting abnormal return. Speculation is based on a strong belief and expectations. It is mostly associated with stock market. Speculation in stock market is an inspiration to **crores** of investors and there is no stock market without it. It is based on mainly from past experience. It is courageous and **costly** decision. Success in speculation requires a highly specialised and talented knowledge. But no speculator can win all the time. No investor ever becomes wealthy without speculating in something. A true investor is interested in a good rate of return earned on a rather consistent basis for a relatively long period of time. Speculation is based on in-depth analysis of share price movements. Investment is different from speculation. Investment is a careful selection of stocks, based on scientific analysis of **intrinsic value**. But speculation is based on **market tips**, hunches and inside dope. Investment involves a moderate risk but speculation provide high risk or high return. Investment activity considers only fundamental factors and evaluation of the performance of the company on regular basis. But the speculation activity considers inside information and market behaviour. Investment uses its own fund and avoids borrowed fund. Speculation uses its own fund and heavily depends upon borrowed resources. The **time horizon** in investment activity may be from **1 year to few years**. But in speculation the holding period is not more than few days to months.

Gambling

A gamble is involved in a game or chance. It is mostly associated with entertainment sector. It is a combination of pleasure and pain. Gamble is a source of easy money for lazy persons. It is usually very short period of investment than the speculation activity. It involves pure element of risk. It does not contain any careful and scientific research. No methods will be adopted in this activity. It is a typical chronic and repetitive experience. The holding period for gamblers is in **"seconds"**. It is involved with **tactics**. Artificial and unnecessary risks are created in gambling. It is a continuous process because the gambler never stops after the winning money. In gambling the results are determined by the roll of dice or the turn of a card. The gambling activity is primarily concerned with entertainment aspect and the money would be the second factor. **Example** for gambling **"Horse raiding, Game of Cards, Lottery"**. Fundamental and financial analysis is only useful for investment activity but it does not meant for **speculation and gambling** activities. Positive returns are expected by the investors in investment activity.

Investment Objectives

Usually every investor expects some return on his investment. Every shareholder will get some amount of money in the form of dividend. The debenture holder or bondholders are entitled to get their interest amount on a specified time from the business concern. The investor expects a regular flow of income and capital appreciation from his committed investment instruments. But some other factors also be considered while making investment decisions by the investors:

(a) Return
(b) Risk
(c) Safety
(d) Liquidity
(e) Hedge

(a) Return

Return is a reward to the investor. Every business activity is based on a desire of earning a reasonable return. The return to the investor may be either in the form of a regular income or capital appreciation. It differs from the nature of the financial instruments, maturity period and a host of other factors. Return is always chased by the risk. Usually, the **higher** the risk, the higher is the return.

(b) Risk

Risk means, a possibility of meeting danger or suffering harm. It can be defined as the change that the expected or perspective gains or profits may not materialise. Risk is an estimation about the degree of happening of the loss. It is a measurable element. The difference between the actual outcome of investment and expected outcome of investment. Basically every investor likes to reduce the risk and maximise his return on his investment. Risk can be avoided by selecting some risk free investments. However, some risks can be controllable and others cannot be. Risk may be arised by various factors such as **wrong decision, wrong timing of investment, type of instrument, quantum of amount, method of investment, nature of the industry, national and international factors.**

(c) Safety

Safety is the most important factor in making investment decisions. The selected type of financial asset should be available under regulatory framework. Investment means just parking of one's own idle fund in a safe place. If the investment is made in a highly regulated environment, adds a flavour of safety. Investment in Government assured securities provide more safety than with the private business concerns. High safety parking places can be ranked as **bank deposits, government bonds, UTI units, non-convertible debentures, convertible debentures, equity shares and deposits with non-banking finance companies**. However, a highly safe investment will generate relatively low return.

(d) Liquidity

Investment in liquid assets attracts more attention by the investors. Liquidity means, easy convertibility of financial asset into cash as and when the investor requires. Hence a liquid investment would enable the investor to encash his investment whenever the need arises. Liquidity of a financial asset will definitely influence the investment decision of the investor. It provides flexibility to the investor in changing economic and political environment. The liquid financial assets provides a easy marketability and trading facility.

(e) Hedge

Inflation is a natural phenomenon in almost all the economies. The rate of return on investment should ensure a cover against the inflation. The return on investment of the investor should be higher the rate of inflation, otherwise the investor will have to face loss in real terms. The bluechip shares can provide a protection against inflation. The return on investment should assure the safety of the principal amount.

Investment Process

A good financial system encourages the saving based investment. Savings are the fundamental factor for making investment decisions. The government should also motivate and educate the public towards the saving habits. Though savings curbs present consumption, but in long-term, it helps the economy. The development of any nation will depend upon the **financial architecture**. The increase of investment in industrial sector leads to capital formation. The rise in capital formation leads to increase in **Gross Domestic Product**. In India, the domestic savings have been categorised into three sectors **households, government and private sector**. The savings from household sector dominate the saving component. The household sector in India is a combination of rural and urban households. Usually the rural people will have much savings potential than urban people. The middle class families in India contributes much amount of resources towards productive ways. The savings of the community will rise to a higher level only when employment opportunities exists to all the public. The fundamental right **"Right to Work"** factor enhances the saving potential of the nation. Generally the savings will be in the form of **"currency, bank deposits, non-bank deposits, life insurance funds, provident funds, pension funds, shares, debentures, bonds, units and trade debt**. The savings in the household sector are mobilised directly in the form of units, premium, provident fund and pension fund. Bank deposits occupies a dominant role in household sector component. However, in India the investment habits among the public should be increased to a higher level. Usually every investor will take some precautionary measures before going to take his investment decisions. The investment decision will depend upon the investment policy of the investor or public. The investment process in the intellectual factor in making of decisions. In India, there is no awareness among the illiterates public where to park their funds for a specific period of time. The government should take necessary measures to follow the strict **financial discipline** among community. A financial discipline may stimulate the growth of potential savings. The investment process involves the selection of better financial asset among various alternatives. The process can be divided into five different stages:

(a) Creation of Investment Policy,
(b) Selection of Investment Options,
(c) Valuation,
(d) Portfolio Construction,
(e) Portfolio Evaluation.

(a) Creation of Investment Policy

Investment policy is the most important factor in making of investment decisions by the individual investors, firms, companies and other organisations. The investor's needs, his objectives, his earning capacity, his future financial plans will influence the investment policy. The financial discipline will stimulate the value of financial assets. The essential ingredients of the investment policy are presented below:

(i) Available surplus funds
(ii) Objectives
(iii) Investment skills

Available surplus funds will influence the investment policy of the investors. Usually in India, the investors are making decisions on the basis of their own funds. The quantum of surplus funds will make a careful selection of different financial assets. If the funds are borrowed, the return on his investment should be higher than the interest he pays. Policy means, a long-term strategy which reflects the investor's needs and dreams. Mutual funds are the bulk buyers and sellers in the stock market. They invest their unit holder's money in different securities in different times. They should work according to the unit holder's investment policies. Their investment policy will be clearly known by their fund managers. However the fund managers should construct their portfolio according to the scheme policies.

(b) Selection of Investment Options

Selection of investment option is another factor in investment process. After the availability of investible funds, the investor should select different financial assets to suit his required rate of return. He must take all precautionary measures before going to make investment such as, regular flow of income, risk perception and liquidity. If the investor is willing to accept the risk, he may choose such type of financial instruments. Some kind of investors are not interested to accept the risk then they should choose liquid financial assets which pays very low amount of return. For choosing the best financial asset, the investor should have some knowledge about the economy, capital market operations, investment tactics, and government policies. In stock market participation, investor should have outstanding skills for parking of his idle funds. But some investors simply handed over the cheque to the broker and left all the things to him. Hence they will burnt their fingers in the stock market. A real investor who thoroughly understands the things about corporate sector performance demand forecasting, consumer behaviour, growth areas, future programmes of the government etc. Investing blindly in the stock market does not generate either return or capital appreciation. A thorough understanding is necessary about the stock market structure, brokers functions, trading methods, insider trading, fundamental analysis, technical analysis and predicting of best growth stocks.

(c) Valuation

Valuation is the another important factor in investment process. Every investor shall know intrinsic value of the perspective financial asset. Before going to purchase the financial instrument, he should know about the book value of the share, price earning ratio, earning per share, reserves of the company. If the investor knows all these things, then he may assess whether the market price of the scrip is **overvalued or undervalued**. It is better to go for purchase of scrips must be undervalued. But in some reasonable extent overvalued scrips may also be selected. In the stock market, some scrips are always available to less than their book value. Investors shall also know about past prices of a particular scrip for 52 weeks. The knowing of higher and lower prices of past can educate the investor for making of investment decisions. However, assessment of intrinsic value of a share is the most important element in becoming success in the stock market. Assessment of present situation and predicting of future will help the investor to get success in the stock market.

(d) Portfolio Construction

Portfolio construction is the important factor in investment process. Portfolio is a combination of different financial assets. It is a basket of different instruments. The portfolio should be constructed according to the needs and goals of investor. The investor tries to attain maximum return with minimum risk. If the investor park his funds in wrong assets, it may leads to getting losses. The risk can be reduced by diversification of portfolio. The diversification can be done either debt to equity or equity to debt. The diversification can also be done either industry or company basis. **Industry diversification means** changing of financial instruments from one industry to another industry. Government policies are most important factors to alter the basket of portfolio. Because sometimes government will encourage a particular type of industry. **For example: Information Technology** sector gets more encouragement from the government presently. **Company diversification** means alteration of the portfolio according to the fundamental analysis. Technical analysts suggest the scrips based on share price movements. Fundamental analysis reflects the performance of the companies. After taking all precautionary measures, the investor select the best scrips and allocate funds for buying of instruments. Therefore the construction of portfolio activity may be completed.

(e) Portfolio Evaluation

Portfolio evaluation is the final step in the investment process. After construction of completion of portfolio, it has to be managed more effectively and efficiently. A continuous monitoring of portfolio may require revision. The evaluation of portfolio consists of **Appraisal and Revision**. Appraisal means interpretation of latest developments of the economy in the portfolio. Usually risk and return performance of the security vary from time-to-time. The variability in returns of the securities can be measured and compared. The appraisal reveals the loss and steps can be taken to avoid such losses. Appraisal of the portfolio needs to make revision. Revision of portfolio means the replacement of financial instruments. The low yielding instruments with high risk can be replaced with high yielding scrips with low risk factor. The portfolio will be under revision upto achieving the desired return of the investor. A detailed discussion will be presented about the **portfolio** aspects in forthcoming chapters.

Investment Media

The objective of any investor is to derive a variety of investment opportunities that meet his preference for risk and expected return. Many types of financial instruments are available in the market. A sound and proper investment programme can be constructed if the investor familiarises the various attractive investments available. There are many alternative investments exist for investors. Investment media is of several kinds. But basically it may categorised in two kinds. It is presented in a chart given below:

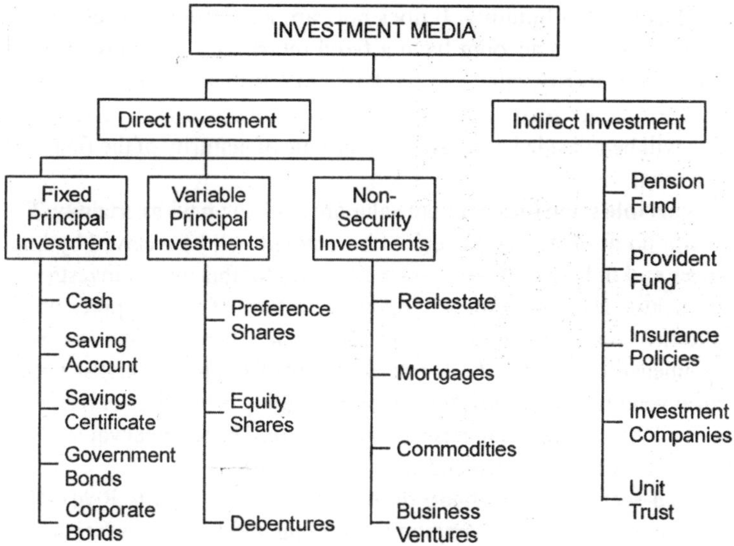

The Investment Media has basically been categorised as below:

1. Direct Investment Alternatives
2. Indirect Investment Alternatives

1. Direct Investment Alternatives

The ultimate objective of the investor is to get a reasonable return on his investment. The individual makes his own choice to make his commitment in this type of investments. The investor will select the portfolio which will maximise his profitability or minimise loss. The financial assets present a wide range of risks such as **risk free instruments, high risk speculative shares and debentures** from availability of all these instruments, he has to select these instruments to minimise his risk. Further the direct investments are classified into:

(a) Fixed Principal Investment
(b) Variable Principal Investment
(c) Non-security Investment

Fixed Principal Investments contains high liquid assets. The principal amount and the terminal value are known with certainty. **Cash, savings account, national saving certificates, Government bonds and corporate bonds** are the best examples for this kind of investment. Cash has its own liquidity. It does not earn any amount of return if it kept idle. Savings account have a fixed return. All other instruments have fixed maturity value and fixed rate of return and a period of time. These assets are guaranteed by the Union government. The terminal value will be refunded accurately on the date of maturity of the financial instrument.

Variable securities terminal value are not known with certainity. The investor do not know how much of his amount will be received by him. **Shares and debentures** are the best examples for this type of investment. Shares provide higher amount of return in the form of capital appreciation, if the investor is willing to accept **high risk**. Therefore, the return of investment is based upon the degree of amount of accepted risk. Risk taking is an adventurous activity. If the investor is willing to take higher risk, then there will be possibility of getting higher return. The terminal value of the share is determined by demand and supply forces.

Non-security Investments differ from securities aspects. Real estate, financing of mortgages, commodities trading and business ventures are examples of this kind of investment. Real estate provides ownership of a house and its terminal value is unknown. But it is a liquid asset. It provides liquidity than the securities form of investment. Mortgage provides a regular fixed income and the principal amount is recovered on a stated maturity date. Commodities are bought and sold in spot markets. The future markets are well-versed with the spot markets. Business ventures sell ownership securities to public. **Art, Antiques**, gold, silver and jewellery are other types of specialised investments which possess the **aesthetic value**.

2. Indirect Investment Alternatives

The investor has no direct hold on the amount of his investment. **Pension fund, provident fund, insurance policies, investment companies, unit**

trusts are the examples of indirect investments. The investor has no control on these financial assets. If he contributes his savings to pension fund, provident fund, the management of resources will be looked after by the LIC or UTI. All these schemes are useful to the investors only after retirement period. These assets are meant for the purpose of **post retirement** life of the investor. These are meant for long-term period of time for the investors. These pool of financial resources are managed by Insurance Companies and Trusts.

Therefore all investors are savers but all savers cannot be good investors. Investment in good kind may generate sufficient amount of returns for the intelligent investor. The emerging trend in growth of urbanisation and levels of literacy have activated the cult of investment.

Financial Instruments

The financial market provides various types of securities. Securities provide property rights to the holders. They provides a claim as an asset. The security holder is entitled to get a regular return on his investment. Usually securities is known as "shares and bonds". Securities may be defined as **"Securities include shares, scrips, stocks, bonds, debentures or other marketable like securities of any incorporated company or other body corporate or government".—Securities Contract Regulation Act, 1956.**

Securities are of different kinds. Companies generally issues various kinds of financial instruments. Securities can be classified on the basis of return and the sources of issue. Securities may be raised by government, semi-government and corporates. The security holders will get different types of returns on various kinds of financial instruments. Securities issued on the basis of return may be classified as **(a) Fixed income securities, (b) Variable income securities.** Fixed income securities provide a fixed amount of return to the security holders. The security holder clearly knows the amount of return at the time of its purchase. **Bonds, debentures and preference shares** are the best examples for fixed income securities. The variable securities provide different amount of income to the security holder. It may vary from year to year. **Equity shares** are the best example for this kind of securities. Dividend is paid by the company to the equity shareholders, depends upon the earnings available to shareholders. Usually the following securities generally issued by almost of all companies in the country:

1. Equity Shares
2. Preference Shares
3. Debentures
4. Bonds

1. Equity Shares

Equity shares are commonly issued by all companies throughout the globe. The owners of the equity shares is known as **"Equity Shareholders"**. They are the actual owners of the company. They have rights and duties in the management of the company. The equity shareholders have the rights according to Section **85(2)** of the Companies Act, 1956. Equity shares have some advantages such as "limited liability, liquidity, capital appreciation, hedge against inflation". Shares are also called as **"stock"**. There is a different between share and stock. Share capital of a company is divided into a number of small units of equal value called as **share**. The stock is known as the aggregate of a member's fully paid up shares of equal value merged in one fund. The stock certificate contains the terms of money and not as many shares. Stock can be divided into share and share may be converted into stock. The recent development in capital market have created **"sweat equity"**. It is introduced by an ordinance in Companies Act, 1998. Section **79(A)** of the Companies Act, 1956 allows issue of sweat equity. This section deals with the all aspects of sweat equity. Sweat equity is a part of equity share capital. These shares can be issued in two situations **(a)** to employees and directors at discount price, **(b)** can be issued for getting technical know-how, or for getting intellectual property rights or value additions. The sweat equity will be offered to the employees and directors for the outstanding contribution made by them to the company. It is an encouragement for their efforts rendered for the development of the company. It is an inspirational instrument to the staff and directors. These shares will offered in recognition of their services rendered to the organisation. At present these shares are mostly offered by **"Software, hardware management consultancies, non-banking finance companies, financial services such as custodians, depositories and credit rating agencies.**

Another recent development occurred in the capital market is issue of **non-voting shares**. The idea was generated for introduction of these shares in 1987 but it was materialised in 1994. The Finance Ministry announced certain broad guidelines in 1994 with reference to issue of non-voting shares. These shares carry no voting rights. These shares attracts additional dividends. These shareholders can enjoy the bonus shares. These shares can be listed and traded in the stock exchanges. Any failure in payment of dividend for two years, these shares would automatically get voting rights. The company can issue these shares to a maximum of 25 per cent of the voting stock. The non-voting shareholders are entitled to get 20 per cent higher than that of voting shareholders.

Bonus Shares are issued to the existing shareholders. These shares will be issued by the companies, when the company get higher amount of profits. The aim of the issue is to capitalise the profits and reserves. Sometime, the company issues bonus shares where it collects hefty amount of premium mobilised from public issues. Bonus shares are the distribution of shares in addition to the cash dividends to the existing shareholders. These shares are issued to only to fully paid up share capital.

Rights Issues are offered to the existing shareholders. Shares offered to the existing shareholders at a price is known as **Right Shares**. It is a matter of legal right to the existing shareholders. Right issues are regulated by the SEBI under the provisions of the Companies Act. Rights issue can be issued by the Public Company only after two years from its formation date or one year from the date of first allotment, whichever is earlier. Hence these shares should be offered at first to the existing shareholders. The shareholders can renounce the right shares in favour of his nominee. If the company fails to get 90 per cent of the subscription. The company shall have to return the entire money received. SEBI, at present removed this condition.

2. Preference Shares

Preference share is also known as **"hybrid security"**. It is a combination of bond and equity. Its features like bond, will get a fixed rate of dividend. In the event of liquidation, it will get priority in getting the principal amount from the company. The dividend will be paid by the company at the discretion of board of directors like as equity shares. These shareholders do not enjoy the benefits like equity shareholders. Preference shares can be classified as **"Cumulative, Non-cumulative, Redeemable-Irredeemable and Convertible"**. Cumulative preference shares will have a right to get their dividends along with all arrears. The unpaid dividends will be paid later when the company has sufficient amount of profits. But arrears of dividend will not get interest. The non-payment of dividend only continues to grow up to **3 years** only. After 3 years accumulative feature ceases. If the Articles of association has no provision about this condition, the arrears of dividend may continue. In case of liquidation, no arrears of dividend will be paid. **Non-cumulative shares** does not accumulate the dividend. The dividend may be paid by the company, only in availability of sufficient profits. If there is no profit in a particular year, the company does not pay the dividend. In the event of liquidation or winding up of a company fully paid up of equity and preference shares have no further rights to claim a part in the **surplus**. If the Articles of Association allows this claim, it will be paid. **Redeemable preference shares** are issued only with the acceptance of Association of Articles. Redeemable means the share capital will be refunded by the Company only after a specified period of time. However the redemption of share capital may be done subject to some conditions such as, the share capital must be fully paid up, redemption fund must be created, etc.

Irredeemable preference shares are not available in India. Section **80A** of the Companies Act, 1956 has not been permitted this type of shares. These shares were available in India till 15-6-1988. Irredeemable preference shares means, the share capital will not be redeemable except on occasion of **winding up** of the business. **Convertible preference shares** are more attractive to the investors. These shares are converted into equity shares after a specified period of time. This financial instrument provides more benefits to the investors such as security and stability of income. It is a privilege of sharing the potential increase in the equity value. The conversion process will take place as in the case of bonds. It is a combination of bond and share capital. **Cumulative convertible preference shares** were introduced in 1984. It failed to attract the interest of the investors, due to the lower rate of interest, and the conversion period is very long. This kind of shares gives a regular return of 10 per cent . According to provisions, these shares must be issue for the purpose of **"new projects, expansion, diversification, modernisation and working capital requirements**. These shares can be converted during gestation period such as **three to five years**.

3. Debentures

Debentures are one of the sources for raising of finance. These are generally issued by the private sector companies. It is a long-term promissory note for raising loan capital. The debenture holders are entitled to get interest on the part of their investment. The company assures to pay interest and principal at a specified period of time. The rate of interest will be fixed at the time of issue. The payment of interest is mandatory. Interest is also known as **"coupon rate"**. Interest may be paid annually, half yearly, or quarterly. The principal amount of debenture will be refunded after 5 years or 10 years. Generally the companies will redeem the fund through a creation of sinking fund. Creation of the sinking fund eliminates the risk of financial difficulties. The debentures are classified on the basis of security and convertibility:

(a) Secured and unsecured debentures
(b) Convertible and non-convertible debentures

Secured debenture means the company will give security for the amount provided by the investors. These debt instruments are secured by a lien on the company's specified assets. They have a charge on the present and immovable assets of the company.

Un-secured debentures are not protected by any security. They are also known as naked debentures. These securities find as difficult to attract the investor because of the risk involved in them. Debentures are rated by the credit rating agencies. Credit rating indicates about the financial quality of a financial asset. Rating creates an idea in the minds of investor about parking place of an idle fund.

Convertible debentures are converted into equity shares after a specified period of time. The conversion process will be done according to the guidelines of the **SEBI**. The convertible debentures can be classified into two kinds **i.e., fully and partly convertible debentures**. Fully convertible debentures are converted into equity shares after a specific period. The entire amount will be converted into shares. Usually these instruments carry a lower rate of interest. Because they will be converted into share in the near future. **Partly convertible** means, some amount of debenture will be converted into equity and remaining amount may be kept in the form of **debenture**. Hence it is a combination of debenture and equity.

Non-convertible debentures are not converted into equity shares. The amount will be refundable after a stipulated period of time. They do not have any right to get shares from the company.

4. Bonds

Bonds are more popular financial products in western countries. In India, they are not attracted by the investors. Bond is a long-term debt instrument. It assures to pay a fixed amount of interest for a specified period of time. Bonds are traded in the stock market just like equity shares. They have face value. They may be issued at par or at a discount.

The interest amount will be paid either annually or half yearly. The interest rate is known as coupon rate. The date of the maturity of the bond is known by the investor. at the time buying the asset. Bonds can be classified into **"secured and un-secured, perpetual and redeemable, deep discount bonds, capital indexed bonds, zero coupon bonds, fixed interest rate and floating interest rate bonds**. Secured bonds are secured by the assets of the issuing company. Un-secured bonds are not assured. They do not get any financial guarantee in the event of insolvency. These bondholders will put their investment on the image of the company. Perpetual bonds never mature. They will never get their investment from the issuing company. The amount of interest will be paid as per the agreed terms. Redeemable bonds are redeemed after a specific period of time. Deep discount bond is one of the kinds of bonds. These bonds are sold to the public at large discount on their nominal value. These bonds are issued on long-term basis say for 25 years. In India the most popular bonds were **"IDBI and ICICI"**. These bonds are more useful for youth. Because the amount invested in these bonds will be refunded only after a long period of time, which is useful for their children's education or marriage purposes. Early redemption is also possible in this kind of bonds. The rural people will like to invest in these kind of assets. Capital indexed bonds are issued on the basis of inflation. The principal amount is adjusted for inflation for every year. In this type of asset, the investor gains the benefit as per **Wholesale Price Index** movements. Inflation will be taken into consideration. The minimum holding period of the instrument is **five years**. These bonds are traded in secondary market. Early exit from these instrument can approach the secondary market. The index rate will be announced by the RBI at regular interval period. **Zero coupon bonds** are sold to the investors at a discount. The face value of the bond will be refunded at the time of maturity. **For example:** A zero coupon bond with 20 years maturity period is available for **Rs. 5185**. The face value of the bond Rs. 50,000 will be repaid at the maturity period. It gives a return of **12 per cent** per annum to the investor. These bonds are more popular in U.S.A. These bond holders will not get any interest from the issuing company. The maturity amount will be adjusted to protect the interest of the investor. These bonds are more useful to the companies because they need not to pay the interest every year during the execution of period of the projects. Fixed interest rate bond indicates a fixed interest rate at the time of the issue of **Floating interest rate bonds**. The interest rates change according to the prefixed norms.

Investment Principles

Investment activities lead the growth of industrial sector. Every country should encourage the sincere and honest investors. Hence the investors want their investments to be more safe and they expect to grow with an increased rate of growth. **Growth** is the most important factor in economy. Growth leads and dictates the life stands of a common man. For increasing standard living of a common, there must be **financial discipline** in the community and in country. Money is a fluid asset. It should be utilised properly to get desired results. The financial discipline is a weapon to counter the poverty. A strict discipline can create a better environment for achieving the destination. The dynamics of economic growth provide various opportunities for investors. For selecting right investment, the investors must follow the principles of investment to reach their financial destination. Before going to make investment decisions they will need to have their own ideas regarding expected return and risk. The investment principles represented below for a successful selection of investment:

(a) Protection
(b) Profit
(c) Liquidity
(d) Income tax
(e) Inflation
(f) Regulations
(g) Tangibility
(h) Transferability

Protection is the most important factor in making investment decisions. Every investor usually needs safety about his invested amount. Adequate protection should exist against the risk of loss. The investor should keep in mind that the safe investment provides a lower rate of return. The investor can protect his investments by diversifying his portfolio. Diversification may reduce the risk of loss of capital. Sometimes it may be reversed. Hence the investor should be more cautious in diversification process.

Profit is the main reason for making investment decisions. Profit is the oxygen to the investors and business concerns. The entire globe is rotating for capturing profit. The investor invest his idle funds for earning a profit. Profit can be realised in the form of **capital appreciation and yield**. Capital appreciation is the difference between purchase and sale price of a financial asset. **Yield** means the earning capacity of a financial asset. Yield is derived from an investment. It is derived in the form of interest or dividend. **Yield** is a reward to investor. The rate of interest is fixed in advance and the rate of dividend may fluctuate from year to year. The dividend depends upon the earning capacity of the company.

Liquidity plays a dominant role in selection of better financial asset. Liquidity means the sale of financial asset arises as per the investor's convenience conversion of the financial asset into cash is known as **liquidity**. Investor always thinks about his investment's liquidity. He thinks about the encashment of his investment whenever the need arises. It also provides the way to sell of an unremunerative investments.

Income tax is one of the factors for making investment decisions. Generally the potential investors will be in tax bracket. Therefore they should make savings in the form of **LIC policies, Provident Fund, National Savings Certificates, Tax Saving Bonds such as IDBI and ICICI, Post Office Savings, Kisan Vikas Patra, Mutual Funds, Medical Insurance, etc.** Important taxation provisions and tax planning possibilities are to be kept in mind while planning an investment strategy.

Inflation means rising of prices. The decline of value in rupees. The investor will lose the real value of money on his invested amount, because every year the purchasing power of rupee declines. So the investor capital is eroded every year to the extent of the rate of inflation.

Regulations in India are strictly implemented by the Government. There are so many rules and regulations controls the activities of the investors. **For example: Gold Control Act, Foreign Exchange Management Act, Income Tax Act, Urban Land Ceiling Act, Companies Act, Contract Act, etc.**

Tangible assets do not yield much returns. But some investors prefer these assets because intangible assets may have lost their value due to price level changes, regulations of law or disturbance in normal peace.

Transferability of financial asset from one person to another is possible in some situations. Among the various financial instruments **equity shares** are more easily transferable in the stock market. Units of the mutual funds have been locked in period of 3 years. National saving certificates are not transferable. Tax saving bonds such as IDBI, ICICI. Infrastructure bonds are also having three year locked in period. Trading of preference shares in India is very negligible in the stock market. Deep discount bonds, and other long-term instruments are not transferable.

Sources of Investment Information

Information is the most important factor in gaining knowledge. Knowledge occupies a dominant role in making of investment decisions. Knowledge based decisions never fails in achieving the goal. Knowledge enhances the skills of a person. The investors should have some basic knowledge about the market in present changed scenario. He must be update about the affairs of the economy. He should know fundamental analysis of the companies. He must know some financial parameters such as **EPS, PE ratio, EBIT, PBT, BEP, Ratio Analysis, etc**. In stock market information about the corporate world plays an important role in making decisions. Investors should react to the tune of present market environment. The investors who have more information can get more benefits from the market. Acquiring knowledge means capturing of the market. An intelligent investor, with higher knowledge gets profit definitely from the market. Following are the best sources of information for acquiring knowledge about the economy:

(a) Global Affairs
(b) National Economic Affairs
(c) Trade Associations
(d) Corporate Information
(e) Financial Periodicals and Journals
(f) Share Price Quotations
(g) Satellite Channels

Global affairs are more useful for assessment of international prices at world markets. A rise in New York stock exchange prices may lead to rise in Bombay stock exchange prices. The rise and fall of oil prices in global markets may influence the financial markets. A rise in gold prices at world markets may leads to a rise in gold prices in India. Therefore, the national markets are reacting to the tune of movements of the world markets. A thorough understanding of all these affairs makes more perfect the investor in predicting the future prices in the domestic market. Sometimes the domestic market may not react pro-actively to the global affairs. Day-to-day developments around globe are published in newspapers and magazines. World information is available in **New York Times, Washington Post, Wall Street Journal, The Economist, Economic Surveys, IMF News Letters, Times Magazine, London Economist far East Economic Review.**

National affairs are useful for predicting the future prices in the domestic market. A thorough understanding of all economic affairs of the nation must be known by the right investor. Simply handing over of a cheque does not mean an investment. The return in the stock market is the barometer for his knowledge and skills of the investor. A combination of money and mind power definitely will get success in the market. The national economic affairs are covered by all the leading financial newspapers and journals such as **"The Economic Times, The Business Standard, Financial Express, Business Line and Journals, Dalal Street, Vikalpa, Intelligent Investor, Capital Market, Business India, Business World, Business Today, Vikalpa Economic and Political Weekly, Finance India, Arthastra, Management Accountant, Money and Indian Management, RBI Bulletins, Fortune India, The Week, India Today.**

Trade associations are known as "Chamber of Commerce, Federation of Indian Confederation of Industries, Bullion Traders Association, Confederation of Indian Industry". They provide first hand information about their activities. Almost many daily newspapers provide regularly the result of studies made on working of industries. The monthly reports of various governing bodies give more upto date information very promptly.

Corporate information is easily available in almost all the newspapers, periodicals and journals. They provide some pages especially for the coverage of day-to-day events occurring in the corporate sector. The media will cover about the performance of various companies, their working results, quarterly results, annual results, conducting of board and shareholders meetings and other needful data. The financial journalists write ups on various companies after interviewing the key executive of the corporate sector. The Bombay stock exchange, National stock exchange and over the counter exchange provide full information about the listed companies in the **"websites".** The media carry out the company analysis and they provide suggestions about the enter and exist of the stock market. They provide hints, rumours, gossips and tactics of the stock markets. Bombay stock exchange publishes directory which contains full information about the trading activities of the stock markets. **Centre for Monitoring Indian Economy** also publishes all the factors about the performance and evaluation of the corporate sector. **National Council of Applied Economic Research** provides a valuable information about the important factors such as **Gross Domestic Product, Net Domestic Product, Purchasing Power, National Income, Consumer**

Behaviour, Per Capita Income and other Valuable Data. Kothari's Economic and Industry provides an insight information about many industrial group and companies. Every year **The Hindu** publishes a yearly supplement edition entitled as **"Survey of Indian Industry"**. It provides a thorough analysis of the various sectors of the Indian economy.

Financial Periodicals and Journals are providing excellent information about the stock markets. They provide information about the fundamental analysis of the companies and suggest for entering and exit from the stock market. The big broker firms are sending newsletters on market information with technical analysis aspects. Almost all broker firms will appoint equity research analysts and research studies are carried out by a team of specialists and experts. **Experts'** advices are necessary for the perspecting investors. Investment should be made on scientific analysis and not on the basis of rumours and gossips. **The Economic Times** established a department of equity research bureau for carrying out of various research aspects relating to stock markets. **Prime Database Management,** a Delhi based organisation provides full information about the primary market operations. The Indian Institute of Finance publishes a journal called as **"Finance India"**. The Institute of Chartered Financial Analyst of India publishes a monthly journal called as **"Chartered Financial Analyst"**. The SEBI also publishes its reports about market activities. Mutual funds also prepares research reports with the help of the fund managers.

Share price quotations are available in almost every daily newspapers of different languages. **Sensex and Nifty** quotions are more popular in India. Capital Market, Dalal Street, Intelligent Investors, Economic Times give company information regarding all financial barometers like "Gross Profit, Net Profit, PBT, EBIT, EPS and PE ratio. The information technology provide all the information regarding financial data at the click of mouse.

Satellite channels are providing excellent information about the corporate affairs on day-to-day basis. Almost all national and regional channels are covering business briefs after the news bulletin. They also telecast the interviews of well-known experts, professional analysts, fund managers, stock analysts and portfolio managers. Some channels like **"CNBC, CNN, Jain TV, Zee News, NDTV, Headlines Today, Star News"**, devote more time for corporate news on global and national basis. **CNBC** provides excellent information and valuable suggestions in all aspects of the business affairs. It provides the information 24 hours on business aspects only.

SECURITY MARKET

Security Market is a combination of trading place of different financial instruments or financial assets. According to the **Securities Contract Regulation Act, 1956** securities includes **"shares, scrips, stocks, bonds, debentures** or other marketable like securities of any incorporated company or other body corporate or government. Security market is broadly known as **"Financial market"**. Financial market is a market, where the financial instruments are traded at a geographic place. The nations' fund requirement is fulfilled by the financial markets. Financial markets can be/classified as **Money market and Capital market**. **Money market** is associated with short-term nature of funds. **Capital market** is known for long-term nature of funds. In financial markets, the funds are available with the savers and there will be demand for funds requirement. In the financial markets, the borrowers are looking for the fund suppliers. It is a place where the suppliers of the fund and borrowers meet in a fixed period of time. Generally the fund suppliers in the market are Individual Investors. Corporates, Firms with large amount of surplus available are investigating about their parking place of their surplus fund. Borrowers are required to refund their debt after a stipulated period of time. In the financial market **reputation** is the most important factor in mobilisation of funds. The quantum of heavy fund is available with the market only for highly reputed, goodwill and financially sound companies. Financial markets are the nerve centres of the economy. The economic development of a nation depends upon the capabilities of financial market. They provide convenience and benefits to the lender and borrowers. The security market can be classified as follows:

(a) Primary Market
(b) Secondary Market

(a) Primary Market

Primary market is also known as **"New Issue Market"**. It is called as **"Initial Public Offer"**. Primary market is most useful to the newly established and existing business concerns. Primary market in India has a vast business potential and can provide higher amount of funds to the reputed business organisations. The household savings will occupy a dominant role in the primary market. Mutual funds, Non-Banking

Financial Companies, Individual Investors, Institutional Investors, Trusts will park their idle funds in primary market. Usually the corporate sector, raise funds to finance their projects through various methods. Primary market is one of the best sources of finance. The promoters can bring their own money in addition to the public issues. In primary market, fund may be raised by issue of shares, preference, debentures, bonds, and global receipts. The primary market is a financial **"Reservoir"**. It provides funds to the needy borrowers throughout the years. The newly established companies approach the primary market. Hence it may be known as **Initial Public Offer**. The main objectives of a capital issues are presented below:

(a) to expansion purpose
(b) for diversification
(c) to meet the working capital requirement
(d) as a seed capital to the newly established companies
(e) to capitalise the reserves and surplus

Relationship between Primary and Secondary Market

The primary market is a dynamic market. It provides funds at any time to the fund raisers. It channelise the funds both for newly established or existing company. All kinds of companies may approach the market. It undertakes the responsibility of selling the stocks to the public. The relation between primary and secondary market is presented below:

(i) There is a strong relation between the two markets. They are interdependent. The primary market cannot function without the secondary market. If the secondary market is more active, there will be higher demand for primary market. The primary market provides funds and the secondary market creates liquidity.
(ii) The primary market provides an indirect link between the savers and the corporate sector. The secondary market creates liquidity and marketability.
(iii) The secondary market controls the primary market through listing of securities. All issues made in primary market shall approach the secondary for listing of securities with the stock exchange. stock exchanges provide oxygen to the primary market. If the secondary market is inactive, therefore there is no buyer in the primary.

Difference between New Issue and Secondary Market

(a) The NIM provides funds directly to the corporate sector but secondary market does not flow any additional fund to the companies.
(b) The NIM deals with fresh equity and secondary market deals with old shares.
(c) The NIM does not have a physical geographical location but the secondary market have excellent physical infrastructure.
(d) The NIM provides a particular scrip during subscription period but the secondary market provide the scrip to the investors at any time.

Features of the NIM

The salient features of the primary market are presented below:

(i) Any company can approach the market for raising funds from the public.
(ii) The premium or discount may be fixed by issuing company, subject to the approval of SEBI.
(iii) Issuing companies need not to approach the financial institutions and for raising of loans.

Classification of New Issues

Primary market facilitates transfer of funds from the saver to the borrower. It can be classified as follows:

(a) First issue of newly established companies (promoters without a track record).
(b) First issue of new companies (set up by existing companies with a track record).
(c) First issue by existing private/closely held company (less than 3 years track record).
(d) First issue by existing private/closely held company (with 3 years track record).
(e) First issue by existing private/closely/existing/unlisted without 3 years track record but promoted by existing companies with 5 years track record.
(f) Existing/private/closely held and other unlisted companies without three years track record of consistent profitability seeking disinvestment by offer to public without issuing fresh capital.

(g) Public issue by existing listed companies.
(h) Existing private closely held or other existing unlisted company with 3 years track record of consistent profitability seeking disinvestment by offer to public without issuing fresh capital.

Functions of New Issue Market

New issue market provide a parking place to the investors for their idle fund. It facilitates the transfer of resources from savers to entrepreneurs. The functions of NIM can be categorised into three ways in view of its operations:

(a) Investigation
(b) Underwriting
(c) Distribution

Generally every company thinks about the low cost of financial resources. At present all companies introduced cost control activities. Therefore every company needs resources for their business expansion or diversification. The requirement of their financial needs must be fulfilled by the cheap sources of finance. Financial cost is an indirect element to the cost of production of the goods. Hence the issuing companies make **investigation** about the financial resources, which are available at lower rate of fund cost. In financial markets, different alternatives are available to the needy companies. The needy companies assign this task to the specialised agencies. The preliminary study will be done by the specialised agencies in terms of **technical, economic, financial and legal** aspects of the issuing company. The specialised agency provide suggestions for improving the quality of capital issues. **Equity** is the best and cheap resources of finance to the corporate world. Therefore the corporate world looks towards primary market. The specialised agency will determine the class of security and price of the issue in the light of changing market conditions. They provide advice regarding timing and magnitude of issues. They will provide best advices regarding **method of flotation and techniques of selling** etc.

Underwriting is one of the functions of NIM. The issuing company will get all the information from specialised agency for raising of equity. After receipt of the information and advices from the agency, the issuing company may decide to go for public issue. It will take all precautions about the uncertainties, which will arise in the market. Therefore the issuing company can eliminate the uncertainties by making an agreement with the underwriters. **Underwriting** is a guarantee about the success of an public issue. The underwriter will assure the issuing company about success of public issue.

Distribution is another important function of new issue market. The success of a public issue depends upon a wide distribution of share application forms to the potential investors. Primary market has unlimited geographic area of operation. Public issue is just like a social event such as performing a **"Marriage"**. It is the combination of different services of agencies. The distribution of application forms will undertaken by brokers. Brokers are most important intermediaries in mobilisation of resources from the market. Brokers are specialised persons in dealing securities and debentures. They maintain regular contacts with the potential investors. The investors are the regular customers. They know about the investment habits and attitudes of their investors. They can influence the investments decisions of the investors. They guide, direct and motivate their clients.

Public Issue Process

Public issue is the most important factor in mobilisation of huge resources from the market. A wide publicity should be done to reach the message of public issue to the general public. The success of an issue depends upon the issue process implementation. In India the issue of shares can be made by any one of the following sources:

(a) Public Issue through Prospectus
(b) Book-building Method
(c) Private Placement
(d) Offer for Sale
(e) Right Issue

(a) Public Issue through Prospectus

Public issue is one of the best sources of raising finance from the market. It is more popular in India. Initial public offer is also known as public issue. Usually all the needy companies can approach the market. In this method, the issuing company invite the public by issue of **"prospectus"**. Prospectus is a document which contains all the particulars about the issuing company. The prospectus is a document, which coordinate the relation between public and issuing company. It is an evidence document to the investors. It indicates the future plan and past performance of the company. The investors will make an investment decisions on the basis of the facts shown in the prospectus. The public issues are generally underwritten to avoid uncertainties in the market. The content of particulars should be correct and no false information allowed by the SEBI. Therefore, the issuing company should take more proper cautions because any false information may attract the civil and criminal liability under the provisions of the Companies Act. The prospectus shall contain the following information:

1. Company name and its registered office address.
2. Present activities and future plans.
3. Location of Industry
4. Date of opening and closing of subscription list.
5. Full information about authorised capital, subscribed and present issue of share capital to public.
6. Name and addresses of all intermediaries involved in issue.
7. Name and address of underwriters along with directors opinion.
8. All information regarding listing arrangements with stock exchange.
9. Minimum amount of subscription.
10. Other legal information about the company.

According to the provisions of Companies Act, 1985, application forms for shares of a company should be accompanied by abridged prospectus. The draft prospectus has to be sent to the **Regional stock exchange** and other stock exchanges where the shares are proposed to be listed. After the receipt of the draft prospectus, the stock exchange **scrutinises** the draft prospectus. After scrutiny of the prospectus, if there is any clarification raised by the stock exchange, the issuing company should respond to the query.

The public issue method has some advantages and disadvantages. The success of the issue will depend upon the wide **publicity**. The shares are allotted to a wide range of the investors either through lottery system or prorata basis. It diffuses the share ownership to a widely scattered investors and prevent the concentration of wealth and economic power. It is a highly expensive method. The cost of flotation involves much expenditure. It is suitable only to large companies for **mega** issue. It is not found suitable to small issues for even large companies. It is a time consuming process. But it provides equal opportunities to all investors irrespective of poor and rich. The **Linking of Rivers, Commercialisation**

of Agriculture, Wasteland development, Power generation, exploration of minerals and natural resources, etc. Projects could be taken with the help of public issues as sources of raising finance. All these activities could be undertaken with private and public sector participation **via public issues.** Mega projects have been financed through public issues.

(b) Book-building Method

Book-building process is another kind of raising of source of finance. It is more popular in United States. In this method, the price of share is determined by the different kinds of investors in the market. The potential investors have an opportunity to place orders at different prices. The price of the issuing company share is quoted by the perspective investors. The issuing company will prepare **"offer document"**. The offer document contains full information about the issuing proposals. The offer document contains the **"Reserve"** or minimum price. This method is not widely accepted in India. It was introduced in the capital market in **October, 1995**. The **Malegaon Committee** made recommendations for the introduction of this method. According to the SEBI guidelines, any company can sell the equity irrespective of size of issue to a group of investors or a syndicate. The investors consortium or syndicate may be created by the lead managers of the issue. **Nirma Company** is the first company in India to adopt this kind of process. In this method, the book runner plays an important role in raising of sources of finance. Book runner is appointed by the issuing company. He is selected from syndicate members of the issue or from lead managers. The book runner name will be indicated in the draft prospectus. The draft copy of the prospectus should be submitted to the **SEBI** for its approval. The issue price will be finalised by book runner in consultation with the issuing company. Underwriting arrangement will be made by the book runner after the fixation of share price. The **SEBI** has full authority to monitor and control the activities of the issuing company. The book runner collects the application forms from the institutional buyers and the underwriters.

(c) Private Placement

Private placement is one of the method of issue of capital. The shares are offered privately to the investors or to the issue houses or to the financial institutions or to the corporate bodies or to **high net worth** individuals. The financial intermediaries purchase the shares and sell them to investors at a later time at a suitable price. Private placement avoids the **underwriting** process. In this method equity shares, preference shares, cumulative convertible preference shares, debentures and bonds are sold. This method reduces flotation expenses. It saves **8 to 10 per cent** of the issue cost. Public issue will take usually **6 months** but the private placement process completes in mostly **2 to 3 months**. Unit Trust, mutual funds, insurance companies, merchant bankers, commercial banks, financial institutions actively participating in private placement. This method provide flexibility to the issuing company and buying parties. It is very popular in abroad. It increased rapidly after 1996, when the primary market was in a state of depression. The public sector has become a major user of private placements.

(d) Offer for Sale

Offer for sale means, the promoter places his shares to the financial intermediaries such as Merchant bankers, investment bankers, firms, stock brokers and issue houses. It is also known as **"bought out deals"**. The intermediaries are called as **sponsor or bought out dealer**. In this method, the promotion off loads, a part of the share capital to a wholesaler. The wholesaler in turn will sell the shares to the retail investors. The sponsor will hold the shares with him for 70 days or more than one year. Pricing of issue is the crucial factor in this process. The sponsor before buying the shares from the issuing company, must take into consideration of the factor such as **financial viability, gestation period, promoters background, and future projections**. This method saves the time and cost of flotation expenses. It possess low risk. The main disadvantage in this process is **Insider trading** and **price rigging**.

(e) Rights Issue

Rights issues are offered to the existing shareholders of issuing company. If a public company wants to increase its subscribed capital, it must offer shares to the existing shareholders. The Companies Act **Section 81** reveals that a company shall issue right shares in the following situations:

(a) The company can issue rights offer after **2** years of its formation.
(b) After one year of first issue of shares.

The rights offer will be made to existing shareholders only by a circular. The company must get special resolution from the shareholders meeting. In this method general investing public has no opportunity to participate in it. It avoids underwriting. It is an economical exercise for issuing companies.

Factors Influencing for Investing in NIM

Primary market provides funds to the corporate sector. It also create an equal opportunity to invest in well-known and good reputed companies. Even a common man can contribute his small savings to a blue chip company. Therefore, it provide better opportunities to the investors irrespective of rich or poor or urban or rural or literate or illiterate. It is the place where fund suppliers and borrowers meet at a fixed time. It is regulated by the SEBI. The issuing company can fix its premium. The SEBI issued guidelines to the corporate sector for raising of funds from the market. The guidelines reveal that the issuer companies shall disclose full information to the investors. The guidelines provide protection to the investors. The investors in stock market shall behave more cautiously. They are responsible for their unscientific decisions which are taken by them with the lack of awareness. In the stock market, the movement of investors is the most important factor and they should acquire some knowledge about the economy, government policies, sectoral analysis, financial parameters and a foresight. Knowledge and gathering of information is the key factors to get success in the stock market. The SEBI framed guidelines to educate the investors about important documents such as **Memorandum of Association** and prospectus. The memorandum of association shall contain all the information of prospectus accompanying application forms. If any information is required by the investors, he may contact the **Company or Merchant banker**. Merchant bankers are the important person in getting success of public issue. Hence the investor shall examine the following factors before going to take investment decision:

(a) Promoters reputation
(b) Objectives of the present issue
(c) Details about project
(d) Market observation
(e) Financial data
(f) Forecasting
(g) Pricing of issue
(h) Disputes
(i) Risk element
(j) Auditor's report

(k) Information about defaults
(l) Fulfillment of formalities
(m) Careful observation
(n) Problems of NIM
(o) Regulatory aspects

(a) Promoters Reputation

Promoter is the most important person to build good reputed organisation. He plays an active role in management affairs of the company. A good reputed company can only get success in the primary market. Primary market scattered throughout the nation, only reputed names of the companies will be known by the investors. The success of the primary market will reflect in the form of number of times over subscribed to the issue. The investors should look into the proper disclosures on all the aspects of promoters involvement in the proposed project. The background of the promoter, his qualification, technical experience, past experience in the industry, business skills, tactics, and their reputation in the market. Past performance is the barometer for future programmes. The investors should collect the information about the promoters work culture attitudes, philosophy and morality. Financial magazines, business journals and media reports enhances the skills and knowledge of the investors. The profitability of the company depends upon the abilities of the board of directors. Introduction of professional management will definitely enhances the growth of a company and will become competent in the market.

(b) Objectives of the Present Issue

The prospectus shall reveal about the needs and purpose of the present issue. The investor shall verify the content of the prospectus. The objectives of the present issue of capital is more important before making investment in that company.

(c) Details about the Project Information

The prospectus contains the information about the proposed or existing project. It is more useful to the investors in evaluating their investment decisions. The prospectus should contain the information such as **Tax holiday benefits, supply of electricity, cost of land, locational advantage of the plant availability of infrastructure facilities, raw material, sources of funding agencies, appraisal methods and agencies etc.**

(d) Market Observation

The investor should know about the brand names of products manufactured by issuing company. **Brand** name reveals the company's earning capabilities. A well established brand assures the guarantee of sales. Sales generate accumulation of profits. Profit is the highly influencing factor in making investment decisions by the investors. The investor should know about the technology adopted by the issuing company. **Technology** is the most important factor in evaluating a business concern. The **latest and sophisticated** technology can reduce the cost of production significantly. Hence it may lead to get higher profits. But the introduction of modern technology may involve with higher amount of capital expenditure. The investor shall observe about the export potential of the product. He should assess the market competition, which is faced by the issuing company. **Competition** in the market may bring pressure on the margins. Competition in the market has some advantages and disadvantages to the corporate world. Competition stimulates the efficiency and capabilities of the corporate sector. In the competitive market, the market leader always enjoys the hefty amount of profits. **The market leader** creates brand loyalty among the customers. Brand loyalty is the highly influencing factor in survival of the company in the intensified competitive environment. The retention of brand loyalty depends upon the customer satisfaction of the product. **Customer satisfaction** is influenced by various factors such as quality, price, features, availability and others. Innovation and creativity is the most important elements in determining the buying habits of the customers. A continuous research on customer satisfaction can reveal their needs and desires. Hence the corporate sector shall make goods to suit the needs and convenient to the customers.

(e) Financial Data

A collection of financial data is necessary before making investment decisions by the investors. The financial data reveals the information about the feasibility of the project. The data reflects the future trend of the company. Past performance is the barometer for the future achievements. The data relating to share capital, reserves, surplus, undistributed profits, sales turnover, distribution of dividend, earning per share, price earning ratio, book value of share, profit before tax, earnings before depreciation, interest and tax, profit after tax, depreciation policy, leverage position, capital structure and other information may help the investor in evaluating the company performance.

(f) Forecasting

Guessing is another important factor in evaluation of a company's future prospects. The guess work about the company activities will influence the investor's decision. The past performance is the indicator of the future prospect.

(g) Pricing of Issues

The issuing company can fix the price of shares either at premium or discount. SEBI has the authority to regulate the primary market activities. The rate of premium or discount must be accepted by the SEBI. The demand and supply of the factors may influence the fixing of premium or discount. A good track record and professional management skills of the company leads to fix hefty amount of premium. The premium must be reasonable with reference to the past performance. A financially healthy company may also command a higher premium amount of the issue. A strong reserves and surplus base may stipulate the issue price.

(h) Disputes

Dispute is a conflict between two parties or two persons. Generally, in business, there is no scope for arising dispute between two parties. Any violation of agreement may leads to arise disputes. Any dispute with another company shall be indicated in the prospectus. The disputes in business may not settle immediately. The disputes will be referred to the court. The pending litigations may likely result for arising of losses or winding up of the company.

(i) Risk Element

The risk is an important factor in the evaluation of a company. Risk means, a future chance of arising loss. Every business concern faces risk. The loss to the business concern may arise in various kinds. Hence the investor must observe the risk component of the issuing company. If the investor is willing to accept high risk, he may get higher return. If he is willing to accept low risk and he may get return. **Return** is reward to the investors. Risk is inseparable. It can be avoided only with outstanding talent and skills. Return is always chased by **Risk element**. The quantum of return to the investor is determined by the level of accepted risk. An intelligent businessman always think about escape of loss and capturing of the profit. The prospectus shall contain the risk factors involved by the issuing company. Reducing risk level and increasing the returns level is the basic intention of any business concern.

(j) Auditor's Report

Every company shall be audited by a chartered accountant. Chartered accountant is an expert relating to verification of financial transactions or accounting system of the issuing company. The statutory auditor of the company will submit an audit report to the shareholders at Annual General Meeting. Auditor's report is one of the sources of information to know about the financial aspects of the issuing company. The highlights of the auditor's report shall contain the offer document. Auditor's remarks should be incorporated in **"offer document"**. The audited figures are the legal evidence of the financial affairs of a company.

(k) Information about Defaults

If any default made by the issuing company, it shall indicate in the offer document. Bank dues and institutions default are known as **"statutory dues"**. The offer document shall also indicate about payment of interest to debenture holders. The SEBI has the authority to take action against issuing company for payment of statutory dues. Hence the investors must be aware about the **financial discipline**. Financial discipline is the most important element in the explosive growth of a business concern. The mobilisation of funds depends upon the financial morality of the company. A prompt repayment of principal and regular interest can boost the confidence and credibility of the investor. **Mega** issues are getting success with the credibility of the business concern. Any default made by the issuing company can make harmful to the public issue. The investors will lose confidence about the issuing company's credibility.

(l) Fulfilment of Formalities

The offer document shall contain about the completion of all legal formalities with the regulating authorities. The position of getting legal formalities should explain in the offer document. The current status of clearances should be indicated to the public. In India there may be a number of legal clearances shall be obtained to commence a project. The issuing company shall have to get clearances from the Central Government and State Government. Any delay in getting of the clearances may badly affect the company's future.

(m) Careful Observations

Finally the investor should come to a conclusion that whether he may invest or not to invest in the particular issue, after reading of the offer document. Offer document is the basis for investment decisions. **Investment** means not simply handover a cheque to the broker, but they should know about the safety of the parking place of their funds. Every shareholders or investors want to make good investment.

(n) Problems of New Issue Market

New issue market in India faces some problems which needs a radical reforms in the market. It plays an important role in capital formation of the nation. It stimulates the growth of **Gross Domestic Product**. An increase of GDP, can boost the national income. The standard of living may be changed. The development of the economy of a nation depends upon the **financial architecture** of the digital economy. India is a country, where the large number of potential individual investors having the much savings at their disposal could not turned up towards the primary market. Hence the NIM is unable to attract the investments from the potential investors due to a wide range of problems in the market. The NIM suffers from functional and institutional gaps particularly in terms of the new financial instruments to appeal the investing community. Merchant bankers play a vital role in the NIM. The success of the issue will be a crucial factor for survival of merchant banking system in India. The **time** factor also disappoint the investor due to a lengthy process and consumption of much time for completion of issue process. The **SEBI** shall take a strong steps to reduce the time gap in completion of issue process. **New issues** should be available to the investors **"on online"** as in the secondary market. The issuing companies shall seek permission in advance period of time and make a chronological order for opening of subscriptions in the market. Another important problem is duping of the investors by establishing fictitious companies and disappearing from the market. Hence SEBI must verify the physical verification of the issuing company's premises and their factories. Another important problem is high flotation cost involved in public issue. It requires an elaborate arrangements throughout the nation. In the public issue, the involvement of many players such as **merchant bankers, underwriters, share brokers, lead managers, registrars, share transfer agents, bankers and publicity agencies** are necessary to make a big success. It requires a physic strain to the small companies. Hence the public issue is not useful to small organisations but useful to mega issues the public issue is a higher expensive affair to the small investors. Because the semi-urban and rural investor has to send the application forms to the collecting centres. Hence the investor has to spend in obtaining a demand draft, postal charges for sending and suffer loss of interest.

(o) Regulatory Framework

The public issues in India require fulfilment of many legal formalities such as Companies Act, Securities Contract Act and SEBI. All the provisions of the acts should be followed by issuing companies:

(a) Companies Act
(b) Securities Contract Act
(c) SEBI

(a) Companies Act

The Companies Act stipulates some rules and regulations regarding issue of shares. The shares are offered to the investors in many kinds. Public issue is one of the sources of raising finance. The issuing company shall have to fulfil some formalities regarding the raising of share capital:

1. Issue of shares
2. Issue of share certificate
3. Buyback

1. Issue of Shares

Public Limited Companies are permitted to raise finance from the market by issue of shares. Every company established in India is required to submit three important documents such as **Memorandum of Association, Articles of Association and Prospectus. Memorandum of Association** contains full information about the company. It states the authorised capital which can be raised at any time according to the needs of the company. The capital clause of the document contains such as **Issued**

capital, paid up capital particulars for raising of finance. The share capital may be refunded by only winding up the company. A share is treated as a movable property and transferable. A company can issue two types of shares such as **equity and preference**. Equity shares are the permanent capital of the company. Equity is the cheapest sources of finance. Preference shares carry a preferential right to fixed dividend and refundable of share capital at winding up of the company. The authorised share capital can be altered by the company according to its convenient. The **capital structure** of the company can be altered with the acceptance of shareholders to meet the needs and convenience of the organisation. The company has the right to issue shares to the public at par, at premium or at discount. The premium amount collected by the Company should be utilised for the purpose of writing of flotation expenses, and preliminary expenses. It can also be used for bonus shares issue and for redemption of redeemable preference shares. The company law board should accept for issue of shares at discount.

2. Issue of Share Certificate

After the completion of issue process, every issuing company shall issue share certificates to the allotted shareholders. It is the basic evidence of the members. The shareholders can use this certificate as a proof of evidence for his ownership claim. The share certificate shall contain the stamp, issued under the common seal of the company. Share certificates should be delivered within **three months** after the allotment of shares and within two months after the application for registration of transfer.

3. Buyback of Shares

Public limited companies are not permitted for purchasing their own shares. After liberalisation, the government made efforts to repurchase of shares by the companies with the following conditions:

(i) Acceptance of Articles of Association.
(ii) A special resolution should be passed in general meeting.
(iii) Buyback process should be completed within a period of 12 months.
(iv) The buyback of shares do not exceed 25 per cent of the total paid up capital including free reserves.
(v) The process shall be completed in accordance with regulations of the SEBI.

(vi) The debt equity ratio does not exceed 2 : 1.

(vii) Shares can be purchased from the employees, open market and from odd lots.

Regulations in Right Issues

Right issue is one of the source of raising finance for the corporate sector. Right issue means, the shares are offered to the existing shareholders. The issue of rights must be made through the rules and regulations of the Companies Act. The Companies Act deals with the issue formalities to be fulfilled by the companies. The right issue may be offered in the following two situations, whichever is earlier:

(a) The company shall offer only after the expiry of two years from the incorporation of a company.

(b) A company shall issue the offer to the existing shareholders after expiry of one year from the first allotment of shares.

A notice shall be given by the company in advance period of time less than 15 days from date of the offer to accept. If there is no response from the existing shareholders, the company has the freedom to fix the future course of action.

Regulations Regarding Issue of Debentures

The board of directors has the powers for issue of debentures after taking the willingness from the shareholders. The shareholders must pass an ordinary resolution to the issue of debentures. Companies can issue different types of debentures such as **Redeemable, Mortgage, Convertible and Non-convertible debentures.** The debenture holders have the following rights which are disclosed in the prospectus:

(a) debentures are transferable;

(b) debentures are transmittable on par with the manner of equity shares;

(c) their rights and privileges can be modified with the consent of at least 3/4th of the amount outstanding or by a special resolution passed at the meeting of the debenture holders.

Regulations Framework in Allotment of Shares

The share allotment process is another important factor in raising of funds from the market. If the company is unable to get minimum subscription from the public, it should not be made allotment of shares, and the collected amount must be refunded. If the company fails to refund the amount within **130 days** after issue of the prospectus, it is liable to pay interest at the rate of **6 per cent** per annum. The company shall commence the allotment process after the completion of **5th day** from the day of the opening of subscription list. If a company violates this rule, it is liable to a fine up to **Rs. 5,000**. The issuing company shall get permission from the concerned stock exchange for making allotment of shares. If the company fails to get permission on expiry of **10 weeks** from the date of the closing of the subscription list. The company is required to refund the amount to the applicants. If refund is not made by the company within **8 days**, it will have to pay interest at 4 per cent and not more than **15 per cent**. The company shall file a return to the **Registrar of Companies** within **30 days** from the date of allotment.

(b) Securities Contract Act

Securities Contract Act provides broad regulations of the present scheme of the stock exchanges functioning in India. The objectives of the act mainly deal with the secondary market operations. The act stipulates rules and regulations regarding primary market operations. The **Sections 21-22A** deals with the process of listing a share with the recognised stock exchange. **Listing** means, an admission of a scrip to trade on stock exchange officially. The listing is not compulsory as per the provisions of the Companies Act, but the Securities Act, **Section 73** indicates, it is necessary. Listing creates ready marketability and liquidity to shareholders of the issuing company. SEBI has the authority to take any action if any one violates the law in listing of shares with the stock exchanges. The rights shares are also necessary to list with the stock exchanges as per the provisions of this act. If any violation is made by the Company, the stock exchange can suspend or withdraw admission to dealings in securities of a company. Delisting of a scrip can also be made by the stock exchange authorities, if the public shareholding falls below **50 per cent** of the public offer.

(c) Securities and Exchange Board of India (SEBI)

Securities and Exchange Board of India was established in April, 1988. It works under the control of Central Government. The activities are monitored by the Ministry of Finance. It regulates primary and secondary market operations. It is the mouth piece of the Central Government. It is the watchdog of the securities markets. The main objectives of the SEBI is **"to protect the investors, to develop the market"**. It has divided into various operational departments such as **primary market department and secondary market department**. Primary market department deals with the aspects of new issue markets. The primary market department involved in regulatory matters with regard to the financial intermediaries, and investor's grievances. It mainly concentrates as non-receipt of dividends, non-receipt of share certificates, non-refund of application money, non-refund of excess money. It also undertakes the scrutiny of offer document. It is empowered with the registration process of financial intermediaries cancellation or suspension of their registration. It has the power to ask additional information from the issuing company. The allotment process will be made in the presence of SEBI officials. Banks, financial institutions, who participate in private placement should regularly furnish the information to the SEBI and RBI.

Public Issue Process

Public issue is one of the important event in the life of a company. Equity is the best and cheapest sources of finance. Traditionally, all companies may go for public issues, whenever, they need finance. In the past, it was handled by the issuing company. But at present, it became very easy to go for public issue to the corporate sector. The services of financial intermediaries are available at the door step of the issuing company. Public issue involves a number of financial intermediaries such as **merchant bankers, lead managers, registrars, underwriters, share transfer agents, collection agents, advertising agencies, brokers, etc.** All of these intermediaries provide specialised, knowledge based work to the issuing company. The present changing scenario of the capital market and the issuing company shall assign all the duties as per the provisions of the Companies Act, and Securities Contract Act. The main agencies involved in the public issue are presented below:

(i) Merchant bankers
(ii) Lead managers
(iii) Underwriters
(iv) Bankers
(v) Brokers
(vi) Registrars

(vii) Debenture trustees
(viii) Portfolio managers

(i) Merchant Bankers

Merchant bankers play an important role in public issue. Public issue is like just a social function. It requires all the services of financial intermediaries. Merchant bankers are one of the intermediary involved in public issue. They work as sponsors of the issue. They render major service to the issuing company. They are involved in the issue, right from choosing best capital structure to get all clearances from the government. They also involved in public issues for appointment of underwriters, bankers, brokers, lead manager and advertising agencies. They must follow the guidelines of the SEBI in issue process.

(ii) Lead Managers

Lead manager is another important financial intermediary in the issue process. They have to be associated with the issuing company, till the despatch of share certificates or the refund of excess application money to the investors. The lead manager should make an agreement with the issuing company and should get approval from the SEBI. The lead managers should accept the minimum underwriting **5 per cent** of the issue or **Rs. 25.00 lakhs** whichever is less. If the lead manager is unable to underwrite the minimum amount, it should be assigned to the merchant banker with an intimation to the SEBI. The number of lead managers will be appointed according to its size of issue.

	Issue size	*No. of Lead Managers*
(a)	Less than Rs. 50 crores	02
(b)	Rs. 50 crores – Rs. 100 crores	03
(c)	Rs. 100 crores – Rs. 200 crores	04
(d)	Rs. 200 crores – Rs. 400 crores	05
(e)	Above Rs. 400 crores	05 and more

They are responsible for the verification. The contents of a prospectus or letters of offer are in respect of an public issue. After the verification of the document he has to submit a certificate to the SEBI at least **two weeks** before the opening of the issue. He has also report the issue information to the **Registrar of Companies** and **Regional stock exchange,** along with the prescribed fee specified below:

	Issue size (Including premium)	*Fee per document*
(a)	Up to Rs. 5 crores	Rs. 10,000
(b)	Rs. 5 crores – Rs. 10 crores	Rs. 15,000
(c)	Rs. 10 crores – Rs. 50 crores	Rs. 25,000
(d)	Rs. 50 crores – Rs. 100 crores	Rs. 50,000
(e)	Rs. 100 crores – Rs. 500 crores	Rs. 2,50,000
(f)	More than Rs. 500 crores	Rs. 5,00,000

The SEBI is the most powerful organisation to control the primary market activities through financial intermediaries. It has the power to **cancel or suspend** the registration of all the financial intermediaries, who are involved in public issue process.

(iii) Underwriters

Public issue involves a number of financial intermediaries. Underwriter is another important intermediary in the public issue process. They assure the guarantee for success of the public issue. It is just like insurance for public issues. They are appointed by the merchant bankers in consultation with the issuing company. The underwriter should get a certificate of registration from the SEBI. The underwriter should pay a fee to the SEBI of **Rs. 2,00,000** for the first and second years and **Rs. 1.00 lakh** for the 3rd year. A renewal fee should be paid Rs. 20,000 for every year, and it is raised to **Rs. 5,00,000**. The underwriter will take the responsibility of **Non-subscription** shares by the public. He will follow the professional code of conduct and abide by all the regulations. He has to maintain a high standard of integrity, dignity and fairness in his all dealings with his clients and fellow professionals. He should not wilfully make untrue statements. He should not make any false representation in the market.

(iv) Bankers to an Issue

Public issue is a combination of different financial intermediaries efforts and skills. Every intermediary has his own role in the issue process. Bankers to issue is one of the important intermediary who collects the application money from the investors through his wide network of branches. They transmit the amount to the company. The SEBI has the authority to grant the certificate of registration to the bankers. The SEBI has right to collect a fee of **Rs. 2,50,000** for the first two years and **Rs. 1,00,000** for the 3rd year to keep the registration in force. The bankers to an issue are required to maintain the books of accounts, records and documents for minimum period of 3 years after the closing of the public issue. He should maintain the books of accounts. Containing about the number of applications received, amount collected, forwarded dates etc., the SEBI is empowered to suspend or cancel the registration.

(v) Brokers to an Issue

Brokers play a vital role in the mobilisation of resources from the market. They know the individual investors and can influence their investment decisions. The brokers to an issue will be selected in consultation with the concerned stock exchanges. The acceptance of the broker should be submitted to the **Registrar of Companies**. The brokers will distribute the share application forms to knoock and corner of the country. They have a wide network of Sub-brokers who spread across the country. It is not possible without the help of the brokers. They will encourage and motivate the investors to participate in public issue. They will bear the distribution expenses. The brokerage rate may be paid in accordance with the provisions of the Act.

(vi) Registrars to an Issue

The registrar to an issue is one of the financial intermediary involved in the public issue. He prepares the records and receives money from the investors. He involved in making allotment process in consultation with the concerned stock exchange. He is involved in processing, despatching allotment letters, refund orders, certificates and other documents related to public issue. He also performs the function of share transfer agent. The share transfer agent is a person who maintain the records of holders of share on behalf of the company. He deals with the transfer of shares. He must get the registration certificate from the SEBI. He may also be renewed every year by the SEBI on the basis of past performance. He must abide by the rules and regulations which are issued by the SEBI from time-to-time.

Public issues are offered to the investors through various methods. The following data reveals the amount mobilised from the new issue market.

Table 1: Public Issues Raised by the Corporate Sector During the Year 1995-2002

(Rs. in crores)

Year	*Amount*	*Number of Issues*
1995-96	11822	1428
1996-97	11687	753
1997-98	3061	62
1998-99	7911	32
1999-2000	7673	65
2000-01	6618	124
2001-02	6423	19

Table 2: Rights Issues During 1995-2002

(Rs. in crores)

Year	*No. of issues*	*Amount*
1995-96	266	6508
1996-97	131	2724
1997-98	49	1703
1998-99	26	568
1999-2000	28	1560
2000-01	27	729
2001-02	13	1041

Sources: Annual Reports, Prime Data Base Management, 1995-2002.

Table 3: Equity and Debentures During 1995-2002

(Percentage)

Types of Issue	*1995-96*	*1996-97*	*1997-98*	*1998-99*	*1999-2000*	*2000-01*	*2001-02*
(a) Equity	75	71	44	66	94	68	18
(b) Debentures	25	39	56	34	06	32	82
	100	100	100	100	100	100	100

Table 4: City-wise Response to Public Issues During 1996-2001

(Percentage)

Rank	*City*	*1996-97*	*1997-98*	*1998-99*	*1999-2000*	*2000-01*
1.	Mumbai	39.4	51.08	54.75	66.53	49.66
2.	New Delhi	12.7	8.41	9.49	3.10	8.23
3.	Kolkata	7.6	6.50	7.54	2.07	4.34
4.	Ahmedabad	6.4	7.92	1.76	12.33	3.34
5.	Hyderabad	2.5	1.85	1.85	2.69	3.27
6.	Bangalore	2.4	1.79	4.10	2.22	3.10
7.	Chennai	3.1	2.59	4.13	2.11	2.89
8.	Pune	1.2	1.99	1.29	1.65	1.08
9.	Vadodara	1.3	1.18	0.60	1.03	1.1
10.	Lucknow	1.24	0.78	0.82	0.10	0.86
11.	Jaipur	1.5	1.16	0.55	0.66	0.81
12.	Kanpur	0.68	0.43	0.63	0.20	0.63
13.	Vijayawada	0.23	0.24	0.13	0.42	0.58
14.	Patna	0.76	0.45	0.37	0.11	0.57
15.	Surat	0.78	0.37	0.53	0.37	0.51
16.	Indore	0.96	0.64	0.33	0.37	0.46
17.	Chandigarh	0.39	0.38	0.35	0.18	0.46
18.	Rajkot	0.43	0.77	0.18	1.40	0.43
19.	Vishakapatnam	0.22	0.16	0.16	0.09	0.42
20.	Bhopal	0.27	0.20	0.18	0.04	0.40
21.	Nagpur	0.40	0.26	0.22	0.13	0.37
22.	Ludhiana	0.49	0.22	0.21	0.13	0.37
23.	Bhubaneswar	0.40	0.10	0.23	0.04	0.35
24.	Guwahati	0.40	0.18	0.64	0.04	0.35
25.	Thane	0.54	0.20	0.18	0.04	0.35
26.	Coimbatore	0.21	0.20	0.30	0.11	0.34
27.	Allahabad	0.28	0.15	0.21	0.02	0.31
28.	Cochin	0.24	0.40	0.29	0.08	0.28
29.	Varanasi	0.42	0.15	0.40	0.03	0.26
30.	Guntur	0.04	0.07	0.02	0.01	0.26
31.	Agra	0.17	0.15	0.12	0.02	0.26
32.	Tiruchirapalli	0.05	0.09	0.10	0.01	0.25
33.	Amritsar	0:19	0.16	0.08	0.02	0.25
34.	Mangalore	0.06	0.19	0.17	0.15	0.24
35.	Dehradun	0.11	0.13	0.11	0.01	0.24
36.	Gandhinagar	0.05	0.11	0.03	0.01	0.24
37.	Nasik	0.20	0.12	0.24	0.02	0.24
38.	Jamshedpur	0.25	0.11	0.11	0.01	0.24
39.	Ghaziabad	0.14	0.09	0.06	0.03	0.23
40.	Meerut	0.28	0.28	0.11	0.03	0.22
41.	Faridabad	1.34	0.28	0.33	0.03	0.22
42.	Gurgaon	0.41	0.07	0.04	–	0.21
43.	Jabalpur	0.14	0.08	0.06	0.01	0.20

(Contd.)

Table 4 (*Contd.*)

Rank	City	1996-97	1997-98	1998-99	1999-2000	2000-01
44.	Jallandhar	0.15	0.09	0.04	0.01	0.20
45.	Panji	0.15	0.16	0.09	0.04	0.20
46.	Noida	0.03	0.34	0.07	0.01	0.19
47.	Ranchi	0.19	0.15	0.13	0.01	0.19
48.	Udaipur	0.17	0.14	0.14	0.01	0.18
49.	Trivandrum	0.17	0.10	0.09	0.02	0.18
50.	Madurai	0.08	0.11	0.11	0.02	0.17

Sources: Prime Annual Reports, 1996-2001.

Table 5: City-wise Response for Public Issues During 1995-2002 (Top 5 cities in India)

(Percentage)

Rank	City	1995 -96	1996 -97	1997 -98	1998 -99	1999-2000	2000 -01	2001 -02
1.	Mumbai	27	39	51	55	67	49	38
2.	Delhi	11	13	08	10	03	08	10
3.	Ahmedabad	19	06	08	02	12	03	02
4.	Kolkata	08	08	06	08	02	04	06
5.	Chennai	05	03	03	04	02	03	03

Table 6: Zone-wise Response to the Public Issues During 1995-2002

(Percentage)

Rank	Zone	1995 -96	1996 -97	1997 -98	1998 -99	1999 -2000	2000 -01	2001 -02
1.	West	56	54	66	61	84	59	47
2.	North	21	25	16	17	05	19	27
3.	East	09	11	10	13	02	15	10
4.	South	14	10	08	09	09	07	16
		100	100	100	100	100	100	100

Table 7: Primary Capital Issues distribution by security and amount

(Rs. in crores)

	Instrument	1995 -96	1996 -97	1997 -98	1998 -99	1999-2000	2000 -01	2001 -02
1.	Equity	21165	17002	16634	10319	27792	16005	7524
2.	Preference	1006	285	2138	1704	730	313	151
3.	Debentures	11,344	17397	31697	49752	41415	61065	39741
	Total	**33515**	**34684**	**50469**	**61755**	**69937**	**77383**	**47419**

Source: Capital Markets, *CMIE Report*, July, 2002, p. 13.

Table 8: Primary Capital Issues Raised from Market

(Rs. in crores)

	Sector	1995-96	1996-97	1997-98	1998-99	1999-2000	2000-01	2001-02
1.	Government	14280	21211	32233	48677	44000	58020	34835
2.	Private	19235	13474	18236	13097	25937	19363	12585
	Total	**33515**	**34685**	**50469**	**61774**	**69937**	**77383**	**47420**

Source: Capital Markets, *CMIE Reports*, July 2002, p. 13.

Table 9: Primary Capital Issues Distribution by Type of Security (Number)

Particulars	1995-96	1996-97	1997-98	1998-99	1999-2000	2000-01	2001-02
1. Equity	1741	943	300	192	365	367	183
2. Preference	75	50	163	100	42	13	07
3. Debentures	126	143	199	167	214	195	219
Total	**1942**	**1136**	**662**	**459**	**621**	**575**	**409**

Table 10: Total Return to the Investors During the Period 1995-2002

Year	Total Return (%)
1995-96	3.24
1996-97	(–) 0.17
1997-98	15.83
1998-99	(–) 3.92
1999-2000	33.73
2000-01	(–) 27.93
2001-02	(–) 3.75

Table 11: Participation of Merchant Bankers in Public Issues (1995-2001)

Year	No. of Merchant Bankers Involved
1995-96	548
1996-97	442
1997-98	99
1998-99	42
1999-2000	58
2000-01	63

Source: Prime Annual Report, 1995-2001.

Table 12: Participation of Underwriters in Public Issues During 1995-2002

Year	*Number of Issues*	*Went for Underwriting*	*Total Issues*
1995-96	437	30%	1428
1996-97	85	8%	753
1997-98	10	9%	62
1998-99	07	2%	32
1999-2000	18	28%	65
2000-01	19	23%	124
2001-02	03	16%	19

Table 13: Top 5 Brokers Participated in Public Issues (by No. of Application)

(Rs. in crores) (2001-2002)

Rank	*Broker*	*No. of Issues*	*Amount Procured*	*% of Total Amount*
1.	JM Morgan	17	1423	23
2.	DSP Merryl Lynch	18	1155	19
3.	Karvy Securities	19	513	08
4.	Bajaj Capital	15	455	07

Table 14: Funds Mobilised by Manufacturing Services and Financial Institutions (1995-2002)

(Rs. in crore)

Year	*Financial Institutions*		*Manufacturing Services*		*Total*
1995-96	6222	53%	5601	47%	11822
1996-97	7895	68%	3753	32%	11648
1997-98	2720	89%	342	11%	3061
1998-99	7708	97%	203	03%	7911
1999-2000	5150	67%	2523	33%	7673
2000-01	4613	70%	2005	30%	6618
2001-02	5155	80%	1268	20%	6423

Source: Prime Annual Reports, 1995-2002.

Table 15: Number of Times Oversubscribed by the Public in Response to the Public Issues (1995-2002)

(Percentage)

	Subscribed	*1995-96*	*1996-97*	*1997-98*	*1998-99*	*1999-2000*	*2000-01*	*2001-02*
1.	Devolved	–	2	07	13	0	10	02
2.	Refunded	–	7	–	0	0	0	04
3.	No response	–	–	–	06	0	0	0
4.	Below 1 – 5	62	82	79	59	20	70	60
5.	1.5 – 3 times	18	06	10	13	08	15	17
6.	3 – 10 times	12	02	03	03	20	05	11
7.	Above 10 times	08	01	02	06	54	0	06
	Total	**100**	**100**	**100**	**100**	**100**	**100**	**100**

Source: Prime Annual Reports, 1995-2002.

> *"Invest for long term. Don't get swayed by day trading. Buy good companies and hold them for long time and invest like great investors"*
>
> **—Warren Buffet and Lynch**

(d) Secondary Market

Secondary market is a place, where the issued shares are available. It is an important component in the capital market. stock exchanges are known as the secondary market. They play an important role in securities market. It is the **resale** market for already issued shares. It is the market for long-term securities. The primary market deals with the issue of fresh capital. Growth of the primary market depends on the secondary market. Equity bonds, debentures and preferred stocks are traded in the secondary market. The investors can sell and buy equity shares in the stock exchange. Government securities, municipal bonds, trust debentures and other financial instruments are also traded in the market. The secondary market does not create any financial claim. The transactions in the secondary market do not provide funds to the corporate sector. But the strong secondary market movements create a high demand for the **New Issue Market**. The stock exchange is an association, or organisation of members to carry on trade in the securities.

Definition

"stock exchange means an association, organisation or body of individuals, whether incorporated or not, established for the

purpose of assisting, regulating and controlling the business in buying, selling and dealing in the securities"

—Securities Contract Act, 1956

According to **J.F. Pyle** "Security exchanges are market places where securities that have been listed thereon may be brought and sold for either investment or speculation".

Origin and Growth

The stock exchange is an organised place for trading in the securities market. They are highly specialised institutions. They are competing with the global stock exchanges. The origin of the stock exchanges in India can be traced back to the latter half of **19th century**. The first stock exchange was set up in India under the name of the **"Native Share and Stock Brokers** Association of Bombay" in 1875. The stock exchanges in India shall follow the legal provisions of the Securities Contract Act, 1956. The Act deals with the administration, control and monitored by thc **SCRA, 1956**. The Act gave powers to the **Central Government** to regulate the stock exchanges. The stock markets in India is in transformation stage and enters into the **digital economy**. It has an excellent technical skill in the Information Technology. Stock markets can become a **24 hours** markets. It can create wonders in the market. It has an excellent potential and talented skilled manpower to construct the **technology bourses**. At present there are **23** recognised stock exchanges in India. The objectives of the Securities Contract Act, 1956 are as follows:

(a) to create an efficient stock market;
(b) to control the malpractices in the stock exchanges;
(c) to protect the investors' interest;
(d) to improve the working conditions of the exchanges;
(e) to regulate the stock markets.

The stock exchanges in India should work within the framework of the Acts such as **Companies Act, 1956; Income Tax Act, 1961;** ***etc.*** They are self-regulatory organisations supervised by the Ministry of Finance. stock exchange regulations cover the entire operations. The regulations involved in **enrolment of members, listing of securities, and the disciplinary actions, trading methods**. Several committees examined and made recommendations to reform the stock exchanges.

1. G.S. Patel Committee (1985)
2. L.C. Gupta Committee (1991)
3. Pherwani Committee (1991)
4. Varma Committee (1997).

Stock Exchanges in India

Bombay stock exchange is the oldest stock exchange. At present there are 23 recognised exchanges functioning in India. stock exchanges will have to get recognition from the government for every five years. Bombay stock exchange is the only permanent recognised organisation in India. The stock exchange does not have any uniform structure. There are different stock exchanges which follow different patterns. Some exchanges are public limited companies and the others are limited by guarantee or as a voluntary non-profit making Organisations. stock exchange is recognised only after the government is satisfied. The Organisation patterns of the recognised stock exchanges in India are presented below:

Sl. No.	*Name of the stock exchanges*	*Year of Estt.*	*Type of Association*
1.	Bombay	1875	Voluntary
2.	Ahmedabad	1894	Voluntary
3.	Calcutta	1908	Public Ltd.
4.	Madras	1908	Public Ltd.
5.	Indore	1930	Voluntary
6.	Hyderabad	1943	Ltd. by guarantee
7.	Delhi	1947	Public Ltd. Co.
8.	Bangalore	1947	Public Ltd. Co.
9.	Cochin	1978	Public Ltd. Co.
10.	Kanpur	1982	Public Ltd. Co.
11.	Pune	1982	Public Ltd. Co.
12.	Ludhiana	1983	Public Ltd. Co.
13.	Guwahati	1983	Public Ltd. Co.
14.	Jaipur	1984	Public Ltd. Co.
15.	Kanara	1985	Public Ltd. Co.
16.	Magadh	1986	Public Ltd. Co.
17.	Bhubaneswar	1989	Ltd. by Guarantee
18.	Saurashtra	1989	Ltd. by Guarantee
19.	O.T.C.	1989	Ltd. by Guarantee
20.	Vadodara	1990	Ltd. by Guarantee
21.	Coimbatore	1991	Ltd. by Guarantee
22.	Meerut	1991	Ltd. by Guarantee
23.	National stock exchange	1992	Ltd. by Guarantee

The regular affairs of the stock exchange are managed by the governing body. The governing body consists of a president, vice-president, executive director, elected directors, public representatives and nominees of the government. The activities will be monitored by a number of various committees. They are known as **"Listing Committee, Clearing House Committee, and Defaulters Committee"**. The growth of stock exchanges depends upon the growth of corporate sector in the country. The stock exchanges follow their own methods of working. The Securities Contract Act stipulates the provisions regarding **"recognition of the stock, control of the government and curbing speculation"**. The stock exchange is a place, where the listed shares are traded regularly at a fixed time. The recognition of the stock exchange depends upon the following factors:

(a) The stock exchange bye-laws should be ensure fair dealings and must be transparent.
(b) The bye-law should protect the interest of genuine investors.
(c) The stock exchange shall follow the rules and regulations which may be imposed by the Central Government from time-to-time.

The Act empowers the Central Government to control the working of the stock exchanges. The Central Government prevents undesirable transactions in the stock exchanges. The government have the full authority in all aspect such as **management, powers, amendments, power to withdraw the recognition granted.** It curbs the speculative transactions of an stock exchange also. It has banned the option dealings in the market. It declared kerb trading as illegal. It transferred the powers to the SEBI. SEBI now regulates the market operations.

Functions of Stock Exchange

The stock exchange provides a geographical place for selling and buying of shares. The shares are transferred one to another investor. It deals with the financial assets according to laid down rules and regulations. It protects the investor's interest. The functions of the stock exchange are as follows:

(a) It provides the liquidity to the financial instruments.
(b) It ensures the safety and transparency.
(c) It creates ready market ability.
(d) It coordinates the companies and the investor.

(e) It facilitates a wider ownership securities.
(f) It facilitates continuous market.
(g) It enhances the goodwill of the company.
(h) It promotes savings and leads to capital formation.
(i) It provides capital to the profitable sectors.
(j) It provides an orderly regulated market for the securities.

Listing of Securities

Listing means an official admission of a scrip to trade as the floor of a stock exchange. Allowing a scrip for buying and selling in the stock exchange are known as **"Listing"**. A company scrip will be admitted in the stock exchange after the submission of information:

(a) Memorandum and association of articles
(b) Prospectus
(c) Audited accounts and balance sheet
(d) Details of capital structure
(e) Information about bonus shares and dividends declared
(f) Agreement particulars with managing director
(g) Consent letter from SEBI
(h) Compliance report regarding various legal provisions
(i) A list of highest top ten holders of each class or kinds of securities of the company.

Kinds of Securities

The admitted scrip in stock exchange will be available to sale and purchase between members. The listed securities can be classified into the following categories:

1. Group A Shares
2. Group B Shares
3. Permitted securities
4. Cleared securities
5. Non-cleared securities.

1. Group A Shares

Group A shares are also known as **"specified securities"**. They are allowed in forward trading. The following conditions should be fulfilled by the companies to admit into **"Group A Shares"**:

(a) The shares should be fully paid up equity shares.
(b) The company's paid up capital should at least Rs. **5 crores.**
(c) The company should have a strong growth potential.
(d) The company should be paid dividend regularly.
(e) The shares should be actively traded on the screen
(f) The company's market capitalisation should be at least Rs. 10 crores.

Group A shares as on 12-2-2005 in Bombay stock exchange **ABB, ACC, Adani Exports, Allahabad Bank, Andhra Bank, Apollo Hospitals, Arvind Mills, Ashok Leyland, etc.**

2. Group B Shares

Group B shares are known as cash scrips. These shares are traded on cash basis. Carry forward trading is not allowed in this group.

3. Permitted Securities

Permitted securities are allowed by some of the recognised stock exchanges. Some stock exchanges will permit the scrips even if they are not listed by them. These scrips are known as permitted securities. They allow the scrips as per the rules and regulations of the stock exchange.

4. Cleared Securities

Cleared securities are also called as specified securities. They are traded for fortnightly settlement. The concerned stock exchange will take a decision from time-to-time include some scrips in this list.

5. Non-cleared Securities

Non-cleared securities are traded among the brokers. These securities are not cleared through the stock exchange clearing house. These securities are not permitted to carry over the facilities.

Services of Stock Exchange

The development of a nation depends upon the speed of industrialisation. The peace will determine the velocity of the growth. Hence it stimulates the growth of stock market. Capital formation enhances the Gross Domestic Product. It leads to accumulate savings from the community. Hence the stock exchange provides the following services:

(a) Services to the Nation
(b) Services to Investors
(c) Services to Corporate Sector

(a) Services to the Nation

The stock exchanges are the financial nerve centres of the economy. The rise in the stock indices reflect the growth and health of the economy. Traditionally Indian economy is strongly supported by the manufacturing, agriculture and services sectors. They strongly form the foundation to the economy. The services are provided by the stock exchanges as follows:

(i) It stimulates the economic growth.
(ii) It creates a good environment for capital formation.
(iii) It diverts the accumulated savings towards productive channel.
(iv) It utilises the better utilisation of financial resources.
(v) It provides liquidity and continuous market.
(vi) It provides a forum for raising public debt for national important projects.

(b) Services to Investors

The following services are provided by the stock exchanges to the investors:

(i) It creates ready market for securities.
(ii) It ensures safe and transparency dealing in securities.
(iii) It provides advice and guidance to the investors.
(iv) It provides the facilities for quick disposal of securities.
(v) The listed securities are useful as collateral security for raising of loans.

(c) Services to Corporate Sector

The stock exchanges provide value addition services to their issued capital. The companies enjoy the following benefits:

(i) It helps to minimise fluctuations in the prices of securities.
(ii) It helps the corporate sector for raising of capital from the public.
(iii) The price reflection in the stock exchange enhances the credit worthiness of the company.

(iv) Active trading in stock exchange and entering into Sensex component are prestigious and status symbol to the corporate sector.

Membership of the Stock Exchange

The stock exchange normally runs the business with the participation of members. The Securities Contract Regulation Act 1956 deals with the granting of membership in stock exchange. It has framed uniform regulations for granting of membership in recognised stock exchanges. The qualifications for becoming a member of a recognised stock exchange are given below:

(a) The minimum educational qualification is a pass in PUC.
(b) He should be an Indian citizen.
(c) He should not be convicted for fraud or dishonesty.
(d) He should not be a defaulter of any other stock exchange.
(e) He should not be a bankrupt.
(f) He should not be engaged in any other business connected with a company.

Though the minimum qualification is PUC, but generally MBAs, CAs, post graduates in finance, area becoming members. Corporate membership is also offered by stock exchanges. The newly entered members will be trained up by the Bombay and Calcutta stock exchanges. These two stock exchanges set-up training institutes to provide an excellent skills to the members of the stock exchange. The training institutes of the concerned stock exchange enhance the abilities and talent of the members. The admitted member is eligible to work as individual or a partner. A member who completed 5 years in a stock exchange is eligible for appointment in other stock exchanges.

Broker

Broker is an important person in the stock market. He occupies a dominant role in selling and buying of securities. He is the financial intermediary both in the new issue market and secondary market. Every broker should get registration from the SEBI. The broker has to abide by the code of conduct laid down by the SEBI. SEBI is the watchdog of the stock market. It controls all the activities and manipulations arised in the market. If any violation of the rules and regulations, the SEBI is empowered to cancel the registration of the broker. The broker should be fair and transparency while dealing with the investors. He should be honest and provide sincere advices to the investors. The broker should be able to confirm the purchase and sale of the securities quickly. He should have a good name in the society. He should have adequate experience in the market to take correct decisions. He should also offer other ancillary services such as arranging for financing the clients' transactions. The brokers are categorised into two:

(a) Indian brokers
(b) Foreign brokers

(a) Indian Brokers

The stock brokers in India should be abide by the guidelines issued by the **SEBI** from time-to-time. SEBI has the powers to prevent malpractices in trading and to protect the rights of the investors. SEBI guidelines are more important and to be followed by the brokers. The broad regulatory framework of the stock exchange contain the major organisational reforms in respect of **Stock brokers, Sub-brokers, Foreign brokers, custodial services, depository system and stock lending scheme**. The following steps are required to meet the legal formalities by the stock brokers:

(i) Registration
(ii) Fee
(iii) Code of conduct
(iv) Capital adequacy norms
(v) Sub-brokers

(i) Registration

As per the guidelines of the SEBI, every broker in India should be registered with SEBI. The broker shall apply for registration through the concerned stock exchange. On receipt of the proposal received from the concerned stock exchange for grant of registration, the SEBI will make enquire into the matters regarding his candidature for stock brokership. The registration certificate will be issued by the SEBI only after satisfaction about the membership in recognised stock exchange, capability of the broker, his manpower and infrastructure facilities, his past experience, his character and suitability. The selected broker has to pay the fee to the SEBI as a registration fee. The annual turnover of the broker will determine the amount of registration fee. The registration of the brokership is valid for 5 years. If the turnover is found less than **Rs. 1 crore**, the registration fee will be **Rs. 5,000**. If the turnover exceeds **Rs. 1 crore, Rs. 5,000+1 per cent** of the excess of **Rs. 1 crore** turnover will be the fee. The auditor of the stock exchange determines the amount of turnover of the broker. The renewal for another 5 years requires to pay Rs. 5,000 as registration fee. If he fails to pay the amount, he would be liable to pay the interest **of 15 per cent p.a.** for each month of delay.

(ii) Code of Conduct

Broker is a professional person. For every profession, there will be a code of conduct and every member shall follow the rules and regulations in force. Hence, the broker should abide by the code of conduct as per the guidelines issued by the SEBI. The broker should maintain good relations with the investors. Investors are the pillars of stock market. He should maintain high standard of integrity, promptness and fairness. He should have adequate skills, intelligence, honest, sincerity and high morality, etc. He should not involve in manipulations or spreading rumours in the market. The role of a broker shall not be neglected in the stock market. He occupies a dominant role in stock market.

(iii) Capital Adequacy Norms

Every stock broker shall maintain the statutory books as per the provisions of the SEBI. The broker should maintain books such as **Sauda book, general ledger, client ledger, cash book, ledger pass book, document register, margin register, Sub-brokers accounts member's agreement book, client consent letters register, confirmation register, agreement register etc**. These books and records must be preserved for **5 years**. SEBI is the watchdog of the stock market. It has full powers in regulating the stock markets. If any broker violates rules and regulations, SEBI has the authority to suspend the registration of a broker in the following situations:

1. If the broker fails to pay the annual fee.
2. If the broker fails to follow the SEBI provisions.
3. If the broker involves in price rigging or concerning.
4. If the broker fails to follow the code of conduct.
5. If the broker submits false information to the SEBI.
6. If the membership of stock exchange is suspended by concerned exchange and SEBI also suspends registration of the broker.

7. If the broker is found guilty, improper business or unprofessional conduct.
8. If the broker fails to resolve the investor's complaints.

(iv) Sub-brokers

The stock brokers do the business, based on the investors' and sub-brokers' requirements. The transactions between the client and broker should be regulated. A reconciliation must be made between broker and sub-broker affairs. The broker shall follow all the legal provisions while maintaining the financial relations with the investors. The broker shall open a separate account and keep the investors' money in separate account. He should not utilise the clients money for his own purpose.

(b) Foreign Brokers

Foreign brokers in India needs to register with the SEBI. Usually **Foreign Institutional Investors** enters the stock market for buying and selling of the shares. The entry of **FIIs** leads to emerge the foreign brokers. The FIIs should disclose all the information regarding his abroad registration particulars. He should not deal the securities on his own.

Steps Involved in Dealing at Stock Exchanges

Generally the shares are available in stock exchanges. The common investor is not allowed to enter into the stock exchange. He has to buy and sell securities through brokers only. Brokers are official members of the stock exchange. They can enter into stock exchange and they involve in stock exchange operations on behalf of his investors. The business in the stock market can do only through recognised brokers. The following steps are involved in buying and selling of the shares at stock exchanges:

(a) Selecting a good broker
(b) Placing order
(c) Making the contract
(d) Contract note
(e) Settlement.

(a) Selecting a Good Broker

Broker is an important person in the stock market. He guides the investors, he is always helpful to the investors in making investment decisions. Every transaction in the stock exchange will be settled through brokers. The investor must select a good broker from the market. He participates in the market through his broker. A common investor can never purchase scrips directly from stock exchange. Therefore the investor should make purchase or sale of the securities through selected broker only.

(b) Placing Order

After selection of a broker, the next step is placing an order for purchase or sale of a scrip. The investor should study about the market position, government policies, primary market movements, Gross Domestic Product information, full knowledge about the economy, an in-depth analysis of companies performance, industry analysis, sectoral analysis, foresight about the market, a strong analysis about fundamentals, a good understanding about technical analysis. All these factors may helpful to the investor for selecting a best scrip from the market. After selection of a best scrip among the alternative, the investor should place an order with the broker. In addition to the investor knowledge, the broker may also provide some useful information. In India, most of the investors following the broker's advice. They simply handover the cheque to the broker for their commitment. Investors should enhance their knowledge, skills, talent by acquiring stock market knowledge. The investment habit should be developed on par with acquiring more knowledge. Knowledge makes more perfect the investor. Knowledge based advice or decision never fails in the stock market. Investment is a knowledge based activity. Knowledge will be acquired through accumulation of information. A lot of information is available with only a wide reading. Reading stimulates the skills of the investor. Therefore investing in stock market is based as many factors such as **Industry growth, company sales, company market share, product portfolio, gross profit, net profit, PBT, PAT, EPS, PE ratio, market capitalisation, 52 weeks lower and higher price levels etc.**

(c) Making the Contract

Making the contract is the another step in the process. Every investor should purchase the scrips through the broker from the market. After selection of a best scrip, the investor place an order with the broker. On the receipt of the various orders from different investors, the broker goes to the stock exchange and fulfills his clients desires by making deals with his fellow brokers. The broker will make bargains in price considerations on behalf of his clients. The broker will prepare after the mutual consent. The seller broker will send the selling note and the buyer will send the buying notes. They provide all the details of trading activities.

(d) Settlement

Settlement is the climax stage in the process of buying or selling of the securities in the stock exchange. It is an activity between two brokers. Any transaction between two brokers will be settled in the stock exchange. Generally the transactions in the stock exchange will be in the form of contracts. Usually contracts are two types in the stock exchange. They are known as:

1. Ready delivery contracts; and
2. Forward delivery contracts.

Ready Delivery Contracts provide a time period of "Three to Seven days in settlement of the transactions. Ready delivery contracts are further classified as liquidation and square up. In liquidation contracts the securities will be delivered on receipt of the cash. In squaring up contracts the dealings are squared up by adjusting by price differences only.

Forward Delivery Contracts are made through stock exchange. These contracts are in speculative nature. In this type of category, the active securities are traded. The forward delivery contracts can be classified into three kinds. They are:

(a) liquidation in full,
(b) liquidation by payment of differences,
(c) carry over.

Liquidation in full: In this category the securities are delivered. The payment will be received immediately. The amount will be adjusted between intermediaries.

Liquidation by payment of differences: In this category, the securities are not delivered. But the difference between purchase and sale price will be adjusted between two parties.

Carry Over: Carry over means the postponement of settlement between two parties for a future date. For this purpose the buying party will pay a certain amount to the selling party. The payment of consideration is known as Badla charges of Contango charges.

Types of Speculators

The purchase of assets for profit is called as the speculation. It is short-term activity. It is an inspiration to the stock market. It is the oxygen to the capital market. We can say that without the speculation, there is no stock market. It is different from investment. Investment is long-term in nature. It creates the capital formation in the country, by encouraging the savings. Investments are useful for the present and future consumption. It leads to more income and longer capital appreciation.

Speculation aims at only short-term trade gains. It involves in buying and selling of the securities for the short purpose. It is double edged sword either to get profit or loss. It may lead to profit sometimes and loss at other times. The persons who are involved in the speculation are called as the speculators. They will balance the share price movements in the mark. They are classified as follows:

(a) Bull
(b) Bear
(c) Stag
(d) Lame Duck

(a) Bull

A bull is also known as Tejiwala. He is an operator who expects a rise in the prices of the securities in the future. He always thinks that the future will be very bright. He makes the purchases of shares with the intention to sell at higher prices in future. He is not interested to take the delivery of shares which he has purchased. He deals only with the differences of prices. The speculator is called a Bull because of resemblance of his behaviour with the bull. He is an optimist. He tries to raise the prices of the securities by making heavy purchases. The market is called as the Bullish market, when all the bulls enter the market at once. In this market, there will be pressure for the buying of the securities. In this market, the supply of shares are scarce and demand will be more. The scarcity of scrips may lead to arise in the share prices. They create liquidity to the market.

(b) Bear

A bear is known as Mandiwala. He expects that prices which fall in future and sells the securities at present. He purchases the securities at lower prices and sells the securities at higher prices. He is interested to purchase in the down market and sell in the up market. He does not have securities at present. But bull sells them in future for higher prices. If all the bears enter the market, it is known as the bearish market. A bear does not take the delivery of securities but takes the difference, if prices fall. In case the prices increases, he will have to pay the difference. If the market is dominated by bears, it is known as the bearish phase. He tends to forced down the prices of different securities. When all the bear operators start selling the securities, the pressure gradually forces down the prices. He is a pessimist. If the prices do not fall they may start spreading rumours to pull the prices down. This situation is known as the bear raid. It is quite opposite to the bull speculator.

(c) Stag

A stag is another speculator in the stock market. He is a cautious speculator. He concentrates on the primary market. He applies for the shares in the new companies and expects to sell them at a premium, if he gets an allotment. He selects only those companies whose shares are in more demand and are likely to carry a higher price. He sells the shares before being called to pay the allotment money. He does not indulge in buying and selling of the shares in the market. He depends on the securities that are allotted to him.

A stag is always expecting a rise in share prices. He behaves same as bull. According to Hartley Withers, "A stag is an applicant for a new issue who applies with a view to prompt resale".

He is called "premium hunter" because he makes sale of the newly allotted shares at a profit like a genuine investor. He expects that the price of the share will soon rise and be sold for a hefty premium.

(d) Lame Duck

Lame duck is a speculator who behaves like a duck. If a bear speculator fails to fulfill his commitments, he is called struggling like a lame duck.

The following transactions reveal the speculative natures of the affairs.

Bull Deal

For example, a bull asks his broker to buy 100 shares of ABC Ltd., at Rs. 10 each, the broker executes the deal. At the time of settlement, the market price of shares of ABC Ltd. is Rs. 35 each. The bull would instruct his broker to sell the shares and takes the difference in prices:

(a) Sale proceeds of 100 shares @ Rs. 35	Rs. 3,500
(b) Purchase consideration 100 × 10	Rs. 1,000
(c) Bull profit	Rs. 2,500

Bear Deal

A Bear is instructed to sell 100 shares of X Ltd., at Rs. 50 each. At the time of settlement of transactions, the actual price of the share is Rs. 40 each. He would instruct the broker to purchase the shares of X Ltd., and enjoys the difference in prices:

(a) Sale proceeds of 100 shares @ Rs. 50	Rs. 5,000
(b) Purchase consideration 100 × 40	Rs. 4,000
(c) Bears profit	Rs. 1,000

Speculation assures the risk of loss with a view to make profits. Speculation needs the full information about the capital market. It requires best expertise on the part of the speculator. The main aim of the speculation is to achieve profits through price changes. Speculation may be categorised as constructive speculation and the destructive speculation. Constructive speculation is based on predicting of future trends of prices. It requires high talent. Skill foresight and intelligent analysis of the security market. Destructive speculation hardly depends on the evaluation of the security market. It has the following advantages and disadvantages:

Advantages

1. It creates liquidity to the market.
2. It tends stability in prices.
3. It encourages forward trading.
4. It provides peace the trading of derivative instruments.
5. It provides continuity in the market.

Disadvantages

Speculation is a high intelligent activity. It requires a lot of skill. It needs a perfect knowledge of the capital market trends. It is useful to us but it creates problems. If the speculators skill do not match with the speculation tool, it may be a misfire. They will have to face many problems.

Speculative Transactions

Speculation is a common phenomenon in stock markets. It creates liquidity to the market. If there is no speculation, there is no growth.

Usually investors will purchase the shares with a view to resale in the up market. The price difference is the consideration for their commitment. The investor should kept his mind about enter and exit of the stock market. The purchase price is the most influencing factor in booking the profits. The speculative activities in the stock market are presented below:

(a) Manipulation
(b) Rigging
(c) Arbitrage
(d) Kerb deal
(e) Cornering
(f) Wash sales

Manipulation is one of the speculative deal in the stock market. It is an intentional activity carried out by a group of members. They create false opinion and spread rumours. They are responsible for artificial increase in prices of some selected scrips. They picturise this situation as a natural phenomenon. Sometimes, the speculators are also face risk in some situations. But innocent investors will get losses in price manipulations.

Rigging is another speculative activity in the stock market. It will be carried out by an individual speculator. In this method the speculator places orders to different brokers at different price levels. He will purchase the same scrip from some brokers and sell them to other brokers. It is done artificially to stimulate the market. It will show an impact on demand and supply position of the securities.

Arbitrage is a highly specialised activity and requires a lot of skill and talent. Arbitrage means purchase of a scrip in cheaper market and sells it in the dearer market. For example: ACC share is available at Chennai market at **Rs. 350** and it commands Rs. 360 in Mumbai market. Hence the arbitrager will purchase in Chennai and sells it in Mumbai at Rs. 360, Rs. 10 will be earned as profit per share. It is based on a price difference between two markets.

Kerb trading is an unofficial trading. It is an unfair practice of dealing. Kerb means sale or purchase of securities before or after official hours of business in the stock exchange. A trading other than stock exchange trading times is known as kerb trading.

Cornering is an unhealthy practice of trading. It is an activity, to create a scarcity for a particular scrip by purchasing a large amount of shares. The circulation of the scrip will be controlled by the speculators.

Capturing a scrip in large amount of shares at lower prices is called as cornering.

Types of Operators

stock exchange activities are the barometer for the development of a nation. It runs with the combination of different players. The following operators are involved in stock exchange operations:

(a) Jobbers
(b) Brokers
(c) Tarawaniwala
(d) Budiwalas
(e) Arbitrageurs
(f) Odd lot dealers

Jobbers are dealers in securities in the stock exchange. They occupy a dominant role in the stock market operations. They buy and sell securities for themselves only. They will not participate purchases for others in the stock market. They buy securities at lower prices and sell them at higher prices. The difference between two prices is known as **Jobbers turn**.

Brokers are another important financial intermediary in the stock exchange. They buy and sell securities for their clients. They are working for commission. They transact the transactions for their clients and for other members. The brokers who work for their clients is called as **Commission brokers**. The brokers who purchase for other members is known as **floor broker**. The floor brokers will get commission from the both parties of the transaction. They occupy a dominant role in the stock exchange. They are well experienced and acquire more knowledge about the economy. Brokerage is a knowledge based activity and it needs a lot of market skills. It is an intellectual based activity. They do the business by appointing sub-brokers throughout the nation. They have a wide network. They can influence the prices of different securities in different phases. Market is consisted of **bull phase and bear phase**. Bull operators dominate the market in bull phase. Bear operators will dominate in bear phase. In bull phase, there will be more demand for buying. There will be pressure on supply of scrips. In bearish phase, there will be demand for selling the scrips.

Tarawaniwalas works for Commission. They render services for other brokers. They purchase and sell the shares for themselves. They do business like jobbers.

Budiwalas provide finance to the needy parties. They make available funds for stock market operations. They are financiers in the stock exchange. They provide loans for a shorter period **2 to 3 weeks**. They charge fee for the granted loan amount. The charge is known as **Contago or undabdla or seedbadla.**

Arbitrageur is a highly specialised activity and requires a great talent. They work for to take the advantage of the price differences in the same market or different markets.

Odd lot means anything less than the market lot. All companies have fixed market lot as **50 or 100**, odd lot dealers specialises in handling the odd lots in stock exchanges. An odd lot arises from the issue of rights or bonus.

Kinds of Orders

The stock brokers will procure orders from their clients in different types of kinds. They are presented below:

(a) Net rate order
(b) Best rate order
(c) Limited order
(d) Stop order
(e) Market rate order
(f) Discretionary order
(g) Matched rate order

Net ret order includes the cost of scrip and brokerage. Net order is a fixed rate of a particular scrip. The order will be placed by the client.

Best rate order will be placed by the clients in actively trading shares. The client gives order to buy or sell at the best price immediately available in the market. If the client placed order for purchases, the broker must try for lowest prices. If the order for sale of shares, the broker must sell at higher possible prices.

Limited order means the client will instruct the broker to buy or sell at a stated price or better price. The order indicates the maximum or minimum price for his trade transactions. In this kind of order the rate depends upon the broker and client relations.

Stop order is associated with restrict the loss to the client. It also protects the amount of capital gains. This kind of order is useful to both parties.

Market rate order indicates the payment of brokerage separately. The investor will place order for a fixed rate which is based on market conditions.

Discretionary order will provide freedom to the broker in respect of purchase price. The client never specify about the price that security to be bought by the broker.

Matched rate order means the client appoints two brokers. He instruct one broker for buying and another for selling.

Settlement Procedure

The stock exchange works with the participation of many members. The member or broker makes purchase or sale from each other and the transactions will be adjusted in a particular day is known as **settlement day**. A settlement cycle consists of 5 days trading period. The settlement day will not be common for all stock exchange. **For example: In Mumbai** stock exchange the settlement cycle starts on **Monday** and ends on **Friday**. Hence the transactions between these days should be settled on Friday. In **NSE**, the cycle starts on **Wednesday** and end on the **Tuesday** of the following week. Settlement cycle is a combination of **pay in day and pay out day**. The pay in day refers to all the buyers brokers shall deposit the money for their purchase of shares. The pay outday means handing over the proceeds to the seller brokers. The settlement cycle is the most important for client and broker. If the investor purchases 100 shares of ACC on Monday, to square up the position by the end of the settlement, the sale will have to take place before Friday, the same week. If the sale has not taken place, he has to pay a consideration for the broker at the end of the settlement period. The broker collects the payments from the clients and deposits it with the exchange on the pay in day. The exchange allows four days, from the end of the settlement cycle. After four days as the pay out day the exchange hands over the proceeds to the seller broker. The settlements will be done in two methods: **(a) Fixed settlement, (b) Rolling settlement**. All of the above transactions and affairs are belonging to **Fixed settlement** cycle. Hence in fixed settlement cycle a fixed cycle starts on a particular day and ends after 5 days.

Rolling settlement is another kind of settlement method in the stock exchange. This method was introduced by SEBI from **Jan 10, 2000**. In this method, the transactions are settled within **five days** from the date of transaction. It is popularly known as **"T+5"**. **For example:** If an investor purchase of 5000 shares of BFL services and sells 3000 shares on Monday he would be asked to settle the net outstanding that is 2000 shares on the following Monday, the fifth or sixth day.

Circular Trading

Speculation in trading generates profits to the investors. Sometimes the share prices will go outstanding levels. No one can control these prices. Abnormal rise or fall in the prices of the securities destroys the investor's confidence. The price fluctuations can lead to high transaction risk. A high price fluctuations create in stability in the market. Stock market is highly volatile market. It is based on market rumours such as **take over bonus issue, financial performance and management problems**. The rumours are two kinds: **(a) Positive, (b) Negative**. Positive rumours leads to increase in share price of a particular company. Once the information is exposed to the market, price can be increased by traders through **circular trading**. Circular trading refers to the trading that takes place among the brokers to manipulate the prices for their personal gain. The issue of bonus share by a company, will take as an opportunity for their personal gain by the brokers. The circular trading is associated with brokers. The innocent investor will burnt his fingers in the market by entering into the market. Traders will exit from the market after profit booking by them. Hence the government introduced price filters to prevent all these consequences happening in the market. Price filters are a controlling tool in hands of stock exchanges. The price filters can be categorised as follows:

(a) Intra day price bands
(b) Inter week price band
(c) Margin

Intra day price band is a tool to prevent the price movement of a scrip during a trading session. In this method, the price range is fixed in advance. For example: Hindustan Lever Ltd. the stock closed on Monday at Rs. 150 at the NSE. It would be allowed to trade between **Rs. 135 and Rs. 165**. It is implemented in all the stock exchanges. It depends upon the price and volatility of the stock. At NSE, the **NIFTY and Junior NIFTY** stocks have 10 per cent and other stocks have 5 per cent range in intra day price band. **At BSE** the filter limit is **5 per cent** in selected stocks of 32 due to the uncertain market conditions. Hence the price filters fix the range of a scrip to be traded in the stock exchange in advance of **24 hours**. If the transactions are arised beyond the limits, are rejected by the system. This price band has certain limitations. It does not allow the proper reaction in prices for the available information. Actual earning capacity of the company performance may not be discounted by the market forces. It is an artificial check as the reaction of the share prices. The intra price band cannot curb the automatic price movements within a day. Some stock exchanges introduced graded price filters. **For example:** Madras stock exchange introduced graded price filters. The graded price filter may allow a scrip to rise 9 per cent at the first instance. If there is no matching orders at this price, the stock price is frozen at this level for the day. If the matching order is found, it would be allowed to rise further by another intermediate price fitter level at 6 per cent. Hence the price movement of a scrip is always controlled by the stock exchange.

Inter week price band is associated with the weekly price movement of a scrip. It is a tool to control the prices of a share on weekly basis. The increase or decrease of a share price would be fixed in advance of a week. The range is fixed in accordance with the price volatility. At NSE the inter week price band is **25 per cent** of the previous week's close on Nifty and Junior Nifty stocks.

Margins are additional filters applied by the stock exchanges. It is a tool to curb the price volatility of a scrip. In this method, the broker has to deposit the margin amount with the stock exchange, where he participated in a transaction. For each and every transaction made by the broker has to deposit margin amount with the stock exchange. The deposited margin amount is used as a tool to discourage the speculative trading activities. The margin amount will be **20 per cent** for each and every transaction of the amount. The following are different kinds of margins imposed by stock exchanges:

(a) Gross exposure margin
(b) Net exposure margin
(c) Market margin
(d) Concentration ratio margin
(e) Special margin

Gross exposure margin is imposed by the stock exchange on individual business of a trader. It is applied to the individual trader, based on his business potential. It makes the trader to reduce his risk exposure. At the NSE, the gross exposure is **7 times** to the traders capital base. If he deposits **Rs. 1,00,000** he can trade up to Rs. 7,00,000. If he exceeds the limit, he has to deposit additional margin to the stock exchange or he may switch over his terminal.

Net exposure margin will be imposed by the stock exchange, only when higher purchases exceeds the sales. It will not be imposed, if a broker made higher sales of securities than purchases. The trader has to deposit margins at a graded basis. It is imposed to curtail the risk. **10 per cent** margin is for net exposure exceeding **Rs. 2 crores** and up to Rs. 5 crores.

Market margin is based on the difference between the closing selling and purchasing price plus outstanding net position at the end of the day. This margin is not imposed on share with market value of Rs. 50 or less.

Concentration ratio margin will be levied on the concentrated shares by the broker. It will prevent the trader showing interest on a few stocks. It reduces the manipulation of the share price. Margin is computed on a graded basis.

Special margin is imposed by the stock exchange to hault the price rigging. If there is a high degree of volatility in a particular scrips price, the exchange even 100 per cent will be imposed. The special margin curbs the price fluctuations. However, all kinds of margins are targeted to arrest the price fluctuations in the stock exchanges.

SEBI is the watchdog of the stock market. It has the full powers and authorities to regulate the capital market operations. Curbing the speculation is the main activity of the SEBI. SEBI has reduced the daily price band from the current level of **10 per cent** to **8 per cent**. It replaced the existing weekly price band of **25 per cent** by a graded margin system linked to price movement stock market is a highly volatile and price fluctuations are very common. The price variation in a security value may be considered as a volatile, if its price varied by ± 16 per cent or more in a single **trading cycle**. The margin rate depends upon volatility of the scrip.

	Volatility		*% of Margin*
(a)	Price variation between	**16% to 24%**	**5%**
(b)	Price variation more than	**24%**	**20%**
(c)	Price variation more than	**32%**	**30%**
(d)	Price variation for	**40%**	**40%**

Carry Forward

Carry forward is related to specified shares. The specified shares are also called as **Group A** shares. Group A shares are selected on the basis of equity market capitalisation and public holding. If a scrip is to be included in a specified group, it must have a good track record and a dividend paying company. The company should have a strong good potential and can be high investor's base. Hence, the Group A shares can enjoy the good reputation and investor's confidence in the market. If any company satisfies these norms, it may be shifted to Group A shares. Carry forward transaction facility is available to **Group A shares only**. The rest of the scrips in the market will be included in **Group B shares**. In specified shares the settlement can be done in three ways:

(a) delivery against payment
(b) squaring up of a transaction
(c) carrying over the settlement to the next settlement period.

Carry forwarding is a complex transaction. It is not a simple method. "The postponement of a transaction from one settlement period to another settlement period". The postponement will be allowed officially up to **90 days**. The carry forward transaction may be carried forward up to **90 days only**. The following aspect will clearly reveal the situation.

Mr. Harish buys 1000 shares on Monday at the price of Rs. 40 but as the settlement day the settlement price is Rs. 50. Hence Mr. Harish has three options before him.

Option A: He should pay Rs. 40,000 and take delivery of shares.

Option B: He may sell the shares at Rs. 50 and gain Rs. 10,000 (10 × 1000).

Option C: He may postpone his transaction for a further rise in selling price. He should forward the transaction with the help of the financier. The financier may charge for the carry ward period of time. It is known as badla charges. The transaction must be settled within 90 days of its origin. In this process four parties are involved. They are investor, brokers, badla financier and the stock exchanges.

Listing of Securities

The equity culture in India has been growing rapidly in the digital economy. Liberalisation, privatisation and globalisation policies stimulated the growth of industrial sector. The rapid industrialisation leads to an increase in growth rate and gross domestic product. An increase in growth of the corporate sector may leads to increase in stock market activities of the economy. The stock market is a part of Indian economy. The development of new issue markets indicate the capital formation and asset creation in the economy. Therefore, a company which approached to the new issue market, for capital raising, it must also enter into secondary markets. After completion of the process of public issue, every public limited shall have to list the share with the recognised stock exchange. Listing means admission of a company scrip in a recognised stock exchange for trading. Listing means, an entry to a secondary market for trading of a share officially. It creates marketability, liquidity and transferability to securities. Listing is helpful to the new shareholders of the company for providing ready market, if they are not interested for holding the equity with them. The Companies Act stipulates compulsory listing of a scrip in stock exchange. In prospectus the company must indicate where the share to be listed. The company shall fulfill legal formalities as per the stock exchange requirements. After the permission is granted by the stock exchange, the becomes eligible to list its securities in the concerned exchange.

Legal Formalities

Every company in India shall follow the legal requirements to list a scrip with the stock exchange:

(a) Capital
(b) Application money
(c) Shareholders
(d) Market maker
(e) Articles of Association
(f) Flotation cost
(g) Size of issue

Capital is the more important factor in smooth functioning of the company. For listing of a scrip with the stock exchange. The minimum public issue offer must be **Rs. 75 lakhs**. The company should have issued capital **Rs. 3 crores**. The Bombay stock exchange raised the limit of issued capital to **Rs. 10 crores**. The other stock exchanges have also increased the limit of issued capital of **Rs. 5 crores**. Hence the listed company should have issued capital to fulfill the requirements of the stock exchange regulations.

Application money is the another important factor in listing of securities. In public issue, the share capital will be collected from the shareholders on instalment basis. As per the SEBI guidelines, the issue process must be completed within 30 days of the closure of the issue. All applications will be received with the application money for purchase of shares. But all applications received will not get shares from the company, if the issue is over subscribed. Hence the company should make refund the excess application money to the non-allottees of the shares with the stipulated period of time. If any company fails to refund within stipulated period, the issuing company should pay an interest rate of **15 per cent p.a.** Bombay and Delhi stock exchanges stipulated these conditions.

Shareholders of a company may spread throughout the nation. For every company issue, there will be a condition for minimum number of shareholders prescribed. The stock exchange present undue concentration of large shareholdings with the company. If the number of shareholders are below the prescribed number, the scrip will be de-listed from the stock exchange.

Market maker is a financial intermediary involved in capital market. He should be appointed, if the company's paid up capital **Rs. 3 crores** but not more than **Rs. 5 crores**. The company should have a commercial operation activities for less than two years. The market maker may provide two way quotes for the concerned stock for a minimum period of 18 months from the date of trading on stock exchange.

Articles of Association shall have a provision about the listing of a security. The listing should be done with the accepting of articles of association. The security is not qualified for listing, if the articles of association does not agree.

Flotation cost should not be exceed as per the guidelines issued by SEBI. The company should adhere to the ceiling in the expenditure of public issue.

Size of the issue should be stated in the first page of the prospectus. All the information regarding issue particulars should be indicated in the prospectus.

Bombay Stock Exchange

Bombay stock exchange was established in 1875. It was organised under the name of **"The Native Stock and Share Brokers Association"** as a voluntary and non-profit organisation. It was recognised as a permanent stock exchange in 1957. It is the premier stock exchange in India. Its business is not confined to Mumbai alone. It covers 100 cities in India. It has introduced **online trading** in 19-1-1995. It is known as **BOLT (BSE Online Trading)**. BOLT has a nationwide network. The business transactions will be transmitted through **"online"**. It has the capacity of

5,00,000 trades per day. It commences the business from **9.30 AM to 3.30 PM**. It provides automated trading facility to the investors. The objectives of the stock exchange are:

(a) to protect the interest of investors;
(b) to provide developed and well regulated market for dealing in securities;
(c) to encourage the capital formation and asset creation in the economy;
(d) to provide world class standard services to Indian investors.

The Bombay stock exchange is the lion of Asia. It is the proud of India. In the stock exchange, three types of securities are allowed for trading such as **A Group, B1 and B Group**. A group shares contains scrips with good track record and large volume of business in the market. A group shares are allowed for carry forward transactions up to 90 days only. B1 group contains relatively liquid securities. The rest of the shares are placed under **"B"** group. Settlements are carried out through the clearing house. The settlement period is **7 days** for all scrips.

Stock market indices are the barometers of the stock market. Bombay stock exchange has listed 7000 scrips. It is not possible to analyse the prices of every stock to find out whether the market movement is upward or downward. Hence the indices provide a meaningful insight about price movements of the market. The indices have always been of great importance in security analysis. People have been observing the stock market fluctuations through market indicators. The investors use the market index as a bench mark. The investors use various indexes for their analytical purpose. They also compete and compel the index numbers. The BSE started publishing an index number of equity prices from 2-1-1986, with the base year 1978-79. It is known as **"Sensex"**. Sensex means sensitive index of 30 scrips selected from the market. The selection is made on the basis of the market activity. The Sensex component of the scrips are always "hot cakes" in the market. They enjoy much status and earn good reputation. Entering into Sensex component means, recording the event in Guinness Book of Records. But it has an outstanding achievement to the corporate sector Sensex is always depends upon the market situations. The movement is based upon many factors such as government policy, global market movements, bullion market prices, political unrest in the country, sectoral fluctuations, fiscal policy of the government, Central Government budget, railway budget, natural calamities, rainfall, agricultural production and other many factors. The component of Sensex is presented below:

Table 16: Statement shows Sensex Components (on 15-2-2005)

(Rs. in crores)

Sl. No.	*Company Sensex*	*Prices on 15-2-2005 6679.33*	*Market Capitalisation 3,88,717*	*Pays Weight 100*
1.	Infosys	2168.85	46,753	12.03
2.	Reliance Industries	543.15	41,648	10.71
3.	ICICI Bank	380.85	28,031	7.21
4.	ITC	1316.55	22,867	5.88
5.	ONGC	823.90	17,622	4.53
6.	TISCO	404.50	16,807	4.32
7.	HLL	151.90	16,718	4.30
8.	HDFC	782.95	16,509	4.25
9.	SBI	665.70	15,766	4.06
10.	Ranbaxy	1050.95	13,678	3.52
11.	HDFC Bank	568.95	13,077	3.36
12.	Satyam Computers	421.45	12,098	3.11
13.	L&T	1001.60	11,710	3.01
14.	Tata Motors	507.60	11,019	2.83
15.	Grasim Industries	1360.40	9,979	2.57
16.	Wipro	711.25	9,970	2.56
17.	Hindalco	1383.40	9,595	2.47
18.	Bharati Telecom	214.80	7,962	2.05
19.	Bajaj Auto	1078.25	7,637	1.96
20.	BHEL	860.30	7,370	1.90
21.	HPCL	369.80	6,274	1.61
22.	ACC	373.75	6,040	1.55
23.	Gujarat Ambuja	446.95	6,020	1.55
24.	Tata Power	408.70	5,662	1.46
25.	Hero Honda	563.75	5,629	1.45
26.	Reliance Energy	574.45	5,331	1.37
27.	Cipla	276.65	4,977	1.28
28.	Dr. Reddy's Lab	742.45	4,261	1.10

Sources: *The Economic Times*, 15-2-2005, p. 11.

Surveillance System in the Bombay Stock Exchange

In stock market, speculation and gambling activities are very common in nature. The rise and fall of the market is a routine programme of the stock markets. But the stock exchange provides a fair and transparent market to the investors. The stock exchange established a separate department for the control of manipulations and speculative activities. This department is known as **"surveillance"** department. The surveillance department can be classified into two kinds:

(a) Price movement
(b) Control on the terminal

(a) Price Movement

The stock exchange is responsible for all the activities carried on by its members. Members are the most important persons in trading of the activities of the stock exchange. The surveillance department is always working for the control of price movement of scrips listed in the stock exchange. It controls and detect the price rigging and manipulations occurred in the stock exchange. It controls the prices in stock exchange through the following methods:

(i) Circuit filters
(ii) Margins

Circuit filter is one of the controlling activity of the stock exchange. The circuit fitter decides in advance, about the range of price of a particular scrip for the next day trading. It decides the maximum price between two trading periods. If any scrips exceeds filter price, it cannot be traded in the stock exchange. Hence the circuit filters can control the high speculation activities in the market. But it is also curb the actual growth and capacity of a particular scrip. The filter percentages for various scrips are changed at the end of the day. According to the situation in the stock exchange, it may be changed even when the trade is going on. The stock exchange has the authority to suspend the trading of a particular scrip, if it violates the percentage of circuit filters.

Margins is one of the methods to detect the manipulations and price rigging in the stock market. The members of the stock exchange deposit part of their trades as a margin to the exchange the margins are levied on scrips depending upon the category of scrips. The members should pay a daily margin of **15 per cent** on their trades both on delivery and carry forward transactions.

(b) Control on the Terminal

Trading in the shares is very easy and now it is available with a click of mouse. Technology has changed the process of trading in stock market operations. Hence the monitoring of the member's activities became very easy to the stock exchange officials. If any violation of law is made by the members, the work stations are **deactivated**. The deactivation of work stations can be done on two situations, (a) if the member fail to pay the fee and violation of trade restrictions framed by the authorities. Generally the member's trade position will be monitored through pay in and pay out settlement method. For this purpose, the stock exchange officials can use various reports prepared by the different departments of the stock exchange. Market Monitoring Reports are available with the Information System using of the exchange for position monitoring purpose. The members' trade exposure beyond a limit is also monitored by the officials of the stock exchange. Generally the members of the stock exchange is allowed to trade up to **Rs. 1 crore** and above for **A and B 1** group scrips. In case of group **B** scrip is **Rs. 50.00** lakhs and **Rs. 10.00 lakhs** for individual scrips. The observation will be made by the exchange authorities about the financial soundness of the members and their credit worthiness. All corrective steps will be taken by the exchange authorities through various kinds of **margins**.

Sometimes, if the exchange officials found any **price rigging** by the member, they take appropriate surveillance against the malpractice. The officials will concentrate about the trading activities, daily turnover of the member are scrutinised. All the transactions and activities are closely monitored by the officials and takes corrective steps. Carry forward transactions are closely monitored by the **Surveillance department**. The disciplinary action committee will take action against any malpractice found in the exchange.

Protection to the Investors

Generally the trading will be carried out by different members of the stock exchange. All the members involve in buying and selling of the shares among themselves. The transactions will be settled through stock exchange clearance house. If any member defaulted to another leads to collapse the market. Hence the stock exchange has set up several funds to protect the investors and trading members from the financial crunch. The following funds have been set up for the protection of the investors:

(i) Investor's protection fund
(ii) Trade guarantee fund
(iii) Broker's contingency fund
(iv) Investor's grievances
(v) Insurance policy

(i) Investor's Protection Fund

This fund has been set up by stock exchange for the safety of the investors. It has been established for the purpose of providing insurance to the investors in case of default by a member. The investor will be protected from default up to **Rs. 3,00,000**. The pool of the fund will be collected from **three** different sources of revenue. The corpus fund will be constructed through:

(a) 2.5 per cent of the listing fee
(b) stock turnover fee, Re. 1 for **Rs. 10,00,000** turnover
(c) half of the interest earned on **1 per cent** of the issue amount deposited at the time of public issue/rights issue.

(ii) Trade Guarantee Fund

This fund has also been established by the stock exchange authorities. The Bombay stock exchange started this fund in 1997. The fund consists of contribution of the members and exchange. The fund has established mainly for the purpose of protecting the investor's money. It provides guarantee the settlement of the bonafide transactions of the members of stock exchange. The fund creates confidence in the minds of secondary market operators. The corpus fund of Rs. 60 crore is supplied by the members and stock exchange. If the corpus fund falls below the level, the exchange has to inform the SEBI and its members. The exchange has authority to call further amount of contribution from the members. The fund has been managed by public representatives. The stock exchange will appoint a defaulters committee to look after the affairs of the fund. The failure of a member of the exchange to meet his obligation on **pay in day** to the clearing house is informed to executive director or the **president** of the exchange. The president of the exchange or governing board or two elected directors of the exchange will give **two hours** notice to the defaulting member declare him as **defaulter**. After confirmation of default, the defaulters committee will pay the unpaid settlement dues to the defaulters to the clearing house before the payout. This arrangement avoids the fear of postponement of the payout.

(iii) Broker's Contingency Fund

The broker's contingency fund has formed by the stock exchange in July, 1997. The fund is useful to help the brokers in financial crunch. It grants refundable advance to members. It is only a temporary adjustment for members. All existing members shall pay **Rs. 1,000** as initial non-refundable contribution to the fund.

(iv) Investor's Grievances

The stock exchange gives top priority to the investor's grievances. It has provided an active and efficient dispute resolving mechanism. It established a separate wing **"Investors service cell"** to resolve dispute between investors and trading members and among trading members also. If any violation of law, the exchange can delist the companies for specific periods. The investor has the right to name the arbitrator. Hence it created the investor's confidence in the market. The arbitration composition will be created as per the provisions of the SEBI. SEBI is the most powerful organisation in the stock market. It is the watchdog of the stock market. It controls and regulates all the participants activities in the stock market.

(v) Insurance Policy

The Bombay stock exchange provides an integrated comprehensive coverage of insurance policy for the exchange, its members and the clearing house. It has made arrangements with **New India Assurance Company Ltd.** It is compulsory for all members of the stock exchange. The insurance policy will cover the infidelity of employees, cyber crime, loss of securities of specified nature and error, omission of professional indemnity. However, the insurance covers all the wings of the stock exchange. The insurance coverage for clearing house to the extent of **Rs. 16 billions**. The member of the stock exchange covers to the extent of **Re. 1 crore**. The insurance company will pay the loss in excess of **Rs. 25,000.**

Stock Market Indices

Indices are barometers of an activity. The index number reveals about the quantitative analysis of the data. The indices provide a direction of price movement of stocks or different commodities. It represent the market movement and reveals the attitude of the market behaviour. The market movement may be upward or downward. The indices provide the following benefits to the investors:

(a) Indices reveal about the trend of the market.
(b) Indices reflect the status of the general economy.
(c) Indices help the investor to allocate funds rationally among various stocks.
(d) Indices are more useful to the fund managers, portfolio managers for taking investment decisions.

(e) Indices are useful in price prediction of the individual shares in technical analysis.

(f) Indices can be used as a benchmark for evaluating the different portfolios.

Computation of Stock Index

Stock market index is the barometer for the measurement of wealth. The prosperity of a nation depends upon asset creation. Asset creation means not only it belongs to real estate but also a reflection of growth of the financial assets. Financial assets are the more important in wealth creation. The growth of the financial assets will be measured in terms of **"Stock Indices"**. Financial assets provide high liquidity position than any other assets. A strong asset creation in the country may leads to prosperity. A stock market index may belong to a price index or a wealth index. The unweighted index is a simple arithmetic average of share prices with a base period. The index may provide a picture about the movement of share prices in the stock market. The **Wealth Index** reflects the market capitalisation. The wealth index will be constructed by taking into consideration of subsequent rights and bonus offers. Market capitalisation is an indication of wealth of a particular company. The wealth index gives an idea abut the real wealth created for shareholders over a period of time. The following method explains about the calculation procedure for the wealth index:

Market Capitalisation = No. of shares × Price of share

For example: 1. Equity of the ACC company Rs. 350 (par value Rs. 10)
2. Equity of the Andhra Bank Rs. 90 (par value Rs. 10)
3. Equity of the Hindustan Motors Rs. 30 (par value 10)

The number of shares:

ACC	100
Andhra Bank	200
Hindustan Motors	300

Market Capitalisation = No. of shares × price of share

MC of ACC	100 × 350 = 35000
MC of Andhra Bank	200 × 90 = 18000
MC of H.M.	300 × 30 = 9000
Aggregate market capitalisation	62,000

Index at period N = 100
Market price at N + 1
ACC share price Rs. 370
Andhra Bank Rs. 100
H.M. Rs. 40

Market capitalisation:

ACC	=	370 × 100	=	37000
A.B.	=	100 × 200	=	20000
H.M.	=	300 × 40	=	12000
Aggregate Market Capitalisation				69000

$$\text{Index at period N + 1} = \frac{69000 \times 100}{62000} = 111.29$$

The market index has always been of great importance in security analysis. The investor community has been observing the stock market fluctuations through market indicators. The indexes are equal weighting approach or price weighted or value weighted approaches. All these methods are used in the calculation of index. The price weighted index is a simple arithmetic average. It involves the comparison of currently computed averages with some base value.

Sensex has been known as the barometer of the Bombay stock exchange. It contains 30 scrips, representations were given to new industrial sectors such as services, telecom, consumer goods and automobiles sectors. The criteria adopted in the selection of **30 scrips** are listed:

(a) Sectoral representation
(b) Market capitalisation
(c) Liquidity
(d) Market depth
(e) Floating stock.

Sectoral representation occupies an important role in construction of index. The ideal index should be able to capture the macro industrial aspects through price movements of individual scrips. The index should accommodate all the major industries which cannot be ignored in the general economy. A strong and potential growth of the companies should be selected among all the major industries. The chosen or selected scrip should be representative of the industry. Keeping in view of the latest economic trends in the economy, the industrial sector representation shall be altered in tune with the winds of the economy. **For example:** Infosys in the Sensex is a representative of the information technology. **ICICI Bank** represents banking sector, **ONGC** represents gas and petroleum sector, **Dr. Reddy's Labs.** is a representative of pharmaceutical sector. The selected company should represent the present state of the industry and its future prospects. Hence the industrial sector representation occupies a dominant role in construction of Sensex.

Market capitalisation is another important factor in formation of index. It indicates the true value of the stock. It is a barometer for performance of a company in the stock market. A high networth of market capitalisation leads to dominate the other scrips in the stock market. It enjoys a good reputation among the millions of the investors. The scrip will become **"Darling of the stock market"**. It may become market leader. It creates a lot of confidence among the investors. It helps to enhance the value addition of the asset creation process. Prosperity of a nation depends upon the capitalisation of the different financial assets. Market capitalisation can be computed by the following formula:

Market capitalisation = No. of shares × market price of shares

Liquidity is other important element in construction of Sensex. It is based on the average number of deals of a scrip. It depends upon the active trading of the shares in the stock market. The trading in high turn over leads to the liquidity position of a scrip. Some scrips will not be sold in the market, due to there is no buyer in the market. Hence liquidity co-ordinate the buyer and seller parties for a agreed price in the market. The average number of deals in the two previous years is taken into account. Generally the blue chip shares are easily sold in the market by the members of the stock exchange. Liquidity provides ready market for the Sensex based scrips.

Market depth is another important component of the Sensex. Market depth means, the average deal as a percentage of company's shares outstanding. Generally the companies may approach the public for issue of shares. The issue of shares will be known as **"Public Issue"**. All the shares which are offered to the public, must be listed in recognised stock exchange within a specified period of time. The listing of a scrip with stock exchange creates an environment for buying and selling among the members. All the shares issued by the company will not be traded in the stock exchange. Some percentage of shares will be held by the long-term investors. The remaining shares are circulating in the market from one investor to another. The market depth depends upon the wide equity base.

The active trading in volume with high turnover leads to market depth of the scrip in the stock market.

- **Floating stock depth** means the supply and demand for a scrip in the market. It is the average number of deals as a percentage of floating stock. Sometimes a low circulation of shares stimulate the growth of the share price. Low floating stock may get a hefty amount of price due to non-availability in the market. If the supply of a particular scrip is very low in the market, automatically it commands high price which is based on companies reputation and brand image. Generally for good scrip, the public holding percentage is very high, may leads to more demand in view of shortage of scrips. Trading volumes are directly linked to the public holding.

Table 17: Statement shows Market Capitalisation Ranking at BSE

Rank	*Company*	*Market capitalisation (as on 14-2-05)*	*Market capitalisation (as on 7-2-05)*	*Market capitalisation (as on 14-1-05)*	*Earning per share*
1.	ONGC	1,17,482.37	1,17,239.96	1,11,151.24	78.35
2.	NTPC	75,817.37	76,353.33	66,953.14	5.93
3.	Reliance Industries	75,723.26	73,910.86	71,683.17	48.05
4.	TCS	67,559.67	62,945.91	62,266.57	0.32
5.	Infosys	58,441.83	54,681.52	53,245.30	62.43
6.	Indian Oil	57,513.30	55,107.18	52,730.26	50.07
7.	Wipro	49,851.51	48,190.30	46,757.04	19.01
8.	Bharati Telecom	39,810.39	40,913.14	38,976.37	0.01
9.	SBI	35,035.79	33,822.67	30,443.82	78.13
10.	Hindustan Lever	33,436.23	35,692.46	30,838.81	5.44
11.	ITC	32,667.56	33,034.79	31,129.11	71.88
12.	ICICI Bank	28,030.94	26,511.08	25,842.70	25.08
13.	SAIL	27,074.77	26,703.04	24,080.23	12.48
14.	TISCO	22,408.96	22,123.62	19,308.99	57.66
15.	GAIL	21,225.82	19,716.33	18,452.08	24.37
16.	BHEL	21,056.70	19,132.89	17,422.02	34.90
17.	Ranbaxy	19,540.31	19,738.33	19,894.51	29.42
18.	HDFC	19,422.64	19,627.75	18,155.17	39.78
19.	Tata Motors	18,364.46	17,810.92	17,360.69	31.54
20.	HDFC Bank	17,436.61	17,191.43	14,758.24	20.16
21.	Maruti Udyog	14,180.19	13,261.43	12,117.30	26.00
22.	BPCL	13,500.00	13,296.00	12,150.00	34.28
23.	Satyam Computers	13,442.15	12,893.55	11,552.88	21.25
24.	L&T	13,010.78	12,662.00	11,320.40	72.08
25.	Hindalco	12,793.68	12,629.53	11,535.96	100.85

Sources: *The Economic Times*, 15-2-2005, p. 11.

Table 18: Statement Shows the Components of Mindex (As on 4-2-2005)

(Rs. in crores)

Sl.No.	*Company*	*Market Capitalisation*	*Days weight*	*PE Ratio*
	Mindex	**3,03,150**	**100**	**48.51**
1.	TCS	67560	22.29	–
2.	Infosys	58442	19.28	34.7
3.	Wipro	49852	16.44	37.4
4.	Bharathi Televentures	39810	13.13	–
5.	Satyam Computers	13442	4.43	19.8
6.	HCL Technology	11379	3.75	35.3
7.	MTNL	8927	2.94	11.0
8.	VSNL	6538	2.16	14.9
9.	Zee Telefilm	6274	2.07	37.7
10.	BHEL	5192	1.71	13.9
11.	I-flex	4806	1.59	29.3
12.	Patni Comp	4739	1.56	20.6
13.	Tata Teleservices	4476	1.48	–
14.	HCL Infosys	2688	0.89	21.5
15.	Moserbaer	2660	0.88	24.9
16.	Mophasis BFL	2014	0.66	43.0
17.	Hughes Software	1839	0.61	18.5
18.	Hexaware Soft	1698	0.56	38.8
19.	Hinduja TMT	1348	0.44	17.2
20.	Polaris Soft	1317	0.43	23.5
21.	E-service	1190	0.39	25.8
22.	GTL	1151	0.38	12.4
23.	NDTV	1077	0.36	55.3
24.	CMC	1032	0.34	17.1
25.	Igate	785	0.26	82.9
26.	Tata Infotech	785	0.25	11.90
27.	NIIT	561	0.19	14.10
28.	TV Today	552	0.18	28.80
29.	Mastek	535	0.18	15.50
30.	Balaji Telefilm	502	0.17	11.40

Sources: *The Economic Times*, 15-2-2005, p. 11.

Table 19: Statement shows the Components of **"Lifex"**

(Rs. in crores)

Sl. No.	*Company*	*Market Capitalisation*	*Days Weight*	*PE Ratio*
	Lifex	**95280**	**100**	**26.51**
1.	Ranbaxy	19540	20.51	35.7
2.	Sunpharma	9268	9.73	28.6
3.	Cipla	8295	8.71	21.6

(Contd.)

Table 19 (*Contd.*)

Sl. No.	*Company*	*Market Capitalisation*	*Days Weight*	*PE Ratio*
4.	Dr. Reddy's Labs.	5681	5.96	66.9
5.	Glaxo	5114	5.37	15.8
6.	Nicholos	5047	5.30	19.6
7.	Biocon	4708	4.94	26.6
8.	Workhardt	4037	4.24	19.4
9.	Cadila Health	3198	3.36	19.8
10.	Matriclab	3143	3.30	23.8
11.	Glenmark Pharma	3138	3.29	49.2
12.	Aventis	2804	2.94	20.3
13.	Lupin	2246	2.36	59.3
14.	Pfizer	1962	2.06	46.9
15.	Novartis	1776	1.86	20.8
16.	Aurobindo	1591	1.67	23.6
17.	Apollo Hospital	1484	1.56	32.5
18.	Devi's Lab.	1435	1.51	22.1
19.	Orchid Cheml.	1084	1.14	48.9
20.	Wyeth	1085	1.14	13.3
21.	Abbott	1054	1.11	10.5
22.	Torrent Pharma	1028	1.08	17.3
23.	FDC	1022	1.07	16.8
24.	IPCA Lab	976	1.02	12.1
25.	Merck	825	0.87	11.6
26.	Dishman Pharma	815	0.86	27.7
27.	Astrazen Pharma	808	0.85	33.0
28.	Strides Àrco	746	0.78	290.9
29.	JB Chemicals	705	0.74	12.1
30.	Unichem Labs	662	0.69	14.4

Source: *The Economic Times*, 15-2-2005, p. 11.

Table 20: Statement shows the Components of Brandex (as on 14-2-2005)

(Rs. in crores)

Sl. No.	*Company*	*Market Capitalisation*	*Days Weight*	*PE Ratio*
1.	HLL	33436	32.57	27.9
2.	ITC	32668	31.82	18.3
3.	Nestle	5641	5.49	25.5
4.	Tata Tea	3144	3.06	25.8
5.	Dabur	3073	2.99	23.0
6.	Nirma	2716	2.65	11.9
7.	Colgate	2617	2.55	22.2
8.	Britania	2219	2.16	13.2
9.	Gillette	2134	2.08	34.9

(*Contd.*)

Table 20 (*Contd.*)

Sl. No.	*Company*	*Market Capitalisation*	*Days Weight*	*PE Ratio*
10.	P&G Hygiene	1948	1.90	19.0
11.	Pantaloon	1606	1.56	62.3
12.	Godrej Consumers	1542	1.50	19.3
13.	Glaxo	1515	1.48	20.7
14.	Marico	1275	1.24	19.2
15.	Pidilite	1089	1.06	15.5
16.	Titan	939	0.91	47.6
17.	Shaw Wallace	897	0.87	–
18.	Mc-dowell Co.	778	0.76	32.6
19.	Trent	775	0.75	47.7
20.	Godrej Philips	603	0.59	10.6
21.	Godrej Industries	536	0.52	6.5
22.	Videocon Int.	471	0.46	2.5
23.	Bata	427	0.42	–
24.	Mirc Elect.	334	0.33	13.5
25.	Henkel Spic	272	0.26	86.5
	Total	**102656**	**100.0**	**22.82**

Source: *The Economic Times*, 15-2-2005, p. 11.

Table 21: Statement shows Turnover of Volume at BSE (As on 14-2-2005)

Sl. No.	*Company*	*No. of Shares Traded*	*Turnover (Rs. in crores)*	*Price as on 14-2-05*
	Group A			
1.	Reliance Industries	1812893	99.45	543.15
2.	SAIL	13113259	86.52	65.55
3.	SBI	1229081	82.20	665.70
4.	TISCO	1704771	69.10	404.45
5.	Infosys	289588	62.82	2168.75
6.	Maruti	1186830	58.56	490.80
7.	Satyam Comp.	1324288	55.78	421.45
8.	TCS	343773	48.29	1407.20
9.	Tata Motors	650106	33.09	507.60
10.	BHEL	357751	30.37	860.30
	B1 Group			
1.	Sesa goa	347068	51.55	1501.85
2.	Jubiliant org.	595677	48.00	804.00
3.	India bulls	3200090	32.07	100.30
4.	Jindal Vijayanagar	13027650	24.27	18.60
5.	NOCIL	8837784	23.38	26.60

(*Contd.*)

Table 21 (*Contd.*)

Sl. No.	*Company*	*No. of Shares Traded*	*Turnover (Rs. in crores)*	*Price as on 14.2.05*
	B2 Group			
1.	Essar Oil	4415685	18.01	40.15
2.	Indian Acrl.	3022652	5.13	16.87
3.	Laxmi Over	221195	3.53	160.85
4.	South Iron	918017	3.30	34.85
5.	Cranes Soft	53425	2.97	540.60

Source: *The Economic Times*, 15-2-2005, p. 11.

Table 22: Statement shows Number of Traded Shares in a Day at BSE (as on 14-02-2005)

Scrips	*Group A Shares*	*Group B1*	*Group B2*	*Others*	*Total*
1. Advances	115	187	245	497	1044
2. Declines	83	327	296	662	1388
3. No change	01	09	014	033	057
Total	**199**	**523**	**555**	**1192**	**2489**

Table 23: Statement shows the Movement of Sensex

Year	*Sensex Average*	*High for the Year*
1986-87	570	659
1987-88	455	536
1988-89	613	719
1989-90	730	798
1990-91	1050	1559
1991-92	1845	4285
1992-93	2899	4286
1993-94	2895	4467
1994-95	3975	4631
1995-96	3289	3598
1996-97	3469	4069
1997-98	3812	4548
1998-99	3295	4281
1999-2000	4659	5934
2000-01	4270	5542
2001-02	–	3742

Source: *The Economic Times*, 15-2-05, p. 11.

Table 24: Statement shows Band Hitters/Circuit Filters at BSE as on 14-2-05

High at BSE		*Previous*	*14-02-2005*	
Sl.No.	*Company*	*Close (13-2-05)*	*High/Low*	*Close*
1.	ABL Biotech	38.80	42.65	40.20
2.	ANG Exports	12.92	13.56	13.56
3.	ASM Technology	13.30	15.96	15.50
4.	Aban Loyd. Chem.	1457.75	1530.60	1523.25
5.	Admoran Fin.	10.99	13.18	13.18
6.	Advani Hotel	34.75	36.45	36.45
7.	Alembic Glass	635.65	667.40	667.40
8.	Alfa Transfo	14.30	15.73	15.68
9.	Alfa Vision	13.91	15.30	14.32
10.	Alfred Herbal	67.00	70.35	70.20
11.	Allianz Capital	11.30	12.43	12.43
12.	Anjani Synthetics	12.81	14.09	14.06
13.	Ansal Builders	15.54	17.09	17.09
14.	Ansal Properties	103.40	113.70	113.70
15.	Arihant Found.	17.50	19.25	19.25
16.	Arrow Coated	27.60	30.35	30.25
17.	Arrow Webtext	36.50	38.30	38.30
18.	Arvind Chem.	39.50	41.45	40.00
19.	Arvind Intl.	22.95	25.20	25.20
20.	Ashirwad	31.40	32.95	32.95
21.	Associated Stone	26.85	28.15	28.15
22.	Astra Micro	880.95	924.95	920.05
23.	Avantel Software	106.45	111.75	111.75
24.	BF Utilities	87.70	71.05	71.05
25.	BSEL Infra	23.85	28.60	28.60
26.	Beck India	245.00	257.25	253.50
27.	Beckons India	12.14	13.35	13.35
28.	Best E Hotel	31.10	32.65	32.65
29.	Bhagira Cement	159.70	167.65	167.65
30.	Bhansali Engg.	32.35	35.55	35.10
31.	Bharat Bijlee	3330.65	3497.15	3497.15
32.	Bharat Fertilisers	15.30	16.83	16.83
33.	Bid Power	58.55	61.45	61.10
34.	Bombay Oxygen	2918.00	3063.90	3063.90
35.	Brady Morris	31.65	34.80	32.55
36.	Caplin Point	17.99	18.88	18.88
37.	Casil Health	49.35	51.80	51.80
38.	Ceenix Expo	10.81	11.89	11.89
39.	Cenlub Industries	13.90	15.29	15.29
40.	Choksi Lab	62.20	68.40	67.85
41.	Cupid Condom	17.70	21.20	18.85
42.	Dagger Frost	41.40	45.50	42.05
43.	Damodar	20.40	22.40	20.65

(Contd.)

Table 24 (*Contd.*)

High at BSE		*Previous*	*14-02-2005*	
Sl.No.	*Company*	*Close (13-2-05)*	*High/Low*	*Close*
44.	Datamat Gl. Sr.	105.90	111.15	111.15
45.	Deccan Poly	10.19	11.20	11.20
46.	Dension Hydro	40.10	154.10	152.00
47.	Dharani Sugar	27.25	27.75	27.75
48.	Dolphin Medicals	17.80	18.65	18.65
49.	Dynamat Tech.	356.65	363.75	363.75
50.	Electro Therm.	62.55	63.80	63.80
51.	Ettrol	1.84	2.20	2.16
52.	Empire Indu.	39.10	43.00	43.00
53.	English ICI	256.00	261.10	261.10
54.	Envair Elect.	14.59	16.04	16.00
55.	FCGL Elect.	42.00	42.80	42.80
56.	Fenoplast	11.63	12.79	12.79
57.	Foods & Inns.	69.85	76.80	76.10
58.	G. Tech.	15.00	16.50	16.40
59.	Gangothri Inno.	12.75	13.38	13.38
60.	Godesic Info.	1251.75	1314.30	1284.75
61.	Golden Camin	13.12	15.74	15.00
62.	Greenplay Ind.	56.90	68.25	68.25
63.	Gujarath State Finance	14.68	15.41	15.41
64.	HFCL Infotech	41.95	44.00	44.00
65.	Hazoor Media	10.03	11.03	10.41
66.	Hellios E Mat	129.65	142.60	142.60
67.	Hester Pharma	80.65	84.65	84.65
68.	High Entr. Bat	228.20	239.60	239.60
69.	Hind. Bio Science	17.70	21.20	21.15
70.	Hind. Nat. Gls.	218.25	222.60	222.40
71.	Hotline Tele	18.00	19.80	18.30
72.	Hyderabad Indust.	166.10	169.40	169.40
73.	ICSA	138.60	145.50	145.45
74.	IFB Ind.	13.15	14.46	14.46
75.	IKF Techno	11.09	11.64	11.64
76.	Impex Ferro	35.80	39.35	39.35
77.	India Bulls	93.85	103.20	100.30
78.	Indian Charg.	202.25	22.27	21.56
79.	Indian Surg.	22.60	23.70	23.70
80.	Indraprastha	34.15	40.95	40.95
81.	Inter World	3.05	3.35	3.35
82.	Invest & Prec.	487.40	536.10	498.15
83.	JK Investors	43.30	45.45	45.45
84.	Javellin Techn.	34.50	37.95	37.95
85.	Jindal Poly.	510.00	535.50	535.40
86.	Kanoria Chem.	86.10	103.30	103.25
87.	Karturi Net	29.20	30.65	30.65

(*Contd.*)

Table 24 (*Contd.*)

High at BSE		*Previous*	*14-02-2005*	
Sl.No.	*Company*	*Close (13-2-05)*	*High/Low*	*Close*
88.	Kesarenter	87.05	91.40	91.40
89.	Laffans Petro.	18.65	22.35	22.35
90.	Lakshmi Over.	157.55	165.40	160.85
91.	Liberty Phosp.	26.60	29.25	29.25
92.	Link Pharma	13.71	15.08	15.08
93.	Livewell Pharma	56.65	59.45	59.45
94.	Lyod Elect.	39.85	41.80	41.80
95.	Lyods Metal	37.30	39.15	39.15
96.	Lok Housing	15.80	17.38	17.38
97.	Mac. Chafes	136.05	138.75	138.75
98.	Magma Leasing	55.55	58.30	58.30
99.	Mahalaxmi Smg.	22.25	24.45	23.20
100.	Mahindra Gesco	93.25	102.55	102.55
101.	Majestic Auto	64.50	67.70	67.45
102.	Mawana Sugar	93.75	98.40	94.45
103.	Mega Corpn.	7.52	8.27	8.27
104.	Millars	22.25	23.35	23.35
105.	Milleu Cyber	33.10	39.70	35.30
106.	Milton Plast	10.20	11.22	10.80
107.	Morarka Fin.	26.95	29.60	29.60
108.	Nagar Agri.	125.05	131.30	131.30
109.	Nagpur Power	25.35	27.85	25.90
110.	National Oxy.	43.80	45.95	44.60
111.	Noble Expl.	39.70	43.65	44.60
112.	Onward Tech.	64.75	71.20	71.20
113.	Orbit Expt.	15.97	17.56	17.56
114.	Organic Coat	25.25	26.50	26.50
115.	Pankaj Policy	11.80	12.98	12.98
116.	Pantaloon	229.05	240.50	240.50
117.	Pasupathi Acrl.	10.21	12.25	10.60
118.	Poddar Pigment	11.84	14.20	14.08
119.	Polar Pharma	11.47	12.61	12.61
120.	Poondal	13.40	14.74	14.00
121.	Pratappur	29.55	31.00	31.00
122.	RTS Power Co.	57.05	59.90	59.90
123.	Radhe Develop.	18.70	19.60	19.60
124.	Rainbow Demn.	16.85	17.65	17.65
125.	Raj Industries	13.40	14.70	14.70
126.	Rathi Ispath	39.80	41.75	41.75
127.	Rathi Udyog	40.85	44.90	44.85
128.	Rishi Laser	19.45	21.35	20.00
129.	Roto Pumps	25.10	27.60	27.60
130.	Saag Prf.	19.07	20.97	20.49
131.	SMZS Chem.	24.15	25.35	25.35

(*Contd.*)

Table 24 (*Contd.*)

High at BSE		*Previous*	*14-02-2005*	
Sl.No.	*Company*	*Close (13-2-05)*	*High/Low*	*Close*
132.	Sanjivani	62.20	65.30	65.30
133.	Saregama	126.05	132.25	132.35
134.	Sayaji Hotel	16.30	17.93	17.93
135.	Shakti Met.	33.35	35.00	35.00
136.	Shiv Bi-metal	346.20	363.50	363.50
137.	Sika Iner	10.79	11.85	11.86
138.	Silicon Valley	5.00	5.25	5.25
139.	Silver Smith	12.75	13.38	13.24
140.	Software Techn.	15.01	16.51	16.51
141.	Soma Papers	10.90	11.99	11.99
142.	SB of Bikaner	2462.75	2585.95	2585.95
143.	Stl. Strips	121.55	127.60	127.60
144.	Stone India	24.47	26.91	26.91
145.	Sudarshan Chem.	157.50	165.35	165.35
146.	Surana Corpn.	11.26	12.38	11.35
147.	Subly Ind.	16.20	17.80	17.55
148.	Systel Info.	15.61	17.17	17.10
149.	TASC Pharma	285.90	300.15	283.30
150.	Tot Chem Polcy.	12.52	15.02	15.02
151.	Titanor Comp.	150.70	167.25	167.25
152.	Toyama Elect.	13.00	15.60	13.43
153.	Triveni Glass	18.25	20.05	20.05
154.	Tycho Indus.	18.15	19.95	18.85
155.	UT	42.55	43.40	43.40
156.	Ugar Supar	213.50	217.75	217.75
157.	Vakrangu	39.50	42.95	42.95
158.	Vapi Paper	14.70	16.17	16.17
159.	Vijay Textile	38.05	41.85	38.80
160.	Vikram Thermo	14.15	14.85	14.85
161.	Visaka Ind.	129.90	142.85	137.50
162.	Vyapar Ind.	176.15	179.65	179.65
163.	Vybra Auto	63.90	70.25	70.20
164.	Walchand Cap.	314.95	346.40	346.40
165.	Welcast Stree	150.00	165.00	165.00
166.	Yukogawa	168.65	185.50	185.50
167.	Zen Techn.	111.65	117.20	117.20
168.	Zentech. Lab.	109.90	115.35	115.35
169.	Zodiac JRD	34.65	38.10	37.90
	Low at BSE			
1.	Aarti Industries	131.85	125.30	125.30
2.	Aimco Pesticides	18.45	17.55	18.00
3.	Alchemist	91.35	86.80	87.45
4.	Alpha Hitech	17.69	16.81	16.85
5.	Amforge Ind.	149.85	142.40	142.45

(*Contd.*)

Table 24 (*Contd.*)

Low at BSE		*Previous*	*14-02-2005*	
Sl.No.	*Company*	*Close (13-2-05)*	*High/Low*	*Close*
6.	Aroni Cheml.	40.00	36.05	37.00
7.	Birla Kenna	65.00	58.55	60.55
8.	Blue Coast	39.00	37.10	37.10
9.	Bombay Swa.	199.40	189.45	189.45
10.	Bright Bros.	31.40	29.85	29.85
11.	Core Health	16.55	15.75	16.45
12.	Doctor Biotech.	5.86	5.59	5.59
13.	ECE Indus.	84.50	80.30	80.60
14.	Elecon. Eng.	171.85	168.45	168.45
15.	Enkel Cast	189.90	180.45	182.40
16.	Ganesh Hsg.	36.95	33.30	35.00
17.	Gujarat Leasing	10.30	9.03	9.25
18.	Gulshan Poly.	13.00	10.41	12.50
19.	Harig. Carnk.	42.35	40.25	40.25
20.	Haryana Ship.	19.20	18.25	18.25
21.	Herc. Hoists	486.10	476.40	476.40
22.	Hitech Enter	48.25	45.85	45.85
23.	Indo Pacific Soft	25.70	24.45	24.45
24.	Indus & Prud.	350.90	280.75	280.75
25.	Jagson Airlines	36.50	32.90	33.75
26.	Janice Textiles	15.40	13.87	13.87
27.	Jolly Board	250.00	237.55	237.55
28.	Jyothi	24.40	23.20	23.20
29.	Karawanwoo	21.88	19.70	20.02
30.	Keynote Corpn.	12.66	12.03	12.24
31.	Kohinoor Bros.	12.10	11.50	11.50
32.	Lahothi Over	54.60	51.90	51.95
33.	Lippi System	10.40	9.40	9.40
34.	Living Room L	21.10	20.05	20.05
35.	Lunax Automo	56.20	53.40	53.40
36.	Mcnally Bahr	38.40	36.50	36.70
37.	Mewar Polytex	11.90	9.53	9.53
38.	Monozyme	22.55	21.45	21.45
39.	Neemtek Org	28.50	25.70	25.70
40.	Nicco Corpn.	12.59	11.97	11.97
41.	Parker Agro	13.26	11.94	12.71
42.	Pharmaids	26.00	23.45	23.50
43.	Polymedicar	100.15	95.15	95.15
44.	Prajay Engg.	10.89	9.81	9.89
45.	RM Mohitex	23.00	21.90	21.90
46.	Ratnabali	41.10	39.05	39.05
47.	Sh. Pacetroni	16.66	15.83	15.83
48.	Shrivastava Intn.	61.45	58.40	58.40
49.	Shukun Const.	14.61	13.88	14.08

(*Contd.*)

Table 24 (*Contd.*)

Low at BSE		*Previous*	*14-02-2005*	
Sl.No.	*Company*	*Close (13-2-05)*	*High/Low*	*Close*
50.	Simbha Sugar	25.55	74.05	74.05
51.	Sinclair Hotels	31.00	29.50	30.00
52.	Sunshield Cheml.	23.95	22.80	22.80
53.	Synergy Meite	41.50	39.45	39.60
54.	TCI Industries	414.75	406.50	406.50
55.	Todays Writing	45.20	42.95	43.65
56.	Tangsune BI	149.05	146.10	146.10
57.	Ushdev Intnl.	42.90	40.80	41.30
58.	Wellswoth One	5.04	4.54	4.74
59.	Western	13.80	12.43	12.50
60.	Yashraj Constn.	13.25	12.60	12.60

Source: *The Economic Times*, 15-2-2005, p. 11.

Table 25: Statement shows "Forward Shares Price Movements" as on 14-2-05

Sl.No.	*Company*	*Price as on 11-2-05*	*Price as on 11-1-05*	*Price as on 11-2-04*
1.	ABB	1268.05	923.45	285.00
2.	ACC	387.70	333.45	174.10
3.	Abbott	687.80	631.79	459.00
4.	Adani Export	77.60	70.70	76.80
5.	Alfalaval	741.35	695.25	162.25
6.	Allahabad Bank	70.20	64.30	–
7.	Alok Industries	66.85	62.85	72.33
8.	Alstom Project	164.45	164.25	–
9.	Andhra Bank	85.45	71.80	–
10.	Apollo Hospital	330.20	246.55	515.29
11.	Apollo Tyres	287.00	250.55	160.00
12.	Arvind Mills	121.90	108.90	20.72
13.	Aashi Industries	168.30	150.05	22.55
14.	Ashok Leyland	24.10	22.80	8.86
15.	Asian Paints	358.80	316.80	165.04
16.	Aurobindo Pharma	308.40	300.35	292.67
17.	Aventis Pharma	1203.50	1223.55	853.50
18.	BASF	201.35	167.60	109.00
19.	BHEL	818.45	732.45	143.55
20.	BPCL	452.20	427.00	158.52
21.	Bajaj Auto	1087.25	1080.30	313.00
22.	Balaji Telefilm	97.30	102.90	–
23.	Ballarpur Industries	88.40	82.80	49.87
24.	Bank of Baroda	208.80	193.85	48.35
25.	Bank of India	85.10	75.59	17.39

(*Contd.*)

Table 25 (*Contd.*)

Sl.No.	*Company*	*Price as on 11-2-05*	*Price as on 11-1-05*	*Price as on 11-2-04*
26.	BEML	357.65	309.55	27.20
27.	BEL	637.05	580.65	117.15
28.	Bharath Forge	1347.75	1027.59	205.75
29.	Bharati Televenture	208.65	195.40	–
30.	Birla Corpn.	188.05	166.85	25.29
31.	Bombay Deying	235.75	202.55	65.00
32.	Bongaigaon Refin	89.30	87.20	11.90
33.	Britania	900.00	893.25	670.00
34.	CESC	168.65	152.80	24.41
35.	CMC	668.25	707.90	671.75
36.	Cadila Health	509.20	504.60	–
37.	Canara Bank	209.40	185.25	–
38.	Castrol	209.40	203.35	307.00
39.	Century Enka	151.10	147.19	55.85
40.	Century Text.	226.05	161.15	39.60
41.	Chambal Fert.	33.30	26.65	13.45
42.	Chennai Petro	217.45	223.85	46.00
43.	Cipla	275.70	252.55	236.55
44.	Colgate	191.45	173.75	161.00
45.	Container Co.	829.25	825.20	245.00
46.	Corpn. Bank	349.00	311.85	108.00
47.	Crompton Greaves	360.45	280.39	45.65
48.	Cummins India	131.60	123.25	100.20
49.	D-Link	123.65	117.60	–
50.	Dabur	104.65	86.95	126.50
51.	Dena Bank	34.40	35.10	12.30
52.	Dr. Reddy's Lab.	742.20	732.70	798.95
53.	Dredding Corpn.	482.05	436.60	224.50
54.	East India Hotels	321.50	261.55	131.00
55.	Engineers India Ltd.	337.35	313.50	261.50
56.	Escorts	70.60	65.55	253.05
57.	Essel Prop.	284.65	268.45	418.82
58.	Excide Indu.	155.80	154.25	76.55
59.	FDC	53.85	52.10	18.76
60.	Federal Bank	155.25	148.00	25.90
61.	FACT	30.65	29.50	–
62.	Finolex Cable	176.25	148.25	257.00
63.	Finolex Indu.	71.60	63.00	29.70
64.	GAIL	247.00	218.25	66.45
65.	GE Shipping	166.40	151.50	19.25
66.	GNFC	74.90	61.60	47.00
67.	GTL	114.40	112.35	910.00
68.	Geometric Soft	443.50	374.40	–
69.	Gillete	653.45	641.79	223.95

(*Contd.*)

Table 25 (*Contd.*)

Sl.No.	*Company*	*Price as on 11-2-05*	*Price as on 11-1-05*	*Price as on 11-2-04*
70.	Glaxosmith Consumer	334.70	319.30	414.30
71.	Glaxosmith Health	680.35	684.80	553.00
72.	Godrej Consumer	277.20	282.95	–
73.	Grasim Indu.	1352.25	1245.70	338.45
74.	Gujarat Ambuja	451.50	400.70	295.00
75.	Gujarat Gas Co.	756.70	588.29	430.00
76.	Gujarat Ind. Power	77.35	67.15	30.05
77.	Gujarat Mineral	342.05	304.55	43.80
78.	HCL Infosys	801.00	790.45	892.50
79.	HCL Techno.	350.60	312.45	1399.02
80.	HDFC	784.40	722.80	161.50
81.	HDFC Bank	574.65	479.45	246.00
82.	HLL	155.30	138.94	249.00
83.	HMT	44.95	40.40	11.50
84.	HPCL	373.80	364.45	152.00
85.	Hero Hond	550.35	547.40	166.20
86.	Heware Technl.	790.45	473.90	1295.00
87.	Hindustan Zinc	174.75	137.19	11.90
88.	Hindalco	1370.45	1240.25	810.00
89.	Hinduja TMT	342.45	283.60	436.45
90.	Huges Soft	549.80	526.75	2124.65
91.	I-Flex	627.95	599.75	–
92.	IBP	590.65	572.60	1475.50
93.	ICI	234.95	225.65	152.00
94.	ICICI Bank	374.85	345.00	175.05
95.	IDBI	108.60	100.90	21.89
96.	IDBI Bank	73.65	61.55	24.92
97.	I-gate Global	262.90	253.75	–
98.	Ing. Vysya Bank	590.90	545.85	121.70
99.	IPCA Lab.	402.30	420.12	111.65
100.	IPCL	185.45	169.00	90.95
101.	ITC	1333.95	1269.30	999.50
102.	India Cement	68.30	58.35	80.75
103.	Indian Hotels	590.70	498.90	244.00
104.	Indian Oil Corp.	488.25	469.00	149.41
105.	IOB	66.85	64.45	–
106.	Indian Rayon	438.45	354.05	69.50
107.	Indo Gulf	131.00	121.45	–
108.	Indo Rama	71.60	67.00	10.30
109.	Indus Ind.	58.30	55.55	37.29
110.	Infosys Techn.	2103.30	1903.55	2460.00
111.	Ingersol Raud	242.85	259.20	238.50
112.	Ispat Ind.	27.40	19.60	6.75
113.	J&K Bank	353.70	342.25	34.00

(*Contd.*)

Table 25 (*Contd.*)

Sl.No.	*Company*	*Price as on 11-2-05*	*Price as on 11-1-05*	*Price as on 11-2-04*
114.	JB Chemicals	441.90	428.85	174.10
115.	Jai Prakash	192.10	172.95	–
116.	Jindal Iron	412.25	311.89	17.50
117.	Jindal Saw	272.50	193.40	35.04
118.	Jindal Stain	98.05	82.40	–
119.	Jindal Steel	1065.25	871.70	172.55
120.	Koch. Ref.	191.50	220.05	56.67
121.	Kotak Mahindra Bank	330.20	263.20	83.50
122.	L&T	991.75	923.30	417.00
123.	LIC Housing	227.15	200.10	30.45
124.	Lupin	557.15	651.90	33.79
125.	M&M	567.50	493.35	507.75
126.	MICO	950.05	1766.70	433.25
127.	MIRC Elect.	24.45	22.55	36.76
128.	MRPL	54.20	48.50	14.50
129.	MTNL	140.30	135.35	312.50
130.	Mah. Seamless	348.80	290.45	21.20
131.	Maruti Udyog	498.35	413.30	–
132.	Mastek	387.80	330.45	2453.00
133.	Merk	487.10	490.40	460.00
134.	Micro Industries	554.75	634.54	258.84
135.	Moser Baer	233.30	218.75	210.00
136.	Mophasis BFL	244.80	241.35	525.25
137.	NTPC	92.10	79.05	–
138.	National Alum.	181.10	170.00	59.05
139.	National Fertl.	38.60	37.60	15.65
140.	Nestle	589.65	543.04	376.15
141.	Neveli Lignite	71.45	65.15	7.65
142.	Nicholas Piramal	265.50	255.65	117.99
143.	Nirma	344.15	323.25	1402.30
144.	Novartis	573.50	622.50	957.85
145.	ONGC	820.70	776.80	174.10
146.	Orchid Chem.	347.95	290.45	458.60
147.	OBC	313.65	290.50	37.15
148.	P&G Hygiene	585.05	568.55	462.30
149.	Pfizer	693.05	712.80	546.50
150.	Pidilite Ind.	429.35	396.30	392.95
151.	Polaris Soft	133.95	139.15	858.75
152.	PNB	420.95	353.55	–
153.	Punjab Tractors	192.95	189.35	270.60
154.	RCF	40.20	37.04	11.75
155.	Ranco System	415.75	393.85	–
156.	Ranbaxy	1045.05	1068.55	612.95
157.	Raymond	321.20	287.20	75.75

(*Contd.*)

Table 25 (*Contd.*)

Sl.No.	Company	Price as on 11-2-05	Price as on 11-1-05	Price as on 11-2-04
158.	Reliance Capital	153.60	135.60	201.35
159.	Reliance Energy	572.60	496.70	272.50
160.	Reliance Indu.	548.55	518.29	350.00
161.	Rolta India	87.25	76.55	806.60
162.	SAIL	64.65	56.30	12.30
163.	SBI	654.15	573.20	240.60
164.	SKF India	188.65	135.55	83.23
165.	Spice	72.00	62.78	–
166.	Satyam Comp.	410.35	356.05	934.51
167.	Shipping Corporation	171.35	144.60	16.05
168.	Siemens	1587.60	1264.30	405.10
169.	Stent Biotech	164.95	156.80	4.10
170.	Sterlite Industries	676.05	560.75	248.33
171.	Steel Optica	80.30	78.95	–
172.	Sun Pharma	498.05	463.55	199.66
173.	Syndicate Bank	57.20	51.40	12.60
174.	Syngeta	413.35	384.70	–
175.	TISCO	398.90	344.15	88.60
176.	TN Newsprint	65.15	60.45	35.40
177.	TVS Motor	74.35	75.95	35.43
178.	Tata Chem.	169.95	147.85	49.50
179.	TCS	1381.85	1292.20	–
180.	Tata Elxi	168.55	145.15	218.00
181.	Tata Infotech	421.55	371.75	650.00
182.	Tata Motors	503.85	474.25	153.60
183.	Tata Power	409.60	339.15	79.09
184.	Tata Tea	546.50	469.30	585.00
185.	Thermax	587.55	488.45	107.50
186.	Titan Industries	223.75	173.00	105.00
187.	Torrent Pharma	487.95	539.85	514.00
188.	UTI Bank	230.70	180.35	35.25
189.	Union Bank of India	117.35	94.15	–
190.	United Phosphorus	688.00	685.65	2.75
191.	VSNL	219.35	214.80	785.40
192.	Videocon Intnl.	67.15	58.60	84.10
193.	Vijaya Bank	59.70	58.80	–
194.	Visual Soft	121.60	120.75	290.40
195.	Welspun Gujarat	45.00	39.79	6.15
196.	Wipro	695.45	656.85	940.82
197.	Wockhardt	377.85	351.05	–
198.	Wyeth	468.55	486.00	407.10
199.	Zee Telefilm	151.7-	154.75	1371.15

Source: *The Economic Times*, p. 10.

Table 26: Statement shows Free Float Stock Market Portfolio as on 31-12-2004

(Rs. in crore)

	Particulars	*Market Capitalisation*	*Percentage*
1.	Foreign institutional investors	2,14,835	29.99
2.	Indian public	1,93,887	27.07
3.	Banks, financial institutions and insurance	1,01,800	14.21
4.	Others	67,471	9.42
5.	Private corporate bodies	53,429	7.46
6.	Mutual funds and UTI	49,094	6.85
7.	Non-resident Indians EOCBs	35,788	5.00
	Total free float market capitalisation	**7,16,305**	**100**

Source: *The Economic Times*, p. 1.

Table 27: Statement shows Bank Stock Performance During a Year 8.2.2004 to 8.2.2005

		Price as on 8-2-05	*Price as on 8-1-05*	*Price as on 8-2-04*
1.	Allahabad Bank	70.95	74.05	28.80
2.	Andhra Bank	84.70	84.25	48.65
3.	Bank of Baroda	209.25	221.30	249.55
4.	Bank of India	86.05	91.00	67.75
5.	Bank of Maharashtra	33.20	38.29	0.00
6.	Bank of Punjab	35.50	35.04	28.55
7.	Bank of Rajasthan	60.75	63.35	43.95
8.	Canara Bank	17.25	19.45	18.10
9.	Centurion Bank	89.55	91.25	68.70
10.	City Union Bank	89.55	91.25	68.70
11.	Corporation Bank	339.65	332.40	244.20
12.	Dena Bank	35.25	39.45	29.35
13.	Dhanalaxmi Bank	29.00	33.20	27.00
14.	Federal Bank	148.50	164.45	93.58
15.	HDFC Bank	560.95	489.50	363.65
16.	ICICI Bank	360.20	358.75	333.30
17.	IDBI Bank	78.20	74.00	51.10
18.	ING Vyasva Bank	563.65	582.85	618.25
19.	IOB	68.55	73.84	38.60
20.	Indus Ind Bank	57.75	61.65	41.95
21.	J&K Bank	341.70	377.30	481.05
22.	Karnataka Bank	82.75	87.76	45.50
23.	KVB	473.85	483.35	359.70
24.	Kotak Mahindra Bank	312.85	282.89	190.90

(Contd.)

Table 27 (*Contd.*)

		Price as on 8-2-05	Price as on 8-1-05	Price as on 8-2-04
25.	OBC	301.25	316.85	268.35
26.	PNB	400.15	402.60	277.20
27.	South Indian Bank	66.20	68.80	72.99
28.	SBI	642.65	615.20	623.54
29.	State Bank of Bikaner	2370.00	2456.40	1718.94
30.	State Bank of Mysore	2101.00	2144.00	2050.00
31.	State Bank of Travancore	1905.25	2002.20	1531.35
32.	Syndicate Bank	56.60	61.80	36.54

Source: *The Economic Times*, 15-2-2005, p. 12.

Table 28: Statement shows Shareholding Pattern of Banks as on 8-2-2005 (percentage)

		Shareholding Pattern in Banks				
		Promoters	FIIS	Public	Others	Total
1.	Allahabad Bank	71.16	0.00	25.07	3.77	100.00
2.	Andhra Bank	62.50	7.03	23.16	7.31	100.00
3.	Bank of Baroda	66.83	17.40	7.54	8.23	100.00
4.	Bank of India	69.47	5.50	14.18	10.85	100.00
5.	Bank of Maharashtra	76.77	0.00	17.67	5.56	100.00
6.	Bank of Punjab	34.47	0.59	44.75	20.19	100.00
7.	Bank of Rajasthan	44.16	0.07	36.28	19.49	100.00
8.	Canara Bank	73.17	13.43	8.88	4.52	100.00
9.	Centurion Bank	0.33	22.13	13.44	64.10	100.00
10.	City Union Bank	0.00	0.00	81.14	18.86	100.00
11.	Corporation Bank	57.17	10.62	2.97	29.24	100.00
12.	Dena Bank	70.99	0.00	19.61	9.40	100.00
13.	Dhanalaxmi Bank	37.01	0.00	52.78	10.21	100.00
14.	Federal Bank	0.00	7.11	44.51	48.38	100.00
15.	HDFC Bank	24.09	26.98	15.12	33.81	100.00
16.	ICICI Bank	0.00	47.15	8.14	44.71	100.00
17.	IDBI Bank	69.39	0.15	17.14	13.32	100.00
18.	ING Vyasva Bank	44.24	19.26	15.55	20.95	100.00
19.	IOB	61.23	5.15	23.97	9.65	100.00
20.	Indus Ind Bank	41.32	8.20	29.16	21.32	100.00
21.	J&K Bank	53.15	21.90	19.23	5.72	100.00
22.	Karnataka Bank	0.00	2.76	77.37	19.87	100.00
23.	KVB	4.84	0.58	73.37	21.21	100.00
24.	Kotak Mahindra bank	60.95	15.91	16.14	7.00	100.00
25.	OBC	66.48	14.29	7.67	11.56	100.00
26.	PNB	80.00	12.82	4.37	2.81	100.00
27.	South Indian Bank	0.00	0.17	65.52	34.31	100.00

(*Contd.*)

Table 28 (*Contd.*)

		Shareholding Pattern in Banks				
		Promoters	*FIIS*	*Public*	*Others*	*Total*
28.	SBI	59.73	11.46	6.71	22.10	100.00
29.	State Bank of Bikaner	75.00	1.90	13.34	9.76	100.00
30.	State Bank of Mysore	92.33	0.21	5.39	2.07	100.00
31.	State Bank of Travancore	75.00	1.73	13.08	10.19	100.00
32.	Syndicate Bank	75.32	0.80	19.97	5.71	100.00

Source: *The Economic Times*, 15-2-2005, p. 12.

Table 29: Statement shows the PSU Stock Performance During the Period 8-2-2004 to 8-2-2005

		Price as on 8-2-05	*Price as on 8-1-05*	*Price as on 8-1-04*
1.	Andrew Yule	26.10	25.80	25.20
2.	BHEL	781.70	737.40	588.40
3.	BPCL	443.20	457.00	475.95
4.	Balmer Lawrence	61.70	49.90	43.00
5.	Balmer Law	208.50	151.19	123.95
6.	BEML	335.65	314.14	191.60
7.	Bharat Electronics	587.10	624.00	563.70
8.	Bharat Immunisation	24.55	24.25	13.35
9.	Bongaigaon Refinery	90.10	93.15	76.05
10.	Chennai Petro	226.75	230.05	88.35
11.	Container Corporation	829.90	890.70	730.00
12.	Dredging Corporation	473.05	454.05	482.25
13.	EIL	330.65	323.50	375.10
14.	GAIL	233.15	235.70	222.25
15.	HMT	44.05	44.45	21.15
16.	HPCL	356.05	392.80	463.95
17.	Hindustan Copper	40.05	38.75	44.75
18.	Hindustan Organics	25.55	24.85	21.00
19.	IBP	575.00	599.04	736.45
20.	ITI	27.25	29.65	17.60
21.	IOC	471.80	497.15	477.15
22.	Kochin Refinery	190.50	226.65	164.70
23.	LIC Housing	220.40	193.15	203.20
24.	MRPL	51.85	52.35	55.55
25.	MTNL	137.10	142.94	136.94
26.	Madras Fertilisers	17.05	16.55	17.10
27.	NTPC	92.60	83.45	0.00
28.	National Aluminium	177.00	179.85	174.25
29.	National Fertilisers	39.60	38.85	42.90
30.	NMDC	1011.00	670.00	468.95
31.	Neyvile Lignite	70.40	72.80	52.60
32.	ONGC	822.20	792.35	744.60

Source: *The Economic Times*, p. 12.

Table 30: Statement shows the Shareholding Pattern of PSUs During the Period 8-2-04 to 8-2-05

Sl.No.	*Company*	*Share Holding Pattern*				
		Government	*FIIS*	*Public*	*Others*	*Total*
1.	Andrew Yule	93.26	0.00	4.80	1.94	100.00
2.	BHEL	67.72	20.56	0.87	10.85	100.00
3.	BPCL	66.20	13.87	3.05	16.88	100.00
4.	Balmer Law	59.67	0.16	16.82	23.35	100.00
5.	Balmer Lawrence	0.00	0.45	14.00	85.55	100.00
6.	BEML	61.23	0.45	18.53	19.79	100.00
7.	BEL	75.86	5.49	4.38	14.27	100.00
8.	Bharat Immunisation	0.00	0.00	16.68	83.32	100.00
9.	Bongaigaon Refinery	74.46	1.38	13.94	10.22	100.00
10.	Chennai Petro	67.27	2.13	8.39	22.21	100.00
11.	Container Corporation	63.09	26.60	1.73	8.58	100.00
12.	Dredging Corporation	78.56	6.96	5.00	9.48	100.00
13.	EIL	90.39	0.16	4.15	5.30	100.00
14.	GAiL	57.34	12.34	5.26	25.06	100.00
15.	HMT	98.19	0.00	0.74	1.07	100.00
16.	HPCL	51.01	19.34	0.60	23.05	100.00
17.	Hindustan Copper	98.95	0.00	0.20	0.85	100.00
18.	Hindustan Organics	58.61	0.04	28.65	12.70	100.00
19.	IBP	53.58	11.86	14.67	19.89	100.00
20.	ITI	77.02	0.07	15.99	6.92	100.00
21.	IOC	82.03	1.02	3.42	13.53	100.00
22.	Kochin Refineries	54.81	3.54	17.17	24.48	100.00
23.	LIC Housing	38.50	15.73	14.54	31.23	100.00
24.	MRPL	88.57	0.01	9.67	1.75	100.00
25.	MTNL	56.25	14.53	1.88	27.34	100.00
26.	Madras Fertilisers	85.27	0.00	11.69	3.04	100.00
27.	NTPC	0.00	0.00	0.00	0.00	100.00
28.	National Aluminiun	87.15	2.1	1.40	9.34	100.00
29.	National Fertilisers	97.64	0.01	0.37	1.98	100.00
30.	NMDC	98.38	0.00	0.17	1.45	100.00
31.	Neyvile Lignite	93.56	0.56	1.74	4.14	100.00
32.	ONGC	74.14	6.36	3.02	16.48	100.00

Table 31: Statement shows Market Capitalisation of Indian National Companies and Multinational Companies During the Period 2004 (1-1-04 to 31-12-04)
Market capitalisation overall increased by INC – 24% MNC – 04%

Sl.No.	*Indian Company*	*Market Capitalisation Change*		
		1-1-04	*31-12-04 (Rs. in crore)*	*Percentage*
1.	Reliance	79566	73743	**–7.3**
2.	Infosys	37428	50039	58
3.	Wipro	40881	52623	29
4.	Bharathi	20572	39282	91
5.	ICICI Bank	18583	27436	48
6.	Ranbaxy Lab.	20479	23127	13
7.	Tata Steel	16444	21638	32
8.	HDFC	15842	18665	18
9.	Tata Motors	14998	18452	23
10.	HDFC Bank	10398	14840	43
11.	Satyam Comp.	11843	13152	11
12.	L&T	13191	13043	**–1.1**
13.	Hindalco	12956	12651	**–2.4**
14.	Grasim Industries	9277	11947	29
15.	Bajaj Auto	11491	11341	**–1.3**
16.	Hero Honda Motors	9132	10999	20
17.	HCL Technology	9187	10523	15
18.	Sun Pharma	5547	10164	83
19.	Reliance Energy	7841	9776	25
20.	Cipla	8101	9331	15
21.	Tata Power	6369	7561	19
22.	Gujarat Ambuja	4931	7139	45
23.	Zee Telefilms	6233	7120	14
24.	VSNL	4493	6668	48
25.	Dr. Reddy's Lab.	10951	6561	**–40**
26.	Sterlite Industries	5034	6512	**29**
27.	Hindustan Zinc Ltd.	5658	6387	13
28.	Mahindra & Mahindra	4560	6350	39
29.	Nicholos Piramal	2999	6039	101
30.	Associated Cement	4435	5804	31
31.	Tata Teleservices	3324	4813	45
32.	IPCL	5717	4440	**–22**
33.	Bharat Forge	2965	4431	49
34.	UTI Bank	3169	4309	36
35.	Workhard	2655	3854	45
36.	Cadila Healthcare	2432	3636	50
37.	Tata Chemicals	2823	3619	28
38.	Kotak Mahindra Bank	2317	3522	52
39.	Matrix Lab	1965	3481	77

(Contd.)

Table 31 (*Contd.*)

Sl.No.	*Indian Company*	*Market Capitalisation Change*		
		1-1-04	*31-12-04 (Rs. in crore)*	*Percentage*
40.	G.E. Shipping	3161	3191	1
41.	Asian Paints	3230	3116	–4
42.	Jindal Steel	1983	2898	46
43.	Lupin	2883	2802	–3
44.	Nirma	3683	2758	–25
45.	Tata Tea	1968	2714	38
46.	HCL Infosystem	1278	2694	111
47.	Arvind Mills	1335	2573	93
48.	Indian Hotels	2007	2474	23
49.	Dabur India	2538	2450	–3
50.	Glenmark Pharma	862	2400	179
51.	Jindal Vijayanagar	1739	2323	34
52.	Indian Rayon	167	2287	41
53.	Britania Industries	1752	2212	26
54.	Essar Steel	1313	2186	67
55.	Jubliant Organosys	1318	2144	63
56.	Raymond	1435	1945	36
57.	TVS Motor	2572	1937	–25
58.	J&K Bank	1862	1756	–6
59.	Godrej Consumer Products	1007	1746	73
60.	DSP Merrill Lynch	1051	1737	65
61.	Davi's Lab	2045	1717	–16
62.	Adani Exports	919	1716	87
63.	Century Textiles	1345	1705	27
64.	Amtek Auto	669	1695	153
65.	Reliance Capital	1732	1694	–02
66.	Micro Inks	1491	1647	10
67.	Polaris Software	2472	1635	–33
68.	Aurobindo Pharma	2028	1627	–19
69.	East India Hotels	1591	1543	–3
70.	Sundaram Clayton	1213	1516	25
71.	Jindal Iron & Steel	1305	1500	15
72.	Crompton Greaves	882	1483	68
73.	Pantaloon Retail	487	1426	193
74.	Ballarpur Industries	1351	1415	05
75.	Hexaware Technology	926	1396	51
76.	Sterling Biotech	867	1372	58
77.	Mathersan Sumi	1047	1304	25
78.	Thermax	1033	1300	26
79.	CESC	876	1287	47
80.	IDBI Bank	1118	1278	15
81.	Sundaram Fasteners	1106	1267	15
82.	Torrent Pharma	861	1228	43

(*Contd.*)

Table 31 (*Contd.*)

Sl.No.	*Indian Company*	*Market Capitalisation Change*		
		1-1-04	*31-12-04 (Rs. in crore)*	*Percentage*
83.	Punjab Tractors	1440	1216	**–16**
84.	Madras Cements	986	1215	23
85.	Tata Finance	1129	1187	05
86.	Centurion Bank	283	1186	319
87.	Exide Industries	1011	1171	16
88.	Birla Corporation	567	164	105
89.	FDC	865	1161	34
90.	Ashahi India Glass	1145	155	01
91.	IPCA Lab.	783	1132	45
92.	Balrampur Chini	531	1128	112
93.	Chambal Fertilisers	966	1123	16
94.	CMC	932	1086	17
95.	Laxmi Machine	608	1068	76
96.	MRF	1000	1066	07
97.	Apollo Hospitals	733	1064	45
98.	Essar Shipping	850	1050	24
99.	Federal Bank	612	1045	71
100.	Jindal Stainless	935	1027	10
	Company (MNC)			
1.	Indian Tobacco Industries	24562	32697	33
2.	Hindustan Lever Ltd.	46798	31621	**–32**
3.	Maruti Udyog	10831	13391	24
4.	Glaxosmith Pharma	4377	6685	53
5.	Motor Industries	5130	6083	19
6.	Nestle India	6750	5667	**–16**
7.	I-flex	6452	4610	**–29**
8.	Siemens	3511	4336	24
9.	ABB	2823	4143	47
10.	Aventis Pharma	1611	3119	94
11.	Ashok Leyland	3497	2961	**–15**
12.	Castrol India	2958	2816	**–05**
13.	Mosarbaer	3400	2568	**–25**
14.	Colgate Palmolive	2292	2457	07
15.	Cummins India	2461	2403	**–02**
16.	Gillette India	2438	2246	**–08**
17.	Novartis India	1376	2158	57
18.	Mophasis BFL	2696	2146	**–20**
19.	Pfizer	1610	2008	25
20.	Sesa Goa	1174	2003	71
21.	Hughes Software	1923	1888	**–02**
22.	P&G Hygiene	1542	1774	15
23.	Ispat Industries	1101	1773	61
24.	Monsanto India	1344	176	31

(*Contd.*)

Table 31 (*Contd.*)

Sl.No.	Indian Company	Market Capitalisation Change 1-1-04	31-12-04 (Rs. in crore)	Percentage
25.	Indus Ind Bank	964	1674	74
26.	Glaxosmith – Health	1484	1511	02
27.	Sygenta India	770	1300	69
28.	Alfa Laval	1038	1298	25
29.	Hinduja TMT	1485	1281	–37
30.	ING Vysya Bank	1271	1279	01
31.	Wyeth	964	1267	32
32.	Abott India	734	1122	53
33.	Alstam Projects	907	1071	18
34.	Indorama Synthetics	1223	1046	–15
35.	Bayor Crops.	1142	1043	–09
36.	Goodlas Nerolac	688	989	44
37.	Merck	719	953	33
38.	ICI	793	949	20
39.	Ingersoll Rand	983	858	–13
40.	Atlas Copco	464	821	77
41.	Igate Global Solutions	936	795	–15
42.	Astazenceca Pharma	544	792	45
43.	Shaw Wallace	338	747	121
44.	Gujarat Gas	787	730	–07
45.	SKF India	517	710	37
46.	Thomas Cook	686	700	02
47.	Kennametal Widia	500	655	31
48.	3M India	578	618	07
49.	Macmillan	465	600	29
50.	Bata	344	492	43
51.	BASF	503	488	–03
52.	ITC Hotels	403	467	16
53.	Timken India	408	451	10
54.	Gainwell Notton	363	425	17
55.	Liba Speciality Chem.	217	415	91
56.	KSB Pumps	226	407	80
57.	VSI Industries	297	387	31
58.	Zensar Techno	320	384	20
59.	Alstom	257	382	49
60.	Vesuil India	310	362	17
61.	Clariant	270	341	26
62.	Colour Chem.	307	334	09
63.	Henkel Spic	363	318	–13
64.	BOC India	288	305	06
65.	Whirlpool	381	294	–23
66.	Saint Gobaint	243	291	20
67.	Mascon Global	96	290	202

(*Contd.*)

Table 31 *(Contd.)*

Sl.No.	*Indian Company*	*Market Capitalisation Change*		
		1-1-04	*31-12-04 (Rs. in crore)*	*Percentage*
68.	Onde Nalco	157	282	80
69.	South East Asia	198	279	41
70.	FAG Bearing	222	274	23
71.	Paper Products	250	269	08
72.	Schendary Herdilla	153	264	73
73.	Aztech Software	137	255	85
74.	Sunflog	196	254	29
75.	Wartsila	255	234	**–08**
76.	Bayer	227	229	01
77.	Solectron Centum	169	220	30
78.	Solvay Pharma	110	220	99
79.	Agro Tech Foods	187	205	10
80.	Wirnco	184	192	05
81.	Denso India	184	192	05
82.	Beck India	61	190	05
83.	Foseco	184	187	02
84.	Timex Watches	216	187	**–13**
85.	FCI	122	178	47
86.	Hindustan Power Plus	183	176	**–03**
87.	Gulf Oil	178	175	**–02**
88.	India Gypsum	135	173	28
89.	Gujjar Sidhee Cement	124	170	38
90.	Fulford	126	167	33
91.	Good Year	125	170	34
92.	Insinco	142	161	14
93.	Itgarshi Motors	128	152	19
94.	Rayban Sun Optics	154	145	**–05**
95.	Fairfield Atlas	54	135	149
96.	Indo Rana Textiles	86	133	53
97.	Goodricke Group	127	131	04

Sources: The Economic Times, 7-1-2005, P. No. 4.

National Stock Exchange

The process of globalisation began with the opening up of the Indian capital markets to the **Foreign Institutional Investors** in 1992. This led the foreign custodians and brokers setting up base in India. They bought their best global practice in the Indian markets. Equity research, portfolio management, gained a prominence. The NSE became operational in the capital market on 3-11-1994 in **Mumbai.** It was set up with a paid up equity capital of **Rs. 25 crores**. It was recognised by the Union government. It has been sponsored by **IDBI, ICICI, IFCI, GIC, SBI, Bank of Baroda, Canara Bank, Corporation Bank, Indian Bank, OBC, UBI, PNB, ILFS, SHCIL**. It was established on the recommendations of the **Pherwani Committee**. The main objectives of NSE are as follows:

(a) to provide national level trading facility for equity debt instruments and hybrid securities.
(b) to provide equal opportunities to investors all over the country.
(c) to provide world standard services to the FIIs.
(d) to provide a fair, efficient and transparent system in market by applying latest information technology methods.
(e) to provide shorten settlement cycle and book entry settlement system.
(f) to encourage debt market.
(g) to prevent the insider trading and price rigging.
(h) to protect the brokers from default.
(i) to provide the listing facilities to public sector undertakings.
(j) to create more employment opportunities in the orbit of capital market.
(k) to professionalise the members to be more competent.
(l) to spread the investment and cult to the savers in rural and urban areas.
(m) to protect the members from the default risk.

The National stock exchange has a fully automated electronic screen based trading system. Trading was done on the computer with the help of the P.C. terminals in broker offices. NSE is India's premier stock exchange at present. Membership in this stock exchange is a great privilege in the orbit of the capital market. It is based on several factors such as capital adequacy, corporate structure, track record, educational qualification and experience in the market. Members will be admitted into the stock exchanges, after completion of **two stages**. The **stage I** requires a written examination. In second stage, the successful applicant will have to face interview. The interview will be conducted by a panel of experts from the industry. The interview will assess the applicants capability to operate as an exchange member. It admits members to the following segments:

(a) Wholesale Debt Market Segment
(b) Capital Market Segment

Eligibility Criteria for Trading Membership of WDM

The WDM deals with large volume of business transactions. It is involved in trading of PSU bonds, treasury bills, government securities, commercial papers, certificate of deposits, etc. In this segment, only **corporate members** are admitted to run the business transactions. The eligibility criteria for trading membership is presented below:

(a) Body corporate, companies, banks and financial institutions are eligible to enter this segment.
(b.) The applicant must possess a minimum networth of **Rs. 2 crores**.
(c) The body corporate should not be engaged in any fund based activities.
(d) The interested company should engage in the business of securities.
(e) Two years experience should possess the board of directors of the body corporate.

Membership Eligibility Criteria for the Capital Market Segment

It involves in trading equity and retail debt. NSE has framed rules and regulations for becoming member in capital market segment. It is based on order driven market. It provides flexibility to the members. The admission process in this segment is based on two stages. The written test and interview shall be faced by the interested applicant. The following are the eligibility norms for becoming members in this segment:

(a) The eligibility conditions should be satisfied as per the Securities Contract Regulation Act, 1957.
(b) Individuals, registered firms, body corporate, companies and other persons are eligible for becoming members.
(c) The interested applicant must be engaged solely in the business of securities and not be engaged in any fund based activities.
(d) The individual and registered firms should have networth of **Rs. 75.00 lakhs** and companies **Re. 1 crore** respectively.
(e) The minimum educational qualification is graduation and two directors must have experience of 2 years in handling securities as a broker or sub-broker or authorised assistant.

Components of the NSE

The NSE provides screen based trading facilities to the investors. It offers national network and more transparency in affairs of the transactions. It ensures cost effective transactions. It has a network of **3075** Very Small Aperture Terminals **(VSAT)** across **379** cities for millions of investors. Information will be carried out with the help of the satellites. The NSE has two separate segments:

(a) The Wholesale Debt Market Segment
(b) The Capital Market Segment

(a) The Wholesale Debt Market Segment

The Wholesale Debt Market Segment is one of the most important segment in the National stock exchange. It deals with banks, financial institutions and other participants. The debt market segment allows to trade treasury bills, PSU bonds, government securities, commercial papers and certificates of deposits. The transactions takes place through computers. The debt market consists of two parties. They are trading members and participants. The trading members are recognised brokers of the NSE. In this segment no individual broker is allowed. Generally the financial institutions, body corporate, banks are eligible to become the trading members. The trading member should pay **Rs. 30 lakhs** towards annual fee. The member should not withdraw his membership up to **five years.** The member can trade on their own purpose or on behalf of their clients. **Participants** are another party in this segment. They involve in buying and selling of the securities. They are the buyers in the market. They are responsible for the settlement of the trade. Their transactions will be settled through trading members. They have access to the trading system. The functioning of the WDM is presented below:

(i) Trading Mechanism
(ii) Settlement Process

(i) Trading Mechanism

Information technology changed the way of trading methods in stock market. NSE is fully computerised stock exchange in India. Trading has become a sophisticated way at present. The revolution in **IT** sector has been made for smooth functioning of the stock market. The trading has now become as **online trading** system. It has increased the trading velocity and reduce the time horizon. NSE provides a facility for the screen based trading with order matching facility. The trading members are scattered throughout the nation and are connected from their respective offices to the main computer at the **National stock exchange**. The NSE centralised premises have a high speed efficient satellite telecommunication network. The trading process is an automated order matching system. It does not reveal the identity of the parties to an executed order or a seller. It is an advantage to the trading members. It operates on a prime time priority. The transactions are matched automatically by the computer. If an order does not find a suitable match, it remains in the system and it will be displayed on the screen till a fresh order matches. The process provides an excellent environment for placing an order several factors like **volume related, price related and time related** can easily be placed on the system. All information regarding a particular scrip or about all scrips will be available in the market. The detailed information regarding the total order in a scrip, **the quantity traded the high, the low** and the last traded prices are available through screen at any time. The WDM is easily accessible to the following types of users:

(i) trader user
(ii) privileged user
(iii) inquiry user

The trading members should keep in touch with the users. The participant parties are allowed as both privileged and inquiry users. The trader user is an important component in the **online trading**. The trader user allowed for entering the order on the trading system. The privileged user has the right to set up a counter party. **The inquiry user** cannot enter orders or trade or set up exposure limits. The inquiry user can have market information and the right to set up the market watch screen. The volume of trade can be executed in the **negotiated or continuous market**. In continuous market, the orders are automatically matched by the computer system. If the order does not find a suitable element, it will be entered in the order book. The entry in the order book is known as **"possible order"**. It may be tallied later with any forthcoming order and result into a trade. The forthcoming order which matches with the existing order is known as the **"active order"**. The WDM system facilitates trading in debt and other instruments as they are outright purchase and sales as **"REPOs"**. Repurchase agreements can be defined as "agreements to buy securities and to resell them at a specified higher price at a later date". The government dealers offer the **"REPOs"** to the corporation the trading members has to indicate the trade type repo/non-repo and the desired settlement term. The NSE permits the settlement term from **"T to T+5"**. The repo term ranges from **3 to 14 days**. The online system works on the basis of price time priority. Generally the trading members can place orders in two kinds such as **"Repo trade and non-repo trade". Repo trade** facilitates the lowest buy rate in case of buying and highest rate for sale transactions. If the buying order in case of non-repo trade is the highest buy price and the best sell order with the lowest price. Hence the orders are matched automatically by the passive method. All the orders should be placed according to the specifications of the NSE. The entered transactions are divided into six parts. This classification is known as **"securities description"**. All the orders are matched on the basis of the descriptions. The transactions are categorised as **security type, security issue, settlement, trade type and repo term**. The order transactions will be filled on the basis of security description, price volume, order type and conditions.

(ii) Settlement Process

The WDM transactions are settled in Mumbai. The segment consists with the participants and the exchange monitors. The traders are settled as per the procedure laid down:

(i) The transactions are settled individually.
(ii) Trades are settled directly between the participants.
(iii) There is no settlement through the clearing house.
(iv) The settlement takes place on rolling basis.
(v) Every order will be settled as per the specified settlement date.
(vi) NSE provides the information to the concerned members regarding the trades to be settled on that day.
(vii) All the government securities are settled by the participants through subsidiary general ledger account with RBI through exchange of physical certificates.
(viii) The cancellation of trade should get prior approval with the NSE.
(ix) The arbitration mechanism has been established by the National stock exchange.

(b) The Capital Market Segment

Capital market segment is another component in the National stock exchange. It consists of trading inequity and the retail debt. This segment is working on the basis of intermediaries. There is a strong need to upgrade the professional standards of the intermediaries. The admission standards to this segment are very rigorous. The rules and regulations are framed by the NSE. The members will be selected on the basis of capital adequacy, good track record, education and experience. Admission into this involves two stages. The applicant is required to go through a written examination followed by an interview. The trading members in this segment are **corporate body, registered firms, individuals and institutional members**. The applicant should engage in fee based services only. The trading members should have a networth of **Rs. 75.00** lakhs. The corporate body should have **Re. 1 crore**. The applicant's minimum educational qualification is graduation and he should have two years professional experience. The experience in financial services or as broker or authorised assistant will get preference in selection.

Trading Mechanism in Capital Market Segment

NSE is working on screen based system. It is fully automated. It works on the basis of an order driven market. The trading method provides flexibility to the members in their placement orders. Order receives for the first time are stamped and immediately processed for a suitable match. If the suitable order is not found, it will be stored in different books. The orders are matched through computer automatically. The orders which are unmatched will be displayed till another party puts in a counter order. The unmatched orders are known as **"passive order"**. The order that match with the existing orders are called active orders. The earlier order will get priority over the orders that come in later. The trading members can enter into various types of orders. There are three conditions in trading process.

(a) Time related conditions
(b) Price related conditions
(c) Volume related conditions

(a) Time Related Conditions

The development of information technology leads to radical changes in trading methods. The traditional trading methods are replaced and the software occupied a dominant role in the matching of orders. The capital market segment transactions are executed on the basis of time conditions. In this type of order, the order will stay in force only for a few days. The time conditions further may be classified as **"day order, a good till order, a good till cancelled, an immediate or cancel"**. **Day order** is valid only for the entered day. If the order is not matched during the day, it gets cancelled automatically. A good till order means, the order allows the trading members to specify the days. It will be kept in the system up to that day. A good till cancelled order means, the order will remain in the trading system until it is cancelled by the member. An immediate order or cancel means, it allows a trading member to sell or buy a particular security when the order is released into the market. If it fails the order will be removed from the system.

(b) Price Condition

It is the most important aspect in this segment. It is known as **"on stop"**. It allows the members to place an order and gets activated only when the market price of the security exceeds a threshold price, until this situation, the order does not focuses in the market. In case, sell order, it gets triggered if the last price will be less than the sell order price.

(c) Volume Condition

The stock exchange may set a minimum disclosed worth from time to time. In this condition, the trading member may disclose only a part of the order value in the market.

Settlement Process in the Capital Market Segment

The National stock exchange provides excellent services for the welfare of the investors. It operates a well planned schedule for speedy settlement in transactions. Trading in this segment facilitate short settlement cycles. The settlement procedure in the NSE is presented below:

(i) The settlement cycles will be announced well in advance by NSE.
(ii) Transactions will be settled through the clearing house.
(iii) There is no settlement among the brokers.
(iv) The settlement will be completed in eight days.
(v) NSE maintains the gap between inflow and outflow of fund is for only one day.
(vi) NSE rectify the bad deliveries.
(vii) NSE assures legal guarantee to the transactions and settlements.
(viii) All the securities are handled by the National Securities Clearing Corporation Ltd. only.
(ix) The Canara Bank is appointed as the clearing bank.

(x) All the transactions are effected through the electronic fund transaction system.

(xi) The clearing house makes short deliveries on Tuesday and auctioned in Wednesday.

(xii) On Thursday pay in for auction takes place and pay out in Friday.

(xiii) All the bad deliveries are required to be reported by Friday.

(xiv) Every member should rectify any problem as delivery of the securities.

(xv) The trading members will be allowed according to the networth of their financial capability.

(xvi) Margins are collected from the members if they reach beyond the limits.

(xvii) The NSE provides prompt settlement process and assures cash settlement.

(xviii) NSE provides additional facilities for its institutional investors.

Institutional Market Segment

Institutional investors will get some privileges in the National stock exchange. It is categorised into two segments: (a) Institutional lot segment, (b) Trade segment. Institutional lot segment provide large volume of transactions. The trade segment is meant to cater to the institutions, which prefer minimising exposure risk. Institution lot segment contains in multiples of **1000** shares irrespective of the securities face value. Institutional investors can enter into the orders separately. The institutional lot trading period commences from **Wednesday to Tuesday**. A trading member may enter and monitor any security in this market. All the pay in and pay out funds are effected on the same day. The institutional market segment contains two conditions in the settlement of securities *i.e.*, **Institutional lots and T.T. segment**. The securities can be delivered in institutional board lots of **1000 shares** and the receiving member has to accept the securities. The custodians should report to the clearing house authorities. The delivered securities should be recorded on the name of delivery member. The T.T. segment transactions are settled on a rolling basis. The transactions are required to be confirmed by **T+3** and will be settled on **T+5**. The delivery of shares are to be accepted by the receiving member. The settlement of the transactions are effected between institutions and custodians through the stock exchange. The custodians occupy an important place in settlement of the transactions.

Advantages of National Stock Exchange

The information technology changed the traditional methods in the stock market. The latest technology made the stock exchanges more competent in rendering the services to the investors. India will definitely compete with world class stock exchanges. BSE and NSE may become as technology bourses. The technology adopted by the exchange made the secondary market operations more simplification. However, India should apply the **IT technique** for primary market. The public issues should also be made on **"on line"** and reduce the time period within one week for completion of all formalities. **On line** public issues can boost the industrial progress in India. Hence the NSE provides the following advantages:

(a) It provides quick trading system through **"V-Sat"**.
(b) It ensures wider accessibility.
(c) It reduces the back office work pressure due to screen based trade.
(d) It provides, any member can place large volume orders.
(e) It provides complete transparency in prices of scrips.
(f) It provides matching of orders through computer.
(g) Any problem to the trading member will be solved by the exchange.
(h) It provides rolling settlement facility which helps the traders to settle the accounts quickly without waiting for a fixed settlement date.
(i) The subsidiary general ledger provides paperless transactions in the debt market.
(j) It provides legal guarantee and protection against risk of loss through insurance.

The computer screen of the trading members is divided into the following major windows:

Major windows:

Windows:	**Display**
Title bar:	Current date, time and trading system
Tool bar:	Inquiry functions
Ticker:	Information about the trades
Market watch:	Market information such as best buy, sell order price cast traded price with order values.

Enquiry of Window: Market by orders, price and outstanding orders.

- **(a) Market by order:** Outstanding order in the trading books.
- **(b) Market by price:** Consolidated orders in trading book at different price.
- **(c) Outstanding order:** Trading members own outstanding buy and sell orders.

National Index for Fifty Shares is known as **"NIFTY"**. It is built by India Index Services Product Ltd. and the Credit Rating Information Services of India Ltd. NIFTY replaced the NSE-100 Index. NIFTY was introduced on April 22, 1996. The index reflect the market movement. It provides information to the fund managers. It is a tool for portfolio managers for measuring returns on his portfolio. It is useful for derivatives market. The index is named as **"S$PCNX 50"**. The Crisil has a strategic alliance with **Standard and Poor Rating Services.** NIFTY is a basket of different composition of scrips. The selection for this index is based on **Market Capitalisation and Liquidity**. The scrips will be selected from the entire universe of securities admitted on NSE. The sample set covers a large number of industry groups. The selected scrips will be given weights in proportion to their market capitalisation.

S $ P NIFTY Junior

It consists of 50 shares among admitted on NSE. These scrips belonged to mid cap companies. The stocks which are having market capitalisation more than Rs. 2 bn. are included in this index. This index objective is to measure the performance of midcap companies. It is an ideal index to be used in derivative trading. It was recasted in 1988. It has been overhauled. Some additions of stock and some deletion of stocks have been made from the index.

S $ P CNX500

It consists of 500 scrips admitted on NSE. The scrips are listed as the basis of their market capitalisation, industry representation, trading activity and financial performance. The base period is 1994. The industry groups are found to be 79 in this index. The index provides a benchmark for comparing portfolio return with market return.

Table 32: Statement shows List of Scrips Admitted in NIFTY (as on 24-2-05)

(Rs. in crore)

Sl. No.	*Company*	*Price as on 24-2-05*	*Market Capitalisation*	*Weight Day*
1.	ONGC	816	116370	13.01
2.	Reliance Industries	547	76260	8.53
3.	Infosys	2164	58319	6.52
4.	Wipro	677	47608	5.32
5.	Bharati	213	39569	4.42
6.	SBI	691	36365	4.07
7.	ITC	1294	32123	3.59
8.	HLI	143	31422	3.51
9.	ICICI Bank	369	27198	3.04
10.	SAIL	63	26228	2.93
11.	TISCO	412	22827	2.55
12.	BHEL	862	21100	2.36
13.	GAIL	234	19797	2.21
14.	HDFC	771	19130	2.14
15.	Ranbaxy Lab.	1000	18604	2.08
16.	HDFC Bank	576	17653	1.97
17.	Tata Motors	472	17069	1.91
18.	L&T	1060	13766	1.54
19.	Maruti Udyog	473	13664	1.53
20.	Hindalco	1375	12714	1.42
21.	Satyam	397	12654	1.41
22.	BPCL	415	12458	1.39
23.	Grasim	1333	12219	1.37
24.	HPCL	347	11780	1.32
25.	PNB	435	11552	1.29
26.	NALCO	173	11163	1.25
27.	Hero Honda	537	10726	1.20
28.	Reliance Energy	563	10449	1.17
29.	HCL Tech.	326	10363	1.16
30.	Bajaj Auto	1013	10250	1.15
31.	Sun Pharma	485	8988	1.01
32.	MTNL	133	8351	0.93
33.	Tata power	403	7975	0.89
34.	Cipla	258	7742	0.87
35.	Gujarat Ambuja	428	7699	0.86
36.	Glaxo	757	6614	0.74
37.	ACC	360	6459	0.72
38.	VSNL	223	6361	0.71
39.	MEM	535	6213	0.69
40.	Zee Telefilm	148	6095	0.68
41.	OBC	305	5877	0.66
42.	Dr. Reddy's Lab.	719	5508	0.62
43.	ABB	1250	5296	0.59

(Contd.)

Table 32 (*Contd.*)

Sl. No.	*Company*	*Price as on 24-2-05*	*Market Capitalisation*	*Weight Day*
44.	SCI	161	4537	0.51
45.	IPCL	175	4358	0.49
46.	Tata Chem.	159	3425	0.38
47.	Dabur	112	3219	0.36
48.	Tata Tea	536	3011	0.34
49.	Indian Hotel	594	2683	0.30
50.	Colgate	187	2540	0.28

Source: *The Economic Times*, 25-2-2005, p. 12.

Table 33: Statement shows Turnover Toppers at National stock exchange

Sl. No.	*Company*	*No. of Shares Traded*	*Turnover (Rs. in crores)*	*Price as on 24-2-05*
	S$P CNX NIFTY			
1.	SBI	50,68,474	348	690.95
2.	RIL	49,71,064	274	547.00
3.	TISCO	59,73,205	248	412.00
4.	Infosys	8,41,927	182	2164.00
5.	ONGC	18,21,481	149	816.10
6.	Tata Motors	28,67,029	136	471.80
7.	Satyam	24,55,001	97	396.75
8.	Ranbaxy	9,12,121	92	1000.60
9.	PNB	19,11,358	83	435.45
10.	Bharati	35,84.828	76	213.50
	S$P NIFTY Junior			
1.	Tata Tolestar	1,80,95,582	57	31.00
2.	IFCI	2,09,33,326	36	17.20
3.	Canara Bank	16,11,912	33	205.40
4.	GE Shipping	15,94,398	28	178.00
5.	Andhra Bank	30,52,553	27	88.25
6.	Syndicate Bank	38,63,011	22	55.70
7.	Iflex Solution	3,53,493	22	617.05
8.	Bank of India	24,06,17	20	84.15
9.	Vijaya Bank	29,96,345	19	64.05
10.	Jaiprakash	9,67,820	19	199.20
	Others			
1.	TCS	13,50,805	185	1367.95
2.	NTPC	1,52,71,545	144	93.85
3.	Bank of Rajasthan	1,21,76,517	87	71.45
4.	Mc-Dowell Co.	46,24,434	79	166.95
5.	Bank of Punjab	1,05,19,449	43	39.95

Sources: *The Economic Times*, 25-2-2005, p. 12.

Table 34: Statement Shows Best Shares at NSE as on 24-2-05

Sl. No.	*Company*	*Price as on 24-2-05*	*Volume*	*Percentage of Change from Previous*
	S$P CNX NIFTY			
1.	HDFC Bank	576.00	3,35,642	3.2
2.	Dabur	112.40	6,93,006	3.0
3.	BHEL	862.05	4,28,183	3.0
4.	PNB	435.45	19,11,358	2.4
5.	Sun Pharma	484.60	13,64,874	2.2
6.	Glaxo	757.40	66,501	1.6
7.	HPCL	347.15	8,98,373	1.5
8.	ABB	1249.75	20,703	1.3
9.	Infosys	2164.30	841,927	1.1
10.	SBI	690.95	50,68,474	2.1
	CNX NIFTY Junior			
1.	Siemens	1668.35	51,720	4.3
2.	Jaiprakash	199.20	9,67,820	4.2
3.	TVS Motor	74.65	12,16,365	4.0
4.	GE Shipping	177.65	15,94,398	3.8
5.	Tata Telestar	31.00	1,80,95,582	3.2
	CNX Midcap 200			
1.	Bata	84.65	20,29,315	12.6
2.	ITI	29.35	34,74,329	9.7
3.	Gujarat Mineral	364.25	1,77,800	6.6
4.	Alstom Prod.	166.20	3,35,360	4.7
5.	EID Parry	500.20	22,636	4.7
6.	Red Infl.	92.80	580,330	20.1
7.	Xero	44.30	379,316	20.1
8.	Vishal Exports	95.60	11,76,057	19.3
9.	Morarjee	94.35	8,04,270	17.6
10.	MSK Projects	51.70	64,63,266	16.3

Source: *The Economic Times*, 25-2-2005, p. 12.

Table 35: Statement shows Circuit Filters at NSE (as on 24-2-05)

Sl. No.	*Company*	*Price as on 22-2-05*	*Day's H/L*	*Close*
1.	Ashapura Ltd.	366.70	385.05	385.05
2.	Astra Microwarve	812.10	852.75	852.75
3.	Bata	75.20	90.25	84.65
4.	Bagyanagar	36.45	28.70	27.55
5.	Bharat Gears Ltd.	55.00	57.75	57.75
6.	Blue Coast Hot	39.90	41.90	41.00
7.	BSEL Infrastructure	33.55	35.25	35.25

(Contd.)

Table 35 (*Contd.*)

Sl. No.	*Company*	*Price as on 22.2.05*	*Day's H/L*	*Close*
8.	Core Healthcare	15.40	16.20	16.20
9.	D.S. Kulkarni	28.50	31.35	31.35
10.	Greenply Industries	62.20	68.45	68.00
11.	Gujarat Flours	325.75	342.05	342.05
12.	Gujarat Base	8.05	8.45	8.25
13.	Haryana Sheet	13.50	14.85	14.85
14.	Hindustan Comp.	60.90	67.00	67.00
15.	Induji Entertech	8.15	8.60	8.60
16.	JBM Auto	90.75	95.30	95.30
17.	JCI Electronic	11.15	12.30	12.05
18.	Keynote Corpn.	12.55	13.20	13.20
19.	Khaitan India	12.80	14.10	13.25
20.	Lyod Electronic	44.10	46.35	45.90
21.	Magma Leasing	68.00	71.40	71.40
22.	Mahindra Geo.	132.05	138.65	138.65
23.	Morarjee Ralt	80.20	96.25	94.35
24.	Motor and General	12.10	12.75	12.75
25.	NEPC India	19.80	20.80	20.80
26.	Orient Press	14.95	16.45	16.45
27.	Petran Engg.	105.20	110.50	110.50
28.	Polar Industries	9.50	10.45	10.45
29.	Praja Indu.	369.70	382.20	381.40
30.	Rai Agro	144.25	151.50	151.50
31.	Rel. Infra.	77.30	92.80	92.80
32.	RPG Life Science	74.75	78.50	78.50
33.	Sambhav Media	141.00	14.70	14.70
34.	Saregama India	144.85	152.10	152.10
35.	Sre Rayalsima	7.55	9.10	9.10
36.	Standard Industries	21.75	23.95	23.95
37.	Subhash Projects	32.20	35.45	35.40
38.	TCI Finance Ltd.	16.45	18.10	18.10
39.	Tikanor Compan	163.85	172.05	172.05
40.	Unitech Ltd.	322.55	354.85	340.00
41.	Videocon Industries	247.35	252.30	252.30
42.	Vishal Exports	80.15	96.20	95.60
43.	Visa Finance	11.95	12.55	12.55
44.	Xpro India Ltd.	36.90	44.30	44.30
45.	Zodiac Ind.	32.75	36.05	36.05
	Low at NSE			
1.	Dharani Sugars	29.90	28.35	28.35
2.	Goetz India	203.60	193.45	193.45
3.	Hyderabad industries	163.95	160.70	160.95
4.	NICCO Corpn.	11.35	10.80	10.85
5.	SMZ Chemicals	19.30	18.35	18.35
6.	Texmaco Ltd.	306.30	291.00	292.25

Sources: *The Economic Times*, p. 12.

Table 36: Statement shows Highest Deliveries at NSE (as on 24.2.05)

Sl.No.	*Company*	*Traded Volume*	*Delivery Volume*	*% Difference to trd. Volume*	*Price as on 24.02.05*
1.	Kothari	57979	57979	100.00	4.90
2.	Container Corporation	51123	50783	99.33	889.35
3.	VLS Finance	72368	69695	96.31	12.25
4.	Motor & General Fin.	104181	99175	95.19	12.75
5.	NIIT	83786	75535	90.15	192.45
6.	Mphasis BFL	78438	70617	90.03	750.20
7.	Vishesh Info.	92989	81921	88.10	17.60
8.	Datamat Tech.	266526	234051	87.82	124.75
9.	Shankar Multi	114418	99072	86.59	7.10
10.	LG Balakrishna	173623	148935	85.78	30.50
11.	Flex Industries	82736	69464	84.33	47.70
12.	Sun Pharma	1374874	1141976	83.67	484.60
13.	Wellwin Ind.	300169	249321	83.06	8.85
14.	Indian Rayon	54779	45185	82.49	438.05
15.	Core Emball	82253	67442	81.99	7.20
16.	Kalpa Power	65347	53369	81.67	289.05
17.	Birla VXL	609448	495828	81.36	19.95
18.	Vashishthi Detergent	184162	148700	80.74	14.00
19.	Morgan Stanley	420532	332193	78.99	20.95
20.	UTI Bank	260015	202393	77.84	228.65
21.	Alcom Techno	53327	41340	77.52	10.25
22.	Computech Ind.	51263	38991	76.06	10.35
23.	Shri Shakti LP	103680	78701	75.91	7.15
24.	ETC Network	57213	43197	75.50	42.10
25.	Polar Industries	62312	46865	75.21	10.45
26.	TN Newsprint	117746	88434	75.11	65.10
27.	Sr. Ray Hitech	294934	220289	74.69	9.10
28.	Hindalco	286599	213381	74.45	135
29.	PNB Gilts	79674	58895	73.92	21
30.	Bajaj Auto Finance	54982	40327	73.35	165

Source: *The Economic Times*, 25-2-2005, p. 12.

Over the Counter Exchange of India (OTC)

Over the counter exchange is associated with the small companies. It fulfils the needs of the small firms. It was set up in 1989 as a company. It has been registered according to the **Section 25** of the Companies Act. It is known as exchange without floor and rings. All activities are computerised. It is promoted by **UTI, ICICI, IFCI, LIC, GIC, SBI capital markets, IDBI and Canara Bank.** It provides global standard services to the small companies in the capital market. It aims at creating a fully decentralised and transparent market. In OTC, the transactions are executed by bids and offers through computer device. The Securities Contract Regulation Act, Section 4 recognises the OTC as a stock exchange.

Players in the OTC Market

The business transactions are carried out by dealers and members. The member should have a networth of **Rs. 2.5 crores**. Members can be scheduled banks, mutual funds, public financial institutions, merchant bankers, venture capital funds, banking subsidiaries and other non-banking financial companies. The annual subscription fee is Re. 1.00 lakh. Every member should pay a non-refundable admission fee of Rs. 10.00 lakhs. The dealers and members will act as brokers. They buying and selling securities according to the instructions of the investors. The dealers should have a minimum networth of **Rs. 5.00 lakhs**. Individuals, partnership firms and companies can become **dealers**. Every dealer should pay one time non-refundable admission fee of Rs. 2.00 lakhs. Every dealer should have sufficient office space and telecommunication facilities. The dealer should pay annual fee of Rs. 5,000. The members and dealers are scattered throughout the nation. The members or dealers work place is a trading floor. Every member/dealer counter refers to the OTC where the investors can buy and sell the securities. The members or dealers and computers are linked to the central OTC computer.

Scrips to be Traded

The Government of India has issued guidelines for trading of scrips in the OTC. The following conditions should be satisfied by the interested companies to trade in the OTC market:

(a) The listed company should have minimum capital of **Rs. 3 crores** and the maximum is **Rs. 50 crores**.
(b) For companies with an issue capital of more than Rs. 30.00 lakhs but less than Rs. 3 crores. The minimum public offer should be 25 per cent of the issued capital or 20 lakhs worth of shares in face value, which ever is higher.
(c) Companies with an issued capital of more than Rs. 30 crores listing requirements should be fulfilled.

Listing Norms

The following norms are to be fulfilled by the perspective companies:

(a) closely held companies interested in listing
(b) new companies with a paid up capital of Rs. 50 crores
(c) venture capital companies (20 per cent shall be issued to public)

Process of Listing

The Government of India has issued certain guidelines for the listing of scrips in OTC. The interested company shall make arrangements for issue of share capital through member of an OTC. The member is called as **"sponsor for the issue"**. The sponsor has full authority in all issue aspects such as technical, managerial, commercial economical and financial appraisals. The sponsor shall submit a report regarding appraisal of the company. The sponsor will fix the issue price. He gets all statutory clearance and compliance as per the SEBI guidelines. He registers with OTC regarding issue of shares. He submits the listing application to the OTC on behalf of the issuing company. All the formalities will be fulfilled by the sponsor and getting the approval, the allotment will be made by the company. Once the allotment is completed the share is listed and trading commences in the OTC market. Hence the role of sponsor cannot be ignored in the issue.

Trading Method

OTC is a floor less exchange. All transactions are computerised. It allows the dealers to operate through their computers. The quotations and transactions are recorded and processed in the OTC. The dealers are scattered throughout the country and have the access to the central computer. The dealers are able to know the best bids and offers the market markers in respect of each scrip. The interested dealer can place his order through computer. If the deal is made, the **counter receipt** will be handed over to the buyer, the counter receipt is like a share certificate. It is a tradable document. The buyer should kept the counter receipt carefully. The sale prices are displayed. If the deal is made sales confirmationship will be issued to the seller. The seller should present the **sales confirmationship** when the payment is made. The counter receipt will be submitted to the OTC counter.

Settlement Cycle

In OTC, the transactions should be settled within 5 days. Forward trading is not permitted on OTC. OTC avoids speculation. The other methods such as short sales and square up have to be done within the trading cycles. The buyer of the shares in OTC must be delivered within a fortnight from the date of purchase. The settlement procedures are different for the listed and permitted securities. In case of listed securities, if the deal is stuck, temporary or permanent counter receipt will be issued to the investors, those purchased the securities. Sales confirmation slip will be issued to the investor for his sale of securities. The settlement agent in OTC will verify the signatures on the counter receipt and store and match the transfer deeds. The transfer process will be carriedout by the **Registrar**. The shares will be transferred within **7 days.**

Market Making System

Market making promotes liquidity to the small investors. It is associated with issue of shares in OTC. It offers two way quotations such as **buy quote and sell quote**. Merchant banker occupies a dominant role in issue of shares. He will be held responsible in this system even after an issue is over. There are three types of market making:

(a) Compulsory market making
(b) Additional market making
(c) Voluntary market making.

Compulsory market making is one of the method of sponsoring. It is associated with the sponsor of the issue for a period of **three years** from the date of public trading. The sponsor cannot transfer his responsibility, even if he assigned to some other members. Hence the sponsor is responsible for the satisfactory discharge of compulsory market making. The sponsor shall bear all the risks associated with the market making system. After completion of three years period, the sponsor can withdraw from compulsory market making system. The sponsor should possess **5 per cent** of the public offer. If he fails to maintain **one per cent**, he should not offer **"sale quotes"**. The market maker can apply for termination of his duty in the following situations:

(a) If the scrip sponsor has incurred cash losses for three years, or
(b) If the company became insolvent, or
(c) If the company's prospects are not bright.

Additional market making is another method of sponsoring. He will be appointed by the sponsor of the issue. He may be permitted to associate for not less than **one year** from the date of public offering.

Voluntary market making is introduced by the member of the exchange. It is offered by voluntarily. Voluntary market maker should continue at least **3 months** from the date of commencement. He can offer buy and sell quotes. He should possess the securities as specified by the OTC. If he fails the specified shares quantity, he should not give sell quotes in the market.

The Current Situation

OTC is a screen based trading. It is a floorless exchange. It helps small companies to raise capital. It covers nationwide market operations. It provides rolling settlements and market making. It also provides services to large capital companies. It provides trading facilities for debt instruments. OTC is not doing well at presently. The main reason for loosing its reputation is, due to dealers disinterest. The dealers are not interested, due to a little scope for speculation. There is another reason behind the fall of OTC is, investor dissatisfaction. Generally investors of the small capital companies prefer to get dividends rather than capital gains. It is in need of upgradation. The NSE is supporting technology to the OTC.

SUMMARY

The post liberalisation era has marked with various stabilisation measures and structural reforms particularly in industrial and trade policies with the broad objective of stronger export performance through liberalised exports and turning domestic industrial sector global.

Deregulation and the delicensing initiatives have been undertaken in India with a view to increase production, improve quality and get access to markets for products and services abroad to competition with others MNCs. After liberalisation, the growth of corporate sector increased tremendously. The **banking sector and the financial system** are undergoing metamorphic changes. The most intractable problem has been one of addressing the question of **Non-performing assets** of banks. **Savings** are the most important factor to any kind of economy. The prosperity of a nation is reflected in the growth of income or **Gross Domestic Product**. The development process involves a large amount of resources pooling for the purpose of **capital formation**. **Investment** is an economic activity. It stimulates the value of wealth. **Speculation** is a dynamic activity. It is a short-term phenomenon. It involves higher level of risk. **Gambling** is involved in a game or chance. It is a combination of pleasure and pain.

Usually every investor expects some return on his investment. Return is the reward to the investor. **Risk** is a possibility of meeting danger or suffering harm. Risk may be arrived by various factors. **Safety** is the important factor in making investment decisions. **Liquidity** attracts more attention by the investors. **Inflation** is a natural phenomenon in almost all the economies. A good financial system encourages the saving based investment. Investment policy is the important factor in making of investment decisions by the individual investors, firms, companies and other firms. Available surplus fund will influence the investment policy of the investors. Selection of investment option is another factor in investment process. Valuation is another important factor in investment process. **Portfolio construction** is one of the important factor in investment process. **Portfolio evaluation** is the final step in the investment process. Investment media have been categorised as **Direct and Indirect** investment alternatives. Investment activities lead the growth of industrial sector. Information is the important factor in gaining of knowledge. **Knowledge** occupies a dominant role in making of investment decisions. **Security market** is a combination of trading place of different financial instruments. **Financial markets** is a market, where the financial instruments are traded at a geographical place. Financial markets can be classified as **Money Market and Capital Market**. Money market is associated with short-term nature of funds. **Capital Market** is known for long-term nature of funds. The security market further can be classified as **Primary and Secondary Market**. Primary market is known as new issue market. It is also called as **initial public offer**. These two markets are parking places of money. Primary market is useful to the newly established and business concerns. It is a dynamic market. All kinds of companies may approach the market. The issue must be get the approval of the SEBI. It provide a parking place to the investors for their idle funds. Underwriting is one of the function of new issue market. Underwriting is a guarantee about the success of the issue. Public issue can be made by prospectus. **Prospectus** is a document which contains all the particulars about the issuing company. **Book building** is another kind of rising of sources of finance. It is more popular in **U.S.A. Nirma** is the first company in India to adopt this method of issue. **Private placement** is one of the method of issue of shares. The shares are offered privately to the investors. **Offer for sale** is another kind of issue. The promoter places his shares to the financial intermediaries such as Merchant bankers, investment bankers, firms, stock brokers and issue houses. **Rights issues** are offered to the existing shareholders of issuing company. The success of public issue depends upon many factors such as "promoters reputation, objectives of the issue, details about the project, financial data etc. New issue market should be done as **"online public issues"**. The online method curbs the consumption of time and money. The public issue requires fulfillment of many legal formalities such as Companies Act, Securities Contract, SEBI. **Rights issue** is another source of raising finance for the corporate sector. The shares allotment process is another important factor in raising of funds from the market. Securities Contract Act provides broad regulations of the present scheme of the stock exchanges functioning in India. **SEBI** was established under the control of Central Government. The activities of the SEBI regulated by the Ministry of Finance. Public issue involves a number of financial intermediaries such as merchant bankers, lead managers, underwriters, bankers, brokers, registrars, debenture trustees and portfolio managers. **Secondary market** is a place where the issued shares are available. stock exchanges are known as **"secondary market"**. The stock exchanges in India should work within the framework of the various acts such as Companies Act, 1956 and Income Tax Act, 1961. **Bombay stock exchange** is the oldest stock exchange. There are 23 recognised stock exchanges functioning in India. The regular affairs of the stock exchange is managed by the governing body. Listing means an official admission of a scrip to trade on the floor of stock exchange. The listed securities can be classified such as **"Groups A, B, permitted cleared and non-cleared securities"**. Speculation and gambling activities are controlled by the stock exchange through a separate department. The stock exchanges give top priority to the investor's grievances. Investor service cell is established for the solving of problems. Stock market indices are barometers of an economic activity. The index number reveals about the quantitative analysis of the data. Market capitalisation is one of the important factor information of index. Liquidity is another important element in construction of Sensex. **Market depth** is another important component of the Sensex. **Floating stock depth** is the supply and demand for a scrip in the market. **National stock exchange** became operational in the capital market in 1994 in Mumbai. NSE has been sponsored by **IDBI, ICICI, IFCI, GIC, SBI, UBI, PNB, etc.** NSE provide national level trading facility for equity, debt and hybrid instruments. The NSE has a fully automated electronic screen based trading system. NSE has two components **wholesale debt market segment and capital market segment**. The WDM deals with banks, financial institutions and other participants. Capital market segment consists of trading in equity and retail debt. This segment is working on the basis of financial intermediaries. The development of information technology lead to radical changes in trading methods. Institutional investors will get same privileges in the NSE. NIFTY stands for National Index for Fifty Shares. NSE also construct CNX Junior and S$P CNX 500 index numbers.

QUESTIONS (PART I)

1. Explain the present situation of the Indian financial system.
2. What are savings? Discuss its role in development of a nation.
3. "Are the saving curbs the present consumption"?
4. What is investment? State the economic and financial meaning of investment?
5. "Investment is a parking place of idle funds". Elucidate.
6. What is speculation? Is it necessary for the stock market?
7. Explain the concept of gambling.
8. What are the investment objectives? Explain as a finance analyst to your client.
9. What is investment process? Explain different stages involved in investment process?
10. What are investment media? Discuss about different investment alternatives?
11. Explain the investment principles? Is it necessary for financial discipline for individuals, companies and a nation?
12. Explain the power of information? Discuss about various sources of investment information available to investors.
13. What is security? Define it?
14. What is primary market? Explain its issue process?
15. What are the factors influencing for investing in new issue market?
16. Explain the regulatory framework involved in new issue market.
17. Explain the role of merchant banker, underwriters, and lead managers with reference to new issue market.
18. What is stock exchange? Explain the origin and growth of the stock exchanges?
19. Explain the various kinds of securities that are traded in the stock exchange.
20. Explain the advantages of stock exchanges in the economy.
21. Who is broker? Explain his qualification and eligibility aspects?
22. What are the steps involved in dealing at stock exchanges?
23. Write an essay on different types of speculators exist in stock exchanges.
24. Explain different kinds of speculative transactions exist in the stock exchanges.

25. Explain various kinds of operators exist in the stock exchange.
26. Explain different kind of orders undertaken by stock brokers in the stock exchanges.
27. Describe the settlement procedure exist in the stock exchanges.
28. What is carry forward? Explain its process in the stock exchange.
29. What is listing? Explain its process involved in trading of a scrip in stock exchange?
30. Describe the importance of Bombay stock exchange in Indian stock market.
31. What is Sensex? List out the components of Sensex?
32. Explain the surveillance system exist in BSE.
33. Write an essay about National stock exchange.
34. Explain the importance of over the counter exchange of India in stock market.

UNIT - II

- Security Analysis
  (a) Objectives of Security Analysis
  (b) Fundamental Analysis
  (c) Technical Analysis
  (d) Dow Theory Oscillators
  (e) Elliot Wave Theory
  (f) Efficient Market Theory

INTRODUCTION

All Investments are risky. The return is always chased by the risk. The difference between return and risk is the gain or loss to the investors. Millions of the investors are entering the stock market for this risk and return relationship. An intelligent investor must escape the risk and capture the return by entering in stock market at right time, at right prices and at right shares. Entering and exit of the stock market are the most important factors in determining the earnings of the investors. It is a simple principle, **buy** at low prices and **sell** at higher prices. The difference between two prices is the return to the investors. Buying at low price of a scrip, requires knowing the actual worth of a scrip. This method is known as **"security analysis"**. Security analysis refers to find out intrinsic value of a security. The intrinsic value represents the true economic worth of a financial asset. Generally every asset has its own value. The Financial assets also hold a face value. An assessment of real worth of a financial asset is called as **"security analysis"**. If you are able to find out the actual value of the asset, we can say whether it is **over priced or under priced**. The common investor does not know these intricacies, and involves in either in profit or loss. Buying a scrip at over priced leads to incurring losses and buying at under priced provides a hefty margin to the investors. The investor always invites return and avoids risk. The behaviour of stock in the market depends upon latest information. Information in the stock market can discount or stimulate the share prices. The intrinsic value of a share depends upon earning potential of the company at present and also in future. Hence the information about performance of a company leads to know the intrinsic value of the share.

The intrinsic value is basically determined by the expected net earnings flow over a number of years. A strong financially sound company will have a potential growth in future. A large resources of reserves, surplus and undistributed profit may strengthen the company activities and leads to get better returns on their investments. Market is a inflow of new and existing scripts. It emerges always flodded with large number of securities. The securities are issued by companies, government, local bodies and public sector undertakings. Securities of more than one year came into the categories of capital and stock. A buyer who visits the shops, always interested to purchase goods at low price and higher quality. In the same way the investor will think about the financial asset, which is available at lower prices and high quality. The selecting process of a best scrip is known as **"security analysis"**. Security analysis refers to analysis of trading securities from the point of view of their prices, returns and risks. It will help in understanding the behaviour of security prices. If it is an analysis of a particular scrip, it is called as **Micro analysis**. If it is an analysis of market of securities, it is known as **Macro analysis**. The analysis of trading securities reveals various facts about the market behaviour. The following factors will influence security market analysis:

(a) Information
(b) Level of savings
(c) Trading methods
(d) Financial instruments
(e) Valuation of financial assets
(f) Market players
(g) Intermediaries

(a) Information

Information is the powerful tool in the hands of an intelligent investor. Information provides a good data and an insight analysis for making investment decisions. A vast resources of information provides a good environment for making right investment decisions. Accumulation of knowledge leads to the better making investment decisions. Knowledge based decision never fails in the prediction. In India, investment means simply handing over of a cheque to the broker. The investors making their decisions based on market tips, rumours and hinches. Stock markets are highly influenced by information and money flow. The flow of information must be perfect and free, the market will adjust to the situation. A wrong information leads to imperfect market and the price formation will be unpredictable and volatile. The published sources of information is available to all the investors. But the investors who respond immediately, may gain advantage from the market. The market is based on demand and supply forces. The information acquired by the investors needs analytical capabilities and future projection. If the information is free and unbiased, the markets behave rationally and nobody can gain additional profits. Hence the investors should be more cautious in the stock market while making investment decisions. The consequences are different when the information is perfect or imperfect or biased or unbiased. Profit booking in the stock market requires a lot of skills such as market behaviours, security behaviours, fundamental analysis, technical analysis and market valuation.

(b) Levels of Savings

Savings are the most important factors in the Capital market. Capital markets will be active, when the level of savings are very high. Market is based on supply and demand forces of the money. The flow of money into the stock market may stimulate the growth of its securities. The micro analysis of saving flow would depend on the objectives such as **return, capital appreciation, hedge against inflation liquidity and safety to the investors.** The level of savings in the country depends upon many factors. The higher level of savings may lead to the growth of capital markets. The interest rates on savings may also influence on the markets. A low rate of interest rates on bank deposits, bonds and debentures leads to increase the secondary market operations because the money will be diverted to the secondary market. If the rate of interest on savings is very high, the secondary market activities will decline significantly. Hence the markets are influenced by the interest rates. The Macro analysis of savings reveal that, the higher level of savings in the community may leads to the Capital formation in the country. Capital formation can boost the growth of the corporate sector. The asset creation in the country is only possible with the primary market or initial public offering. The higher level of asset creation enhance the purchasing capacity of the Community. A high rate of savings in the economy curtails the present consumption. A reduction in present consumption leads to fall of a industrial production. A fall of industrial production leads to closure of many units. The economy will be disturbed.

(c) Trading Methods

Trading means buying and selling of a financial product in the market. Market is a place, where buyers and sellers meet at a fixed place in a fixed time. Market is a coordinator between seller and buyer. It is influenced by the forces of supply and demand factors. These factors determine the volume of **trading turnover** and also the prices. The trading turnover is one of the macro indicator for studying the market behaviour. **Market behaviour** reveals about the movement of the share prices in the capital market. There will be two pressures in the market such as **buying pressure** and **selling pressure.** The buying pressure in the stock market arises in the **bear phase**. The bear phase requires more supply of scrips. If the prices are falling, the bears will enter into the market and makes purchases. Hence the market will stabilise and protection will be made from the falling of prices. If the prices are increasing, there will be more demand for scrips. The bulls enters into the market is known as **bullish phase**. The trading in scrips will be analysed in the form of deals per day, or deals per hour. The scrips which are regularly traded in the stock exchange with high volume is known as **"Active scrips"**. The active scrips will command goodwill and enjoys reputation in the market among the millions of investors. These scrips are being sold in the market as hot cakes. These scrips will be available for sale or purchase at any time in the market. These scrips are treated on par with the cash. They are treated as current assets in the market by the corporate sector. These scrips provide liquidity to the investors and market. It is related to the intrinsic value of the company and other internal factors of the company.

(d) Financial Instruments

The mobilisation of resources from the market by the corporate sector can be done through issue of various financial instruments. The issuing company has to select a best financial instrument among the various alternatives. The selection of financial instruments depends upon many factors. The capital structure of the company plays an important role in selection of financial instrument. **Debt-equity** ratio occupies a dominant role in selection of financial instrument. It is a statutory ratio, which determines the company either go for equity or debt. A number of different instruments which are available in the market presented in the following:

(i) Equity shares
(ii) Preference shares
(iii) Debentures
(iv) Bonds
(v) Convertible preference shares
(vi) Fully convertible debentures

(vi) Partly convertible debentures
(viii) Non-convertible debentures
(ix) Zero coupan bonds
(x) Warrants
(xi) Deep discount bonds
(xii) Option bonds
(xiii) Secured premium notes
(xiv) Non-voting equity shares

(e) Valuation of Financial Assets

The aim of the security analysis is to find out the real worth of a financial asset which is available at a market price. The market price can be either excess price or lower price is known by the investors for making their investment decisions. Sometimes, the shares are available in the market at lower prices. The market consists of thousands of securities whose prices change from day-to-day and from time-to-time. The detailed information about the share prices makes the investors to take a decision regarding buying and selling of securities. Hence it is necessary to make security valuation as important part of market analysis. The trends of prices and volume of trading are inter-related. The investors should know full information about the market indicators such as **price, volume of trading, velocity of price changes and intensity of trading** etc. All the information enables the investor to take a right investment decisions. The valuation of a financial asset can be categorised into two kinds. (a) **Market valuation,** (b) **scrip valuation**. Market valuation is associated with the macro level of analysis. The macro level analysis is done with the help of suitable price indices of the reputed scrips in the market and their **PE ratio**. The details of various indices for different scrips are prepared by the BSE National Index. The investor can use all these informations for making his investment decision. It is an open published source of information. It is available to all investors in the market. The information is a powerful tool in the hands of an intelligent investor. Published information is a public property to all the investors. Participation in stock market is an adventurous activity which shall be carried out by a skilful person. Now-a-days, the investors simply ignoring the analytical tools and making investment decisions based on market tips and rumours. It is highly impossible to get success in the stock market without a basic knowledge and proper skills. Ability to provide the money is not the criteria in the stock market, but identification of best scrip is the most important factor to get success. The best scrips which are unexposed to the market is mixed with thousands of securities. The intelligent investor has to pick up the best scrip from the market himself.

Scrip valuation is another important factor in the security valuation. It refers to study about the behaviour of a particular scrip. It is associated with the micro level of analysis. Micro level of analysis deals with the intrinsic value of a security. **The intrinsic value** of the security reveals that the market price of a security is either **over priced or undervalued**. This determination enables the investor to take a decision regarding his investment. The instrinsic value of a share can be determined by the expected net earnings flow over a number of years discounted to the present time by a suitable discount rate. But it is difficult to project future earnings of a company. Hence the analysts will take **PE ratio** for future earnings of the company. Traditionally there are three approaches to market valuation. They are presented below:

(i) Efficient Market Hypothesis
(ii) Fundamental Analysis
(iii) Technical Analysis

The above valuation models are dealt with in detail in subsequent chapters. Further the valuation models in shares have three approaches. These are presented below:

(i) Discount of future inflows
(ii) Payback period (PE ratio)
(iii) Conceptual framework.

Discount of future inflows is the most important factor in valuation approach. The earning capability in future of a scrip command a good reputation and it is hidden talent. We may assess a best scrip based on not only on present capabilities but also in future course of time. Talented people who are not exposed and the society will not recognise them. Like in the same way some scrips which are having good potential growth in future is ignored by the normal investors. An intelligent investor must findout such scrips from the market. The value of future income streams can be assessed as follows:

(i) Compound method,
(ii) Discounting method.

In valuation of compound method takes 6 per cent interest rate and capital of Re. 1.

In one year, it becomes Rs. $(1+0.06) = 1.06$
In two years, it becomes Rs. $(1+0.06)^2 = 1.1236$
In three years, it becomes Rs. $(1+0.06)^3 = 1.2624$

In discounting method for example:

(a) the present value of Rs. **100**, 10 years will be Rs. 39 at a discount rate of **10 per cent.**
(b) the present value of the principal of Rs. **100** after 5 years at **8 per cent** will be Rs. 68.

The process will apply to valuation of debt instruments. It will be discussed in latter chapters.

Payback period is associated with one of the valuation approaches. It is also known as **Multiplier approach.** It is useful for valuation of equity shares. It is used in the form of PE ratio For example A company's earning is Rs. 20 and the scrip price is Rs. 100.

∴ PE ratio = 100/20 = 5

Hence the payback period is 5 years.

Conceptual framework is related to study about investment decision activities influencing the productive process of the economy. Investment enhanced the output level of a nation and strongly influence the income component in the economy. According to **Keynes,** Investment is an income multiplier in the economy. An additional investment may leads to an addition to output and Income. The following factors reveal the theoretical framework regarding investment decisions:

(a) Savings Investment Theory
(b) Participants in trading
(c) Fundamental in trading
(d) Technical analysis
(e) Risk and Return relation.

Savings Investment Theory

It is the most important theoretical tool to study about the flow of investment. The savings flow into investments enhance the output and income levels. It is called as the capital output ratio or investment multiplier. Hence the savings promote capital formation and economic growth. Economic growth stimulates the GDP level and influences per capita income of the public. A growth in purchasing power stimulates the demand for more additional and quality goods. The standard of living of a common man increases and his lifestyle will also be changed significantly. **For example:** At present a common man, who is in below poverty line uses **cellular services**. He wants more comforts for his life. The savings will be attracted towards productive way by the capital market. The capital market is a vehicle, to provide sufficient resources for the corporate sector by issuing a number of financial assets. The **capital market** comprises new issue and secondary markets. The new issue capital provides **oxygen** to the newly established concerns. The primary market should be strengthened and it must be flexible to the market. The primary market in India has vast potential capabilities to meet the requirement of the corporate sector. The public issue should be made as **"online"** issues. The investors allotment of shares should be finalised within **48 hours** of the closing of issue. There is a strong need to make structural changes in the public issue. The investors should also be opened "Demat" accounts for participation in the primary market. The SEBI should take steps to reduce the time in public issues. The primary market can create winders in the world of finance. It must be technologically updated Purchasing shares at primary market should done on par with secondary market operations. The IPOs should be available in **"Internet"**. The procedure for applying and allotment of shares should be completed within **48 hours** after the closure of issue. All these transactions must be carried through the application of Information Technology. The Primary market can be utilised for the commencement of **Mega project "Linking of Rivers"**. The mega project of the decade requires an amount of **Rs. 6,00,000 crores**. It can be raised through public issue very easily and the block money can be diverted towards this mega project. This project will change the lives of 100 crore people of India. H_2O is the basic factor for all developmental activities. The Indian economy depended upon agriculture. The cultivation of agriculture needs H_2O. The water can solve all the problems of the modern **India**. If this project materialises, the citizen of India is no more less than **American Citizen**. India will definitely grow with the **prosperous countries**. The project should be taken up as a **patriotic** movement. Every citizen of India should contribute as per his financial capability in the form of shares. The project cost is an equivalent to the market capitalisation of the Indian stock market.

Participations in trading is another important factor in making of the investment decisions made by the investors. The market behaviour depends on the market players and their role in trading. The trading in stock exchange is publicly available information to each and every interested investors. The volume of trading in a particular scrip, the value of trading in a counter, the trading per hour, intra-day trading information, and all other information is available to the public. The free flow of correct and unbiased information is always available in the market. The market absorbs all the information available in the market. Hence the investor will know about the market behaviour immediately. **The Capital Market Efficiency Theory Random Walk Theory** and many other theories will clearly explain about the price behaviour in the market. Sometimes the share price movements may be **erratic and biased**. They may be overvalued or undervalued at any point of time. The market is consisting of various factors such as **"rumours, inside information, cornering, price rigging and other malpractices"**, which are unrelated to the prevailing fundamentals of the company. The theoretical analysis of the market would enable the investor to understand the movement. Hence the investor can take a decision regarding his investment commitments towards future for entering the stock market.

Fundamental analysis is one of the most important tools in investment analysis. It deals with the factors affecting the market in the **Macro and Micro sense**. In **macro analysis**, a close observation will be made about economic, industry and company aspects of the regular activities. All about these factors will be discussed in latter chapters. The **micro analysis** reveals the intrinsic value of a share through security valuation models. It indicates whether a share is **overvalued** or **undervalued**. It will examine the balance sheet and profit and loss account of the company, whose share is being examined. **Ratio analysis** is the powerful tool to analyse the Company performance. However the fundamental analysis will enable us to decide what shares to buy and what shares to sell. The conceptual framework reveals about the factors influencing the market behaviour:

(a) External factor (environmental, economic and political development)
(b) Internal factors (financial performance of the company)
(c) Capital structure
(d) Investment habits of the public.

The market price depends on the supply and demand forces of the share. The security is valued in terms of the returns or earnings of the Company. The following factors influencing share prices in the market:

1. Market efficiency theory (Fundamental Analysis)
2. Random walk theory (Fundamental Analysis)
3. Capital asset pricing method (Fundamental Analysis)
4. Trend walk theory (Fundamental Analysis)

5. Dow theory (Technical Analysis)
6. Elliot's wave theory (Technical Analysis)

In addition to the above factors, a lot of other factors such as **psychological and emotional** elements, will influence the share prices in the stock market.

Technical analysis is another important factor in conceptual framework. It reveals about the price behaviour of the aggregate market and of individual share. It is a knowledge based activity. It requires a lot of skill to understand the situation. It indicates the information with the help of the charts about share prices, trading volume and moving averages. It will help us to know about trends in price changes and suggest buy and sell points in the charts. It informs us the past price of the individual scrip to take a good investment decision. **The Dow and Elliot Wave Theory** is the part of technical analysis. These two theories will explain the price behaviour in the past and help us to guide the future. A detailed discussion will be made available in latter chapters.

Yet another kind of analysis is the observation of **Risk and Return**. The risk and return is the most important factor in determining the amount of investment. **Return** is always chased by the **risk. Risk** is an estimated future loss of the business activity. Risk cannot be avoided. It is an escapable element. But in same situations, it cannot be escaped. It is an accepted level of loss by the investor. The return is always depended upon the level of accepted risk. If the investor is willing to take more risk, the higher return is waiting for the investor. The risk and return analysis to be achieved by the use of **portfolio theory and portfolio management**. The degree of risk depends upon the financial asset preferences, income requirements and other investment characteristics. The portfolio theory always thinks about the minimisation of risk and maximisation of return. All the theories are integrated to help decision-making by investors. The valuation is an important aspect of security analysis. Security valuation is an important part of market analysis.

(f) Market Players

The capital market provides long term funds to the corporate sector. It co-ordinates the suppliers and borrowers at a fixed place and time. The fund suppliers are generally consists of individual investors, companies, firms, finance companies and non-banking finance companies. **The borrowers** include companies, finance companies, governments and other organisations. Recently a number of mutual funds, public financial institutions, non-resident Indians have also started as players in the market.

(g) Intermediaries

Intermediaries are co-ordinators between fund suppliers and borrowers. They act as mediator for the both parties in the financial market, brokers, merchant bankers, financial institutions and investment consultancy firms. They are active in primary market and secondary market. The number of players are more in primary market. The success of public issue mainly depends upon the assistance of intermediaries. Brokers will play an important role in the new issue market. Investors are regular clients of the brokers. The brokers will guide, motivate and inspire the millions of investors through their wide network. Hence the brokers are powerful financial intermediaries in mobilisation of resources in the primary market. Secondary market operations are also handled by the brokers. Basically the secondary market operates through brokers only. They work for the clients on a commission basis. They render the services to the clients in buying and selling of shares in the market. The brokers occupy a dominant role in the secondary market. The primary market is involved with many intermediaries such as merchant bankers, registrars, underwriters, share transfer agents and collecting bankers. The success of public issue is depended upon these financial intermediaries services.

Hence all the above aspects are integrated to help in decision-making by investors scientifically. **Scientific analysis** is the most important factor before going to make investment. **Profit booking** in stock market is possible only with proper careful analysis. But in practice, investment in stock market is made by investors blindly by handing over a cheque to the broker. They simply do not know about the company reputation, brand image, financial performance of the company, EPS, PE ratio, past price, relation to government policy etc. Therefore the **savings investment theory** explained the flow of savings into investment which helps the growth process in the economy.

Time Value of Money

Time is the most important factor in stock market. Today is more valuable than the same tomorrow. The time factor determines the enter and exit of stock market. Money has alternative uses and opportunity costs. The present value of a delayed pay off may be found by multiplying the pay off by discounting factor, which is expressed as the reciprocal of 1 plus a rate of return.

(a) Present value method
(b) Discounted cash flows method

The present value can be computed by the following formula:

$$PV = \frac{1}{1+r} \times C$$

C = expected cash flow
r = rate of return to the investor
If there are more than one period,

$$PV = \frac{C_1}{(1+r)} + \frac{C_2}{(1+r)^2} + \frac{C_3}{(1+r)^3} = \Sigma \frac{Cr}{(1+r)^t}$$

$C_1 C_2 C_3$ = expected cash flow in periods 1, 2, 3.
r = remains as the same rate of return during all these periods.

The following formula can be applied through **discounted cash flow method.**

$$DCF = \frac{C_1}{(1+r)} + \frac{C_2}{(1+r)^2} + \frac{C_3}{(1+r)^3}$$

$C_1 C_2 C_3$ = expected cash in flow
r = rate of return.

Security analysis reveal about the behaviour of the market. It finds out the true value of a security. The **intrinsic value** is also known as real value of a security. The following topics will be covered in this Unit.

(1) Fundamental Analysis
(2) Technical Analysis
(3) Dow Theory
(4) Elliot Wave Theory
(5) Efficient Market Theory.

1. FUNDAMENTAL ANALYSIS

Introduction

Fundamental analysis is one of the tools for a scientific analysis in stock market operations. Any investor or any analyst can not ignore the importance of fundamental analysis. It relates to an examination of the intrinsic value of the share. It is a powerful tool to measure the efficiency of a company. The state of the economy can show an impact on the profitability of a company. The economic policy of the government, political stability, good labour legislations, good infrastructure facilities, a strong and efficient capital market can **boost** the **Gross Domestic Product** of the nation. The speedy industrialisation process in the nation will stimulate the growth in all aspects. An economy with favourable savings, investments, stable prices, balance of payments provides a good environment for common stock investment. The prosperity of a nation depends upon the economic freedom of a country.[1] According to **Swaminathan S. Anklesaria Aiyar,** the laissez faire is the proven path to prosperity. The **freest economies** have a per capita income of **$ 29,219,** more than twice that of the "most free" category and more than **four times** that of the mostly unfree category. Every year, the **Wall street journal** and Heritage foundation bring out a book called **"The index of economic freedom",** the centre piece of which is an index ranking countries by the extent of freedom in **10 economic dimensions.** The economic dimensions are presented below:

(a) Trade policy
(b) Fiscal burden
(c) Government intervention
(d) Monetary policy
(e) Foreign investment policy
(f) Banking and Finance
(g) Wages and prices
(h) Property rights
(i) Regulation and informal markets

Table: Index of Economic Freedom 2005

Rank	*Country*	*Rank*	*Country*
	I. Free		
1.	Hongkong	2.	Singapore
3.	Luxumbourg	4.	Estonia
5.	Ireland	6.	Newzeland
7.	United Kingdom	8.	Denmark
9.	Iceland	10.	Australia
11.	Chile	12.	Switzerland
13.	United States	14.	Sweden
15.	Finland	16.	Canada
17.	Netherlands		

(Contd.)

1. Many different paths to prosperity, *The Economic Times*, 19-1-05, p. 8, Swaminathan S. Anklesaria Aiyar.

(Contd.)

Rank	*Country*	*Rank*	*Country*
	II. Mostly Free		
18.	Germany	19.	Austria
20.	Bahrain	21.	Belgium
22.	Cyprus	23.	Lithunia
24.	Elsalvador	25.	Bahamas
26.	Italy	27.	Taiwan
28.	Latavia	29.	Malta
30.	Norway	31.	Spain
32.	Barbados	33.	Czec Republic
34.	Israel	35.	Hungary
36.	Solvak Republic	37.	Bostwana
38.	Portugal	39.	Japan
40.	Trinidad	41.	Poland
42.	Armenia	43.	Oruguay
44.	France	45.	South Korea
46.	Solvenia	47.	Beilire
48.	Magadaskar	49.	UAE
50.	Bolivia	51.	Mangolia
52.	Bulgaria	53.	Panama
54.	Costarica	55.	Kuwait
56.	Peru	57.	South Africa
58.	Jordan	59.	Greece
60.	Jamaica	61.	Oman
62.	Cape Verde	63.	Cambodia
64.	Mexico	65.	Mauritius
66.	Nicaragua	67.	Albania
68.	Maurtiana	69.	Macedonia
70.	Malaysia	71.	Thailand
72.	Saudi Arabia	73.	Senegal
	III. Mostly Unfree		
74.	Croatia	75.	Uganda
76.	Lebanon	77.	Moldova
78.	Swaziland	79.	Guyana
80.	Sri Lanka	81.	Namibia
82.	Qator	83.	Tunisia
84.	Bosnia	85.	Gautemala
86.	Mali	87.	Morocco
88.	Colombia	89.	Ukraine
90.	Brazil	91.	Philippines
92.	Ivory Cost	93.	Burkina Faso
94.	Fiji	95.	Guinea
96.	Kenya	97.	Kyrgyztsan

(Contd.)

(Contd.)

Rank	Country	Rank	Country
98.	Dijihouti	99.	Ghana
100.	Georgia	101.	Mozambique
102.	Lesotho	103.	Azerbajan
104.	Chad	105.	Egypt
106.	Gabori	107.	Gambia
108.	Zambia	109.	Tanzania
110.	Handanaus	111.	Paraguay
112.	China	113.	Turkey
114.	Algeria	115.	Argentina
116.	Ecudor	117.	Central African Republic
118.	Eql. Guinea	119.	**India**
120.	Niger	121.	Dominician Republic
122.	Indonesia	123.	Rwanda
124.	Russia	125.	Romania
126.	Cameron	127.	Nepal
128.	Benjin	129.	Malawi
130.	Kazikisthan	131.	Togo
132.	Yeman	133.	Ethipoia
134.	Pakisthan	135.	Sierra Leone
136.	Republic of Congo	137.	Vietnam
138.	Guinea-Bissasu	139.	Suria
140.	Suriname	141.	Bangladesh
142.	Nigeria	143.	Belaraus
	IV. Repressed		
144.	Tajikisthan	145.	Haiti
146.	Venezula	147.	Uzbekisthan
148.	Iran	149.	Cuba
150.	Laos	151.	Turkemenistan
152.	Zimbabwe	153.	Libya
154.	Burma	155.	North Korea

Source: *The Economic Times*, 19-1-05, p. 8.

The index itself shows that the fastest growing countries are mostly unfree. **China**, the miracle economy of the last two decades, ranks 112 out of 155 rated countries. It has moved up 16 places in 2005. Yet its low position after **25 years** of Deugist reform shows that relative unfreedom can produce the fastest growth rise in history. **Vietnam** enjoyed average **GNP** growth of **7.9 per cent** in 1999-2000, the second highest in the world. This sterling performer comes **137th.**

The countries of the sub-continent have done well in recent years, growing at 5-7 per cent, yet come in **"mostly unfree"** category. India has been growing at around 6 per cent annually. **Sri Lanka and**

Bangladesh have achieved around 5 per cent annually. **Pakistan** is back of **5-6 per cent** growth after a difficult time in the 1990's. Yet the index ranks **Sri Lanka** at 79, **India** at 112, **Pakistan** 133, and **Bangladesh** at 141 second last among the mostly unfree countries. So this part of the index could be used by **left wingers** to claim that **prosperity** lies in being mostly unfree. **Hongkong and Singapore** continue to be the top of the list. These are developing countries that have become the **richest** in the world. They have done so by creating **open economies** with low **taxation and strong property rights**. The index also drives having the point that the **United States** is not exactly the land of the free, having slipped from **5th position** in **1998 to 12th today**. Its corporate tax is high by world standards and it ranks 112 in this respect. Hence the world is a complex place where there are many paths to **success and failure**. Economic freedom by itself does not tell enough. **Hongkong** is top of the list, but public spending accounts for **half** its housing and most of its education, and a good chunk of its infrastructure. Its tax rates are very low mainly because the government owns most of the land and makes millions through land sales. **Singapore** has focussed on attracting foreign investment, and the biggest locally owned companies are public sector giants, providing infrastructure very efficiently. These two most free countries actually run on the basis of excellent public/private sector partnerships not pure **laissez faire**.

The political economy of **small countries** seems very different from that of large countries. Small countries know that they cannot aim for self sufficiency or create national champions behind protectionist barriers. They tend to be countries where lobbies for trade, banking and shipping are more powerful than for industry and this facilitates an open economy. They see foreign investment as a **fertiliser** for growth, not an instrument of foreign domination. So it is no surprise that the **06 freest** economies as measured by the index are all small countries **Hongkong, Singapore, Luxemburg, Estonia, Ireland and New Zealand**. By Contrast, large countries tend to have industrial and agricultural lobbies equating protectionism with patriotism. Their internal trade greatly exceeds external trade, so they entertain delusions about self sufficiency. The mind set created by such institutions makes it impossible to move rapidly towards economic freedom.

The fundamental analysis allows for selection of securities of different sectors of the economy. The Indian economy is mainly depended upon agriculture. Agriculture is based on monsoon. The following factors are considered to be essential for the better performance of the corporate sector:

(a) Good monsoon
(b) Performance of agriculture sector
(c) Monetary policy
(d) Economic system
(e) Political stability
(f) Economic policy
(g) Business cycles
(h) Labour legislations

The security analysis will be made by the investor before making an investment decisions. It will be useful for understanding business and market environment in the country. It enables the investor to assess the potentiality of the particular company's earning capacity. The total analysis of the investment environment can be categorised into the following three types:

(a) Economic Analysis
(b) Industry Analysis
(c) Company Analysis.

(a) Economic Analysis

The state of economy is most important factor in the fundamental analysis. Indian economy is basically agriculture dominated market. The mixed economy is a participation of public and private sector. The government shall have co-ordinate the intricacies of the both sectors. The government should encourage the private sector and also protect the public sector. The encouragement of the private sector depends upon the government industrial policy. The industrial policy is greatly helpful in formation of capital in the country. The capital formation is the **most important** factor in the development of a nation. The capital formation leads to asset creation in the economy. Asset creation is the indicator for measuring the **prosperity of a nation.** The **prosperity** of a nation depends upon the level of economic activity played by different forces. If the economy grows rapidly, industry can also be expected to show rapid growth. Growth is a strong and powerful element in the development of a nation. **Growth** is an element for assessing the efficiency and capabilities of a nation. It depends upon the efforts made by the economy. If the level of economic activity is **high**, the stock prices are **high** and if the level of economic is low, stock prices are also in low. Hence the stock prices in stock market is a reflection of levels of economic activities. Higher stock prices is a reflection of **prosperous** outlook for sales and profits of the corporate sector. The analysis of **macro-economic** environment enables to understand the behaviour of the stock prices. **Macro analysis** deals with the following factors:

(i) Gross domestic product
(ii) Savings potential
(iii) Monsoon
(iv) Taxation
(v) Foreign exchange
(vi) Inflation
(vii) Budget
(viii) Infrastructure
(ix) Prediction
(x) Interest rates
(xi) Economic assessment
(xii) Economic indicators.

(i) Gross Domestic Product

Gross domestic product is a tool for analysis of the level of economic activities in the country. It represents the aggregate value of the goods and services produced by a country. It indicates all efforts made by a nation of people. It is the society contribution. It takes all factors into consideration for arriving the value of amount of goods and services produced by a whole nation. It is the most important factor in the **Macro analysis.** It consists of personal consumption, expenditure, gross private domestic investment and government expenditure and net exports of good and services. The estimates are available on annual basis. It is a combination of all sectors of the economy. The contribution of GDP is presented below:

Table: Statement shows Various Sector's Contribution of GDP (Percentage)

	93-94	*94-95*	*95-96*	*96-97*	*97-98*	*98-99*	*99-2000*	*2000-01*	*01-02*	*02-03*	*03-04*	*04-05*
1. Agriculture	30.97	30.28	28.00	28.46	26.50	26.42	24.99	23.92	24.03	21.50	21.71	20.53
2. Mining	2.57	2.62	2.59	2.41	2.52	2.44	2.37	2.33	2.26	2.37	2.32	2.29
3. Manufacture	16.06	16.74	17.94	18.25	17.68	17.05	16.71	17.20	16.85	17.27	17.01	17.34
4. Power	2.43	2.48	2.47	2.41	2.48	2.49	2.47	2.47	2.42	2.40	2.29	2.28
5. Construction	5.20	5.10	5.06	4.79	5.04	5.02	5.12	5.23	5.14	5.30	5.23	5.17
6. Trade	12.72	13.11	13.99	13.97	14.35	14.49	14.65	14.59	15.02	15.63	15.67	26.60
7. Transport	6.54	6.69	6.93	6.95	7.18	7.29	7.63	8.20	8.47	9.17	9.89	–
8. Finance	11.53	11.33	11.43	11.34	12.08	12.18	12.70	12.59	12.44	13.01	12.84	12.87
9. Community	11.98	11.52	11.59	11.43	12.18	12.62	13.36	13.46	13.37	13.36	13.03	12.92

Table: Statement shows Contribution of Different Industry to GDP Growth (Percentage)

	93-94	*94-95*	*95-96*	*96-97*	*97-98*	*98-99*	*99-2000*	*2000-01*	*01-02*	*02-03*	*03-04*	*04-05*
1. Agriculture	–	21.4	**-3.6**	34.3	**-14.4**	25.3	1.4	**-0.6**	26.0	**-42.2**	24.3	3.3
2. Mining	--	3.3	2.1	0.2	4.9	1.1	1.3	1.3	1.0	5.1	1.8	1.8
3. Manufacture	–	26.5	34.0	22.1	5.8	7.4	11.2	28.4	10.8	27.7	14.0	22.0
4. Power	–	3.2	2.3	1.7	4.0	2.7	2.2	2.5	1.6	1.9	1.0	2.10
5. Construction	–	3.9	4.3	1.4	10.2	4.8	6.6	7.8	3.6	9.4	4.4	4.30
6. Trade	–	18.7	25.8	13.7	22.2	16.7	17.3	13.4	22.4	31.0	16.1	41.80
7. Transport	–	8.9	10.0	7.3	11.9	8.9	13.3	21.3	13.10	26.8	18.3	–
8. Finance	–	8.8	12.6	10.1	27.5	13.8	21.3	10.0	9.9	27.20	10.90	13.3
9. Community	–	5.4	12.4	9.3	27.9	19.4	25.5	15.9	11.8	13.1	9.20	11.40

Sources: The Economic Times, 19-02-05, P. No. 14.

The contribution of the manufacturing sector to GDP growth has increased sharply in **2004-2005**. According to the advance estimate of **Central Statistical Organisation (CSO)** the share of **manufacturing sector in GDP** growth has increased from **14 per cent** in **93-94** to **22 per cent** in the current year.

The index of **manufacturing** production has infact been rising consistently since the beginning of **2004-2005.** The index has grown by **9 per cent** during the first nine months of the current year. April–Dec. 2004 compared to **7.2 per cent** in the corresponding period last year. The strong performance of manufacturing sector has pushed up the index of industrial production from **6.6 per cent** during the first nine months of **2003-2004 to 8.4 per cent** now.

Higher industrial growth has prompted CSO to revise upwards the GDP growth rate too. It has estimated a **6.9 per cent** GDP growth for 2004-2005 against 6 to 6.5 per cent growth projected by the RBI and 6.2 per cent projected by **CMIE.**

GDP growth at 6.9 per cent will still be lower than the annual growth target of the 10th plan. But what is significant is that this has come despite a sharp fall in agricultural contribution. Agriculture's share in incremental GDP is just about 3.3 per cent in 04-05 against 24.3 per cent in the previous year. Hence the **higher** growth rate is more favourable to the stock market.

(ii) Savings Potential

Savings are the most important element in the economy. They influence the present level of investment. Though savings curb the present consumption but in long term nature they help to grow the economy. The savings will be directed towards various financial assets such as **equity shares, deposits mutual fund units, real estate and bullions.** India has a strong savings potential and the middle class families commands the higher level of savings. Savings towards new issue market leads to capital formation. Capital formation stimulates the value of assets. Asset creation is the most important factor in the **prosperity** of the nation. Prosperity is the barometer of the development. It is the indicator of the efforts made by a human resources of a nation. **China and Japan** are the best examples for the development of their economy. The patterns of savings in society will be highly influenced by various factors such as **Interest rates, taxation, purchasing power, disposable income etc.** If the interest rates are at lower levels in the economy, the investors are not interested to save the money. The low rate of interest may curtail the savings habits in the economy. The debt market will be inactive but equity market can grow higher level due to funds available at cheaper rate of interest. Hence the level of rate of interest will influence the level of savings. **Tax system** in the economy is one of the factor to increase the level of savings. Tax payers in India are encouraged to save upto **Rs. 1.00 lakh** for reducing their tax burden. Hence the direct tax can also influence the level of savings. **Purchasing power** in the community is another important factor in influencing the investment levels. Higher income with low spending habits may arise to increase the level of savings. **Disposable income** at higher level with the community helps to mobilise the savings. The savings mobilised through various factors may useful to produce more goods to the economy. Higher level of production is an value addition to the worth of assets. Higher level of asset creation in the economy may leads to better living standards to the citizens of their country. A better quality of living standards can reduce the citizen's problems. We can construct the **modern India** and can affordable better quality of living standards on par with **American citizen**. For achieving this purpose India should concentrate on **Political reforms** rather than **economic reforms**. India can create miracles in the economy. Politicians in India should change their mind set. They should be trained in economic aspects. They should be in a position to run the government with corruption free environment. The economy should be **"Free economy"** to achieve the goal like in China. We can do lot of things by observing of the developed economy. But we should not copy them or theft. Development enhances the capabilities and efficiency. The **restricted economy** will halt the development and progress. Hence the power of savings will be useful to construct the **modern India**. The **digital economy** can enhance the living standards of the poor citizens. The below poverty line people are facing many problems on the earth. Their problems will be solved with the proper careful financial planning of the economy. The poverty can be attacked with the change in mindset of the society. Development is not involved with the monetary help. It is achieved with the proper utilisation of available financial resources. The proper utilisation of funds can definitely achieve the growth.

(iii) Monsoon

Agriculture is occupying a dominant role in the economy. It is based on rainfall in India. The rainfall depends upon good climate and pollution, non-pollution environment, free environment. It is directly and indirectly linked with the industries such as **sugar, cotton, textiles, food processing** etc. These industries depend upon agriculture for raw material. Fertilisers and chemical industries are supplying inputs to the agriculture. **A good monsoon** leads to higher demand for input and results in heavy crop. This situation enables the stock market to activate more and more. The higher level of stock index performance leads to a good healthy environment in the country and it may attract more **foreign direct investments**. If the monsoon is very bad, agricultural and hydel power production would suffer a lot and leads to industrial **unrest** in the economy. A disturbance in the industrial process leads to a fall in the level of **GDP**. A negative growth in **GDP** is a dangerous situation. Hence the monsoon is the most important factor in the Indian economy. The good rainfall depends upon the environment. The encouragement of **Eco-friendly** Industries leads to non-pollution environment. The government is also taken steps to create pollution free environment through various legislations and statutory clearences.

(iv) Taxation

In India, every year in the month of **February**, the government presents its budget in the parliament by the Finance Minister. The business community and the whole of India eagerly awaits the government's announcement regarding the tax policy. Tax policy is the part of the Finance act. **Finance act** is the part of the Union Government's budget. **Budget** is the most important tool to the Central Government to change the lives of crores of people. Budget is a document consisting of Income and Expenditure of the government. The government collects its revenues through direct and indirect taxes. Direct taxes are regulated in India by the **Central Board of Direct Taxes.** The indirect taxes are controlled by Central Board of Excise and Customs Duties. Both of these wings are working under the control of Finance Ministry. They make arrangements to give tax relief to various industries in the form of concessions and incentives. **Direct taxes** are levied and collected by the Central Government. **Income tax, Gift tax and Wealth tax** are the best examples for Direct taxes. **Central excise, customs** and **central sales tax** are the examples for indirect taxes. Tax reliefs given to savings for encouragement. A lower rate of corporate tax is offered in the latest budget, 2005. The minimum alternate tax levied by the government in 1996 adversely effected the stock market. Customs duty on fabrics down

5 per cent and Central excise on **polyster filament yarn** down 8 per cent in the latest budget 2005. The highlights of the budget 2005 is presented below which shows impact as corporate sector:

(a) Apparel prices, domestic and imports likely to drop by **6 per cent.**

(b) A reduction in customs duty on refrigerated vans from **20 per cent to 10 per cent.**

(c) A reduction in customs duty on machinery of leather and footwear industry from **20 per cent to 5 per cent.** The duty on ethyl vinyl acetate, an input for the footwear industry is also proposed to be reduced from **20 per cent to 10 per cent.**

(d) A reduction in customs duty to pharmaceuticals and bio-technology sectors. Customs duty reduced on **nine** specified machinaries used in these two sectors to **5 per cent.**

(e) A reduction in customs duty on specified parts of battery operated road vehicles and for printing presses from **20 per cent to 10 per cent.**

(f) A reduction in customs duty on primary and secondary metals from **15 per cent to 10 per cent**. Similarly industrial raw materials such as catalysts, refractory raw materials basic plastic materials, molasses and industrial ethyl alcohol will now be liable to a reduced customs duty rate of **10 per cent.**

The following table indicates the reduction in custom duties:

(i) Lead proposed to reduce the duty to **5 per cent.**

(ii) Cocking coal with high ash content reduced from **15 per cent to 5 per cent.**

(iii) Proposed to remove the customs duty on specified capital goods and all inputs required for the manufacture of information technology agreement bound items.

(iv) An increase in the customs duty on **cut flower** from **30 per cent to 60 per cent.**

(v) A reduce in the duty on cloves to **35 per cent.**

(vi) A reduction in the customs duty on atmospheric drinking water generators from **20 per cent to 5 per cent.**

(g) The following items reveal about the aspects of **central excise duty** regarding on various items:

(i) Government's intention is to bring as many goods as possible to the **CENVAT** rate of **16 per cent**. Today **05** items attract **24 per cent** out of the **5,** three items selected

PFY, tyres and air conditioners, reduced excise duty to **16 per cent**.

(ii) Imitation Jewellery now attracts an excise duty of **16 per cent.**

(iii) A levy of excise duty on branded jewellery is **2 per cent.**

(iv) A levy of excise duty on mosaic tiles at **8 per cent** and on road tractors for semi-trailers of engine capacity exceeding 1800 cc at **16 per cent**. Agriculture tractor will continue to remain exempt.

(v) Abolition of surcharge on tea, refined edible oils, and vanaspati.

(vi) Hand made matches are fully exempt from excise duty. Machine made matches reduced from **16 per cent to 12 per cent.**

(vii) The ceiling for SSI exemption based on turnover from the level of Rs. **3 crores to Rs. 4 crores**.

(viii) Iron and steel attract the normal level of tax **16 per cent**.

(ix) An increase in the specific duty on molasses from **Rs. 500** per MT to **Rs. 1000** per MT and in case of Cement clinkers from **Rs. 250** per MT to **Rs. 350** per MT.

(x) An increase in the specific rate on cigarettes by about **10 per cent** and impose a surcharge of **10 per cent** an *ad volorem* duties on other tobacco products including gutka, chewing tabacco, snuff and panmasala.

(xi) The corporate tax for domestic companies is **30 per cent** with a surcharge of **10 per cent.** The rate of depreciation will be **15 per cent** for general machinery and plant but the initial depreciation rate will be increased to **20 per cent**.

(xii) To encourage technological upgradation, tax on technical services have been reduced from **20 per cent to 10 per cent**.

(xiii) There is no change in taxation regarding foreign companies.

(xiv) Weighted deduction of **150 per cent** of expenditure on in house research and development facilities of companies engaged in business of **bio-Technology Pharmaceuticles electronics, telecommunications chemical and any other notified product.**

(xv) Deduction of profit of new industrial Undertakings in **Jammu and Kashmir.**

(xvi) 100 per cent deduction of profits of companies carrying on scientific research and development and approved by the department of scientific and industrial research.

Table: Statement shows the Budget for the Year 2005-06

(Rs. in crores)

Particulars	*2005-06*
1. Revenue receipts	3,51,200
2. Tax revenue	2,73,466
3. Non-tax revenue	77,734
4. Capital receipts	1,63,144
5. Recoveries of loans	12,000
6. Borrowings	1,51,144
7. Total receipts (1+4)	5,14,344
8. Non-plan expenditure	3,70,847
9. On Revenue A/c of which	3,30,530
10. Interest payments	1,33,945
11. On capital A/c	40,317
12. Plan expenditure	1,43,497
13. Total expenditure	5,14,344
14. Revenue deficit	95,312
15. Fiscal deficit	1,51,144
16. Primary deficit	17,199

Source: *The Economic Times*, 1-3-2005, p. 16.

(v) Foreign Exchange

Foreign exchange is the most important element in the economy. A favourable balance in foreign exchange reserves will stimulate the growth of the Indian economy. The foreign exchange relates to the country's receipts earned through exports by the corporate sector. The country also requires the payments to other nations for import of goods for the domestic consumption. The difference between receipts and payments may be surplus or deficit. Balance of payment is a measure of the strength of rupee on external account. If the **deficit** increases, the rupee may depreciate against other currencies. The depreciation in rupee value leads to the weakening of the economy. The imports may become more costly. The companies which are involved in export and import business will be affected by the changes in foreign exchange rate. The volatility of the foreign exchange rate severely affects the flow of foreign currency into the stock market through **foreign institutional investors**. The stock markets will activate by the entry of **FIIs**. FIIs will occupy a dominant role in the stock market. The enter and exit of the **FIIs** from the stock markets will greatly influence the prices of Indian stock market. A favourable balance of payments in foreign exchange balances can create a positive effect on the Indian stock market.

(vi) Inflation

Inflation is another important factor in the economy. It refers to increasing the prices of different commodities and services available in the market. It increases along with the growth of GDP. Hence the real rate of growth would be less. The demand in the consumer product industry is significantly affected. The growth in demand for more products will stimulate the production levels of the Industry. Hence the industries will come under the price control of the government. They may loss the market. **For example: Sugar**. The profitability of the industry depends upon the government price control. **Inflation** is useful to the economy upto some extent but higher rate is harmful to the stock market.

(vii) Budget

Budget is an important tool to the government. It can influence the lives of crores of people. It contains the receipts and payments of the Central Government for a specific period. It is a guiding force to the government machinery. The budget may show either **defeat or surplus** balance. Deficit budget may lead to high rate of inflation which adversely affect the cost of production. **Surplus** budget leads to deflation. Deflation result a lower level of prices for all commodities. Profits will be low and production levels declines. Therefore, balanced budget is more useful to the stock market.

(viii) Infrastructure

The development of the economy depends upon the good infrastructure facilities. Infrastructure is an essential for the growth of-industrial and agriculture sector. It is useful for overall development of the nation. The government need not to develop the every sector, but creation of better infrastructure facilitates automatically stimulate the growth of every sector. Providing good transport mode, quality supply of power, provision for better natural resources, good communication facilities, better legislation, good labour relations will enhance the Industrial productivity. Hence the Central Government made a provision in the 2005-06 budget, with a massive new outlays for **National highways and Urban renewal**. A **special purpose vehicle (SPV)** that will raise Rs. 10,000 crores for various projects, and a subsidy fund of Rs. **1500 crores**, will fill the viability gap of infrastructure projects that may need bids for minimum subsidy. The Central Government budget also made provisions for rural villages.

The villagers will be provided **one crore** additional hectares under irrigation. All villages to be connected by road, telecom, electricity and drinking water supply to additional **74000** villages. The budget envisaged the telecom sector by removing mobile subscribers from **1/6** criteria for filing of income tax returns. It was earlier a major deterrent for the growth of services. The budget also stressed development of the telecom network in rural areas and makes a provision of **Rs. 1200 crores** in the **Universal service obligation** fund for 2005-06. Development of rural telephony would help in the overall growth of India's economy. The budget envisages **BSNL** would provide telephony in **66,882** villages in next three years. The cost of setting up networks is also likely to be reduced due to reduction in the prices of equipment. The budget also envisages reducing to **zero duty** on raw material and components required to manufacture equipment. The budget made provision for a rural electrification scheme for villages. The scheme that covers **1.25** lakh villages in a five year period and a 4 per cent cut in customs duty on capital goods have generated same sparks to keep the power sector going this budget. The finance minister has also promised an 11 KV substation in each block and a distribution transformer in every village. In the next **five years** investment in infrastructure through the **Rs. 33000 crore** outlay for 2005-06, will be a growth driver for the sector. The budget also made big plans about surface transportation especially on roads. There will be roads and more roads both **highways, roads in villages** and in the remote North-east. Initiatives are currently on to improve the **National Highway Network** including NHDP. Under this scheme **13,146 kms** of National highway will be converted to **4 lanes or 6 lanes** track at an estimated cost of **Rs. 54,000 crores**. National highway authority revenues are derived from fuel costs less and tolls. There was a rapid growth in collections from Rs. 85 crores in 1999-2000 to Rs. 371 crores in 2003-2004. The government is also looking at special purpose vehicles and viability gap funding for infrastructure projects.

Forex for Infrastructure[1] is a novel and innovative concept proposed recently by the **Planning Commission**. A key concern raised in the debate is that dollars can be spent only on imports while infrastructure largely requires the acquisition of domestic resources. Careful analysis reveals that at least this concern is without foundation. The import intensity of infrastructure is virtually irrelevant to the final outcome.

---

1. "Maddled on Forex for Infrastructure" Arvinda Paragaria, *The Economic Times* 17.1.2005, p. 2.

Thus, **a $ 5 billion dollars** can be utilised for import of prefabricated power station. The money supply unchanged, the price level remains unchanged, no change occurs in the GDP, incomes, consumption levels or exchange rate. Hence the government will take a decision regarding this innovative concept.

(ix) Prediction

Prediction is one of the important factor in assessing market situation. Assessment of future in a right way enable the investors to book the profits in the stock market. The assessing capabilities depends upon many factors such as **Foresight, good understanding of the economic environment, rapid changes in the technological** aspects etc. A change in customers attitudes, a change in government policy etc. must be known by the predictor. The success of the prediction is basically depends upon the abilities of the predictor.

(x) Interest Rates

Interest is the reward to the fund owner. It is treated as an expense in cost of production of a commodity. The rate of interest can show impact on cost of production of a commodity. Interest rates are fluctuating in the market, which is determined by the RBI. Reserve Bank is the full authority in determining the interest rates in the country. If the interest rates decreases, the profitability of the firms will be increased. A lower rate of interest will be stimulate the earning capacity of the commercial enterprises. A flow of higher amount of money is available at lower interest rate for the **brokers** may stimulate the speculative activities in the secondary market. A rise in share prices encourages more investors towards stock markets. The availability of resources at lower rate of interest will definitely stimulate the growth of the stock markets. A rise in secondary markets leads more demand for the **New Issues**. The demand for new issues creates capital formation. Capital formation is the indicator of the development of economic progress. Economic progress creates more employment opportunities to the **100 crores** people of India. A good government can provide job opportunities in the corporate sector by providing funds at lower rate of interest. A rise in interest rates leads to **higher** cost of production. The goods are sold in the market at higher prices reduces the demand. A fall in demand for goods will decline the sales of the corporate sector and profitability will be decline. Hence the interest rates are influencing factor in determining the growth of the corporate sector. The government will take a decision regarding the rate of interest in the market according to its monetary policy. The decisions of the government will be implemented by the Reserve Bank of India. Reserve Bank is the supreme authority in determination of supply of money in the market.

(xi) Economic Assessment

A study of economic environment is necessary for the success in the stock market. The macro economic analysis is more useful to book the profits in the stock market. The economic activities of the country affect the corporate profits and show an impact on the economy. **Gross Domestic Product** is the most important influencing factor in determining security prices. A fall in **GDP** may lead to a fall in corporate profit and consequent by in the security prices. The success in stock market depends upon the correct forecasting techniques. The investor or analyst should know advantages and dis-advantages of various techniques. The general techniques which are usually used by the analyst is presented below:

(a) Economic Barometer,
(b) Statistical Techniques.

Acquiring of various techniques by the investor for investment purpose will definitely conquer the success. The techniques will help him to decide the right time to invest and the type of security to be purchased. Stock market is not a ordinarily involved business, it requires intelligency analytical skills, talent, expertise, scientific analysis and good understanding about various economic aspects and its intricacies arise in the economy. Statistical techniques will be useful for analysing the situation to take a good investment decisions in the stock market.

(xii) Economic Indicators

Economic development is the most important factor to a nation. The development of a nation can be measured through powerful economic indicators. The economic indicators indicate the present status of the economy. It reveals about the progress or slow down the economy. The indicators are the barometres of the economy. They reveal the actual situation which is involved the many factors such as **capital investment, business profits, money supply, gross national product, interest rate and unemployment rate etc.** All these indicators inform about what is going to happen in the economy. The indicators show a signal to predict the way of the economy. The popular indicators in our economy are **Fiscal policy, monetary policy rainfall index, productivity, capital formation, Foreign Direct Investments and the stock indices**. The fiscal policy is related to the central government affail. The aim of the policy is to reduce the fiscal deficit or increase the surplus balances in the economy. The Indian economy has always a deficit balance in its balance sheet. The Central Government will take measures to reduce the deficit in the economy. In order to increase the revenue of the government, a levy of direct and indirect taxes are necessary. Hence the tax policy of the government may enhance the revenue levels of the economy. The reduction in expenditure levels of the government is not possible in the democratic country. Hence the government is always trying to boost its revenue and reduces deficit in the economy. The tax policy of the Central Government will be reflected in the Finance bill. Finance bill is the part of the Union Budget. The budget of the Union Government decides the taxation rates in India. The budget also contains about the incentives provided to the export oriented units in order to encourage the exports contribution in the global economy. After globalisation process, every nation is trying to capture the **global market**. The global markets provide excellent opportunities to the competitive nations. The global market requires a high quality of goods with lower prices. Hence those countries are able to meet these standard parameters can export their goods and earn foreign exchange. The commendable and favourable balance of the foreign reserves will make the **"Rupee"** more strong in the global market. Generally the global market is dominated by the **Dollar**. The dollars are more powerful weapons in the global market. The global market is an indicator to the efficiency of a nation. The major contribution of the global business is influenced by efficient utilisation of resources by a nation. Competition in the global market is very high and the efficient countries only can capture the business. The efficiency is the barometre in the global market. **The Monetary policy** is also related to the central government aspect. The RBI is the official agency to prepare the monetary policy on behalf of the Union Government. Monetary policy is associated with the money supply in the economy. The cheap money or the tight money policy adopted by the authorities will show impact on the industry. The stock market will discount all the affairs of the policy matters of the Central Government. Any aspect in the government's policies will observed by the stock market participants. The rise of **BSE Sensex and NSE NIFTY** will indicate trend of the economy. **Sensex and NIFTY Index** are the delicated tools and they will react for every small incident occurred in the economy of the country. A significant rise in these two index numbers will reflect the economic strength of India. India will definitely become a strong nation. If it utilises the available manpower in a right way. It should encourage research activities and a sophisticated legislation towards corporate sector will reach the goal. The development of India is not based on finance, but depends upon the attitude of the 100 crores public. Development is only a psychological aspect not a financial problem. The government is only a weapon to counter the poverty. Development activity should be taken as a patriotism. Every citizen attitude should be changed to work hard for the building of **Modern India**. China is the guiding force for development of our nation. The patriotic adventure should be initiated by the government by creating an awareness in the population. The other indicators are identified in our economy such as **unemployment rate, consumer price index and flow of foreign funds**. The predictions of the indicators can be constructed with the help of **Mathematics** is known as **Econometrics**.

2. INDUSTRY ANALYSIS

Industry is a group of firms producing similar characteristics goods. The firms are producing goods to meet the requirements of their customers. The commercial firms will survive in the market upto **patronage** of the customers. The consumers' tastes are changing, their needs are flactuating, their buying habits are highly **volatile**, all these factors will show a strong impact on the growth of an **Industry**. Industry is consisting of a number of companies. Companies are classified as per their activities of manufacturing goods. The **Reserve Bank of India** has classified the following industry groups:

(a) Food products
(b) Textiles
(c) Beverages, tobacco
(d) Wood and wood products
(e) Rubber and plastic products
(f) Transport equipment and parts
(g) Basic metals, alloys and metal products
(h) Machinery and machinery tools
(i) Non-metallic mineral products
(j) Other manufacturing industries
(k) Chemical and chemical products.

The industries are different from one another. They are classified on the basis of the business cycles. The business cycle is a combination of different phases:

(1) Growth Industry
(2) Cyclical Industry
(3) Industry Life Cycle.

Growth Industry is a combination of different companies producing similar characteristics of the goods. The **growth industries** have some special features in the business cycle. They have a **high rate of earnings**, high brand loyalty growth in expansion. They are independent of the **business cycle**. They are well established and stabilised in the market. They are ready to face any situation that exist in the market. The Industry will go for expansion with the help of **latest technology. Technology** is the most important and influencing factor in the business sector. The latest technology reduces cost of manufacturing expenses very significantly. Now-a-days all industries are taking **cost reduction measures** in order to get substantial savings of expenses. But the technology involves higher amount of **capital expenditure**. The **Information Technology** created a new wave in the corporate sector. The **IT** provides solutions to many business enterprises to attract the customers. **For example:** the commercial banks attracting the customers by providing **ATM services** throughout the nation. **ATM** facility provides flexibility to the customers for their withdrawal of cash. At the same time the banks also getting substantial savings in the form of salaries to their limited workforce. **E-commerce** is a sophisticated technology which saves time and money of the customer. It is also a cost effective tool to counter the cost of finished products. Business cycles continued to grow in the economy such as colour television, Telecommunications, Drugs and Pharmaceuticals. These industries have shown remarkable growth recently. The liberalisation policy created a best environment to grow in the economy for the **corporate sector**. Some industries move alongwith business cycles such as **Boom and Depression. White goods** command a good market in the boom period and demand declines during **depression** period. Hence the refrigerators, washing machines and home appliances enjoy a higher growth in the boom time. Some industries differ from the movement of business cycles. They are known as **Defensive Industry**. The basic needs of the human being is associated with this industry. Generally food and housing sectors will come under this classification. The food industry commands a good demand during recession and depression. The defensive industry scrips may be purchased by the investors for income earning purpose. Sometimes the government protection is available for this sector. Some industries are based on cyclical and at the same time growing concept. The industries are known as **cyclical growth industry**. They are technology based performance sectors. They will face stagnation period and experiences decline in sales. But they grow immediately with the changes occurred in the technological aspects. **For example: Automobile sector** introduces new models to help the industry for the growth of its firms. Hence, the investor should always think about the latest changes occurring in the market. **Industry life cycle** is the most important theory in the **Fundamental analysis**. This theory is contributed by Julius Gordensky. The study of different stages spread over of a firm's life period. Generally all companies are entering in every stage of the industry life cycle. The life cycle of the industry can be classified as follows:

(a) Preliminary stage
(b) Growth stage
(c) Stability
(d) Declining stage.

(a) Preliminary Stage

Preliminary stage is initial period for the newly established companies. Manufacturers try to develop brand name. In this stage prospective demand for the product is promising and the technology of the finished product is low. There are many producers exist in the market producing the same quality of goods and creates a tough competition. The demand for that products attracts many entrepreneurs to survive in the market. The market creates a severe competition and only fittest companies survive in the market. Every company in the market wants to capture the market share. The major portion occupied by a company is known as **market leader**. In this stage, survival is the most critical and influencing factor in the life of a business concern. The producers will provide heavy amount of budget for advertising to push the product at the disposal of the customers. Hence in this stage it is difficult to recommend the companies for investment purpose. Hence the survival is not known and the investor is unable to select companies. The competition in the market will change the positions of the firms. The changing environment in the market creates uncertainty. Therefore the business in this stage is involved with high risk. Risk is always haunting the businessmen. Risk is inescapable. Risk can be countered by the skills and intelligency of the business concern.

(b) Growth Stage

Growth stage is another important position in the industry life cycle. The preliminary stage eliminates some inefficient companies which are unable in better performance. The survived companies can only enter into this stage. In this stage the companies must face heavy competition for capturing the market share of the product. **Technology** occupies an important position to get higher margins from the market. The latest technology will provide a substantial savings of expenses and generates more quality products. **Quality and price** dictates the market. Every company should provide goods with high quality of goods and lower prices. The companies have stable growth rate in this stage and they show the best financial performance to the share holders in the form of declaration of higher rate of **dividend. Dividend** is the reward to the share holders. It is advisable to invest in these company's shares. The **pharmaceutical industry, Telecommunications industry** are the best examples for this stage. The growth rate is generally higher than the industry's average growth rate. It is the dynamic stage. The future will be decided and determined in this stage.

(c) Stability

Maturity position will revel all the consequencies to the industry. It is the perfection stage and the growth rate tends to moderate. The growth rate would be more or less equal to the **Gross domestic product growth rate**. The technology adopted by the industry may become **obsolete**. Technology must be upgraded and new products should be introduced in this stage. It is also a cautious positions to the industry. The investors have to closely observe the series of events that occurs in this stage. Hence the investors should take an investment decision after a careful study of the events occurred in the industry.

(d) Declining Stage

Declining stage is the end of the industry life cycle. In this stage demand for the specified product in the industry will be declined. The sales of firms will be fall. The earnings of the companies reduces drastically. The margins are under pressure. The product will become outdated. New products are replaces the old brands. Innovative products will appear in the market. **For example:** At present there is no demand for **black and white TVs**. There is no demand for **VCRs, VCPs** and replaced by **CD players and DVD players**. There is no demand at present for **Mopeds**.

After the liberalisation, automobile industry produces and provides a number of models in the **Motorcycle category**. The rural market of the mopeds are replaced by the motorcycle vehicles. There is less demand for **Ambassador** product of four wheelers and entering of new branded cars in the market. All these changes occurred due to changes in consumer's preference. Hence the consumer behaviour is the most important factor in determination of future. Even in the boom period, the growth of industry is negligible and leads to declining position. Any product, any company will survive in the market upto the **patronage** of consumers. Hence the investors are more to be cautious and investment in this kind of companies shares leads to erosion of capital. The investment decisions in these kind of shares are involved with **high risk.**

Industry analysis is a reflection of all aspects regarding different stages in the economy. All Industries are the part of **Gross Domestic Product**. GDP is the most important factor in our mixed economy. GDP occupies a dominant role in economic development of our country. An increase in GDP stimulates the value of prosperity and leads to asset creation. **Asset creation** in the country enhances the richness of a nation. GDP is an indicator of the efficiency of a nation and it reveals the historical cost of different products manufactured by various kinds of industries. In addition to the above factors, the investors in India has to analyse some other influencing elements. They are presented below for acquiring more knowledge about the Indian Industry. These factors are only helpful in prediction of the different alternatives available in the market at the disposal of the investors:

(a) Growth of the Industry
(b) Earning capabilities
(c) Product
(d) Competition
(e) Research
(f) Industrial peace
(g) Government policies.

(a) Growth of the Industry

Industry is a combination of different firms producing similar characteristics of products. GDP is a combination of various industries efforts. Economy constitutes various factors. The performance of various industries are monitored by different agencies. The research agencies and regulatory organs of the various industries closely observes the situation that arises in the economy and publishes different reports. The reports are more useful in analysing and assessment of the stock markets for the investors. The common investor in India should make careful analysis about the market movements before making his investment decisions. For this purpose he has to search for valuable information. The industry-wise information is published periodically by different agencies such as **"The centre for monitoring Indian Economy", "National Council of Applied Economic Research", "Indian Statistical Institute", "Central Statistical Organisation", "RBI bulletins", "National Institute of Financial Management", "Society for Capital Market Research" etc.** In the marketing aspects of the corporate world, various research organisations conducts surveys and makes periodical reports about the sales of different companies. **Indian Market Research Bureau, Operations and Research Group, Marketing and Research Group** publishes various periodical reports. Information provides knowledge. Knowledge about the economic environment creates an indepth analysis about the functioning of the corporate world. The past earnings and present growth stimulates the economic value of the corporate sector. Macro economic factors provide an **Insight** into the future. Past performance is not repeated in the business but it can show a direction to predict the future. The **Information Technology** created a wave in the Indian economy. A tremendous growth in **IT scrips** occurred and created history in the stock markets. The **IT** sector dominates in other industries and play a vital role in all sectors. The computerisation process has introduced by all most all industries including government departments. Hence the future of **GDP** is based on utilisation of IT sector. Indian is becoming a **knowledge** based economy. The digital economy will completely change the corporate sector. Therefore the investors should observe all these changes occurring in the economy and they should make investment decisions according to the latest situation in the market.

(b) Earning Capabilities

Profit is glamour to the corporate sector. The efficiency of a business concern can be measured through the quantum of money earned as profit. The sale price of a commodity by the manufacture includes **fixed and variable cost**. The ratio of fixed and variable cost affects the cost of production, which ultimately fell on the profitability of a company. The fixed cost is different from one industry to another. **For example:** the fixed cost is very high in case of Oil and Natural Gas Industry and Iron and Steel etc. **High fixed cost** requires a greater sales volume to meet the firm's **break even**

point (BEP). The break even point is the most influential factor in determining the volume of profit available to the company. If the company crosses **BEP** and the production is going on, the margins can be increased naturally. Hence the plant capacity utilisation indicates the actual earnings made by the company. The full utilisation of installed capacity needs additional capital to be invested for fixed equipment. Therefore lower the fixed cost will definitely shows impact on the corporate earnings. The variable expenses will be fluctuated according to the production schedule of the company. The latest situation in the market, reveal that the quality of goods must be high and price should be at low. Hence in order to meet such situation, every company is trying to cut the costs substantially by adopting innovative techniques. For this purpose the companies are introducing **cost reduction programmes** in order to reduce the pressure on the earnings of the company. Hence the investors must observe all these factors while taking investment decisions.

(c) Product

The goods which are demanded by the consumers in the market are manufactured and delivered by the corporate sector. Now-a-days the goods should be manufactured according to the needs and convenience of the customers. The customer is king in the market. He dictates the terms to the corporate sector. The products may be classified as **Industrial and Consumer goods**. **For example:** Cement, Steel and Iron goods are produced. The demand for them depends on the construction industry. The automobile component sector depends upon the growth of the automobile sector. Hence there will be a relation between these two factors. The investors have to make careful observation analyse the conditions for related goods producing industry and the ultimate and uses of the product. The nature of the product is also occupying an important role in investment decisions of the investors.

(d) Competition

Competition in the market is a common phenomenon in the business. The demand and supply of the goods are based on the several factors. High competition in the market reduces margins to the companies. Competition enhances the skills and abilities of the corporate sector. There will be competition between domestic and multinational companies. The competition may be in organised and unorganised sector. The competition would lead to a decline in the price of the product. The investors should be careful before investing in this type of scrips.

(e) Research

Technology occupies a vital role in the manufacturing goods. Traditional method of production of goods require an higher amount of expenditure and time consuming process. The manufacturing of goods at factory levels are changing very fast by adopting latest technology methods. Latest technology saves time and money. The technology will be available only on a continuous efforts made towards research and development. The **R&D** facilitate to acquire new method of manufacturing process in order to reduce the expenses. The economies of scale and new markets can be obtained through R&D. The higher percentage of allocation of budget for **R&D** leads to the emerging new methods of process.

(f) Industrial Peace

The Labour relations in the industrial sector is also occupying a vital role in the performance of corporate world. Good labour relations and labour legislation may helpful for the smooth functioning of the production of goods. The trade unions activities and attitudes will have impact on the labour productivity. Any disturbance in industrial peace leads to the interruption of the production of goods. The production targets of the industry will be fulfilled with the support of labour trade unions. The availability of adequate skilled persons may stimulate the productivity of the industry. An increase in productivity reduces the cost of production substantially. Therefore the investor must observe these things before making his investment decisions.

(g) Government Policy

Policy is a long term strategy. The government policies affect the profitability of the various industrial sectors. Government will give protection to some kind of units such as **tax holidays and subsidies** are provided for export oriented units. Every government policy will effect an any industrial sector either positively or negatively. **For example: control and de-control** of sugar prices affect the profitability of the sugar industry. Fertilisers are subsidised by the government **Pharmaceutical** prices are also under the control of government. The government provides tax incentives for companies which are established in backward areas. The Tourism department will provide tax incentives for the **five star hotels**. The domestic industries are protected by the government by way of giving incentives and subsidies. Hence the investors are required to analyse themselves by observing all these factors. The government policy regarding aviation sector is quite encourage and more aviation companies are entering into this segment. At present new companies are entering into this sector such as **Sahara airlines, Jet airways, Deccan aviations etc.** with the intensified competition, the private airlines offering a lower prices of tickets to their passengers. It is surprising that **Rs. 500** can afford air travel to the common man in India by the **Deccan aviations.** Hence the aviation sector gets full support from the government.

(h) Company Analysis

A knowledge about companies performance and their working environment is helpful to the investors in evaluating the performance of different companies. Stock market activities are involved with **knowledge** based skills and persons those who are fully equipped with a lot of information may become the stars of the stock market. Hence acquiring of information about corporate sector is necessary. From the available information, the investor assimilates the related Company's data and evaluates the present and future value of a stock. **The risk and return** is associated with the purchase of financial asset from the stock market. **Risk** is always chased by the return. **Return** is always haunted by **risk**. The investor must get better returns by avoiding risk. The valuation of financial asset process depends upon the investor's skills, abilities, knowledge foresight, analytical process to elicit information from various related variables. Any decision in company's board room will definitely show an impact on the company's earning capabilities. There are so many factors which influencing the corporate profits. The evaluation of share prices can be classified as follows:

(i) Future price
(ii) Present price.

Any major decision of the company management can influence the share price either in present or in future. The selected company may be a good company in now but it will be turned into a obsolete in tomorrow.

(i) Future Price

The investors in the stock market are searching for a good company. They collect the information about the various companies which shows better performance and achieving their targets and goals. But they are not in focus but tomorrow they will become **blue-chip company**. The companies which are working silently and without much publicity can explore the hidden talents. They provide much returns to their shareholders. The companies which perform very well and maintains good labour relations with their workforce, can be turned tomorrow as blue-chip organisations. Hence the investor must assess the capabilities of different companies by keeping not only present situation but also in future aspects. The following factors are affects share prices in future:

(a) Capabilities
(b) Profits
(c) Capital structure
(d) Board skills
(e) Operating efficiency
(f) Financial analysis.

(a) Capabilities

Economy is consisting of a number of industries. Industry is consisting of a number of individual firms producing similar characteristics of the goods. Hence the market contains thousands of individual organisations. Eventhough a large number of organisations exists in the market, but a few companies will become more popular and enjoys a lot of goodwill. The popular and good reputed companies control the major market share. In all industries some companies rise to the position of excellence and dominance. **Heavy** companies are successful in facing the severe competition. Once the companies occupy the market leadership position, they will have to retain and keep their position in the market. Companies working in the market will have to prove their efficiency with the existed competition and to capture a sizeable share in the market. The abilities and skills, competitiveness of the companies can be with the help of the following factors:

(i) Market position
(ii) Sales performance
(iii) Stability.

Market position or Market share is an important factor in evaluation of a company's performance. All companies are working for the desired targets of the sales. They work for becoming market leader in the market. The market share occupied by the company helps to determine the companies abilities and competitive edge. If a company capture higher rank in market share, the organisation would be able to meet the severe competition successfully. **For example: Hero Honda** topped the list in terms of sales in 2004 in automobile sector for two wheeler sector. In evaluation of the market share, the size of the company should be considered. The smaller companies in the market have less scope for survival in the future in market. The large companies have higher potential to face any situation in the market, even for a long period of time. The **star companies** of today's market will continue to retain the position in the future. The investors should make a comparison before taking investment decision between companies in the market. **For example: An automobile** company should be compared with other automobile companies to choose the best company in that industry. A comparison between two companies in the same industry would draw a better conclusions in the analysis. The skills, efficiency and capabilities of an organisation will be exposed in comparison of the company's performance. A well reputed company always occupy the market share and stood at **Number one position.** A leading company will always have competitive edge over other companies. The reputation and brand image will be achieved by the companies by putting many efforts in reaching of its destination.

Sales performance is one of the important factor in capturing market share. **Sales** is the oxygen to any commercial enterprises. The basic activities of the commercial enterprise involves buying and selling of the goods. All leading companies may not be showing higher sales. The growth in sales is different from one company to another. Market is just like a game of **musical chair**. All participants in the game requires more attention and cautious towards reaching their destination. Any negligence in market leads to decline in sales and loosing its market share and giving a chance to grow in the market for competitor. Hence the companies are required to move in the market with more attention. The remarkable growth in sales is happy movement for company shareholders. The shareholders will become prosperous due to a growth in sales, because the value of a scrip in the stock market increases tremendously. The scrip will be sold in the market with higher prices and its market capitalisation will be stimulated. Generally the large companies with inadequate growth in sales will not be preferred by the investors. The sales in the market is highly influenced by the **brand loyalty. Brand** name is the most important factor in the world of **marketing.** Brand loyalty creates a guaranteed sales to the company. Brand image is the basis for establishing the brand loyalty relation. The satisfaction of a customer for a brand is reflected in the form of brand loyalty. Hence if any company wants to become market leader, it should be remembered about the brand positioning. Once the customer satisfied with the particular brand, he may not change his attitude. The ranking of brands in the market is presented below for more clarity of information about the sales position in the market.[1]

Table: India's Top Brands

Rank	*Product/Company*	*Rank*	*Product/Company*
1	Colgate	2	Lux
3	Rin	4	Dettol
5	Tata salt	6	Ponds
7	Fair & Lovely	8	Britania
9	Vicks	10	Bata
11	Pepsodent	12	Close-up
13	Lifeboy	14	Surf
15	Horlics	16	Zandubalm
17	Titan	18	LIC
19	Parle	20	Tata Tea
21	Good Knight	22	Thumps-up
23	Pepsi	24	Fevicol
25	Philips	26	Clinic Plus
27	Vim	28	Bournvita
29	Maggi	30	Moov
31	Videocon	32	Ariel
33	Complan	34	Johnson & Johnson
35	Coca Cola	36	Dabur
37	Iodex	38	Wheel
39	LG	40	Amul
41	Nirma	42	HMT
43	Rasna	44	Onida
45	Godrej	46	Parachute
47	Frooti	48	Vaseline
49	Liril	50	Limca
51	Mirinda	52	Sony
53	Sunsilk	54	Cadbury Dairy Milk
55	Ujala	56	Amrutanzan balm
57	Band aid	58	Head & Shoulder
59	Crocin	60	BPL
61	SBI	62	Mortein
63	Cinthol	64	Nescafe
65	All out	66	Hamam
67	Pears	68	Hero Honda Splender
69	Asian Paints	70	Fanta
71	Nokia	72	Raymond

(Contd.)

(*Contd.*)

Rank	*Product/Company*	*Rank*	*Product/Company*
73	Samsung	74	Vicco
75	Vimal	76	5 Star
77	Brooke Bond	78	Kitkat
79	Boroline	80	Whirlpool
81	Tata Sumo	82	Pantene
83	Tide	84	Lakme
85	Eveready	86	Bajaj Chetak
87	Palmolive	88	Burnol
89	Maruthi 800	90	BSNL
91	Timex	92	Saffola
93	Godrej No. 1	94	Bisleri
95	D'cold	96	ICICI Bank
97	Uncle Chips	98	Saradon
99	Robin blue	100	Hero Honda Passion
101	Dispirin	102	Boost
103	Lijjat	104	Santoor
105	Haldirams	106	Breeze
107	LG Mobile Phone	108	Kissan
109	Whisper	110	Bank of India
111	Bombay Dyeing	112	Sundrop
113	Perk	114	Liberty shoes
115	Reliance India mobile	116	Sprite
117	Lipton	118	Maruthi Zen
119	Cibaca	120	7 up
121	Action shoes	122	Tata Indica
123	Keo Karpin	124	Airtel
125	Samsung Mobile	126	Bajaj Pulsar
127	Himami Navratan	128	Nivea
129	Hero Honda Dawn	130	Lays
131	Central Bank of India	132	Sansui
133	Anchor toothpaste	134	Topaz
135	PNB	136	Alpenlibe
137	Indian Bank	138	Bru
139	Stayfree	140	Fairglow
141	Rexon Deo	142	IOC
143	Bajaj Calibre	144	Indian airlines
145	Maruthi esteem	146	LIC Mutual Fund
147	Gillettes	148	Tata Indicom
149	Akai	150	Harpic

1. All in the gain, *The Economic Times*, Brand Equity, 15.12.2004, p. 1.

Most trusted brand survey conducted by the **Economic Times** found the above 150 brands. The emerging power houses that are the **superbrands** of tomorrow. It is the fourth year of publishing the brand equity survey. They have been adding to this survey, and extending its scope even since it was launched. Last year **(2003)** they incorporated rankings of the white hot services sector and this year, they have increased the number of categories in the survey. The most trusted brands survey aims to identify the brands that bond the best with consumers. They are not just the brands that are most familiar. They are the brands that consumers believe provide **Quality and reassurance**. The Survey conducted by the research agency **"AC Nielsen ORG-MARG**, the survey is the largest of its kind in India, with a sample of over **7000** distributors across socio-economic class, age, income and geography. The research agency taken into consideration of **275 brands** (195 consumer products, and 80 service brands) for the research purpose. The evaluation of brand image was based on the following characters:

(a) Quality
(b) Perceived Popularity
(c) Value for Money
(d) Feeling of friendliness
(e) Repurchase intention.

The final brand rating is arrived at in four steps. **(brand attributes):**

(a) Always maintains a high level of quantity
(b) It is worth the price it commands.
(c) It is going to be a popular brand for many years.
(d) It evokes a feeling of confidence and pride among users.

Stability is most important for survival in the market. If a firm has stable sales, the earnings of that firm also will have stable profits. A continuous and constant profits are more useful for a company which enjoys brand reputation and market leader position. A wide variation in sales leads to fluctuation in **Capacity utilisation, financial planning and dividend**. An indication of **100 per cent** capacity utilisation leads to better sales performance. The investor can assume that 100 per cent capacity utilisation is an indication of growth in sales regularly. Generally all the financial newspapers, Journals and Magazines publish information about the **market share** of different organisations in an industry. A rise in market share indicates, more profit is available that company. A decline in the market share shows the declining trend of the company. If a company shows stability in sales, it should be compared with its market share and the competitor's market share. A right direction to the marketing department stimulate the sales volume of a company. The sales performance of a company mainly depends upon accurate **"sales forecast"**. Sales forecast means a prediction about the process of market capturing by the concerned organisation. A good reputed company enjoys a superior position capturing more sales but the investors in the stock market should have an idea whether the sales will continue in future or not. Hence the study about future sales can be made in different methods. The investor can apply the trend line method either **linear or non-linear** which even is found more suitable for his sales forecasting. Another method can be used for finding sales forecast by the investors is known as **"Least square"** technique. A comparison will be made about **historical sales** of the company and Industry sales. This method of comparison easily reveal about the company's position in the market. According to macro economic analysis technique. The sales volume of the company can be compared with **Gross Domestic Product, per Capita Income and population growth**. According to demand analysis technique, a product is demanded by many different sources such as from customers and direct from Industries. Hence the total demand for a product should be taken into consideration. **For example: Steel and Petroleum Products** are demanded by Consumers and Industries.

(b) Profits

An increase in sales may not reflect in increase of profits levels. The cost and expenses of the company influence the levels of earnings. Sometimes sales will decline, but profits will be at stimulating levels. In some situations, the sales performance of the company is very good but the level of profits declines. Hence the expenses occupy a dominant role in earnings part of the company's profit. A rise in costs and expenses shows impact on earnings of the company. Hence the investor needs a careful analysis regarding sales volume, because the earnings are most important factor rather than sales. The earnings of the Company is a combination of operating and non operating sources. **Operating Income** is the basic earning of the Company. Operating income is involved with sales activities of the produced goods by the Company. This sources of income vary from Industry to Industry. **For example:** the **Cement Industry** generates operating income from sales of manufactured Cement. **For example:** The Income of a Commercial bank arises from lending the loans on Interest basis. Basically every Company gets operating income through the business activities i.e. buying and selling or purchasing raw material and selling finished products. The operating income is also known as

"Revenue". Usually Companies gets revenue either from sales or from other sources. The **Revenue from other sources** is known as **"Non-operating Income"**. The corporate sector generally acquires non-operating income from various sources. There are many sources for getting non-operating income which are presented below:

(i) Interest from debentures and bonds.
(ii) Rents from buildings etc.
(iii) Sale of assets.
(iv) Dividends from securities.

The investor should be more cautiously while analysing the data for his reference. He should know particularly about the operating and non-operating incomes of a company. Sometimes the earnings of the company appear more, due to dominants factor of the non-operating income. But earnings must be more generated through the business activities of the company. The investor should know that the earnings of the company may have highly influenced by such factors as **"Change in sales, cost reduction programme, the method of depreciation adopted, change in direct and indirect taxes."**

(c) Capital Structure

Capital structure is another important and influencial factor in determining the earnings of the company. Now-a-days, earning of profit by increasing **selling price** is not possible due to severe competition exists in the market. Hence the companies are forced to reduce their revenue expenses substantially. A reduction in expenses may stimulate the earnings level of the company. Capital is necessary for every business enterprise. Capital is available at a specified cost. The cost of capital is a financial expenses, which is chargeable to the **profit and loss A/c**. A higher amount of financial expenses leads to show impact on earnings of the company. At present environment, only share capital is not sufficient to run the company smoothly. In addition to equity, **Debt** is necessary for the smooth functioning of the company. **Debt** is compulsory like death is natural to human being. All Companies exist in market, may not be in a position to avoid the debt content in their capital structure. The combination of debt and equity is known as capital structure. The debt-equity mix ratio is necessary for all legal formalities as per the provisions of the companies Act. A high debt composition in the capital structure may show pressure on earnings of the company.

(d) Board Room Skills

The company is managed by the board of directors. The board of directors are the legal organs to run the business enterprise. The board is a combination of different persons, those who acquired a lot of skills in all aspects of the business. Hence the efficiency of the top level management is one of the influencing factor in determining the earnings of the company. A strong top level management can easily generates more revenue with their experience, talent and expertism. Now-a-days all companies are running with **professional managers**. Hence professionalisation of the company activities will definitely stimulate the levels of earnings. The basic objectives of the management is to **maximise return and minimise risk**. The business is a game between risk and return the efficient management escape the risk and capture return. The good management have some essential characteristics which are presented below:

(i) getting the things with people
(ii) leadership qualities
(iii) analytical skills
(iv) influencing behaviour

In professional management environment, every level of managerial performance is evaluated against targets and objectives. The investor further analyse the capabilities and abilities of managerial personnel are presented below:

(i) Background, educational qualifications and experience of the managers.
(ii) The review of top level managements record over the past years.
(iii) The managerial skill can be found by observing the market share of the business.
(iv) The investor should verify about the company's future plans of expansion. He must notice the strength of the company either in expansion or diversification. The **horizontal or vertical expansion** is a good sign of an efficient management.
(v) The investor further analyse about the management's capacity in carrying out of proper production schedules and maintaining of good level of inventory stocks.
(vi) The financial strength of the company should also be analysed. The management should have capabilities to raise resources from the market to meet the growing needs of the business.

(vii) The relationship between employees and management of the company may also be analysed. A good relations between workforce, employees, and management enhances the productivity of the company.

(viii) The adoption of scientific management techniques also influence the profitability of the company. The techniques are the methods to increase the productivity among the human resources.

All the above factors will influence the level of profitability of the entire corporate sector. Hence the investor should analyse all the influencing factors to boost the Company's earnings.

(e) Operating Skills

The earnings of a company depend upon operating skills of a business concern. The growing company must work for utmost satisfaction of the consumers. A high operating efficiency company produces goods at lower cost. A stable firm concern stable profit. Efficient use of assets may generate more earnings. The operating efficiency can be measured through **operating leverage.** Operating leverage means, involving fixed cost component in the company's total cost. Hence the contribution of fixed cost in the total cost is called as **operating leverage**. If the fixed cost is high in the total cost of a production, it is said to be **high degree of operating leverage**. Hence the operating efficiency of a firm determines the earning capabilities of the company.

(f) Financial Performance

Financial performance occupies a dominant role in making investment decisions by the investors. It can be observed with the help of the **financial analysis**. An analysis of a business concern with reference to the financial efficiency is called as **Financial analysis**. Analysis means methodical classification of the given data. The data is more useful in analysis of a business concern. Financial statements are the main ingredients in study of financial performance. Financial statement is an organised collection of data according to logical and accounting procedures. The aim of the financial analysis is to know whether the firm is working in efficiently or not? Financial statements provides historical and present information about the Company's operations. Historical data helps to predict the future. **Financial statements** can be classified into the following aspects:

(i) Income statement
(ii) Balance sheet
(iii) Statement of retained statement
(iv) Statement of changes in financial position.

(i) Income Statement

Income statement is also known as **profit and loss A/c**. It is associated with the financial data. It reveals the result of operations between two balance sheet dates. It consists revenue expenditure and revenue receipts. It shows the net profit earned or net loss earned by a firm during a particular period. The excess of revenue expenditure is known as net profit. **Net Profit** earned by the company during a financial year is the barometre for study of analysis.

(ii) Balance Sheet

Balance sheet is a document which contains liabilities and assets of a business organisation. It reflects the financial position of a company at a specified moment of time. Every commercial enterprise should prepare balance sheet to fulfill the legal provisions of the various acts. It represents all assets owned by the business at a particular moment of time and claims of the owners. It shows all the financial information related to the company during a particular period of time. **Financial strength** of a business concern can be observed from balance sheet. Balance sheet is an accumulation of fact data. It consists of historical data. Historical data is more useful for prediction.

(iii) Statement of Retained Earnings

The accumulation of excess earnings over expenses is known as **"retained earnings"**. The available net profit is transferred from income statement to balance sheet is called as **"retained earnings"**. It is relational factor between income statement and balance sheet. The large amount of retained earnings shows the financial muscle of the company. A vast amount of reserve, rètained earnings makes a company to grow substantially for expansion and diversification. Every year the available surplus amount of profits will be transferred to balance sheet. The pool of funds can be utilised by the company for business purpose. A higher amount of surplus funds will halt the borrowings of the company. The reduction of borrowing saves substantial amount of revenue expenditure.

(iv) Statement of Changes in Financial Position (SCFP)

The income statement exposes the net profit earned by a company. The balance sheet reveals the financial status of a commercial enterprise at a specified moment of time. But these two statements never show about the movement of **circulating capital**. Hence the SCFP reveals about the movement of working capital. It also reveals about the flow of cash from the business. The changes in working capital position reflects in the SCFP. The SCFP is popularly known as **"funds flow statement"**. The funds flow statement reveals the moment of funds. A change in cash position reveals in the **cash flow statement**. A charge in overall financial position will be reflected in **"SCFP"**.

Financial statements are indicators of the two significant factors such as **profitability and financial soundness**. Profitability can be procured from the income statement. Financial soundness will contain by the balance sheet. The balance sheet exposes the financial soundness of a commercial enterprise.

Types of Financial Analysis

Financial analysis can be made through the study of various financial statements. Financial analysis can be done by various persons for various purposes. It can be classified into different categories depending upon the following sources:

(i) Information
(ii) *Modus operandi*

Financial analysis which is based on information can be further classified into the following types:

(a) External analysis
(b) Internal analysis

(i) External Analysis

External analysis is made by the outsiders of the company. Investors, credit agencies, government organisations, Financial institutions and creditors are interested towards external analysis. All these persons have no access to the internal records of the company. They rely on the published financial statements. The **external analysis** will be carried out for a specific purpose by the outsiders. The increased level of government control over the business enterprises requires to do this kind of analysis. This kind of analysis provides a detailed and elaborative financial data made easy for thorough understanding of the concerned business enterprises progress. The development or progress can be traced out with this kind of analysis.

(ii) Internal Analysis

Internal analysis will be made by the company executives and employees of the organisation. They have access to the records of the company. This analysis can also be done by officers appointed for this purpose by the **Government or the Court**. This analysis requires not only business information but also other information related to the company business. This analysis will be carried out by the persons for a specified purpose. The top level management acceptance is necessary for carrying this kind of analysis.

Modus Operandi

Financial analysis can also be done as various kinds of methods. *Modus operandi* analysis can be done through the following methods:

(a) Horizontal analysis
(b) Vertical analysis.

Horizontal analysis is associated with the review and analysis of financial statements for a number of years as desired by the analyst. In this kind of analysis the present year's data will be compared with the base year or the standard year. The **base year or standard year** will be selected by the analyst according to his objectives. The analysis can be carried out for two years or more years and the changes are recorded in the form of **percentage**. The horizontal analysis can also be called as **"Dynamic analysis"**. This analysis explores the facts about the strength and weaknesses of the organisation. It completely related to analysis of financial data for a number of years to meet the specific purpose.

Vertical analysis is associated with quantitative relationship of the various items in the financial statements on a particular date. It is also known as **"Static analysis"**. It is frequently used for referring ratios. This analysis is useful in comparing the several companies performance in the same group or divisions or departments in the same company.

Analysis of Financial Statement

Financial statement contains available information regarding the worth of a company. A statement can be analysed in different ways as per the intention of the analyst. Hence the financial statements exposes a number of **hidden facts** about the organisation. The statements deals with the financial aspects of a company during a particulars period of time. The following steps are involved in financial statement analysis:

(a) Methodical classification
(b) Financial tools.

(a) Methodical Classification

Analysis requires a careful study of data in a chronological order. In order to have a meaningful analysis, it is necessary that the data should be arranged in a systematic manner. The statements are prepared in a manner to suit the needs and convenience of the analyst. The data will be arranged in two kinds of statement which are presented below:

(i) Income statement/operating statement
(ii) Balance sheet.

The proforma of **income statement** is presented below for quick reference of the study.

Operating Statement
for the year ending..................

Particular	**Rs.**	**Rs.**
Sales	......	......
Less: Sales returns	......	......
Sales tax/excise	......	......
Net Sales for the year (1)		
Less: Cost of sales (2)		
Raw material consumed	......	
Direct wages	......	
Manufacturing wages	......	
Add: Opening stock of finished goods	......	
	——	——
Less: Closing stock of finished goods	......	......
	——	——

	Rs.	Rs.
Gross profit (1) – (2) = (3)		......
Less: Operating expenses		
Administration expenses	......	
Selling and distribution expenses	......	
Net Operating Profit (3) – (4) = (5)		......
Add: Non-trading income		
Dividends		
Interest received		
Less: Non-trading expenses	......	......
	......	
Income before interest and tax (6)		......
Less: Interest on debentures **(7)**		......
Earnings before interest and tax (8)		......
Less: Income tax (9)		......
Profit after tax (10)		......

Balance Sheet As on.....

Cash in hand	......
Cash in bank	......
Bills Receivable	......
Books debts **(less provision for bad debts)**	......
Marketable trade investments	......
Liquid Assets **(1)**	......
Inventories **(Stock of raw materials, finished goods etc.)**	......
Prepaid expenses	......
Current Assets **(2)**	......
Bills payable	......
Trade creditors	......
Outstanding expenses	......
Bank overdraft	......
Other liabilities payable within a year	......
Current liabilities **(3)**	......

	Rs.
Provision for Tax	......
Proposed Dividends	......
Other provisions	......
Provisions **(4)**	......
Current liabilities and provisions (3) + (4) = **(5)**	......
Net working capital **(6)**	......
Liabilities and provision (2) – (5)	......
Goodwill at cost	......
Land and Building	......
Plant and Machinery	......
Loose Tools	......
Furniture and Fixture	......
Investment in subsidiaries	......
Patents, copyright etc.	......
Fixed Assets **(7)**	......
Capital employed (6) + (7) = **(8)**	......
Other Assets **(9)**	......
Investment in government securities unquoted investments, etc.	......
Other investments **(non-trading)**	......
Advances to directors	......
Company's Net Assets (8) + (9) = **(10)**	......
Debentures	......
Other long-term loans (payable after a year)	......
Long-term loans **(11)**	......
Share holder's net worth (10) – (11) = **(12)** **(or total tangible net worth)**	......

	Rs.	Rs.
Preference share capital **(13)**		......
Equity shareholder's net worth (12) – (13) = **(14)**	......	
Equity shareholder's net worth is represented by:–		
Equity share capital	......	
Forfeited shares	......	
Reserves	......	
Surplus	......	
Equity share holder's claims	......	......
Less: Accumulated losses		
Miscellaneous Expenditure		
(Such as preliminary expenses, discount on issue of shares or debentures not written off)		
Equity shareholder's net worth	......	......

(a) Financial Tools

The analyst can make analysis with help of the company data. There are many several financial techniques available to make a more meaningful comparison:

(i) Comparative financial statements
(ii) Common size financial statements
(iii) Trend percentage
(iv) Fund flow analysis
(v) Cash flow analysis
(vi) Cost volume profit analysis
(vii) Ratio analysis

Comparative financial statement reveals about the financial position of the company. In this statements data for two or more periods are placed side by side to facilitate comparison more meaningful. The statements consist of **comparative income statement and comparative balance sheet. The income statement** reveals the net profit or net loss from business activities of the company. The statement indicates the absolute data for two or more periods. The analyst can make a comparison between two periods about the profitability of the company. The analyst can understand the performance of the company by seeing the statement which arranged by a meaningful way. Hence it will be more useful to the reader. **Comparative balance sheet** is useful to study about the trends in a business enterprise. The statement indicates about changes in increase or decrease in assets and liabilities of the company. A single balance sheet is enough for study about the financial performance of the company during a particular period of time.

Common size financial statement is another kind of financial technique. In this statement figures are converted into percentages to some common base. The base is assumed to be 100 and all figures are expressed as a percentage of the total. This statement is useful for studying percentage of the total. These statements are useful for studying the **comparative financial position** of two or more businesses.

Trend percentages are useful in making a comparative study of financial statements for several years. Any year will be taken as base year. It is useful for highlighting of the important changes arised in the company. An adjustment should be made in the light of price level changes arised during a specified period of time.

Funds flow analysis is one of the important tool to the financial analyst. Funds flow statement reveals the changes in working capital position. It reveals about the utilisation and procurement of funds. The analysis will useful in estimating about the company's financial position and policies.

Cost volume profit analysis is another important tool of profit planning. It realises that, this technique is not used for analysis of financial statement. But it is an important tool for the management for decision-making. It indicates about the relationship cost, volume of production, sales and profit. It further indicates about the **break even point, cost of production, volume of sales, selling price and cost.** It also reveal about the quantity to be produced and sold in order to get the desired profit levels of the company.

Ratio analysis is the most important tool available to the analysts. Ratios are the powerful tools in analysing the two figures. Ratios are calculated for different purposes. Ratios indicates a mathematical relationship between two figures. **Gross profit ratio, Current asset ratio etc.** They are used as a **yardstick** for evaluating the financial status and performance of a business concern. There are many ratios which expresses information about the financial performance of a commercial enterprise. They are expressed it in two ways: **(a) times, (b) percentage**. They can be classified into different categories depending upon the basis of classification. Basically they are classified into two kinds:

(a) Traditional
(b) Functional

(a) Traditional

Ratios are the tools for financial analysis. The traditional ratios are further classified as follows:

(i) Profit and Loss A/c ratios
(ii) Balance sheet ratios.

(iii) Composite ratios

Profit and Loss A/c ratios will be calculated from the items of Income statement. Income statement is also called as **Profit and Loss A/c**. These items are drawn from the P & L A/c only. **For example: Gross profit ratio, stock turnover ratio, net profit ratio.**

Balance sheet ratios are related for balance sheet items. The components of balance sheet items will be taken for calculation purpose. **For example: current ratio debt equity ratio etc.**

Composite ratios are also called as Inter statement ratios. Ratios are related to Profit and Loss A/c and Balance sheet. **For example: Fixed assets turnover ratio, overall profitability ratios.**

(b) Functional

Functional classification of ratios are another kinds of a tool for financial analysis. They have to be studied together in order to determine the **profitability and solvency** of the business. According to functional classification of ratios, they are presented below:

(i) Profitability ratios
(ii) Coverage ratios
(iii) Turnover ratios
(iv) Financial ratios

Profitability ratios are useful to bankers, financial institutions and other creditors. It shows the efficiency of a company regarding its performance. The operational performance can be measured through this kind of ratios. Poor operational performance reveals the poor sales and lower profits. A lower profit is an indication of the lack of control over **expenses**. The top level management and owners of the firms are interested to know the profitability regarding deployment of their funds and efforts. They are further classified as follows:

(a) Overall profitability ratio
(b) Earning per share
(c) Price earning ratio
(d) Gross profit ratio
(e) Net profit ratio
(f) Operating ratio
(g) Payout ratio
(h) Dividend yield ratio.

Overall profitability ratios are also called as **return on investment**. The Return on investment is also known as **Return on Capital Employed**. It reveals the efficient utilisation of funds by the company during a particular period of time. The return on capital employed can be computed by the following formula:

$$\text{Return on capital employed} = \frac{\text{Operating profit}}{\text{Capital employed}} \times 100$$

Capital employed I = Total value of all assets
Capital employed II = Total of fixed assets
Capital employed III = Share capital + Reserves and surplus + Long term loans – (Non-business assets + fictitious assets)
Operating Profit = Profit before interest and tax.

The return on capital employed can be further classified as follows:

(a) Return on shareholder's funds
(b) Return on equity shareholder's funds
(c) Return on total assets
(d) Return on gross capital employed

Formulas:

Return on total capital employed =

$$\frac{\text{Net operating profit before interest and tax}}{\text{Total capital employed}} \times 100$$

(a) Return on shareholder's fund =

$$\frac{\text{Net profit after interest and tax}}{\text{Shareholderis funds}} \times 100$$

(b) Return on equity shareholder's funds =

$$\frac{\text{Net profit after interest, tax and preference dividend}}{\text{Equity shareholder's funds}} \times 100$$

(c) Return on total assets is computed to know about the utilisation of the total assets of the company. It can be computed in three methods:

(i) $$\text{Return on total assets} = \frac{\text{Net profit after tax}}{\text{Total assets}} \times 100$$

(ii) $$\text{Return on total assets} = \frac{\text{Net profit after tax + Interest}}{\text{Total assets}} \times 100$$

(iii) Return on total assets =

$$\frac{\text{Net profit – tax + Interest}}{\text{Total assets – Fictious assets}} \times 100$$

(d) $$\text{Return on Investment} = \frac{\text{Net profit before interest and tax}}{\text{Average capital employed}} \times 100$$

Earning per share is the most important ratio in the stock market. It is more useful to the investors in the stock market for taking a decision regarding his investment. It is the part of the overall profitability ratio. It can be computed by the following formula:

$$\text{Earning per share} = \frac{\text{Net profit after tax + Preference divident}}{\text{Number of equity shares}} \times 100$$

The EPS helps in assessment of a market share price of the equity share of the company. It measures the capacity of the earning power of a company. **A high EPS** is the measurement of better uitlisation of resources of the company.

Price earning ratio is another important ratio in the stock market. The ratio indicates the number of times the earning per share is covered by its **market price.** It helps the investors in making investment decisions in the stock market. It indicates about a particular share, whether the share price is **overvalued or under priced.** It can be calculated with the following formula:

$$\text{PE ratio} = \frac{\text{Market price per equity share}}{\text{Earning per share}}$$

Gross profit ratio is another important ratio to measure the operating efficiency of the company. It reveal relationship between gross profit and net sales of the company:

$$\text{Gross profit ratio} = \frac{\text{Gross profit}}{\text{Net sales}} \times 100$$

Net profit ratio indicates about the capability of the earning power by a commercial enterprises. The ratio is more useful to the investors in the stock market for taking investment decisions. An increase in the net profit over the previous year indicates the efficiency of the company. An investor can take a decision whether to buy a scrip or not:

$$\text{Net profit ratio} = \frac{\text{Net operating profit}}{\text{Net sales}} \times 100$$

Operating ratio deals with the operating expenses of a company. It is also known as **expenses ratio.** It indicates about the expenses incurred by a company with high or low leverage. The operating costs included the cost of material, direct labour, and factory or office or selling **overheads.** Financial expenses such as **taxation and interest** elements will be excluded. It gives cautions to the to level management regarding control of expenses:

$$\text{Operating expenses} = \frac{\text{Operating costs}}{\text{Net sales}} \times 100$$

Payout ratio is associated with the payment of dividend to shareholders. The dividend will be paid by the company as per the profits earned by it. If the retention ratio is low, naturally the payout ratio will be more, and shareholders enjoy the dividend amount. The payout ratio is also called as **Retained earnings ratio:**

$$\text{Payout ratio} = \frac{\text{Dividend per equity share}}{\text{Earning per share}}$$

$$\text{Retained earnings ratio} = \frac{\text{Retained earnings}}{\text{Total earnings}} \times 100$$

Dividend yield ratio is associated with investor's interest. A high rate of dividend may keep pleasure the investors to patronage the company in future. It can be computed by the following formula:

$$\text{Dividend yield ratio} = \frac{\text{Dividend per share}}{\text{Market price per share}} \times 100$$

II. COVERAGE RATIOS

Coverage ratios are associated with either shareholders or debentureholders of the company. It indicates about the repayment of agreed interest amount or dividend. The interest or dividend may be paid as per the agreement made by both parties. It can be further classified into three types, such as:

(a) Fixed interest cover ratio
(b) Fixed dividend cover ratio
(c) Debt service coverage ratio

Fixed interest cover ratio is related to the payment of interest to lenders of the company. It reveals that if the business earn sufficient profits, the lender's will be happy, otherwise they involved in **risk.**

$$\text{Interest coverage ratio} = \frac{\text{Net profit before interest and tax}}{\text{Interest changes}}$$

$$\text{Fixed dividend cover ratio} = \frac{\text{Net profit after interest and tax}}{\text{Preference dividend}}$$

$$\text{Debt service coverage ratio} = \frac{\text{Net profit before interest and tax}}{\text{Interest} + \dfrac{\text{Principal payment instalment}}{1 - \text{tax rate}}}$$

III. TURNOVER RATIOS

Turnover ratios are related to the efficient utilisation of funds by the company. It reveals about the efficiency regarding the capital employed deployed in the business. It indicated about the overall profitability of the business enterprise. The turnover ratios can be classified into two methods:

(a) Net profit ratio
(b) Turnover ratio

The turnover ratios further can be divided into two kinds. They are:

(1) Fixed assets turnover ratio
(2) Working capital turnover ratio

Fixed assets turnover ratio = Net sales/Fixed assets

Working capital turnover ratio = Net sales/Working capital

Working capital turnover ratios can be further classified into **five methods.** They are presented below:

(i) Debtor's turnover ratio
(ii) Debt collection period ratio
(iii) Creditor's turnover ratio
(iv) Debt payment period enjoyed ratio
(v) Stock turnover ratio

(i) Debtor's turnover ratio = Credit sales/average accounts recievable

(ii) Debt collection period ratio = Accounts recievable/monthly credit sales.

(iii) Creditor's turnover ratio = Total purchases/Accounts payable

(iv) Debt payment period enjoyed ratio = Months in a year/Creditor's turnovers

(v) Stock turnover ratio = Cost of goods sold/Average inventory.

IV. FINANCIAL RATIOS

Financial ratios are the most important tools in financial analysis. They indicate about the financial status of the company. They are classified into two kinds:

(a) Liquidity ratios
(b) Stability ratios

Liquidity ratio is related to the solvency of a business concern. Liquidity ratio is also called as **short term solvency ratio.** They are further classified into the following kinds:

(1) Current ratio
(2) Quick ratio
(3) Super quick ratio
(4) Defensive interval ratio

(1) Current ratio = Current assets/Current liabilities
(2) Quick ratio = Liquid assets/Current liabilities
(3) Super quick ratio = Cash and marketable securities/Quick liabilities

(4) Defensive interval ratio = Quick assets/projected daily cash requirement

Stability ratios are related to long term solvency of the company. It can be classified as follows:

(a) Fixed assets ratio
(b) Capital structure ration

(a) Fixed ratio = Fixed assets/Long term funds
(b) Capital structure ratio can be further classified as follows:
   (i) Capital gearing ratio.
   (ii) Debt equity ratio.
   (iii) Proprietary ratio

(i) Capital gearing ratio $= \dfrac{\text{Funds bearing fixed interest}}{\text{Total capital employed}}$

(ii) Debt equity ratio $= \dfrac{\text{External equities}}{\text{Internal equities}}$

Debt equity ratio I $= \dfrac{\text{Total long term debt}}{\text{Total long term fund}}$

Debt equity ratio II $= \dfrac{\text{Shareholder's funds}}{\text{Total long term fund}}$

Debt equity ratio III $= \dfrac{\text{Total long term debt}}{\text{Shareholder's funds}}$

(iii) Proprietary ratio $= \dfrac{\text{Shareholder's funds}}{\text{Total tangible assets}}$

The ratios are power tools in the hands of financial analysts or researchers. A purposewise classification of ratios are presented below for ready reference:

1. Liquidity ratios
2. Assets utilisation ratios
3. Profitability ratios
4. Appropriation ratios
5. Capitalisation ratios
6. Coverage of senior charges
7. Financial stability ratios.

Hence the ratios have some advantages and dis-advantages. But simply the ratios are conveying more message to the analyst and the future of a particular company. However it is more useful for prediction.

Present Price

The share prices in the stock market is highly influenced by a number of factors. The share value of a particular company depends upon the following factors:

(i) Past price
(ii) Price earning ratio
(iii) Economic environment
(iv) Stock market situation.

Past price of stock is the most important factor before going to buy a particular scrip. Though past performance is not guarantee for the future price of the stock, but it reveals about the attitude of the stock market. The **historical price of stock** reveals about the **52 weeks** with high and low price ranges of a scrip. It enables the investor whether to buy a share or not to buy a scrip.

Price earning ratio is the most common financial parametres used in the stock market. It associate the share price with **earning per share**. The media will provide the PE ratios for all traded shares in the stock market. The past performance is the basis for future performance of the company. A **high PE ratio** reveals high expectation of the market regarding the growth of future earnings of the company. The PE ratio is influenced by other factors such as **dividend payout, dividend growth rate and the financial expenses.** A **high PE ratio** arises due to large dividend pay outs, high dividend growth rates and low cost of funds. It plays an important role in portfolio management. Generally the common investor will make a comparison about the PE ratio with the Company and Industry. It is better to purchase the scrip when it is available in **under priced**. A PE ratio lower than industry ratio is known as **under price** valuation of performance. If the current PE ratio is larger than the **expected PE ratio**, the stock is **overpriced**. Therefore it is better to sell when the share commands overprice. However the investor should know about the **intrinsic value** of the share. The true economic worth of the share is called as **intrinsic value of share**. The intrinsic value of a share can be computed by the following formula:

Intrinsic value of a share = Normal EPS × Expected PE ratio

$$\text{Expected PE ratio} = \frac{\text{Dividend/Expected EPS}}{\text{Discount rate} - \text{Growth rate}}$$

Economic environment is another important factor in determination of present price levels of a share in the stock market. The monetary policy, the fiscal policy, finance bill, industrial policy and legislation of various acts can influence the stock market prices immediately. The routine activities of the **RBI, SEBI, Department of company affairs, Company Law Board, Ministry of Finance** is also influence the present prices of shares in the stock market.

Stock market environment is one of the influencial factor of the share prices. Stock market is a highly volatile market. The share prices are fluctuated for a small incidence in the economy. **For example:** A change in interest rates, A change in oil prices, A changes in gold prices, A change in Foreign exchange prices etc. Hence the investor should be more cautious in the stock market.

Shareholder Value Creation

The concept of **Finance** has been changed at present due to liberalisation, globalisation and privatisation. All these policies have been putting pressure on money. These policies encourages the industrialists to deploy their financial resources in the business environment. Hence a lot of pressure arised on the supply of money. Hence the importance of finance has been noticed and recognised by the business sector on global basis. The globalisation policy has changed the situation in reduction of distance between two nations by providing international Communication, global transport and foreign technological collaboration etc. The aviation policy of the Central Government has shown a great impact on business environment. The flights of International carriers became just like **City bus services**. Therefore availability of transportation made the foreigners to think about investments in India. The Central Government is also in proactive to attract the **FDI**. The globe is rotating on the supply of money. The **digital economy** requires higher skills, talent, expertism in all aspects of the business. **Privatisation** policy aims to encourage the private persons in the business aspects to meet the growing needs of the **global citizens**. In the same situation the government reduces its role from the business environment due to its inefficient management of business enterprises under their control. **A loss** making public sector enterprises forced the government to dis-appear from the market and pushing the private parties before the customers. **Privatisation** will make some benefits to the customers due to heavy competition in the market. Therefore, the government occupied a place only as a industry regulator. It is the better situation to the customers to enjoy the benefits from the market due to competitive environment. The government need not to do business, but only encourages more players in the market. **Competition** is the most important factor in the business aspects. The government should create a good healthy competitive environment in the market. In the competitive world, only efficiency will get success. **Liberalisation** policy provides a good environment for establishing the industries. It encourages entrepreneurs by removing unnecessary clearances from the government. The time for clearance of the licences and all legal formalities have been reduced drastically. Now the Central Government and all State Governments are approaching the **Big Industrial Houses** for setting up of units in their respective states. Therefore all State Governments are maintaining good relations with perspective entrepreneurs. After implementation of these policies, a lot of demand for finance has been increased. India has a strong potential investors base to develop the industrial sector. The power of middle class family **savings** cannot be ignored. They contribute higher amount of financial resources in the form of shares and debentures. All **Initial Public Offerings** are making over subscriptions in the primary market. All companies are raising financial resources from the market for their expansion or diversification process. A lot of competition emerged among the companies to attract the public money. Hence the companies are giving assurance to their shareholders for stimulating the value for their money. All financial and corporate policies have been framed according to the needs and convenience of the shareholders. The corporate sector has been forced to create more value for their shareholders. The financial policies and strategy are directed towards the shareholders value creation. The traditional method of management techniques have been replaced by the modern and innovative technology. The latest technology and trends have changed the way of corporate sector. The corporate finance policy should be developed in the context of the **strategic decision-making** power. **Strategy** is a plan for achieving a major goal. The corporate sector at present is always think about the shareholder value creation. The shareholder value can be created by the following factors:

(a) Strategic decision-making framework
(b) Financial goals of the firms.

(a) Strategic Decision-Making Framework

Strategy consists of multiple goals and objectives pursued by the corporate sector to satisfy its desires. The success of the corporate sector depends upon competitive edge and resources deployment of the firms. The shareholder should examine about the competitiveness, capabilities and managerial skills of the company before going to purchase the scrip. The firm's effectiveness is determined by the efficiency. Financial policies can influence the efficiency of a business enterprise. The primary focus on strategy is an efficiency and it depends upon the following factors:

(i) Strategic choices
(ii) Strategic financial management
(iii) Strategic investment policy
(iv) Strategic financing policy.

(i) Strategic Choice

Strategic Choice is one of the important factors in strategic decision making framework. It consists of various portfolio models. The business portfolio models are more popular and understand market situation. The investor should observe about the understanding capabilities of the market situation by the company. The existence of the firm is based on **market growth, market share, cost and cash flow patterns, capital intensity and product maturity**. The assessment of market growth is an important factor which influences the market capture. **The market growth, market share model** is the simple model of business portfolios. It is popularised by the **Boston Consulting Group**. The business enterprises are grouped in a specified categories. They are presented below for further discussions:

(a) Stars
(b) Cows
(c) Wild cats
(d) Dogs.

Star category companies are well known companies. They are well reputed and regulated brands in the market. They are best performers and showing higher capabilities, efficiency in capturing market. They earn super profits and growth opportunities in a rapidly growing market. Their brands are well established and well recognised in the market. They acquired customer satisfaction by providing higher quality goods, lower prices, sales after service etc. They are generally financial muscle companies. They acquire large amount of profits and having large amount of reserves and accumulated surplus.

Cows are another category companies which are declining stars. They provide cash to be utilised in the firm.

Dogs are one of the grouped companies and financially a weak competitive position held in the market. There is as little chance to grow in the market. They are facing many problems to generate little amount of profit. Existence and survival in the market is not a simple task for these companies. They would attempt to liquidate or selling their assets to survive in the market.

Wild cats category companies are attempting to become as **star companies**. They are trying to capture the market in a rapidly growing market. They are waiting for bigger opportunities. They are interested to enhance the firms abilities skills, efficiency and talents. They require higher amount of funds to achieve desire goals. These firms are mostly concentrated on reducing inefficiency and enhancing the efficiency.

The Boston Consulting Group developed a model to achieve the desired goals by the companies. The model implies that cash surplus from **cash cows** should be transferred to wild cats, for achieving their financial goals. The BCG indicates that dogs have no chance of improvement. The group reveals that experience in business stimulates the market share. The market leader usually have a competitive dominance. They enjoy the lower cost due to mass production undertaking. It is not a simple task to get dominant role in the market from competitors. It is generally difficult and expensive to **seize** market share from competitors. Every company shall deploy its abilities and resources to capture the market from its competitors. The high competitive environment in the market forces the firms to reduce the prices substantially. A pressure on profits is necessary in the competitive environment. The success of a business firm needs a balanced portfolio of products or business. The strategic position of a firm is determined by market share, and profitability.

(ii) Strategic Financial Management

The basic task of a finance manager involves in **acquisition** of funds and **allocation of** resources. The main aim of the business is to maximise the wealth of shareholders. The finance manager shall make decisions that will increase the shareholder's stake in the firm. The efficient capital markets enable investors to lend or borrow funds. The capital markets are always discounted by the information.

Strategic management considers all markets, including product, labour and capitals as imperfect and changing. Strategies are made to manage the firm in uncertain situations. Therefore the management has to analyse changing market conditions and environment to make **predictions** and allocation of resources. The shareholders are not only interested in the firms activities but also other many influential constituents such as **lenders, employees, customers, suppliers, competitors, government and society**. The strategic management focuses on **growth, profitability and flow of funds** rather than on the maximisation of the market value of share.

(iii) Strategic Investment Policy

Investment decisions shows impact on the profitability of the firm. Strategic investments are generally involve large amount of expenditure. Strategic investment decisions are based on both **Quantitative and Qualitative analysis**. The business portfolio approaches can be very useful in identifying investment opportunities. A balanced portfolio of projects can create a lot of **synergistic values**. The financial theory reveal that the firms diversification is not useful to shareholders. In un-developed capital market diversification is an appropriate **corporate strategy.** It reduces corporate risk. **Risk** is an important aspect in the business. Its analysis is an important task of **strategic management**. Strategic management is involved in managing **total risk**. At present, the survival in the business is a successful phenomenon in the corporate environment. A commercial enterprise is always threatened by many factors such as **Competition, Technological obsolence, labour relations, government policies etc.** Hence the investment policy may stimulate the shareholders value by making appropriate decisions in the business.

(iv) Strategic Financing Policy

Finance is the provision of money. Money is the essential element on the earth. Money is a facilitator for the smooth functioning of the firms. Money earns money and rotates with commercial motive. The procurement and allocation of financial resources depends upon the firm's policies. Generally all firms will depends upon the following financing aspects:

(a) External financing
(b) Internal financing.

External financing means, procuring financial resources from outsiders of the firm. The procurement of funds depends upon the **debt policy** of the firm. Borrowing from the capital market or money market is known as external finance. Usually every company desires to keep high credit worthiness for their issuing financial assets. The firms will generally avoid debt competent if their capital structure. But **debt** is necessary in changing business environment. At present debt component dominates the capital structure of the corporate sector. Debt threatens the profitability of the company.

Internal financing is the reflection of financial soundness of the firm. The reserves and surplus accumulated profit un-distributed profits, depreciation fund are best examples of internal finance. A large amount of earnings may not be distributed by the company to its shareholders. A high retention policy of the company facilitate for provisions of internal finance. A low payout ratio dissatisfies the shareholders. But high retention policy may stimulate the shareholders values with a large amount of savings in the form of financial costs. Internal financing is the cheapest and best sources of the money supply.

(b) Financial Goals of the Firm

Goal is a long term phenomenon. Financial goals are framed by the company itself. It is associated with the quantitative expressions of a company's mission. The empirical research in America reveals that profit is not always a priority element. Financial priorities are changed due to changes in economic and competitive environment. Financial goals are changeable and unstable. The finance managers find it difficult to understand and accept the goal. There are demand related goals and supply related goals. Demand related goal is associated with sales growth of a company. **Supply related** goals concentrates on earning of **better returns.** It also focuses on payment of dividend to shareholders and reduction of financial cost through internal financing. The **Indian companies** are rotating in the market for achieving the following financial goals:

(i) Maximising the levels of networth, profit and market value.
(ii) Maximising the ROI, net profit, market share.
(iii) Maximising the growth in assets and sales.
(iv) Sufficient funds at disposal.

However the common investor should observe the following parameters before making his investment decisions in a specified company scrip:

(1) Cash flow per share
(2) Price earning ratio
(3) Market value of per share
(4) Book value of networth
(5) Operating profit
(6) Market rate of return
(7) Net profit to networth
(8) Earning per share
(9) Market share
(10) Return on investment

Monetary Policy 2005-06

The policy statements of the Reserve Bank provide a framework for the monetary, structural and prudential measures that are taken from time to time against the background of an assessment of macroeconomic and monetary developments.

The policy statement consists of two parts. **Part I**: Annual statement on monetary policy for the year **2005-06. Part II:** Annual statement on Development and Regulatory policies for the year **2005-06**.

Monetary Policy for 2005-06

During 2004-05, monetary policy faced difficult challenges which prompted a change in the stance in the mid term review of **October 2004**. First, there was a carry forward of excess liquidity of over **Rs. 81,000** crores. Second, the headline wholesale price Index inflation accelerated beyond the anticipated level during the first half of the year. Third, the seasonal decline in food prices did not materialise fully, perhaps stemming from deficient monsoon. Fourth, International commodity prices remained high and volatile. Fifth, internationally, monetary policy stance in a number of countries was transiting from highly accommodative to a neutral level. Sixth, the pass through of international commodity price pressures to domestic inflation had implications for inflationary expectations. Seventh, given the uncertainties, the reaction of financial market was advance. As interest rates were at historically low levels, the upside risk was high. There was sharp upward movement in interest rates towards the middle of the year which ensured a selling pressure in government securities market. Eighth, the equity markets touched a low on May 17 which had an adverse impact on sentiments very temporarily and markets bounced back very quickly thereafter. Finally, these developments occurred at a time when Industrial growth was looking up after a prolonged period of sluggishness and non-food credit was also picking up. In the event, the RBI had to balance the considerations of growth while containing inflationary expectations. Given the role of supply factors in the nature of inflation. The response was in concert with the government. In signalling its commitments to price stability. The RBI switched its stance from a very close watch on the movements in the price level in the annual policy statement to equal emphasis on price stability in the mid term review. Similarly liquidity management for the purpose, was emphasised with a switch from a provision of adequate liquidity to appropriate liquidity. The policy measures were also calibrated to evolving circumstances with a view to stabilising inflationary expectations.

Source: "Captain keeps ship at steady dip", *The Economic Times*, 29-4-05, p. 12.

During 2004-05, the following steps were taken in a measure and calibrated manner:

(a) The Reserve Bank communicated its assessment of the supply induced nature of inflation to the market on several occasions.
(b) The market was sensitised to the differential behaviour of inflation at the producer's and the consumer's level, the former being higher as observed in a number of other oil importing countries.
(c) The government responded with fiscal measures, particularly by reducing customs and excise duties on oil.
(d) Corporates also responded positively by moderating the exercise of their pricing power.
(e) In order to enable the RBI to address the overhang of liquidity, the government raised the ceiling of **MSS** from **Rs. 60,000 crores** to **Rs. 80,000 crores**.
(f) For a more flexible management of liquidity, overnight fixed rate reverse repo under **LAF** was introduced.
(g) CRR was raised by one half of one percentage point to **5 per cent**.
(h) The remuneration of CRR was delinked from the bank rate and was reduced to **3.5 per cent** to enhance its effectiveness as a monetary instruments.

(i) Banks were also allowed to transfer their investment into **HTM** category upto their statutory minimum **SLR** requirement after providing for depreciation while this measure provided an opportunity to banks to interface with interest rate cycles, at a macro level, it helped in maintaining financial stability.

Finally the fixed reverse reporated under LAF was raised by 25 basis points to **4.75 per cent**. However, the repo rate and the bank rate were left unchanged at 6 per cent signalling the short term nature of upward inflationary pressures. The financial markets responded positively to the package of measures and consequently, interest rates stabilised towards the last quarter of the year, albeit at higher levels, but lower than their intra year higher registered during the middle of the year. Moreover credit flow to the commercial sector remained uninterrupted and the government borrowing programme could be completed smoothly.

In the conduct of monetary policy, RBI was faced with the challenge of reconciling two domains crimes. As inflation was supply induced, it was argued that direct monetary policy action may be premature keeping in view the fact that industry was coming out of a sluggish phase. On the other hand, the deterioration in inflation expectations on the basis of observed acceleration in headline inflation, accompanied sharp movements in market interest rates, tested the resolve of the Central Bank on price stability. Since such a deterioration occurred under conditions of overhang of excess liquidity, strong credit growth, incomplete pass through of oil price shock and uncertainties about its second round effects, the other arguments were in favour of monetary policy response to contain inflationary expectations.

The received wisdom, with the hindsight of oil price shocks of the **1970s and the 1980s**, is that in the face of a significant supply shock, it is not prudent for monetary policy to be overly accommodative. Moreover, globally, monetary policy was transiting in a number of countries from excessive accommodation towards a neutral position on inflation concerns. On balance of considerations, the RBI raised **CRR** and the reserve reporate moderately to signal its strong commitment to price stability. In this context, it is important to note that higher levels of sustainable growth is feasible only in an enabling environment of stable prices.

Monetary Management during second half of 2004-05 was conducted broadly in confirmity with the stance of the policy set out for the second half of the year. In terms of macroeconomic outcome during 2004-05:

(a) The GDP growth rate turned out to be better than anticipated largely on account of higher than expected growth from agricultural sector. More importantly, **GDP** growth was characterised by a pick up in industrial activity which. If sustained, could left India to a higher growth trajectory.

(b) The inflationary outcome, though consistent with the anticipation at the beginning of the year turned out to be more favourable than the perception of the mid term review due to moderation in prices of primary and manufactured products as well as cushioning of the oil price impact.

(c) The interest rates in money and government securities markets rose intra year, they stabilised during the later part of the year albeit at higher levels.

(d) The pick up in non-food credit growth was generally sustained and distribution of credit became broad based across sectors during the later past of the year. More importantly, the expansion of credit did not trigger an increase in lending rates.

(e) The term deposit rates showed some increase.

(f) Money supply growth turned out to be lower than the projections made at the beginning of the year.

(g) Though the exchange value of the rupee vis-à-vis the US dollar depreciated at the beginning of the year, it recovered and exhibited greater two way movement.

(h) The trade deficit widened significantly reflecting a deficit on non-oil trade balance and higher oil imports.

(i) Though the net invisible receipts are buyonant, the current account of balance of payments which remained in surplus for consecutive three years is turning into a deficit during **2004-05** reflecting adverse trade balance. While invisibles, such as private remittances have lent support to the current account, the trade account has particular relevances as it reflects the competitiveness of the underlying industrial structure and the degree of openness.

(j) Capital flows resumed after a brief pause resulting in significant increase in foreign exchange reserves during the year. Finally corporate results and the domestic business outlook continue to remain positive.

Against the background of developments during 2004-05, the stance of monetary policy will depend on several factors, including macroeconomic prospects, global developments and the balance of risks:

(1) The outlook for growth in 2005-06, which should be noticeably better than previous year, may get moderated by the conditions in oil markets which remain tight.

(2) If the impact of mineral oil prices on whole sale prices is isolated, the underlying inflationary pressures appear moderate. The supply factor will continue to dominate the price situation, while demand management seems to invite close attention.

(3) The non-food credit during 2004-05 recorded its second highest growth in **55 years**. There is evidence of increase in credit elasticity of GDP and credit penetration. Hence adequate credit growth needs to be ensured for productive sectors and the borrowing programme of governments accommodated, while closely assessing the implications for demand management to maintain macro and price stability. In these circumstances the liquidity management becomes critical. The interest rate outlook should take into account. These domestic challenges but the increasing integration warrants same attention to global factors.

(4) The borrowing programme of the Central Government was unusually low in **2004-05**. While the borrowing programme for **2005-06** is significantly higher than the previous year, it is in line with the magnitudes in **2002-03** and **2003-04.** Though the credit growth was sluggish in those years.

(5) The current account was in surplus for three consecutive years, is turning into a deficit. The capital account continues to be in surplus in a significant way. Current indications are that these trends will continue in **2005-06** and consequently. The external sector will exhibit strength and resilence, though unanticipated, globally transmitted shocks cannot be ruled out.

The **India Meteorological Department** in its forecast of **south-west** monsoon for the current year has placed the expected rainfall at **98 per cent** of its long period average. With a normal monsoon the growth in agriculture can be assumed to be around **3 per cent**. Further, it is expected that industry and service sectors would maintain their current growth momentum while absorbing the impact of oil prices. The real GDP growth during **2005-06** on the basis of above assumptions, could be placed around **7 per cent** for the purpose of monetary policy formulation.

A factor that complicates the conduct of monetary policy during certain periods is the difficulty encountered in precisely assessing the potential inflationary pressures based on the available data for the current period:

(1) The liquidity overhand which was reduced to a significant extent by **December 2004**, has since increased to levels witnessed at the beginning of **2004-05**.
(2) The international oil prices have again turned volatile with an upward pressure.
(3) Besides oil, the other primary commodity prices remain firm in international markets.
(4) The full pass through of international prices of oil to domestic price has not taken place and fiscal maneuverability on this front is getting limited.
(5) Credit growth continues to remain buoyant. Finally as against these factors, it must be recognised that there is evidence of increasing productivity in several sectors in the economy that could moderate pressure on prices. The level of food stocks and forex reserves provide cushions against some price increases.

Further, the contextual analysis of wholesale price index excluding mineral oils, on a point-to-point basis in 2004-05, worked out to **3.5 per cent** as against **4.7 per cent** in the previous year, which gives same indication of supply shock elements of WPI as distinct from what may be constructed as core components of inflation. In view of these considerations governing current trends, the inflation rate in 2005-06 on a point-to-point basis, may be placed in a range of **5–5.5 per cent** subject to the growing uncertainties on the oil front both in regard to global prices and their domestic absorption.

Consistent with the real growth of GDP and inflation, the projected expansion of money supply **(M3)** for 2005-06 is placed at **14.5 per cent**. In tune with this order of growth in **M3**, increase in aggregate deposits of scheduled commercial bank is set at **Rs. 2,60,000 crores** which is higher by **15 per cent** over its level in the previous year. Non-food bank credit including non-SCR investments of banks is projected to increase by around **19 per cent**. The magnitude of credit expansion is expected to meet adequately the credit needs of all the productive sectors of the economy.

For the year **2005-06**, the union budget has placed the fiscal deficit at **4.3 per cent** of GDP and the net market borrowing programme of the centre is budgeted at **Rs. 1,10,291 crores** as compared with **Rs. 46,050 crores** in the previous year. While the borrowing programme of the centre much higher than that in the previous year, taking into account the normal market borrowing programme of status and the comparable level of borrowings of centre and states in the years prior to **2004-05**, the RBI expects to conduct debt management within the monetary projections for **2005-06** barring unexpected developments. In this regard, there is scope for accommodating continued growth in credit needs as well as higher borrowing programme to the extent it is possible to unwind MSS to provide appropriate liquidity consistent with macro objectives.

Monetary policy would continue to enhance the integration of various segments of the financial market, improve credit delivery nurture credit culture and enhance the quality of financial services. Eventhough volatility in the inflation rate during **2004-05**, there is also a need to consolidate the gains obtain in recent years from raining in inflationary expectations. It is important to appreciate that while sustained efforts overtime have helped to build confidence in price stability, inflationary expectations can turn adverse in a relatively short time, if noticeable adverse movements in prices takes places. In the world economy after a prolonged period of low inflation there are signs that inflation may be edging up. The global oil markets continue to remain tight with higher prices and increased volatility. Credible commitment of policy to fight inflation is critical to stop the translation of higher prices into wage-price spirals. In addition, the international prices of non-oil primary commodities may continue to remain firm. On the domestic front, the maneuverability on oil prices is getting limited and corporates have a higher probability of the gaining their pricing power with a better industrial outlook. The pricing pressure, if it were to occur from the supply side, could get complicated by continuing overhang of excess domestic liquidity. While the economy has the residence to withstand supply shocks, the upside risks do exist. As such, the inflationary situation needs to be watched closely and there could be no room for complacency on this count. In the context of current inflation scenario, and issue of policy interest for financial management by banks and other market participants is whether the interest rate cycle has turned from the low observed during **2003-04**. As it is well known, the outcome for interest rate depends mainly on the outlook for inflation, growth, prospects and investment demand and it is not possible to predict short-runs movement in interest rates either up or down, without taking cognizance of possible movements in all other macro economic variables. These variables are also subject to unanticipated changes because of unforeseen, domestic or external developments. However, the system has to recognise interest rate cycles and strengthen risk management processes took cope with eventuality. So that financial stability could be maintained and interest rate movements could be transited in a known-disruptive manner. In this regard it is instructive to observe global trends as the Indian economy is progressively getting linked to the world economy. While there is an overhang of domestic liquidity partly mirroring abundant global liquidity, the trends in global interest rate inflation expectations and investment demand would also have some relevance in the evaluation of the domestic interest rates. It will, therefore, be desirable to contain inflationary pressures to stabilise domestic financing conditions both for the government and the private sector.

The RBI will continue to ensure that appropriate liquidity is maintained in the system so that all legitimate requirements of credit or met, consistent with the objective of price stability towards this end. RBI will continue with its policy of active demand management of liquidity through **open market operations** including **MSS, LAF** and **CRR**, and using the policy instruments at its disposal flexibly and when the situation warrants.

In sum, darring the emergence of any adverse and unexpected developments in various sectors of the economy and keeping in view of the inflationary situation, the overall stance of monetary policy for the year **2005-06** will continue to be as set out in the mid term review of October 2004, namely:

(a) Provision of appropriate liquidity to meet credit growth and support investment and export demand in the economy while placing equal emphasis on price stability.
(b) Consistent with the above, to pursue an interest rate environment that is conducive to macro economic and price stability, and maintaining the momentum of growth.
(c) To consider measures in a calibrated manner in response to evolving circumstances with a view to establishing inflationary expectations.

Monetary Measures

The following measures have been initiated by the RBI:

(a) Bank rate
(b) Reserve repo rate
(c) Cash reserve ratio.

(a) Bank Rate

In the mid-term review of October 2004, the bank rate was kept unchanged at **6 per cent.** On a review of the macroeconomic developments, it is considered desirable to leave the bank rate stable at **6 per cent** at present.

(b) Reserve Repo Rate

In view of the current macroeconomic and overall monetary conditions, it has been decided to increase the fixed reserve repo rate by **25 basis points** under the liquidity adjustment facility of the RBI effective from April 29, 2005 to **5 per cent** from **4.75 per cent**. The repo rate will continue to be linked to the reserve repo rate as at present. However, the spread between the reserve repo rate and the repo rate is reduced by **25 basis points** from **125 basis points** to **100 basis** points with effect from April 29, 2005. Accordingly the fixed repo rate under CAF will continue to remain at 6 per cent.

(c) Cash Reserve Ratio

The cash reserve ratio of scheduled banks is currently at **5 per cent.** While the RBI continues to pursue its medium term objective of reducing the CRR to the statutory minimum level of **3 per cent** on a review of the current liquidity situation, it is felt desirable to keep the present level of **CRR 5 per cent** unchanged.

First Quarter Review

The first quarter review of this part of the annual policy statement will be undertaken on July 26, 2005 and will contain such other changes measures as may be necessary.

Unit II: Annual Statements on Developmental and Regulation Policies for the Year 2005-06

A stable and efficient financial sector is essential for sustained economic growth. In this context, the annual policy statements as well as mid-term reviews of RBI have been continuously focussing on the developmental and regularity measures to strengthen the financial system. The policy statements also discern the links among the monetary credit and regularity policies involving the overall structural transformation of the real and financial sectors. The emphasis has been on safeguarding the financial stability of the overall system through effective monitoring and assurance of implementation of regulations. In this direction, the overall approach has been that of re-orienting the role of RBI for improving institutional soundness, strengthening the regulatory and supervisory process in alignment with international practices and developing the necessary technological and legal infrastructure while the approach towards the reforms has been gradual and relevant to the context, consultative process and appropriate sequencing of measures have succeeded in aiding growth avoiding crisis, enhancing efficiency and imparting resilience to the system. The aim is to move towards a system that is responsive to the needs of the common person.

In order to reinforce stability of the overall system and to serve the common person, the emphasis of the policy statement, at this stage is on certain key areas:

(a) It is useful to debate the current regulation on interest rates and stipulations relating to priority sector in terms of their contemporary effectiveness in delivering adequate credit at appropriate prices.
(b) To facilitate a balanced development of the financial system, it is necessary to further develop money, forex and government securities markets.
(c) There is a need to bridge the financing gaps in agriculture and in small and medium enterprises in order to enhance credit delivery.
(d) From a systematic point of view, sound corporate governance practices, better risk management and adherence to prudential norms within the financial sector needed to be encouraged.
(e) In order to strengthen the payment and settlement systems, a road map and development and application of technology in the financial sector in the medium term becomes important.
(f) As financial institutions expand and become more complex, it is imperative to ensure availability of quality services to all sections of the population.

In order to have focussed attention on the identified areas for policy purposes this annual statement on developmental and regulatory policies for the year **2005-06** consist of **five sections**:

(1) Interest rate prescriptions
(2) Financial markets
(3) Credit delivery mechanism
(4) Prudential measures
(5) Institutional developments.

1. Interest Rate Prescriptions

The deregulation of financial markets in the recent years has improved the competitive environment in the financial system and strengthened the transmission mechanism of monetary policy. Sequencing of interest rate deregulation has been an important component of the reform process which has imparted greater efficiency in resource allocation. The process has been gradual and predicated upon institution of prudential regulation of the banking system, market behaviour, financial opening and above all, the underlying macroeconomic conditions. The interest rates have been largely deregulated except for (i) savings deposit A/c, (ii) Non-resident Indian deposits, (iii) small loans upto **Rs. 2 lacs,** (iv) export credit.

The annual policy statements of 2002 had weighed the option of deregulation of interest rate on savings accounts but the time was not considered opportune considering that bulk of such deposits are held by households in semi-urban and rural areas. It has, however, been argued that regulation will facilitate better **Asset-Liability Management** for banks and competitive pricing to benefit the holders of saving accounts. As regards **NRI** deposits, interest rate ceilings on **FCNR (B)** deposits are linked to **LIBOR/SWAP** rates of corresponding foreign currencies, while NRE deposit rates are linked to US dollar **LIBOR/SWAP** rates. These stipulations have been put in place taking into account their implications for the banking system and the management of the capital.

As regards lending rates, given the limited ability of small borrowers to manage interest rate risk and for ensuring availability of credit at reasonable rates, interest rate, ceiling on small loans upto **Rs. 2 lacs** is linked to BPLR. The contrary view is that given the competitiveness in the credit market, high share of sub-**BPLR** lending and increasingly broad based credit structure, availability of credit to all segments of the economy at a price consistent with their risk profiles becomes important. Further, it is argued that lending rate regulation has dampened larger flow of credit to small borrowers. In addition the current regulation seems to have imparted an element of the downward rigidity to **BPLR**. It may be noted that RRBs and co-operative banks are free to determine their lending rates and these are no restrictions on lending rates of **micro finance institutions**.

Interest rate regulation on export credit has been favoured for making available credit to exporters at internationally competitive rates. The annual policy statement of April 2002 had indicated that "Linking of domestic interest rates on export credit to PLR has become redundant in the present circumstances as 'effective interest rate on export credit in rupee terms is substantially lower than the PLR". The mid-term review of October 2002 had mooted deregulation of interest rate on rupee export credit in faces to encourage greater competition in the interest of exports. One view is that in the light of competitive lending rates in the economy, it is important to ensure that regulated interest rates should not restrict credit flow of all the segments of the exporters with different risk profiles.

While there is merit in moving forward to impart greater competitiveness and depth to the activities of the financial system by further deregulating interest rates in some segments which have hitherto remained regulated for various reasons found relevant at different stages, it is proposed to continue with *status quo* as various issues pertaining to above regulations on interest rates are being debated.

2. Financial Markets

Financial markets can be studied through the following classification:

(a) Money Market
(b) Government Securities Market
(c) Foreign Exchange Market.

(a) Money Market

Money market provides a focal point for the central bank's operations in influencing system liquidity and thereby transmitting the monetary policy impulses. The broad policy objectives that are being pursued for the development of money market include ensuring stability in short term interest rates, minimising default risk and achieving a balanced development of various segments of the money market. In order to review the recent developments and current status of money market in the context of evolving monetary policy framework, fiscal scenario, regulatory regime and extent of financial integration, both domestic and external, a technical group on **Money Market** was constituted. The report of the group was discussed in the **Technical Advisory Committee on Money, Foreign Exchange and Government Securities Markets** and certain recommendations have been accepted for implementation. Accordingly, the following measures are proposed:

(i) Call money market
(ii) Market Repo
(iii) Certificate of Deposit.

(i) Call Money Market—With effect from the fortnight beginning June 11, 2005 non-bank participants except PDs, would be allowed to lend on average in a reporting fortnight, upto **10 per cent** of their average daily lending in call money market during 2000-01.

With effect from **August 6, 2005** non-bank participants, except PDs, would be completely phased out from the call money market.

With effect from the fortnight beginning **April 30, 2005**, the bench mark for fixing prudential limits on exposures to call money market in the case of scheduled commercial banks would be linked to their capital funds. **(sum of Tier I and Tier II Capital)**

From April 30, 2005 all NDS members are required to report their term money deals on NDS platform.

A screen based negotiated Quote driven system for all dealings in call and term money market transactions is proposed.

(ii) Market Repo—An electronic trading platform for conduct of market repo operations in government securities in addition to the existing voice based system to be facilitated.

Participation in market repo facility in government securities for non-scheduled urban co-operative banks and listed companies having gilt accounts with scheduled commercial banks will be allowed subject to eligibility criteria and safeguards.

(iii) Certificate of Deposits—The minimum maturity period of certificates of deposits reduced from **15 days to 7 days** with immediate effect. The recommendations of the group on introduction of asset backed commercial paper to further deepen the CP market and additional Intra day LAF to stablise short term rates would be considered in future in consultation with market participants. In addition, optionalise in OTC rupee derivatives would be considered, once legal clarity to OTC derivatives is provided and appropriate accounting standards are put in place.

(b) Government Securities Market

The government securities can be observed as follows:

(i) Central Government Securities Market
(ii) Sale of Government Securities.

Central Government Securities are related to medium term. In terms of the stipulation of **FRBM Act,** RBI will not be participating in primary issuance of government securities with effect from **April 1, 2006**. In this context, the mid-term review of **October 2004** emphasised that open market operations would become a more active policy instrument necessitating review of processes and technological infrastructure consistent with market advancement. In order to address these emerging needs and equip RBI as well as the market participants appropriately, a technical group on Central Government securities market was constituted. Earlier another group had examined the role of primary dealers in the government securities market. The report was discussed in TAC and certain recommendations have been accepted for implementation. Accordingly, the following measures are proposed.

The number of actively traded securities need to be enlarged to enhance liquidity and improve pricing in the market. It is proposed to consolidate debt and build up large liquid securities in consultations with the government while continuing the programme of reassurances.

Post-FRBM, RBI will reorient government debt management operations while simultaneously strengthening monetary operations. This will entail functional separation between debt management and monetary operations within RBI. For this purpose, RBI will have discussions with market players on the modalities and procedures of market operations.

The settlement system for transactions in government securities will be standardised to **T+1** basis.

The RBI would continue to resort to multiple and uniform price methods, flexibly in the auction of government securities.

Permitted structures of **PD** business will be expanded to include banks which fulfil certain minimum criteria subject to safeguards and in consultation with banks, PDs and the government.

The recommendations of the technical group on re-structuring the underwriting obligations of **PDs,** allowing **PDs** exclusively in primary auctions, introduction of when issued market and limited short selling in government securities would be considered in consultation with the government.

Sale of government securities relaxation at present, sales allotted in primary issues can be entered into on the same day only between entities maintaining **SGL** account with RBI. In order to facilitate further deepening of the government securities market. It is proposed:

To permit sale of government securities allotted in primary issues with and between **CSGL** account holders also on the same day.

Market borrowings of state governments, the **12th Finance commission** recommended that the centre should not act as a financial intermediary for future lending to the states. The centre would release only the grant portion of central assistance of state plan to state and allow them to approach the market directly to raise the loan portion of the funds. In case same fiscally weak states are unable to raise funds from the market, the centre could borrow for on lending to such states. The centre has accepted in principles the recommendations and has proposed to implement in it phases, in consultation with RBI. As the implementation of the recommendations of **TWFC** would have major implications for the market borrowing programmes. RBI would facilitate smooth transition of the process in consultation with the Central and State Governments. As a first step, consultations were held with state finance secretaries on **April 8, 2005.**

(c) Foreign Exchange Market

This segment can be studied through the following process:

(i) Forex Market
(ii) Overseas Investment
(iii) Foreign Currency Accounts.

(i) Forex Market—Since the on set of reforms in the early 1990s, significant liberalisation of the foreign exchange market has taken place and the process gained momentum after Sodhani Committee recommendations were accepted for implementation by RBI. The foreign exchange market is now deeper and wider as gauged in terms of parameters such as the range of products, participation, liquidity and turnover. As indicated in the mid-term review of October 2004, an internal group was set up to review comprehensively the initiatives taken by RBI in the Forex market and identify areas for further improvements. The group reviewed Forex market liberalisation in select emerging markets and examined the current regulatory regime in the light of liberalisation in related sector to identify areas for further liberalisation. The report of the group was discussed in **TAC**, as recommended by the group. The following measures are proposed:

(a) Cancellations and re-booking of all eligible forward contracts booked by residents, irrespective of tenor, to be allowed.
(b) Banks to be allowed to approve proposals for commodity hedging in international exchanges from their corporate customers.

(c) The closing time for interbank forex market in India to be extended by one hour upto **5.00 pm.**

(d) Dissemination of additional information including traded volumes for derivatives such as foreign currency rupee options to the market.

The other recommendations of the group pertaining to writing of covered options by corporates and hedging of economic risks of corporates in respect of their domestic operations arising out of changes in the landed cost of the imported substitutes of the commodities. They consume produce would be considered. The sequencing with regard to implementation of these measures will take into account the enabling conditions for further progress towards capital account convertibility, liberalisation in other sectors of the economy and trend in overall balance of payments.

(ii) Overseas Investment—At present, under the automatic route, Indian entities are permitted to invest in overseas joint ventures and/or wholly owned subsidiaries upto **100 per cent** of their net worth. With a view to promoting Indian investments overseas, it is proposed.

To raise the ceiling of overseas investment by Indian entities in overseas joint ventures and/or wholly owned subsidiaries from **100 per cent to 200 per cent** of their networth under the automatic route.

(iii) Foreign Currency Accounts—At present, authorised dealers are required to obtain RBI approval for opening of foreign currency accounts of the project officer set up in India by foreign companies. In order to further liberalise the procedure, it is **proposed.**

To accord general permission to ADs to open foreign currency accounts of the project officer set up in India by foreign companies and operate the accounts flexibly.

3. Credit Delivery Mechanism

The credit delivery mechanism can be studied as follows:

(a) Flow of Credit to Agriculture.

(b) Micro Finance.

(c) Flow to Small Scale Industries.

(d) .Flow to Medium Enterprise.

(e) Development of RRBs.

(f) Priority sector lending.

(a) Flow of Credit to Agriculture

The union budget has proposed to increase the flow of credit to agriculture by **30 per cent** during the year **2005-06**. It has been the RBI endeavour to enhance credit flow to agriculture by removing bottle necks in credit delivery. In this direction, as indicated in the annual policy statement of May 2004 and the mid-term review of October 2004, most of the recommendations of the advisory committee on flow of credit to agriculture and related to activities from the banking system have been implemented by RBI and NABARD. Other recommendations covering the target for direct and indirect lending for agriculture under priority sector lending, negotiable warehousing receipt system, setting up of agri-risk fund computerisation of land records, permitting access to external commercial borrowing and granting autonomy of **NABARD** are under examination of the government. As at the end of December 2004, PSBs have issued **167.9 lakhs** Kisan credit cards with limits amounting to about **Rs. 46,000 crores**. Cumulative sanctions and disbursements under various branches of **RIDF** amounted to about **Rs. 42,000** crores and **Rs. 24,000 crores** respectively by February 2005. With a view to further increasing, the flow of credit to agriculture, the following measures have been initiated.

The RBI has enabled non-governmental organisations engaged in micro finance activities to access ECBs upto US dollars **5 millions** during a financial year for permitted end use, under automatic route, as an additional channel of resource mobilisations.

(b) Micro Finance

As a follow up of the budget proposals, modalities per allowing banks to adopt the agency model by using the infrastructure of civil society organisations, rural iciosics and village knowledge centres for providing credit support and rural and farm sectors and appointment of micro finance institutions, as the banking correspondence are being worked-out.

(c) Credit Flow to Small Scale Industries

The SSIs sectors plays a very important role in the development of the economy. While large industries have assess the various sources of finance. The SSI sector had to primarily depending on finance from banks and other financial institutions. With a view to further smoothening the flow of credit, the following measures have been initiated.

(i) The Credit Information Bureau of India Ltd., is working out a solution that would provide comprehensive credit reports on SSIs.

(ii) The RBI is reviewing all its existing guidelines on financing small sect or, Debt restructuring, nursing of sick units etc. With a view to rationalising, consolidating and liberalising them. Banks are argued to take the revised guidelines and indicative minimum requirement and the boards of the banks are expected to formulate more liberal schemes as appropriate.

(iii) Under a scheme to be drawn up by the RBI, banks will be encouraged to establish mechanisms for better coordination between their branches and branches of **SIDBI** which are located in 50 dusters that have been identified by the Ministry of Small Scale Industries, Government of India. Under the scheme of strategic alliance (1) the existing branches of SIDBI re-designated as **"small enterprises financial centres"** (SEFC), will take up co-financing of term loan requirements of SSI units along with bank branches and the working capital requirements of these units will be met by the banks. (2) the expertise of SIDBI in appraisal of credit requirements of SSI units will be leveraged by the branches of commercial banks by payment of nominal fee. (3) SIDBI will provide other expert services to help the banks in simplifying the application form, documentation and disbursement procedure etc., and (4) the working of the scheme may be monitored and modified to suit the local conditions by the state level bankers committee SLBC and depending on the experience, the coverage of the scheme may be extended to the more clusters. The services of SEFCs will be available for tiny industrial units also.

(d) Credit Flow to Medium Enterprises

In view of the fast changing markets conditions and increasing competitiveness, there is a urgent need to upgrade the technology of small scale industries and their graduation to medium enterprise sector. The RBI will explore modalities to meet their growing financial needs. A simplified debt restructuring and rehabilitation mechanisms is also being considered for the sector.

(e) Restructuring and Development of RRBs

The Regional Rural banks are conceiving as institutions that combine the local feel and familiarity with rural problems, which are co-operatives process, and the degree of business organisation as well as the abilities to mobilise deposits, which the commercial banks possess. In view of their importance as purviewers of the rural credit, the union budget 2004-05 emphasised that the sponsor banks will be accountable for the performance of their RRBs. An indicated in mid-term review of October 2004 sponsored banks are being encouraged to emerge the RRBs sponsored by them statewise. A few proposals in this regard are at various stages of consideration. While the sponsoring banks were advised that the appointment of chairman of their RRBs should be approved by the management committees of their boards, the government was requested to ensure that independent and professionally qualified persons are nominated to the boards of RRBs to make them more vibrant and pro-active.

In order to reposition RRBs as an effective instrument of credit delivery in the Indian financial system, RBI is in the process of reviewing the performance of RRBs, exploring restructuring of RRBs through merger/consolidation, changing of sponsor banks, reviewing minimum capital requirement and suitable measures have been suggested for regulation and supervision and governance of RRBs.

(f) Priority Sector Lending

Prescriptions relating to priority sector lending have been modified from time-to-time, and generally the eligibility criteria have been enlarged to include several new areas. In December 2004 it was decided that only advances will be eligible, thus, beginning a phased withdrawal of eligibility of investments in bonds. There have been suggesting for a further review of the eligibility criteria and other related aspects.

One view is that lending to any infrastructure project should be made eligible for priority sector lending, while making, sub-targets fungible within the overall target. There is another view that enlargement of areas has resulted in loss of focus. It is also held that credit growth in housing, venture capital and infrastructure has been strong while it has been sluggish in agriculture and small industries. Further, it is argued that only sectors that impact large population, weaker section and are employment intensive such as agriculture, tiny and small industry should be eligible for priority sector. Since, there are several issues that need to be considered in this regard, it is appropriate that these are debated and examined in depth.

(g) Prudential Measures

The RBI has taken several steps to strengthen the regulatory and supervisory framework of the financial sector. Further developments in this area as under:

(a) Policy on M&A of banks
(b) Supervision of financial conglomerates
(c) Interests of the depositors
(d) Financial exclusion
(e) Customer advice
(f) New capital adequacy
(g) Ownership and Government in private banks
(h) Guidelines on securitisation of standards assets
(i) Modification of CDR Mechanism
(j) Working group-financial services sector

(a) Policy on MEA of Banks

In pursuance of the recommendations of the Joint Parliamentary Committee, a working group was constituted by **RBI** to evolve guidelines for voluntary merger of banking companies. Based on the recommendations of the group and in consultation with the Government.

It is proposed:

> To issue guidelines on M&A between PSBs and with **NBFCs**. The guidelines would cover process of merger proposal, determination of Swap ratios, disclosures, norms for buying/selling of shares by promoters before and during the process of merger and the boards involvement in the merger process. The principles underlying these guidelines would also be applicable as appropriate to PSBs subject to relevant legislation.

(b) Supervision of Financial Conglomerates

As indicated in the annual policy statement of May 2004, the working group on financial conglomerates has identified 22 FCs. With a view to monitoring intra group transactions and exposures, a pilot process was initiated to obtain information from the designated entities of each FC by the principal regulators. Such information was analysed and discussed amongst the principal regulators and a system for exchange of information among them has been put in place. In order to appropriately focus on monitoring of the process, in consultation with chairman SEBI and chairman, **IRDA**.

It is proposed:

> To hold a half-yearly discussion with the CEO of the designated entity, which would be convened by the lead regulator with other regulators, on the basis of available information for review and addressing concerns, if any.

(c) Interests of the Depositors

Depositor's interests form the focal point of the regulatory framework for banking in India and it has been appropriately enshrined at several places in the Banking Regulations Act, 1949. In **Section (5) (ca)** of the Act, banking policy has been defined as **"any policy which is specified from time-to-time by the RBI in the interest of the banking system or in the interest of monetary stability or sound economic growth, having due regard to the interests of the depositors, the volume of deposits and other resources of the bank and the need for equitable allocation and the efficient use of these deposits and resources".**

Furthermore, as per the Act, some of the considerations that are required to be taken into account while granting licence for banking business, in addition to ensuring the capacity of the bank to pay present and potential depositors in full, is whether the affairs of the company are not being or are not likely to be detrimental to the interest of the depositors or pre-judicial to public interest. A licence to do banking business provides the entity the ability to accept deposits and access to deposit insurance for small depositors. Similarly, regulations supervision by RBI enable these entitles to access funds from a wider investor base and the payment and settlement systems provide efficient payments and funds transfer services. All these services, which are in the nature of public good, involve significant costs and are being made available only to ensure availability of banking and payments services to the entire population without descrimination.

Against this background, while policies relating to credit allocation, credit pricing and credit restructuring should continue to receive attention, it is an inappropriate to ignore the mandate relating to depositors interests. In our country the socio-economic profile for a typical depositor who seeks safe avenue for his savings deserves special attention relating to other stakeholders in the banks.

In the observations and recommendations of the committees on procedures and performances of audit on public services **(CPPAS)** on **"Banking operations: Deposit accounts and other facilities relating to individuals (non-business)".** It was indicated "the banks offerings are generally "opaque" what is not charges is mentioned but what is charges is not mentioned high hidden costs appear rampart and unjustified, thus banks enjoy under enrichment. If a small customer goes to a bank and has a technical problem, anecdotal evidence suggests that he runs into enormous difficulties. The committee notes with some sadness that there is substance in the widespread impression among the small depositor community that one needs to know some one higher-up forgetting his/her job done intense depositor loyalty is the only plank on which the Indian banking system is surviving. The banks have to understand that depositors are at the end of their tether and banks providing poor customer service will be punished by switching loyalty. The information suggests that in recent years banks are taking increasing recourse to non-deposit resources to fund their assets. Against this background:

(i) Banks are urged to refocus on deposit mobilisation and empower the depositors, by providing wider access and better quality of banking services.
(ii) RBI will persist with its efforts to ensure quality of banking services in particular to small individual depositors.

(d) Financial Exclusion

There has been expansion, greater competition and diversification of ownership of banks, leading to both enhanced efficiency and systematic resilience in the banking sector. However, there are legitimate concerns in regard to the banking practices that tend to exclude rather than attract vast sections of the population. In particular pensioners self employed and those employed in unorganised sector. While commercial considerations are no doubt important, the banks have been bestowed with several privileges, especially of seeking public deposits on a highly leveraged basis, and consequently. They should be obliged to provide banking services to all segments of the population, on equitable basis. Against this background:

(i) RBI will implement policies to encourage banks which provide extensive services while disincentivising those which are not responsive to the banking needs to the community, including the underprivileged.

(ii) The nature, scope and cost of services will be monitored to assess whether, there is denial, implicit or explicit of bank banking services to the common man.

(iii) Banks are urged to review their existing practices to align them with the objective of financial inclusion.

(e) Customer Service

Liberalisation and enhanced competition accord immense benefit but experience has shown that consumer's interest are not necessarily accorded full protection and their grievances are not properly attended to several representations are being received in regard to recent trends of living unreasonably high services/user charges and enhancement of user charges without proper and clear intimation. Among the complaints received are charges for balance enquiry cheque status verification, signature verification, address confirmation, photograph verification, punitive services charges for non-maintenance of minimum balance in savings accounts, transaction charges for re-order of cheque book and for cash transactions at the branch beyond a stipulated number and diversion of customer to usage of ATMs including payment for cash transaction.

It is instructive in this regard to note that in **Canada**, the issue of bank service charges was the subject of a 1988 investigations conducted by the house of commons standing committee on finance. The committee reports set out a number of recommendations, which have subsequently been reflected in the market practice. The committee recommendation resulted in improved disclosure of service charges and the designation of Office and the Superitendent of Financial Institutions (**OSFI**)to handle and report on service charges complaints.

In the **U.S.A.** organisations such as consumers union are fighting to create legislation that will help protect vulnerable. Consumers from price gouging on checking accounts. American consumer groups are against what they call is the "trap of never ending bank fees that is impossible to escape". They are demanding lifeline banking legislation which will give consumers assess to basic banking services and protect them frame exorbitant fees and surcharges for providing information such as signature and photograph verification. Several Americans states have implemented legislation for minimum no frills services. Some states prohibit ATM surcharges.

In the **UK**, there exists an institutional arrangement whereby a separate board has been set up to oversee the code drawn up by the banks association. The banking code of the British Bankers Association (**BBA**) is a voluntary code, which sets standards of good banking practices for financial institutions to follow when they are dealing with personal customers in the UK. It provides valuable protection for customers on day-to-day basis as also in the times of financial difficulty. The code applies to savings deposits and current accounts, card products and services, loans and overdrafts and payment services including foreign exchanges. Taking account of all these considerations it has been decided.

(i) To set up and independent banking codes and standards board of India on the model of mechanism in the UK in order to ensure that comprehensive code of conduct for fair treatment of customers are evolved and adhered to.

(ii) To issue appropriate guidelines to banks to ensure transparency and disclosure of information by the card issuing banks and customer rights protection including facilitating enforcement of such rights.

(iii) To widen the scope of the banking on budsman *inter alia* to cover all individual cases/grievances relating to non-adherence to the fair practices code evolved by IBA and adopted by individual banks.

(f) New Capital Adequacy Framework in India

As indicated in the mid-term review of October 2004 draft guidelines or implementation of the new capital adequacy framework were formulated and placed on the RBI website. In order to maintain constancy and harmony with international standards banks were advised to adopt standardised approach for operational risk with effect from 31-3-07. The RBI may consider allowing some banks to migrate to internal rating based approach after developing adequate skills both in banks and at supervisory levels. As banks would be allowed to adopt/migrate to the advanced approached only with the specific approval of RBI, as a first step, banks which are aiming at adopting the advanced approaches should make an objective self assessment of their fulfillment of the minimum criteria prescribed under **Base II.**

As banks have two years lead time to prepare themselves for **Base II**, they are encouraged to focus on capacity building and undertake impact analysis. On the basis of the out come of the impact studies, banks may put in place appropriate strategies and plans for raising fresh capital or argument capital through internal resources. Banks may also re-define their business strategy with a view to attaining their profile of risk exposure or adopt a combination of both these approaches to meet the capital requirement.

Under the new framework, banks adopting standarised approach would the ratings as signed only by those credit rating agencies which are identified by RBI. The new framework also recognises the responsibility of bank management in developing an Internal Capital Adequacy assessment process that is commensurate with banks risk profile and control environment. Banks are therefore, required to focus on formalising and operationalising their ICAAP which will serve as a useful benchmark while undertaking the parallel run with effect from 1-4-2006.

(g) Owernship and Governance in Private Banks

It was indicated in the mid-term review of October 2004 that the second draft on the policy framework for ownership and governance in private sector banks would be put in public domain. Based on the feedback received on the draft guidelines and in consultation with the government, RBI has since issued final guidelines. These guidelines focus on ensuring fit and proper criteria, on a continuous basis in respect of investments restructuring and consolidation in the banking sector and provide for observance of sound corporate governance principles. The Reserve Bank would enter into bank wise dialogues to ensure a time bound frame work for compliance.

(h) Guidelines on Securitisation of Standard Assets

In the recent period the market for securitisation of standard assets has grown significantly. In order to ensure orderly development of the market, draft guidelines on securitisation of standard assets by banks/financial institutions and **NBFCS** were issues and placed on the RBI website for comments. On the basis of the feedback, the draft guidelines would be finalised.

(i) Guidelines on Purchase/Sale of non-performing Assets

With a view to further increasing the options available to banks for effectively addressing the issue of non-performing assets, draft guidelines were issued on sale/purchase of NPAS and comments there on were sought from the banks by end April 2005. The guidelines broadly cover the areas on procedure for purchase/sale of NPAS by banks including valuation and pricing aspects, prudential norms, and disclosure requirements and would be finalised on the basis of feedback.

(j) Modification of CDR Mechanism

Performance of the corporate debt restructuring mechanism has been reviewed and it has been decided to make changes in regard to criteria for the minimum exposure and number of lenders for deciding on CDR package; rationalisation of regulatory concessions a applicability of the extant instructing relating to asset classification only for the first restructuring of debt; and flexibility in exit option by allowing one time settlement, draft circular is being put in the public domain for wider dissemination before taking final decisions.

(j) Working Group Financial Services

As indicated in the mid-term of review of October 2004, RBI has constituted a working group on conflicts of interest in the Indian financial services sector. The report of the group is expected by July 2005, which would be put in the public domain for wider dissemination before recommending for adoption.

4. Institutional Developments

The following aspects have been observed by the Reserve Bank of India:

(a) Payment and settlement systems
(b) Board for regulation
(c) Electric payment product
(d) Reinforcing of information.

(a) Payment and Settlement System

As indicated in the mid-term review of October 2004 a vision document for payment and settlement systems were prepared by RBI under the guidance of the National Payment Council and was placed on the RBI website. Based on the feedback, a road map for upgradation of payment systems was drawn up for implementation in the next three years 2005-08. Some of the key action plans of the document relate to a new umbrella organisation for retail payment systems, regulation for various modes of electronic credit transfers, risk migration measures, customers rights and services and rural reach. The vision document indicating action points would be placed in the public domain for wider dissemination by June 2005.

(b) Board for Regulation and Supervision

In continuation of the steps initiated by RBI for developing institutional framework for payment and settlement systems, a board for regulation and supervision of payment and settlement systems were constituted as a committee of the Central Board of RBI as notified in the Gazette of India on February 18, 2005. The BPSS would prescribe policies relating to the regulations and supervision of all types of payment and settlement systems, set standards for existing and future systems authorise the payment and settlement systems and determine criteria for membership to these systems.

In order to assist BPSS in performing its functions, RBI constituted a new department, the department of payment and settlement system with the constitution of DPSS, the functions of the department of information technology would be to formulate and to implement information technology policies for RBI as well as the banking and financial systems in the country.

(c) Electronic Payment Products

The coverage of RTGS and ECS has increased significantly during last year. As on **25-4-05**, RTGS connectivity was available in **4776** bank branches at 398 centres of the country. It is expected that about **10,000 branches** would be covered by the end-March 2006.

The RBI proposes operationlisation of National Electronic Fund transfer systems, which would enable **T+O** settlement for all networked branches of banks all over the country for electronic transfer of funds. In order to facilitate non-networked branches of banks to transfer funds electronically, the NEFT system would be implemented under which these branches could access NEFT enabled branches of banks for transfer of funds.

(d) Re-inforcing of Information Security

In view of the increasing dependence of the financial sector on internal and external networked for their operations, information security has assumed greater importance. In this direction, RBI has initiated several measures to ensure information security in banks. As indicated in the mid-term review of October 2002, banks were encouraged to use public key infrastructure to protect information security. Since then inter banks systems like **RTGS, PDO/NDS/SSS SFMS and CFMS** have been made

PKI compliant. Banks are encouraged to make increasing use of SFMS which is PKI enabled for inter/inter bank transactions.

Information Technology

The RBI has been guiding banks in implementation of information technology so as so to provide for seamless integration across various entities in the financial sector. In order to facilitate the technology plans of the financial sector. RBI is preparing a financial sector technology vision document, covering the medium term policy perspectives. The draft of the vision document would be put in the public domain for under dissemination. Based on the feedback, action points would be finalised.

Urban Co-operative Banks

Urban Co-operative Banks are functioning under the control of RBI. As indicated in the mid-term review of October 2004 a draft vision document for Urban Co-operative Banks were prepared keeping in view the heterogeneity of the sector in terms of size, area of operation, performance and strength and was placed on the RBI website. Based on the feedback, a medium-term framework for **Urban Co-operative Banks** upto 10 is being drawn up in order to facilitate the development of this sector into a strong and vibrant system comprising entities conforming to all prudential requirements. The medium term framework would be placed in the public domain for wider dissemination and for implementation as appropriate. The standing advisory committee for Urban co-operative banks is increasingly being used for continuous dialogue with the various stakeholders of the sector.

Restructuring of Weak Scheduled UCBs is another aspects in the monitoring activities of the RBI. RBI has began a consultative process involving officials of the concerned state governments and banks for revitalising and rehabilitating the weak scheduled UCBs. The emphasis is on a time bound programme for restructuring of UCBs by identifying the contours of their rehabilitation plan and setting up monitorable milestones. The RBI would be closely monitoring the achievements of the banks vis-à-vis the targets at regular intervals and initiating appropriate action with a view to protecting depositors interests and avoiding systematic problems. The issues relating to large depositors part conversion of deposits into equity reduction of NPAs, human resources and technological development as also support from the state government would be examined. The option of merger/amalgamation could also be explored wherever necessary.

Non-banking Financial Companies

NBFCs play a critical role as an instrument plays a critical role as an instrument of credit delivery, particularly, in the small scale and retail sector in the remote areas. The emphasis has been on developing NBFCs into a financially strong sector with improved skills and technology. In this context, RBI is examining the issue of smooth flow of bank finance to **NBFCs**.

Working Group on Computerisation of State Treasuries and Online Connectivity

The RBI has constituted a working group on computerisation of state treasuries and online connectivity to gather information on government receipts and payments with members drawn from four state governments and RBI to study the existing practices in treasury functions of various states, system of accounting of receipts and payments, level of computerisation in treasuries, scope for further computerisation and issues relating to uniform application software for treasury operations.

Standing Committee on Procedures and Performances Audit on Public Services

As indicated in the mid-term review of November 2003, the standing committee on procedures and performances audit on public services constituted by RBI has submitted 14 reports. Six reports submitted the committee deal with matters relating to foreign exchange, government transactions, banking operations, currency management, regional assessment and benchmarking. Eight special reports were submitted dealing with specific references made by RBI. Banks and RBI have implemented most of the recommendations of the committee. The standing committee ceased its operations in March 2005. In order to facilitate regular monitoring. Adhoc committees in banks have been converted to permanent standing committee on customer service. A system for monitoring on a regular basis the customer services rendered by RBI offices is being put in place.

Legal Reforms: Review of Developments

The RBI in co-ordination with the government, has taken initiatives for necessary changes in the legal structure to strengthen the functioning of the financial system. The Credit Information Companies (Regulation)

Bill, 2004 and Government Securities Bill, 2004 were introduced in the Parliament. As indicated in the budget 2005-06, certain amendments to the Banking Regulation Act, 1949 and the RBI Act, 1934 will be considered by the government. In addition, the payment and settlement bills is being finalised by the board for regulation and supervision of payment and settlement systems.

Mid-term Review

A review of the annual policy statement will be undertaken on October 25, 2005 and will contain such other changes/measures as may be necessary in regard to developmental and regulatory policies for the second half of the year.

Illustration 1

From the following Profit and Loss Account and the Balance Sheet of Karthik Textiles Ltd. for the year ended 31st March, 2004 and 2005. You are required to prepare a comparitive Balance Sheet and a comparitive income statement.

(Rs. in lakhs)

P/S	*2004*	*2005*	*P/S*	*2004*	*2005*
To cost of Goods Sold	1200	1500	By net sales	1600	2000
To operating expenses					
Administrative expenses	40	40			
Selling expenses	60	80			
To net profit	300	380			
	1600	2000		1600	2000

Balance Sheet as on 31st March

(Rs. in lakhs)

Liabilities	*2004*	*2005*	*Assets*	*2004*	*2005*
Bills payable	100	150	Cash	200	280
Sunday creditors	300	400	Debtors	400	600
Tax payable	200	300	Stock	400	600
6% Debentures	200	300	Land	200	200
6% preference capital	600	600	Building	600	540
Equity capital	800	800	Plant	600	540
Reserves	400	490	Furniture	200	280
	2600	3040		2600	3040

Solution

Karthik Textiles Limited
Comparitive Income Statement
For the year ended 31st March, 2004–2005

(Rs. in lakhs)

Particulars	*2004*	*2005*	*Absolute increase or decrease in 2005*	*Percentage of increase or decrease in 2005*
Net sales	1600	2000	+400	+25
Cost of goods sold	1200	1500	+300	+25
Gross profit	400	500	+100	+25
Operating Expenses				
Administration Expenses	40	40	–	–
Selling expenses	60	80	+20	+33.3
Total operating Expenses	100	120	+20	+20
Operating profit	300	380	+80	26.6

Karthik Comparitive Balance Sheet
as on 31st March, 2004-05

(Figures in lakhs)

Assets	*2004*	*2005*	*Absolute increase or decrease during 2005*	*Percentage increase (+) or decrease (–) during 2005*
Current Assets				
Cash	200	280	80	+40
Debtors	400	600	200	+50
Stock	400	600	200	+50
Total Current Assets	1000	1480	480	48%
Fixed Assets				
Land	200	200	–	–
Building	600	540	–60	–10%
Plant	600	540	–60	–10%
Furniture	200	280	+80	+40%
Total Fixed Assets	1600	1560	–40	–2.5%
Total Assets	2600	3040	440	+17%

(Contd.)

(Contd.)

Assets	2004	2005	Absolute increase or decrease during 2005	Percentage increase (+) or decrease (–) during 2005
Liabilities & Capital:				
Current Liabilities				
Bills payable	100	150	+50	+50%
Sundry creditors	300	400	+100	+33.33%
Tax payable	200	300	+100	+50%
Total current liabilities	600	850	+250	+41.66%
Long term Liabilities				
6% Debentures	200	300	100	+50%
Total liabilities	800	1150	+350	+43.75%
Capital & Reserves				
6% Pref. capital	600	600	–	–
Equity capital	800	800	–	–
Reserves	400	490	+90	22.5
Total Shareholders funds	1800	1890	+90	5%
Total Liabilities & Capital	2600	3040	440	17%

Illustration 2

Balance Sheet of Harish Textiles Ltd. as on 31st March, 2005 from the following information prepare common size balance sheet of Harish Textiles Ltd.

Liabilities	2004	2005	Assets	2004	2005
Share Capital			**Fixed Assets less:**	2,40,000	2,20,000
Equity	20,000	40,000	Depreciation		
Preference	40,000	20,000	**Current Assets:**		
Reserves & Surplus	60,000	60,000	Inventories	88,000	80,000
Profit & Loss Account	99,650	80,000	Sundry debtors	66,050	60,000
Loan Funds:			Marketable	21,600	30,000
12% Debentures	76,000	80,000	Securities		
Term loans	38,000	40,000	Cash	16,000	10,000
Current Liabilities					
Bills payable	18,000	16,000			
Sundry creditors	30,000	24,000			
Other current liabilities	50,000	40,000			
	4,31,650	4,00,000		4,31,650	4,00,000

Solution

Common size Balance Sheet of Harish Textiles Ltd.
as on 31st March, 2005

(Rs. in lakhs)

Liabilities	As on 31-3-2004 Amount	% of Total	As on 31-3-2005 Amount	% of Total
Capital and Reserves				
Share Capital	20,000	5%	40,000	9.3%
Preference Capital	40,000	10%	20,000	4.6%
Reserves	60,000	15%	60,000	13.9%
P/L account	80,000	20%	99,650	23.1%
	2,00,000	50%	219650	50.9%
Long-term debt				
12% Debentures	80,000	20%	76000	176%
Term loans	40,000	10%	38000	8.8%
	1,20,000	30%	114000	264%
Current liabilities				
Bills payable	16,000	4%	18,000	4.1%
Sundry Creditors	24,000	6%	30,000	7.0%
Other Current Liabilities	40,000	10%	50,000	11.6%
	80,000	20%	98,000	22.7%
Total	4,00,000	100%	4,31,650	100%
Assets				
Current Assets				
Cash	10,000	2.5%	16,000	3.7%
Investment	30,000	7.5%	21,600	5.0%
Debtors	60,000	15.0%	66,050	15.3%
Inventory	80,000	20%	88,000	20.4%
Total Current Assets	1,80,000	45%	1,91,650	44.4%
Fixed Assets				
Gross Fixed Assets	4,40,000		4,80,000	
Less: Accumulated depreciation	2,20,000		2,40,000	
	2,20,000	55%	2,40,000	55.6%
Total	4,00,000	100%	4,31,650	

Illustration 3

From the following Profit and Loss Accounts and the Balance Sheet of Swadeshi Polytex Ltd. for the year ended 31st December, 2003 and 2004, you are required to prepare a common-size Financial statements.

Profit and Loss Account

(Rs. in lakhs)

Particulars	*2003* *Rs.*	*2004* *Rs.*	*Assets*	*2003* *Rs.*	*2004* *Rs.*
To Cost of Goods sold	1200	1500	By Net Sales	1600	2000
To Operating Expenses					
Administrative Expenses	40	40			
Selling Expenses	60	80			
To Net Profit	300	380			
	1600	2000		1600	2000

Balance Sheet as on 31st December

(Rs. In lakhs)

Liabilities	*2003* *Rs.*	*2004* *Rs.*	*Assets*	*2003* *Rs.*	*2004* *Rs.*
Bills Payable	100	150	Cash	200	280
Sundry Creditors	300	400	Debtors	400	600
Tax Payable	200	300	Stock	400	600
6% Debentures	200	300	Land	200	200
6% Preference Capital	600	600	Building	600	540
Equity Capital	800	800	Plant	600	540
Reserves	400	490	Furniture	200	280
	2600	3040		2600	3040

Solution

Swadeshi Polytex Ltd.
Common-size Income Statement
For the Year ended 31st December, 2003–2004

(Figures in percentage)

	2003	*2004*
Net Sales	100	100
Cost of Goods Sold	75	75
Gross profit	25	25
Opening Expenses		
Administration Expenses	2.50	2
Selling Expenses	3.75	4
Total Operating Expenses	6.25	6
Operating Profit	18.75	19

Swadeshi Polytex Ltd
Common-size Balance Sheet
As on 31st December, 2003–2004

Assets	*2003* % 100	*2004* % 100
Current Assets		
Cash	7.70	9.21
Debtors	15.38	19.74
Stock	15.38	19.74
Total Current Assets	38.46	48.69
Fixed Assets		
Building	23.07	17.76
Plant	23.07	17.76
Furniture	7.70	9.21
Land	7.70	6.68
Total Fixed Assets	61.54	51.31
Total Assets	100	100
Liabilities and Capital	100	100
Current Liabilities		
Bills payable	3.84	4.93
Sundry Creditors	11.54	13.16
Taxes payable	7.69	9.86
Total Current Liabilities	23.07	27.95
Long-term Liabilities		
6% Debentures	7.69	9.86
Capital & Reserves		
6% Preference share capital	23.10	19.72
Equity share capital	30.76	26.32
Reserves	15.38	16.15
Total Shareholder's Fund	76.93	72.05
Total Liabilities & Capital	100	100

Illustration 4

From the following Balance Sheets of **Vani Textiles Ltd.** . You are required to prepare **(a) A schedule of changes in working capital, 31st March, 2004–2005, (b) A funds flow statement.**

Liabilities	2004	2005	Assets	2004	2005
Share Capital	2,00,000	2,00,000	Goodwill	24,000	24,000
Reserves	28,000	36,000	Building	80,000	72,000
P&L A/c	32,000	26.000	Plant	74,000	72,000
Creditors	16,000	10,800	Investments	20,000	22,000
Bills Payable	2,400	1,600	Stock	60,000	46,800
Provision for taxation	32,000	36,000	Bills receiveables	4,000	6,400
Provision for doubtful debts	800	1,200	Debtors	36000	38000
			Cash at Bank	13,200	30,400
	3,11,200	**3,11,600**		**3,11,200**	**3,11,600**

Adjustments:

(a) Depreciation charged on plant was Rs. 8,000 and on buildings Rs. 8,000.

(b) Provisions for taxation of Rs. 38,000 was made during the year 2005.

(c) Interim dividend of **Rs. 16,000** was paid during the year 2005.

Solution

Statement of Changes in Working Capital

P/S	*2004*	*2005*	*(+) increases*	*(–) decreases*
Current assets				
Cash at bank	13,600	30,400	17,200	
Debtors	36,000	38,000	2000	
Bills receivables	4000	6400	2400	
Stock	60,000	46,800		13,200
Current Liabilities				
Provisions for doubtful debts	800	1200		400
Payable bills	2400	1600	800	
Creditors	16000	10800	5200	
			27,600	**13,600**

Net increase in working capital (27600 – 13600) = 14000

Funds Flow Statement

Sources:	Funds from operations[1]	72000
	Total sources	72000

Applications

Purchase of Plant[2]	6000
Tax paid[3]	34000
Investments purchased[4]	2000
Interim dividend paid	16000
Total application	58000
Net increase in working capital	14,000

Working Notes

Funds from operations[1]		
P & L A/c balance as on 31-3-2005		26,000
Add: Items which do not decrease funds from operations		
(a) Transfer to general reserve	8000	
(b) Provision for tax	38000	
(c) Depreciant on plant	8000	
(d) Depreciation on building	8000	
(e) Interim dividend paid	16000	78000
		104000
Less: Profit and Loss A/c balance on 31-3-2005		32,000
Funds from operations		72,000

Working Notes:

Purchase of plant[2]	
Opening balance	74,000
Add: Purchases (balancing figures)	6000
	80,000
Less: Depreciation	8,000
Closing balance	72,000

Tax adjustments[3]	
Opening balance	32,000
Add: provisions made during the year 2005	38,000
	70,000
Less: Tax paid during the 2005	34,000

Closing balance 36,000

Investments[4]

A change in investment value reflects the purchase value 22,000–20,000 = 2,000

Illustration 5

The Balance Sheets of Nitheesh Textiles Ltd. as at the end of 2004 and 2005 are given below:

Liabilities	*2004*	*2005*	*Assets*	*2004*	*2005*
Share Capital	2,00,000	3,00,000	Freehold land	2,00,000	2,00,000
Share premium	—	10,000	Plant at cost	2,08,000	2,00,000
General reserve	1,00,000	1,20,000	Furniture at cost	14,000	18,000
P & L A/c	20,000	34,000	Investments at cost	1,20,000	1,60,000
12% Debentures	1,40,000	1,00,000	Debtors	60,000	1,40,000
Provision for depreciation for plant	1,00,000	1,12,000	Stock	1,20,000	1,30,000
			Cash	60,000	90,000
Provision for depreciation on furniture	10,000	12,000			
Provision for taxation	40,000	60,000			
Creditors	1,72,000	1,90,000			
	7,82,000	9,38,000		7,82,000	9,38,000

Adjustments:

(1) Provision for taxation should be assumed as Non-current liabilities.

(2) A plant purchase for Rs. 8,000 (depreciation Rs. 4,000) was sold for cash for Rs. 1600 on September 2004.

(3) On June 30, 2004 an item of furniture was charge for Rs. 4000.

(4) A dividend of **22.5 per cent** on original shares was paid.

(5) Tax paid as per last year.

You are required to prepare a funds flow statement and verify the results by preparing a schedule of changes in working capital.

Solution: Funds Flow Statement

	Rs.
Sources of Funds:	
Share Capital (including premium)	1,10,000
Sale of plant	1,600
Funds from operations[2]	1,59,400
Total Sources	2,71,000
Applications of Funds:	
Redemption of Debentures	40,000
Purchase of Furniture	4,000
Dividend paid	45,000
Investments purchased	40,000
Tax paid[1]	40,000
Total uses	1,69,000
Increase in Working Capital	1,02,000

The increase in working capital can be verified by preparing a schedule of changes in working capital.

Schedule of Changes in Working Capital

	2004	*2005* *Rs.*	*Increase (+)* *Rs.*	*Decrease (–)* *Rs.*
Current Asset				
Debtors		60,000	1,40,000	80,000
Stock		1,20,000	1,30,000	10,000
Cash		60,000	90,000	30,000
Current Liabilities				
Sundry Creditors		1,72,000	1,90,000	18,000
			1,20,000	18,000
Increase in working capital			1,02,000	

Working Notes:

(1) Provision by taxation has been taken as a non-current liability. Moreover, in the absence of any specific instructions in the

question, it is safe to presume that tax must have been paid equivalent to last year's provision for taxation.

(2) Funds from operations have been calculated as follows:

Adjusted Profit & Loss Account

Dr.			*Cr.*
To Dividend paid	45,000	By Balance b/d	20,000
To provision for taxation	60,000	By Funds from operations	1,59,400
To Transfer to General Reserve	20,000	(Balancing figure)	
To Depreciation:			
Plant	16,000		
Furniture	2,000		
To loss on sale of plant	2,400		
To Balance c/d	34,000		
	1,79,400		1,79,400

(3) Loss on sale of plant and provisions for Depreciation on Plant and Furniture made during the year have been found out by preparing different accounts:

Plant Account

To Balance b/d	2,08,000	By Bank	1,600
		By P & L (Loss on sale of plant)	2,400
		By Provision for depreciation (on plant sold)	4,000
		By Balance c/d	2,00,000
	2,08,000		2,08,000

Furniture Account

To Balance b/d	14,000	By Balance c/d	18,000
To Bank (Balancing Figure)	4,000		
	18,000		18,000

Provision for Depreciation on Furniture

To Balance c/d	12,000	By Balance b/d	10,000
		By P & L A/c (depreciation charged the year balancing figure)	2000
	12,000		12,000

Provision for Depreciation on Plant

To Plant A/c (dep. on plant sold)	4,000	By Balance b/d	1,00,000
To Balance c/d	1,12,000	By P & L A/c (Balancing figure- depreciation Charged during the year)	16,000
	1,16,000		1,16,000

Illustration 6

Following are data for Anand Products

(Rs. in lakhs)

2005			*2005*
Assets	12000	Revenues	13,200
Short term liabilities	900	Operating Exp.	11,900
		EBIT	1,300
8% Debenture	2500	Interest	300
10% Bonds	1,000	EBI	1,000
Common stock (Rs.10 par)	7,000	Taxes	400
Surplus	600	Dividend	100

(a) Find out the following ratios
- (i) Asset turnover
- (ii) Effective interest rate
- (iii) Effective tax rate
- (iv) Debt/equity ratio
- (v) Dividend payout rate

(b) What growth rate of EBIT can be expected?

Solution

Asset turnover = 13,200/12000 = 1.1

Effective interest rate = 300/4400 = 0.068

Effective tax rate	= 400/1000	= 0.4
Debt/Equity	= 4400/7000	= 0.628
Dividend payout	= 0.14/0.86	= 16.28 per cent
Earnings per share	= 600/700	= 0.857
Dividend per share	= 100/700	= 0.142
Growth in EBIT	= Retention rate × Return on assets	
ROA	= EBIT/Assets	
	= 1300/12000	= 0.108
Growth in EBIT	= Retention rate × ROA	
Retention rate	= 1 – 0.16	= 0.84
	= 0.84 × 0.108	= 9.07

Illustration 7

The capital structure of the Kalyani Corporation Consists of as ordinary share capital of Rs. **20,00,000** (shares of Rs. **100** par value) and Rs. **20,00,000** of **10 per cent** debenture. Sales increased by **20 per cent** from **2,00,000** units to **2,40,000** units, the selling price is Rs. 20 per unit; variable cost amounts to Rs. 12 per unit and fixed expenses amount to Rs. **4,00,000**. The income tax rate is assumed to be **50** per cent.

You are required to calculate the following:

(i) The percentage increase in earnings per share;
(ii) The degree of financial leverage at **2,00,000** units and **2,40,000** units;
(iii) The degree of operating leverage at **2,00,000** units and **2,40,000** units.

Comment on the behaviour of operating and financial leverage in relation to increase in production from **2,00,000** units to **2,40,000** units.

Solution

Kalyani Corporation

Statement showing EPS and operating and Financial leverages at two levels of operation:

	2,00,000 units	2,40,000
Sales (@ 20 per unit)	40,00,000	48,00,000
Less: Variable costs	24,00,000	28,80,000
Contribution (c)	16,00,000	19,20,000
Less: Fixed expenses	4,00,000	4,00,000

Operating profit (EBIT or Op)	12,00,000	15,20,000
Less: Interest	2,00,000	2,00,000
Profit before tax (PBT)	10,00,000	13,20,000
Less: Tax 50 per cent	5,00,000	6,60,000
Profit after tax or Net profit	5,00,000	6,60,000

(i) EPS: $\frac{\text{Profit after tax}}{\text{No. of ordinary shares}}$ $\frac{5,00,000}{20,000} = \mathbf{25}$ $\frac{660000}{20,000} = \mathbf{33}$

Percentage increase in EPS

(ii) Operating leverage

$\frac{(c)}{(op)}$ $\frac{16,00,000}{12,00,000} = \mathbf{1.3}$ $\frac{19,20,000}{15,20,000} = \mathbf{1.26}$

(iii) Financial leverage

$\frac{(op)}{(PBT)}$ $\frac{12,00,000}{10,00,000} = \mathbf{1.2}$ $\frac{15,20,000}{13,20,000} = \mathbf{1.15}$

Illustration 8

The following data relate of Company Praveen Ltd.

Sales	4,00,000
Less: Variable expenses (30%)	1,20,000
Contribution	2,80,000
Fixed operating expenses	2,00,000
EBIT	80,000
Less: Interest	10,000
Taxable income	70,000

(1) Using the concept of leverage, by what percentage will taxable income increase if sales increase by 6 per cent.

(2) Using the concept of operating leverage by what percentage will EBIT increase if there is a 10 per cent increase in sale.

(3) Using the concept of financial leverage, by what percentage will taxable income increase if EBIT increases by 6 per cent.

Solution

(1) Degree of composite leverage on sales level of Rs.

$$\frac{\text{Contribution}}{\text{Taxable income}} = \frac{2,80,000}{70,000} = 4$$

If sales increase by 6 per cent, taxable income will increase by **4 × 6 = 24** per cent.

$$\frac{16,800 \times 100}{70,000} = 24\%$$

Workings

Sales	4,24,000
Less: Variable expenses (30%)	1,27,200
Contribution	2,96,800
Less: Fixed expenses	2,00,000
EBIT	96,800
Less: Interest	10,000
Taxable Income	86,800

Income in Taxable Income Rs. **16,800** i.e. **24%** over Rs. **70,000.**

(2) Degree of operating leverage on sales level of Rs. **4,00,000**

$$\frac{\text{Contribution}}{\text{Operating income}} = \frac{2,80,000}{80,000} = \mathbf{3.5}$$

If sales increase by **10%** EBIT will increase by **3.5 × 10 = 35%**

Workings

Sales	4,40,000
Less: Variable expenses	1,32,000
Contribution	3,08,000
Less: Fixed expenses	2,00,000
EBIT	1,08,000

Increase is Rs. 1,08,000 – 80,000 = 28,000

(3) Degree of financial leverage if EBIT increase by

$$\frac{\text{EBIT}}{\text{Taxable income}} = \frac{80,000}{70,000} = 1.14$$

If EBIT increase by 6 per cent, taxable income will increase by **1.14 × 6 = 6.84%**

Workings

EBIT	80,000
Add: 6%	4,800
	84,800
Less: Interest	10,000
Taxable income	74,800

Increase is Rs. **74,800 – 70,000 = 4,800**

Illustration 9

From the following data relating to the accounts of Alpha Ltd., comment upon the present state, trend in respect of profitability, solvency and capitalisation of the company. Consider only two significant ratios under each head.

	2002-03 *Rs.*	*2003-04* *Rs.*
Sales	24,00,000	30,00,000
Net Block	10,00,000	16,00,000
Receivables	4,00,000	5,90,000
Payables	2,00,000	4,00,000
Cash and Bank	1,00,000	40,000
Closing stock	4,00,000	8,00,000
Bank O/D	2,00,000	5,00,000
Purchases	18,00,000	24,00,000
Expenses	2,00,000	3,00,000
Depreciation	1,50,000	2,40,000
Interest on O/D	30,000	80,000
Loan	—	4,00,000
Interest on Loan	—	70,000
Share Capital	8,00,000	8,00,000
Reserves & Surplus	3,80,000	4,15,000
Provision for Income tax	2,40,000	3,95,000
Proposed Dividend	80,000	1,20,000
Stock on	3,60,000	—

Solution

Basic Calculations

(i) Profit and Loss Statement

		Rs.		Rs.
Sales (1)		24,00,000		30,00,000
Less: Cost of Goods sold (2).				
Operating stock	3,60,000		4,00,000	
Add purchases	18,00,000		24,00,000	
	21,60,000		28,00,000	
Less: closely stock	4,00,000	17,60,000	8,00,000	20,00,000
Gross profit (1) – (2) = (3)		6,40,000		10,00,000
Expenses	2,00,000		3,00,000	
Depreciation	1,50,000		2,40,000	
Interest on overdraft	30,000	3,80,000	80,000	6,20,000
Profit before Interest and Tax (3) –(4) = (5)		2,60,000		3,80,000
Less: Interest on Loan (6)		—		70,000
Profit before Tax (PBT) (7)		2,60,000		3,10,000
Provision for Taxation (8)				1,55,000
Profit after Tax (PAT) (9)				1,55,000
Proposed Dividend (10)				1,20,000
Transfer to Reserve (11)				35,000

Alpha Ltd.

(ii) Balance sheet as on 31st March.

		Rs.		Rs.
Net Block:		10,00,000		16,00,000
Net current Assets:				
(a) – (b)				
Receivable	4,00,000		5,90,000	
Cash at bank	1,00,000		40,000	
Quick assets	5,00,000		6,30,000	
Stock	4,00,000		8,00,000	
(a)	9,00,000		14,30,000	
Liabilities other than overdraft:				
Payables	2,00,000		4,00,000	

Provision for taxation	2,40,000		3,95,000	
Proposed Dividend	80,000		1,20,000	
	5,20,000		9,15,000	
Bank overdraft	2,00,000		5,00,000	
(b)	7,20,000	1,80,000	14,15,000	15,000
Capital Employed (1) + (2) = (3)		11,80,000		16,15,000
Represented by:				
Share Capital		8,00,000		8,00,000
Reserve & Surplus		3,80,000		4,15,000
		11,80,000		12,15,000
Loan		—		4,00,000
Capital Employed		11,80,000		16,15,000

At the end of March 2003 the provision for taxation appears to be dis-proportionate to the amount of the profit before tax of Rs. 2,60,000. It may be possible that the figure of tax provision includes an amount in respect of unassessed income of previous years or provision made in excess of what is genuinely required.

(i) Profitability 2002-03 2003-04

(1) Gross profit ratio = $\frac{\text{Gross profit}}{\text{Sales}} \times 100$ $\quad \frac{6,40,000 \times 100}{24,00,000}$ $\quad \frac{10,00,000 \times 100}{30,00,000}$

= 26.7% **= 33.3%**

(2) Return on Capital Employed = $\frac{\text{Profit before interest and tax}}{\text{Capital employed}} \times 100$

$$\frac{2,60,000}{11,80,000} \times 100 \qquad \frac{3,80,000}{16,15,000} \times 100$$

= 22.03% **= 23.53%**

(ii) Solvency

(1) Current Ratio= $\frac{\text{Current Assets}}{\text{Current Liabilities}} = \frac{9,00,000}{7,20,000} =$ **1.25**

$= \frac{14,30,000}{14,15,000} =$ **1.01**

(2) Liquidity Ratio $= \dfrac{\text{Liquid Assets}}{\text{Current Liabilities}} = \dfrac{5,00,000}{7,20,000} = \mathbf{0.69}$

$= \dfrac{6,30,000}{14,15,000} = \mathbf{0.45}$

(3) Fixed Assets Ratio $= \dfrac{\text{Fixed Assets}}{\text{Long term Funds}} = \dfrac{10,00,000}{11,80,000} = \mathbf{0.85}$

$= \dfrac{16,00,000}{16,15,000} = \mathbf{0.99}$

(iii) Capitalisation

(1) Debt Equity Ratio

(ignoring bank overdraft as debt) $= \dfrac{\text{Long term loans}}{\text{Shareholder's funds}}$

$\dfrac{0}{11,80,000} = 0 \quad \dfrac{4,00,000}{12,15,000} = \mathbf{0.33}$

(2) Capital Gearing Ratio

$\dfrac{\text{Preference share capital + Debentures + Loan}}{\text{Equity share capital}}$

$\dfrac{0}{11,80,000} = 0 \quad 0.33 : 1$

(3) Fixed Assets Ratio $= \dfrac{\text{Fixed Assets}}{\text{Long-term funds}} = \dfrac{10,00,000}{11,80,000} = 0.85$

$= \dfrac{16,00,000}{16,15,000} = 0.99$

Illustration 10

A Ltd. has a share capital of Rs. **2,00,000** divided into share of Rs. **10** each. It has a major expansion programme requiring an investment of another Rs. **1,00,000**. The management is considering the following alternatives for raising this amount:

(i) Issue of **10,000** equity shares of Rs. **10** each.
(ii) Issue of **10,000,** 12 per cent preference shares of Rs. **10** each.
(iii) Issue of **10 per cent** debentures of Rs. **1,00,000.**

The company's present earnings before interest and tax (EBIT) are Rs. **80,000** p.a. You are required to calculate the effect of each of the above modes of financing of the earnings per share (EPS) presuming:

(a) EBIT continues to be the same even after expansion.

(b) EBIT increase by Rs. **20,000**.

Solution

(a) When EBIT is Rs. **80,000** p.a.
Present and projected earning per share.

	Present Capital Structure (All Equity)	*Proposed Capital Structure* (i) (All Eqty)	(ii) (Eqty + Pref)	(iii) (Eqty + Debt)
EBIT	80,000	80,000	80,000	80,000
Less: Interest	—	—	--	10,000
PBT	80,000	80,000	80,000	70,000
Less: Tax	40,000	40,000	40,000	35,000
PAT	40,000	40,000	40,000	35,000
Less: Pref. dividend	—	—	12,000	—
Profit for equity share-holders	40,000	40,000	28,000	35,000
No. of equity shares	20,000	30,000	20,000	20,000
EPS	2	1.33	1.44	1.75
Dilution against initial EPS of Rs. 2	—	0.67	0.56	0.25

The above table shows that dilution of earning per share has been the least when funds have been raised by issue of debentures:

(b) When EBIT is Rs. **1,00,000** p.a.
Present and projected earning per share.

	Present Capital Structure (All Equity)	*Proposed Capital Structure*		
		(i) (All Eqty)	(ii) (Eqty + Pref)	(iii) (Eqty + Debt)
EBIT	80,000	1,00,000	1,00,000	1,00,000
Less: Interest	—	—	—	10,000
PBT	80,000	1,00,000	1,00,000	90,000
Less: Tax	40,000	50,000	50,000	45,000
PAT	40,000	50,000	50,000	45,000
Less: Pref. dividend	—	—	12,000	—
Profit for equity share-holders	40,000	50,000	38,000	45,000
No. of equity shares	20,000	30,000	20,000	20,000
EPS	2	1.66	1.9	2.25
Change in EPS as against initial of Rs. 2.	—	(–) 0.33	–0.10	+ 0.25

Illustration 11

The summarised Balance Sheets of a company which has a good record of expansion are as under:

(Rs. in lakhs)

	2004	*2003*		*2004*	*2003*
Liabilities			**Assets**		
Share capital	336.00	192.00	Land	67.20	72.00
Reserves	280.96	376.24	Buildings	388.80	268.80
Provision for Depreciation	130.16	86.88	Machinery	158.40	96.00
Debentures	72.00	48.00	Tools	19.20	33.60
Bank overdraft	4.56	3.26	Investment in Associated companies	8.64	7.20
Trade creditors	12.54	29.76			
Interest accrued	4.80	2.88	Stock	100.80	104.64
Doubtful Debts	2.16	1.10	Prepaid Expenses	0.58	0.68

Provision for taxation	2.56	1.44	Debtors	96.48	57.12
			Cash & Bank balance	4.64	4.32
			Discount on Debentures	1.00	1.20
			Goodwill	—	96.00
	845.74	741.56		845.74	741.56

Summarised Profit and Loss Account for the year ended 31 Decembers 2004 as follows:

		(Rs. in lacs)
Sales		622.00
Manufacturing & other expenses	329.92	
Selling & Distribution expenses	141.60	
General expenses	75.40	
Interest on Debentures	3.60	
Depreciation on Building, Machinery and Tools	59.28	609.80
Net profit before tax		12.20
Provision for taxation		4.00
Net profit after taxation		8.20

The chairman of the company is unable to determine the reasons for the charges in working capital. You are requested to assist him and prepare a statement of sources and application of funds for the year 2004 together with supporting schedules. On a scrutiny of records, the following information relating to 2004 accounts are found to be relevant for the purpose of your work:

(1) Machinery costing Rs. 2.16 lacs was scrapped and written off. Accrued depreciation on this machinery was Rs. **1,60,000**.
(2) There was as issue of share capital during August 2004 at par.
(3) An interim dividend of **3.5 per cent** was paid in January 2004.
(4) There were no purchases or sales of tools during 2004.
(5) A small piece of land was sold for Rs. **4.80 lakhs**.

Solution

Schedule of Changes in Working Capital

(Rs. in lakhs)

Assets	2003	2004	Increase in WC	Decrease in WC
Currents Assets				
Stock	104.64	100.80	—	3.84
Prepaid expenses	0.68	0.58	—	0.10
Debtors	57.12	96.48	39.36	—
Cash and bank	4.32	4.64	0.32	—
	166.76	202.50		
Current Liabilities				
Bank overdraft	3.26	4.56	—	1.30
Creditors	29.76	12.54	17.22	—
Interest accrued	2.88	4.80	—	1.92
Provision for doubtful debts	1.10	2.16	—	1.06
Provision for taxation	1.44	2.56	—	1.12
	38.44	26.62		
Working Capital	128.32	175.88	—	—
Net increase in W.C.	47.56	—	—	47.56
	175.88	175.88	56.90	56.90

Statement of Sources and Application of Funds

(Rs. in lakhs)

Sources		Applications	
Issue of Share Capital	144.00	Purchase of Investments in associated companies	1.44
Issue of debentures	24.00	Purchase of building	120.00
Sale of land	4.80	Purchase of machinery	64.56
Funds from operations	67.48	Dividend paid	6.72
		Net increase in W.C.	47.56
	240.28		240.28

Workings

Funds from operations	*(Rs. in lakhs)*
Net profit after tax (as given)	8.20
Add: Depreciation on buildings, machinery and tools	

(non-fund item)	59.28
Funds generated	67.48
Purchase of Buildings	
Opening balance (at cost)	268.80
Closing balance (at cost)	388.80
Purchase during the year	120.00
Purchase of Machinery	
Opening balance (at cost)	96.00
Less: Scrapped and written off (at cost)	2.16
	93.84
Closing balance	158.40
Purchase during the year	64.56
Purchase of Investments	
Opening balance	7.20
Closing balance	8.64
Purchased during the year	1.44

Note: (1) Bank overdraft and provision for taxation have been considered as current liabilities.

(2) Net profit after tax has been taken from Profit and Loss Account which has been arrived at without debting non-funds and non-operating items: hence Goodwill written off, discount on debentures written off, Machinery scrapped and Interim Dividend have not been added back while finding funds from operations. Depreciation on Building. Machinery and Tools which has already been debited to Profit and Loss A/c has been added back while finding Funds from operation, being a non-fund charge.

Illustration 12

Below are given summarised Income Statement and Balance Sheet of Vasu Textiles Ltd.

Income Statement for the year ended on 31-12-2004

(Rs. in thousand)

	Rs.
Sales	3200
Less: Cost of goods sold	2620
Gross Margin	580
Less: Selling and administration expenses	80

Net operating Income (EBIT)	500
Less: Interest	90
Earnings before tax	410
Tax paid	164
Net Income after Tax	246
Earnings per share (EPS)	3.07

Balance Sheet
As on 31-12-2004

(Rs. in thousands)

Liabilities	Rs.	**Assets**	Rs.
Paid up Capital (80,000 shares of Rs. 10 each fully paid)	800	Net Fixed Assets	1600
		Inventory	800
Retained earnings	240	Debtors	350
Debentures	1400	Marketable Securities	150
Creditors	360	Cash	100
Bills payable	40		
Other Current Liabilities	160		
	3000		3000

Price per share	15.00
Industry's average ratios are:	
Current Ratio	2.40
Quick Ratio	1.50
Sales to Inventory	8.00
Average Collection Period	36 days
Price per share/Book value of the share	1.6
Debts to Assets	40%
Times Interest Earned	6%
Profit Margin	7%
Price to earning ratio	15%
Return to Total Assets	11%

(a) Vasu textiles would like to borrow Rs. 10,00,000 from a bank for less than a year. Evaluate the firm's current financial position by calculating ratios, that you feel would be useful for the bank's evaluation.

(b) What problem areas are suggested by your ratio analysis? What are the possible reasons for them?

(c) Do you think bank should grant the loan?

Solution

Vasu Textile Ltd.
Computation of Ratios for Evaluation

(*Rs. in thousands*)

	Firm's Ratio	Industry Average
(a) **Current Ratio** $= \dfrac{\text{Current Assets}}{\text{Current Liabilities}}$		
Current Assets = 800 + 350 + 150 +100 = 1400		
Current Liabilities = 360 + 40 + 160 = 560		
Current Ratio $= \dfrac{1400}{560}$	2.50	2.40
(b) **Quick Ratio** $= \dfrac{\text{Liquid Assets}}{\text{Current Liabilities}}$		
Liquid Assets = 350 + 150 + 100 = 600		
Quick Ratio $= \dfrac{600}{560}$	1.07	1.50
(c) **Sales to Inventory** $= \dfrac{\text{Sales}}{\text{Inventory}} \; \dfrac{3200}{800}$	4.00	8.00
(d) **Average Collection** Period $= \dfrac{\text{Debtors}}{\text{Average daily sales}} = \dfrac{350}{\frac{3200}{720}}$	= 4.00	3.60
(e) **Price per share to book value of the share:** $= \dfrac{\text{Price per share}}{\text{Book value of share}}$		
Book value $= \dfrac{1040}{80} = 13 \quad \dfrac{15}{13} = 1.15$	1.15	1.60
$\left[\text{Book value of share} = \dfrac{\text{Paid up capital + Retained earning}}{\text{No. of shares}}\right]$		
(f) Debts to Assets $= \dfrac{\text{Debts}}{\text{Assets}} = \dfrac{1400}{3000} \times 100$	= 46.6%	40%
(g) Times EBIT $= \dfrac{\text{Earnings before interest \& tax}}{\text{Interest}} \dfrac{500}{90}$	= 5.56%	6%

(h) Profit Margin = $\frac{\text{Net profit}}{\text{Sales}} \times 100 = \frac{246}{3200} \times 100 = 7.66\%$ 7%

(i) Price to earning ratio = $\frac{\text{Price per share}}{\text{EPS}} \frac{15}{3.075} = 4.88\%$ 15%

(j) Return on Total Assets = $\frac{\text{N.P.}}{\text{Total Assets}} = \frac{226}{3000} \times 100 = 8.2\%$ 11%

(a) Various ratios have been computed and given in the table for analysis purpose. A final word about further borrowing will be decided only after discussing various ratios and problem areas of the firm.

(b) The current ratio of the firm is above than that of the industry but quick ratio is much less in comparison. The difference between current and quick ratios reveal the value of inventory in hand. Out of Rs. **14,00,000** in current assets, inventory accounts for Rs. **8,00,000**. The average collection period of the firm is more than that of industry. If the average collection period has been rising in the past then it is an alarming situation for the firm. The slow movement of the stock may be due to absolute or demaged goods. The credit policy of the firm should also be reviewed to expedite debt collection.

The debt/assets ratio is higher for the firm than the industry average. It shows that the firm has comparatively borrowed more money in relation to its assets. Interest coverage of the firm is slightly lower for the firm in comparison to industry. The creditors may not like to lend more money to the firm at prevailing interest rates. The firm may be required to pay higher rates of interest for future borrowings.

The price earning ratio and price to book value are much below the industry averages. It may be due to more debt funding and lower use of assets. The investment in the firm looks risky and it may adversely affect the future growth of the firm.

(c) By keeping in view the above analysis, the bank may not grant loan to the firm. Even if the bank decides to give loan, it may ask for higher rate of interest.

PONDS

Illustration 13

Financial Data
for the year ending on March 31, 2005

(Rs. in lakhs)

	2004	*2005*
Revenue (REV)	13122	19546
Operating profit (PBOIT)	1250	1678
Depreciation	176	230
PBIT	1074	1448
Interest	432	752
Tax	0	130
Profit after Tax (PAT)	642	566
Share Capital	632	632
Reserve and Surplus	2260	2528
Borrowings	2946	3060
Capital employed	5838	6220
Gross fixed assets	2672	3178
EPS	10.17	8.97
DPS	5.00	5.00

Comment on Pond's performance. Show computations to support your answer.

Solution

Financial Analysis

Ratio	*Financial dimension*	*2004*	*2005*	*Change*
REV/CF	Turnover	2.25	3.14	Increase
PBIT/REV	Margin	8.20	7.40	Decrease
PBIT/CE	RoI	18.40	23.30	Increase
PAT/PBIT	Tax leverage	59.80	39.10	Decrease
CE/NW	Finance leverage	2.02	1.97	Decrease
PAT/NW	RoE	22.20	17.97	Decrease

Pond's registered on impressive growth in revenue. Although revenue increased by **49 per cent** operating profit increased by **34 per cent** and PBIT increased by **35 per cent**. However, PAT declined by **12 per cent** due to **74 per cent** increase in interest and **31 per cent** increase in depreciation. As a result EPS reduced to Rs. **8.97** in 2005 from Rs. **10.17 in 2004**. The company maintained DPS at Rs. **5**, which tended to increase payout ratio to **50.8 per cent** from **44.3 per cent** in 2004.

Pond's margin reduced in **2005**, but was more than compensated by improved utilisation of capital; its turnover increased to **3.14** in **2005** from **2.1** in **2004**. This resulted in an impressive improvement in before tax return on investment. However, the company paid more interest and tax in **2005**, while maintaining debt equity ratio. The resided in about **4 per cent** drop in its RoE in **2005**. Lower RoE and lower retention (or higher payout) in **2005**, reduced the company's equity growth.

Illustration 14

From the following particulars of Mr. Harish, prepare fund flow statement on (i) Working Capital Basis, and (ii) Cash Basis.

	1st Jan. 2004 *Rs.*	*31st Dec. 2004* *Rs.*
Cash	10,000	8,000
Debtors	80,000	90,000
Stock	60,000	50,000
Land	60,000	80,000
Building	1,00,000	1,10,000
Machinery	1,40,000	1,60,000
	4,50,000	4,98,000
Current Liabilities	70,000	80,000
Land from Mrs. Vani	—	50,000
Bank Loan	80,000	60,000
Capital	3,00,000	3,08,000
	4,50,000	4,98,000

During the year, Mr. Harish brought an additional capital of Rs. **20,000** and his drawings during the year were Rs. **62,000**.

Provision for depreciation on machinery—opening balance Rs. **60,000**, closing balance Rs. **80,000**. No depreciation need be provided for other assets.

Solution

(i) Working Capital Basis

Schedule of Changes in Working Capital

	Jan. 1, 2004 *Rs.*	*Dec. 31, 2004* *Rs.*	*Increase in W.C.* *Rs.*	*Decrease in W.C.* *Rs.*
Currents Assets:				
Cash	10,000	8,000		2,000
Debtors	80,000	90,000	10,000	
Stock	60,000	50,000		10,000
	1,50,000	1,58,000		
Current Liabilities:				
Current Liabilities	70,000	80,000		10,000
	70,000	80,000		
Working Capital (CA–CL)	80,000	68,000		
Net Decrease in W.C.			12,000	12,000
			22,000	22,000

Funds Flow Statement (on working Capital Basis) for the year ended December 31, 2004

Sources	*Rs.*	*Applications*	*Rs.*
Additional Capital Introduced	20,000	Purchase of Land	20,000
Loan Raised from Mrs. Vani	50,000	Purchase of Building	10,000
Cash operating profit	70,000	Purchase of Machinery	40,000
Net Decrease in W.C.	12,000	Drawings	62,000
		Repayment of Loan	20,000
	1,52,000		1,52,000

(ii) Cash Basis

Funds Flow Statement on Cash Basis for the year ended 31st December 2004

Sources (Inflows)	*Rs.*	*Application (Outflow)*	*Rs.*
Opening Balance of cash on January 1, 2004	10,000	Purchase of Land	20,000
Additional Capital	20,000	Purchase of Building	10,000

Introduced			
Decrease in stock	10,000	Purchase of Machinery	40,000
Increase in Current Liabilities	10,000	Increase in Debtors	10,000
Loans raised from Mrs. Vani	50,000	Repayment of Bank Loan	20,000
Cash operating profit	70,000	Drawings	62,000
		Closing Balance of Cash on December 31, 2004	8,000
	1,70,000		1,70,000

Workings

1. Land A/c

	Rs.		Rs.
To Balance b/d	60,000	By Balance c/d	80,000
To cash-purchases (bal. fig.)	20,000		
	80,000		80,000

2. Building A/c

	Rs.		Rs.
To Balance b/d	1,00,000	By Balance c/d	1,10,000
To cash-purchases (bal. fig.)	10,000		
	1,10,000		1,10,000

3. Machinery A/c

	Rs.		Rs.
To Balance b/d	1,40,000	By Depreciation	20,000
To cash-purchases (bal. fig.)	40,000	By Balance c/d	1,60,000
	1,80,000		1,80,000

4. Capital A/c

	Rs.		Rs.
To Cash (drawings)	62,000	By Balance b/d	3,00,000
To Balance c/d	3,08,000	By Cash (addition)	20,000
		By Profit (bal. fig.)	50,000
	3,70,000		3,70,000

5. Cash Operating Profit

	Rs.
Profit mode during the year	50,000
Add: Depreciation charged during the year being non-cash item	20,000
Cash Operating Profit	70,000

Illustration 15

From the following Comparative Balance Sheet and Income Statement of Janardhan Ltd., prepare a statement of changes in financial position:

Janardhan Limited

Comparative Balance Sheet

For the year ended 31st December, 2004 and 2003

Particulars	**2004**	**2003**
Current Assets:		
Cash	1,40,000	1,00,000
Debtors	80,000	90,000
Stock (Inventory)	2,50,000	1,80,000
Total Current Assets	4,70,000	3,70,000
Fixed Assets:		
Land and Building	3,00,000	2,00,000
Plant and Machinery	4,40,000	4,00,000
Less: Accumulated depreciation	(–1,64,000)	(–1,60,000)
Total Fixed Assets	5,76,000	4,40,000
Total Assets	10,46,000	8,10,000
Current Liabilities:		
Creditors	50,000	60,000

Salaries payable	30,000	20,000
Provision for tax	1,00,000	1,20,000
Provision for dividend	80,000	80,000
Total Current Liabilities	2,60,000	2,80,000
Long-term Liabilities:		
Bank Loan	46,000	30,000
Debentures	2,40,000	3,00,000
Total Long-term Liabilities	2,86,000	3,30,000
Total Liabilities	5,46,000	6,10,000

Solution

Statement of Changes in Financial Position

Sources:	
Funds from operations	2,42,000
Sales of plant	72,000
Loan from bank	16,000
Issue of shares:	
for cash	1,10,000
as stock dividend*	40,000
to convert debentures*	60,000
(A)	5,40,000
Applications	
Purchase of land and buildings	1,00,000
Purchase of plant and machinery	1,40,000
Payment of dividend:	
in cash	80,000
as stock*	40,000
Redemption of debentures by conversion into shares	60,000
(B)	4,20,000
Increase in working Capital **(A) – (B)**	1,20,000

Working Notes

Adjusted Reserves and Surplus Account

To proposed Dividend	1,20,000	By Balance b/d	35,000
To Accumulated Dep. A/c	44,000	By Plant Machinery A/c (Profit on sale)	12,000
To Balance c/d	1,25,000	By Funds from operations (bal. fig.)	2,42,000
	2,89,000		2,89,000

* **Proposed dividend has been added back to find out real funds from operations.**

	2004	2003
Owner's Equity:		
Share capital	3,50,000	1,50,000
Share premium	25,000	15,000
Reserves & Surplus	1,25,000	35,000
	5,00,000	2,00,000
Total Equities	10,46,000	8,10,000

Janardhan Limited Income Statement
for the year ended 31st December, 2004

Sales		10,00,000
Less: Cost of goods sold		4,20,000
Gross profit		5,80,000
Less: Operating Expenses:		
Office and Administration Expenses	90,000	
Selling and Distribution	50,000	
Interest	24,000	
Depreciation	44,000	2,08,000
Operating profit		3,72,000
Add: Gain on sale of plant		12,000
Total profit		3,84,000
Less: Income-tax		1,70,000
Net profit		2,14,000

Additional Information

(1) During the year plant Rs. 1,00,000 (accumulated depreciation Rs. 40,000) was sold.
(2) The debentures of Rs. 60,000 were converted into share capital at par.
(3) The company declared a cash dividend of Rs. 80,000 and a stock dividend of Rs. 40,000 for year.
(4) The company issued 10,000 additional shares, par value Rs. 10 per share, at a premium of 10 per cent during the year.

Plant and Machinery Account

To Balance b/d	4,00,000	By Accumulated Dep. A/c	40,000
To Adjusted Reserves and surplus A/c	12,000	By cash (sale)	72,000
To cash (purchase—bal. fig.)	1,40,000	By Balance c/d	4,40,000
	5,52,000		5,52,000

Accumulated Depreciation Account

To Plant A/c	40,000	By Balance b/d	1,60,000
To Balance c/d	1,64,000	By Adjusted Reserves and Surplus A/c (Dep.)	44,000
	2,04,000		2,04,000

Illustration 16

Laxmi Narayan Trading Co. Ltd. provides the following information.

1,60,000 equity shares of Rs. 10 each	16,00,000
9 per cent 60,000 preference shares of Rs. 10 each	6,00,000
	22,00,000

Profit after tax at 60 per cent	Rs. 5,40,000
Depreciation	Rs. 1,20,000
Equity dividend paid	20%
Market price of equity share	Rs. 80

You are required to calculate:

(a) Dividend yield on equity share
(b) Cover for the preference dividend
(c) Cover for the equity dividend
(d) Earnings per share

(e) The price earnings ratio
(f) Net cash flow.

Solution

(a) Dividend yield on equity share $= \frac{\text{Dividend}}{\text{Market price}} \times 100$

$$= \frac{2}{80} \times 100 = 2.5\%$$

(b) Cover for the preference dividend $= \frac{\text{Profit after tax}}{\text{Preference dividend}}$

$$= \frac{5{,}40{,}000}{54{,}000} = 10 \text{ times}$$

(c) Cover for the equity dividend $= \frac{\text{PAT-Preference dividend}}{\text{Equity dividend}}$

$$\frac{5{,}40{,}000 - 54{,}000}{32{,}000} = \frac{4{,}86{,}000}{32{,}000} = 1.518$$

(d) Earning per share $= \frac{\text{PAT} - \text{Preference dividend}}{\text{Number of equity shares}}$

$$= \frac{5{,}40{,}000 - 54{,}000}{1{,}60{,}000} = \frac{4{,}86{,}000}{1{,}60{,}000} = 3.03$$

(e) Price earnings ratio $= \frac{\text{Market price per share}}{\text{Earnings per share}} = \frac{80}{3.03} = 26.40$

(f) Net cash flow = Total cash flow – Dividend
Total cash flow = Net profit + Depreciation – Dividend
= 5,40,000 + 1,20,000 – 3,20,000 + 54,000
= 6,60,000 – 3,74,000 = 2,86,000

Illustration 17

Kasturi Textiles Ltd. provides the following information relating to last year earnings:

(a) Income tax 60 per cent
(b) PBT Rs. 48,92,000
(c) Proposed dividend 20 per cent
(d) Preference share capital (9%) Rs. 20,00,000

(e) Equity share capital 60,000 shares 100/- each Rs. 60,00,000.
(f) Reserves and surplus in the beginning of the year Rs. 44,00,000.

From the above information, calculate (for equity share):

(i) Earnings per share
(ii) Book value per share
(iii) Earnings yield ratio
(iv) Price earnings ratio
(v) Dividend payment ratio
(vi) The current market price of the equity share is Rs. 400.

Solution

(a) Calculation of earnings per share

$$= \frac{\text{NP available to equity share holders}}{\text{No. of equity shares}}$$

PBT	
48,92,000	
(–) Tax 60 per cent	29,35,200
	19,56,800
(–) Preference dividend:	1,80,000
(9% on 20,00,000)	
Earnings available to equity shareholders	17,76,800

EPS = 17,76,800/60,000 = **29.60**

(b) Book value per share

$$= \frac{\text{Earnings available to equity share holders}}{\text{No. of equity shares}}$$

Net profit	17,76,800
(–) Proposed dividend	12,00,000
Rs. 60,00,000 (20%)	5,76,800
Add: Reserves	44,00,000

49,76,800 + 60,00,000 = 1,09,76,800

$$= \frac{1,09,76,800}{60,000} = 182.95$$

(c) Earnings yield ratio

$$= \frac{\text{Net profit available for equity holders}}{\text{Amount available for equity share holders}} \times 100$$

$$= \frac{17,76,800}{1,09,76,800} \times 100 = 16.19\%$$

(d) Price earnings ratio $= \dfrac{\text{EPS}}{\text{Market Price per share}} \times 100$

$$= \frac{29.61}{400} \times 100 = 7.40\%$$

(e) Dividend payment ratio $= \dfrac{\text{Proposed dividend}}{\text{Net profit}} \times 100$

$$= \frac{12,00,000}{17,756,800} \times 100 = 67.54\%$$

Illustration 18

Mahesh Textiles Ltd. engaged in capital Intensive industry and it has been in operations for 15 years. The company deployed capital employed **Rs. 340 lakhs**. The equity share capital and reserves **Rs. 200 lakhs**. The company has raised **Rs. 100 lakhs** from debentures and **Rs. 40 lakhs** from cash credit from banks. Annual sales is **Rs. 160 lakhs**. The working capital of the company is provided as below:

(a) Stock Rs. 60 lakhs
(b) Stores Rs. 28 lakhs
(c) Debtors Rs. 70 lakhs
(d) Advance Rs. 12 lakhs

Calculate six financial ratios from the above for the use of company management.

Solution

The liquidity ratios and solvency ratios are useful to the management.

(Rs. in lakhs)

Liabilities		**Assets**	
Share capital and reserves	200	Stock	60
Long term borrowings	100	Stores	28
Bank overdraft (cc)	40	Debtors	70
		Advances, Deposits	12
		Fixed assets (assumed)	170
	340		340

Liquidity ratios

(a) Current ratio, (b) Liquidity ratio

(a) Current ratio = Current assets/Current liabilities

= 170/40 = **4.25**

(b) Liquidity ratio = Liquid assets/Current liabilities

= 41/20 = **2.05**

Solvency Ratios: (a) Debt equity ratio, (b) proprietory ratio, (c) Fixed assets to proprietors funds, (d) Fixed assets ratio:

(a) $\text{Debt equity ratio} = \dfrac{\text{Outsiders funds}}{\text{Shareholders funds}}$

$$= \frac{100{+}40}{200} = \frac{140}{200} = 0.7$$

(b) $\text{Proprietary ratio} = \dfrac{\text{Shareholders fund}}{\text{Total assets}}$

$$= \frac{200}{60 + 28 + 70 + 12 + 170}$$

$$= \frac{200}{340} = 0.58$$

(c) $\text{Fixed assets to proprietors funds} = \dfrac{\text{Fixed assets}}{\text{Shareholders fund}}$

$$= \frac{170}{200} = 0.85$$

(d) $\text{Fixed assets ratio} = \dfrac{\text{Fixed assets}}{\text{Total long term funds}}$

$$= \frac{170}{200+100} = \frac{170}{300} = 0.56$$

Illustration 19

Suresh Polysters Ltd., provides the following information for your analysis. As a financial analyst you are called upon to make a comparative assessment of the following **three** possible positions for a certain period.

P/S	*Position I*	*Position II*	*Position III*
(a) Debt	2,00,000	5,00,000	8,00,000
(b) Equity	8,00,000	5,00,000	2,00,000
	10,00,000	10,00,000	10,00,000

(i) Calculate the Debt equity ratio
(ii) The rate of Interest on Debt is 10 per cent.
(iii) Calculate the maximum rate of dividend payable to its shareholders, when the rate of earnings is:–
   (a) 8 per cent (under position I, II, and III)
   (b) 16 per cent (under position I, II, and III)
   (c) 24 per cent (under position I, II, and III)

Solution

(i) **Calculation of Debt equity ratio**
Debt equity ratio = Debt/equity

Particulars	*Position I*	*Position II*	*Position III*
(a) Debt equity ratio	0.25	1	4
(b) Maximum rate of dividend (8%)	7.50%	6%	—
(c) Maximum rate of dividend (16%)	17.50%	22%	40%
(d) Maximum rate of dividend (24%)	27.50%	38%	80%

(e) Income tax has been ignored due to non-disclosure of tax rate.

(a) Debt equity ratio Position I 2,00,000/8,00,000 = **0.25**
Position II 5,00,000/5,00,000 = **1.00**
Position III 8,00,000/2,00,000 = **4.00**

Maximum rate of dividend

Earnings 8 per cent on Rs. 10,00,000	80,000
Position I (–) Interest on debt 10 per cent	20,000
Surplus available for dividend	60,000

$$\therefore \frac{60{,}000}{8{,}00{,}000} \times 100 = \mathbf{7.5\%}$$

Position II Earnings	80,000
(–) Interest on debt 10 per cent	50,000
Surplus available for dividend	30,000

$$\frac{30{,}000}{5{,}00{,}000} \times 100 = 6\%$$

Position III Earnings			80,000
(–) Interest on debt 10 per cent			80,000
			00,000

	I	II	III
Maximum rate of dividend (Earnings 16%)	1,60,000	1,60,000	1,60,000
(–) Interest on debt 10%	20,000	50,000	80,000
	1,40,000	1,10,000	80,000
	$\frac{140000}{800000}\times 100$	$\frac{110000}{500000}\times 100$	$\frac{80,000}{200000}\times 100$
	17.5%	**22%**	**40%**

	I	II	III
(Earnings 24%)			
Maximum rate of dividend			
Earnings	2,40,000	2,40,000	2,40,000
(–) Interest on debt 10 per cent	20,000	50,000	80,000
	2,20,000	1,90,000	1,60,000
Maximum rate of dividend	$\frac{2,20,000}{8,00,000}\times 100$	$\frac{1,90,000}{5,00,000}\times 100$	$\frac{1,60,000}{2,00,000}\times 100$
	= 27.5%	**38%**	**80%**

Illustration 20

Narmada Polysters Ltd. provides following data relating to its competitors in the industry. You are requested to analyse the inter firm comparison study and comment on the financial performance of the companies.

(Rs. in crore)

Company	*Sales*	*Total assets*	*Net Profit*
(1) Nithish Polysters Ltd.	20	16	0.14
(2) Dinesh Polysters Ltd.	40	20	4.0
(3) Sowmya Polysters Ltd.	16	12	1.6
(4) Ramya Polysters Ltd.	10	05	1.0
(5) Supriya Polysters Ltd.	24	08	3.0
(6) Srinath Polysters Ltd.	34	16	2.0

From the available data you are required to calculate:

(a) Assets turnover ratio
(b) Net profit margin ratio
(c) Earning power

Solution

Statement showing calculations of assets turnover ratio, net profit margin, and earning power:

(a) Assets turnover ratio = $\frac{\text{Sales}}{\text{Total assets}} \times 100$

(b) Net Profit Margin ratio = $\frac{\text{Net profit}}{\text{Sales}} \times 100$

(c) Earning Power = $\frac{\text{Net profit}}{\text{Total assets}} \times 100$

Name	*Assets turnover ratio*	*NP Ratio*	*Earning Power*
1. Nithish Polysters Ltd.	20/16 × 100 = 125%	14/20×100 = 0.7%	0.8%
2. Dinesh Polysters Ltd.	40/20×100 = 200%	4/40×100 = 10%	4/20×100 =20%
3. Sowmya Polysters Ltd.	16/12×100 = 133%	1.6/16×100 = 10%	12%
4. Ramya Polysters Ltd.	10/5×100 = 200%	1/10×100 = 10%	20%
5. Supriya Polysters Ltd.	24/8×100 = 300%	3/24×100 = 12.5%	37.5%
6. Srinath Polysters Ltd.	34/16×100 = 212.5%	2/34×100 = 6%	12.5%

Comments

The performance of Supriya Polysters Ltd. is **the best all.** Nithish Polyster Ltd. is the worst performance. Ramya Polyster Ltd., and Sowmya Polyster Ltd. performance is identical.

Illustration 21

Below is given the Balance Sheet of Gowthami Ltd. as at 31st March, 2005 together with the Profit and Loss Account.

(Rs. in thousands)

Liability	*Rs.*	*Assets*	*Rs.*
Equity share capital	1000	Trade Investment	400
Dividend Equilisation		Patents	60
Reserve	140	Land & Building (at cost)	640

General Reserve	220	Plant & Machinery (at cost)		1300
Profit & Loss A/c	380			
6% Debentures	500	Cash at Bank		176
Bank Overdraft	300	Stock	*Rs.*	
Staff provident fund	160	Materials	180	
Creditors	420	Finished Goods	320	
Unpaid Dividend	20	Work-in-progress	120	620
Proposed Dividend	120	Sundry Debtors	460	
Provision for Taxation	340	**Less:** Provision for doubtful debts.	**16**	444
Provision for Depreciation	500			
		Bills Receivable		60
		Staff Provident Fund Investment		160
		Deposits with Customs Authorities		60
		Advance for purchase of Machinery		120
		Preliminary Expenses		60
	Rs. 4,100			Rs. 4,100

Profit and Loss Account for the year ended 31st March, 2005

(*Rs. in thousands*)

To Stock	180	By Sales		4,000
Materials	240	By Stock	180	
Finished Goods	80	Materials	320	
Work-in-progress	500	Finished Goods	120	
To Purchase of Materials	1700	Work in Progress		620
To Wages	560	By dividend on Investment		60
To Power	80	By Sales of Scrap		16
To Misc. Factory Expenses	220			
To Office Salaries	160			
To Miscellaneous Expenses	180			
To Selling and Distribution Expenses	240			
To Advertisement	160			
To Preliminary Expenses	10			

To Debenture Interest		30	
To Depreciation			
Plant	120		
Land and Building	24	144	
To provision for taxation		340	
To proposed dividend		120	
To Balance of Profit		252	
		4696	4696

You are required to present the information aptly summarised in single-column statement (vertical form) showing distinctly the following:

(i) Total Capital Employed
(ii) Shareholder's Funds.
(iii) Gross Profit
(iv) Net operating profit.
(v) Cost of goods sold.

Solution

Gowthami Limited
Balance Sheet as on 31st March, 2005

Cash at Bank			176
Book Debts (net)			444
Bills Receivable			60
Liquid Assets		**(1)**	**680**
Deposit with Customs			60
Stock:			
Materials	180		
Finished Goods	320		
Work-in-Progress	120		620
Current Assets		**(2)**	**1360**
Bank Overdraft			300
Creditors			420
Unpaid Dividend			20

Current Liabilities	**(3)**		**740**
Proposed dividend			120
Provision for Taxation			340
Current Liabilities and Provisions	**(4)**		**1200**
Net working capital **(2)–(4)**			160
Land and Building (at cost)		640	
Plant and Machinery (at cost)		1300	
Patents		60	
Fixed Assets	**(5)**	**2000**	
Less: Provision for Depreciation		500	
Net Fixed Assets		1500	
Advance against Machinery		120	
Trade Investments		400	**2020**
Total Fixed Investment	**(6)**		
Staff Provident Funds Investments		160	
Less: Staff Provident Funds		160	—
Total Capital Employed	**(7)**		**2180**
Less: 6% Debentures	**(8)**		**500**
Shareholder's Funds	**(9)**		**1680**
Represented by:			
Equity Share Capital			1000
General Reserve			220
Dividend Equalisation Reserve			140
Profit & Loss A/c			320
(**Less:** Preliminary Expenses)			
			1680

Profit and Loss Account
For the year ended 31st March, 2005

	(*Rs. in Thousands*)
Sales:	40,000
Less: Cost of Goods Sold	2568

Gross profit		1432
Less: Operating Expenses		
Salaries	160	
Miscellaneous Expenses	180	
Selling Distribution Expenses	240	
Advertisements	160	740
Net operating profit		692
Add: Non-operating income (Dividends on Investments)	60	
Less: Non-operating Expenses (Interest on Debentures)	30	30
		722
Less: Preliminary Expenses written off		10
Profit before Tax		712
Less: Income Tax payable		340
Profit after Tax		372
Less: Proposed Dividend		120
Profit retained in the business		252

Statement of Cost of Goods Sold
for the year ended March 31, 2005

(*Rs. in thousand*)

Cost of Goods Manufactured:		
Work-in-progress on 1-4-2004		80
Materials consumed: Opening stock	180	
Purchases	1700	
	1800	
Less: Closing stock	180	1700
Wages		560
Power		80
Miscellaneous Factory Expenses		220
Depreciation		144
		2784

Less: Sale of Scrap	16	
Work-in-Progress on 31-3-2005	120	136
Cost of Goods Manufactured		2648
Add: Opening stock of Finished Goods		240
		2888
Less: Closing stock of Finished Goods		320
Cost of Goods sold		2568

Case Studies

HERO HONDA

Still Leading Two-Wheeler Race

The domestic two-wheeler market has seen a shift in consumer preference in recent years. In 1998-99, motorcycles overtook scooters to emerge as the largest product segment in the auto industry. Hero Honda is uniquely placed to expand and thrive in the two-wheeler market. The company retained its position as the single largest manufacturer of two-wheelers in the world for the third year in a row in 2003. Its best selling model Splendour is the world's largest selling motorcycle brand and has sold 10 lakhs units.

The domestic motorcycle market has expanded in the past few years due to easy availability of loans and falling interest rates. At the same time, competition among two-wheeler manufacturers has intensified. Motorcycle manufacturers have been launching a variety of models across all segments, and product launches are after accompanied by heavy discounts on new as well as existing models.

Hero Honda performed very well in fiscal 2003-04. Net profit increased by 25 per cent over the previous fiscal, and its market share in motorcycles increased by 4 percentage points to 48 percent. Net profit in the first quarters of 2004-05 increased by 20 per cent and sales volume was up 33 per cent over that in the corresponding year ago period.

But the company still faces huge challenges. The motorcycle market in India has become extremely competitive with technology evolving constantly. Hero Honda's domestic competitor's like TVS and Bajaj have launched or they are planning to launch a slew of models in the executive (mid-priced bikes in the 125-135 cc range) segment. This segment is now dominated by Hero Honda's Splendour and Passion models and account for 58 per cent of total two-wheeler sales. The company will find it increasingly difficult to withstand this onslaught without cutting prices, a difficult proposition given that input costs are rising.

Competition is also expected to intensify with the entry of foreign companies. The most significant from Hero Honda's perspective, is its own joint venture partner Honda through its Indian subsidiary, Honda Motorcycles and Scooters (India). Though both companies maintain that their models will complement, and not compete, with each other it is difficult to predict which way things will go.

Source: *Economic and Political Weekly*, January 1-7-2005, p. 9.

But the feature is not so gloomy for Hero Honda either. Though the company became somewhat complacent, allowing competitors to reduce the gap, it still would be competing from a position of strength. It is the market leader by a wide margin and has a very good distribution network. It also has a large cash hoard to face competition. The company is also entering the scooter segment, and increasing experts to hedge it bets.

(*Rs. in Lakhs*)

Financial Indicators	*Hero Honda*	
	2003-04	*2002-03*
Income/Appropriations		
1. Net sales	583243	510171
2. Value of Production	581084	512279
3. Other income	5675	2583
4. Total income	586759	514862
5. Raw materials/stores and spares/ power and fuel consumed	425596	373593
6. Other manufacturing expenses	0	0
7. Remuneration to employees	23152	20163
8. Other expenses	34988	33330
9. Depreciation	7333	6339
10. Gross profit	95690	81437
11. Interest	–135	–102
12. Operating profit	95825	81539
13. Non-operating surplus/deficit	11421	6917
14. Profit before Tax	107246	88456
15. Tax provisions	34414	30380
16. Profit after Tax	72832	58076
17. Dividends (Include tax on Dist profit)	39938	35944
18. Retained profits	32894	22132
Liabilities/Assets		
19. paid-up capital	3994	3994

(*Contd.*)

(Contd.)

Financial Indicators	*Hero Honda*	
	2003-04	*2002-03*
20. Reserves and surplus	109887	82109
21. Long-term loan	—	—
22. Short-term loan	13428	11644
(i) of which, bank borrowings		
23. Gross fixed assets	91691	78629
24. Accumulated depreciation	34579	27842
25. Inventories	18820	20092
26. Total assets/liabilities	140353	107247
Miscellaneous Items		
27. Excise duty	0	0
28. Gross value added	121412	106576
29. Total foreign exchange earnings	–	–
30. Total foreign exchange outgo	–	–
Key financial and performance ratios		
31. Turnover ratio (Sales to total assets)	4.7	5
32. Gross value added to gross fixed assets (%)	142.6	143.0
33. Return on investment (gross profit to total assets) (%)	77.3	86.9
34. Gross profit to sales (gross margin) (%)	16.4	16.0
35. Operating profit to sales (%)	16.4	16.0
36. Profit before tax to sales (%)	18.4	17.3
37. Tax provisions to profit before tax (%)	32.1	34.3
38. Profit after tax to net worth (return on equity) (%)	72.8	75.1
39. Dividend (%)	999.9	899.9
40. Earnings per share (Rs.)	36.5	29.1
41. Book value per share (Rs.)	57.0	43.1
42. P/E ratio (multiple)	11.3	10.5
43. Debt-equity ratio (adjusted for revaluation)	0.12	0.14
44. Short-term book borrowing to inventories (%)	0.0	0.0
45. Sundry Creditors to sundry debtors	1414.2	234.2
46. Total remuneration to employees to value added (%)	19.1	18.9
47. Total remuneration to employees to value of production (%)	4.0	3.9
48. Gross fixed assets formation (% growth)	16.6	11.6
49. Growth in inventories (%)	–6.3	12.6

GAIL

Energised Expansion

The Gas Authority of India (GAIL), a leading public sector 5 enterprises, is the largest gas transmission and marketing company in the country. GAIL is ranked among the 10 companies in India. Its activities range from gas marketing and distribution through trunk and regional systems, to retailing of natural gas and procession gas for production, and marketing of liquefied petroleum gas (LPG), liquid hydrocarbons and petrochemicals. The Indian gas market has traditionally been supply constrained. However, the supply side scenario is changing rapidly. The intensification of domestic exploration activities and the new exploration and licensing policy has led to the discovery of new oil and gas reserves. The current share of gas in primary energy consumption is 8 per cent. This is bound to increase as supplies emerge in geographically dispersed areas of the country. Macro economic policies would drive the demand for gas in the coming years. The industrial sector also has a large appetite for gas, and the new supplies would satisfy its need to a certain extent. Similarly, the growing urban pollution will require greater availability of compressed natural gas for the transport sector as well as for other forms of energy.

While supply sources of gas are geographically dispersed. India locks interstate pipeline infrastructure for supply of gas to the markets. In this context, the natural gas grid, conceptualised by GAIL, represents a huge opportunity for growth. The company has made some progress in the implementation of the grid, covering acquisitions, preparing feasibility studies, identification of markets and procurement of gas management systems.

GAIL has recently ventured into the telecom sector, diversification has two major aims: obtaining category A internet service provider license from Department of Telecom for leasing bandwidth to the corporate sector and signing a contract with Bharti Telescopic. However, the Oil Ministry has reportedly asked the company to stick to its core competency.

Exploration, production, import of gas and other technology-oriented projects make up the bulk of GAIL's business development plans for the coming years. GAIL is likely to focus mainly on growth in the gas sector to maintain its dominant position in the domestic market. It aims to transform itself into an integrated energy company with involvement in the upstream and downstream power sector, and also undertake projects in the countries in West Asia and South-East Asia in gas infrastructure development and processing. The company is also likely to play a pivotal role in augmenting gas supplies. It is already associated with various transnational gas pipeline projects in India and is also invalued in LNG import projects. It also plans to interface with other companies with similar initiatives for increasing gas supplies in the market. It would undertake a low-cost expansion of its infrastructure of gas pipelines and networks to increase gas usage in the market. As India has large coal and lignite deposits, GAIL is also exploring the possibility of deriving benefits from these energy resources.

Source: *Economic and Political Weekly*, January 1-7, 2005, p. 9.

(Rs. in lakhs)

Financial Indicators	*GAIL*	
	2003-04	*2002-03*
Income/Appropriations		
1. Net sales	1053918	999077
2. Value of production	1057779	999818
3. Other income	164738	167120
4. Total income	1222517	1166938
5. Raw materials/stores and spare/power and fuel consumed	808004	773631
6. Other manufacturing expenses	0	0
7. Remuneration to employees	17418	15847
8. Other expenses	35478	29903
9. Depreciation	66397	64259
10. Gross profit	294980	269640
11. Interest	13797	18637
12. Operating profit	281183	251003
13. Non-operating surplus/deficit	259	826
14. Profit before tax	281442	251829
15. Tax provisions	94508	87918
16. Profit after tax	186934	163911
17. Dividends (includes tax on Dist profit)	33826	33826
18. Retained profits	153108	130085
Liabilities/Assets		
19. Paid-up capital	84565	84565
20. Reserves and Surplus	659950	549348
21. Long-term loan	165552	16395
22. Short-term loan		
(i) of which bank borrowings	47796	18837
23. Gross fixed assets	1358473	1104871
24. Accumulated depreciation	544185	478661
25. Inventories	47491	41859
26. Total assets/liabilities	1222517	1166938

(Contd.)

(Contd.)

Financial Indicators	*GAIL*	
	2003-04	*2002-03*
Miscellaneous Items		
27. Excise duty	47183	42446
28. Gross value added	215886	184426
29. Total foreign exchange earnings	2171	14671
30. Total foreign exchange outgo	171809	67232
Key Financial and Performance Ratios		
31. Turnover ratio (sales to total assets)	0.9	1.0
32. Gross value added to gross fixed assets (%)	17.5	17.0
33. Return on investment (gross profit to total assets) (%)	24.7	26.3
34. Gross profit to sales (gross margin) (%)	28.0	27.0
35. Operating profit to sales (%)	26.7	25.1
36. Profit before tax to sales (%)	26.7	25.2
37. Tax provisions to profit before Tax (%)	33.6	34.9
38. Profit after tax to net worth (return on equity) (%)	27.1	28.1
39. Dividend (%)	40.0	40.0
40. Earnings per share (Rs.)	22.1	19.4
41. Book value per share (Rs.)	88.0	75.0
42. P/E ratio (multiple)	9.7	7.9
43. Debt-equity ratio (adjusted for revaluation)	0.29	0.32
44. Short-term bank borrowings to inventories (%)	0.0	0.0
45. Sundry creditors to sundry debtors (%)	176.0	167.2
46. Total remuneration to employees to value added (%)	8.1	8.6
47. Total remunerations to employees to value of production (%)	1.6	1.6
48. Gross fixed assets formation (% growth)	23.0	3.2
49. Growth in inventories (%)	13.5	−1.3

THERMAX

Single-Window Energy Solutions

Thermax is a leading player in the energy and environment management business. It offers a wide range of boilers, that can operate with as many as so different kinds of fuels (mainly biomass). The company has forward and backward integration in this domain to offer innovative solutions in heating, cooling water and waste management, chemicals, air pollution control and co-generation.

During the course of fiscal 2003-04 sales increased by 9.8 per cent to Rs 564 crores and net profit improved by 12.1per cent to Rs 54 crores.

This is the second successive year of profit after its turnaround in 2001-02. The company also unstressed a record order intake of Rs. 867 crores, an increase of 86 per cent over the previous year.

There was some cause for concern during the course of fiscal 2003-04. The continued rise in the cost of key inputs such as Petroleum, Steel, Copper and Styrene put pressure on the company's margins. Thermax has had to take resource to alternative global sourcing to mitigate the effects in cost competitiveness. Another factor of concern was the appreciation of the rupee against the dollar, which affected its export.

Source: *Economic and Political Weekly*, 1-7-2005, p. 9.

The Management has identified their drivers for growth in energy, which have significantly influenced the company's competitive advantage. First, there has been a distinct fuel shift from volatile and price sensitive fuels like oil and gas to locally available fuels like pet coke and biomass. This has created new opportunities for Thermax's boilers and power business lines. The second driver has been the emergence of a favourable policy environment for captive power generation. This has become a preferred method because it guarantees fixed cost, fast-track completion besides ensuring optional plant performance. Lastly, there is a strong trend towards combined heating, power and cooling processes, which optimises the use of energy in industries and commercial establishment. Thermax is well positioned to provide integrated and single-window solutions to its customers and thereby improve the latter's cost competitiveness with a right choice of fuels, equipment and value added services.

In order to realise its full potential, Thermax has hired consultancy firm Mckinsey for a transformation process designed to make it a competitive player in the global market place and significantly improve its topline and bottomline. The company is also simultaneously working on evolving into a global organisation with cost leadership.

The company is also trying to tap markets in China and Brazil for which it has set up wholly owned subsidiaries. China offers enormous potential for growth, as it consumes 50 per cent of the estimated 5600 millions worth of absorption chillers sold every year. Thermax might export to China in the first phase, and might later consider setting up an assembly unit and eventually a manufacturing facility. It is also looking at China as a sourcing base for a variety of material.

Financial Indicators	*Thermax*	
	2003-04	*2002-03*
Income/Appropriations		
1. Net Sales	56329	51271
2. Value of Production	56343	51675
3. Other income	3993	3893
4. Total income	60336	55568
5. Raw materials/Stores & Spares/ Power & Fuel consumed	36207	33591
6. Other manufacturing expenses	0	0
7. Remuneration to employees	6804	5935
8. Other expenses	8543	7900
9. Depreciation	878	969
10. Gross Profit	7904	7173
11. Interest	40	65
12. Operating Profit	7864	7108
13. Non-operating surplus/deficit	–619	–758
14. Profit before tax	7245	6350
15. Tax Provisions	1836	1526
16. Profit after tax	5409	4824
17. Dividends (includes tax on Dist profit)	3010	2860
18. Retained Profits	2399	1964
Liabilities/Assets		
19. Paid-up Capital	7149	2383
20. Reserves and Surplus	31917	34670
21. Long-term loan	—	—
22. Short-term loan		
(i) of which bank borrowings	—	—
23. Gross fixed assets	16523	16584
24. Accumulated depreciation	8443	8621
25. Inventories	5951	4696
26. Total assets/liabilities	39843	37994
Miscellaneous Items		
27. Excise duty	59	89
28. Gross value added	11524	10182
29. Total Foreign exchange earnings	11308	12091
30. Total Foreign exchange outgo	1541	1669
Key Financial and Performance Ratios		
31. Turnover ratio (Sales to total assets)	1.4	1.4
32. Gross value added to gross fixed assets (%)	69.6	61.2
33. Return on investment (gross profit to total assets) (%)	20.3	18.9
34. Gross profit to sales (gross margin) (%)	14.0	14.0
35. Operating Profit to Sales (%)	14.0	13.9
36. Profit before tax to sales (%)	12.9	12.4
37. Tax Provisions to Profit before tax (%)	25.3	24.0
38. Profit after tax to net worth (return on equity) (%)	14.2	13.3
39. Dividend (%)	42.1	120.0

(*Contd.*)

(Contd.)

Financial Indicators	*Thermax*	
	2003-04	*2002-03*
40. Earnings per share (Rs.)	22.7	20.2
41. Book value per share (Rs.)	163.9	155.5
42. P/E ratio (multiple)	22.2	13.7
43. Debt-equity ratio (adjusted for revaluation)	0	0
44. Short-term borrowings to inventories (%)	0	0
45. Sundry creditors to sundry debtors (%)	55.6	76.6
46. Total remuneration to employees to value added (%)	59.0	58.3
47. Total remunerations to employees to value of production (%)	12.1	11.5
48. Gross fixed assets formation (% growth)	–0.4	–0.5
49. Growth in inventories (%)	26.7	3.0

ITC

Looking Beyond Tobacco

Indian Tobacco Company (ITC) is a subsidiary of the global tobacco giant British American Tobacco. Its mainstay is the tobacco and hotels business. In recent years, it has been diversifying into areas like retailing, greeting cards and stationery, biscuits and confectionery, hospitality, inscense sticks and agribusiness. This may be ITC's strategy to spread risk as tobacco companies the world over are facing litigation from government and health groups. The Indian government has banned effective May 2004, tobacco advertising through the print media and hoardings. This move could work both for and against ITC. The company may benefit from the fact that since it is already dominant in India, its rivals may find it difficult to promote their products. ITC may thus actually save money on advertisement expenses. However, it may also have to disassociate some of its popular cigarette brands, such as Wills, for instance, from its tobacco business so that its apparel retail venture. Wills Lifestyle, can be promoted without invoking charges of surrogate advertising.

Over the past 17 years, ITC's turnover and profits have soared, and the company has pulled out of its old business and launched new ones. Its corporate strategy aims at creating multiple drivers of growth anchored in its core competency. The company has four main business segments: FMCG (divided into cigarettes and 'others'), hotels, agricultures and paper and packaging. The FMCG division has seen the launch of new products like branded packaged foods, lifestyle retailing, greeting cards and incense sticks. In the cigarettes segment, ITC is the market leader in India with brands positioned across the price spectrum. In the hotels segment, the company has decided to merge its subsidiary, ITC Hotels, with itself. This business requires the largest investment, although it also offers the largest margins. The agribusiness initially only had leaf tobacco and commodity trading, but has now expanded to providing an internet-based network called e-choupal for farmers.

Source: *Economic and Political Weekly*, December 11-17, 2004, p. 5281.

For fiscal 2003-04, ITC's net sales rose by 10 per cent, and net profit was upto 16 per cent. The company also reported a healthy 16 per cent growth in profit after tax for the first quarter of 2004-05. Except for the agribusiness, all other segments saw an increase in profitability. The Supreme Court recently ruled in favour of ITC in a 17 years old. Rs. 800 crores law suit relating to excise duty evasion. The company will now get a Rs. 300 crores refund from the Finance Ministry and it can also show the Rs. 800 crores provision made for the lawsuit as profits in its books. It can also fulfil a long list of investment demands from the funds released. Plans are afoot to expand ITC's hotel chain internationally.

ITC's long-term plan is to shrink the share of its tobacco business as a proportion of its total business. This can only be done gradually, because the cigarette business still contributes around 80 per cent of the company's total business. The merger of the hotels division with the parent company could help share up ITC's bottom line. However, there could also be significant managerial difficulties thrown up by the merger. Since ITC started diversifying into non-tobacco businesses, the company structure has become more complex. In this context, the question that arises is whether a bigger entity would lose focus and market agility.

Financial Indicators	*ITC*	
	2003-04	*2002-03*
Income/Appropriations		
1. Net Sales	647044	586578
2. Value of production	672287	585278
3. Other income	17391	18134
4. Total income	689678	603412
5. Raw materials/stores & spares/ Power and fuel consumed	227338	178055
6. Other manufacturing expenses	56475	69927
7. Remuneration to employees	41648	34612

(*Contd.*)

(Contd.)

Financial Indicators	*ITC*	
	2003-04	*2002-03*
8. Other expenses	104277	90707
9. Depreciation	24162	23734
10. Gross profit	235778	206377
11. Interest	2479	2984
12. Operating profit	233299	203893
13. Non-operating surplus/deficit	–1393	2226
14. Profit before tax	231906	205619
15. Tax provisions	72621	68484
16. Profit after tax	159285	137135
17. Dividends (includes tax on Dist. profit)	49536	37127
18. Retained profits	109749	100008
Liabilities/Assets		
19. Paid-up Capital	24768	24751
20. Reserves and surplus	616238	511811
21. Long-term loan	3156	4652
22. Short-term loan		
(i) of which bank borrowings	8929	6932
23. Gross fixed assets	505468	441561
24. Accumulated depreciation	144263	124564
25. Inventories	153421	125222
26. Total Assets/Liabilities	661865	554618
Miscellaneous items		
27. Excise duty	534460	515910
28. Gross value added	285985	248110
29. Total Foreign exchange earnings	107751	129400
30. Total Foreign exchange outgo	3476	3910
Key Financial and Performance Ratios		
31. Turnover ratio (sales to total assets)	1.9	2.2
32. Gross value added to gross fixed assets (%)	60.4	61.2
33. Return on investment (gross profit to total assets) (%)	38.8	40.3
34. Gross profit to sales (gross margin) (%)	36.4	35.2
35. Operating profit to sales (%)	36.1	34.7
36. Profit before tax to sales (%)	35.8	35.1
37. Tax provisions to profit before tax (%)	31.3	33.3
38. Profit after tax to net worth (return on equity) (%)	27.1	28.8
39. Dividend (%)	200.0	150.0
40. Earnings per share (Rs.)	64.3	55.4
41. Book value per share (Rs.)	—	—
42. P/E ratio (multiple)	18.6	14.5
43. Debt-equity ratio (adjusted for revolution)	0.02	0.02
44. Short-term bank borrowings to inventories (%)	5.8	5.5

(Contd.)

(Contd.)

Financial Indicators	*ITC*	
	2003-04	*2002-03*
45. Sundry creditors to sundry debtors (%)	1218.5	992.1
46. Total remuneration to employees to value added (%)	14.6	14.0
47. Total remunerations to employees to value of production (%)	6.2	5.9
48. Gross fixed assets formation (% growth)	14.5	19.5
49. Growth in inventories (%)	22.5	6.1

TATA TEA

Brand Potion

Tata Tea is the leading tea plantation company in India and the largest integrated tea producer in the world. The company and the Indian tea industry in general have been troubled by falling prices. Bulk tea prices have been declining steadily in recent years and tea companies in India are finding it ever harder to maintain their tea estate. Even well-entrenched players like **Tata Tea** are finding the market conditions difficult. The strategy of many Indian companies was to supply unbranded tea in bulk. They are now realising that they must move out of the commodities business and start building brands.

The year **2004** began positively for the tea industry. There was very little stock carried over from the previous year and export business from West Asia has been trickling back, after a temporary slowdown due to strife. The best news may be from the domestic front. The tea market in India is growing steadily from **65 crore kg in FY03 to 70 crore kg in FY04**, and is estimated to touch **72 crore kg** in the coming fiscal.

Tata Tea has been transforming itself from being primarily in the plantation business into a player in the international branded tea market. A major step forward in this direction was when it acquired the UK-based Tetley group in **2000**. This propelled the company overnight to number two position globally in the branded tea segment. The company sells branded tea under different names in India. At the national level, it has brands like **Tata Tea, Tetley and Agni**. It also has a number of regional brands that have carved outniches in certain pockets.

The company is putting into place a strategy for the future. It is adopting managerial procedures used by Tetley in its International operations. For instance, there will be different brand managers so that the levels of control are better organised. **Tata Tea** is also looking towards cutting costs to improve competitiveness. It is estimated that employee costs account for **60 per cent** of the total costs. In order to cut costs, Tata Tea is mulling over a plan to exit most of its plantations, possibly through sale. Alternatively, it could offer the managers the opportunity of an executive buyout.

Net sales of Tata Tea improved by **4 per cent** in **2003-04** from that in **2002-03** significantly, profit after tax increased by **30 per cent**, from **Rs. 70 crore to Rs. 91 crore**. In the quarter ended June 30, 2004. The company registered a marginal increase in net profit to Rs. 22.45 crore from Rs. 22.33 crore a year ago.

Source: *Economic and Political Weekly*, December 11-17, 2004, p. 5281.

Tata Tea is planning to venture into new international markets like China, one of the largest tea drinking countries. It has also decided to go for business acquisitions globally and domestically. The company is looking for acquisitions only in markets where there is potential for growth in the black tea segment. One of the considerations is that the acquisition should come with a huge brand size.

Financial Indicators	*Tata Tea*	
	2003-04	*2002-03*
Income/Appropriations		
1. Net sales	77002	74168
2. Value of production	75066	73990
3. Other income	6313	5780
4. Total income	81379	79771
5. Raw materials/Stores and Spares/ Power and fuel consumed	22024	21651
6. Other manufacturing expenses	10662	11009
7. Remuneration to employees	16097	16144
8. Other expenses	17737	17980
9. Depreciation	2204	2265
10. Gross profit	12657	10721
11. Interest	994	1439
12. Operating profit	11663	9282
13. Non-operating Surplus/deficit	360	728
14. Profit before tax	12023	10010
15. Tax provisions	2870	2950
16. Profit after tax	9153	7060
17. Dividends (includes tax on dist profit)	4779	3935
18. Retained profits	4374	3124

(*Contd.*)

(Contd.)

Financial Indicators	*Tata Tea*	
	2003-04	*2002-03*
Liabilities/Assets		
19. Paid-up Capital	5622	5622
20. Reserves and Surplus	91903	92241
21. Long-term loan	1650	5703
22. Short-term loan		
(i) of which, bank borrowings	—	—
23. Gross fixed assets	51709	51914
24. Accumulated depreciation	20586	18960
25. Inventories	10949	11275
26. Total assets/liabilities	120796	124189
Miscellaneous Items		
27. Excise duty	—	—
28. Gross value added	25769	24433
29. Total Foreign exchange earnings	11870	13330
30. Total Foreign exchange outgo	497	396
Key Financial and Performance Ratios		
31. Turnover ratio (sales to total assets)	0.6	1
32. Gross value added to gross fixed assets (%)	49.7	47.9
33. Return on investment (gross profit to total assets) (%)	10.3	8.8
34. Gross profit to sales (gross margin) (%)	16.4	14.5
35. Operating profit to sales (%)	15.1	12.5
36. Profit before tax to sales (%)	15.6	13.5
37 Tax provisions to profit before Tax (%)	23.9	29.5
38. Profit after tax to net worth (return on equity) (%)	9.4	7.5
39. Dividend (%)	85.0	70.0
40. Earnings per share (Rs.)	16.3	12.6
41. Book value per share (Rs.)	173.5	174.1
42. P/E ratio (multiple)	25.7	20.0
43. Debt-equity ratio (adjusted for revaluation)	0.20	0.23
44. Short-term bank borrowings to inventories (%)	–	–
45. Sundry creditors to sundry debtors (%)	288.3	187.7
46. Total remuneration to employees to value added (%)	62.5	66.1
47. Total remuneration to employees to value of production (%)	21.4	21.8
48. Gross fixed assets formation (% growth)	–0.4	3.5
49. Growth in inventories (%)	–2.9	1.4

WEST COAST PAPER MILLS

Cost Concerns

West Cost Paper Mills is the flagship company of the SK Bangur Group, and one of the country's leading paper mills. The company manufactures writing and printing paper, kraft paper and simplex boards. The domestic paper and paper boards industry can be classified on the basis of capacities, raw material used and type of paper produced. Paper and paperboards can be classified into cultural and industrial paper. Cultural paper (writing and printing paper) accounts for 40 per cent of the total paper produced.

In fiscal 2003-04, West Coast paper's profit after tax fell by 21 per cent, even though net sales increased by 12 per cent. One reason for this may be that the tax amount between FY03 and FY04 increased by 91 per cent. Moreover, it had to deal with the shutdown of a part of its machinery for as long as 45 days, and also an increase in the cost of production. The sharp rise in production cost was due mainly to the increase in raw material rates and maintenance expenses.

The company implemented a restructuring strategy that has brought some benefits. Rise in the cost of inputs has been offset to some extent by the completion of an expansion programme as part of the restructuring exercise.

West Coast Paper Mills has two divisions: the paper and duplex board division and cable division. The paper division produced 1,63,714 metres of paper, paper board and duplex board in 2003-04 against 1,51,477 meters in the previous fiscal. Overall production in the current fiscal is expected to improve over that the previous fiscal because of optimum utilisation of machinery. One cause for concern, however is the increase in coal prices, which may push up input costs. The cable division manufactured 6,230 km.of cable in 2003-04, against 6,319 km. the year before. Sales turnover for 2003-04, at Rs. 991 lakhs was lower than 1,408 lakhs. Demand for fiber-optic cable has been declining due to the adoption of wireless technology. Since the industry capacity is more than the domestic demand, downward pressure on prices is likely to continue. The company acquired a controlling interest in Rama Newsprint and papers in 2003 by buying 33.85 per cent of the share capital.

Financial Indicators	*West Coast Paper Mills*	
	2003-04	*2002-03*
Income/Appropriations		
1. Net sales	51492	46130
2. Value of production	51486	46185

(Contd.)

(Contd.)

Financial Indicators	*West Coast Paper Mills*	
	2003-04	*2002-03*
3. Other income	367	365
4. Total income	51853	46550
5. Raw materials/stores and spares/ power and fuel consumed	26818	23090
6. Other manufacturing expenses	0	0
7. Remuneration to employees	4616	3783
8. Other expenses	14182	12374
9. Depreciation	1689	1823
10. Gross profit	4548	5480
11. Interest	320	773
12. Operating profit	4228	4707
13. Non-operating surplus/deficit	141	–306
14. Profit before tax	4369	4401
15. Tax provisions	1524	797
16. Profit after tax	2844	3604
17. Dividends (includes tax on dist profit)	894	760
18. Retained profits	1950	2844
Liabilities/Assets		
19. Paid-up capital	894	894
20. Reserves and surplus	14036	12935
21. Long-term loan	10196	9117
22. Short-term loan		
(i) of which, bank borrowings	1000	111
23. Gross fixed assets	35761	28469
24. Accumulated depreciation	11479	9806
25. Inventories	9581	9343
26. Total assets/Liabilities	39019	34156
Miscellaneous Items		
27. Excise duty	6236	5728
28. Gross value added	10239	10620
29. Total Foreign exchange earnings	2855	–2406
30. Total Foreign exchange outgo	25	–49
Key Financial and Performance Ratios		
31. Turnover ratio (sales to total assets)	1.6	3.0
32. Gross value added to gross fixed assets (%)	31.9	74.6
33. Return on investment (gross profit to total assets) (%)	12.4	32.1
34. Gross profit to sales (gross margin) (%)	8.8	11.9
35. Operating profit to sales (%)	8.2	10.2
36. Profit before tax to sales (%)	8.5	9.5
37. Tax provisions to profit before tax (%)	34.9	18.1
38. Profit after tax to net worth (return on equity) (%)	19.8	52.1

(Contd.)

(Contd.)

Financial Indicators	*West Coast Paper Mills*	
	2003-04	*2002-03*
39. Dividend (%)	100.0	85.0
40. Earnings per share (Rs.)	31.8	40.3
41. Book value per share (Rs.)	167.0	154.7
42. P/E ratio (multiple)	6.1	5.5
43. Debt-equity ratio (adjusted for revaluation)	1.18	1.04
44. Short-term bank borrowings to inventories (%)	10.4	1.2
45. Sundry creditors to sundry debtors (%)	212.6	191.2
46. Total remuneration to employees to value of production (%)	45.1	35.6
47. Total remunerations to employees to value to production (%)	9.0	8.2
48. Gross fixed assets formation (% growth)	25.6	—
49. Growth in inventories (%)	2.5	—

Source: *Economic and Political Weekly*, December 11-17, p. 5282.

ISPAT INDUSTRIES

Foreign Ahead

Ispat Industries, after years of dismal performance, is making a strong come back booking profits during the year under review. The company recorded a 64 per cent increase in net sales from Rs 1,756 crores during 2001-02 to Rs. 2,880 crores in 2002-03. It fully capitalised on the available export opportunities and increased its export earnings to Rs. 799 crores as against Rs. 201 crores in the previous year. Exports accounted for 30 per cent of its turnover during 2002-03, as against 10 per cent in 2001-02. With the current rally in demand for steel expected to remain firm, the company is ramping up its production activities and aggressively looking forward to maximise its turnover by focusing on exports.

The ongoing capacity enhancement project completed its first phase of expansion of hot rolled coil plant during the year under review. During this first phase, operational capacity of hot rolled coils was increased to 1.5 million tonnes per annum. Capacity enhancement is on progress to increase it to 2.4 million tonnes per annum. Further increase in capacity upto 3 million tonnes per annum is expected to be fully completed in the financial year 2004-05. Simultaneously, the operation of blast furnace carried out by its subsidiary. Ispat Metallics India (IMIL), was ramped up, keeping in mind the increasing requirement of hot metal for production of hot rolled coils. To synergies operations, IMIL is in the process of being merged with the parent company. The merger will streamline related processes leading to savings in the cost of production. Additional power requirement is to be supplied by the proposed 110 MW power plant. The primary fuel for the power plant would be blast furnace gas, which will be provided by IMIL. As the other phases of the capacity enhancement project gets commissioned, additional oxygen will be required. For this purpose, an oxygen plant is expected to be commissioned during 2004-05. Completing these projects on scheduled time will crucially depend on availability of required funds. The Company which had earlier invested in Hughes Telecom (India) has sold around 97 per cent of its holding in an open offer.

Source: *Economic and Political Weekly*, March 20-26, 2004, p. 1188.

The recent introduction of the debt re-structuring package is expected to improve the financial position of the company. This package for re-structuring of its financial liabilities through the corporate debt re-structuring mechanism instituted by the Reserve Bank of India, *inter alia*, includes conversion of equity into preference shares, reduction of interest rate, conversion of loans to either foreign currency loans or low cost rupee loans. With the re-structuring package put into place, interest cost has come down from the earlier 13 per cent to 10 per cent and will bring down its interest burden substantially.

Financial Indicators	*Ispat Industries*	
	2002-03	*2001-02*
Income/Appropriations		
1. Net Sales	288036	175621
2. Value of production	282906	174323
3. Other income	25300	9229
4. Total income	308206	183552
5. Raw materials/Stores and Spares/ Power and Fuel consumed	217903	151852
6. Other manufacturing expenses	7635	6928
7. Remuneration to employees	5194	3800
8. Other expenses	35058	21066
9. Depreciation	21012	21250
10. Gross profit	21404	–21344
11. Interest	32756	36693
12. Operating profit	–11352	–58037
13. Non-operating surplus/deficit	18004	–6878
14. Profit before tax	6652	–64915
15. Tax Provisions	–1631	–20630
16. Profit after tax	8283	–44285

(Contd.)

(Contd.)

Financial Indicators	*Ispat Industries*	
	2002-03	*2001-02*
17. Dividends (includes tax on dist profit)	0	0
18. Retained Profits	8283	–44285
Liabilities/Assets		
19. Paid-up Capital	98175	98175
20. Reserves and Surplus	96923	101640
21. Long-term loan	631019	642293
22. Short-term loan	20766	30971
(i) of which bank borrowings	20766	30451
23. Gross fixed assets	607410	613230
24. Accumulated depreciation	115875	93163
25. Inventories	31329	22996
26. Total assets/liabilities	874839	898818
Miscellaneous Items		
27. Excise duty	30721	24726
28. Gross value added	24001	–4192
29. Total Foreign exchange earnings	79929	20104
30. Total Foreign exchange outgo	22708	12436
Key Financial and Performance Ratios		
31. Turnover ratio (Sales to total assets)	0.4:1	0.4:1
32. Gross value added to gross fixed assets (%)	3.9	–1.4
33. Return on investment (gross profit to total assets) (%)	2.4	–4.7
34. Gross profit to sales (gross margin) (%)	6.7	–10.7
35. Operating profit to sales (%)	–3.6	–29.0
36. Profit before tax to sales (%)	2.1	–32.4
37. Tax provisions to profit before tax (%)	–24.5	31.8
38. Profit after tax to net worth (return on equity) (%)	4.2	–44.3
39. Dividend (%)	0.0	0.0
40. Earnings per share (Rs.)	–0.9	–7.7
41. Book value per share (Rs.)	28.2	28.9
42. P/E ratio (multiple)	2.9	—
43. Debt-equity ratio (adjusted for revaluation)	3.3:1	3.4:1
44. Short-term bank borrowings to inventories (%)	66.3	132.4
45. Sundry creditors to Sundry debtors (%)	177.7	228.9
46. Total remuneration to employees to value added (%)	21.6	–90.6
47. Total remunerations to employees to value of production (%)	1.8	2.2
48. Gross fixed assets formation (% growth)	–0.9	—
49. Growth in inventories (%)	36.2	—

ZUARI INDUSTRIES

Shaping Up

Zuari Industries a member of the K K Birla promoted Zuari-chambal group, is in the business of manufacturing fertilisers and agro chemicals. Formerly known as Zuari Agro Chemicals, the company over the period has been exiting its non-core areas to focus on its core businesses. In pursuance of this strategy, the furniture products division of the company was demerged to become a subsidiary with effect from 2002-03. However, Zuari Leasing and Finance Corporation was amalgamated with the company with operations mainly for its group companies. The failure of monsoons led to a decline in the consumption of fertilisers by 7.4 percent to 16.08 million tonnes from 17.36 million tonnes during 2001-02. Despite declining consumption of fertilisers and severe competition, the company has reported to have handled a volume of 11,83,845 tonnes of fertilisers as against 11,41,721 tonnes during the previous year. Sales of agro chemicals dropped to Rs. 16.32 crores compared to Rs. 17.38 crores in the previous year. As a whole, sales turnover for 2002-03 at Rs. 1,178.67 crores showed a decrease of 4.06 per cent over Rs. 1,228.58 crores for the previous year.

The company's cash flow from operating activities during 2002-03 was almost half of its last year's figure. Overall cash flow turned negative to the tune of Rs. 2.53 crores as against positive cash flow of Rs. 2.27 crores during 2001-02. Book debts outstanding for more than six months as on March 31, 2003 stood at Rs. 3.27 crores as compared to Rs. 1.80 crores in the previous year. As a result, there were severe constraints on it working capital management, which entailed the company to borrow funds from banks. The company was not able to cash in on the prevailing lower interest rate structure to its advantage. Interest expenses were higher from Rs. 26 crores in 2001-02 to Rs. 39.5 crores in 2002-03. The Company is confident of realising the debts from its customers and perform better in the coming years.

The present challenge for the company will be its strategy to align itself with the new pricing policy for urea units. The new pricing policy encourages efficiency parameters of international standards based on the most efficient feed stock and state of the art-technology. Based on the recommendations of Expenditure Reforms Commission, the Union Government has announced a new pricing policy, which replaced the unit specific retention pricing scheme by a group concession scheme with effect from April 1, 2003. Units are grouped into six groups based on the feedstock and vintage, with the company being placed in 'pre-1992 naphtha based unit' group. The new pricing scheme will be implemented in stages. The first stage will be of one-year duration from April 1, 2003 to March 31, 2004 after which the second stage would be implemented for two year duration. Modalities of subsequent stages will be decided after review of the first and second stages. Along with the new pricing policy, partial decontrol of distribution of urea has been allowed under 'Government Concession Scheme'. In the first stage, the allocation of urea under Essential Commodities Act, 1955 will be restricted upto 75 per cent and 50 per cent of production capacity in Kharif 2003 and Rabi 2003-04 respectively. During the second stage, urea distribution will be totally decontrolled after having evaluated the first stage.

Source: *Economic and Political Weekly*, March 20-26, 2004, p. 1188.

Financial Indicators	*Zuari Industries*	
	2002-03	*2001-02*
Income/Appropriations		
1. Net sales	117867	122858
2. Value of Production	118042	121438
3. Other income	1595	1402
4. Total income	119637	122840
5. Raw materials/stores and spares/ power and fuel consumed	91928	96881
6. Other manufacturing expenses	3269	3661
7. Remuneration to employees	4961	4186
8. Other expenses	12323	12422
9. Depreciation	1282	1525
10. Gross profit	5873	4186
11. Interest	3957	2602
12. Operating Profit	1917	1584
13. Non-operating surplus/deficit	39	137
14. Profit before tax	1956	1722
15. Tax provisions	–128	457
16. Profit after tax	2084	1265
17. Dividends (includes tax on dist profit)	498	294
18. Retained Profits	1586	971
Liabilities/Assets		
19. Paid-up Capital	2944	2944
20. Reserves and Surplus	31217	33606
21. Long-term loan	35210	31153
22. Short-term loan	15043	5829
(i) of which bank borrowings	15043	5829
23. Gross fixed assets	33152	39149

(Contd.)

(Contd.)

Financial Indicators	*Zuari Industries*	
	2002-03	*2001-02*
24. Accumulated depreciation	16152	16147
25. Inventories	15179	16934
26. Total assets/liabilities	118495	96520
Miscellaneous Items		
27. Excise duty	0	467
28. Gross value added	11041	9011
29. Total Foreign exchange earnings	0	320
30. Total Foreign exchange outgo	40747	40751
Key Financial and Performance Ratios		
31. Turnover ratio (Sales to total assets)	0.6:1	0.8:1
32. Gross value added to gross fixed assets (%)	30.5	23.7
33. Return on investment (gross profit to total assets) (%)	5.5	4.5
34. Gross profit to sales (gross margin) (%)	8.9	5.7
35. Operating profit to sales (%)	2.9	2.2
36. Profit before tax to sales (%)	3.0	2.3
37. Tax provisions to profit before tax (%)	–6.5	26.5
38. Profit after tax to net worth (return on equity)(%)	5.9	3.5
39. Dividend (%)	15.0	10.0
40. Earnings per share (Rs.)	7.1	4.3
41. Book value per share (Rs.)	116.0	124.1
42. P/E ratio (multiple)	5.5	4.8
43. Debt-equity ratio (adjusted for revaluation)	1.5:1	1.0:1
44. Short-term bank borrowings to inventories (%)	99.1	34.4
45. Sundry creditors to sundry debtors (%)	207.5	153.3
46. Total remuneration to employees to value added (%)	44.9	46.2
47. Total remunerations to employees to value of production (%)	4.2	3.4
48. Gross fixed assets formation (% growth)	–15.3	6.4
49. Growth in inventories (%)	–10.4	–12.9

FINOLEX CABLES

Focus on Exports

Finolex Cables, the flagship company of the Pune based Finolex Group, had a difficult year during 2002-03 with sales turnover of Rs. 433.92 crores and profit after tax of Rs. 24.71 crores being lower than its previous years figures of Rs. 555.96 crores and Rs. 65.94 crores, respectively. The company is engaged mainly in the manufacture and marketing of cables that are used in a wide range of electrical and telecommunication applications. It is the market leader in the domestic cable industry providing a range of products. During the year under review, the company suffered a major setback from dwindling demand for its jelly filled telephone cables (JFTC). As a result, production of communication cables was of 3,154 TCKM (Thousand Crore Kilometres) against production of 6,674 TCKM in the previous year. Sales were at Rs. 153 crores for the year under review against Rs. 361 crores for the previous year. Production and sales were lower mainly due to substantial reduction in the procurement quantity of JFTC by its major customer, Bharat Sanchar Nigam (BSNL). The company manufactures optic fibre and was able to increase optic fibre sales from Rs. 16 crores during 2001-02 to Rs. crores in 2002-03 but is suffering from capacity bottlenecks. Looking into the increasing demand, the company undertook an ambitious programme to enhance its optic fibre capacity. To overcome domestic stagnation in demand for JFTC, the company is looking to export this product into potential overseas markets. It has already been according higher attention to the overseas markets in the recent years. During the year under review, total foreign exchange earned showed a quantum jump to Rs. 87.38 crores from Rs. 47.31 crores in the previous year.

Financial Indicators	*Finolex Cables*	
	2002-03	*2001-02*
Income/Appropriations		
1. Net sales	43393	55596
2. Value of production	43393	55596
3. Other income	2483	2932
4. Total income	45876	58528
5. Raw materials/stores and spares/ power and fuel consumed	30640	38615
6. Other manufacturing expenses	964	1709
7. Remuneration to employees	2511	2607
8. Other expenses	4686	4931
9. Depreciation	2352	2220
10. Gross profit	4722	8447
11. Interest	2671	1636
12. Operating profit	2051	6811
13. Non-operating surplus/deficit	771	433
14. Profit before tax	2822	7245
15. Tax provisions	350	650
16. Profit after tax	2472	6595
17. Dividends (includes tax on dist profit)	1035	2575
18. Retained Profits	1437	4019

(*Contd.*)

(Contd.)

Financial Indicators	*Finolex Cables*	
	2002-03	*2001-02*
Liabilities/Assets		
19. Paid-up Capital	3059	3434
20. Reserves and Surplus	49228	55252
21. Long-term loan	11632	9391
22. Short-term loan	8725	2846
(i) of which, bank borrowings	5454	1521
23. Gross fixed assets	45963	42103
24. Accumulated Depreciation	15222	13388
25) Inventories	8893	9268
26. Total assets/liabilities	75495	73051
Miscellaneous Items		
27. Excise duty	5242	8441
28. Gross value added	7204	10468
29. Total Foreign exchange earnings	8738	4731
30. Total Foreign exchange outgo	6928	4818
Key Financial and Performance Ratios		
31. Turnover ratio (sales to total assets)	0.7:1	0.9:1
32. Gross value added to gross fixed assets (%)	16.4	28.6
33. Return on investment (gross profit to total assets) (%)	6.4	11.9
34. Gross profit to sales (gross margin) (%)	9.7	13.2
35. Operating profit to sales (%)	4.2	10.6
36. Profit before tax to sales (%)	5.8	11.3
37. Tax provisions to profit before tax (%)	12.4	9.0
38. Profit after tax to net worth (return on equity) (%)	4.5	11.2
39. Dividend (%)	30.0	75.0
40. Earnings per share (Rs.)	7.8	19.2
41. Book value per share (Rs.)	165.7	170.9
42. P/E ratio (multiple)	13.8	3.9
43. Debt-equity ratio (adjusted for revaluation)	0.4:1	0.2:1
44. Short-term bank borrowings to inventories (%)	61.3	16.4
45. Sundry creditors to sunday debtors (%)	48.8	30.0
46. Total remuneration to employees to value added (%)	34.9	24.9
47. Total remuneration to employees to value of production (%)	5.8	4.7
48. Gross fixed assets formation (% growth)	9.2	35.7
49. Growth in inventories (%)	–4.1	15.9

Source: *Economic and Political Weekly*, March 20-26, 2004, p. 1189.

INFOSYS

Expanding Via Consultancy

Infosys Technologies is India's second largest IT services company. It is mainly engaged in customised software development maintenance, re-engineering services, e-commerce and internet consulting as well as dedicated offshore Software development centres. Infosys also develops and market company owned software products. It has 17 offshore development facilities throughout India.

Infosys has become a byword for Indian Software development. It was the first Indian Company to be listed on the New York Stock Exchange in 1999. Infosys posted a net profit of Rs. 1,243 crores for fiscal 2003-04 (on sales of Rs. 4,760 crores) against Rs. 951 crores in 2002-03, a rise of 30 per cent. In the process, it became the first listed Indian IT company to gross more than a billion US dollars in sales. Infosys once again beats expectations to post a hefty 39 per cent increase in revenues and a 39 per cent increase in net profit to Rs. 388 crores in the first quarter of 2004-05.

Infosys intends to expand from being on IT services company to a full service software company that offers consultancy services as well. In April, it announced the launch of Infosys Consulting, a separate global company. In offering an integrated consultancy service along with its software services business. Infosys may angle for a unique value proposition. For example, a company that wants to implement strategic changes has to hire the services of management consultancy firms to draw up a blue print and then approach another company for the technology implementation. The whole process is expensive. What Infosys plans to do is to combine both services so that clients save on costs. Infosys did a lot of due diligence and decided to expand the consultancy business organically and not through acquisitions.

During fiscal 2003-04, Infosys faced some challenges. The outery raised in the US against outsourcing of services to India has the potential to hurt Infosys, given that a lot of the company's clients are based in the US. The movement against outsourcing has picked up momentum, given the current tumultuous trends in US politics. The others issue of concern to Infosys was the appreciation of the rupee vis-à-vis the US dollar in fiscal 2003-04. Since, a lot of Infosys revenue is earned in foreign currencies, particularly US dollars, an appreciation of the rupee would eat into its earnings. The trend has reversed now.

Infosys has good HR management techniques in place and is regarded as a good employer. However, the framed employee stock option programme (ESOP), which was pioneered by the company and made many of its employees millionaries, was suspended earlier this year.

Source: *Economic and Political Weekly*, November 6-12, 2004, p. 4870.

Financial Indicators	*Infosys*	
	2003-04	*2002-03*
Income/Appropriations		
1. Net sales	476089	362269
2. Value of production	476089	362269
3. Other income	12739	9961
4. Total income	488828	372230
5. Raw materials/stores and spares/ power and fuel consumed	2872	2260
6. Other manufacturing expenses	0	0
7. Remuneration to employees	236586	167712
8. Other expenses	78236	65711
9. Depreciation	23090	18895
10. Gross profit	147047	115893
11. Interest	0	0
12. Operating profit	147047	115893
13. Non-operating surplus/deficit	0	0
14. Profit before tax	147047	115893
15. Tax provisions	22700	20100
16. Profit after tax	124347	95793
17. Dividends (includes tax on Dist profit)	86246	17881
18. Retained Profits	38101	77912
Liabilities/Assets		
19. Paid-up capital	3332	3312
20. Reserves and surplus	322011	282753
21. Long-term loan	—	—
22. Short-term loan		
(i) of which, bank borrowings	—	—
23. Gross fixed assets	157023	127331
24. Accumulated depreciation	80341	57715
25. Inventories	—	—
26. Total assets/liabilities	325343	286065
Miscellaneous Items		
27. Excise duty	0	0
28. Gross value added	398567	296122
29. Total Foreign exchange earnings	453256	337787
30. Total Foreign exchange outgo	192664	153540
Key Financial and Performance Ratios		
31. Turnover ratio (Sales to total assets)	1.6	2.5
32. Gross value added to Gross fixed assets (%)	280.3	465.1

(*Contd.*)

(Contd.)

Financial Indicators	*Infosys*	
	2003-04	*2002-03*
33. Return on investment (gross profit to total assets) (%)	48.1	81.0
34. Gross profit to sales (gross margin) (%)	30.9	32.0
35. Operating profit to sales (%)	30.9	32.0
36. Profit before tax to sales (%)	30.9	32.0
37. Tax provisions to profit before tax (%)	15.4	17.3
38. Profit after tax to net worth (return on equity) (%)	40.7	67.0
39. Dividend (%)	2256.8	502.7
40. Earnings per share (Rs.)	186.6	—
41. Book value per share (Rs.)	488.2	—
42. P/E ratio (multiple)	32.7	25.4
43. Debt-equity ratio (adjusted for revaluation)	0.00	0.00
44. Short-term bank borrowings to inventories (%)	—	—
45. Sundry creditors to sunday debtors (%)	68.0	46.2
46. Total remuneration to employees to value added (%)	59.4	56.6
47. Total remunerations to employees to value of production (%)	49.7	46.3
48. Gross fixed assets formation (% growth)	23.3	—
49. Growth in inventories (%)	—	—

LARSEN & TOUBRO

Going Global

Larsen and Toubro (L&T), the engineering and construction conglomerate, is making its mark in the international arena. After years of drifting away from its core business of engineering and construction, the company now appears to have acquired a new vision and seems determined to establish its presence internationally. A product and portfolio review was undertaken to decide which businesses to retain and which to give up. Manpower-positioning HR policies were initiated to retain talent, and a process of developing and grooming global leaders who would lead the company's international forays was put into place. A new system that rewarded performance was among the many programmes devised to retain talent. Voluntary retirement schemes and outplacement services were offered to trim the workforce. The aim was to have a committed cadre of employees and weed out the redundant staff.

Initially, L&T started to look beyond India to compensate for the Nagaries of the domestic market. In the past 18 months, L&T has been one of the most aggressive Indian Companie in the International market.

The company plans to increase revenue earned from its international business, from 17 per cent of total revenues at present to 25 per cent by 2009. To make this happen, L&T will have a mixed bag of international businesses, including joint ventures, exports and turnkey projects. It is also armed with a war chest of Rs. 500 crores for acquisitions. L&T is on the look out for high technology process engineering companies to help it moves up the value chain. It has already bagged orders to construct a process platform on an oilfield in the UAF. It has won a contract to supply coal gasification equipment for a Chinese company. Earlier this year, it bagged a $30 millions order to upgrade its facilities in Abu Dhabi. In the past one year, it has bagged over Rs. 2,700 crores of international orders.

As the scale of its international operations improves, L&T is redrawing its plans for the future. Over the next five years, the company is aiming to reduce its reliance on some markets, hike off unwanted business and improve its profitability at home and abroad. It has also changed its strategy for the global markets in recent years. When it first ventured outside India, it focussed on small orders, in the process foregoing profitability to establish credibility.

Last year, L&T demerged its cement division into a separate company, Ultra Tech Cemco, which was eventually sold to the Aditya Birla Group. It exited from the metal packaging business as it was unprofitable, and shut down its glass container division, which was identified as a non-core business. With the dermerger of the cement business and streamlining of its other units, the company can now focus on its core engineering business. But the move saw a 30 per cent decline in L&T's net worth even as its liabilities were shaved off by 55 per cent.

L&T's margins are on the lower side. While the company averages around 8.5-9 per cent, the margins of its close competitor Bharat Heavy Electrical margins are around 14 per cent. In comparison, margins on international projects range from 6 per cent for construction projects to 12 per cent for heavy engineering and electronics projects. The company aims to improve its average margins to 11 per cent.

Source: *Economic and Political Weekly*, November, 6-12, 2004, p. 4870.

Financial Indicators	*L&T*	
	2003-04	*2002-03*
Income/Appropriations		
1. Net Sales	951633	936012
2. Value of production	999392	935897
3. Other income	38302	23802
4. Total income	1037694	959699
5. Raw materials/stores and spares/ power and fuel consumed	499710	437772
6. Other manufacturing expenses	25896	12079
7. Remuneration to employees	67808	66810
8. Other expenses	359413	347165
9. Depreciation	8609	31355
10. Gross profit	74806	64449
11. Interest	3656	17699
12. Operating profit	71150	46750
13. Non-operating surplus/deficit	5733	4270
14. Profit before tax	76883	51020
15. Tax provisions	23608	7710
16. Profit after tax	53275	43310
17. Dividends (includes tax on dist profit)	19904	18680
18. Retained profits	33371	24630
Liabilities/Assets		
19. Paid-up capital	2488	24867
20. Reserves and surplus	275016	331387
21. Long-term loan	104525	270311
22. Short-term loan		
(i) of which, bank borrowings	5463	6373
23. Gross fixed assets	196631	608932
24. Accumulated depreciation	94400	219421
25. Inventories	181230	151582
26. Total assets/liabilities	433691	766452
Miscellaneous Items		
27. Excise duty	24543	50971
28. Gross value added	123911	149243
29. Total Foreign exchange earnings	—	—
30. Total Foreign exchange outgo	—	—
Key Financial and Performance Ratios		
31. Turnover ratio (sales to total assets)	1.6	3
32. Gross value added to gross fixed assets (%)	30.8	49.0
33. Return on investment (gross profit to total assets) (%)	12.5	16.8
34. Gross profit to sales (gross margin) (%)	7.8	6.9
35. Operating profit to sales (%)	7.4	5.0
36. Profit before tax to sales (%)	8.0	5.5
37. Tax provisions to profit before tax (%)	30.7	15.1
38. Profit after tax to net worth (return on equity) (%)	16.8	24.3
39. Dividend (%)	697.3	65.5

(*Contd.*)

(Contd.)

Financial Indicators	*L&T*	
	2003-04	*2002-03*
40. Earnings per share (Rs.)	42.8	—
41. Book value per share (Rs.)	223.1	—
42. P/E ratio (multiple)	20.8	15.2
43. Debt equity ratio (adjusted for revaluation)	0.40	0.78
44. Short-term bank borrowings to inventories (%)	0.0	0.0
45. Sundry creditor to sundry debtors (%)	61.6	66.2
46. Total remuneration to employees to value added (%)	54.7	44.8
47. Total remunerations to employees to value of production (%)	6.8	7.1
48. Gross fixed assets formation (% growth)	–67.7	–
49. Growth in inventories (%)	19.6	–

ELECTROSTEEL CASTINGS

Building Project Capacity

Electrosteel Castings is a kolkata-based water infrastructure company that provides technological solutions in water supply and sewage systems. The company manufactures ductile iron pipes, ductile iron fittings and cast iron pipes. These pipes are mainly used in the transportation of water and sewage.

Net sales registered a 10 per cent increase in 2003-04 at Rs. 672 crores from Rs. 589.8 crores in 2002-03. However, net profit declined by 24 per cent to Rs. 73 crores in 2003-04 from Rs. 97.5 crores in 2002-03. Margins were also under pressure due to an increase in input costs, particularly in electric power and imported coke. Cost of imported coke almost doubled due to rising demand in 2002-03 continue to stay strong. The company has also improved its operating efficiency significantly through backward integration and low cost expansion projects that have improved its cost structure significantly. The company has also introduced concepts such as hot charging of iron to reduce energy costs.

Electrosteel, having established itself as a leading players in the domestic market, is now positioning itself as an international manufacturer of ductile iron pipes. With products comparable with the best in the world, the company has already fulfilled export order requirements for a varied clientele in the Gulf, South Asian and African markets. It also expects to expand its market in Europe substantially.

Source: *Economic and Political Weekly*, November 6-12, 2004 p. 4870.

The company envisions itself as a total water and waste management origanisation. The engineering, procurement and construction (EPC) division is helping it in the objective to evolve from being a mere manufacturer and supplier of DI pipes to a complete infrastructure erection service provider from water and sewage projects. Commissioned in 1996, the EPC division has been emerging as a growing revenue earner, contributing nearly 10 per cent of the total revenues during 2002-03. The company believes that through composite contracts, which involve assembling, erecting and testing to actually delivering water over distances or disposing of waste, it will be able to create a stronger brand name for itself.

Financial Indicators	*Electrosteel Castings*	
	2003-04	*2002-03*
Income/Appropriations		
1. Net sales	67210	58984
2. Value of production	68625	60199
3. Other income	2617	5337
4. Total income	71241	65536
5. Raw materials/stores and spares/ power and fuel consumed	36350	32679
6. Other manufacturing expenses	0	0
7. Remuneration to employees	3757	3406
8. Other expenses	18055	14173
9. Depreciation	2279	2039
10. Gross profit	10801	13240
11. Interest	503	1431
12. Operating profit	10297	11809
13. Non-operating surplus/deficit	554	4
14. Profit before tax	10851	11813
15. Tax provisions	3483	2067
16. Profit after tax	7368	9746
17. Dividends (includes tax on dist profit)	1619	1619
18. Retained profits	5749	8127
Liabilities/Assets		
19. Paid-up capital	1619	1615
20. Reserves and surplus	45999	40457
21. Long-term loan	28634	16816
22. Short-term loan	6487	10225
(i) of which, bank borrowings	2487	2000
23. Gross fixed assets	30204	27940
24. Accumulated depreciation	12383	10432
25. Inventories	17499	9646
26. Total assets/liabilities	85358	71792

(*Contd.*)

(Contd.)

Financial Indicators	*Electrosteel Castings*	
	2003-04	*2002-03*
Miscellaneous Items		
27. Excise duty	5235	6702
28. Gross value added	14580	13620
29. Total Foreign exchange earnings	11889	12110
30. Total Foreign exchange outgo	10940	9624
Key Financial and Performance Ratios		
31. Turnover ratio (sales to total assets)	0.9	1.0
32. Gross value added to gross fixed assets (%)	50.2	49.2
33. Return on investment (gross profit to total assets) (%)	13.7	19.4
34. Gross profit to sales (gross margin) (%)	16.1	22.4
35. Operating profit to sales (%)	15.3	20.0
36. Tax before tax to sales (%)	16.1	20.0
37. Tax provisions to profit before tax (%)	32.1	17.5
38. Profit after tax to net worth (return on equity) (%)	16.4	25.5
39. Dividend (%)	87.2	87.4
40. Earnings per share (Rs.)	45.5	60.2
41. Book value per share (Rs.)	294.1	259.8
42. P/E ratio (multiple)	—	—
43. Debt-equity ratio (adjusted for revaluation)	0.74	0.64
44. Short-term bank borrowings to investment (%)	14.2	20.7
45. Sundry creditors to sundry debtors (%)	58.0	4.1
46. Total remuneration to employees to value added (%)	25.8	25.0
47. Total remunerations to employees to value of production (%)	5.5	5.7
48. Gross fixed assets formations (% growth)	8.1	1.9
49. Growth in inventories (%)	81.4	10.7

BHARTI TELE-VENTURES

Expanding Bandwidth

Bharti Tele-ventures is one of India's largest telecom companies and the largest provider of GSM mobile service. It has over 8 lakhs mobile and fixed-line customers. Bharti also provides fixed line local access, national and international long-distance telephony, VSAT, Internet service and corporate data network solutions.

Bharti's business has been organised into two strategic units, mobile service and infotel service. The mobile service (Airtel) provides GSM mobile service in 16 of India's 23 telecom circles. Bharti has applied for licences to commence operations in the other seven circles. The infotel group provides fixed line, long distance, and group data and enterprise services. The company owns a 23,000 km. national fibre optic back bone and substantial international band width.

The company registered robust growth in 2003-04 and has posted, for the first time on a full year basis, a net profit (Rs. 583 crores) of this, the mobile business contributed 65 per cent, or Rs. 328 crores. This is significant considering that in 2002-03, it posted a net loss of Rs 205 crores. The Indian telecom sector has seen extensive regulatory changes and intense competition. Despite this and the fact that telecom tariffs in India are said to be among the lowest in the world, Bharati joined the 'billion dollor' club in revenue terms in 2003-04.

The Indian telecom industry experienced unprecedented growth in 2003-04, and according to analysis, this trend is expected to continue. Bharti has invested Rs. 11,700 crores in building telecom infrastructure in India. It has also acquired Hexacom and is now well on its way to being an all India operator.

Looking forward, Bharti's aim is to capitalise on the growth opportunities that the India Telecommunications market throws up and to consolidate its position as an integrated telecom services provider. Its focus will be to implement a modular rollout of its cellular network to attain an all India presence and introduce fixed line and data networks to meet the needs of high-end corporate customers. Since tariffs are low in India, the only way companies can compete in the market, and retain and attract customers, is by offering innovative services. To this end, Bharti proposed to unveil innovative, value added services in terms of content, speed and comfort. Since the company plans to be a national level player, it will be relying on economics of scale in operations to standardise services.

Financial Indicators	*Bharti*	
	2003-04	*2002-03*
Income/Appropriations		
1. Net sales	500248	304994
2. Value of production	493708	299273
3. Other income	7076	4449

(Contd.)

Source: *Economic and Political Weekly*, November, 20-26, 2004, p. 4952.

(Contd.)

Financial Indicators	*Bharti*	
	2003-04	*2002-03*
4. Total income	500783	303723
5. Raw materials/stores and spares/ and fuel consumed	9087	6167
6. Other manufacturing expenses	0	0
7. Remuneration to employees	37208	27541
8. Other expenses	238725	162097
9. Depreciation	68474	48011
10. Gross profit	81132	10709
11. Interest	32530	31302
12. Operating profit	48602	–20593
13. Non-operating surplus/deficit	6669	2969
14. Profit before tax	55272	–17624
15. Tax provisions	–3220	18
16. Profit after tax	58369	–20506
17. Dividends (includes tax on dist profit)	0	0
18. Retained profits	58369	–20506
Liabilities/Assets		
19. Paid-up Capital	185337	185337
20. Reserves and surplus	306125	297281
21. Long-term loan	—	—
22. Short-term loan	—	—
(i) of which, bank borrowings		
23. Gross fixed assets	1121916	869170
24. Accumulated depreciation	261148	174129
25. Inventories	3168	2090
26. Total assets/liabilities	962416	857171
Miscellaneous Items		
27. Excise duty	0	0
28. Gross value added	186152	83537
29. Total Foreign exchange earnings	—	—
30. Total Foreign exchange outgo	—	—
Key Financial and Performance Ratios		
31. Turnover ratio (sales to total assets)	0.5	0.7
32. Gross value added to gross fixed assets (%)	18.7	19.2
33. Return on investment (Gross profit to total assets) (%)	8.9	2.5
34. Gross profit to sales (gross margin) (%)	16.2	3.5
35. Operating profit to sales (%)	9.7	–6.8
36. Profit before tax to sales (%)	11.0	–5.8
37. Tax provisions to profit before tax (%)	–5.8	–0.1
38. Profit after tax to net worth (return on equity) (%)	12.0	–8.5
39. Dividend (%)	0.0	0.0
40. Earnings per share (Rs.)	3.1	–1.1

(Contd.)

(Contd.)

Financial Indicators	*Bharti*	
	2003-04	*2002-03*
41. Book value per share (Rs.)	26.5	26.0
42. P/E ratio (multiple)	—	—
43. Debt-equity ratio (adjusted for revaluation)	0.0	0.0
44. Short-term bank borrowings to inventories (%)	0.0	0.0
45. Sundry creditors to Sundry debtors (%)	270.0	350.0
46. Total remuneration to employees to value added (%)	20.0	33.0
47. Total remunerations to employees to value of production (%)	7.5	9.2
48. Gross fixed assets formation (% growth)	29.1	—
49. Growth in inventories (%)	51.6	—

APOLLO TYRES

Taking JV Path to Growth

Apollo Tyres is engaged in the manufacture of automobile tyres and tubes. It has a leadership position in the truck tyre replacement market, besides having a strong presence in the commercial vehicle original equipment manufacture (OEM) segment. The Company also supplies to car and tractor OEM majors.

The company's performance in 2003-04 did not match that in the previous year. Though net sales increased by nearly 19 per cent from Rs. 1,608 crores to Rs. 1,910 crores, this did not translate into higher profits. In fact, profit after tax slipped by 41 per cent to Rs. 70 crores in FY04, from Rs. 120 crores in the previous fiscal. What is worse, the company's evokes have continued. In the first quarter of 2004-05, Apollo Tyres reported a 16.5 per cent drop in net profit to Rs. 15.6 crores from Rs. 18.7 crores in the corresponding quarter of the previous year. The reason for this is a steep increase in input cost. Rubber prices have increased and so have prices of other petro-based inputs. There has also been a rise in the interest burden of the company to Rs. 11.68 crores in 2003-04 from Rs. 3.55 crores in the previous year. Apollo tyres had foreign currency loans worth Rs. 115 crores at the end of FY04. Added to this is the fact that the rupee depreciation in the last quarter led to additional burden on interest payments.

Source: *Economic and Political Weekly*, November, 20-26, 2004, p. 4952.

In FY04, the company's three plants increased capacity by 14 per cent. This should help profitability by 14 per cent. This should help profitability by increasing product supply. Apollo Tyres has also decided to reduce worker strength in its two factories in Kerala by introducing a VRS package, to cut staff from 2,500 to 1,900. Once the VRS is implemented, monthly outgo on salary will comedown by 50 per cent, also leading to substantial savings.

Apollo announced a joint venture with Michelin, the largest tyre maker in the world, to develop tyres using Michelin technology and its own distribution net work. The joint venture company is called Michelin Apollo Tyres and will import tyres from China till production starts at its own plant in 2005. Investment in the plant by Apollo and Michelin would be of the order of $75 million, in the ratio of 51:49 and the target is to produce 3.5 lakh truck and bus radial tyres by 2007.

One of the key areas of growth and Apollo has identified is passenger car radials. The company is working on a strategy that will stimulate it into the leadership position in this category.

Financial Indicators	*Apollo*	
	2003-04	*2002-03*
Income/Appropriations		
1. Net sales	191075	160833
2. Value of production	194866	163542
3. Other income	603	139
4. Total income	195469	163681
5. Raw materials/stores and spares/power and fuel consumed	159532	110612
6. Other manufacturing expenses	0	0
7. Remuneration to employees	13753	11498
8. Other expenses	25379	20691
9. Depreciation	4459	3423
10. Gross profit	12433	17544
11. Interest	1863	2486
12. Operating profit	10570	15058
13. Non-operating surplus/deficit	-47	-67
14. Profit before tax	10523	14991
15. Tax provisions	3481	4651
16 Profit after tax	7042	12002
17. Dividends (includes tax on dist profit)	0	0
18. retained profits	7042	12002
Liabilities/Assets		
19. Paid-up capital	3834	3632
20. Reserves and surplus	53359	38312

(*Contd.*)

(Contd.)

Financial Indicators	*Apollo*	
	2003-04	*2002-03*
21. Long-term loan	37641	21614
22. Short-term loan	4500	6862
(i) of which, bank borrowings	-	3271
23. Gross fixed assets	97587	72003
24. Accumulated depreciation	32779	28767
25. Inventories	26266	21648
26. Total assets/liabilities	108823	78468
Miscellaneous Items		
27. Excise duty	40356	41729
28. Gross value added	31388	35100
29. Total Foreign exchange earnings	–	–
30. Total Foreign exchange outgo.	–	–
Key Financial and Performance Ratios		
31. Turnover ratio (sales to total assets)	2.5	5.2
32. Gross Value added to gross fixed assets (%)	37.0	97.5
33. Return on investment (gross profit to total assets) (%)	13.3	44.7
34. Gross profit to sales (gross margin) (%)	6.5	10.9
35. Operating profit to sales (%)	5.5	9.4
36. Profit before tax to sales (%)	5.5	9.3
37. Tax provisions to profit before tax (%)	33.1	31.0
38. Profit after tax to net worth (return equity) (%)	14.2	57.2
39. Dividend (%)	0.0	0.0
40. Earnings per share (Rs.)	18.4	33.0
41. Book Value per share (Rs.)	149.2	115.5
42. P/E ratio (multiple)	12.3	6.0
43. Debt-equity ratio (Adjusted for revaluation)	0.74	0.68
44. Short-term bank borrowings to inventories (%)	–	16.0
45. Sunday creditors to sunday debtors (%)	303.9	286.8
46. Total remuneration to employees to value added (%)	43.8	32.8
47. Total remunerations to employees to value of production (%)	7.1	7.0
48. Gross fixed assets formation (% growth)	35.5	–
49. Growth inventories (%)	21.3	–

ASIAN PAINTS

Pan-Asian Plans

Asian Paints are India's largest domestic paints company and the market leader in decorative paints. Its brands, Royal in the premium segment. Apcolite in the middle segment and Gattu, Tractor, Utsav, 3-Mango, and others in the lower segment are all well established.

The company declared respectable results for the first quarter of FY05. The topline grew by 10 per cent year-on-year during the quarter. Despite strong crude prices, operating margins have improved which are reflected in a healthy bottomline. Profit after tax for 2003-04 was Rs. 147 crores against Rs. 142 crores in the previous year a rise of 4 per cent.

Asian Paints are an overall market share of around 30 per cent and a 50 per cent share in the decorative paints segment. Through a 50:50 joint venture with PPG Industries of the US, it also has a presence in the automotive paints segment of late, the company has gone on an acquisition spree that would increase contribution from its international operations significantly in the coming years.

Asian Paints business can be classified into two divisions, namely, paints and chemicals on a stand-alone basis, revenues have increased by 10 per cent, comprising a 9 per cent growth in paint sales and around 23 per cent growth in chemical division sales. The latter had a poor FY04 and it is expected that this division will post better result in FY05 due to better petrochemicals prices.

Operating margins have improved slightly because of the reduction in material consumed. The percentage of raw materials and packaging materials consumed in total sales has come down marginally, but volatile crude prices in the global market and the recent rupee depreciation remain matters of concern.

Asian Paints are pursuing a three-pronged strategy to increase its export business to a quarter of its sales turnover within the next five years. The strategy is to identify markets where it could gain leadership position, countries where it sees opportunities for growth and nations where licensing agreement possibilities exist.

In the longer term, Asian Paints management expects Sri Lanka, Nepal, Fiji and the upcoming operations in Bangladesh to be key potential growth drivers for its international operations.

Financial Indicators	*Asian Paints*	
	2003-04	*2002-03*
Income/Appropriations		
1. Net sales	174246	157542
2. Value of production	174834	160703
3. Other income	1675	1139
4. Total Income	176509	161842

(*Contd.*)

Source: *Economic and Political Weekly,* November 20-26, 2004, p. 4952.

(Contd.)

Financial Indicators	*Asian Paints*	
	2003-04	*2002-03*
5. Raw materials/stores and spares/ power and fuel consumed	102986	91357
6. Other manufacturing expenses	1073	829
7. Remuneration to employees	10156	10642
8. Other expenses	33630	30718
9. Depreciation	4801	4852
10. Gross profit	23863	23445
11. Interest	527	835
12. Operating profit	23377	22610
13. Non-operating surplus/deficit	–224	–125
14. Profit before tax	23113	22485
15. Tax provisions	8355	8148
16. Profit after tax	14779	14201
17. Dividends (includes tax on dist profit)	8153	7061
18. Retained profits	6625	7140
Liabilities/Assets		
19. Paid up capital	9592	6419
20. Reserves and surplus	43562	41243
21. Long term loan	6139	7898
22. Short-term loan	908	2464
(i) of which, bank borrowings		
23. Cross fixed assets	65119	63056
24. Accumulated depreciation	31065	26618
25. Inventories	21149	20690
26. Total assets/liabilities	65067	63840
Miscellaneous Items		
27. Excise duty	26463	23520
28. Gross value added	40014	40077
29. Total foreign exchange earnings	1026	717
30. Total foreign exchange outgo	286	390
Key Financial and Performance Ratios		
31. Turnover ratio (sales to total assets)	3.1	3
32. Gross value added to gross fixed assets (%)	62.4	65.4
33. Return on investment (Gross profit to total assets) (%)	37.0	40.4
34. Gross profit to sales (gross margin) (%)	13.7	14.9
35. Operating profit to sales (%)	13.4	14.4
36. Profit before tax to sales (%)	13.3	14.3
37. Tax provisions to profit before tax (%)	36.1	36.2
38. Profit after tax to net worth (return on equity) (%)	29.3	32.0
39. Dividend (%)	74.1	101.7

(Contd.)

(Contd.)

Financial Indicators	Asian Paints	
	2003-04	2002-03
40. Earnings per share (Rs.)	15.4	—
41. Book value per share (Rs.)	55.4	—
42. P/E ratio (multiple)	18.7	19.2
43. Debt-equity ratio (adjusted for revaluation)	0.13	0.22
44. Short term bank borrowings to inventories (%)	0.0	0.0
45. Sundry creditors to sundry debtors (%)	100.9	134.5
46. Total remuneration to employees to value added (%)	25.4	26.6
47. Total remunerations to employees to value of production (%)	5.8	6.6
48. Gross fixed assets formation (% growth)	3.3	5.8
49. Growth in inventories (%)	2.2	32.7

MARUTI UDYOG

Networked Sales and Services

Maruti Udyog (MUL) began its production in 1983, and has come a longway since then MUL is the market leader among automobile companies in India. The Government of India, which was a partner in MUL, divested its stake to the public in 2003-04. The public issue was over subscribed 10 times.

Though the improved economic environment in the country has led to an increase in automobile sales, the going has not been entirely smooth for the Indian auto industry one main reason is competition, which have intensified with the increase in the number of auto companies, which has introduced several models in the market and driven down prices in all segments. The industry has also witnessed a significant increase in raw material prices, which has put profit margins under pressure.

Maruti's net sales increased by 31 per cent between FY03 and FY04 from Rs. 7,126 crores to Rs 9,345 crores. Profit after tax increased by 270 per cent, from Rs. 146 crores to Rs. 542 crores.

One of MUL's strengths is its strong leadership and service network. The company has a network of 280 sales outlets and 1,900 workshops. This ensures that customers have no problem either in buying cars or

Source: *Economic and Political Weekly*, November 27-December 3, 2004, p. 5072.

getting their cars serviced. Maruti has also launched other services under new business initiatives. This includes a consortium of finance companies called Maruti Finance, Maruti Insurance and Maruti Truevalue, a preowned car business.

The last financial year was significant for MUL for a number of resins. The company recorded its highest ever sales of 4.7 lakh vehicles in the domestic and export markets secondly.

This sales growth, coupled with improvements in operational efficiencies, resulted in significantly higher returns on investment. Earnings per share increased from Rs. 5.14 in 2002-03 to Rs. 18.8 in 2003-04 MUL's exports grew by 51 per cent, from Rs. 620 crores to Rs. 941 crores. The Company exported over 50,000 vehicles.

However, a major source of concern last year was the continuous and steep increase in the prices of all categories of steel products, which added significantly to raw material costs. Further, there was a shortage of steel supplies in the open market through out 2003-04. MUL overcome this problem in two ways. First, the company entered into long-term contracts with domestic and international parties, which helped it minimise the impact of hardening steel prices and also ensured availability of steel. Second, to meet the requirements of its vendors, Maruti engaged in consolidated buying of steel. It also held direct negotiations with steel mills to fix prices and ensure availability of material.

MUL's future looks bright according to industrial analysis, India could become a production hub for small cars. If this happens Maruti could benefit immensely.

Financial Indicators	*Maruti*	
	2003-04	*2002-03*
Income/Appropriations		
1. Net sales	934560	712650
2. Value of production	934880	703160
3. Other income	40540	29010
4. Total income	975420	732170
5. Raw materials/stores and spares/ power and fuel consumed	713350	568710
6. Other manufacturing expenses	—	—
7. Remuneration to employees	29750	22120
8. Other expenses	102140	71870
9. Depreciation	49490	32210
10. Gross profit	79760	33520
11. Interest	4570	5180

(Contd.)

(*Contd.*)

Financial Indicators	*Maruti*	
	2003-04	*2002-03*
12. Operating profit	75190	28340
13. Non-operating surplus/deficit	–770	–950
14. Profit before tax	76980	28210
15. Tax provisions	22770	13570
16. Profit after tax	54210	14640
17. Dividends (includes tax on dist profit)	4330	4270
18. Retained profits		
Liabilities/Assets		
19. Paid up capital	14450	14450
20. Reserves and surplus	344670	295350
21. Long term loan	30000	30000
22. Short term loan		
(i) of which, bank borrowings	1190	15600
23. Gross fixed assets	456670	451380
24. Accumulated depreciation	273590	225810
25. Inventories	43980	48700
26. Total assets/liabilities	408640	376110
Miscellaneous Items		
27. Excise duty	193840	184140
28. Gross value added	109580	60080
29. Total foreign Exchange earnings	94180	62050
30. Total foreign exchange outgo	10740	14660
Key Financial and Performance Ratios		
31. Turnover ratio (sales to total assets)	2.9	4.8
32. Gross value added to gross fixed assets (%)	24.1	26.6
33. Return on investment (gross profit to total assets) (%)	20.3	17.8
34. Gross profit to sales (gross margin) (%)	8.5	4.7
35. Operating profit to sales (%)	8.0	4.0
36. Profit before tax to sales (%)	8.2	4.0
37. Tax provisions to profit before tax (%)	29.6	48.1
38. Profit after tax to net worth return on equity (%)	16.2	9.5
39. Dividend (%)	30.0	29.6
40. Earnings per share (Rs.)	18.8	5.1
41. Book value per share (Rs.)	124.3	107.2
42. P/E ratio (multiple)	17.4	26.0
43. Dept-equity ratio (adjusted for revaluation)	0.1	0.1
44. Short-term bank borrowings to inventories (%)	2.7	32.0
45. Sundry creditors to sundry debtors (%)	110.2	92.3
46. Total remuneration to employees to value added (%)	27.1	36.8
47. Total remuneration to employees to value production (%)	3.2	3.1
48. Gross fixed assets formation (% growth)	1.2	—
49. Growth in inventories (%)	–9.7	—

COLGATE-PALMOLIVE

Pricing Strategy

Colgate-Palmolive (India) is an oral care and hygiene products company that has managed to increase its net profit for fiscal 2003-04 despite a decline in net sales during the year, from Rs. 947 crores to Rs. 939 crores. Net profit, however, increased by 22 per cent, from Rs. 88 crores in 2002-03 to Rs. 108 crores in 2003-04.

A drop in tax provisions had a big role to play in this increase. But that is not the only reason. Margins before accounting for advertisement expenses fell by almost 200 basis points. Due to the drop in prices, the company could cut down on advertising and promotion. Cost of advertising fell by nearly 380 basis points as percentage of sales in fiscal 2003-04. Colgate is setting up a manufacturing centre in Himachal Pradesh, which should help to lower costs because of the tax benefits available.

Much of the expansion in profits has thus been funded by a cut back in advertising expenses. This strategy of cutting back on advertisement spending, and passing on the savings to consumers through price cuts, might have as impact on the visibility of Colgate's brands in an increasingly crowded market place over the long-term. Part of the savings from the cutback in advertisement spending has been absorbed by rising procurement costs. One positive trigger for Colgate's stock could come from its emergence as a sourcing base for its US-based parent.

The market environment remained extremely competitive during the year and Colgate pursued an aggressive pricing strategy to spur demand for its products. Prices of various brands were reduced by an average of 17 per cent. The cuts were targeted at low-priced competitors, and affected around 65 per cent of the company's sales. The price reduction strategy was successful in re-igniting volume growth.

The results for the first quarter of 2004-05 have been good. Revenues grew by 7 per cent year-on-year (y-o-y) to Rs. 242 crores, and profit after tax grew by 23 per cent in the same period. The company also reported a three-fold jump in operating profit. During the quarter, staff and raw material costs fell by 140 and 266 basis points respectively, on a y-o-y basis. The productivity gains so accrued saw operating expenses fall by 410 basis points. Advertising expenses declined by 11.2 per cent to Rs. 39 crores. The company's top brands, Colgate Dental Cream and Colgate Cibaca, emerged as market leaders in the economy segment.

Source: *Economic and Political Weekly*, November 27-December 3, 2004, p. 5072.

The personal care business, where Colgate has introduced new brands at the premium end, such as the Palmolive Naturals soap range and the Aromatherapy range of shower gels, has the potential to improve its sales mix and profit margins. But the pay-off from this diversification may take some time to materialise.

Financial Indicators	*Colgate-Palmolive*	
	2003-04	*2002-03*
Income/Appropriations		
1. Net sales	93919	94744
2. Value of production	93919	94744
3. Other income	2992	3576
4. Total income	96911	98320
5. Raw materials/stores and spares/ power and fuel consumed	48713	46435
6. Other manufacturing expenses	67	113
7. Remuneration to employees	6952	6951
8. Other expenses	23502	27567
9. Depreciation	2426	1947
10. Gross profit	15251	15308
11. Interest	59	24
12. Operating profit	15192	15284
13. Non-operating surplus/deficit	–44	–636
14. Profit before tax	15148	14648
15. Tax provisions	4348	5782
16. Profit after tax	10800	8866
17. Dividends (includes tax on dist profit)	8160	5780
18. Retained profits	2640	3086
Liabilities/Assets		
19. Paid-up capital	13599	13599
20. Reserves and surplus	10832	13903
21. Long-term loan		
22. Short-term loan	217	214
(i) of which, bank borrowings	—	—
23. Gross fixed assets	32123	31969
24. Accumulated depreciation	23144	16359
25. Inventories	6168	5332
26. Total assets/liabilities	25832	30370
Miscellaneous Items		
27. Excise duty	10289	10945
28. Gross value added	22168	21102
29. Total Foreign exchange	1999	2269

(Contd.)

(Contd.)

Financial Indicators	*Colgate-Palmolive*	
	2003-04	*2002-03*
30. Total Foreign exchange outgo	2525	1432
Key Financial and Performance Ratios		
31. Turnover ratio (sales to total assets)	3.7	3.6
32. Gross value added to gross fixed assets (%)	69.2	66.7
33. Return on investment (gross profit to total assets) (%)	54.3	52.2
34. Gross profit to sales (% gross margin)	16.2	16.2
35. Operating profit to sales (%)	16.2	16.1
36. Profit before tax to sales (%)	16.1	15.5
37. Tax provisions to profit before tax (%)	28.7	39.5
38. Profit after tax to net worth (return on equity) (%)	41.6	33.7
39. Dividend (%)	60.0	42.5
40. Earnings per share (Rs.)	7.9	6.5
41. Book value per share (Rs.)	18.0	20:2
42. P/E ratio (multiple)	17.7	21.3
43. Debt-equity ratio (adjusted for revaluation)	—	—
44. Short-term bank borrowings to inventories (%)	—	—
45. Sundry creditors to sundry debtors (%)	469.5	431.8
46. Total remuneration to employees to value added (%)	31.4	32.9
47. Total remunerations to employees to value of production (%)	7.4	7.3
48. Gross fixed assets formation (% growth)	0.5	2.1
49. Growth in inventories (%)	15.7	–27.1

ESSAR STEEL

Demand Boost

Essar Steel is the flagship company of the Ruiafamily-promoted Essar Group. It is based in Hazira in Gujarat and manufactures hot rolled coils, sponge iron and liquid steel.

Essar Steel posted a net profit of Rs. 60 crores for the fiscal ended March 31, 2004, against a loss of Rs. 562 crores for the previous fiscal. The company has a huge amount of debt, which is not unusual among private sector steel companies in India. Steel deregulation in 1991 resulted in a massive. Capacity build-up, and support from financial institutions enabled private players to enter the market. However, this brought with is attendant debt problems when the industry slumped. Essar Steel's interest and depreciation for FY04 stood at Rs. 397 crores and Rs. 403 crores respectively, against Rs. 393 crores and Rs. 367 crores for the previous year.

The improved performance has been due to persistent attempts to reduce debt, an increase in volumes and an improved product mix, coupled with buoyancy in the steel markets. The company plant to clear Rs. 460 crores of debt by handing out cumulative convertible preference shares that can be converted into equity within about 18 months. It also plants to raise $200 millions to replace its high cost debt and meets working capital needs. Another plan, mooted by the corporate debt-restructing of the company by writing down its equity by 40 per cent.

To increase shareholder value, Essar Steel is implementing a three-point programme: raise production volumes, improve operating margins and reduce finance costs. This strategy has already begun to pay-off through increased profitability. The company aims to raise its hot-rolled coils capacity from 2.4 mn tonnes per annum (mtpa) to 3 mtpa, with only a marginal additional investment, lowering pertonne costs and raising profits. Simultaneously, it is squeezing improved productivity out of all its operations.

Essar Steel has been the largest exporter of hot-rolled coils for the past five years, exporting over 40 per cent of its production. However, due to shrinkage of the export market, exports have registered a substantial decline. Owing the past four years, the global steel industry went through a recession. Most developed nations raised trade barriers, making export of steel unviable. In India itself, steel was considered a sunset industry and a value destroyer. The turnaround has therefore been gradual. Over the past six months, Indian steel companies have been gearing themselves for expansion and increased demand. Investments in the steel industry total to over Rs. 1,00,000 crores. Domestic consumption of steel is expected to rise from the current level of 35mn tonnes to 60 mn tonnes by 2012. A second factor is the strong demand for the steel from China.

Domestic demand is also expected to play an important role. Infrastructure growth in India will ensure a good pick up in demand for steel products. The automobile sector, white goods and oil and gas pipelines are also expected to fuel demand for steel, thus further shoring up the bottomlines of steel companies.

Source: *Economic and Political Weekly*, November 27-December 3, 2004, p. 5972.

Financial Indicators	*Essar Steel*	
	2003-04	*2002-03*
Income/Appropriations		
1. Net sales	370095	162802

(*Contd.*)

(Contd.)

Financial Indicators	*Essar Steel*	
	2003-04	*2002-03*
2. Value of production	372034	161119
3. Other income	1670	659
4. Total income	373704	161778
5. Raw materials/stores and spares/power and fuel consumed	257133	109246
6. Other manufacturing expenses	—	—
7. Remuneration to employees	4831	2320
8. Other expenses	19358	–1268
9. Depreciation	40327	21789
10. Gross profit	53686	29691
11. Interest	46226	25349
12. Operating profit	7640	4342
13. Non-operating surplus/deficit	1947	–4191
14. Profit before tax	9407	151
15. Tax provisions	3408	0
16. Profit after tax	5999	151
17. Dividends (includes tax on dist profit)	0	0
18. Retained profits	5999	151
Liabilities/Assets		
19. Paid-up capital	50797	33035
20. Reserves and surplus	144296	142149
21. Long-term loan	397761	356890
22. Short-term loan	69736	122509
(i) of which, bank borrowings	—	—
23. Gross fixed assets	680254	664776
24. Accumulated depreciation	331701	291414
25. Inventories	69428	58098
26. Total assets/liabilities	740385	749387
Miscellaneous Items		
27. Excise duty	32365	13676
28. Gross value added	98062	53434
29. Total Foreign exchange earnings	—	—
30. Total Foreign exchange outgo	—	—
Key Financial and Performance Ratios		
31. Turnover ratio (Sales to total assets)	0.5	0
32. Gross value added to Gross fixed assets (%)	14.6	8.0
33. Return on investment (gross profit to total assets) (%)	7.2	3.9
34. Gross profit to sales (gross margin) (%)	14.5	18.2
35. Operating profit to sales (%)	2.0	2.7
36. Profit before tax to sales (%)	2.5	0.1
37. Tax provisions to profit before tax (%)	36.2	0.0
38. Profit after tax to net worth (return on equity) (%)	3.2	0.1
39. Dividend (%)	0.0	0.0

(Contd.)

(Contd.)

Financial Indicators	*Essar Steel*	
	2003-04	*2002-03*
40. Earnings per share (Rs.)	1.2	0.0
41. Book value per share (Rs.)	38.1	52.4
42. P/E ratio (multiple)	14.2	—
43. Debt-equity ratio (adjusted for revaluation)	2.4	2.7
44. Short-term bank borrowings to inventories (%)	—	—
45. Sundry creditors to sundry debtors (%)	128.5	199.5
46. Total remuneration to employees to value added (%)	4.9	4.3
47. Total remunerations to employees to value of production (%)	1.3	1.4
48. Gross fixed assets formation (% growth)	2.3	0.2
49. Growth in inventories (%)	19.5	31.7

NATIONAL ALUMINIUM COMPANY

Expansion Drive

The Public Sector aluminium behemoth National Aluminium Company (Nalco) is on an expansion drive awaiting approval from the government for the planned second phase of investments. The Central Government earlier had chalked out a plan for disinvesting Nalco to bring down its holding in the aluminium major from 87.15 per cent to 26 per cent, after factoring a 2 per cent reservation for employees. Now, with the stalling of the disinvestments proceedings, the company wants to go ahead with its expansion programme. The previous phase of expansion was accomplished during 2002 increasing aluminium smelter capacity by 1.15 lakh tonne per annum (tpa) and adding two 120 MV each captive power plants. During this round of expansion the company intends to invest a total of Rs. 4,000 crores, of which Rs. 1,200 crores will be utilised to further expand alumina refinery capacity by 5.25 lakhs tonne per annum. This will increase the total capacity of alumina refinery at Damonjodi in Orissa to 21 lakh tonnes. The remaining amount will be utilised to further increase the aluminium smelter capacity at its Angul plant in Orissa from 3,45,000 tonnes to 4,60,000 tonnes, expansion of bauxite mines from 48 lakh tonnes to 63 lakh tonnes and addition of two more captive power plants of 120 MW each. This will increase Nalco's installed power generation capacity up to 1200 MW.

Source: *Economic and Political Weekly*, May 8-14, 2004, p. 1868.

The other to bigwigs in this non ferrous metal business, Balco and Hindalco, are also involved in similar expansion programmes with the latter in the process of completing its expansion project. This industry wide expansion of capacities by primary producers in the country has been driven by the upsurging in demand for aluminium. Although current supply is higher than demand, most producers believe that the current upsurging is going to be sustained, particularly due to the strong demand emanating from China. During April—December 2003 there has been a robust 23.5 per cent increase in production of aluminium as compared with 7 per cent increase recorded in the corresponding period last year. Recently, aluminium majors in the country have increased the domestic prices of aluminium products by about Rs. 3,000 per tonne.

Nalco has started full-fledged production and marketing of value added special alumina/hydrate (alumina chemicals) zeolite-A and cold rolled products. This has been made possible with the completion of the special grade alumina project and commissioning of the cold rolled products plant in 2002. The company entered into rolled products through the acquisition of International Aluminium products (IAPL) in 2001. It was subsequently merged with the smelter unit at Angul and latter commissioned in March 2002. This 50,000 tpa plants is well-equipped to produce a variety of rolled products like foil stock, finstock, can stock circles, cable wraps and standard sheets having wide applications in consumer durables and packaging industry. Among traditional products, Nalco produces aluminium ingots, sows, billets, wire rods, alloy wire rods and cast strips. Among alumina and hydrate products, the company produces calcined alumina and alumina hydrate. The company reported Rs. 520.93 crores of net profit on a turn over of Rs. 2,739.67 crores in 2002-03 and in the third quarter ended December 31, 2003, it has posted a net profit of Rs. 167.09 crores as compared to Rs. 127.67 crores in the corresponding quarter last year.

Financial Indicators	*Nelco*	
	2002-03	*2001-02*
Income/Appropriations		
1. Net sales	256430	222510
2. Value of production	253186	222969
3. Other income	22302	14466
4. Total income	275488	237435

(Contd.)

(*Contd.*)

Financial Indicators	*Nelco*	
	2002-03	*2001-02*
5. Raw materials/stores and spares/ power and fuel consumed	90629	76379
6. Other manufacturing expenses	8739	6746
7. Remuneration to employees	26551	34604
8. Other expenses	28941	24964
9. Depreciation	35957	31237
10. Gross profit	84671	63505
11. Interest	12045	11690
12. Operating profit	72626	51815
13. Non-operating surplus/deficit	2517	746
14. Profit before tax	75143	52561
15. Tax provisions	23051	11626
16. Profit after tax	52092	40935
17. Dividends (includes tax on dist profit)	43612	25773
18. Retained profits	8480	15162
Liabilities/Assets		
19. Paid-up capital	64431	64431
20. Reserves and surplus	266573	258093
21. Long-term loan	86833	122921
22. Short-term loan	45611	33424
(i) of which bank borrowings	45611	13787
23. Gross fixed assets	875862	819856
24. Accumulated depreciation	374701.	338813
25. Inventories	48925	48432
26. Total assets/liabilities	621925	600002
Miscellaneous Items		
27. Excise duty	17537	16064
28. Gross value added	125209	115163
29. Total foreign exchange earnings	153279	123542
30. Total foreign exchange outgo	27656	45145
Key Financial and Performance Ratios		
31. Turnover ratio (sales to total assets)	0.4:1	0.4:1
32. Gross value added to gross fixed assets (%)	14.8	15.0
33. Return on investment (gross profit to total assets) (%)	13.9	11.4
34. Gross profit to sales (gross margin) (%)	33.0	28.5
35. Operating profit to sales (%)	28.3	23.3
36. Profit before tax to sales (%)	29.3	23.6
37. Tax provisions to profit before tax (%)	30.7	22.1
38. Profit after tax to net worth (return on equity) (%)	15.9	12.0
39. Dividend (%)	60.0	40.0
40. Earnings per share (Rs.)	8.1	6.4
41. Book value per share (Rs.)	51.4	50.1
42. P/E ratio (multiple)	14.9	10.3
43. Debt-equity ratio (adjusted for revaluation)	0.40:1	0.48:1

(*Contd.*)

(Contd.)

Financial Indicators	Nelco	
	2002-03	2001-02
44. Short term bank borrowings to inventories (%)	93.2	28.5
45. Sundry creditors to sundry debtors (%)	288.4	83.3
46. Total remuneration to employees to value added (%)	21.2	30.0
47. Total remuneration to employees to value of production (%)	10.5	15.5
48. Gross fixed assets formation (% growth)	6.8	13.8
49. Growth in inventories (%)	1.0	18.9

ADANI EXPORTS

Diversifying Product Range

Adani Exports is a global trading organisation engaged in export and import of commodities. The Company over the period has been successfully diversifying its portfolio of commodities and now covers more than 40 products comprising broadly in Agro, Energy, Textiles and precious goods. Trading in precious goods, mainly diamonds, started during 2002-03 in the markets of China and Taiwan. It is now considering exporting cut and polished diamonds to these countries and also to Dubai and European countries to enlarge the business. Focus continues to be on agro commodities and during the year under review, the company emerged as one of the largest exporter of wheat from India. It has introduced trading of rice and is planning to export sugar in a big way. Similarly, in textiles, new products like cotton grey, knitted fabrics, bed sheets and raw silk have been added.

Performance of the company is intricately linked to the volume of global trade of the country. Although, exports from the country continue to be under 1 per cent of the total global market share, it remains one of the swiftest and lucxative sectors of the economy and performance over the recent years have been commendable. During 2002-03 exports increased by 17.8 per cent as against a decline of 0.4 per cent in the previous year. Imports also increased by 16.9 per cent as compared to the marginal increase of 1.7 per cent in the previous year.

Against the backdrop, Adani Exports during 2002-03 earned a total income of Rs. 2,853.36 crores registry a net profit of Rs. 88.33 crores as

Sources: *Economic and Political Weekly*, May 8-14, 2004, p. 1868.

against Rs. 65.67 crores in 2001-02. Profit before depreciation, interest and tax was Rs. 130.91 crores as compared to Rs. 109.64 crores in the previous year. Earning in the form of other income through sale of investments was Rs. 60 crores. Other income for the company has been flowing from its investments in infrastructure development projects. As a developer, it has been involved in infrastructure ventures and has recently signed a memorandum of understanding with the Orissa Government to develop the Gopalpur port on a build, own, operate and transfer basis. Gujarat Adani Port at Mundra, a joint venture with Wilmar Holdings Private Limited of Singapore, is now fully functional. The company during 2002-03 divested part of its holdings in this infrastructure facility to P and O Ports and derived Rs. 44.2 crores. It is likely to derive a significant portion of its profits in the form of other income through sale of investments in 2003-04 as well through divestment of around 25 per cent stake in Adani container (Mundra) Terminals.

Financial Indicators	*Adani Exports*	
	2002-03	*2001-02*
Income/Appropriations		
1. Net sales	272797	277385
2. Value of production	272810	276937
3. Other income	18434	8688
4. Total income	291245	285625
5. Raw materials/stores and spares/ power and fuel consumed	261608	258648
6. Other manufacturing expenses	1298	1322
7. Remuneration to employees	573	664
8. Other expenses	9546	9711
9. Depreciation	186	189
10. Gross profit	18034	15091
11. Interest	7810	7696
12. Operating profit	10223	7396
13. Non-operating surplus/deficit	–1132	–799
14. Profit before tax	9092	6597
15. Tax provisions	258	30
16. Profit after tax	8834	6567
17. Dividends (includes tax on dist profit)	746	695
18. Retained Profits	8087	5872
Liabilities/Assets		
19. Paid-up capital	3205	4205
20. Reserves and surplus	51863	47406
21. Long-term loan	10855	16196
22. Short-term loan	21236	31351
(i) of which bank borrowings	31088	30523

(Contd.)

(Contd.)

Financial Indicators	*Adani Exports*	
	2002-03	*2001-02*
23. Gross fixed assets	4616	4682
24. Accumulated depreciation	924	786
25. Inventories	7746	12526
26. Total assets/liabilities	97444	99490
Miscellaneous Items		
27. Excise duty	0	0
28. Gross value added	641	7417
29. Total Foreign exchange earnings	37743	86996
30. Total Foreign exchange outgo	76518	75546
Key Financial and Performance Ratios		
31. Turnover ratio (sales to total assets)	2.8:1	2.7:1
32. Gross value added to gross fixed assets (%)	13.8	169.2
33. Return on investment (Gross profit to total assets) (%)	18.3	14.6
34. Gross profit to sales (gross margin) (%)	6.6	5.4
35. Operating profit to sales (%)	3.7	2.7
36. Profit before tax to sales (%)	3.3	2.4
37. Tax provisions to profit before tax (%)	2.8	0.4
38. Profit after tax to net worth (return on equity) (%)	16.6	12.8
39. Dividend (%)	20.6	16.5
40. Earnings per share (Rs.)	39.4	28.3
41. Book value per share (Rs.)	249.8	234.1
42. P/E ratio (multiple)	10.1	4.8
43. Debt-equity ratio (adjusted for revaluation)	0.76:1	0.92:1
44. Short-term bank borrowings to inventories (%)	401.3	243.7
45. Sundry creditors to sundry debtors (%)	63.5	67.2
46. Total remuneration to employees to value added (%)	89.4	9.0
47. Total remunerations to employees to value of production (%)	0.2	0.2
48. Gross fixed assets formation (% growth)	–1.4	14.6
49. Growth in inventories (%)	–38.2	—

GUJARAT ALKALIS AND CHEMICALS

Turnaround

Gujarat Alkalis and Chemicals (GACL) is a diversified and integrated producer of chemicals with leadership position in production of caustic soda and caustic chlorine in the country. It has successfully turned into

Sources: *Economic and Political Weekly*, May 8-14, 2004, p. 1869.

itself during 2002-03 after four years of successive losses, recording a net profit of Rs. 28.04 crores on a total income of Rs. 923.43 crores. During the year under review net sales shot up to Rs. 924.03 from Rs. 817.52 crores in 2001-02, improving turnover ratio from 0.6 per cent to 0.7 per cent. Production of major chemicals recorded a rise of 5.03 per cent during 2002-03 as against last year's aggregate production. It has continued with its improved performance to record net sales of Rs. 717.70 crores and profit of Rs. 40.03 crores for the completed three quarters of the current financial year 2003-04.

During the year under review, the company went through overall debt restructing under the corporate debt restructing system instituted by the Reserve Bank of India. The comprehensive debt-restructing package classified the debts into four different series. Debts under the first series are repayable in three years without any interest and 75 per cent of overdue interest and liquidated damages have been waived. Under the second series, the rate of interest on the loans/debentures has been reduced to 8 per cent with effect from April 1, 2002. Redemption shall be in 12 quarterly instalments commencing from April 1, 2005. Under the third series, interest has been raised up from 10.5 per cent to 11.5 per cent over the period from 2003 to 2010 and the repayment shall be in 26 quarterly instalments commencing from October 1, 2003. The last series debts have been fixed with tenure of 10 years from April 1, 2002 with step-up interest from 10.5 per cent to 14 per cent over the period from 2003 to 2012. The repayment shall be in 24 instalments commencing from October 1, 2003. Besides, the unpaid penal charges have been waived in case of all the four series. The company has now decided to make a rights offer to the shareholders to cater to its financial requirements. It will be issued in the ratio of three equity shares for every five equity shares held, at a price of Rs. 12.50 per share aggregating Rs. 34.43 crores. The Company has already received Rs. 10.39 crores from the government of Gujarat as advance for share application money.

Financial Indicators	*GACL*	
	2002-03	*2001-02*
Income/Appropriations		
1. Net sales	92403	81752
2. Value of production	91721	83246
3. Other income	623	1000
4. Total income	92344	84247
5. Raw materials/stores and spares/ and fuel consumed	60156	59595

(Contd.)

(Contd.)

Financial Indicators	*GACL*	
	2002-03	*2001-02*
6. Other manufacturing expenses	1001	1085
7. Remuneration to employees	3802	3370
8. Other expenses	5662	3911
9. Depreciation	7910	7865
10. Gross profit	13813	8420
11. Interest	9315	12418
12. Operating Profit	4498	–3998
13. Non-operating surplus/deficit	830	–80
14. Profit before tax	5328	–4078
15. Tax provisions	2524	0
16. Profit after tax	2804	–4078
17. Dividends (includes tax on dist profit)	0	0
18. Retained profits	2804	–4078
Liabilities/Assets		
19. Paid-up capital	4590	4590
20. Reserves and surplus	27288	28154
21. Long-term loan	81380	90366
22. Short-term loan	7401	12428
(i) of which bank borrowings	6901	8028
23. Gross fixed assets	161219	159247
24. Accumulated depreciation	58034	49703
25. Inventories	5041	5815
26. Total assets/liabilities	140722	146431
Miscellaneous Items		
27. Excise duty	9889	8961
28. Gross value added	25286	18678
29. Total Foreign exchange earnings	1782	2214
30. Total Foreign exchange outgo	4182	5323
Key Financial and Performance Ratios		
31. Turnover ratio (sales to total assets)	0.7:1	0.6:1
32. Gross value added to gross fixed assets (%)	15.8	12.1
33. Return on investment (gross profit to total assets) (%)	9.6	5.7
34. Gross profit to sales (gross margin) (%)	13.5	9.3
35. Operating profit to sales (%)	4.4	–4.4
36. Profit before tax to sales (%)	5.2	–4.5
37. Tax provisions to profit before tax (%)	47.4	0.0
38. Profit after tax to net worth (return on equity) (%)	8.7	–11.7
39. Dividend (%)	0.0	0.0
40. Earnings per share (Rs.)	6.1	–8.9
41. Book value per share (Rs.)	69.4	71.3

(Contd.)

(Contd.)

Financial Indicators	*GACL*	
	2002-03	*2001-02*
42. P/E ratio (multiple)	5.1	3.8
43. Debt-equity ratio (adjusted for revaluation)	2.78:1	3.14:1
44. Short-term bank borrowings to inventories (%)	136.9	138.1
45. Sundry creditors to sundry debtors (%)	37.6	30.0
46. Total remuneration to employees to value added (%)	15.0	18.0
47. Total remunerations to employees to value of production (%)	4.1	4.0
48. Gross fixed assets formation (% growth)	1.2	6.9
49. Growth in inventories (%)	–13.3	38.9

HLL

Toughing it Out

Hindustan Lever Limited (HLL) is India's largest FMCG Company, with a dominant presence in almost all consumer categories. Its turnover, at Rs. 10,000 crores, is nearly half that of the total organised FMCG business in the country. In recent times, HLL's brand equity, which used to be unrivalled in India, has eroded to a certain extent.

The past four years have been tough for the company. Since 2000, sales have shrunk and profits have grown at 14 per cent annually, compared with an annual sales growth of 31 per cent and profit growth of 45 per cent in the preceding four years. Market capitalisation has shrunk steadily from Rs. 48,000 crores in 2001 to Rs. 29,000 crores in May 2004. In fact, HLL, which was ranked third among Indian corporates in terms of market capitalisation in August 2003, has now slipped to eighth place. The share price of HLL, once an integral part of an investor's portfolio, has taken a severe beating the stock price hit a seven-year low of Rs. 113 in August 2004.

The company's price wars in detergents and shampoos with Proctor and Gamble and other players like Cavinkare have cost it heavily. Also, several small players have emerged and created regional brands, eating into HLL's market share. These small players have proved to be more adopt at reacting quickly to changes in market conditions than has HLL. Adding to its list of woes in the fact that consumer goods sales are stagnating and there is intense competition in a significantly penetrated market.

In response to changing market conditions, HLL undertook a restructing exercise in April 2004, in order to make the organisation learner and fitter. It split its FMCG business into two separate divisions: home and personal care and foods. The home and personal care divisions integrated the soaps, detergents and personal products business, while the foods division integrated the beverages, foods, icecreams and confectionery units. The company has also announced a plan to reinvent its distribution model, to create new ways to reach consumers and redefine current channels.

HLL has, in a SWOT analysis, identified its complex supply chain configuration, price positioning in some categories and high social costs in the plantation business as its weaknesses. HLL is aware of the fact that increased consumer also spending on education, consumer durables, entertainment and travel has resulted in lower spending on FMCG goods. Among the threats that it has identified are aggressive price competition from local and multinational players, grey imports, spurious and counterfeit products in rural areas and small towns, changes in fiscal benefits, and unfavourable raw material prices in oils, tea and other commodities.

The analysis seems to be tough, but HLL's management is confident that with the strategies that it has put in place, it can restore the company to its former glory.

Financial Indicators	*HLL*	
	2003	*2002*
Income/Appropriations		
1. Net share	1012444	993160
2. Value of production	1024464	993544
3. Other income	40054	37959
4. Total income	1064518	1031503
5. Raw materials/stores and spares/ power and fuel consumed	560584	539956
6. Other manufacturing expenses	13953	16567
7. Remuneration to employees	57863	59911
8. Other expenses	194181	183851
9. Depreciation	12478	13410
10. Gross profit	225457	217809
11. Interest	6676	918
12. Operating profit	218781	216891
13. Non-operating surplus/deficit	2460	6662
14. Profit before tax	221241	223553
15. Tax Provisions	44061	46580

(Contd.)

(*Contd.*)

Financial Indicators	*HLL*	
	2003	*2002*
16. Profit after tax	177180	176973
17. Dividends (includes tax on dist profit)	66037	66037
18. Retained Profits	111142	110935
Liabilities/Assets		
19. Paid-up capital	22012	22012
20. Reserves and surplus	191860	343875
21. Long-term loan	160370	1962
22. Short-term loan	457	3868
(i) of which bank borrowings	9604	
23. Gross fixed assets	214172	199436
24. Accumulated depreciation	84609	77890
25. Inventories	139263	127874
26. Total assets/liabilities	384303	371717
Miscellaneous Items		
27. Excise duty	95766	99676
28. Gross value added	273048	266733
29. Total Foreign exchange earnings	127882	124120
30. Total Foreign exchange outgo	19701	18726
Key Financial and Performance Ratios		
31. Turnover ratio (sales to total assets)	2.9	3.2
32. Gross value added to gross fixed assets (%)	132.0	135.7
33. Return on investment (gross profit to total assets) (%)	59.6	63.6
34. Gross profit to sales (gross margin) (%)	22.3	21.9
35. Operating profit to sales (%)	21.6	21.8
36. Profit before tax to sales (%)	21.9	22.5
37. Tax provisions to profit before tax (%)	19.8	20.8
38. Profit after tax to net worth (return on equity) (%)	61.1	52.8
39. Dividend (%)	300.0	300.0
40. Earnings per share (Rs.)	7.9	8.0
41. Book value per share (Rs.)	9.5	16.6
42. P/E ratio (multiple)	23.7	—
43. Debt-equity ratio (adjusted for revaluation)	0.75	0.02
44. Short-term bank borrowings to inventories (%)	6.9	0.0
45. Sundry creditors to sundry debtors (%)	390.9	563.3
46. Total remuneration to employees to value added (%)	21.2	22.5
47. Total remunerations to employees to value of production (%)	5.6	6.0
48. Gross fixed assets formation (% growth)	7.4	3.0
49. Growth in inventories (%)	8.9	3.1

PFIZER

Global R & D Hub

Pfizer is a 40 per cent subsidiary of Pfizer Inc, a US multinational. Recently, the parent company and Warner Lambert (the parent company of Parke Davis) agreed on a $90 billion merger to create the World's fastest growing pharmaceuticals company. Pfizer Inc has also finalised a deal to buy rival company Pharmacia for $60 billions.

Pfizers pharmaceuticals product portfolio spans a wide range of therapeutic classes from vitamin supplements and nutritionals to antibiotics and cardiovasculars. The company's products include protinex (protein supplement). Isoniazid (anti-TB drug), Becasules (B-complex supplement) and Corex (cough syrup). Pfizer India, which is also into the animal healthcare business, entered into a strategic marketing alliance for animal health products with Bayer last year.

Pfizer India has reported impressive results for the quarter ended May 31, 2004. Net profit surged nearly sevenfold to Rs. 9.35 crores. It posted an operating profit of Rs. 7.89 crores during the three months against an operating loss of Rs. 5.42 crores in the corresponding year ago period. The company has been selling unviable plants and employees' strength has also been reduced to lower costs. Synergies in the form of marketing efficiencies, and an efficient supply chain due to the integration of Parke Davis (India), should further boost profitability.

Pfizer India is planning a major rejig of its product portfolio, which could see many of its older, low-volume products hived off either for co-marketing with Indian Companies or be sold off. This will also see the subsidiary finalising a list of products from its parent's stable for introduction into the Indian Market.

India is fast emerging as a low-cost manufacturing hub for global pharma majors. Manufacturing costs of drugs in India are almost half those in Europe and the US, and the cost of drug discovery is one-tenth that in the Western World. India also boasts a large pool of talented scientists and technicians. Pfizer has, therefore, identified its Indian clinical research set up as one of the prime global hubs for its new drug development activity. Pfizer India is strengthening its clinical research team to cope with the added responsibilities. Currently, the team has more than 100 scientists and the company has planned to expand its human resource base in phases. Pfizer India has begun to figure high on the priorities of Pfizer Inc, because in the three phases of clinical research (start-up, execution and close-out) the company has found that its Indian operations have a competitive advantage against other global hubs. This advantage helps it in getting drugs to the market sooner from the time of inception.

Financial Indicators	*Pfizer*	
	2002-03	*2001-02*
Income/Appropriations		
1. Net sales	47463	54243
2. Value of production	46673	53959
3. Other income	3915	5635
4. Total income	50588	59594
5. Raw materials/stores and spares/ power and fuel consumed	26647	23159
6. Other manufacturing expenses	0	0
7. Remuneration to employees	7942	8784
8. Other expenses	15191	15717
9. Depreciation	1083	1064
10. Gross profit	6207	10869
11. Interest	39	76
12. Operating profit	6168	10793
13. Non-operating surplus/deficit	137	372
14. Profit before tax	6305	11164
15. Tax Provisions	3554	3570
16. Profit after tax	2751	7594
17. Dividends (includes tax on dist profit)	2160	2160
18. Retained profits	591	5434
Liabilities/Assets		
19. Paid-up capital	2880	2344
20. Reserves and surplus	27960	27923
21. Long-term loan	0	0
22. Short-term loan	0	0
(i) of which bank borrowings	0	0
23. Gross fixed assets	13683	13687
24. Accumulated depreciation	8022	8527
25. Inventories	8658	8484
26. Total assets/liabilities	30840	30803
Miscellaneous Items		
27. Excise duty	8432	10884
28. Gross value added	12273	16282
29. Total Foreign exchange earnings	1149	939
30. Total Foreign exchange outgo	462	309
Key Financial and Performance Ratios		
31. Turnover ratio (sales to total assets)	1.8	2.7
32. Gross value added to gross fixed assets (%)	89.7	141.2

(*Contd.*)

(Contd.)

Financial Indicators	*Pfizer*	
	2002-03	*2001-02*
33. Return on investment (gross profit to total assets) (%)	20.1	45.5
34. Gross profit to sales (gross margin) (%)	11.1	16.7
35. Operating profit to sales (%)	11.0	16.6
36. Profit before tax to sales (%)	11.3	17.1
37. Tax provisions to profit before tax (%)	56.4	32.0
38. Profit after tax to net worth (return on equity) (%)	9.0	32.1
39. Dividend (%)	65.4	80.3
40. Earnings per share (Rs.)	9.6	32.4
41. Book value per share (Rs.)	107.1	129.1
42. P/E ratio (multiple)	15.8	15.2
43. Debt-equity ratio (adjusted for revaluation)	—	—
44. Short-term bank borrowings to inventories (%)	—	—
45. Sundry creditors to sundry debtors (%)	134.2	70.0
46. Total remuneration to employees to value added (%)	64.7	53.9
47. Total remunerations to employees to value of production (%)	17.0	16.3
48. Gross fixed assets formation (% growth)	0.0	45.9
49. Growth in inventories (%)	2.1	50.3

VSNL

More Bandwidth

Videsh Sanchar Nigam Limited (VSNL) provides public international telecommunication services, directly and indirectly, linking the Indian domestic telecommunications network to 237 territories worldwide. VSNL offers both basic and spcialised services. Basic services include telephony, telex and telegraph. Specialised services include gateway packet data transmission, electric data interchange, e-mail, internet, international maritime satellite mobile services, leased channel, transmission of signals for international television broadcasts, and video conferencing. The company has three operating segments: international telephony, Internet and leased line services.

VSNL is no longer the sole provider of international long-distance services in India. That lucrative monopoly once provided about 90 per cent of the company's sales. VSNL hopes to enter the domestic long-distance phone market, and is building up its network infrastructure. It has been ranked the third largest Internet service provider (ISP) in Asia. Before opening up the international long distance market to competition, the government sold a 25 per cent stake in VSNL, with management control, to the Tatas conglomerate in 2002. The Tatas subsequently hiked their stake to 45 per cent.

Over the last financial year, falling rates ate into VSNL's margins and increased competition led to a loss in market share. Unlike in the days when it was a monopoly, the lower rates have not been offset by an increase in volumes. Thus, in the nine months to December 2003, VSNL's revenues fell by 34 per cent while profit before tax fell by 58 per cent. However, VSNL has since recorded on amazing turnaround. It registered a rise of almost 93 per cent in net profit for the quarter ended June 30, 2004, at Rs. 127 crores, against Rs. 66 crores in the corresponding year ago period.

VSNL has announced plans to make a capacity expansion investment of Rs. 2,000 crores during the current year. On the anvil are plans to consolidate its presence in the broadband business and to offer telephony services in Hong Kong. VSNL acquired Dishnet-DSL's narrow band and broadband business for Rs. 270 crores earlier this year, which will give its operations a significant presence in the ISP and broadband business.

VSNL's basic business of providing international long distance services has fallen in revenue terms. It has been aggressively persuing other business areas. VSNL is keen on focusing on broadband and has launched high speed internet over cable networks in some parts of Mumbai. It has also commissioned a submarine link between Chennai and Singapore, which is expected to generate a large amount of band width. It has also made sizeable investments in the current fiscal on infrastructure and broadband services. The enhancement in capacities should lead to growth over time.

Financial Indicators	*VSNL*	
	2003-04	*2002-03*
Income/Appropriations		
1. Net sales	316354	453855
2. Value of production	316354	453855
3. Other income	20105	26784
4. Total income	336459	480638
5. Raw materials/stores and spares/ power and fuel consumed	3200	3227
6. Other manufacturing expenses	0	0

(*Contd.*)

(Contd.)

Financial Indicators	VSNL	
	2003-04	2002-03
7. Remuneration to employees	13824	15364
8. Other expenses	246606	321806
9. Depreciation	17207	14702
10. Gross profit	53716	124837
11. Interest	44	327
12. Operating profit	53672	124510
13. Non-operating surplus/deficit	655	930
14. Profit before tax	54326	125440
15. Tax Provisions	16561	47433
16. Profit after tax	37766	78007
17. Dividends (includes tax on dist profit)	12825	24225
18. Retained profits	24941	53782
Liabilities/Assets		
19. Paid-up capital	28500	28500
20. Reserves and surplus	488218	526542
21. Long-term loan	0	35400
22. Short-term loan	6300	0
(i) of which bank borrowings	0	0
23. Gross fixed assets	256517	340446
24. Accumulated depreciation	59081	101519
25. Inventories	241	68
26. Total assets/liabilities	523729	622468
Miscellaneous Items		
27. Excise duty	0	0
28. Gross value added	118858	186176
29. Total Foreign exchange earnings	138357	284995
30. Total Foreign exchange outgo	69748	97594
Key Financial and Performance Ratios		
31. Turnover ratio (sales to total assets)	0.6	1
32. Gross value added to gross fixed assets (%)	39.8	59.7
33. Return on investment (gross profit to total assets) (%)	9.4	20.6
34. Gross profit to sales (gross margin) (%)	17.0	27.5
35. Operating profit to sales (%)	17.0	27.4
36. Profit before tax to sales (%)	17.2	27.6
37. Tax provisions to profit before tax (%)	30.5	37.8
38. Profit after tax to net worth (return on equity) (%)	7.0	14.7
39. Dividend (%)	39.2	74.1
40. Earnings per share (Rs.)	13.3	27.4
41. Book value per share (Rs.)	181.3	194.8
42. P/E ratio (multiple)	15.5	2.7
43. Debt-equity ratio (adjusted for revaluation)	0.01	0.06
44. Short-term bank borrowings to inventories (%)	0.0	0.0

(Contd.)

(Contd.)

Financial Indicators	*VSNL*	
	2003-04	*2002-03*
45. Sundry creditors to sundry debtors (%)	237.0	109.2
46. Total remuneration to employees to value added (%)	11.6	8.3
47. Total remunerations to employees to value of production (%)	4.4	3.4
48. Gross fixed assets formation (% growth)	–24.7	20.1
49. Growth in inventories (%)	256.1	33.8

TATA MOTORS

Going Global

Tata Motors is on its way to being a global automobile manufactures like General Motors, Toyota Motors and others. The company has recently changed its name from Tata Engineering and Locomotive Company Limited to reflect its core business of design development and marketing of automobiles. The company made its first mart on a major international market with its passenger car, 'Indica'. It has come up with an agreement with MG Rover, the UK-based auto major, to supply Indica for the latter's requirement of a small car in its portfolio. Although the car will be sold with the brand name 'City Rover' and with some modifications, it marks a significant milestone in terms of acceptability in the international market Tata Motors will be supplying one lakh 'City Rover' over the next five years to be sold in the UK and other European markets. This apart, the parent company of MG rover, Phoenix Holdings, has decided to market other vehicles of Tata Motors like 'Tata Safari' and 'Tata 207 DI' pick-up vehicles in the European markets.

In its strides towards globalisation, the company recently acquired Daewoo Commercial Vehicle Company (DWCV), the truck-making unit of the Korean company Daewoo Motors. With this acquisition, Tata Motors will make its foothold in the South Korean market and will spread to the neighbouring countries, particularly the booming Chinese market. DWCV is the second largest truck maker in South Korea with an annual production of 20,000 vehicles and controlling around 25 per cent of the market sharp in the Korean heavy trucks segment. The products of both the companies are complementary as Tata Motors manufactures vehicle under 200 hp range, while DWCV makes vehicles in the 200 hp to 400 hp range. Besides this complementary range of products, the integration process on completion will provide muscle to product development and also international marketing. Both the companies have already joined hands to accelerate the development of new generation commercial vehicle. Tata Motors initiated the 'Global Truck Project' a year ago and now with Daewoo offering its technical competencies is expecting to launch these vehicles by 2007.

With its turnaround during 2002-03 the company has strengthened its market leadership in commercial vehicles. Sales of commercial vehicles improved from 1,46,700 vehicles in 2001-02 to 1,91,200 vehicles in 2002-03 giving it a share of 55 per cent of the total market share. Commercial vehicles can be classified into three segments based on gross vehicle upright as heavy, medium and light vehicles. Market share of the company in the first two segments improved from 63 per cent in 2001-02 to 64 per cent in 2002-03. Although Tata Motors is also the largest player in the light commercial vehicle segment, its share has been on the decline in the recent years. The market share, which was 46 per cent in 2001-02, has declined to 43 per cent in 2002-03. The company during 2002-03 launched its new models with high standards of safety features, comfort and aesthetics—the Ex-series of medium and heavy commercial vehicles and 207 DI pick-up vehicles in the light commercial vehicle segment. The company launched the 'Indigo' Sedan as its first offering in the mid segment of passenger cars during 2002-03.

Financial Indicators	*Tata Motors*	
	2002-03	*2001-02*
Income/Appropriations		
1. Net sales	886025	724742
2. Value of production	897999	719839
3. Other income	23917	18454
4. Total income	921916	738293
5. Raw materials/stores and spares/ power and fuel consumed	609320	506661
6. Other manufacturing expenses	46041	33631
7. Remuneration to employees	72037	69164
8. Other expenses	81932	73463
9. Depreciation	35951	35468
10. Gross profit	76635	19906
11. Interest	27895	38223
12. Operating profit	48740	–18317
13. Non-operating surplus/deficit	2297	7396

(Contd.)

(*Contd.*)

Financial Indicators	*Tata Motors*	
	2002-03	*2001-02*
14. Profit before tax	51037	–10921
15. Tax Provisions	21026	–5548
16. Profit after tax	30011	–5373
17. Dividends (includes tax on dist profit)	14430	0
18. Retained Profits	15581	–5373
Liabilities/Assets		
19. Paid-up capital	31983	31982
20. Reserves and surplus	227733	214524
21. Long-term loan	139590	200887
22. Short-term loan	6241	29609
(i) of which bank borrowings	6241	2003
23. Gross fixed assets	601703	591006
24. Accumulated depreciation	271045	243172
25. Inventories	115929	98751
26. Total assets/liabilities	761865	745889
Miscellaneous Items		
27. Excise duty	174379	138929
28. Gross value added	164147	108718
29. Total Foreign exchange earnings	0	0
30. Total Foreign exchange outgo	0	0
Key Financial and Performance Ratios		
31. Turnover ratio (sales to total assets)	1.4	1.1
32. Gross value added to gross fixed assets (%)	27.5	18.4
33. Return on investment (gross profit to total assets) (%)	10.2	2.4
34. Gross profit to sales (gross margin) (%)	7.2	2.3
35. Operating profit to sales (%)	4.6	–2.1
36. Profit before tax to sales (%)	4.8	–1.3
37. Tax provisions to profit before tax (%)	41.2	50.8
38. Profit after tax to net worth (return on equity) (%)	0.1	0.0
39. Dividend (%)	40.0	0.0
40. Earnings per share (Rs.)	9.2	–2.0
41. Book value per share (Rs.)	79.8	90.8
42. P/E ratio (multiple)	26.1	—
43. Debt-equity ratio (adjusted for revaluation)	0.56	0.94
44. Short-term bank borrowings to inventories (%)	5.4	2.0
45. Sundry creditors to sundry debtors (%)	0.0	0.0
46. Total remuneration to employees to value added (%)	43.9	63.6
47. Total remunerations to employees to value of production (%)	8.0	9.6
48. Gross fixed assets formation (% growth)	1.8	–0.1
49. Growth in inventories (%)	17.4	–10.6

MICRO INKS

Making a Mark

Hindustan Inks and Resins (HIR) which has been recently renamed as Micro Inks, is fast printing its marks across the world. Started in 1992 by the lesser known Bilakhia Group based in Vapi, Gujarat. The company has been growing rapidly at a compound annual growth rate of more than 50 per cent. The company quickly mastered the art of making ink with ingenious process innovations and by adhering to quality standards has been luring customers world wide. It has been able to enjoy cost competitiveness in the overseas market. The net sales during 2002-03 were Rs. 563.86 crores from Rs. 492.28 crores in the previous year. HIR is the domestic market leader accounting for about 40 per cent of the aggregate market share. Having established its dominance in the country, the company embarked on its export-led growth strategy. This started three years back initially targeting the US market, which is the largest market for inks and resins in the world. For this a wholly owned subsidiary, Micro Inks Corporation was created and it has now completed two years of operation. Sales during the second year stand at US$57 million from US$36 million in 2001-02. According to the company, performance during 2002-03 was adversely affected by the sluggish economic condition in the US and the weak level of confidence prevailing the post-September 11, 2001 period. Although the subsidiary is yet to two into black, the parent company is confident about its prospects and has infused additional Rs. 80.4 crores of investments during 2002-03 by way of preferred stocks. The company is now focusing on expanding its territorial markets in the rest of the world. This endeavour has already resulted in the company's presence in more than 50 countries, spreading over Africa, Europe, West Asia and Latin America. Sales in the rest of the world (excluding India and the US) during 2002-03 grew to Rs. 69 crores from last year's figure of Rs. 19 crores. Net foreign exchange earnings during 2002-03 were Rs. 124 crores.

Hindustan Inks is an integrated manufacturer of inks and resins with backward linkages supplying critical raw materials, *viz*. pigments, flush pigments, resins and varnishes, and additives. It has been on a capacity expansion programme since the last couple of years. The company now has five units, which includes the recently commissioned 100 per cent export-oriented unit of Vapi. With expansion and de-bottle necking of its plants, total installed capacity stands at 2,76,440 MT from 1,12,990

MT as of March 2001. During the year under review, a captive power generation plant has been commissioned in the export-oriented unit. According to the company, total investments stand to generate sales of more than Rs. 2,000 crores. To facilitate these initiatives, the promoters during 2002-03 infused Rs. 500 crores in addition to the previous Rs. 1,000 crores. The company has proposed to raise capital through rights issue and adjust the above amount on the other hand, advantage was taken of lower interest rates to replace high cost borrowings with low cost rupee/foreign currency borrowings. It also availed working capital facilities in foreign currency resulting in lower cost of capital of funds on account of rupee appreciation and lower interest rates. The weighted average cost of debt works out to 89 per cent per annum from 11 per cent per annum in the earlier year.

Financial Indicators	*Micro Inks*	
	2002-03	*2001-02*
Income/Appropriations		
1. Net sales	56386	49228
2. Value of production	56069	47866
3. Other income	2307	3397
4. Total income	58376	51262
5. Raw materials/stores and spares/ power and fuel consumed	39459	32609
6. Other manufacturing expenses	0	0
7. Remuneration to employees	2536	2226
8. Other expenses	6737	5468
9. Depreciation	1668	1290
10. Gross profit	7975	9669
11. Interest	4411	4221
12. Operating profit	3565	5448
13. Non-operating surplus/deficit	1951	566
14. Profit before tax	5516	6013
15. Tax provisions	1112	1183
16. Profit after tax	4404	4831
17. Dividends (includes tax on dist profit)	617	547
18. Retained Profits	3788	4284
Liabilities/Assets		
19. Paid-up capital	5716	5866
20. Reserves and Surplus	39247	32643
21. Long-term loan	23411	19900
22. Short-term loan	13814	18137
(i) of which bank borrowings	13314	17132
23. Gross fixed assets	32557	30615
24. Accumulated depreciation	4822	3201

(*Contd.*)

(Contd.)

Financial Indicators	*Micro Inks*	
	2002-03	*2001-02*
25. Inventories	7102	5753
26. Total assets/liabilities	99246	87619
Miscellaneous Items		
27. Excise duty	4414	4139
28. Gross value added	10023	9952
29. Total Foreign exchange earnings	27009	22214
30. Total Foreign exchange outgo	14603	10145
Key Financial and Performance Ratios		
31. Turnover ratio (sales to total assets)	0.7	1
32. Gross value added to gross fixed assets (%)	31.7	38.4
33. Return on investment (gross profit to total assets) (%)	8.5	14.0
34. Gross profit to sales (gross margin) (%)	13.1	18.1
35. Operating profit to sales (%)	5.9	10.2
36. Profit before tax to sales (%)	9.1	11.3
37. Tax provisions to profit before tax (%)	20.2	19.7
38. Profit after tax to net worth (return on equity) (%)	10.6	15.9
39. Dividend (%)	9.6	9.3
40. Earnings per share (Rs.)	26.6	31.6
41. Book value per share (Rs.)	329.2	281.9
42. P/E ratio (multiple)	22.5	—
43. Debt-equity ratio (adjusted for revaluation)	0.83	0.99
44. Short-term bank borrowings to inventories (%)	187.5	297.8
45. Sundry creditors to sundry debtors (%)	56.0	34.6
46. Total remuneration to employees to value added (%)	25.3	22.4
47. Total remunerations to employees to value of production (%)	4.5	4.7
48. Gross fixed assets formation (% growth)	6.3	44.0
49. Growth in inventories (%)	23.5	–16.5

MAHAVIR SPINNING MILLS

Upgradation and expansion

Vardhman Group's Mahavir Spinning Mills is a major player of cotton yarn and polyester sewing threads in the Indian Textile Industry. The company also has presence in the production of steel. During 2002-03, turnover increased to Rs. 906.06 crores from Rs. 780.91 crores, a growth of 16 per cent as against 2 per cent is the previous year. With a turnover ratio of 0.9 per cent as compared to the previous year's 0.8 per cent, the company has been able to cash in from its capacity expansion programme. It has been on a capacity expansion drive since the last few years. Fixed assets are at Rs. 774.94 crores from Rs. 616.48 crores in 2000-01. Last year fixed asset worth Rs. 40.83 crores were added through the expansion-cum upgradation programme. During the year under review, the company acquired Arisht Spinning Mills to its fold thereby increasing fixed assets by Rs. 95 crores. Both production and sale of cotton yarn were higher during 2002-03 with production increasing from 30,532 MT to 37,727 MT. Production of thread was 5,412 MT as against 5,202 MT in the previous year. On the other hand, though production of steel ingots/billets and rolled products were lower than in the previous year, realisation was higher on the back of rising prices of steel. Profits for the year 2002-03 were to the tune of Rs. 42.52 crores, a growth of 67 per cent from the previous year's figure of Rs. 25.41 crores. Export earnings increased from Rs. 199.06 crores in 2001-02 to Rs. 235.91 crores in 2002-03. So far, during 2003-04, performance of the company has been favourable with sales during the quarter ended December 2003 being at Rs. 284.2 crores as compared to Rs. 237.0 crores in the corresponding period last year. The area of concern has been the increasing prices of raw materials world-wide. The upsurging in the cotton prices has been persisting since the first quarter of the current fiscal and its being aggravated by the growing demand from China. World cotton production during 2003-04 is expected to be 20.18 millions tonnes, while present cotton consumption is estimated at 20.87 million tonnes.

Financial Indicators	*Mahavir*	
	2002-03	*2001-02*
Income/Appropriations		
1. Net sales	84179	72782
2. Value of production	85600	73298
3. Other income	1095	645
4. Total income	86695	73943
5. Raw materials/stores and spares/ power and fuel consumed	51592	44351
6. Other manufacturing expenses	2182	1964
7. Remuneration to employees	4955	4590
8. Other expenses	13397	11061
9. Depreciation	5117	4328
10. Gross profit	9452	7649
11. Interest	3882	4165
12. Operating profit	5570	3484
13. Non-operating surplus/deficit	260	170
14. Profit before tax	5830	3654

(Contd.)

(Contd.)

Financial Indicators	*Mahavir*	
	2002-03	*2001-02*
15. Tax Provisions	1578	1113
16. Profit after tax	4252	2541
17. Dividends (includes tax on dist profit)	1220	1082
18. Retained Profits	3032	1460
Liabilities/Assets		
19. Paid-up capital	2575	2575
20. Reserves and surplus	42770	39630
21. Long-term loan	28366	27552
22. Short-term loan	18351	12127
(i) of which bank borrowings	18115	11856
23. Gross fixed assets	77494	64852
24. Accumulated depreciation	30865	26538
25. Inventories	31172	21418
26. Total assets/liabilities	110328	94243
Miscellaneous Items		
27. Excise duty	6428	5309
28. Gross value added	18740	16176
29. Total Foreign exchange earnings	23592	19906
30. Total Foreign exchange outgo	8553	11825
Key Financial and Performance Ratios		
31. Turnover ratio (sales to total assets)	0.9	0.8
32. Gross value added to gross fixed assets (%)	26.3	25.6
33. Return on investment (gross profit to total assets) (%)	9.2	8.2
34. Gross profit to sales (gross margin) (%)	10.4	9.8
35. Operating profit to sales (%)	6.1	4.5
36. Profit before tax to sales (%)	6.4	4.7
37. Tax provisions to profit before tax (%)	27.1	30.5
38. Profit after tax to net worth (return on equity) (%)	9.7	5.8
39. Dividend (%)	42.0	42.0
40. Earnings per share (Rs.)	2.8	1.6
41. Book value per share (Rs.)	29.4	27.1
42. P/E ratio (multiple)	8.2	4.3
43. Debt-equity ratio (adjusted for revaluation)	1.03	0.94
44. Short-term bank borrowings to inventories (%)	58.1	55.4
45. Sundry creditors to sundry debtors (%)	13.7	14.1
46. Total remuneration to employees to value added (%)	26.4	28.4
47. Total remunerations to employees to value of production (%)	5.8	6.3
48. Gross fixed assets formation (% growth)	19.5	5.2
49. Growth in inventories (%)	45.5	2.9

TECHNICAL ANALYSIS

Stock market is a highly volatile market. It requires higher talent, skills, imagination, foresight and risk bearing attitude by the investor. The share prices movement can be analysed in two approaches. They are **"Fundamental and technical analysis"**. The fundamental analysis reveals about the intrinsic value of a share. It also analyses various factors such as economic environment of the nation. Industry position and company efficiency. Therefore the intrinsic value of a share is influenced by these factors. The investor should buy shares when the share price is available at less than intrinsic value. The investor should sell the shares when the share price is higher than in intrinsic value of the scrip. In stock market, knowing the intrinsic value of a scrip is the most important factor. If any investor ignored this element, he will fall in risk. **Technical analysis** is associated with the study of price movement of the security. It deals with the trend position of the market. The investor can know the market trend whether the prices shows **up trend** or **down trend.** The investor will make purchases. If the share prices reveal uptrend, the investor may sell his shares in the down trend for avoiding his risk position from the portfolio. It is helpful information of buying and selling strategy of the scrips in stock market: It analyses the relationship among **price, volume supply and demand** factors. The market is based on supply and demand forces. The volume of share business in the market influences for further trading in the market. Hence the technical analysis will help when to buy or sell the scrips. In stock market investment timing is the most important factor to get success. Enter and exit in the stock market involves either risk or return. It is based on the following **assumptions**:

(a) The share prices are determined by the interaction of supply and demand factors.
(b) The market knows everything.
(c) The market always reveals the trend position.
(d) The market is based on past prices to predict the future.

The above assumptions are considered while making technical analysis. The market discounts every information about the business environment, and corporate financial performance. **Technical analysis** is based on **Dow theory**. Charles H. Dow wrote a series of articles in the Wall Street Journal in 1984. Dow theory was closely associated with the share price movement analysis. However, the technical analysis consists the following aspects:

(1) Dow theory
(2) Technical Indicators
(3) Triangles.

1. Dow Theory

Dow theory was proposed by Charles H. Dow. He was the first editor of the Wall Street Journal. The Theory reveals about the movement of prices of securities on the stock exchange. The stock prices can be studied in the following ways:

(a) Primary movements
(b) Secondary movements
(c) Daily movements.

Primary movements are related to study the share price movements for a period of three years. It is associated with the study of share prices on long term movements. The market is balanced by **bulls and bears.** If the market is dominated by bull operators, then it will be called as **"bull phase"**. In bull phase the share prices are increasing and demand for more scrips. Hence the demand for more scrips during the bulls phase period. If the market is dominated by the bears, then it will be known as **bear phase.** The share prices are declining and more supply of shares exist in the market. The full supply of scrips reduces the market prices. If the share prices increases, it will be called as **Bullish market.** If the share prices declines marginally, it will be known as **Bearish market.** Hence the primary movements may be upward or downward. The trend between upward and downward is called as **"Intermediate trend"** or corrective movements. This corrective movement is related to **3 weeks to 3 months.**

Secondary movements are related to study the share price movements for short term period. The share prices will be closely observed in stock exchanges from **three weeks to three months.** They are opposite in direction to the primary movements. In the **bullish market** the secondary trend would result in the fall of share prices. In the **bearish market** the secondary trend carries the price upward and corrects the main trends.

Daily movements are associated with the observation of share prices for each and every day. It represents irregular fluctuations in the stock exchange prices. They move without any definite trend. The fluctuations do not show any particular trend. These movements will be arised due to speculative transactions. Speculation is **oxygen** to the stock market. These fluctuations arised due to participation of the speculators in the stock exchange. Some investors will make gains out of these fluctuations is only by a chance factor. Winning in the stock market is a chance of factor for same situations. **A Finance Manager** should not depend upon these movements because he is basically an investor and not a **speculator**. Generally speculators will depends upon these movements for a short term gains. They are making buying and selling shares on daily basis for even a small amount of margins. In stock market, times is the most important element for enter and exit. An intelligent investor may purchase shares at lower prices and will be sold at market price rises. Hence the investor should be in a position to identify exactly position of the period. This is technically termed as identification of the turn in the stock exchange prices. Identification of the **"turn"** is a difficult task. If you are able to identify the turn position, you may get success in the stock market. **Primary, secondary and daily movements** are part of the **Dow Theory**. In stock market, the investors can depend upon primary and secondary movements. **Speculators** can depend upon daily movements, because they accept the **risk**. Technical analysis is the important tool in analysing the **support and resistance level** of the stock market. **Support level** is associated with individual stock prices. A considerable demand for a particular stock is expected to prevent further fall in the price level. Hence the fall of a share price can be halted for time being. In this situation demand for the particular share is expected in the stock market.

Resistance level is associated with reduction of share price from further increase in share price. The share price can be halted for the time being is called as **Resistance.** In this situation the supply of shares would be more greater than demand. The increased supply of shares will halt the further increase in share price. These two levels occupy an important role in the stock market. If a particular scrip reaches a certain level and then automatically drops, this situation is called as **Resistance** level. If a particular share price reaches down to a certain level and then its rises is called as **support level**. Hence these two levels may switch over from one level to another levels. They need not be formed only on tops or bottoms. They can be depicted on the graph. It is known as trend lines or **Gaps** of the **Chart**. **Gaps** means a difference in price level between two trading days. **For example:** If the high price of the **ACC** scrip on **April 2nd** is **Rs. 350** and on **April 3rd** low is **Rs. 375**, a gap is said to have occurred on the chart. It indicates that the share is not traded between the level **Rs. 375 and Rs. 350**. This gap indicates further rise in price level. The same situation is applicable in falling price levels of the share prices. A gap is formed if the low price on **May 2nd** is Rs. **200** and the high price on **May 3rd** is Rs. **180**. It indicates that there was no transaction between 200 and 180.

2. Technical Indicators

Technical indicators are one of the important aspect in the technical analysis. The indicators provide a valuable information about the stock market. They will indicate about the direction of the overall market. It reflects the overall market situation. It indicates about macro aspects of the secondary market operations. The overall market movements will show greater impact on the individual share price. In the stock market macro analysis is useful than micro analysis of the environment. **Forecasting** is an important factor in the stock market. Aggregate forecasting is considered to be more reliable than the individual forecasting. Technical indicators are **price and volume of trade, and short sales.**

Volume of Trade

Technical analysis is the study about the market data. It provides full information about the stock market operations. The investors will generally collect the data before making investment decisions. They collect the past share prices, past volume of business done in a particulars scrip will make the investor to take decisions. Investors will get confidence in a particular scrip trading volume. The trend is based on the volume of trade for a particular scrip. In bullish market, large volume of trade will be occurred. Volume expand in bullish market and down in the bearish market. The volume of trade is influenced by the price behaviour of the stock. It is a matter of concern for the investor and the trend may not continue for a longer time. If the share prices rises or fall leads to large increase in volume. The volume of trade can be studied in the Bombay stock exchange in preceding pages.

Statement shows Volume of Trade in BSE on 15-4-2005
Turnover Toppers at BSE

Sl. No.	*Name of the Company*	*No. of shares traded*	*Turnover (Rs. in crores)*
1.	Infosys Technology	7,51,652	147.81
2.	TISCO	27,14,022	100.08
3.	Reliance Industries	18,02,986	529.70
4.	SBI	12,35,575	621.75

(Contd.)

(*Contd.*)

Sl. No.	Name of the Company	No. of shares traded	Turnover (Rs. in crores)
5.	Tata Motors	18,59,412	410.25
6.	TCS	4,80,063	1319.00
7.	LIC Housing Finance	20,99,712	252.25
8.	Satyam Computers	11,91,082	382.75
9.	SAIL	70,85,929	58.70
10.	ONGC	3,21,110	846.45
11.	Essar Steels	77,86,626	54.50
12.	Jindal Photo	8,26,510	296.35
13.	Alstom	15,31,089	153.10
14.	M.C. Dowell Co.	8,37,188	285.15
15.	Sesa Goa	3,26,035	686.05
16.	Interlink Financial	1,23,521	246.50
17.	Energy Development	7,75,485	29.70
18.	Essar Oil	5,37,121	34.15
19.	Cranes Software	33,843	516.15
20.	Transparent Biological	1,18,362	121.40
21.	Mega Corpn.	34,56,568	28.95
22.	Hellos & Maths	2,32,416	169.75
23.	Bhansali Engg.	7,93,819	40.75
24.	Alphangeo.	2,21,285	88.35
25.	Ankur Drugs.	2,81,145	68.90
26.	VXL Instruments	3,01,343	58.60
27.	Zigma Software	10,09,745	17.00
28.	United Breweries	38,698	420.20
29.	JMC Project	1,26,190	112.60
30.	Encove Software	4,71,842	30.90

Source: *The Economic Times*, 16-4-2005, p. 8.

Statement shows Turnover Topper at National Stock Exchange (Volume of Trade)

Sl. No.	Name of the Scrip	No. of Shares Traded 15-4-2005	Turnover (Rs. in crore)
S&P CNX NIFTY			
1.	Infosys Technology	21,82,500	429.24
2.	TISCO	60,61,247	223.44
3.	Reliance Industries	39,12,912	208.54
4.	TCS	12,32,810	163.93
5.	Satyam Computers	37,04,816	143.39
6.	Tata Motors	32,48,965	133.68
7.	SAIL	2,18,41,721	130.92
8.	ONGC	14,90,685	127.66
9.	SBI	19,24,131	124.06
10.	Wipro	9,22,352	56.42
S&P NIFTY Junior			
1.	Canara Bank	11,24,751	21.22
2.	Union Bank	15,57,198	17.06

(*Contd.*)

(*Contd.*)

Sl. No.	Name of the Scrip	No. of Shares Traded 15-4-2005	Turnover Rs. in crore
3.	Tata Tele Services	53,95,376	14.15
4.	Nicholas Piramal	5,13,312	10.92
5.	Jaiprakash Associate	5,56,216	9.95
6.	IDBI	11,12,739	9.65
7.	Banagaion Refinery	9,98,406	9.37
8.	Mphasis BFL	3,63,524	8.91
9.	Vijaya Bank	14,62,621	8.83
10.	Andhra Bank	8,10,268	8.39
Others			
1.	Jindal Photo	22,83,206	67.99
2.	MC Dowell Co.	20,15,988	56.88
3.	NTPC	58,67,194	49.51
4.	Hindustan Oil Expo.	35,33,434	48.98
5.	TV 18	15,71,304	38.53
6.	Jet Airways	2,23,648	27.87
7.	Aztec Software	20,60,365	22.50
8.	Tale Data	39,91,254	22.36
9.	Gateway Dist.	16,52,300	18.43

Source: The Casino Effect, *The Economic Times*, 16-4-2005, p. 8.

Statement shows High Volume and Low Price Stock at BSE on 15-4-2005

Sl. No.	Name of the Scrip	Volume on 15-4-2005	Previous volume 14-4-2005
1.	GV Films	30,10,000	46,05,000
2.	Oasis Media	9,61,000	13,26,000
3.	Dynacon System	5,42,000	2,10,000
4.	Kanika Infotech	4,22,000	2,57,000
5.	Penta Software	4,05,000	2,63,000
6.	Kashyap Radiators	3,51,000	4,35,000
7.	Ocean Infrastructure	3,06,000	1,82,000
8.	Systematrix	2,53,000	3,20,000
9.	SVC Supertech	2,47,000	2,42,000
10.	Lyods Finance	2,34,000	71,000
11.	VFL Software	2,30,000	48,000
12.	Khyathi Multimedia	2,16,000	6,65,000
13.	Krishna Life	1,95,000	1,02,000
14.	Futuristic	1,63,000	85,000
15.	Estar Infotech	1,58,000	1,94,000
16.	Consortek	1,45,000	44,000
17.	SRG Infotech	1,22,000	1,35,000
18.	Datapro Infotech	1,15,000	81,000

(*Contd.*)

(Contd.)

Sl. No.	Name of the Scrip	Volume on 15-4-2005	Previous volume 14-4-2005
19.	Ras Propack	1,04,000	21,000
20.	Onida Saivak	1,02,000	33,000
NSE			
1.	Penta Soft Technology	14,34,000	8,94,000
2.	LCC Infotech	6,77,000	6,28,000
3.	Maars Software	4,67,000	3,98,000
4.	Lyods Finance	3,92,000	6,45,000
5.	Dynacons	2,85,000	2,14,000
6.	SRG Infotech	1,63,000	1,02,000
7.	Sri Shakthi	1,34,000	2,63,000
8.	ATN Intnl.	84,000	65,000
9.	Mardia Chemicals	51,000	35,000
10.	Nuchem	34,000	22,000
11.	Peakock Industries	26,000	19,000
12.	Steel Tubes	25,000	14,000

Source: *The Economic Times*, 16-4-2005, p. 8.

Statement shows Highest Deliveries at National Stock Exchange 15-4-2005

Sl. No.	Company Name	Traded Volume	Delivery Volume	% Delivery to Trade Volume	Day's Close
1.	Asian Paints	85,008	83,963	98.77	389.95
2.	Indian Rayon	98,113	96,610	98.47	420.00
3.	Shri Shakthi	1,33,637	1,29,768	97.10	4.10
4.	JCT Electronics	6,03,530	5,84,496	96.85	8.45
5.	Hotel Leela	51,921	50,238	96.76	156.05
6.	Birla Corpn.	1,34,833	1,24,884	92.62	174.70
7.	Ultra Tech Cement	2,55,614	2,33,180	91.22	370.20
8.	Mardia Cement	50,707	46,005	90.73	2.05
9.	Sun Pharma	86,228	75,273	87.82	461.60
10.	Maharastra Seamless	2,69,273	2,35,969	87.63	343.85
11.	Amtek Auto	1,61,122	1,38,203	85.78	159.55
12.	Morgan Stanley	6,17,749	5,29,408	85.70	21.25
13.	CCL Products	59,352	50,358	84.85	198.35
14.	Kit Ply Industries	63,106	52,606	83.36	9.55
15.	BAG Films	59,303	49,350	83.22	9.90
16.	Dynacon System	2,85,106	2,34,525	82.26	0.45
17.	NIIT	55,487	45,520	82.04	193.65
18.	JK Industries	3,15,663	2,58,305	81.83	99.10
19.	Lyods Finance	3,92,076	3,19,010	81.36	3.60
20.	Dewan Housing	1,06,357	85,712	80.59	37.70
21.	Jindal Stainless	97,386	78,844	80.59	96.65
22.	Tourism Finance	99,021	78,586	79.26	17.65
23.	Deccan Chronicle	87,184	68,516	78.59	153.05

(Contd.)

(Contd.)

Sl. No.	*Company Name*	*Traded Volume*	*Delivery Volume*	*% Delivery to Trade Volume*	*Day's Close*
24.	TVS Motor Co.	1,50,300	1,16,842	77.74	69.55
25.	TN Newsprint	1,92,208	1,48,834	77.43	60.60
26.	Tata Tea	1,94,277	1,50,099	77.26	510.15
27.	Vardhaman Acr.	1,96,361	1,49,380	76.07	13.75
28.	South Indian Bank	1,14,741	86,023	74.97	65.80
29.	Sundaram Finance	89,798	67,320	74.97	108.30
30.	Adlabs Films	85,917	64,091	74.60	125.10

Source: Casino Effects, *The Economic Times*, 16-4-2005, p. 8.

The Breadth of the Market

Stock market is a highly volatile narket. The prices are changing on daily basis, and some times even on hourly basis. Hence the investors should be always cautious before making investment decisions. The breadth of the market is associated with the study of price changes in the stock exchange. The **breadth** of the market consists of **Advances, Declines and Net.** Advances mean the number of shares whose prices have increased from the **previous day's trading. Decline** means the number of shares whose prices have fallen from the previous day's trading. All these information is available on all business dailies. **The Net** is the difference between the number of stock advanced and declined during the same period is the **breadth** of the market. A cumulative index of net differences measures the market breadth. The analysis can be presented on graph.

Statement shows Breadth of the Market (BSE)

Trading Date 15-4-2005	
Advances	457
Declines	1858
Unchanged	43
	2358
At NSE	
Advances	89
Declines	719
Unchanged	06
	814

Short Selling

Short selling is one of the technical indicator. It is known as **short interest**. It refers to the selling of shares which are not owned. It is a speculation activity.

The bears are the short sellers who sell now in the hope of purchasing at a lower price in the future to acquire profits. A demand for a particular share indicates future rise of prices. This position shows the general business situations. It requires higher talent and knowledge of the investors.

Oddlot Trading

Shares are generally sold in a denomination of **100**. The shares, which are sold below 100 is called as **oddlot**. The buyers and sellers of small lots is known as oddlot traders. The buying and selling oddlots make **oddlot index**. The oddlot index will be constructed on the basis of volume of business. An increase in purchase of oddlots increases the value of **Oddlot Index**. Selling of oddlots leads to fall in the index. All these information is known by the professional investors. Professional investors are stranger than the oddlotters. If professional investors dominates the market, it is called as strong market. If the oddlotters dominate the market, it is known as **weak market.** The big oddlot purchases make a fall in the market price.

Moving Average

Generally the share prices are moving towards either increasing or decreasing way. Market indices are constructed by with selected share prices. Moving means a change in mobility of a particular thing. Moving average means that the body of data moves a head by absorbing latest things. The trend can be studied by smoothing of the data. The moving average is useful to study movement of the stock market. It also reveals the individual scrip price movement. It indicates the underlying trend in the scrip price. Trend can be determined on the basis of the period. **The short term trend** is associated with the study of moving averages for **10 days to 30 days.** In case of medium-term trend **50 days to 125 days**. The long-term is related to **200 days.** Hence the study can be made for the factors i.e. index and individual stock prices. The professional investors will observe the individual stock prices before making investment decisions. They will compare the individual stock price with the indices to know the bullish or bearish trend. The technical analysts may plot the movements on graph paper. If NSE or BSE index is above stocks moving average line, it indicates **bullish trend**. If the BSE or NSE is below the stocks moving average, it indicates the **bearish market**. If the moving average of the individual stock is above the index average, it indicates **sell signal** and the same situation in reverse indicates **buy signal**. The moving average is useful when to buy and sell shares in the stock market. A comparison should be made between stock price and stock prices moving average. A comparison can also be made between long-term and short-term moving averages. The comparison will reveal the buy or sell signal.

Oscilators

Oscilator means moving from one place to another place. The share prices are changing in the stock market on day-by-day basis. The investor should always be cautious in the stock market before making his investment decisions. Oscilators indicate the market momentum or scrip momentum. It refers to the velocity of price changes. It is measured by the rate of change of prices. It covers the short or a longer period. The short-term oscilators may reveal the price change for **5 or 10 days**. The long-term period for **3 to 6 months** may also be covered by oscilators. The oscilators may move in the same direction, either **positive or negative** depending on the trends of the market.

Relative Strength Index

Relative strength index is one of the oscilator. It is used for identifying the inherent strength or weakness of a particular scrip. This theory was developed by **Wells Wilder**. It can be calculated for a particular scrip by applying the following formula:

$$RSI = 100 - \frac{100}{1 + RS}$$

$$RS = \frac{\text{Average gain per day}}{\text{Average loss per day}}$$

It is calculated for **5, 7, 9 and 14 days.**
A case study of Siemens India presented below:

Date	*Price*	*Gain*	*Loss*
8-4-05	1690.60	—	—
11-4-05	1701.35	10.75	—
12-4-05	1715.20	13.85	—
13-4-05	1742.20	27.00	—
15-4-05	1744.75	2.25	—
		53.85	—
		53.85/4 = 13.46	

$$\text{RSI} = 100 - \frac{100}{1 + 13.46} = 100 - 7.42 = 92.58.$$

Source: *The Economic Times*, 16-4-2005, p. 8.

If the RSI reaches seventy may be down turn and it is time to sell. If the RSI falls below thirty it is time to pick up the scrip.

Charts

Charts are one of the tools in the Technical analysis. They represent the information more easily to understand by a layman. It is easiest tool to analyse the data. It helps to know the trend of the share prices. It reveals the current situation of the stock market. It shows the past movements of a particular scrip. The analysts can use these charts according to their needs and convenience. The charts require higher skills to handle the situation, otherwise they will become dangerous. The charts can be classified as follows:

(a) Figure Charts
(b) Bar Charts
(c) Triangles.

Figure Charts help the investor to find out the trend of the price without any difficulty. They are useful for technical analysts. The share price movement of a particular stock or market indices can be found with the help of these charts. They are one dimensional presentation of data. They are unable to indicate about time or volume. A comparison of current price with previous prices can be made with the help of figure charts. They are drawn in the ruled paper. They are in simple but have certain limitations such as non-indication of intra day price movement. Volume will not be taken into consideration in picturisation of charts. Volume and trend of direction is the most important for taking investment decisions by the investors. In bull market price rise is accompanied by **high volume of trading**. The bear market is related to low volume of trading due to decrease in share prices. **Bar chart** is another kind of charts. It is the simplest and most commonly used tool of a technical analysis.

Triangles are one of the tool in technical analysis. They are easily predictable and popular method. They can be classified into three kinds: **(a) Symmetrical, (b) Ascending, and (c) Descending**. Symmetrical triangle is built up with series of fluctuations. It does not have any bias towards the bull and bear operators. **Ascending triangle** reveals about the upward movement of the share price. **Descending triangle** indicates downward movement of the share price. It is associated with the bear operators movement.

ELLIOT WAVE THEORY

Stock market is a highly volatile market. The investors should always be cautious in the stock market. The behaviour of the stock market can be studied through various number of theories. Technical analysis is the study of data regarding stock market prices. It is fully involved in analysis of the stock market behaviour. Ralph Elliot was introduced a theory about the stock market behaviour. He conducted various empirical studies and tested rules for his theory. According to this, the stock market is unfolded through the basic **rhythm or pattern**. The basic rhythm consists of **five up waves and three down waves** to form a complete cycle of 8 waves. The **rhythm** is reflected in various cycles and waves. One complete cycle consists of **bullish and bearish** phases. Hence the waves are balancing each other and the stock market will be in stabilised manner. In a complete cycle there are **5 bullish and 3 bearish** waves occur. The cycle consists total number of 8 waves. The waves are based on the principle that **action is followed** by reaction. After the completion of 8 waves, there will be a fresh cycle starting with similar impulses arising out of market trading, change of sentiment in the market. The stock market is continuously rotating like these cycles consisting of 8 waves. This theory was empirically tested and found accuracy and timeliness of arising waves. The waves and cycles are useful in identifying the buy and sell signal in the stock market. A lot of empirical study has been carried out by the researchers about the waves and cycles. It is found in the result of the research that the behaviour of prices on the stock market confirms to the cycles and waves. It is proved that the theory has acceptable to predict the prices of shares. **The wave** is the most important element in this theory. The wave indicates the movement of the market price. The waves are emerging from the demand and supply pressures on the market. A demand exceeds supply, there will be a rise in share prices. A supply exceeds demand, there will be a chance leading to a down trend in the prices. **Bullish** phase occurs when demand exceeds supply position. **Bearish** phase arises when supply exceeds demand position of the market. Hence the waves are generated depending upon the pressure of the situation. This theory had also explained that the stock market behaviour was in a consistent manner. Therefore, wave theory is fully based on waves and cycles. The waves are an integral part of the reflection of mass psychology. In same situations, these waves counts are not clear, the shape and length may vary depending on the **buying and selling pressures**. But an experienced analyst can discern the waves in both upward and downward directions. This theory offers the tools of identifying the market turns and their approach. It has some limitations that, the rhythms may not be consistent and the count number may not be possible.

EFFICIENT MARKET THEORY

Markets are generally dynamic. They are influenced by many factors. Stock markets are very delicate and they will react even to a small incident occurred in the Economic, Political, and Business environment. They are influenced by money flows and information flows. Information is most powerful tool in the hands of experts. The market prices are determined by the supply and demand factors. Hence **demand and supply** elements in business can not be ignored. They are the basic foundation for growing dynamic market. The markets are becoming more competitive and they discount every information. The prices are the reflection of the present situation after absorbing the latest information. Hence this situation is called as **"efficient market"**. The free flow of information is discounted by the market and absorbed by it in the form of reflection of price changes. Efficiency means abilities and acquiring skills. The efficient market theory is based on free flow of information and there is no scope for insider information and malapractices. Malpractices in the market exists in many ways. There are no monopoly elements in the market. Information flow is free and costless. In the normal business environment, money flows towards profit. Profitability is the indication of efficiency and competitiveness. Money flows from **less profitable to more profitable avenues.** Hence the **profit** element dictates the flow of money. The information is available to all the investors, which is immediately reflected in the stock prices and nobody can gain additional profit. All financial instruments will be correctly priced and all the information is absorbed by then and any investor entering the market at anytime will have the same advantage. There is no excess profit is available to any investor. If the information is exposed to the public, there is no extra profit is waiting for any investor. The profit is available to those who react immediately to the latest information available in the market. The risk or return depends upon the reaction of the exposed market information content and the investors acceptance level of risk. If the demand and supply forces are playing their role freely, the price are reflecting suitable to the situation. The prices are fair and move in a random manner. Prices are changing in the market on day-to-day forces and move in an independent and random manner. This situation has been lead to concept of **Randomness**. The randomness leads to **Random Walk Theory. Random Walk Theory** is associated with market price behaviour. It is better to understand the Random Walk Theory before going to study about the **Efficient Market Theory**.

Random Walk Theory

Random Walk Theory explains that changes in stock prices are independent and no factor can be influenced. The current prices are independent of the past trends. The information can influence the price levels. This theory was tested by researchers on the basis of empirical work on the market price behaviour. The equilibrium price of a stock is determined by demand and supply forces. This theory is based on the following assumptions:

Assumptions

(1) Market is dynamic and no one can influence it.
(2) Market knows all current information and prices are reflected by absorbing latest development.
(3) All investors have free access to the same information and no one can gain additional profits.
(4) Market prices are changing due to changes in fundamentals.
(5) There is no scope for insider information.
(6) Market can not be influenced by Institutional investors and bulk purchasers.
(7) There is no scope for manipulations in the market.
(8) Competition in the market exists in all times.

The prices are changing in the market due to change in the fundamental factors. Fundamental analysis is associated with the assessment of Intrinsic value of a share. The fundamental factors influence the equilibrium prices. This theory is based on the capital market efficiency theorem. It is considered as restatement of Efficient Market Theory by some analysts. According to this Theory stock exchange prices can never be predicted since they are based on statistical ups and downs. Therefore, the behaviour of stock prices are absolutely unpredictable. Information is a powerful weapon in the hands of professional investors and fund managers. Usually there are three kinds of information affecting the market, **past prices and trends, public information and inside information**. All these sources of information is same to all kinds of investors but all these types are not absorbed perfectly by the market. There is a possibility of some gaining return from the investment.

A lot of research has been carried out to test Random Walk Theory. Empirical tests were conducted both in the past and present in India and abroad. These tests to some extent support the theory. The price changes of today are independent of the past price. The following tests have been carried out by researchers in connection with the validity of **Random Walk Theory**:

(a) Filter Test
(b) Run Test
(c) Correlation Test
(d) Other Tests

Filter means fixing of a ceiling rate in price variation of a scrip. The change in prices are permitted to a particular level i.e. 10 per cent. Hence the increase or decrease of prices of a particular scrip must be in the horizon of 10 per cent. The scrips are not permitted to grow beyond the certain levels of prices. Filtering is the observation of important information affecting the prices from unimportant things. Filter tests were conducted by well known researchers **Fama, Blume and Alexander**. They found that filter tests did not give conclusive proofs.

Run test is associated with the study of price changes in same direction. This test is conducted by **Fama**. It is based on time series data and used to test the theory. Run tests are conducted by the following method.

For example: Associated Cement Company share prices.

350, 352, 356, 356, 362, 360, 360, 365, 370, 360–**10**

An increase in price change in the same direction shows + sign. The count number of signs with no change will be assigned **0**. The changes in price declines will be assigned with – **sign**. The above data shows that there are no price dependencies. As per the test, yesterday's prices neither indicate today's price nor today's price of tommorrow's prices. Several research works have been conducted and found that security prices moved in a random manner.

Correlation Test

Correlation test is associated with the study of movement of stock prices. It is used to measure the extent of association of one series of security prices with a series in the past. Moore is associated to test this theory. He measured the correlation coefficient of price changes of a particular scrip for one week. He also measured the changes for later week of a particular same scrip. He found that a price rise did not show the tendency to the price fall in any predictable manner.

Other Tests

Several empirical studies have been conducted to test the hypothesis. **Brownian** is one of the person to study motion of a share price. Several persons involved in research to study the price changes in the market. **Levy, Jensen, Bennington and Osborne** was associated with the tests. All these tests reveal that price changes in the present period are independent of the past trends. Similarly some of the authors conducted empirical tests in mutual fund performance. **Sharpe, Jenson** were associated with the study of mutual fund performance. They found that insider information is not found to earn any additional profits.

Efficient Market Theory

Efficient market theory is the study about price behaviour of the market. A market in which asset prices reflect all available information quickly and accurately. The market efficiency theory reveals that prices are the result of free flow of information which the market absorbs quickly and efficiently. It is based on correct information. In stock market, information plays a vital role in making investment decisions. Information provides a clear picture about future trend. Professional investors must acquire information to update their portfolio. Information enhances the skills and provide a confidence way. It is a value addition factor. There are three types of information which affect the market *i.e.* past prices, public information and inside information. These three types of information may show impact on the stock prices. The analyst have placed the market absorption under the following heads:

(a) Weak form
(b) Semi-strong form
(c) Strong form.

(a) Weak Form of Efficient Market Hypothesis

The weak form absorbs only market price information. A lot of research has been carried about the weak form. The research proves that the weak form holds good as it is not possible to gain more from the price information of the market. The weak form is closely related to **The Random Walk Hypothesis.** The past prices are not necessarily represent the present prices. The present prices move independently and there is no relation to predict the future.

(b) Semi-strong Form

Semi-strong form is the second component in the information content. It is associated with price information and also other public information. According to this formula, the market absorbs quickly and efficiently not only the **Price Information** but also **publicly** available information. We have already discussed about the power of information. Information in India is easily available in the market. Public Information is available to the investors in the form of **Financial reports Balance Sheet, P & L A/c, earnings, dividend reports, financial results etc.** A number of financial dailies, magazines, journals carries a wide variety of reports concerning financial aspects. A plenty of information is available at the disposal of investors. The success of the stock market depends upon the utilisation of available information. The extraction of information stimulates the level of knowledge of the investors. All information relating to corporate activities are published in the media. Every incident of corporate activity is published in the media and immediately reported in business channels. After the spread of satelite channels, communication flow is very easy to the investors. **The Mega business channel CNBC** provides an excellent source of information. CNBC is providing reports with analytical content and interviews with experts, General Managers, Managing Directors, Board of Directors, Finance Managers and Professionals etc. The media also report such material like financial structure, liquidity, solvency and absorbed by the market in the price information. In the flow of information, some wrong notions, rumours can also be spread. Biased information would also flow in as news affecting the market. Any revision of data or changes in functioning of the company affect the share prices. Some aspects like earnings reports, bonus issues, right issues affect the market even in before official announcement. Empirical research has been conducted to test the effect of any public information released, on the share prices. The studies found absorption of the information on share prices was inefficient and varied from scrip to scrip and the time period. Hence the semi-strong form is empirically not well supported. But in abroad, it is found to be applicable and markets quickly absorb all published information. The public information effect has been tested through **Capital Asset Pricing Model** or some econometric models. However the investors behaviour should be changed. All these theories, bars, charts are ignored by them and blindly they are investing in the stock market. They simply handover the cheque to the broker and they did not know about the company activities, brand names, product line, EPS, dividend declaration, experience of top level management, skills of employees, market share of the company, market potential of the company, capital structure of the company, Industrial relations, consumer behaviour, government policies etc. The revolution in information and communication technology has changed the common man life style significantly.

(c) Strong Form

Strong form is the one of the tools in flow of information. This hypothesis study about the **private information, insider information and unpublished data**. These sources of information is absorbed by the market and represents in stock prices. If any unknown information is exposed to the public, the profit are waiting for all the investors equally. The reaction to the exposed information content is most in factor in getting the success of highly volatile market. Any investor can gain the average return from the market. Acquiring latest information and superior analysis by professional investors can make better returns. It is also possible to get good returns for **inside traders, floor brokers, and institutional investors**. The price movements can be forecast only result in superior return.

The Efficient Market Theory in its strong form is not applicable in the market. In India it is not useful to the investors for same factors. In the Indian capital market, prices are rigged up, manipulation of prices, lack of knowledge of the investors, unqualified empirical analysis had made the failure of this theory. Institutional investors, professional investors can make use the strong form of information by appointing qualified equity market analyst. Equity market research is one of the tools for forecasting prices and identification of undervalued scrips. **Equity research analysts** are the right persons to capture the strong form contents. In Indian market speculation carries **80 per cent** of transactions and markets are not perfect and the absorption of all types of information is also not timely and efficient. The fundamental analysis is useful for the assessment of over valuation and under valuation of the scrip. Investment analysis contains market research, fundamental analysis and technical analysis. **Fundamental analysis** is useful to a large extent and technical analysis occupies a lesser role in the context of market situations. However the **Efficient Market Hypothesis** is based on certain limitations. They are presented below for a wide discussion of this topic:

(1) Random walk hypothesis holds good.
(2) Semistrong form has found less useful to the investors.
(3) The perfect markets do not exist in India.
(4) The stocks are not representing the intrinsic value of a share.
(5) Speculation and sentiment occupies a dominant role in the stock prices.
(6) Information does not spread evenly among all segments of the market.
(7) Investors' knowledge is very low level in the stock market aspects.

Suggestions

SEBI is the most powerful organisation in the capital market. It is conducting investor's conference for primary market operations. But it should provide training facilities to the secondary market investors. Empirical studies have been encouraged by the foreign markets. In India, the focus on research studies should be made by the government. Research organisations should be established and **R&D** wing is necessary for enhancing the levels of knowledge of the investors.

CASE STUDIES

Technical Analysis

Two is better than one

Eveready Industries has kicked off a restructuring exercise that would unlock the value hidden in its related yet diverse lines of business, namely

FMGC and bulk tea. The company has decided to demerge its bulk tea business in to a separate company. The timing is important as its dry cells and packaged tea businesses, comprising the FMCG line, no longer need the support of its cash rich division.

The bulk tea business too is witnessing an up trend over the past nine months and therefore, it can yield handsome value to the company's shareholders. As per plans, if would behaved off into a separate company, Mcleod Russel.

The company's management believes that the demerger would enhance shareholder value over the medium term. The company has already obtained the necessary court approvals for the split

Post-split, equity of Eveready Industries (carrying on the business of dry cells and packaged tea) would be halved to Rs **29.89 crores**, and the shareholders would be offered shares of Mcleod Russel, which would have the bulk tea business. The latter would also have an equal equity capital.

In another move, the company's management has initiated transfer of its dry cells plant from Chennai to the site where its other unit is located. This has offered the company an opportunity to encash the real estate released by the shifting of the plant.

The company's stock trades at Rs. 67 on the bourses.

Reality Boom

Eveready Industries has obtained **8.4 acres** of land near Chennai Airport by trnasferring its dry cells unit. It has tied up with a develops in the area to hand over the released land in exchange for **Rs. 25 crores** up front payment. A part from this sum, the developer would also develop an information technology sector with **10 lakhs** square feet of space in the area. Eveready would be entitled to sell **20 per cent** of this space upon the completion of the project. Therefore, while Eveready Industries would immediately get Rs. 25 crores as up front payment, it would receive more cash flow from sale of developed land in another **15 to 18 months**. It would also manage to reduce operating costs at the consolidated dry cells plant.

Tea Business

Until the beginning of the year the tea sector was not doing too well. Thus, the bulk tea division of Eveready Industries was contributing around

30 per cent of the company's annual revenues. However, with tea prices picking up by **25-30 per cent** profitability has risen hand somely.

The company has **60,000** hectares of land under tea cultivation with better cash flows and a pick-up in sentiment, the company could raise its land usage substantially. Assurances from government on relief measures for the tea sector and waiver of some state imposed levies and taxes like octroi, local taxed and introduction of VAT may prove hopeful with the opening up of markets in Egypt, Iran, Russia etc, the company hopes to explore the export markets for tea in a more effective manner.

FMCG Business

The Company's FMCG operations have dry cells business, flash lights and packaged tea business. After the demerger of the bulk tea business and thanks to cash flow from sale of land, the company plans to reduce debt burden and expand its revenues.

Financials

In the current financial years, due to better performances of **FMCG** and tea divisions, net profit has risen to Rs. 40.59 crores in the April–December 04 period, a shade better than Rs. 38.78 crores profit it earned in the same period last year.

However, last year it had suffered badly during Q4 due to a bad tea season. That had pushed the company into losses during FY04. However, the current year Q4 may be much better due to a stable tea season and the company may end the year with profits close to Rs. 45 crores.

Eveready Industries

	'04'	*'03'*	*FY04*
Net sales	744.41	687.57	868.22
Other income	23.03	19.82	40.07
Expenditure	647.9	595.5	814.08
Operating profit	119.54	13.39	94.21
Interest	52.36	49.79	74.26
Gross profit	67.18	63.6	19.95
Depreciation	23.5	23.72	31.98
Profit before tax	43.68	39.88	–12.03
Tax	3.09	1.1	0.35
Net profit	40.59	38.78	–12.38
Equity capital	55.78	55.78	55.78

Source: The Economic Times, 31 January2005-6 February 2005, p. 3.

Out Look

As per the scheme of arrangement, the splitting of FMCG and bulk tea businesses into separate entities would become effective retrospectively from April 2004, and both—Eveready Industries as well as Mcleod Russel-would be listed independently on the stock exchanges.

With the business out look for both entities appearing positive at the movement, the combined value of the two could easily exceed the current valuation of the merged entity.

ALL CHARGED UP

Eveready Industries
Technical: Eveready Industries
Long-term Trend: Market performer
Medium-term Trend: Market performer
Short-term Trend: Out performer

Price Movement

The current upward movement in the scrip started from a level of Rs. 19 as it moves up while forming higher tops and bottom. The scrip, after touching a high of Rs. 72, is currently quoting at around Rs. 67 levels. Volumes have been shrinking and the scrip's has been forming bottoms, which is an indication that traders are not interested in selling the scrip at lower levels.

Oscillator Charts

The moving average convergence divergence (MACD) on the weekly charts is currently in the positive territory and has come into buy mode once again On the daily charts also it is on the verge of giving a buy signal as it takes support from the equilibrium line. The 12th week rate of change (ROC) is in the positive territory and is showing strong divergence on the daily charts, this oscillator is currently placed in the positive territory but is not showing any strong negative divergence. The 14th week relative strength index (RSI) is just below the over bought territory but is showing strong negative divergence on the daily chart, it is currently placed in the equilibrium territory and is also showing negative divergence. The extreme short-term oscillators of the scrip have started moving upward from the over

sold territory. This indicates that the upward movement of the scrip has still minor strength left.

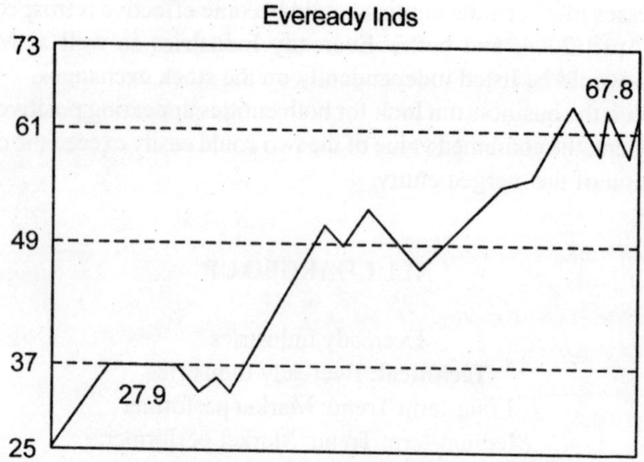

Source: The Economic Times, 31 January2005-6 February 2005, p. 3.

Inference

The scrip has been out performing the market for the last 12 months, but the current oscillator charts are indicating divergence. While investors holding the scrip may stay put, and fresh investment would only be seen when the scrip moves southward.

FREEZING THE DOWNSIDE

As the sensex makes new heights, market participants are wondering when this bullrally will come to a halt. There is a lot of apprehension over making fresh purchases, as analysts suggest partial profit booking. Though this may be a prudent strategy in most cases, there are few sectors that are still undervalued and if investors have a long-term view, buying at these levels is recommended. One such sector is the banking sector. This sector is set to outperform in the next year, once the interest rate overhang and the move to held to maturity (HTM) category is out of the picture. The reason for this beliefs is that almost all banks are witnessing margin expansions and growth in retail portfolio.

One bank that is set to capitalise on the retail in the country is UTI Bank. And, since the bank has shifted most of its securities to the **HTM**

category, the coming quarters will reflect the effect of increasing margins. We take a look.

Investment

With India witnessing a huge pick-up in credit demand, all banks are trying to take a share of this pie. **UTI Bank**, till a few years back, was focussed on corporate banking. It is only in the past three years that the bank has aggressively started increasing its retail presence. This shift in focus has helped the bank improve profitability and margins.

The bank's margins were **1.7 per cent** in **FY02, 2.8 per cent in FY04** and **3.1 per cent** for the quarters ended September 2004. That the focus is now on retail can be gauged from the fact that in March 2002 retail loans constituted only **5 per cent** of the total loan book and by end September 2004, retail loans were **26 per cent** of the total book. It was not only the loan side that was dominated by corporate loans; even the fundling side had a non retail focus. That has now changed, as low-cost deposits are now 32 per cent of total deposits; this figure was just 16 per cent in March 2002.

Because of the retail shift, the bank has not only witnessed margin expansion but core earnings have grown as well. Core fee income grew by **91 per cent** Y-O-Y in the second quarter of 2004-05 with retail fee being the key driver.

Another point in the bank's favour is its Superior asset quality. The bank has among the lowest NPAS in the industry. The gross NPL ratio is just **2.5 per cent** while net NPL is below 1.5 per cent. This is despite the fact that bank has a low coverage ratio of just **59 per cent**.

The bank has one of the largest net worked distribution infrastrucures in the country, with **297 branches** and **1,415 ATMs**. And, since all these branches and ATMs are net worked, implementing new schemes and initiatives is cost effective.

Concerns

TILL recently, bulk of the bank's earnings came from treasury gains. Now, with interest rates going up, treasury gains have totally dried up and so has the major source of bank's income. Public sector banks have been more badly hit than their private sector counterparts, as they had close to 50 per cent of investments in government securities. In addition, they were maintaining very high durations of **5 to 6** years. UTI Bank, on the other hand, had the stipulated **25 per cent** invested in government securities and was maintaining duration of 2 to 3 years.

A commendable point is that the bank has shifted almost its entire portfolio to the HTM category, thereby immunising its portfolio from any interest rate movement. Though the shift to HTM category entailed a one-time hit, UTI Bank is better off than most banks, which still to shift their securities to the HTM category.

Another concern is the **15 per cent** stake that HSBC picked up in UTI Bank. HSBC picked this stake in **December 2003** and in **July 2004**, the RBI came out with a draft guideline stating that any foreign bank with an existing branch network in India cannot hold more than 5 per cent stake in private sector bank. This created havoc in the market and all banking stocks took a beating. But the finance minister recently stated that foreign banks would be allowed to follow the creeping acquisition route and take up to 10 per cent stake in a bank every year. This issue of the 15 per cent stake of **HSBC** is still not clear but it is expected that **HSBC** will be allowed to keep the stake, as it picked up the stake before the guidelines were made.

BANK WITH THE BEST

UTI Bank

	12 Months	
	March 2003	*March 2004*
Income	1875.28	2126.86
Operating Income	1464.81	1586.71
Other Income	410.47	540.15
Non-Recurring Income	0	0
Expenditure	1574.08	1697.45
Interest Expended	1142.41	1021.45
Personnel Cost	85.23	121.25
Other Expenses	346.44	554.75
Profits/Losses		
PBDT	301.2	429.41
Depreciation	0	0
Provisions and Contingencies	0	0
PBT	301.2	429.41
Tax	109.02	151.1
Deferred Tax	0	0
PAT	192.18	278.31

Source: *The Economic Times*, 12 December, 2004, p. 13.

Outlook

The bank is expected to come out with an equity issue in the new year to increase its tier-1 capital to help sustain growth in the next few years. The bank is financially sound and has been reporting good results year after year. The service standards of this bank are among the best in the industry and the new thrust on retail will help the bank in the long run.

With no tension of shifting securities to the **HTM** category, UTI Bank will score over other banks in the coming quarters. The bank is all poised to mark its presence in all retail sectors. Its valuations look attractive; investors can look at the stock for the long-term.

Technical
Quite bankable UTI Bank
Long-term Trend: Out Performer
Medium-term Trend: Market Performer
Short-term Trend: Market Performer

Price Movements

It's among the few banking stocks that has been able to beat the index in the last one year forming a new high along with the sensex. Its post May 17 upward journey started from Rs. 115 as formed higher tops and bottom. It is currently quoting at a new high Rs. 189. The strong intermediate upward movement of the scrip is being followed by a strong correction move, which has a long time frame.

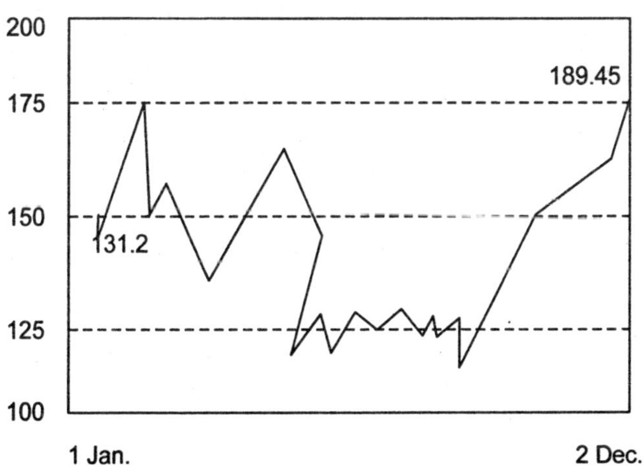

Oscillator Charts

The moving average convergence divergence (MACD) on the weekly charts is currently in buy mode in the positive territory. On the daily charts also, this Oscillator is placed in the positive territory and is moving upward. Though the first signs of negative divergence have appeared on this chart, it is still not being reflected on the price of the scrip. The 14th week relative strength index (RSI) is currently placed in the over fought territory but has still not given a sell signal on the daily charts also this Oscillator is currently in the over fought territory, but has not given a sell-signal. The 12th week rate of change (RoC) is in the over fought territory and is moving in tandem with the scrip. The Oscillator on the daily charts is also indicating a similar trend as it moves upward while forming higher tops and bottom. The weekly stochastic is in buy mode just below the over fought territory. The daily stochastic, on the other hand, is on the verge of giving a buy signal as both the average and trigger lines are converging.

Inference

The scrip seems to be in strong hands as it forms a new high. While in the short-term it might witness a correction, but as far as long-term investors are concerned, they should stay invested.

ENJOYING THE PIGGYBACK RIDE

Haryana Based Omax Autos is a Tier-I vendor of sheet metal, tubular and machined components for two wheelers and sprockets for cars. It is a key vendor to Hero Honda with around **75 per cent** of its revenues coming from the company and some **10 per cent** from Maruti of late, the company is working on widening its client box, leveraging its product range and making intiatives to move up the product value chain.

The company, promoted by the Mehtal Brothers and managed by the Omax Group **(47 per cent stake)**, has six manufacturing facilities and is in the process of setting up new facilities in Bangalore and Haryana.

Financials

A look at Omax's number shows that the performance has been steady in **FY04**. Net sales have moved up **12.6 per cent** to Rs. 366.9 crores in **FY04**. Despite higher cost of raw materials, a trend likely to continue net profit has risen by **2.9 per cent to Rs. 14.3 crores** in FY04. The company expects net profit figures to move to around is 18 crore in **FY05** and around Rs. 22 crores in FY07.

Rising raw material costs has resulted in shrinking of operating margins, which have fallen to 8.3 per cent in FY04, from 9.3 per cent in the previous year.

The company has seen a marginal fall in its return on capital employed to 22.7 per cent from 23.2 per cent in FY04, and its return on equity too has declined from **34.4 per cent to 29.7 per cent** company officials feel that rising raw material cost and capital expenditure, plans have strained the RoCE and RoE measures.

Things could look up in the next two years as exports are expected to be higher. It customers include Delphi, Tenneco (suppliers to Ford), Cummins and Ikea of Sweden. The company expects exports to grow to Rs. 100 crores in the next few years. Capital expenditure plans for Bangalore and Haryana are in progress. The Bangalore plant is expected to go fully on stream in the next three years for production of sheet metal components.

Though company officials are non-committal about fund raising, analysts expect the company to raise capital. It might see an equity dilution of about **10 per cent** (**2 million** new shares being added to the 20.31 million existing shares outstanding) over the next two years. In February 2004, Omax had obtained shareholder approval for issue of 2 million convertible warrants to a promoter company at a price of Rs. 90 each **(as per SEBI guidelines),** to be convertible in two stages of 1 million each in FY05 and FY06.

Subsequently on February 19, 2004, the board of directors issued the first stage of 1 million warrnats to the promoters. With further dilution highly likely. It would be a matter of concern for investors interested in the Omax scrip.

On Auto Pilot

	FY04	*% change*
Net Sales	366.9	12.6
Total Expenditure	336.5	13.8
Net profits	14.3	2.9
Interest	5.2	16.5
Depreciation	10.4	2
Operating Margins	8.3	—
RoCE	22.7	—
RoE	29.7	—

Source: *The Economic Times*, 12 December, 2004, p. 3.

M and As

Omax is also looking at acquisition opportunities abroad. Company officials had visited an Australian plant some months back and are considering other options as well Omax officials claim that they are aiming at a Rs. 100-150 crores acquisition using Rs. 25 crores from surpluses and the balance from debt. Besides acquisition plans, the company also got Indital Tintoria amalgamated with itself in end September 2004.

Omax plans to increase its press shop facilities with some 20 imported presses, by the end of this year or beginning of next year.

Outlook

The Omax scrip has seen a rise in its earnings year end EPS of the share rising to Rs. 9.2 from Rs. 6.4 last year. The company is hopeful of a 20-30 per cent annual growth over the next couple of years. The amalgamation with M/s Indital Tintoria might have an impact on Omaxs Financials in the coming year though.

Given its plan for capital expenditure and overseas acquisition, Omax has to tackle its problem of falling operating margins and financial ratios. However, it can hope to gain from the positive sentiment for the automotive components sector.

FULFILLING A PIPES DREAM

Maharashtra seamless is the Rs. 800 crores flagship company of the DP Jindal Group. The company is in the business of manufacturing seamless pipes and electric resistant welded (ERW) pipes. It is emerging as a major player in the liquid logistics industry and caters to the high growth oil-drilling sector, which is a major customer. The company is a market leader in seamless pipes of up to 14" diameter, and a leading player in ERW pipes as well.

Having established its presence in both these segments, where the clientele is mainly from the petroleum and power sectors, the company has undertaken backward integration to grow exponentially and increase margins. The company has initiated a Rs. **550 crores** backward integration project to manufacture steel billets in the State of Orissa. This will help the company bring down its cost of raw-materials, increasing margins substantially in the future.

Source: *The Economic Times*, 27 December, 2005, p. 3.

The company is a big gainer from the increasing opportunities being presented by the scaling up of activities in the offshore drilling sector, focus on gas and oil transport through pipelines, LPG distribution through pipelines and massive thrust on infrastructure by the government.

The Company has also recently entered into a **50:50** joint venture with Hydril Company LP of the US to from Hydril Jindal. International for the manufacture of premium connections, supplied exclusively by Maharashtra seamless to local and export markets.

There is significant business upside for the company from enhanced oil exploration activity under the new exploration licensing policy and the thrust on infrastructure spending that would require increased transportation of liquids and gas.

Therefore, visibility for earnings growth is pretty high for MSL and the future looks promising for the debt-free company.

Products

The company manufactures seamless pipes, which are used for high pressure and high strength applications. Such applications find use in oil and gas drilling gas transport, boilers, refineries, etc. The company has leading multinational oil companies as its customers.

Approval to the new exploration licensing policy and subsequent award of various projects has vastly increased the activity in the petroleum and gas sector, as well as drilling. This has raised the usage of seamless pipes in the recent past and demand is likely to rise sharply in future.

Being a market leader in the seamless pipes segment, MSL should be the biggest beneficiary of this explosive growth in oil exploration.

The company's other major product line is the manufacturing of ERW pipes, used mainly in moderate to low pressure applications like transport of crude oil, petroleum products and water, etc. The growth in this segment is strong, yet moderate composed with the pace in seamless pipes.

Backward Integration

Over the past year and a half, price of main raw material steel has been soaring. MSL uses steel billets as a key raw material. Rising steel prices eroded the company's margins, as most of its supplies were on a long-term contract basis.

To tackle the menace of fluctuation in raw material prices and also to achieve lower cost of production, MSL has initiated moves to backward integrate operations by setting up a steel billets plant in Orissa.

The project estimated to require a Rs. **550 crores** out lay would ensure that the company starts saving on its raw material costs within a year from now. This backward integration could prove to be a big forward for improving the company's profit margins going forward.

Financials

In the current financial, Maharashtra seamless clocked net sales of Rs. **548.7 crores, up 63.67 per cent** from the comparative period's net sales of Rs. **335.24** crores last year. Operating profit in the first nine months of FY05 moved up to Rs. **91.74** crores, up 18.05 per cent from **Rs. 77.7** crores in the comparative period of **FY04.**

Operating profit margin during FY04 slipped almost 600 basis points compared with the first nine months of FY04. This was caused by the steep rise in raw material costs, part of which the company had the bear in the current financial.

The gross profit rose to Rs. 89.47 crore in the first nine months of FY05, up **17 per cent**. Rise in raw-material costs was the only dampened for the company's performance as its growth otherwise remained very strong. Still, the company managed a higher profit before tax of Rs. 82.07 crores for the first nine months of FY05 compared with Rs. 71.57 crores last year.

Outlook

The company is likely to end the current financial with a net profit of nearly Rs. 80 crores, translating into an earnings per share (EPS) of around Rs. 28 for FY05 on a conservative basis. However, next year, FY06 earnings are likely to be significantly higher. The company can see a growth of nearly 40 per cent annually over the next three years thanks to higher volumes, product price hikes and lower input costs.

The PE multiple on current year earnings is close to 12 times, while on a one year forward earnings basis it is around nine times with high earnings visibility the present valuation appears low.

Once the company gets fully integrated after completion of its steel billets manufacturing project it would enjoy significant cost advantage with opportunities for growth continuing to rise in oil and gas exploration and in other infrastructure areas, the company is poised for growth in the medium a long-term.

Maharashtra Seamless

	Apr-Dec 04	*Apr-Dec 03*	*FY 04*
Net sales	548.7	335.24	491.1
Other income	4.38	9.84	6.76
Expenditure	461.34	267.38	390.77
Operating profit	91.74	77.7	107.09
Interest	2.27	1.05	1.97
Gross profit	89.47	76.65	105.12
Depreciation	7.4	5.08	6.99
Profit before tax	82.07	71.57	98.13
Tax	28.27	19.23	33.62
Net profit	53.8	52.34	64.51
Equity Capital	28.82	28.82	28.82

Technical

GET A GRIP

Maharashtra Seamless

Long-term Trend	:	Out performer
Medium-term Trend	:	Market performer
Short-term Trend	:	Out performer

Price Movements

After coming out of hibernation in 2003, the scrip has continued to out perform the market, whenever the market has been in a strong bull phase, the scrip has moved up while forming higher tops and bottom. And, during corrections and bearish phases, it has moved in a side ways direction. Volumes in the scrip have been improving too. After touching a high of Rs. 375, the scrip is currently quoting at Rs. 345. The scrip's up move has been in shorts and spurts. The secondary correction, which set into the scrip, was in a sideways form with volumes decreasing sharply. This is an indication of the strength in the scrip, as before bears take control of a stock, the secondary correction tends to become very long.

Source: *The Economic Times*, 27 December, 2005, p. 3.

Maharashtra Seamless

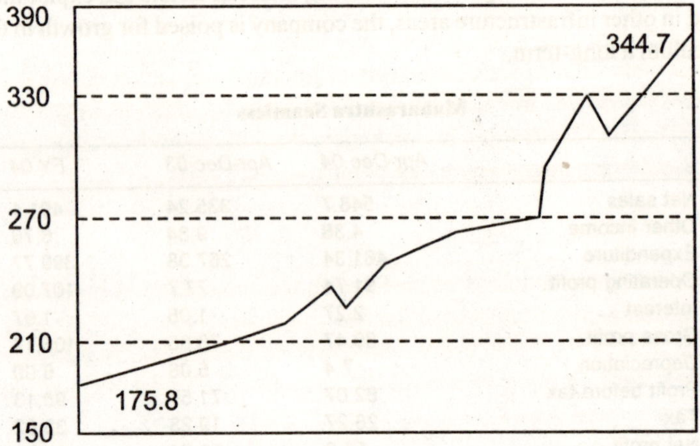

Osillators Charts

The moving average convergence divergence (MACD) on the weekly charts is in buy mode as it inches up without showing any negative divergence. On the daily charts, though the MACD is in buy mode, the average and triggers lines are converging, as it gets ready to give a sell signal. In the past this oscillator has given false buy signals. The 12th week rate of change (RoC) is in the positive territory and is currently moving up while forming higher tops and bottom. On the daily charts also, this oscillator is in the positive territory and is moving in tandem with the scrip. The 14th week relative strength index (RSI) is in the over bought territory but is yet to give a sell signal. On the daily charts, RSI is placed in the equilibrium territory, but is not showing any major divergence. The weekly stochastic is in the over bought territory but is yet to give a sell signal. On the daily charts the oscillator is currently placed in the over sold territory but has also not given a buy signal.

Inference

The scrip is in the strong grip of bulls and the short-term correction too seams to be getting over. Investors may look at the scrip with a medium to long-term perspective.

JUST AT RANDOM

Wanderlust took a strong hold over Indians and foreigners alike in the past year. That's music to the ears of International Travel House (ITH), which provides travel and tourism services for individuals as well as corporates. There was a big pick up in the tourism trade in 2004, which should bring in good times for companies like ITH.

Financials

All the major concerns of past year have been effectively addressed. The company's net sales for quarter ended December 2004 were up **16 per cent to Rs. 11.76 crore,** while total expenses, chiefly wages, rose **8 per cent** on plans to control the costs ITH MD Anil Bhandari said, "Salaries and wages are likely to go up Travel House is automating all its work processes as well as launching its own travel portal to distribute its products, which would result in controlling the wage cost". A rising top line yielded operating margins for the latest quarter at 25.4 per cent compared with **20.3 per cent a year ago**. This quarter is one of the indicative months for the travel trade, since bookings for the peak winter months, October–February, for in found tourism are made several months in advance.

However, Bhandari adds a note of caution, "Operating margins are likely to come down during 2005 but we plan to counter the same by increasing sale volumes."

The company has been focusing on the high margin MICF (Meetings, Incentives, Conferences and Exhibitions) segment over the past year for the individual traveller, ITH had launched over 100 plans as well as niche plans which are expected to drive growth for 2005-06. Presently, the strategy seems to be working. Net profit for December 2004 quarter was Rs. 1.19 crores, a growth of 38 per cent over December 2003 quarter. For the year ended March 2004, ITH's net sales were Rs. 38 crores against Rs. 33 crores in the previous year. For the year ended March 2004. PAT was Rs. 2.87 crore, though not really comparable to March 2003 results since there was a non-recurring income of Rs. 4.09 crores as ITH divested its 49 per cent stake in lease plan India, making it a fully travel tourism focussed company now.

Outlook

Going forward, all indicators suggest tourism growth should be robust in

2005, says Bhandari, "The outlook for tourism industry is good. We expect 3.3 million in bound tourists this year. For the year 2005-06 we expect a growth of 15 per cent. In respect of out bound, we presently have 5 million tourists. We expect a growth of 20 per cent in the year 2005-06. Presently, we have 300 million domestic travellers and we expect a growth of 15 per cent during the year 2005-06."

The 'incredible India' compaign to promote India as a safe and diverse tourist destination has started paying off. Coupled with this campaign, the open sky policy that now allows more Indian and international carries to operate from various airports in India is also a positive step. The increase traffic should offset decrease in commissions that many airlines have implemented. ITHS billings rose 16 per cent in 2003-04. Says Bhandari, "The FIT Luxury Segment appears to be the key growth area and this is the reason for the launch of the Travel House luxury vacations package. The outlook appears good for the rest of the current financial year. We expect a growth of 25 per cent during 2005-06, on the down side, however, factors that can impact ITH's future performance are outside its control. This means past performance may not necessarily be maintained in case of disruptions. Added to this is the continued non-availability of hotel rooms and shortage of air seats, which remain a different to growth.

Valuations

The company's share price is currently around Rs. 80. Its stock price has consistently ranged between Rs. 75-80 over the past three months, which have otherwise been volatile for the Bombay Stock Exchange (BSE) sensex.

ITH presently trades at a P/E ratio of 14.59. Dividend yield is not too good currently at about 2 per cent but with rising profits it could rise in future. Its industry peer, Thomas cook India, trades at P/E of 24.69, with a yield of less than 1 per cent.

Given the likelihood that tourism business in India could boom for years to come, ITH is in the right business at the right time. It can expect a double digit growth for the near future. The management too is strong. It belongs to the ITC group, which directly holds 3.6 per cent in ITH and another 58 per cent *via* subsidiaries Russell credit, Russel Investments and Peninsular Investments. This takes its stake to over 62 per cent. The Indian public holds 30.68 per cent with the rest of the stake held by foreign institutional investors and others.

ITS a Wander World

	2000	*2001*	*2002*	*2003*	*2004*
Operating income	13.8	32.4	29.9	33.5	38.1
PBDIT	3.9	15.7	7.3	13.7	9.6
PAT (Rs. Cr.)	0.7	8.1	0.9	6.6	2.9
EPS (Rs)	0.91	9.88	–0.19	8.80	3.59
Dividend Ratio (%)	20.0	25.0	10.0	25.0	15.0

Source: *The Economic Times*, 14-20 February, 2005, p. 3.

NO RIPPLES OF DISCONTENT

Varun Shipping has been moving ahead with confidence over the past year and a half, ever since the shipping freight rates cycle has started moving northwards. This is well reflected by the fact that the company has just ended FY05 by rewarding its shareholders with a handsome dividend of 30 per cent in a period, in which the company's equity base has shot up by almost 60 per cent as compared to its equity base at the end of **FY04**. This is against the **16 per cent** dividend it distributed on a much lower equity base in **FY04** over and above the **10 per cent** interim dividend that the company distributed during FY05, it has just proposed a final dividend of 20 per cent on its expanded equity base of Rs. **113 crores** last week. This effectively means that the company even if required to bring down the dividend rate to **20-25 per cent** in FY06 due to a bleated equity base, would offer a dividend yield of at least 10 per cent per annum to an investor who chooses to invest in the stock at its present price of Rs. **38.5**, and chooses to stays on till the distribution of FY06 dividend payouts.

This would be considering the fact that he would then be entitled to Rs. 2 final dividend for **FY05**, which he would receive in a couple of months, and the subsequent Rs. **2-2.5** in another **15 months** time. Thus at Rs. **28-39**, the Rs. **400 crores** company, Varun Shipping appears to be a perfect dividend yield play from the mid cap sector.

Comforting Factors

The major comforting factor regarding Varun Shipping is that the Company, operating with a fleet of **15 ships** including eight LPG carriers is now eyeing higher volumes at a time when wet-cargo rate cycle has yet peaked out, and stability has been witnessed even for right rates for dry commodities over the past three months. The company has already acquired three LPG carriers over the past six months to ensure that the company's growth is maintained. Besides, the company, which has raised plenty of funds over the past year to expand its fleet at the right time, is still flush with funds. The company has ended FY05 with an operating income of Rs. **388.96 crores, up 32.8 per cent** against the operating income of Rs **292.87 crores for FY04** and its net profits have surged in the same period to Rs **81.69 crores,** from Rs 35.8 crore that it posted in **FY04.** Despite a sharp rise in the equity to Rs **113.65 crores** at the end of FY05, the profits translated into a much-improved earnings per share (EPS) of Rs. 7.18 on a diluted basis, compared to Rs. 4.93 in FY04.

The major reason for the company's equity base surging to Rs. **113 crores from Rs. 72.5 crores** at the end of FY04 is that during the last financial, the company not only come out with a rights issue of one share for every two shares at a premium of Rs. 8, but also subsequently made a preferential allotment of equity shares to some FIIs at Rs. **32.09**. Besides, it has allotted optionally fully convertible warrants to promoters in the fourth quarter of **FY05**. The funds raised, so far, have mainly been used to purchase crude carriers, two of which have come in the past two months.

Outlook

By purchasing three crude carriers over the past few months, thus expanding its fleet size to 15, Varun Shipping has now entered into a high growth zone where it's no longer left very far behind majors like GE Shipping, Essar Shipping, and SCI. Since it has also been regularly retiring its comparatively old vessels, it has now ensured that its fleet now appears much improved. All this has been made possible due to higher internal accruals due to a shipping cycle reversal towards positive trends, and the subsequent raising to funds at regular intervals. This has ensured that the company's operating income has picked up by almost 32.8 per cent in FY05 alone over the FY04 numbers and its gross profits have surged by almost 64 per cent in the same period.

On a year-on-year basis, its net profits for FY05 of Rs. **81.69 crores** have shot up by almost 129 per cent over the FY04 net profits. The company has reported a handsome EPS of Rs. **7.18 for FY05**. Its stock, now trading around Rs. 38, has still got some upside potential considering that it offers an annualised dividend yield of over 10 per cent (annualised basis) on a forward basis. If an investor considers remaining invested for the next 14-15 months.

Carrying on Varun Shipping Financials

	FY05	*FY04*	*Cha %*
Operating Income	389.0	292.9	32.8
Other Income	1.6	1.5	—
Expenditure	222.5	185.1	20.2
Operating Profit	168.0	109.2	53.8
Interest	17.5	17.5	—
Gross Profit	150.5	91.8	64.0
Depreciation	67.0	53.7	24.9
Profit Before Tax	83.5	38.1	119.0
Tax	1.8	2.3	—
Net Profit	81.7	35.8	128.2
Equity Capital	113.7	72.5	—
Re-saving	294.6	—	—

Source: *The Economic Times*, 2-8 May, 2005, p. 3.

STEERING NORTH AT TOP SPEED

The Indian auto-components and manufacturer's association reported an estimated revenue of $5.4bn for the country's auto-comp industry, growing at **18-20 per cent**. Some 15 per cent comes from drive transmission and steering parts out of this industry estimates put the steering market at Rs. **930 crores,** a huge captive business for steering makers to make money on.

Pune-based ZF Steering Gear (ZFSG) is one of the few power steering gears manufactures in the country. It's only around 20 years old and was set up in technical collaboration with ZF fried rich shaten AG of Germany, ZFSG (part of the Robert Bosch Group).

Current Financials

Financials for the nine months ended FY05 portray an improving picture for ZFSG. Its net sales, at Rs. **116.1 crore, were 37.1 per cent** higher than that during the corresponding period last year. The company's net profit also rose by 77.5 per cent to Rs. 12.4 crores during the nine months of FY05. At the same time ZFSG managed to keep its raw material costs in check raw material costs went up 39 per cent to Rs. 77.9 crore. This also meant that total expenditure was in control it was **34 per cent** higher than the Rs. 93.7 crores incurred last year. The company was thus able to increase its operating margins by two percentage points to 19.3 per cent from 17.5 per cent for the corresponding period last year. Coming at a time in contrast to the shrinking operating margins of its auto component pears facing the brunt of rising steel prices ZFSG is apparently at an advantage.

Industry Outlook

ZF makes power steering for commercial vehicles. The other large steering system manufacturer, Sona Koyo focuses on passenger cars. In the CV Market, ZF has very little competition in the domestic market. The CV market has done well this year. In fact, commercial vehicles saw a 14 per cent rise in production for the period April 2004-February 2005 to 312,440 units tarned out by Indian manufacturers. Among companies Ashok Leyland, with whom ZFSG has had a long-standing business, witnessed a 23 per cent increase in net sales and a 45 per cent hike in net profit in its FY05 Financials.

Beside CVS, tractor sales are on a rise too April 2004 to February 2005 data from industry sources shows that the production of tractors has grown to 18,867 in February 2005 from 15,714 in April 2004 a 20 per cent risc in monthly production. Between the period February 2004 to February 2005, the total tractor production also rose to 243,903, a 28 per cent increase over the corresponding period last year, obviously, with customers like Eicher Tractors, International Tractors, New Holland Tractors and Punjab Tractors in its kitty—this upturned in the tractor production bodies well for ZFSG.

ZFSG should be inspired by the growth in light medium and heavy commercial vehicles. It supplies both manual steering gears (150,000 units) and power steering gears (75,000 units) to its customers though out of its net sales of Rs. 125 crores in FY04 only about 10 per cent of the total steering sales come from manual steering the rest accrue from sales of power steering for commercial vehicles on Indian roads—especially after CVMR rules incorporating the usage to conserve fuels ZFSG should be able to cash in on the increased power steering business.

Source: *The Economic Times*, 2 May-8 May 2005, p. 3.

Valuations

The market seems to be approving of all the above. In the last six months till April 29, ZFSG's market capitalisation increased by 44 per cent to Rs. 195 crore. EPS for the ZFSG scrip for the first three quarters of FY05 stands at 27.3, 79 per cent higher compared to 15.2 for the some period in FY04. The downside can come from its P/E ratio starting at 10.6 beginning November 2004 reaching levels of 14 by end-January 2005, and thereafter it started to fall again, though, it has again bucked the trend and is at 12 levels.

When one puts this in perspective to ratios like RoCE (at 37.7 per cent in FY04 compared to 24.6 per cent in FY03) and the debt/equity ratio of 0.48 (in FY03 ZFSG's debt stood at Rs. 21.1 crore 43 per cent higher than FY04 debts of Rs. 14.7 crore) things look consistent for the scrip. The only point worth noting here is that the promoter holding in the company is around 70 per cent. So, the company's floating stock on the bourses in minuscule. And as ZFSGs compensates that with its healthy dividend policies over the years, investors would be wise to take a look at this scrip.

Crive Me a Look

	9 months		
	FY05	*FY04*	*Chg (%)*
Net sales	116.1	84.7	37.1
Total expenditure	93.7	69.9	34.1
Net Profits	12.4	6.9	77.5
Operating Margins	19.3	17.5	—
Interest	0.09	0.02	350.0
Depreciation	6.3	3.2	93.8
EPS	27.3	15.2	79.6

COLOURFUL DESIGNS

S. Kumar's Nationwide Ltd. (S. Kumars Synfabs Ltd.) has initiated a move to showcase its new business model in fabrics/readymades by making an entry into the buzzing retail business. Adding to its 16-odd exclusive stores, the company recently opened four exclusive showrooms for fabrics/readymades in Mumbai. It is now eyeing Delhi as the next stop with more retail showrooms.

The company is benefiting from the marketing rights of the global brand 'Reid and Taylor' besides its own readymades/fabrics brands. S Kumar's and Tamarind on the cards is a women's wear brand called Balmool which will be added to the collection in its exclusive stores. The company is a strong player in the school uniforms segment.

Its entry into the retail sector through exclusive showrooms comes at a time when the government is looking at throwing open the sector to foreign direct investment (FDI) in retail. Such a step would augur well for companies like S. Kumar's and its competitions Pantaloon, Trent etc.

Meanwhile, S Kumar's has received approval for a corporate debt restructuring (CDR). Also, this Rs. 600 crores giant has tied up with overseas investor to raise funds for repayment of past dues. Now with the company having get almost 10 years funded interest term loan (FITL) to repay its past interests dues as per the CDR, it can work fully towards exploiting future opportunities in the buzzing textile sector.

S. Kumar's nationwide has started showing positive signs and is nearing a turnaround. After a gap of almost two years, it has ended the December 2004 quarter with cash profits.

Replica of Arvind Mills

The case of S. Kumar's nationwide is almost like that of Arvind Mills three years back. At that time, this global denim player was facing similar problems. It was not the result of a faulty business model, but due to ambitious expansion targets which resulted in heavy borrowings and consequent huge losses. Arvind Mills too had submitted adept restructuring plan, which gave it time to clean up its balance sheet, with several interest waiver clauses thrown in. The company has done well since then and is currently placed in a select rank of denim global players. Since approval of the CDR, Arvind Mills has never let down its investors FIs or Banks.

S. Kumar's too could shine on the strength of marketing rights of the international brand 'Reid and Taylor', its own brands and entry into exclusive retailing. Since CDRs are approved by FLs/banks for only those companies whose business models are strong and who hold potential for repayment of dues, the case for S.Kumar's gets only stronger.

CDR Package

The CDR package of S. Kumar's nationwide envisages the conversion of outstanding interest costs of the company into funded interest term loan

(FITL) for a period of not less than 10 years. This would bring down the interest costs of the company. Interest costs were the main factor for S. Kumar's downfall. Besides, through a fresh preferential allotment the promoters would raise fresh funds. The company has approved the raising of funds through financial instruments worth Rs. 500 crores on private placement basis. Erstwhile lenders of the company have agreed to provide guanrantee of upto $50 mn which would very soon be raised through foreign currency from Exim Bank.

Improved Performance

With all the tie-ups for loans and the CDR in place, the company has started showing signs of healthy growth. In the quarter ended December 2004, S. Kumar's clocked net sales of Rs. 148.33 crore, up 23 per cent against the comparative quarter last year operating profits in the same period picked up by over 163 per cent to Rs. 9.58 crore in October-December 2004 quarter with literally no interest costs to serve the company's gross profit shot up to Rs. 8.83 crore, as against losses in the comparative quarter a year before. Effectively, the company ended the quarter with cash profits. It is now just a short distance from recording a turn around at the net profit level.

S. Kumars Synfabs

	October-December		*Oct 2003-Sep 2004*
	2004	*2003*	
Net Sales	148.33	120.55	615.16
Other Income	0.86	0.9	6.92
Expenditure	139.61	117.81	582.75
Operating Profit	9.58	3.64	39.33
Interest	0.75	28.35	1.87
Gross Profit	8.83	–24.71	37.46
Depreciation	14.65	14.75	58.6
Profit before Tax	5.82	–39.46	21.14
Tax	—	—	2
Net Profit	–5.81	–39.46	19.14
Equity Capital	154.67	154.67	154.67

Outlook

The company has already up graded its capacities at various locations. The only area where it may have to spruce up. Some of its facilities would be in the ready mades space. In the past, CDR packages allowed to textile companies and other industries have been a win-win proposition for companies FIS and investors. The case of S. Kumar's nationwide may be no different. The stock is poised at around Rs. 24. It could yield handsome returns to investors willing to wait for the medium term in this stock.

Technical

LOOKING UP

S. Kumar's Nationwide

Long-term Trend	:	Out performer
Medium-term Trend	:	Market Performer
Short-term Trend	:	Out performer

Price Movements

Though the scrip has started moving upward recently with strong volumes, it was in early 2004 that the scrip showed first signs of revival. After forming a rounding bottom formation, the scrip has started moving upward very sharply while forming higher top and bottom. After touching a high of Rs. 28 it is currently ruling at Rs. 23. The formation of the bar chart of the scrip during the last 12 months is normally found in scrips which are turnaround cases. In such cases, the scrip witnesses a long consolidation phase and then it breaks out.

Oscillator Charts

The moving average convergence divergence (MACD) on the weekly charts is currently placed in buy mode as it moves upward in positive territory. Though the MACD daily chart is placed in sell mode, it currently moving in tandem with the scrip as it moves upward forming higher top and bottom. The 12-week rate of change (RoC) is placed in positive territory thought it moves southward. The 12-day RoC is currently showing very volatile movements as it criss crosses between the positive and negative territories. The 14-week relative strength index (RSI) is currently placed in overbought territory but is yet to give a sell signal. The daily oscillator also shows a similar trend as it moves near the over bought territory without showing signs of negative divergence. The stochastic on the weekly charts is currently placed in the sell mode in the equilibrium territory but on the weekly charts, this oscillator is placed in buy mode as it inches upward in positive territory. The extreme short term oscillators have again reached oversold territory during the correction seen by the sector senses.

Inference

The scrip has come out of hibernation after a long period of time and the long-term oscillators are currently showing strength as they move upwards sharply in positive territory. One may enter the scrip at current levels with a short to medium-term perspective.

S. Kumar's

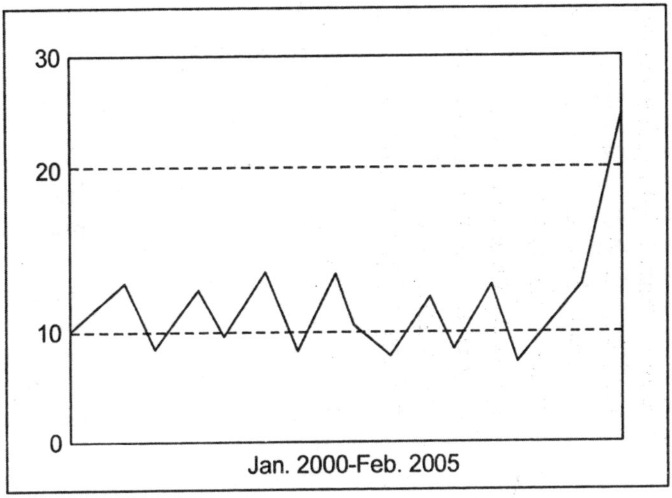

SWEET SUCCESS

During the past four years, India had surplus, production of cane crop, which resulted in a glut in sugar due to this sugar mills were unable to get remunerative prices, which in turn resulted in their being unable to pay farmer's dues. This situation has now changed.

The economic survey has estimated sugar production. In India during 2004-05 at 125 lakhs tonne against consumption of 180 lakhs tonne (production during 2003-04 was 145 lakhs tonne). This is because of drought in sugar-producing states of Maharashtra, AP and Karnataka. With the Sugar Industry seeing supply falling short of demand and sugar mills now able to get good prices for their produce, sugar companies fortunes have looked up sharply. EID Parry (I) Ltd. is gaining significantly from this situation as 60 per cent of sugar produced in Tamil Nadu comes out of this company's sugar mills.

Revamp

During Fy 2003-04, EID Parry (I) sharpened its focus by existing the seeds, tiles and electronics businesses. The farm inputs division was demerged into its subsidiary Coromandel Fertilisers (CFL). EID holds 68.69 per cent stake in CFL. The wholly owned subsidiaries, Parry and Co. and Mofussil Warehouse and Trading Co. were amalgamated with EID Parry. Lastly, EID Parry sold its holdings in Parrys Confectionary, to Lotte Group Korea. The revamp has seen EID's debt levels fall and consequently interest costs have reduced significantly.

Operations

In the sugar space, EID Parry is seeing continuous reduction in operating costs combined with a rise in cane crushing. Use of imported raw sugar is resulting in higher margins. Its move into high grade sugar will further add to margins.

Manufacturing of ethanol for blending with petrol is another significant business opportunity being exploited at EID Parry's distillery at Nellikuppam. Its power co-generation plant at Pugalur helps slash energy costs. EID Parry's bio-products business is centred around the Neemazal® range of products manufactured from neem seed Kernel produced at its unit at Thyagavalli (TN) and supported by its R and D group in Bangalore. Neemazal ® products are sold in 23 countries including the US and Europe.

Its 'Parry ware' and 'Johnson' pedder range of bathroom accessories are well known with a market share of around 38 per cent, this ISO 9001:2000 and ISO 14001:1996 business is growing aggressively on the bank of a construction boom in the country.

Financials

Due to demergers and hiving off of units, FY 2003-04. Financials are strictly not comparable with that of the previous year yet, net profits were higher. For FY 2003-04, sales were Rs. 609.79 crores (Rs. 1,346.83 crores in the previous year). PBDIT was Rs. 102.5 crores (Rs. 122.72 crores). Interest charges were sharply lower at Rs. 18.84 crores (Rs. 40.67 crores) consequently, PBDT was higher at Rs. 83.66 crores (Rs. 82.05 crores). PBT too was sharply up at Rs. **53.29 crores** (Rs. **37.03** crores). PAT shop up to Rs. **43.23** crores from Rs. **26.83 crores** in the previous year.

Financials for the nine months ended December 2004 have zoomed. Total income at Rs. 494.74 crore was up **12.3 per cent** from Rs. **440.44 crores** in December 2003. PBDIT was sharply up at **Rs. 106.95** crores

(Rs. 46.48 crores). PBIT too was up at Rs. **82.02 crores** (Rs. **20.06 crores**). Duc to falling interest costs, PBDT was up sharply from Rs. **37.78 crores** in December 2003 to Rs. **104.31 crores** in 2004. Despite tax provisions of Rs. **15.66 crores** (Rs. **7.69 crores** in December 2003) PAT zoomed to Rs. **67.72 crores** in December 2004 (Rs. 3.67 crores).

EID Parry (India)

	FY ending	9 months ended	
	March 04	Dec. 03	Dec. 04
Income	595.17	440.44	494.74
Net Sales	560.70	426.91	450.4
Other Income	34.37	13.28	28.19
Expenditure	503.98	393.96	387.79
PBDIT	91.19	46.48	106.95
Interest	7.53	8.7	2.64
PBDT	83.66	37.78	104.31
Depreciation	30.37	26.42	20.93
PBT	53.29	11.36	83.38
Tax	10.06	7.69	15.66
Deferred Tax	3.16	—	—
PAT	43.23	3.67	67.72
Capital	17.85	17.84	17.85

Outlook

EID Parry is now focussed on three business lines. Not only are all three lines of business growing strongly, their prospects too look bright on annualised nine months figures, PAT will be at least Rs. 90 crores on a small equity base of Rs. **17.85 crores.** EPS should be over Rs. 50. At a current market price of Rs. 488, the PE is a low 9.8. The industry PE is 16.8 with the sugar story just beginning to unravel investors would gain substantially by remaining invested in this scrip.

RANE UNRAVELLED

Rane Madras Ltd. is the flagship company of the Rs. **750 crores**. Rane Group, which is a leading manufacturer of automotive components in India. The other group companies are Rane Brake Linings, Rane Engine Valves, Rane Investments. Rane N&K and Rane TRW of these companies only Rane Madras, Rane Brake Linings and Rane Engine Valves are listed.

There exists a complex web of cross holding between these companies and the Rane Group is undergoing a rigorous restructuring exercise to unbundle this structure. The result of this restructuring will be that Rane Madras will be renamed as Rane holdings and all holdings of the other group companies will be routed through this company. A new company known as Rane Madras Manufacturing will come into existence which will take over the current manufacturing business of Rane Madras.

Products and OPS

Rane Madras produces steering linkages, ball joints, axial joints, suspension joints, manual steering gears, hydrostatic steering gears among other things. The products can be categorised into two segments, namely steering and suspension linkage products and steering gear products. The company is a market leader in both these product categories with a market share of more than **50 per cent** in the linkage product category and **70 per cent** in the latter.

Most of the Company's sales come from the domestic market with exports forming a small part of total turnover. Over the years, the company has been trying to increase its share of sales from exports and the effort have paid off. From a mere 5 per cent till last year, the contribution of sales from exports has gone up significantly to 14 per cent this year and is expected to rise further in the years ahead on the other hand, imports as a percentage of sales have been steadily declining and this will lead to an expansion in margins. The company has also undertaken extensive cost-cutting initiatives, which will give a further boost to margins.

Restructuring

The aim behind the restructuring exercise is to consolidate the economic ownership of the group with Rane Madras. For this purpose, the promoters have sold their holdings in Rane Engine Valves to Rane Madras, Rane Brakes Linings and Rane Investments. The valuation of each share is Rs. 410 and the promoter has received for every share of Rane Engine Valve, two shares of Rane Madras and Rs. 118 in cash. The promoters also made an open offer of 20 per cent for the shares of Rane Brake Linings. In addition, Rane Madras, Rane Brake Linings and Rane Investments made an open offer of 20 per cent for Rane Engine Valves.

After all these cross holdings are unbundled, Rane Madras will be renamed as Rane Holdings after getting the requisite approvals from the authorised courts. The shareholding and Investments will consolidate into this company. The manufacturing activity of Rane Madras will be transferred to a new company called Rane Madras Manufacturing existing shareholders of Rane Madras will get one share of Rane Madras Manufacturing for every share held by them. In the end, instead of three there will be four listed companies from the group. These companies will be Rane Brake Linings, Rane Engine Valves, Rane Holdings and Rane Madras Manufacturing.

Outlook

Rane Madras has been showing encouraging results lately. The full year profits for the year ended march 2004, showed a 132 per cent increase over the previous year. The restructuring exercise will help in improving the image of the Rane Group on the whole and will make the holding structure transparent. This will help in improving the perception and valuation.

Rane Madras has proved its worth and is a market leader in the segment that it operates in and is committed to maintaining high quality standards of production. The company is now aggressively targetting the export market and is on a strong growth trajectory. The restructuring exercise will help shareholders create substantial value. One should take a long-term view on the company.

Source: *The Economics Times*, 14-20 March, 2005, p. 3.

GETTING READY FOR A GOOD HARVEST

KRBL is among the world's largest exporters of basmati rice with a turnover close to Rs. **520 crores per annum**. The company earns nearly 50 per cent of its total revenues from exporting rice to different regions across the world. By expanding into areas of farm processing, the company has managed to retain its leadership position in the industry with peers like Satnam overseas and REI Agro.

The company has established its presence in the seeds segment, acquire a rice mill in Punjab and promoted contract farming at the grass roots level for procuring paddy. Most of these steps have been rolled out over the past one year when government was promoting for farm related processing activities.

These steps should enable the company to grow rapidly over the next few years in terms of revenues as well as profitability by improving margins. The stock has been re-rated over the past year and is now quoting at close to Rs. 126.

At this price, the company is evolved at close to 2.25 times of its projected sales turnover in FY05. Even in terms of price to book value, the stock trades just **1.45 times** of its book value of Rs. 88. This is far cheaper compared with valuations of peer group companies.

KRBL's brands like India Gate Royal, Doon and others have found wide acceptance in American chain stores including Walmart and Sams club in addition to the traditional demand from middle-east markets like Kuwait, and Yemen considering that KRBL is a large exporter of basmati rice and would have a higher milling capacity after acquisition in Punjab, its growth outlook appears good.

The Competitive Edge

Over the past year, KRBL underlook a diversification strategy that should benefit the company in the future KRBL has made concentrated efforts to ensure that its revenue mix does not get dominated by rice exports alone.

The Company has tried to capitalize on the thrust provided to the farm sector by the UPA Government by getting into new areas of agri-related activities like seed marketing, promoting contract farming for improving its feed stock and other value added services. Such moves are likely to improve KRBL's profit margins and also ensure that its revenue stream is not dominated by a signal product or service which may have cyclical fluctuations. KRBL has also finalised a deal in Dhuri in Punjab for acquiring a rice will with a co-generation power capacity (out of husk) of **10 MW**. With the deal close to completion the company should gain a rice milling capacity of **120 MT** per hour. It is also is in the process of raising the rice milling capacity of its existing plant at Dadri in Uttar Pradesh to 38 MT per hour from 30 MT per hour.

These added capacities could ensure that KRBL is placed well to gain substantially in terms of sales and is eyeing the Rs. 1000 crores turnover mark in the next couple of years. It is also stepping up its presence in the domestic markets.

Financials

The Company's turnover has remained stagnant in the first nine months of FY05 compared with the previous year's turnover. However, its sales are projected to nearly double in the FY06.

Also, while sales have been marginally down in the first three quarters, the operating profit has improved to Rs. 32.23 crores in April-December 2004 from Rs. 29.9 crores, in the comparative period last year. Its profit before tax climbed to Rs. 21.04 crore in this period against Rs. 19.2 crores it posted in April-December 2003 period.

It is expected that the Company may end the current year with a sales turnover of Rs. 520 crore and net profit of Rs. **19 crores in FY05** on its equity base of Rs. **17.9 crores** this would translate into an earnings per share of around Rs. 10.5 to Rs. **11 per share for FY05**. This year ahead should see substantial growth with its latest acquisition contributing significant revenue growth.

KRBLS Financial	*April-Dec.*		
	2004	*2003*	*FY04*
Net Sales	333.4	366.0	478.1
Other Income	2.7	1.5	10.4
Expenditure	303.9	337.6	451.6
Operating Profit	32.2	29.9	36.8
Interest	5.6	5.8	8.2
Gross Profit	26.6	24.2	28.6
Depreciation	5.6	5.0	7.2
Profit Before Tax	21.0	19.2	21.4
Tax	6.7	5.1	6.7
Net Profit	14.3	14.1	14.8
Equity Capital	17.9	13.7	17.7

Outlook

After the completion of this acquisition and addition of new capacities, KRBL should post gains from the first quarter of FY06. Revenues from other farming services should also improve its sales and bottom line in the next financial year. At current valuations the stock is fully priced for the current year earnings.

If the company manages to achieve growth from new initiatives, its valuation could see a re-rating in the next 12 months.

TECHNICAL
REACHING FOR THE TOPS

Long-term Trend	:	Bullish
Medium-term Trend	:	Bullish
Short-term Trend	:	Sideways

Price Movements

Though the scrip has been listed for a long period of time, it caught the attention of the market in early 2003 only. The initial part of the upward movement was not very strong and the volumes were not very high.

However, after March 2004 the scrip has been able to move upward on much stronger Fundamentals and is currently out performing the market. The scrip is currently moving upward while forming higher tops and bottom. After touching a high of Rs. 140 the scrip underwent a correction and is currently quoting at the level of Rs. 130.

Oscillator Charts

The moving average convergence divergence on the weekly charts is currently in the buy mode as it inches upward in the positive territory. On the daily charts also this oscillator is in the buy mode as it moves upward in the positive territory but it is showing negative divergence, which indicates that the upward movements is likely to be in the form of higher tops and bottom. The 12th week rate of change (RoC) is currently placed in the positive territory but at the same time it is slipping southward. The 12th day RoC is currently placed in the positive territory and is not showing any kind of divergence which is indicative that the chances that the rally will continue are very high. The 14th week relative strength index (RSI) is currently placed in the over bought territory but has still not given the sell signal on the daily charts, this oscillator is currently placed in the equilibrium territory and is moving in tandem with the scrip. The extreme short-term oscillators of the scrip are currently placed in the overbought territory but are yet to give the sell signal.

KRBL

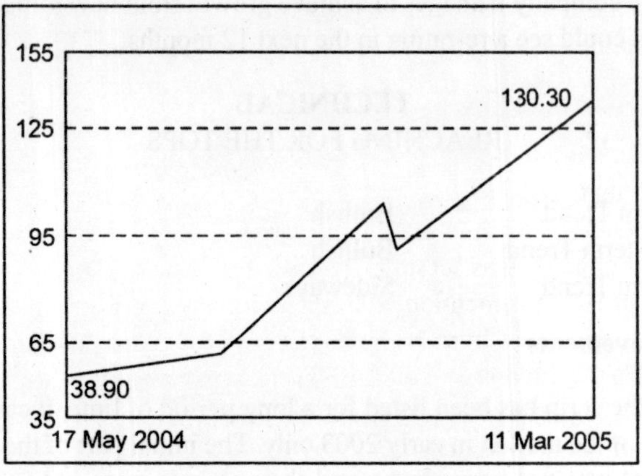

Inference

The current movement of the scrip seems to have some more strength in it Investors should hold on to the scrip.

SAVE THE BEST FOR LAST

Jaiprakash Hydro Power Limited is the kind of stock not commonly encountered on the Indian market safe and guaranteed returns but few growth prospects by and large, a utility company. Given the nature of the stock, it may be interesting for a very long term investor looking for stable returns over a long period.

JHPL operates a **300 MW** run of the river hydel power plant in Himachal Pradesh, which can produce **1213.18 million units of** power annually. The company has a power purchase agreement with the Himachal Pradesh SEB for a period of **40 years. 88 per cent** of the power sold is paid for while 12 per cent is given to HPSEB free of charge. In the first half of FY05, the company generated 853.8 MW against a designed 780.7 MW. This implies that the designed generation for the second half of the year would be about 432 MW for the second half. The net income of the company for the first half of FY05 was **Rs. 198.33 crores** while the net profit was **Rs. 64 crores**. The major expenses were interest costs. Rs. 71.2 crores and depreciation at Rs. 42 crores for the period.

JHPL is not vulnerable to fluctuations in raw material prices as the power production depends on the flow of water which is free. The company has a long-term (40 years) power purchase agreement (PPA) with its single customer. A return on equity of 16 per cent is guaranteed to the company along with some incentives that can take it up to **20-21 per cent**. Moreover, it sells a commodity that's in short supply (power) and whose demand is set to increase. Income of the company is also protected upto 2010 in case the water availability in the river is lower than that envisaged in the PPA. However, growth prospects aren't there since the company was set up to execute a single project.

The prospectus mentions that the company has brought down the cost of its rupee debt from **16.5 per cent to 10.5 per cent** which would bring down the interest cost by Rs. **50 crores per annum**. However, this saving will be passed on to the Himachal Pradesh State Electricity Board and isn't of concern to investors.

The first half number translate into an EPS of Rs. 1.30 for the first half of the year. Since a return-on-equity of 16 per cent is guaranteed. This implies that there is a floor of Rs. 1.6 on the EPS. Given the incentive structure, this also means that EPS could go up to Rs. 2.1 or Rs. 2.2. The payment from HPSEB shouldn't be a problem, since proceeds from power sales in some circles are to be put up in an escrow account. However, this return is on a share price of Rs. 10. The selling price band for JHPL ranges from Rs. 27.32 giving a rather steep PE ratio of 15-20. At this range, the issue size could be Rs. 486 is 76 crore. JHPL will not receive any of the proceeds. post issue, the promoter holding will some down to 63.34 per cent.

Jaiprakash Hydro Power

	FY05 (6 months)	*FY04 (Full year)*
Total Income	198.33	296.61
Interest and Finance charges	71.23	131.24
Depreciation	42.06	71.26
PBT	69.47	62.89
PAT	63.98	57.91
EPS	1.30	1.24

Source: *The Economic Times*, 14-20 March, 2005, p. 3.

UNIT II
SUMMARY

All investments are risky. The return is always chased by the risk. Security analysis refers to find out intrinsic value of a share. Instrinsic value is basically determined by the expected earnings flow over a number of years. Security market is influenced by various factors such as information, levels of savings, trading methods, Financial instruments valuation of financial assets etc. Investment enhances the productive process of the economy. **Fundamental analysis** is one of the tools for a scientific analysis in stock market operations. It allows for selection of securities of different sectors of the economy. **Economic analysis** is one of the important component of fundamental analysis. Capital formation is the most important factor in the development of a nation. **Industry analysis** is another tool useful for fundamental analysis. **Company analysis** is the most important factor in fundamental analysis. The share prices in stock market are influenced by capabilities, profits, capital structure, board skills, operating efficiency and financial analysis. **Technical analysis** is associated with the study of the share price movement. **Dow Theory** reveals about the movement of prices of securities on the stock exchange. **Technical indicators** are one of the important aspect in the technical analysis. The indicators are **volume of trade and short sales.** Charts are one of the tool in the technical analysis. Elliot Wave Theory study about the stock market behaviour. **Efficient Market Theory** is based on free flow of information and assumed that there is no scope for insider information, and malpractices. **Random Walk Theory** is associated the study of price changes in stock market.

QUESTIONS: ESSAYS TYPE

1. What is meant by security analysis?
2. What is fundamental analysis? Explain its role in selection of a scrip.
3. What is economic analysis? What are the factors influencing it?
4. What is Industry analysis? How it is useful in making investment decisions?
5. What is meant by financial performance? How is it useful in analysis of data?
6. What is ratio? How they are useful to the investors in the context of stock market operations?
7. What is meant by Technical analysis? How it is differ from the fundamental analysis?
8. Explain the concept of Dow Theory. How is it useful in stock market operations?
9. What is short selling?
10. What is meant by oddlot trading?
11. What are Oscillators?
12. What is a point and figure chart? and how is it used?
13. What is chart? How are they useful in predicting the stock price movement?
14. What is Elliot Wave Theory? Explain how is it useful to the investors.
15. What is efficiency? Explain Efficient Market Theory.
16. What is form? How they show impact on the stock market operations?
17. "Stock Prices are like random numbers" Explain.
18. What is Random Walk Theory? State the various empirical evidences to reject the random walk theory?

QUESTION 1

The Finance Manager of **Kinetic Engineering Ltd.** provides the following financial information related to **2001-02 and 2002-03**. You are required to analyse the data and calculate the following financial ratios:

(a) Profit before tax to sales.
(b) Return on equity.
(c) Return on Investment.
(d) Short term bank borrowing to investories.
(e) Gross value added to gross fixed assets.
(f) Total remuneration to employees to value added.
(g) Total remuneration to employees to value of production.
(h) Operating profit to sales.

(Rs. in crores)

	Financial Indicators	*2001-02*	*2002-03*
Income/Appropriations			
1.	Net Sales	304	258
2.	Value of Production	318	267
3.	Other Income	03	03
4.	Total Income	321	268
5.	Raw materials/stores/ spares power and fuel consumed	208	156
6.	Other manufacturing expenses	05	05
7.	Remuneration to employees	29	25
8.	Other expenses	47	58
9.	Depreciation	12	13
10.	Gross profit	19	10
11.	Interest	08	13
12.	Operating profit	11	–03
13.	Non-operating surplus	–0.05	02
14.	Profit before tax	11	–01
15.	Tax provisions	39	–01
16.	Profit after tax	07	0
17.	Dividends	01	0
18.	Retained profits	06	0
Liabilities/Assets			
19.	Paid up caital	04	04
20.	Reserves and surplus	118	118
21.	Long term loan	128	113
22.	Short term loan	92	86
	(i) of which bank borrowings	67	86
23.	Gross fixed assets	231	249

(Contd.)

(Contd.)

	Financial Indicators	*2001-02*	*2002-03*
24.	Accumulated depreciation	134	146
25.	Inventories	57	69
26.	Total assets/liabilities	398	378
Miscellaneous Items			
27.	Excise Duty	50	39
28.	Gross value added	58	49
29.	Total foreign exchange earnings	08	14
30.	Total foreign exchange outflow	27	07

Ans.

	2001-02	*2002-03*
(a)	3.1%	**–0.4%**
(b)	5.8%	**–0.3%**
(c)	5.4%	2.6%
(d)	119%	124%
(e)	26.7%	20.6%
(f)	50.2%	50.9%
(g)	9.2%	9.4%
(h)	3.2%	–1.0%

QUESTION 2

The following data is available for you, please analyse the financial performance of **"JCT Ltd."** which is a popular and well established company. You are required to calculate the parameters:

(a) Profit before tax to sales
(b) Return on equity
(c) Return on Investment
(d) Short-term bank borrowing to investories
(e) Gross value added to gross fixed assets
(f) Total remuneration to employees to value added
(g) Total remuneration to employees to value of production
(h) Operating profit to sales.

(Rs. in crores)

	Financial Indicators	*2001-02*	*2002-03*
Income/Appropriations			
1.	Net Sales	483	531
2.	Value of Production	479	531
3.	Other Income	08	08
4.	Total Income	487	539
5.	Raw materials/stores/spares/ power/fuel/consumed	359	389
6.	Other manufacturing expenses	01	03
7.	Remuneration to employees	61	55
8.	Other expenses	48	51
9.	Depreciation	46	30
10.	Gross profit	–27	12
11.	Interest	32	26
12.	Operating Profit	–59	–14
13.	Non-operating surplus	15	17
14.	Profit before tax	–44	03
15.	Tax provisions	0	0
16.	Profit after tax	–44	03
17.	Dividends	0	0
18.	Retained profits	–44	03
Liabilities/Assets			
19.	Paid up capital	128	128
20.	Reserves and Surplus	115	115
21.	Long-term loan	171	156
22.	Short-term loan	72	77
	(i) of which bank borrowings	72	73
23.	Gross fixed assets	562	577
24.	Accumulated depreciation	358	383
25.	Inventories	91	92
26.	Total Assets/Liabilities	486	475
Miscellaneous Items			
27.	Excise duty	64	60
28.	Gross value added	77	94
29.	Total foreign exchange earnings	63	80
30.	Total foreign exchange outflow	13	15

Ans.

	2001-02	*2002-03*
(a)	**–8.1%**	0.5%
(b)	**–11.3%**	1.2%
(c)	**–4%**	2.4%
(d)	79.4%	79.1%
(e)	13.8%	16.5%
(f)	78.6%	58.6%
(g)	12.7%	10.4%
(h)	**–10.7%**	–2.4%

QUESTION 3

The following information was related to **Tata Chemicals Ltd.** for the years **2002-03 and 2001-02** respectively you are requested to calculate the following ratios:

(a) Profit before tax to sales
(b) Return on equity
(c) Return on Investment
(d) Short term bank borrowing to inventories
(e) Gross value added to gross fixed assets
(f) Total remuneration to employees to value added
(g) Total remuneration to employees to value of production
(h) Operating profit to sales.

(Rs. in crores)

Financial Indicators	*2001-02*	*2002-03*
Income/Appropriations		
1. Net Sales	1311	1521
2. Value of Production	1282	1525
3. Other Income	52	31
4. Total Income	1335	1557
5. Raw materials/stores/spares/ power/fuel/consumed	544	617
6. Other manufacturing expenses	61	65
7. Remuneration to employees	60	70
8. Other expenses	279	358
9. Depreciation	133	137
10. Gross profit	257	310
11. Interest	119	98
12. Operating Profit	138	211
13. Non-operating surplus	62	51
14. Profit before tax	200	262
15. Tax provisions	73	65
16. Profit after tax	127	197
17. Dividends	90	99
18. Retained profits	36	97
Liabilities/Assets		
19. Paid up Capital	181	181
20. Reserves and Surplus	1371	1455
21. Long-term loan	755	468
22. Short term loan	306	348
(i) of which bank borrowings	81	318
23. Gross fixed assets	2860	2835

(Contd.)

(*Contd.*)

	Financial Indicators	*2001-02*	*2002-03*
24.	Accumulated depreciation	1045	1150
25.	Inventories	198	181
26.	Total Assets/Liabilities	3493	3173
Miscellaneous Items			
27.	Excise duty	76	92
28.	Gross value added	407	492
29.	Total foreign exchange earnings	21	53
30.	Total foreign exchange outflow	92	91

Ans.

	2001-02	*2002-03*
(a)	14.4%	16.3%
(b)	7.3%	12.3%
(c)	7.3%	9.3%
(d)	40.7%	176.1%
(e)	14.4%	17.3%
(f)	14.8%	14.2%
(g)	4.7%	4.6%
(h)	9.9%	13.1%

UNIT - III

❖ Portfolio Theory

INTRODUCTION

Stock market is a highly volatile market. The share prices are fluctuated on daily basis. The Innocent Investor will loss his money in the stock market due to lack of expertism and stock market skills. A careful scientific analysis and observation will provide good returns to the investor. Enter and exit from the stock market is the most important factor in getting success from highly volatile market. It is not possible to a common investor to acquire the intricacies of the stock market. A professional investor can understand upto some level of market intricacies, but he may not know all the things. Perfection in the stock market is only possible to experts such as **Fund managers, Equity analysts, Stock brokers, Merchant bankers, Underwriters, Lead managers, Registrars, Market analyst and Financial advisors.** All these experts are highly paid employees. Hence the common investor is unable to benefit from these professionals advice. Therefore, he approaches **Mutual Funds.** Mutual funds are now becoming very popular in the market. They are established for the purpose of providing best expertism to small investors/unitholders. They will pool the small amount of resources from unit holders and deploy the fund at the disposal of experts. The experts will run the scheme by providing stock market advices. They operate the fund to the utmost satisfaction of the unitholders. They construct best **"portfolio"** for providing good returns to the unitholders. Portfolio means, a set of different assets. It is a combination of different financial instruments. It will be constructed by stocks bonds and money market instruments. **Portfolio** is managed by an expert is called as **"portfolio managers".** Portfolio managers are professionally qualified and competent skilled persons to manage crores of rupees. Portfolio management is still in infancy stage in India. After the setting up of public sector mutual funds, the importance has been growing steadily. The investors are recognized its importance in the market. Investment consultants some of them are transformed as portfolio managers. They manage the funds of clients on both **discretionary and non-discretionary** basis. Mutual funds have guaranteed a minimum return or capital appreciation. Any issuance to the unitholders are prohibited by the SEBI. **SEBI** is the regulatory authority in the stock market. It is a most powerful organization. It is a watchdog of the security market. The portfolio managers, share brokers, merchant bankers, lead managers, underwriters, registrars, bankers to the issue, fund managers *etc.*, should be followed by the SEBI guidelines. All the financial Intermediaries will have to get the registration certificate from the SEBI. SEBI has the full authority to check any malpractice by any intermediary in the market. The SEBI has imposed stricter rules, code of conduct, minimum infrastructure, experience and expertise *etc.,* are required to be fulfilled by the upcoming financial intermediaries. At present it is not possible without SEBI's acceptance to work as a portfolio manager. The guidelines of the SEBI had fixed the responsibility for each and every category of financial intermediary.

Basics of Portfolio Management

Portfolio is a combination of different financial assets. The aim of the portfolio manager is to minimise the risk and maximise the return to the investor. The success of the stock market is not a permanent element, because if you win at one time, another day risk awaiting you. **Risk** plays an important role in the stock market. Any investor cannot escape risk. It is an intelligent activity. Return is always chased by the risk. **Risk and Return** is an important phenomenon in the stock market. Hence portfolio is a basket of Investment. The assets can be mobilized according to the wish of the investors. **Risk** is uncertainty of the income or capital appreciation or loss of both. Risk can be classified as **"systematic and unsystematic risk."** The systematic risk arises due to several factors such as **raw material supply, taxation, government policy, inflation and financial risk.** The unsystematic risks are associated with **mismanagement, increasing inventory, wrong financial policy and defective marketing.** Investors making their investments to make a provision for future. They acquire different sets of assets in order to gain more returns. Investors are more freedom to select different kinds of financial assets available in the market. They are **gold, silver, real estate, buildings. Insurance policies, post offices, certificates. National saving certificates, equity, debt and bonds.** All of these assets having their own limitations and advantages. In India, the householder keeps most of his income in cash or in bank.

They are safe and least risky. But there will be a little fear for storage of cash in the house due to theft or any other loss. Indian housewife is the best finance expert in the world. She can manage her house with little amount of husbands income. The basics of portfolio management can be known through the following factors:

(a) Strategy
(b) Objectives
(c) Time
(d) Risk
(e) Guidelines

(a) Strategy

Strategy is a plan for achieving goal. It is released to long-term period. A common man needs to prepare his different strategies to meet goals in all walks of life. **Investment strategy** is one of tool to reach his goals. Investment is made by the ordinary man for his future. It is the reflection of savings. It is influenced by savings. Savings are most important for capital formation. Capital formation is the main ingredient in development of a nation. India is a developing country with vast majority of middle class families who have large amount of small savings at their disposal. Savings curb the present consumption. Savings means, post payment of current **desires, dreams and development.** A high levels of investment may not generate reasonable return due to **poor investment strategy.** A rich investment strategy can yield better returns. It is surprising that savings rate is high in India and it contributes more than 27 per cent of GDP. But the return in the form of output growth is low as **5 per cent to 7 per cent** per annum. The use of money in India is wasteful and not properly utilised by the corporate sector. India is rich in labour and poor in capital. There is a strong need for the services of portfolio managers in order to gain benefits from the financial markets. The services, expertism and experience of portfolio managers will stimulate the growth of returns from the stock market.

The savers in India withhold money 60 per cent in the kind of financial form and 40 per cent in physical form. The financial form contains nearly **42 per cent** is held in cash and bank deposits which provide returns less than inflation rates. There are so many financial instruments are available to the investors in the market. The financial savings in India can be found in the form of Insurance, provident fund, government securities, post office savings deposits, National Savings Certificates, public provident fund, National saving scheme. All of these investments yield a lower rate of return, and even less than average inflation rate. Tax incentives have been removed by the Union government to some of these investments, become **less attractive** to the investors. The investors objectives are fulfilled by only the capital market instruments. The investors with good knowledge and stock market skills can definitely yield high returns.

(b) Objectives

Every man has his own objectives. He makes plans to achieve the desired objectives. Financial objectives are the most important for the development of a common man. Financial objectives may not be fulfilled very easily. Generally every investor will have objectives such as **regular income, capital appreciation, liquidity, marketability, safety of the principal amount and hedge against inflation.** Among all of the available financial instruments, **"Equity"** shares provide higher returns, if the investor is accepted for risk. The return from equity depends upon the level of accepted risk by the investor. In this context, the abilities, expertism, stock market tactics, fundamental analysis, technical analysis is more useful to the investors to get success in the stock market. All investments may not involve risk. Some risk free investments are available like **bank deposits, post office deposits.**

(c) Time

The return on Investment indicates the efficiency of the financial instrument. The earning capacity of the financial asset can be measured through **time factor**. In portfolio management time occupies an important role in order to assess the capabilities of a portfolio. Portfolio refers, a basket of different kinds of investments. Time and time value of money are very relevant in portfolio management. Liquidity is another important factor in investment. Investment means, "Just parking place of your idle money." Investor prefers today's return than tomorrows return. **"A bird in hand is worth two in the bush."** The money received in future is less valuable than what it is today. Time value of money is one of the central idea in finance. Individuals and business firms frequently involve in cash crisis over several period of time. The time value of money becomes more important in decision making. Time factor will occupy a dominant role in recovery of investment from Mega projects. Cash inflows and outflows are closely monitored by the time factor from a particular project. The cash flows which accrue from different projects over different time periods, should be converted to sums of money at a common point of time.

According to this concept **"a person will have to pay in future more for a rupee received today."**[1]

"A person may accept less for a rupee to be received in future".

Hence, the time factor cannot be ignored in making investment decisions by a professional or an investor. The time valuation can be studied through the following ways:

(a) Compound value concept.
(b) Present value concept.

(a) Compound Value

Generally a common man is interested to receive money at present instead of waiting for future. But he will wait, if he is duly compensated for the waiting time by way of providing more money in future. The additional amount paid by the borrower is known as **"Interest"**. Interest is a reward to the owner of money. He will be compensated by way of interest. **For example:** A person being offered **Rs. 1000** today may wait for a year, if he is ensure of **Rs. 1100** at the end of one year (taking his preference for an interest of **10% p.a.**). The cash flow of **Rs. 1000** at present or **Rs. 1100** after one year will be the same. The value of money at future will be found by the following formula:

$$V_1 = V_0 (1 + i)$$

V_1 = Future value of the period 1
V_0 = Value of money at time o.
i = Interest rate

Sometimes the money will be paid after a longer period of time. For example: **Rs. 1000** will be paid by the borrower after 10 years to the lender. Then the future value of money at the end of **10 years** at **10 per cent** rate of interest shall be:

$$V_N = V_0 (1 + i)^n$$

1. S.N. Maheswari, *Financial Management*, S. Chand and Sons, p. A-19.

$$V_{10} = 1000\,(1+10)^{10}$$
$$V_o = 1000\,(1+.10)^{10}$$
$$= 1000\,(1{:}10)^{10}$$
$$= 1000 \times 2.594 = 2594$$

The calculation for larger period will be computed on the basis of compound factor table. The table shows factors for a period of ten years.

Period	*2%*	*4%*	*6%*	*8%*	*10%*
1	1.020	1.040	1.060	1.080	1.100
2	1.040	1.082	1.124	1.166	1.210
3	1.061	1.125	1.191	1.260	1.331
4	1.082	1.170	1.262	1.360	1.464
5	1.104	1.217	1.338	1.469	1.611
6	1.126	1.265	1.419	1.587	1.772
7	1.149	1.316	1.504	1.714	1.949
8	1.172	1.369	1.594	1.851	2.144
9	1.195	1.423	1.689	1.999	2.358
10	1.219	1.480	1.791	2.159	2.594

Sometimes factor table can be easily used to calculate the doubling period. It is very popular among the literate and illiterate investors to get the double amount in a specified period of time. For example: If an investor deposited Rs. 5000 today at present at 6 per cent rate of Interest will become Rs. 10,000 in 12 years. It can be computed as follows. 72 is a Thumb rule for 6 per cent. Interest

$$\text{Doubling period} = \frac{72}{\text{Rate of Interest}}$$

$$= \frac{72}{6} = 12 \text{ years}$$

The time value of money can also be computed through **Multiple compounding period.** The interest amount will be paid in different modes. *i.e.*, month by quarterly, half yearly, yearly basis. Generally all commercial banks may allow interest on quarterly basis. Companies usually allow compound of interest twice a year on **30th June and 31st December every year.** The future value of money can be computed as follows:

$$V_n = V_o\left(1+\frac{i}{m}\right)^{m\times n}$$

V_n = Future value of money after n years.
V_o = Value of money at time
i = Interest rate
m = Number of times of compounding per year.

Illustration

Calculate the compound value of Rs. 1000 at the end of 3 years at 12 per cent rate of interest when interest is calculated on (a) yearly basis, (b) Quarterly basis.

Solution

Calculation of compound value when interest is computed on yearly basis:

(a) $\mathbf{V_n = V_o (1 + i)^n}$
$V_n = 1000\ (1+0.12)^3$
$= 1000\ (1.405)$
$= 1450$

(b) Interest is compounded on quarterly basis:

$$V_n = V_o\left(1+\frac{i}{m}\right)^{m \times n}$$
$= 1000\ (1 + 0.12/4)^{4\times3}$
$= 1000\ (1.03)^{124}$
$= 1426$

In sometimes, the principal amount will be refunded at series of different periodical times. Then the future value can be computed by the following formula:

$V_n = R_1\ (1+I)^{n-1} + R_2\ (1+i)^{n-2} + \ldots\ldots\ldots (R_{n-1})\ (1+i) + R_n.$
V_n = Future value at period N
R_1 = Payment after period 1
R_2 = Payment after period 2
R_n = Payment made after period n
I = Rate of Interest.

Illustration

Calculate the future value at the end of **five** years of the following series of payments at **10 per cent rate of Interest:**

R_1 = Rs. 100 at the end of the first year.
R_2 = Rs. 200 at the end of the second year.
R_3 = Rs. 300 at the end of the third year.
R_4 = Rs. 200 at the end of the fourth year.
R_5 = Rs. 150 at the end of the fifth year.

Solution

The future value of this series of payment will be computed by the following formula:

$$V_5 = R_1 (1+I)^{n-1} + R_2 (1+i)^{n-2} + R_3 (1+I)^{n-3} + R_4 (1+I)^{n-4} + R_5 (1+I)^{n-5}$$
$$V_5 = 100 (1.10)^4 + 200 (1.10)^3 + 300 (1.10)^2 + 200 (1.10) + 150$$
$$V_5 = 100 (1.464) + 200 (1.331) + 300 (1.210) + 200 (1.10) + 150$$
$$146.40 + 266.20 + 363 + 220 + 150 = 1145.60$$

This can also be calculated as given in the following Table.

End of Year	*Amount of Payment*	*No. of Years Compounded*	*Interest Factors*	*Future Value*
(1)	*(2)*	*(3)*	*(4)*	*(5) = 2 × 4*
1	100	04	1.464	146.40
2	200	03	1.331	266.20
3	300	02	1.210	363.00
4	200	01	1.100	220.00
5	150	0	1.000	150.00

Annuity

Annuity means an equal amount of payment for some specified duration. For example: The **premium** amounts will be collected by LIC in the form of annuity. It can be calculated as follows:

$$\mathbf{V_n = R (1+i)^{n-1} + (1+i)^{n-2} + (1+i)^{n-3} + 1}$$

Annuities can also be computed with the help of Annuity compound factor tables. A simple presentation of the annuity compound factor table is given for clear understanding of the computations.

	Percent				
Period (n)	*2*	*4*	*6*	*8*	*10*
1	1.000	1.000	1.000	1.000	1.000
2	2.020	2.040	2.060	2.080	2.100
3	3.060	3.122	3.184	3.246	3.310
4	4.122	4.246	4.375	4.506	4.641
5	5.204	5.416	5.637	5.867	6.105
6	6.308	6.633	6.975	7.336	7.716
7	7.434	7.898	8.394	8.923	9.487
8	8.583	9.214	9.897	10.637	11.436
9	9.755	10.583	11.491	12.488	13.579
10	10.950	12.006	13.181	14.487	15.937

Illustration

Mr. Sriharsha deposits Rs. 100 at the end of every year for 4 years and the deposit earns a compound interest 10 per cent per annum. Determine how much money he will get at the end of **4 years?**

Solution

The amount can be found in two methods:

(a) **Using compound factor table**

$$V_n = R\,(1+i)^{n-1} + (1+i)^{n-2} + (1+i)^{n-3} + 1$$
$$V_n = 100\,(1+.10)^{4-1} + (1+.10)^{4-2} + (1+.10)^{4-3} + 1$$
$$V_n = 100\,(1.10)^{3} + (1.10)^{2} + (1.10)^{1} + 1$$
$$V_n = 100\,(1.331 + 1.210 + 1.100 + 1)$$
$$V_n = 100\,(4.64)$$
$$V_n = 464.10$$

The amount can also be computed through the following annuity compound factor table:

$$\mathbf{V_n = R\,(ACF_{i,n})}$$
$$V_n = 100\,(4.641)$$
$$V_n = 464.10$$

Sometimes, the cash flows occur at the beginning of each period, the annuity is called as an annuity due. The future value of an annuity due can be computed as below:

$$\mathbf{V_n = (R)\,(1+i)^n + (R)\,(1+i)^{n-1} + (R)\,(1+i)^1}$$

With the help of annuity compound factor tables, it can be calculated the future value of an annuity due as:

$$V_n = (R)\,(ACF_{i,\,n})\,(1 + i)$$

Illustration

Mr. Srinath Jakka deposits **Rs. 500** at the beginning of each year for 5 years in a bank and the bank pays a compound interest at **8 per cent p.a.** Determine the future value of money at the end of **5 years.**

Solution

The future value of an annuity due can be computed in two methods:

(a) Using compound factor tables:

$V_n = (R)\,(1+i)^n + (R)\,(1+i)^{n-1} + (R)\,(1+i)^1$

$V_n = 500\,(1+0.08)^5 + (1+0.08)^4 + (1+0.08)^3 + (1+0.08)^2 + (1+0.08)^1)$

$= 500\,(6.335)$

$= 316.75$

(b) The annuity due can be calculated by the following formula:

$V_n = (R)\,(ACF_{\,i,\,n})\,(1+i)$

$V_n = 500\,(5.867)\,(1.08)$

$= 316.75$

(B) Present Value Concept

It is the another method of valuation of time value of money. It is also known **"Discounting value concept"**. It is quite opposite to the compound value of money. The future value of money concept reveal how much a sum of money becomes at a specified period of time. The present value concept indicates what the value is today of some future sum of money. The present value of money to be received in future will always be less. It can be computed in two ways:

$$V_n = V_o\,(1+i)$$

Or

$$V_o = \frac{V_n}{(1 + i)}$$

Illustration

Mr. Srinivas Jakka find an opportunity to buy a debenture today and he will get back **Rs. 1000** after one year. He is entitled to get interest **10 per cent p.a.** Calculate the present value of the debenture after one year.

Solution

$$V_o = \frac{V_n}{(1+i)}$$

$$V_o = \frac{1000}{(1+0.10)}$$

$$V_o = \frac{1000}{1.10} = \text{Rs. } 909.00$$

Sometimes the present value of money or discount concept of money can be computed with the help of the **"present values Discount factor tables."** A part of the factors are presented below for quick understanding.

	Percent				
Period	*2*	*4*	*6*	*8*	*10*
1	0.980	0.962	0.943	0.926	0.909
2	0.961	0.925	0.890	0.857	0.826
3	0.942	0.889	0.840	0.794	0.751
4	0.924	0.855	0.792	0.735	0.683
5	0.906	0.822	0.747	0.681	0.621
6	0.888	0.790	0.705	0.630	0.564
7	0.871	0.760	0.665	0.583	0.513
8	0.853	0.731	0.627	0.540	0.467
9	0.837	0.703	0.592	0.500	0.424
10	0.820	0.676	0.558	0.463	0.386

$\therefore$ Present value $(V_o) = V_n \times DF_{i,n}$

Illustration

Smt. Janaki Jakka is to receive Rs. 500 after 5 years from today. She is entitled to get 10 per cent p.a. Calculate its present value by using discount factor tables.

Solution

Present value V_o = Future value × $DF_{i,n}$

= 500 × 0.621

= 310.50

In sometimes, we may have to calculate present value of several sums of money, each occurring at different points of time. The present values can be computed through the following formula:

$$V_o = \frac{R_1}{(1+i)} + \frac{R_2}{(1+i)^2} + \frac{R_3}{(1+i)^3} + \frac{R_{n-1}}{(1+i)^{n-1}} + \frac{R_n}{(1+i)^n}$$

Or

$$V_o = \sum_{t=1}^{n} \frac{R_t}{(1+i)^t}$$

Illustration

From the following information calculate the present value of the following cash flows. The interest rate is **10 per cent:**

Year	*Cash Flows*
1	500
2	1000
3	1000
4	300
5	200

Solution

The present values can be computed as follows:

Year	*Cash Flows*	*PV Factor 10%*	*PV of Cash Flows*
1	500	0.909	454.50
2	1000	0.826	826.00
3	1000	0.751	751.00
4	300	0.683	204.90
5	200	0.621	124.20
Total present value of cash flows			**236.60**

Present value of an Annuity

Annuity means a series of equal payments for some specified period. The present value of an annuity can be presented as follows:

$$V_o = R\left[\sum_{i=1}^{n}\frac{1}{(1+i)^t}\right]$$

Or

Using discount factors it can also be computed as follows:

$$V_o = (R)\,(ADF_{\,i,\,n})$$

Illustration

Mr. Kiran has to receive **Rs. 200 per** year for **5 years.** Calculate the present value of the annuity assuming that he can interest on his investment **at 10 per cent p.a.**

Solution

Present value $V_o = 200 \times 3.791 = 758.20.$

Annuity Discount Factor Table

Period	P2	E4	R6	C8	E10 N T
1	0.980	0.962	0.943	0.926	0.909
2	1.942	1.886	1.833	1.783	1.736
3	2.884	2.775	2.673	2.577	2.487
4	3.808	3.630	3.465	3.312	3.170
5	4.713	4.452	4.212	3.993	3.791
6	5.601	5.242	4.917	4.623	4.355
7	6.472	6.002	5.582	5.206	4.868
8	7.325	6.733	6.210	5.747	5.335
9	8.162	7.435	6.802	6.247	5.759
10	8.983	8.111	7.360	6.710	6.145

Illustration

Mr. Nitish Babu has to receive Rs. 100 at the beginning of each year for **10 years.** Calculate the present value of the annuity due assuming **8 per cent rate of Interest.**

Solution

The present value of annuity due will be calculated as follows:

$$
\begin{aligned}
V_o &= (R)\,(ADF_{i,n})\,(1+i) \\
&= 100\,(6.145)\,(1+0.8) \\
&= 100\,(6.145)\,(1.8) \\
&= 100\,(11.06) \\
&= 1106
\end{aligned}
$$

Present value can also be calculated in following ways:

(a) Infinite life annuity

(b) Annuity at constant growth rate.

(a) The present value of an infinite life annuity can be computed by the following formula.

$$V_o = (R)\,(ADF_{i,\alpha})$$

Or

$$V_o = \frac{R}{i}$$

Illustration

Calculate the present value of Rs. 10,000 received in perpetuity for an infinite period, with discount rate 8 per cent.

Solution

$$V_o = \frac{R}{i}$$

$$V_o = \frac{10{,}000}{0.8} = 12{,}500$$

Illustration

Mr. Sridhar has rented out a portion of his house for 5 years at an annual rent of **Rs. 8000** with a condition that rent will increase by **10 per cent** every year. If the required rate of return is **15 per cent**. What is the present value of the expected series of rent?

Solution

The present value of expected series of rent can be calculated in two steps.

(a) Calculation of rent (10% increase every year).
(b) Calculation of present values.

Rent:

Year	Amount of Rent
1	8000
2	8800
3	9680
4	10648
5	11713

(b) Calculation of present values.

Year Ended	Cash Flows	PV Factor 15%	PV of Cash Flows
1	8000	0.870	6960
2	8800	0.756	6653
3	9680	0.658	6369
4	10648	0.572	6090
5	11713	0.498	5833
			31905

Techniques of Time Value of Money

Finance is a provision of money, when it require. In financial management, the time factor occupies an important role in decision making. The financial manager can also take some important applications into consideration. They are presented as below:

(a) Sinking fund method,
(b) Capital recovery method,
(c) Compound growth rate method, and
(d) Interest rate method.

(a) Sinking Fund Method

Sinking of method is associated with making a provision of money at future. It is related to determine the amount of annual payments. It also undertake to redeem an existing liability. It provides funds for replacement of an existing asset. It can be computed by the following formula:

$$V_n = (R)(ACF_{i,n})$$

Or

$$R = \frac{V_n}{ACF_{i,n.}}$$

Illustration

Voltas Ltd., has Rs. 4,00,000 6 per cent debentures outstanding at present. It has to redeem the debentures after 5 years and establishes a sinking fund to provide funds for redemption. Sinking fund investments earn interest **10 per cent p.a.** The investments are made at the end of each year. What annual payment must the firm make to ensure that the required Rs. 4,00,000 is available on the designated date?

Solution

The time value of money can be computed by the following formula:

$R = V_n/ACF_{i,n}$
i = 10 per cent,
n = 5 years. Compound value of an annuity
R = 4,00,000/6.105 = **65520** of Re. 1 is 6.015 for 5 years.

Therefore, the company should make annual payment of **Rs. 65520** for 5 years.

(b) Capital Recovery Method

Capital recovery method is one of the technique of time value of money. A company is in interested to know about the amount of equal instalment to be paid every year. The debt amount should be refunded by the company at a specified period of time. For this purpose the firm should make the annual instalment for a duration of time to redeem debt promptly. Hence the following formula can be applied for determining the amount of annual payment towards a provision of time.

Illustration

Krishna Textiles Ltd., has raised a loan of Rs. 10,00,000 from a financial institution at **8 per cent p.a.** rate of interest. The amount has to be paid back in **5 equal annual** instalments how much amount shall make instalment?

Solution

The instalment amount can be determined as follows:

$$R = V_o/ADF_{i,n}$$

$$R = \frac{10,00,000}{3.993} = 2,50,438$$

Hence the company should make a provision for redeem debt within 5 years. The annual instalment is Rs. 2,50,438.

(c) Compound Growth Rate

It is another method of technique to determine the amount of instalment. It can be calculated by the following formula.

$$V_n = V_o(CF_{i,n})$$

Illustration

From the following information for xyz Ltd., you are required to calculate compound rate of growth in profits.

Years	*Profit Rs. in Lakhs*
2000	60
2001	65
2002	75
2003	87
2004	98
2005	100

Solution

$$V_n = V_o(CF_{i,n})$$
$$V_n = 100 \quad V_o = 60$$
$$100 = 60\,(CF_{i,n})$$
Or
$$(CF_{i,n}) = \frac{100}{60} = 1.666$$

Using compound factor table for 6 years it found that 1.67 at **9 per cent**. Therefore, the compound rate of growth is nearly 9 per cent.

(d) Interest Rate Method

It is the last method of technique to explicit the interest in certain situations. It can be computed by the following formula.

$$V_n = (R)(ACF_{i,n})$$

For example: A company offers to pay Rs. 20,304 at the end of 10 years to investors who deposit annually Rs. 1000. What interest rate is implicit in the offers?

Solution

$$V_n = (R)(CF_{i,n})$$
$$V_n = 20{,}304$$
$$20{,}304 = 1000\,(ACF_{i,n})$$
$$ACF_{i,n} = 20.304$$

By using annuity compound factor tables we find that for 10 years, the rate of interest is **15 per cent.**

(d) Risk

Risk is a chance of loss. It is allowed to some extent of level in the business. The return is always haunted by Risk. Every business involves risk. It can be avoided in some situations but cannot be escaped by anyone. It is an expected rate of loss. A high risk component involves in business may generate higher profits. Low risk may provide lower amount of profits. The return depends upon the level of accepted risk. The return is a reward to the investor. In some situations risk may be reduced by combining various kinds of securities. Portfolio is a different sets of assets. Diversification reduces risk. Risk can be classified as **"systematic risk and unsystematic risk".** The systematic risk can be called as **market risk.** It cannot be reduced through diversification. It arises on account of the economy. Market is a combination of different factors. The **systematic risk** arises due to the following factors:

(i) the interest rate policy according to the government policy.
(ii) an increase corporate taxes.
(iii) government policy reflecting deficit financing.
(iv) credit policy by the RBI.
(v) a rise in inflation.

Unsystematic risk is also called as **Unique risk.** It is reduced through diversification, the following factors causes to raise unsystematic risk. They are:

(i) industrial unrest in the organisation.
(ii) an increase in attrition rate in case of experts from **RED wing.**
(iii) the degree of competition in the market.
(iv) fail in winning of mega protects.
(v) adoption of latest technology in process of innovation methods.
(vi) inferior quality of raw materials introduced by the company.

Total risk: Systematic risk + Unsystematic risk.

Therefore, risk is uncertainty of the income/capital appreciation or loss of both. The systematic risk is managed by the use of **Beta** of different company shares.

Beta

Beta is per cent change in the scrip return divided by the percentage change in the market return. The appreciation in the share prices will be reflected by a number of factors. There are two kinds of risk. **(i) scrip risk, (ii) market risk.** Scrip risk is related to the fluctuations of the market prices. Stock market is a highly volatile. The share prices are fluctuated even for small incident of things. Market risk is associated with the market index. If the **beta is** greater than **1**, the scrip risk is more than the market risk. It is better to select beta less than **1**. Risk takers would prefer scrips with beta greater than **1**. Beta measures sensitivity of the return of one asset to the market return. Usually all financial assets will have a total return consisting of two factors **(a) Risk free return, (b) Risk premium.** Return is a reward to the investors. The return received from a financial asset without any risk element is known as **Risk free return.** Some assets may generate more return for risk taking is known as **Risk premium.** It varies from asset to asset. Some kind of financial assets involves no risk. They provide risk free return. For example: Bank deposits, treasury bills, Government securities *etc*.

(e) Guidelines of the SEBI

Portfolio Management is a professional assignment. In India, it is in infancy stage. It is more popular in western countries. It requires a professional talent, high degree of integration, professional skills, expertism, and code of discipline. It has become, a complex and responsible job. It requires an in depth training and expertise. The entry into this service is not very easy. It is an art and requires high **degree** of expertise. The Merchant banker has been authorised to do these services. Category-**I** merchant bankers only one is eligible to do the business. No one can do portfolio management without **SEBI** registration and licence. **SEBI** is the regulatory authority to appoint the portfolio managers in India. It has issued guidelines regarding the appointment of portfolio managers. It has the licensing authority. A code of conduct was laid down for this position. **SEBI** is the most powerful organisation in the capital market segment. Portfolio management is a service for management of **portfolios** for others *i.e.*, clients or customers. The interested person, who wants to become portfolio manager, should have necessary infrastructure with professionally qualified persons with experience in the business. The person should have a minimum net worth of money as stipulated by the SEBI from time to time. The selected person should pay registration fee as stipulated by the SEBI from time to time. The **certificate** once granted is valid for three years. Afterwards, he has to pay a renewal fee for every year. The rates are changed by the SEBI from time to time. SEBI has imposed a number of obligations and a code of conduct on them. The portfolio manager should have a high standard of integrity, sincerety and honesty and should not have been convicted of any economic offence or moral turpitude. He should not participate or encourage in malpractice. They should submit books of accounts, are subject to inspection and audit by the SEBI. The activities of the portfolio managers are monitored by the SEBI. SEBI has powers to inspect and levy penalties for violation of rules and regulations. The portfolio manager has to submit periodical return and documents as may be required by the SEBI from time to time. The portfolio manager should not give assurance to the clients about return on portfolio. SEBI has prohibited the portfolio manager to assume any risk on behalf of the client. The client provides sufficient funds to the portfolio manager, the investments made or advised by him are subject to **risk.** The risk should be borne by **client.** The relation between client and portfolio managers is a contractual element. The portfolio manager will charge a fixed rate of fee as per the contract. The fee charged by him should be transparent as per the contract. The portfolio manager should not misuse the funds which are provide by the clients. According to the **SEBI** guidelines, the contract period between portfolio manager and client should be less than a year. The portfolio manager should not use the clients money for lending, badla financing and bill discounting. He should not deploy the clients money against the contract. The money should be used as per the provision of contract. The portfolio manager should keep the money in a separate account in public sector bank. He should not mix the money with his own funds or investments. All the financial affairs of the client should entered in his name. Contract notes, bills are passed in clients name. A separate ledger should be opened and maintained for each client. All the affairs between client and portfolio manager should be done as per the **agreement.** The termination of the contract, final settlement should be made as per provision of the contract. Usually the investments can be put in both money market and capital market instruments. The portfolio manager will accept the management of portfolio of client on discretionary or non-discretionary basis as per the provisions of the contract. The management of client's portfolio is influenced by many factors such as **objectives, composition of assets, proportion of financial instruments** ***etc.*** The portfolio will be managed as per preference of the client. The portfolio manager will construct the client's database such as income basis, assets types, needs, risk bearing capacity, personal details. According to the available data, the portfolio manager will design a **"proper investment strategy"** for each and every client. The portfolio should have a **time horizon.** Time is the most important factor in investment strategy. An ideal time for better portfolio return is **3 to 5 years.** While designing the portfolio, the manager should keep in mind about tax benefits. The portfolio manager should take consideration into tax advantages and investment incentives. Return is a reward to the investor. Returns are enjoyed by the investors. After tax payment, the return will be enjoyed by the client. The net return includes inflation risk. These are called net real rates of returns. The tax benefits are highly influencial factor for **high networth individuals.** Hence it is worth while to know about the tax implications effect as the portfolio. Usually real rates of return excludes taxes. Investors are interested in real returns. Hence it is necessary for investors to learn the tax provisions relating to different financial assets. The income tax provisions are changing from year to year according to the **finance act.** The finance act is introduced in the parliament by the **Finance Minister.** Finance act is a part of the budget. Budget is a reflection of government's receipts and payments. It is an estimation of government income and expenditure. The tax rates in India are changed every year and is based as government policy. Hence the tax incentives are provided to the investors by the government policy. Government policies are changing according to political strategies. Now-a-days all political parties are in run race to attract the mass for gaining popularity.

Political strategy of the government is followed by populist methods rather than stricter financial discipline. **Discipline** is the most important factor for development. Financial discipline is necessary for any common man or any country. If any person/country does not follow the financial discipline, they should pay the cost. Hence financial discipline can be utilised as a instrument to counter the poverty. Any violation of financial discipline can be treated as a **beautiful lady** without moral values. Therefore the political leaders, who play with the lives of crores of public should be provided with proper financial management techniques. Because, they are running the government according to their strategies. Government is a powerful machinery to counter the **poverty.** Poverty can be attacked with suitable weapons such as various government policies. Government policies are framed with a strong perception of all factors. But the problems are arised at various stages of implications. If the effective utilisation and implementation of the policies will show a distinct impact on the common mans life. However, it should be noted that, creation of work for all will stimulate the growth of the economy. India also become another **America.**

Finance Act 2005—The present tax system is indicated in the finance act 2005. The act deals with the direct and indirect taxes of the country. The present tax system provides some benefits to tax paying investors. Investors usually need to make tax planning in advance to avoid last minute problems and financial crisis. A well tax planning system makes for easy payment of tax. A tax liability or burden will be reduced by adopting a strategy. The basic aim of tax planning is reducing tax liability of the investor. The following aspects will be observed in tax implications of finance act:

(a) Dividends and Interest.
(b) Brokerage Income.
(c) Business profits.
(d) Income tax.
(e) Corporate tax.
(f) Capital gains.
(g) Wealth tax.
(h) Gift box.
(i) NRIs.
(j) Investments.
(k) Recent trends.
(l) Transaction cost.

(a) Dividend and Interest

Dividend and interest is reward to the investors. Investors are risk takers and return gainers. They will get income in two ways *i.e.*, revenue income and capital appreciation/capital loss. Generally the bank depositors will get income in the form of **Interest.** The amount of interest is tax able in the hands of the depositors subject to conditions. Any revenue income from the units of mutual funds, shares will be liable to pay tax by the shareholders. **Bonds and Debentures** are another kind of financial assets. The bond holders and debenture holders are entitled to get the interest from issuing agencies. The receipt of interest will attract the income tax in the hands of bond/debenture holders. The more radical changes have been in the way breaks for investment have been handled. No more tax breaks under Section **88 or 80L**, both sections are abolished. The finance act also provided a overall limit of **Rs. 1.00 lakh** for a basket of investments at the convenience of the tax payer. It is a very good idea and it encourages for construction of new houses. All of these payments include for **public provident fund, mutual fund investments, repayment of housing loan principal, approved pension funds, premiums paid for pension plans etc. Rs. 12,000** will be allowed as a deduction under Section 80L from the **GTI** of an individual and HUF.

(b) Brokerage Income

The financial intermediaries earns income by the way of brokerage. Share consultants, firms which deals in securities are required to pay tax on their earnings. They earn commission or brokerage by charging from the investors or client's. They provide services to them according to their convenient and flexibility.

(c) Business Profits

The business profits or trading profits are subject to normal rates. Speculation is an activity involved for profit element. But there is also involvement of **risk** component. Risk is in reflection of **capital loss.** Return reveals capital appreciation. The loss/appreciation of capital can be classified as **short and long-term capital gains.** The short-term capital gains and speculative losses can be carried forward to be offset by only short-term speculative gains.

(d) Income Tax

Income tax is an example of direct tax. The tax rates are fluctuated every year. According to the finance act 2005, the income tax rates are presented below for easy reference:

(i) **Individuals, Hindu undivided families.**
(ii) **Cooperative societies.**
(iii) **Firms.**
(iv) **Local authorities.**
(v) **Companies.**

(i) Individuals

The finance act, 2005 specifies the rates of income tax for individuals, Hindu undivided family and association of persons. The basic exemption is allowed for **Rs. 1,00,000.** Therefore no tax is levied on income below Rs. 1,00,000. The tax rate slabs are presented below for the assessment year 2006-07.

Income Slab	Rates
(a) Upto Rs. 1,00,000	Nil
(b) Rs. 1,00,001 to Rs. 1,50,000	10%
(c) Rs. 1,50,001 to 2,50,000	20%
(d) Above Rs. 2,50,000	30%

Persons having income exceeding **Rs. 8,50,000** in this slab would be required to pay **10 per cent surcharge** on the total income tax payable after rebate. Education cess at the rate of **2 per cent.** On Income tax and surcharge continues to believed in the proposed rate structure persons in this slab having income exceeding **Rs. 10,00,000** would be required to pay **10 per cent** surcharge on the total income tax payable after rebate, if any under chapter VIII A. Marginal relief on such tax is also provided for.

(ii) Cooperative Societies

In case of cooperative society, the following rates are applicable for the assessment year 2006-2007:

(a) where the total income does not exceed **Rs. 10,000** : **10% of the total income.**

(b) where the total income exceeds **Rs. 10,000** but does not exceed **Rs. 20,000** : **1000 + 20 per cent** of the amount by which the total income exceeds **Rs. 10,000.**

(c) where the total income exceeds **Rs. 20,000** : **3,000 + 30%** of the amount by which the total income exceeds of **Rs. 20,000.**

Surcharge: 2.5% on Income tax.

(iii) Firms

In case of every firm, the computation of total income attracts **35 per cent.** The amount of income tax computed at the rate herinbefore specified or in section III A or section 112, shall in case of every firm, be increased by a surcharge for purpose of the union calculated at the rate of **2.5 per cent** of such tax.

(iv) Local authorities

In case of local authority, the income tax is levied on the whole total Income of **30 per cent**. Surcharge will be levied on income tax at 2.5 per cent.

(v) Companies

For domestic companies, the corporate income tax rate will be **30 per cent.** There will also be a surcharge of **10 per cent.** In the case of a company other than a domestic company, the following classification will be applied:

(i) on so much of the total income as consists of:

(a) royalties received from government or an Indian concern in pursuance of an agreement made after 31-3-1961 but before 1-4-1976.

(b) Fee for rendering technical services received from government or an Indian concern in pursuance of an agreement made by it with government after **29-2-1964 but** before **1-4-1976.**

} **50 %**

(ii) On the balance, if any of the total income : **40%**
Surcharge will be levied at **2.5%.**

(e) Corporate Tax

The Union budget assumes a nominal GDP growth rate of **13.7 per cent** for 2005-06. If the average rate of inflation is taken at 6 per cent, then the real growth of GDP is projected at nearly 8 per cent. The corporation tax is projected to grow over **33 per cent** for 2005-06. The following table will clearly explains about the various aspects of the tax levels:

	Rupee comes		*Rupee goes*	
(a)	Income tax	0-11	Interest	0-22
(b)	Customs duty	0-08	Defence	0-14
(c)	Excise duty	0-20	Other non plan exp.	0-12
(d)	Other taxes	0-03	Subsidies	0-07
(e)	Non tax revenue	0-13	State share of taxes	0-16
(f)	Non-debt capital	0-02	State EVT plan assist	0-05
(g)	Borrowings	0-25	Central plan	0-18
(h)	Corporate tax	0-18	Non plan assist and to states	0-06

The budget has also taken important steps for promotion and welfare of the industries. The following are the important provisions introduced in the present budget[1]:

(a) Measure to promote regional development **(Section 80-I B).**
(b) Rationalization and simplification measure for **SEZs.**
(c) Revival of exemption on lease rentals on aircraft engines.
(d) Reduction in rate of tax on Royalty and fees of technical services.
(e) Extension of tax benefits for developing infrastructure.
(f) Depreciation on new machinery.
(g) Utilisation of reserves for purchase of a slip.
(h) Deduction of payment of VRS.

(a) Measure to Promote Regional Development (Section 80-I B)

Under the existing provisions contained in sub-section **(4)** of Section 80-I B, industrial undertakings engaged in manufacture or production or operation of a cold storage unit and set up during the period **1-4-1993 to 31-3-2005** in the state of **J&K** are eligible for a **100 per cent** deduction of profits for a period of **five years** followed by **25 per cent (30% in case of companies)** for the next five years. The deduction is subject to a negative list of commodities included in the **13th** schedule which should not be manufactured or produced by such industrial undertakings. The deduction is not available to industries in the state set up after **31-3-2005.**

1. *The Economic Times,* 1 March, 2005, p. 15.

With a view to promote the industrial development of the state of **J&K**, it is proposed to extend the terminal date for setting up of industrial undertakings and commencement of eligible business in the state by two more years from 31-3-2005 to 31-3-2007. The amendment will take effect from 1-4-2006 and will accordingly, apply in relation to the assessment 2006-07 and subsequent years.

(b) Special Economic Zones

Under the existing provisions of sub-section **(1A)** of Section **10A**, an undertaking set in a special economic zone, which begins to manufacture or produce articles or things or computer software after **31-3-2002**, is allowed a **100 per cent** deduction of export profits for a period of **five years** and **50 per cent** for the next two years followed by a **50 per cent** deduction of export profits credited to a special reserve account for the next **Three years.**

With a view to rationalise the provisions of this section, it is proposed to insert a sunset clause so as to provide that no deduction under the sub-section shall be allowed to any undertaking which begins to manufacture or produce such articles or things or computer software after **31-3-2009**, in a special economic zone.

The proposed amendment will take effect from **1-4-2006** and will, accordingly, apply in relation to assessment year 2006-07 and subsequent years.

(c) Lease Rentals for Aircraft

Clause (15A) of Section 10 provides for exemption from income tax of the lease payment received in respect of a lease of an aircraft or an aircraft engine by the government of a foreign state or foreign enterprise from an Indian company engaged in the business of operation of aircraft. This exemption is available subject to the condition that the agreement for such lease is entered into prior to **1-4-2005.** It is proposed that the exemption for lease payments shall continue with regard to agreements entered into on or before 30th September 2005.

However, the benefit of exemption from tax on tax will be available in respect of lease rent payments made in pursuance of agreements entered in or after 1-10-2005. These amendments will take effect from 1-4-2006 and will, accordingly, apply in relation to the assessment year 2006-07 and subsequent years.

(d) Royalty or Technical Services

The finance act 2005, proposed a reduction in rate of tax on royalty and fees for the technical services in the case of a **non-resident** from **20 per cent to 10 per cent.** This amendment will take effect from **1-4-2006** and will, accordingly, apply in relation to the assessment year 2006-07 and subsequent years.

(e) Tax benefits to Infrastructure Activities

Under the existing provision of clause (i) of sub-section (4) of section **80-I A,** an enterprise carrying on the business of developing or operating and maintaining or developing, operating and maintaining any infrastructure facility, which commences such operation and maintenance on or after 1-4-1995, is eligible for a **100 per cent** deduction of profits for a period of **10 years.** Sub clause (a) provides that the enterprise should be owned by a company registered in India or by a consortium of such companies.

It is proposed to amend the above condition so as to enable an authority or a board or a corporation or any other body established or constituted under a central or state act which is not incorporated under the Companies Act, 1956 to take advantage of the benefits provided under the said section. The proposed amendment will take effect from 1-4-2006 and will accordingly, apply in relation to the assessment year 2006-07 and subsequent years.

(f) Depreciation on Machinery

Under the existing provisions of Section 32 of act, depreciation on capital assets is allowed as a deduction at the accelerated rates specified in the appendix to Income tax rule, 1962. The accelerated rate of depreciation on general machinery and plant is **25 per cent.** Further, section 32 also provides for an initial depreciation of **15 per cent** on new machinery and plant subject to *inter alia* the condition that the installation of new plant and machinery result in a **10 per cent** increase in the installed capacity.

In view of the above, it is proposed to amend the income tax act and the rules thereunder so as to reduce the rate of depreciation for general machinery and plant to **15 per cent** from the existing rate of **25 per cent.** Rates of depreciation of other capital assets are also being rationalized in line with the reduction in the rate for general machinery and plant.

Further, in order to encourage new investments, the initial depreciation on new machinery and plant is proposed to be increased to **20 per cent** from the existing level of 15 per cent. The requirements of creating a minimum increase of 10 per cent in installed capacity for availing the initial depreciation is also proposed to be eliminated. Consequently, the initial depreciation will be available to all new plant and machinery except those referred in provision to the proposed clause (iia) of section 32 of the income tax act. This amendment will take effect from 1-4-2006 and will, accordingly apply in relation to the assessment year 2006-07 subsequent years.

(g) Tax Treatment of Reserves Utilised for Purchase of a Ship

Under the existing provisions of Section 33AC a shipping company is allowed a specified deduction in respect of amounts credited to a reserve account to be utilised for acquiring a new ship. The acquisition of a new ship is generally financed by debt and internal accruals. These internal accruals could be from general reserves or special reserves created for this purpose. Further, the law provides that if a company sells or transfers the ship after the three years' lock-in period and the sale proceeds are not utilised for the purpose of acquiring a new ship within a period of one year from the end of the previous year in which such sale or transfer took place, the sale proceeds are deemed to be the profits of the assessment year immediately following the previous year in which the ship was sold or transferred.

As stated above, a new ship is acquired by a shipping company by utilising both the reserves and borrowed capital. The existing law provides that if a ship is sold or transferred, the whole of the sale proceeds would be subject to tax. This implies that both borrowed capital and amount withdrawn from reserves would bear, the burden of tax. The real intend is to restrict the incidence of tax on the amount utilised from the reserve account for acquiring the ship. The proposed amendment seeks to clarify this real intend, whereby only so much of the sale proceeds which represent the amount credited to the reserve account and utilised for acquisition of the ship would be deemed to be the profits.

This amendment will take retrospective effect from 1-4-2004 and will, accordingly apply in relation to the assessment year 2004-05 and subsequent years.

(h) Deduction for the Payments under the Voluntary Retirement Scheme

During the last decade, a number of companies have embarked on a programme of restructuring which *inter alia* includes the reviewing the size of its workforce. As a result such companies have introduced voluntary retirement scheme for its employees. The companies are allowed to amortize the payments to its employees at the time of their voluntary retirement under any scheme framed in accordance with the prescribed guidelines.

The existing provisions do not fully reflect this intent. Under the existing provisions, **1/5th** of the amount paid to an employee at the time of VRS is allowed as deduction and the balance is allowed to be deducted in **Four equal** instalments in four succeeding years. Where part payments are made at the time of voluntary retirement, only the payment made in the first year is allowed to amortized over five years. The balance paid in instalments in subsequent years is not allowed as deduction. The proposed amendment seeks to provide for amortization of the amount of the payment made in any year, each such payment independently admissible for amortization over a period of **Five years.**

These amendments will take retrospective effect from 1-4-2004 will, accordingly, apply in relation to the assessment year 2004-05 and subsequent years.

(f) Capital Gains

The finance act 2005, reveals the tax benefits regarding capital gains. The existing provisions contained in the provision to clause **(42A)** of the said section provides that, if a share in a company or any other securities listed in a recognised stock exchange in India or units of UTI or unit of a mutual fund specified under clause **(23D)** of section 10, is held for not more than twelve months, it shall be in nature of **short-term capital asset.** It is proposed to amend the said provision so as to treat **zero coupon bond** held not for more than 12 months as a short-term capital asset. Clause **17** seeks to amend section **54EC** of the Income tax act relating to capital gain not to be charged on investment in certain bonds. The existing provisions provide that the capital gain arising from transfer of a long-term capital asset shall be exempt from tax if such capital gain is invested, within a period of **six months** after the date of transfer, in a long-term specified asset being any bond redeemable after **three years** issued by NABARD or National Highways Authority of India, NHB, REC, SIDBI. If part of the capital gain is so invested in acquiring the long-term specified asset, proportionate exemption will be available. The exemption is available subject to the condition that, the said long-term specified assets are held for a minimum period of three years, failing which the exemption allowed on the basis of such investment will be disallowed and the amount so disallowed will be deemed to be the income chargeable to tax under the head capital gains of the previous year in which such long-term assets are sold otherwise transferred.

(a) **Wealth tax**—In India, there are two kinds of taxes. (i) **Direct Taxes,** (ii) **Indirect taxes.** Direct tax consists of Income tax, Wealth tax, and Gift tax. The finance act 2005 deals with the tax proposals of direct and indirect taxes. Income tax is levied by the central government. It collects from the public and the accruals will be utilised for welfare of the public. Wealth tax is levied by the government in acquiring assets by the citizens, firms, societies and companies. The rates are applied as per the provisions of the act.

(h) Gift Tax

Gift tax is another part of the Direct taxes. It will be levied and collected on gifts made by the people. The Donor is responsible for payment of tax.

(i) Non-Residents

Under the existing provisions of sub-clause (ii) of clause (4) of **Section 10** of the Income tax act, any income by way of interest on many standing to the credit of an individual in a **"Non-Resident (External) account"** in any bank in India, is exempt from Income tax. However, this exemption is not available in respect of such interest income after 31-3-2005. It is proposed to amend the said sub-clause (ii) to provide that such income by way of interest on moneys standing to credit of individual in a Non-Resident external account shall continue to be exempt from tax even after 31-3-2005. This amendment will take effect from **1-4-2006**, and will accordingly apply in relation to the assessment year **2006-07** and subsequent years. Another important development is **"revival of exemption of Interest on Foreign currency deposits".** Under the existing provision of item (fa) of sub-clause (iv) of clause (15) of section 10, the interest payable by a scheduled bank before **1-4-2005** to a Non-resident or to a person who is not ordinarily resident on deposits in foreign currency where the acceptance of such deposits by the bank is approved by the RBI is exempt from income tax. It is proposed to amend the said item (fa) to provide that such income payable by way of interest to a Non-Resident or to a person who is not ordinarily resident shall continue to be exempt on or after the 1-4-2005. This amendment will take effect from 1-4-2006, and will, accordingly, apply in relation to the assessment year 2006-07 and subsequent years.

(j) Investments

Investment is the paramount requirement of consolidate the growth process. In **agriculture**, we shall enhance public and private investment in the infrastructure required to support expansion diversification and value addition. In the **Industrial sector**, both the public and private sector will be allowed the space to grow and compete with each other. Government will play the leading role in providing and facilitating investment in public goods such as roads, railways, power, seaports and airports. In the **service sector**, Government will recognise the leading role played by the private sector and provide a supportive policy environment and stable tax policies. In the financial year **2005-06**, the government will provide equity support of **Rs. 14,040** crore and loans of **Rs. 3554** crore to public sector enterprise. Success will ultimately depend upon our ability to finance the growth. Government will, therefore, through a mix of right policies and prudent taxes, promote savings and devise ways and means to channel these savings into productive investment. The capital market banks, insurance companies, pension funds, and superannuation funds would have a crucial role in mobilizing and disbursing the financial resources required to sustain high investment.

(k) Recent Trends

The investment boom in infrastructure, industry and service needs to be nurtured through further reforms in the financial sector including reforms in the following sector:

(a) Banking sector.
(b) Capital market.

(a) *Banking Sector*—The banking sector presents a picture of paradoxes. There are many banks in India but none among the top twenty in the world our largest bank, SBI, ranks **82** in terms of business. It is universally acknowledged that the key drivers of the banking sector in the future will be **"competition, consolidation and convergence"**. RBI has prepared a road map for banking sector reforms and will unveil the same. RBI on its own authority, some legislative changes would be required to be made. A bill to amend the Banking Regulation Act, 1949 will be introduced in the budget session. The following proposals have been made to amend the act:

(i) To remove the lower and upper bounce to the statutory liquidity ratio and provide flexibility to RBI to prescribe prudential norms.
(ii) To allow banking companies to issue preference shares, since preference share capital can be treated regulated capital under specified circumstances as per **Base 1** norms.
(iii) To introduce specific provisions to enable the consolidated, supervision of banks and their subsidiaries by RBI in consonance with the International best practices in this regard.
(iv) To remove the limits of the cash reserve ratio to facilitate more flexible conduct of monitory policy.
(v) To enable RBI to lend or borrow securities by way of repo, Reserve repo or otherwise.

(b) *Capital Market*—Capital market has emerged as a measure vehicle for converting savings into investments. It is also the preferred investment destination of foreign savings. The RBI had initiated steps in July 2004 to strengthen the capital market. It is time for more measures and hence the RBI proposed:

(i) authorised Securities and Exchange Board of India to set up a national institute of security markets for teaching and training intermediaries in the securities markets and promoting research.
(ii) permit **FIIs** to submit appropriate collateral, in cash or otherwise as prescribed by SEBI, when trading in derivatives on the domestic market.
(iii) amend the definition of "securities" under the Securities Contracts (Regulation) Act, 1956, so as to provide a legal framework for trading of securitized debt including mortgaged backed debt.
(iv) appoint a high level expert committee on corporate bonds and securitisation to look in to the legal regulatory tax and market design issues in the development of the corporate bond market.
(v) **over the counter derivatives** play a crucial role in mitigating the risks of corporate, banks and other financial entities, there is, however some ambiguity regarding legality of **OTC** derivatives contracts which has inhibited their growth. RBI proposes to take measures to provide legal validity of such contracts.
(vi) stamp duty on stock exchange corporation the SCRA, 1956 as amended recently requires all stock exchanges to be corporatised

and demutilised. **Three stock exchanges** are not yet corporatised. In order to facilitate their corporatisation, the RBI proposed to grant a **one time exemption** to the from stamp duty on the notional transfer of assets.

(vii) stamp duty on commercial paper. In order to create a level playing field for banks and non-bank entities to issue commercial paper and to bring the Indian commercial paper market closure to International standard, RBI proposed to rationalised the stamp duty so that it applies uniformly regardless of the issuing entity.

(viii) **Mumbai,** a regional financial centre is placed in between **London and Tokyo** of two nerve centres of global finance. Mumbai is home to **NSE and BSE** ranks No. 3 and No. 5 among the stock exchanges of the world by the number of trades per year. The time has come to begin work on making Mumbai a regional hub for finance. RBI propose to appoint a high powered expert committee to advise the government for making Mumbai a regional financial centre.

(ix) Ten years ago, the gold inflows are through the official channels alone. At present we are now in a position to introduce gold units and create a market for such units. RBI proposed the SEBI to establish a gold exchange trade fund. The fund should be available to common man to buy the gold at even for small amount. Such units could be traded in the some manner as units of mutual funds.

(l) Transaction cost

The finance act 2005, provides measures for additional resources mobilisation through levy of transaction tax in a recognised stock exchange. The existing provisions of chapter VII of the finance No. 2 act, 2004 provide for levy of a securities transaction tax on the value of transactions in respect of specified securities. The securities transaction tax shall be charged in respect of the following transactions at the rates as under:

(a) **0.0075 per cent** on the value of transactions of delivery based purchase of an equity share in a company or a unit of an equity oriented fund, entered in a recognised stock exchange, to be paid by **the buyer**.

(b) **0.0075 per cent** on the value of transactions of delivery based purchase of an equity share in a company or a unit of an equity oriented fund, entered in a recognised stock exchange, to be paid by the **seller**.

(c) **0.0015 per cent** on the value of transactions of Non-delivery based sale of an equity share in a company or a unit of an equity oriented fund, entered in a recognised stock exchange, to be paid by the **seller**.

(d) **0.01 per cent** on the value of transactions of derivatives being option or future entered in a recognised stock exchange.

(e) **0.15 per cent** on the value of transactions of sale of units of an equity oriented fund to the mutual fund with a view to raise additional resources and also plug the leakage of a tax revenue, it is proposed to enhance these rates. The proposed new rates shall be as under:

  (i) **0.01 per cent** on the value of transactions of delivery based purchase of an equity share in a company or a unit of an equity oriented fund, entered in a recognised stock exchange, to be paid by **the buyer.**

  (ii) **0.01 per cent** on the value of transactions of delivery based sale of an equity share in a company or a unit of an equity oriented fund, entered in a recognised stock exchange, to be paid by the **seller**.

  (iii) **0.02 per cent** on the value of transactions of delivery based sale of an equity share in a company or a unit of an equity oriented fund, entered in a recognised stock exchange, to be paid by **the seller**.

  (iv) **0.0133 per cent** on the value of transactions of derivatives being option or future entered in a recognised stock exchange.

  (v) **0.2 per cent** on the value of transactions of sale of units of an equity oriented fund to the mutual fund. The proposed amendment will take effect from **1-6-2005.**

Speculation

Speculation is the oxygen to the stock markets. Stock markets convert the savings into productive investment channels. Savings flow will be diverted towards productive ways. This flow of money is useful for capital formation. A strong capital formation leads to **Asset creation.** Generally investors first start with making applications in primary market. After allotment of shares, keeping with some time and will be disposed in the stock market at the convenient of investors. In this juncture, investor is interested in speculation and not in investment. If the issue is not appreciating after listing, or if he is a long-term investor, he will keep such investments. Enter and exit in the stock market is a adventure activity for the innocent investors. A professional investor, who moves intelligently in the stock market can win the situation or otherwise burnt his fingers. He may lose his wealth for his wrong investment decisions.

Precautions for Investment

Investment is a curb in the present consumption. The curb in consumption leads to enhancing the investment levels. All investors should make proper planning of their investments first to provide for their requirements of comfortable life with a basic need of house, real estate, physical assets *etc.* He should also take care about comforts and insurance for life and make a provision for a provident fund and **pension fund** for a future day. Before entering into stock market, the investor should think about his prior commitments by avoiding financial crisis in his life period. They make investments in the stock market on the advise of friends, relative, agents or brokers. Hence they should take all precautions prior to enter into the stock market. The risk and return are two important factors in the Portfolio Management. If we want more return, we must accept for more risk and if no risk is taken, simply bank deposits are opted for investment. The return is a reward to the investor. Portfolio is a combination of different financial assets. The ratio of different combination of financial instruments. Portfolio is just like a **"cocktail"**. The combination of different kinds of ingredients stimulates the taste of the drink. The portfolio return is related to **risk.** In the market the risk free return assets are also available to the investors. **Bank deposits, post office deposit or certificates** are the best examples for risk free assets. Hence the investors may also keep these assets in their portfolios to reduce the risk levels of portfolio. There are also high return assets available in the market. The higher return depends upon many factors like accepted level of risk, expertise in selection of financial assets, return due to diversification *etc*. The return in stock market depends upon many factors.

Portfolio is a combination of different financial assets such as shares, bonds and money market instruments. The aim of the portfolio management is to **minimise the risk** and maximise **return**. The mix of blending different broad assets will provide better return with minimum risk is known as **"portfolio construction"**. The risk can be reduced through diversification. The return can be found by altering the original portfolio. Portfolio can be classified as family. The family's goodwill will be enhanced by some members and at the same time, it will be damaged by the other members. Hence the portfolio return can also be enhanced through some assets. The other assets will pull down the asset values of the portfolio. In portfolio, some securities may not show performance as expected by the portfolio managers. Some other securities may show excellence performance as expected by the portfolio manager. A single security may lead to a greater actual return.

Approaches in Portfolio Construction

Portfolio is a mix of different kinds of financial instruments. All of these assets combinations may generate return. That return is reward to the investor. The return earned through portfolio indicates the capacity abilities and skills of the portfolio manager. Hence the construction of portfolio is the most important factor in portfolio management. A well structured portfolio may generate sufficient and expected return. Construction of portfolio can be done in two methods:

(a) Traditional Method.
(b) Modern approach.

(a) Traditional Method

Portfolio theory is the basis of portfolio management. It relates to the construction of a good portfolio. It is associated with efficient portfolio management in financial and physical assets including shares, debentures and bonds of various companies. A portfolio mean holding of different kind of physical assets with a view to earn return from them. In this approach, the portfolio manager needs some information about the client. He considers the needs of client in terms of income and capital appreciation. The collected information about the clients position enables the portfolio manager to frame a good portfolio to satisfy the needs of his client. In this **traditional approach,** the portfolio manager will evaluate the entire financial plan of the individual or client. The **traditional approach** is related to construction of a good portfolio by considering the following factors:

(i) Objectives of the portfolio.
(ii) Composition of securities.

(i) Objectives of the Portfolio

Portfolio is a combination of different kinds of financial assets. Financial assets will generate some rate of return or arises some risk. Hence the investors intelligence is to **avoid risk or escape risk** and capture the return. The game of risk and return is the yield of portfolio. The return is the barometer of efficiency. The efficiency of portfolio manager is reflected in the returns of portfolio. **Minimise** the risk and **maximise** the return is the main motive behind in construction of best portfolio. The construction of best portfolio is influenced by many factors. Before formulating the objective of the portfolio, the hurdles faced by the client should be analysed. Hence the portfolio manager should frame the portfolio within the hurdles faced by the Investor. The hurdles of the investors should be compensated with efficient portfolio construction. The following are the important factors in traditional approach:

(a) Hurdles.
(b) Time.

(a) **Hurdles**—Generally, the investors will invest their amount of savings in the **form of portfolio**. Portfolio is a combination of financial instruments which generate appropriate returns. A common man should have to face many hurdles to pool his investment in the form of portfolio. The following hurdles faced by the common investors:

(i) Revenue
(ii) Safety
(iii) Liquidity
(iv) Time horizon.

(i) **Revenue**—It is very common to expect a regular revenue from his investment by the investor. Every investor expect some return from his commitment. Every investor needs some income to meet all or part of the **living expenses.** The inflation also erodes the purchasing power. The investor need to set off the effect of the inflation and needs income in **constant rupees.** Generally investors need money in two situational factors:

(a) Desire for present revenue.
(b) Regular flow of income.

Generally, common investors desires some amount of money for present consumption. He fulfills all his needs with the availability of present income levels. The current income levels depends upon the current financial plan of the investors. He needs some money to cover his certain level of standard of living expenses. He needs some amount of money for his routine expenditure. Once the information is arrived at, it is very easy to assess the needs of money. It enables the portfolio manager to decide how much income must be provided for the construction of portfolio. The design of portfolio can be made very easily to achieve the clients financial goals.

Another important aspect is inflation. Inflation reduces the purchasing power of money. The rupee value is determined by the levels of inflation. A low level of inflation in the economy stimulates the value of **Rupee.** A high level of inflation exists in the economy reduces the value of **Rupee**. Therefore, the investor should take all considerations while designing the portfolio for his investment process. He must try to build a best portfolio which could offset the effect of inflation. The portfolio manager should take a decision and funds should be invested according to the impact of inflation. Hence the inflation element cannot be ignored in portfolio management. In order to achieve the goals of the client, the portfolio manager should invest the funds in **growth stocks**. Identification of growth stock is the main important task in the portfolio management. The growth stock may also be known as **Sunrise Industries stocks.** They are also known as **Blue chip shares**. A strong earning potential, large amount of reserves, undistributed amount of profits, Retained' earnings are the main characteristics of the blue chip companies. Hence the selection of growth stocks can show impact on the portfolio.

(ii) **Safety**—Investment means, just parking one's idle fund. The investors will invest the fund for time being. After the completion of their time, they demand their amount of money from the parking place. Hence the investor always think about the safety of his investment rather than return. Investment in debentures and bonds are safer than equity. Investing in regularly trading securities are not risky. Investing in unquoted, less traded, on traded may not provide adequate safety to the investors. Investing in **blue chip company shares** will enhance the safety levels of investment.

(iii) **Liquidity**—Liquidity is the most important factor in the stock market operations. Some kind of financial assets provide high liquidity. High quality short-term debt instruments provide higher liquidity. Money market instruments, commercial papers and shares that are widely traded creates high liquidity. Active trading, large volume of trading securities indicates the levels of liquidity in the market. Some sectors lack liquidity due to their nature of business. **For example, Real estate**. Some kind of shares are poorly traded in stock market creates no liquidity to that financial instruments. The portfolio manager should design the portfolio according to the needs of the levels of liquidity as desired by the investor or client.

(iv) **Time Horizon**—Time is the essential important factor in designing best portfolio in order to meet the financial goals of the client or investor. Generally investors are making their investment for a special purpose for their future. After a specific period of time, they pull their investment from the portfolio. Hence the **push and pull strategy** will be applied by the common investor. He will **push** the funds when it is available freely at his disposal for a specific period of time. After the expiry of time he will **pull** his money from a basket of investment. Portfolio means a basket of different kinds of financial assets. The **time horizon** varies from individual to individual. Investment planning periods known as **"Time horizon".** Gaining in the stock market is a game of **Risk and Return elements.** The mix of risk and return is the pleasure of the investor. The enjoyment of risk and return depends upon the life cycle of the common investor. The **life cycle of the** Investor can be studied in the following ways:

(a) Career stage.
(b) Mid-career level stage.
(c) Retirement stage.
(d) Tax considerations.

Career stage is an early stage of life cycle of a common man. The stage of the life cycle determine the nature of investment. A student of higher education/lower education enters into life cycle of a common. He will be placed in a suitable career according to his qualifications and capabilities. A bright future awaits him. His talent, skills, abilities may be exposed more if he settle early in a better career. At the early stage, the investor will have less assets than their liabilities. He wants to purchase more goods for his comfortable life. He needs more money for his consumption of goods. He will in making of construction of own house. In order to fulfill his dreams he may avail the housing loan scheme. The **housing loan scheme** deduction from the salary reduces the level of flow of money. The salary amount will be declined to the extent of level of finance taken by home. A regular **EMIs** to be paid from his salary in order to get the own house. His next priority is towards savings for liquidity purpose. He provides a shelter for his family by way of taking insurance policies for protecting his life members from financial crisis on his expiry or death. In this stage, the time horizon has long life expect any with a possibility of higher growth income. Hence this stage is more important in designing the portfolio for his clients by the portfolio manager. It is more important that the average life expect any of the common man have been increased experientially. The level of increase in life expectancy of the man stimulate the value of money due to longer period of holding time. The holding period of long-term nature of portfolio leads to the higher levels of income.

Mid-career stage is another important factor in time-horizon factor. At this period the investor acquires more assets than his liabilities. The balance sheet of the individual reflects with surplus amount. He has limited time period to invest in this stage. He needs to think about potential pension benefits at this stage. At this stage he has limited period to invest in the stock market instruments. He has to invest his money to invest in **high risk** and **high return securities**. Mid-career is a chance of opportunity to invest in the form of portfolio.

The **third and final stage** is retirement stage. In this period of time horizon investment is very much limited. At this final stage, he needs stable way of income because he looses his regular salary income. He thinks about the alternative regular flow of income. In this stage all this financial resources may be exhausted and all his loans must be cleared off by him. He will take utmost care about financial planing to end his life. He is in completion of all life insurance policies and shifts his investments to low return and low risk category of investments. At this stage he gives priority to the safety of the principal amount.

Tax is an element which changes from year to year. The direct taxes in India changes in every budget period. The taxation system will be indicated through **finance act**. **Finance act** deals with direct and indirect taxes in India. Income tax is one of the most influencial factor in determining of the investment decisions. Investors in Income tax horizon always considers to reduce the tax liability. The finance act provides some savings for getting tax exemption under the law.

The finance act provides some tax concessions to the tax payers for investing in savings instruments. The investors always think about to reduce the tax liability by investing in provisions of the act. All the latest topics related to income tax aspects have been presented in earlier pages for ready reference. Hence the investors should make their tax planning according to the latest provisions of the act. The interest or dividend will be tax able under the head of Income from other sources. The **profit or loss** will be shown as capital gains or capital loss. The capital gains will be taxable as per the existing income tax rates. The capital appreciation will be liable to taxable as per the Income tax act. The loss on capital may also to be adjusted from capital gains. Hence any appreciation or depreciation in capital should be adjusted as per the provisions of the Income tax act. Investing in government bonds and **National Saving Certificates** can avoid taxation. If the investor wants to reduce tax burden, he can invest in these securities in addition to his portfolio.

Investment decisions are based on some times on psychological factors. The temparament of the investor is one of the important factor in framing investment objectives. Investors are different kinds. Some of them **risk takers**. They would like to take up higher risk in order to earn more return from portfolio. Some of them are not interested towards risk. They would like to deploy the funds in risk free return instruments. Hence the temparament of the investor occupies an important role in framing the portfolio for the clients.

(b) Composition of Securities

Portfolio is a basket of different kinds of investments. It has the basic objective of financing current and future expenditures from a part of assets. The **pool of assets** are called portfolio. The investors return is based on acceptance level of risk by the client. The basic intention of construction of a portfolio is to get a regular revenue and capital appreciation. Generally all the investors have the following objectives in construction of a portfolio:

(i) Revenue income.
(ii) Accumulated growth.
(iii) Capital appreciation.
(iv) Provision for future.

Revenue income is a regular flow of income to the investors. Generally the regular flow of income is an additional sources of income to the client. He will depend upon the additional income to meet the livelihood expenses. This additional sources of income stimulates the level of clients income. It is a value addition activity.

Accumulated growth of shares reflects the wealth of the investors. A long-term strategic investor can invest in growth oriented scrips. Risk will be balanced in long-term nature of investments. Identification of the growth scrip is the important task of the portfolio manager.

Capital appreciation means, an appreciation in the value of financial asset. Every asset has either appreciation or depreciation in its value. Investors will enter into stock market at lower prices and the securities will be sold in higher price market. The difference between purchase and sale price during the holding period is known as **capital appreciation**. The investor will gain in the stock market in the form of capital appreciation. The appreciation in value is based on market situations. Market is a combination of various factors. It will be fluctuated according to the situation. But in the stock market, there will be equal likelihood of loosing the **capital.**

Provision for future is an essential element for every investor. Generally investors will have some idle fund for saving purpose. They think that future will be not so bright and the stored money will help them in old age. **Old age** is the most important stage in the man's life for financial needs. He will be in a good position to store the money for his old age period. Hence investment vehicle is a **reservoir of finance**.

As per the life cycle of a investor, objectives of Investment, the portfolio manager should select a best portfolio in order to get the financial needs of the client. The **selection of portfolio** depends upon the following factors:

(a) Asset composition.
(b) Diversification.

(a) **Asset composition**—The portfolio manager will make a good portfolio for his client. He select the portfolio in accordance with the needs and convenience of the client. The abilities, skills and capabilities of the portfolio manager shall be reflected in the appreciation value of a selected portfolio. The asset composition will be based on clients preference. If the client requires in getting adequate amount of current income, **60 per cent** of funds should be invested in **Debt** instruments and **40 per cent** on equities. The combination of debt and equity depends upon the individuals preferences. If the client objective is stable income and safety of capital, the funds will be invested in **short-term bonds**. The bonds provide a stable return and safe custody of principal amount. The asset proportion in portfolio is based on the factors:

(i) Asset mix (Income based).
(ii) Asset mix (Capital appreciation).
(iii) Asset mix (Safety of principal).
(iv) Asset mix (Risk and Return).

(i) **Asset mix (Income based)**—Already, we discussed that, the asset combination is prepared by the portfolio manager as per the desire of his client. If the investor requires a regular flow of income from his investment the portfolio may consist of **60 per cent to 100 per cent in** equities and **0 to 40 per cent** in debt instruments. The proportion of the asset mix is known as portfolio. The debt composition of the portfolio can attract Income tax exemption. The equity component enhances the value of portfolio. For example: Non-conventional energy companies, computer software, and hardware company shares *etc*.

(ii) **Asset mix (Capital appreciation)**—The portfolio manager will keep the asset composition as per the intention of the client. Capital appreciation means, the value of the original investment increases over the years. Some investments may provide a faster rate of capital appreciation. **For example: Real estate.** Stock markets are also provide much higher than their original issue prices. The market capitalization has also increased exponentially. Now-a-days stock market is becoming more popular formulating investments in the capital market. A careful analysis and observation of stock market movements can definitely achieve the desired goal of the client. The portfolio manager shall prepare the portfolio for capital appreciation motive and the funds must be invested **in equity from 90 per cent to 100 per cent.** Equity consisted portfolio may generate sufficient and reasonable return through **capital appreciation.**

(iii) **Asset mix (Safety of the principal)**—Risk is a future chance of loss. The return is based on level of accepted risk. Normally, all investors are very particular about the safety of principal amount. No investor likes to loose his capital. In this kind of portfolio, debt instruments dominate the asset composition. The investment in short-term debt instruments will keep the principal amount more safely. Debt based portfolios may generate a regular flow of income by way of interest but lack in capital appreciation.

(iv) **Asset mix (Risk and Return)**—Risk and Return are two important factors in stock market. Risk is always involved in the market. Return is chased by the risk. The yield earned by an investor is the game of risk and return. The traditional approach is based on some assumptions such as **risk, return and non-risk factors.** Generally the individual investors prefer more returns from the equity. Hence the investors has involved in **high risk** in order to get more returns. The return is based on the accepted level of risk. The following diagram will analyse the relation.

I. High Risk ↑	→	High return ↑
II. No Risk	→	No return
III. Low Risk ↓	→	Low return ↓

The risk factor in stock market cannot be ignored. The risk cannot be escaped. But it can be avoided in some situation. It depends upon the efficiency of **Risk Management.** The risk can be classified in many ways. They are Interest rate risk, purchasing power risk, financial risk, and Market risk. The portfolio manager should also take into consideration of Non-risk factors such as taxation, marketability *etc*. The ability of the portfolio manager can be assessed through the earning capacity of asset composition.

(b) **Diversification**—The portfolio will be designed as per the intention and wishes of the client. The portfolio manager will take all precautions before finalizing the construction of a portfolio. Once the asset mix and combination is determined and the **risk and return** are analyzed, the final step is the **diversification of portfolio. Risk** is a future chance of loss. Return is always haunted by risk. The investor should escape the **risk** and capture the **return**. The yield or appreciation in portfolio value is the indication of efficiency of the portfolio manager. **Risk** can be minimised and **Return** may be **maximised**. In the stock market, there will be a chance to arise **financial risk**. Financial risk can be reduced by introducing top quality bonds. Bonds will provide poor resistance or **Inflation**. Inflation in the economy is a continuous phenomenon, and it cannot be avoided. Shares will provide better protection from inflation effect. But they are more vulnerable to **financial risk**. There are many kinds of debentures available in the market. But good convertible debentures may balance the **financial risk** and **purchasing power risk**. The portfolio can be categorized as **bond portfolio, and stock portfolio. Bond portfolio** may be constructed with long-term and short-term bonds. The investor should make a chance of balance between these two term bonds. **Short-term** bonds offers more risk to income. **Long-term bonds** involves more risk to principal. In the category of stock portfolio, the investor has to follow the steps.

Ist Step	→	**Sectorial analysis → Selection of Industry.**
IInd Step	→	**Selection of companies in the Industry.**
IIIrd Step	→	**Size of the portfolio.**

The portfolio should be constructed ultimately within the goals of the investor. The needs of the financial goals must be reached through better construction of good portfolio. Portfolio is a mix of different kinds of securities drawn from the capital market. Capital market provides a number of kinds of different financial assets. The investor has to choose among them to his needs and convenient. The **portfolio manager** should take all precautions about the safety and liquidity of the different kinds of financial assets. The portfolio manager should tune the portfolio according to the dreams of the investor. The investor has to analyse about the **fundamental factors** of the industry and company. There are so many industries exist in the Indian economy. **For example**: Manufacturing Industry, Coal Steel, Automobile, Consumer durable goods, Heavy machinery engineering, Cement, Aluminum, Banking, Insurance, Hotel, Shipping, Transport, Healthcare, Pharmaceuticals, Drugs and Fast moving consumer goods. Each and every industry exist in the economy with business cycles. All industries move according to cyclically. The investor should know about the intricacies of the economic principles such as business cycles, demand and supply factors and life cycle of various industries. The investor should know about the industries advantages and disadvantages regarding the economic cycles. The investor has to select **Industry** at first moment, **company at second moment** and the size of portfolio at final stage. The investor has to select two scrips from each industry. The selection of company is the most important factor in the portfolio construction. The selection of a scrip is influenced by many factors such as **growth, yield, expected earnings, past profits, reserves, assets, price earning ratio, earning per share, dividend rate, Retention ratio, expenditure on research and development etc.** Selection of best scrip is the ability and expertism of the investor. It reflects the investors knowledge and perception regarding the corporate sector. Investors knowledge about the various companies functioning, performance reports, studying and news gathering from the financial periodicals, observing expects interviews with business channels will make him more perfect about the stock market. The investor's knowledge and perception has no horizon in the stock market. After acquiring knowledge, and other information about the corporate sector, the investor has to select the **number of shares** of each stock to be purchased. It involves the diversification process of the portfolio management. The portfolio manager has to build the portfolio as per the goals of the client. The investors selection of different kind of **financial assets** enables the portfolio to balance the **risk and return forces.**

(b) ***Modern Approach***—The traditional approach undertakes all background factors of the investors. It think about the pre and post-investment conditions of the investor. It focusses more on individual needs of the financial plan. But modern approach is different from traditional method. The modern approach focusses on equity based portfolio. Let us study more about modern approach in the forthcoming chapters.

B. Arbitrage Pricing Theory

Arbitrage means getting a price advantage in two different markets for the same financial asset. The share prices are quoted regularly in news papers at different stock exchanges in India. The share prices are determined by the number of factors. **For example:** The share price of ACC may be quoted in BSE at **Rs. 350, at NSE Rs. 360** at Hyderabad stock exchange **Rs. 345.** Hence the investor may parchase at Hyderabad Stock Exchange and sell at NSE for **Rs. 360** by taking on advantage of prices in different markets at the same time for the same **financial asset.** Arbitrage is a process of earning profit. It is a specialized activity. It requires a lot of buying and selling skills. It is an advantage of differential pricing for the same financial asset. It is one of the tools used by the individual investors and portfolio managers. Arbitrage pricing theory is developed by **"Stephen Ross."** It is a less complicated manner in asset pricing model. It explains the nature of equilibrium in asset pricing with fewer assumptions. Profit earned through arbitrage process is **riskless.** In this arbitrage process, the investor should be more active to undertake the price advantage exist in the market. The person who undertake this activity is known as **"Arbitrager".** He earns through price advantage only. He brings the price levels at equilibrium stage.

Assumptions

1. The investors are risk averse.
2. The Investors have homogeneous expectations.
3. There is no transaction cost exist in the market.
4. Market prevails perfect competition.

The arbitrage price theory does not assume the following factors:

(a) No taxes exist.
(b) Funds are available at risk free rate of interest.
(c) Selection of portfolio is based on mean and standard deviations.

Arbitrage price theory is an equilibrium model of asset pricing. It assumes that returns are acquired by a **factor model.** In this model, the investor do not look at expected returns. He concentrates only on price advantage exist in the market. It is based on the return generated by following factors:

(a) Single factor model.
(b) Multiple factor model.

(a) Single Factor Model

Market is a combination of different factors. It reflects various forces and pressures in the market. The investor should know about the asset price before going to buy it. The prices are fluctuating in the market that absorb everything. The market discounts everything and influenced by all the factors exist in the market. The market is a very dynamic and it reacts for every small incident that exist in the economy. **For example:** A slight change in interest rates will be absorbed by the market. Hence the following factors will influence the single factor model:

(i) Gross National Product.
(ii) Interest rates.
(iii) Money supply.
(iv) Inflation rates.

Gross National Product is the barometer of industrial productivity. The process of manufacturing, services sector reflects the GNP. GNP indicates the development of the economy. A rise in GNP is reflection of prosperity. The prosperity is the wealth creation. The wealth will accumulated in the form of **capital base.** The capital formation is the most important and crucial factor in the economy. The capital formation creates assets. A strong asset base is necessary for development of a nation. An increase in GNP reflects the full employment to the nation. Work creation to all stimulates the purchase levels of the population. An increase in purchasing capacity will stimulate the higher level of production. An increase in Industrial level of factors leads to show an impact on the economy. The Industrialization peace will decide the guiding factor of the stock markets. GNP is the basic factor, that everyone should know before going to the stock market. The industrial level of activity will reflect in the stock market prices. As per the recent survey conducted by **Morgan Stanley**

Capital International, the Geneva based agency has found the following information.

	Country	*New*	*Old*
1.	Taiwan	23.5	18.3
2.	Korea	22.4	24.9
3.	Hongkong	16.9	18.0
4.	China	10.2	10.4
5.	Singapore	8.5	9.0
6.	India	7.2	7.5
7.	Malaysia	5.1	5.2

Sources: "Marginal change for India in MSCI recast," *The Economic Times.*

The **Geneva** based agency manages regional and country specific **benchmark Indices** for global fund managers. It has announced a re-**balancing** of some indices. The Index has witnessed significant changes due to a substantial change in the **Taiwan country** weightage.

Taiwanese equities will now have a **23.5 per cent** weight in the index against **18.3 per cent** earlier. As a result, India's weightage falls marginally to **7.2 per cent** from **7.5 per cent.** Korea's weightage falls to **22.4 per cent** against **24.9 per cent** earlier. These changes will take effect from 1-6-2005. The agency has added **13 new** Indian scrips to the index and deleted **Punjab Tractors. The 13 scrips** added included **Reliance Energy, UTI Bank, Jet Airways, Glenmark Pharma, Jindal Steel, Matrix Laboratories, Bharat Electronics, Arvind Mills, Kotak Mahindra Bank, Oriental Bank of Commerce, Bharat Forge, Nicholas Piramal and Biocon.** Market players are surprised at the exclusion of heavy weights like Bharathi Televentures, National Thermal Power Corporation. Over the past two years, India has seen over $ 17.5 billion invested in Indian equities. Nearly **70 per cent** of the amount is through allocation money.

India is the biggest recipient of **FII** money after Korea, and Taiwan in the emerging markets category. Over the past two years, FIIs reported a net inflow of **$ 75** billion into emerging markets. Korea, Taiwan and India accounted for over **80 per cent** of those inflows. Fund managers have put more money into Indian equities than that mandated by the Morgan Stanley Capital International Index.

Interest rates are another important factor in the economy. Interest is a reward for the fund owner. It is a price for utilisation of others money. Financial resources are transferred from one place to another.

The funds will move from surplus to shortage area of place. Interest rate is the price where the borrower and lender accepts for transfer of resources. The fund is like a commodity. It has its own price. It will be based on supply and demand factor. The Monetary policy of the government reflects the rates of Interest. The Central Government will implement its policy through **RBI**. **RBI** is the powerful organisation to move according to the government policy regarding interest rates. A reduction in interest rates will result in emerging **equity portfolios.** An increase in Interest rates leads to emerging **bond portfolios**. A low rate of interest attracts the investors towards stock market. Funds are available for lower rate of interest. The spending habits of the society will be increased. Then it will be known as **push economy.** Credit flow of money is easily available to all sectors. A financial help to all sectors will definitely show impact on the economy. An increase in interest rates will lead to raise the bank deposits, small savings, Debt instruments *etc*. Hence the Interest rates will show an impact on the economy.

Money supply is one of the factor influences the economy development. The velocity of the money is more important factor for the overall development of a nation. The velocity of money is influenced by a number of factors. Money supply to all sectors of the economy leads to development. Economic development will be reflected in the form of standard of living cost, life style, purchasing capacity, rotation of money, provision of finance act.

Inflation is another important factor in asset pricing theory. It indicates the healthy levels of the economy. It is necessary for the economy to develop more and more. It refers to an increase in price levels of commodity in the economy. An increase in price levels to a certain limit is acceptance. It refers to chasing of money for goods. Goods are available at limited quantum but the money supply is more. It undertakes all factors into consideration. Inflation index is calculated on the basis of **whole sale prices**. The wholesale price Index is useful to construct and valuation of price indices. It is calculated by the government. It is calculated on the week basis. At present the inflation rate has touched[1] basis points to **5.67 per cent** in the week ended April, 30, 2005.

1. Inflation rate softens down to touch 5.67%, *The Economic Times*, 14-5-2005, p. 3.

As per the forecast of the **Delhi** based Institute of Economic Growth, the rate is expected to hover at about **5.77 per cent** in May because of the hard international crude prices and the temporary dislocations in trade caused by the introduction of state level value added tax. The index rose by **0.1 per cent** to **192.1 per cent** points due to a surge in the index of heavy weighted manufactured products, though fuel prices have remained unchanged. The index for the manufactured products rose by **0.2 per cent to 170.8 per cent points.** The index was **162 points** a year ago.

(b) Multiple Factor Model

Arbitrage pricing theory is an equilibrium model of asset pricing. A number of variables are taken into account for the asset price model. The **macro economic factors** are taken into consideration. It is very closer to reality. The objective of the asset pricing model is to identify the **equilibrium** asset price for expected return and risk. If the asset prices are not equal, there is a **scope** for arbitrage.

Arbitrage portfolio Theory—Arbitrage means, the price advantage of a financial asset in different market at the same time. All investors will pour their money for earnings from the portfolio. Portfolio is a cocktail. A mix of different blend of financial assets. The portfolio will be constructed for the purpose of getting expected returns. The ABT aims to find out the possibility to increase returns from the portfolio without increasing the amount of funds in the portfolio. It also focusses on increasing the return without additional risk. It always think about to keep the risk at the same level. **For example:** A common investor holds a portfolio and he wants to change the proportion of the securities without any additional financial resources. Hence the ABT reveals that returns will be acquired without introduction of additional capital. It also inform that profits will be gained with an alteration of the proportion of the securities in a portfolio. After alteration of changes of proportion should not be changed to the extent of original portfolio. A number of alterations, can be changed in order to gain the benefits. But the changes in different securities will add up to **zero.** It is the basic requirement of an arbitrage portfolio theory. The following illustration will clearly reveal about the **Arbitrage price theory**.

Illustration

Mr. Tejaswani provide the following information:

	Scrip	*Return*	*B*	*Original Weight*
1.	India cements	18%	0.45	0.33
2.	Associated cements	13%	1.35	0.33
3.	Nagarjuna cements	10%	0.55	0.34

Now the proportions changed
The changes are:

$$\Delta X_A = 0.2$$
$$\Delta X_B = 0.025$$
$$\Delta X_C = -0.225$$

The total amount invested Rs. 3,00,000.

Solution

For an arbitrage portfolio:

$$\Delta X_A + \Delta X_B + \Delta X_C = 0$$
$$0.2 + 0.025 - 0.225 = 0$$

The sensitivities also become zero:

$$\Delta X_A\, b_A + \Delta X_B\, b_B + \Delta X_c\, b_c = 0$$
$$0.2 \times 0.45 + 0.025 \times 1.35 - 0.225 \times 0.55 = 0$$

In an arbitrage portfolio, the expected return should be greater than 0:

$$\Delta X_R\, R_A + \Delta X_B\, R_B + \Delta X_c\, R_c > 0$$
$$0.20 \times 18 + 0.025 \times 13 + -0.225 \times 10 > 0$$
$$3.6 + 0.325 + -2.25$$
$$3.925 - 2.25 = 1.675 \text{ per cent.}$$

The investor may increase his investment in India cement, Associated cement by selling Nagarjuna cements Ltd. The new composition of weights are as follows:

$$X_A = 0.33 + 0.20 = 0.530$$
$$X_B = 0.33 + 0.025 = 0.355$$
$$X_C = 0.34 + -0.225 = 0.115.$$

The portfolio allocation of stocks:

India cement	3,00,000 × 0.53 =	1,59,000
Associated cement	3,00,000 × 0.355 =	1,06,500
Nagarjuna cement	3,00,000 × 0.115 =	34,500
		3,00,000

The sensitivity of the new portfolio:

$$0.45 \times 0.53 + 1.35 \times 0.355 + 0.34 \times 0.115 = 0.781$$

Old portfolio

$$0.45 \times 0.33 + 1.35 \times 0.33 + 0.55 \times 0.34 = 0.781$$

Old portfolio return:

$$18 \times 0.33 + 13 \times 0.33 + 10 \times 0.34$$
$$5.94 + 4.29 + 3.4 = 13.63 \text{ per cent}$$

The new portfolio return:

$$18 \times 0.53 + 13 \times 0.355 + 10 \times 0.115$$
$$9.54 + 4.61 + 1.15 = 15.30 \text{ per cent}$$

This is equivalent to the old portfolio return

$$13.63 + 1.675 = 15.30 \text{ per cent.}$$

Arbitrage Price Theory Model

Arbitrage is an advantage price in differential market. This theory was introduced by **Stephen Ross.** He found that earnings on portfolio are influenced by a number of **Macro economic factors.** Arbitrageur should know about economy before involving in this adventural activity. He should know about the general states of the economy. The growth rate of the economy such as **Gross domestic product, National Income, per capita income, purchasing capacity, Inflation, Regional development, Infrastructural development, Flow of foreign exchange, Reserves and surplus, household savings, Investment patterns, Fiscal deficit, Monetary policy** *etc.* The arbitrage theory is represented by the equation:

$R_i = \alpha_o + \alpha_1 bi_1 + \alpha_2 bi_2 + \alpha_j bi_j$
R_i = average expected return
α_1 = sensitivity of return to bi_J
bi = the beta co-efficient relevant to the particular factor.

Illustration

Mr. Akhil provides the following information relating to his portfolio. Calculate the average expected return of the portfolio:

Risk free rate α_0 = 14 per cent

$\alpha_1 = 3.60$	$b_1 = 2.4$
$\alpha_2 = 2.50$	$b_2 = 3.0$
$\alpha_3 = 1.00$	$b_3 = -1.5$

Solution

Expected return on Investment $= \alpha_0 + \alpha_1 b_1 + \alpha_2 b_2 + \alpha_3 b_3$

$= 14 + 3.6\ (2.4) + 2.50\ (3.0) + 1.00\ (-1.50)$
$= 14 + 8.64 + 7.50 + (-1.50)$
$= 30.14 - 1.50$
= 28.64 per cent.

Illustration

From the following information, using Arbitrage pricing theory, calculate expected return on Investment. The risk free rate is **6 per cent.** What is the expected return. If two stocks are equally weighted.

Solution

Factor	α	b_a	b_b
1	0.18	1.00	1.40
2	–0.06	0.80	1.60
3	0.08	2.40	0.40

$Er_a = \alpha_o + \alpha_1 b_1 + \alpha_2 b_2 + \alpha_3 b_3$
$= 0.06 + 0.18\ (1.00) + -0.06\ (0.8) + 0.08\ (2.40)$
$= 0.06 + 0.18 + -0.048 + 0.192$
$= 0.24 - 0.048 + 0.192$
= 0.192 + 0.192 = 38.4 per cent.

Expected Return B = 0.06 + 0.18 (.14)–0.06 (.16) + 0.08 (.4)
= 0.06 + 0.0252–0.0096 + 0.32
= 0.06 + 0.0252–0.0096 + 0.32
= 0.0852–0.0096 + 0.32
= 0.0756 + 0.32
= 0.3956 or 39.56 per cent

If they are equally weighted (0.5 and 0.5)

ER_p = 0.5 (38.4) + 0.5 (39.56)
= 19.2 + 19.78 = 38.78 per cent

Illustration

From the following information, calculate the expected return through Arbitrage pricing theory. The **risk free rate at 7 per cent.** What is the expected return. If two stocks are invested 1/3rd in X stock 2/3rd in.y

Factor	α	b_x	b_y
1	0.09	0.50	0.7
2	–0.03	0.40	0.8
3	0.04	1.20	0.2

Solution

$\bar{R}_x$ = 0.07 + 0.09 (.5)–0.3 (0.4) + 0.04 (1.2)
$\bar{R}_x$ = 0.07 + 0.045–0.012 + 0.048
R_x = 0.115–0.012 + 0.048
0.151 or 15.1 per cent
$\bar{R}_x$ = 0.07 + 0.09 (0.7)–0.3 (.8) + 0.04 (.2)
= 0.07 + 0.063–0.24 + 0.008 = 0.099 or

If we invest in the ratio **of 1:2**

ER_p = 0.333 (15.1) + 0.666 (9.9)
= 5.028 + 6.59
= 11.62 per cent

If we invest in the ratio **1:3** in the securities x and y

ER_p = 0.25 (15.1) + 0.75 (9.9)
= 3.775 + 7.425
= 11.2 per cent.

C. Modern Portfolio Theory

Traditional approach undertakes the individuals all needs such as housing, pension plan and other domestic affairs. It focusses more an individuals background. It takes into consideration of other financial needs of the individual. But all these aspects are not covered by the **Modern Portfolio Theory**. The Modern Portfolio theory gives top priority to select the best scrips in portfolio.

Savings will stimulate the higher levels of investments. The savings will depend upon many factors. Savers are generally risk averse and try to reduce risk by all sources. It is assumed that the markets are perfect and knows every aspect perfectly. The returns are the same whenever you enter the market. Hence the **selection of securities** is the key point in portfolio formation. The basis of selection of securities depends upon the following factors:

(a) Diversification.
(b) Concept of Dominance.
(c) Beta.
(d) Duration.
(e) Risk.
(f) Asset allocation.
(g) Expected return.
(h) Borrowed funds.

(a) Diversification

Diversification means investing in more than one security, asset, Industry with a view to reduce risks. Generally the investors are always think about reduction of risk. The aim of the portfolio management is minimising the risk and maximising the **return**. Risk and return is the game of stock markets. Risk can be reduced by the simple kind of diversification. The group of assets may consist with **stocks** and different types of **bonds**. The portfolio may contain an equity dominated or **debt dominated**. If equity portfolio has been formed by the investor. It contains shares of different industries when different kinds of shares added to the original portfolio, the **total risk** tends to decrease.

The risk taken would choose high risk portfolio. Investors with low risk tolerance may select low level risk portfolio. The shares are not selected on the basis for Income or appreciation. But the selection of portfolio is based on **Risk and Return relationship**. The Investor needs return either in the form of dividend or capital appreciation.

(b) Concept of Dominance

All investments are risky. Equities are **more risky**, debentures are less risky and public sector bonds or government securities are **least risky**. Hence the portfolio manager has the opportunity to include **risk free assets** such as government bond or bank deposits in the portfolio. When the portfolio manager insert the risk free assets in the portfolio, the risk level will be reduced. Hence the equities can be combined with bonds and risk free assets.

(c) Beta

Beta is a measure of sensitivity of the return of one asset to the market return. It describes the relationship between the stocks return and index return. It can be positive and negative. It is the indication of the percentage change in the price of the stock related to the percentage changes in the market index. It can be studied in three ways. If **Beta is zero,** the stock price is unrelated to the market index. **If Beta** is **1**, a one percentage change in market index will lead to one percentage change in price of stock. **If the Beta-1,** it indicates a negative relationship with the market index. It measures the systematic market related risk. It cannot be eliminated by diversification. It can be calculated by the following formula:

$R_j = a + B_j\, RM + U$

R_j = Return on security

RM = Return on market index

B_j = Measure of the risk

a = Intercept term

U = Error term.

Or

Beta = Risk free rate +**B** (Expected return on market portfolio–Risk free rate).

For example: If the risk free rate is **12 per cent**. The expected market return is **17 per cent** and B is **1.5**, the expected return on the security should be as follows:

Risk free rate + B (expected return on market portfolio—Risk free rate)

12 + 1.5 (17–12)

12+1.5 (5)

12+7.5 = 19.5 per cent.

(d) Duration

Duration means, the life period of the portfolio. Portfolio means a combination of different kinds of financial assets. Every constructed portfolio should have time period. The portfolio will be constructed for a particular financial goal and for a particular period of time. The maturity period of the portfolio is known as "Duration". The assets are two kinds *i.e.*, equity and debentures. The duration of the equity is infinity but the debenture has some maturity period say *i.e.*, for 5 years, 10 years or 15 years. The time horizon set for a particular constructed portfolio is called as Duration. The Money Market instruments and cash has no duration period. Duration is a measure of average time prior to receipt of payment. It can be computed by the following formula:

$$\text{Duration (years)} = \sum_{t=1}^{n} \frac{\text{PVCf} \times t}{\text{TPV}}$$

cf = cash flows

t = Time period

TPV = Total present value

n = number of years.

$$\text{Duration of equity} = \frac{\text{Market price}}{\text{Earning per share}}$$

Or

$$= \frac{\text{Market price}}{\text{Dividend per share}}$$

For example 18 per cent in Equity (25 years)	**0.18 × 25 = 4.5**
70 per cent in Debentures (3 years maturity)	0.7 × 3 = **2.1**
30 per cent in Money market instruments	0.30 × 0 = **0**
Total duration is 6 years approx.	**6.6**

(e) Risk

In the stock market, **risk is allergy** and **return is energy**. The stock market is a game of risk and return. The investor always thinks about minimise the **risk** and maximise the **return**. Risk can be classified as **diversifiable** and **non-diversifiable**. It can also be further classified as **systematic** and **unsystematic risk**. Risk is a chance of future loss. It always chase the investor. The portfolio risk can be managed by diversification, management of duration and utilisation of **Beta** for management of systematic risk.

Risk can be defined as the degree or **probability** of loss. Risk is different from uncertainity. Uncertainity does not know the possible events. But risk knows possible events. Risk is interchangeably used with uncertainity. Hence risk and uncertainity are different from each other. Risk has two components (a) systematic, (b) unsystematic. **Systematic risk** is uncontrollable. It is caused by the external factors. It affects the market. It cannot be avoided by the investor. It is unavoidable. It is further classified as **Market risk, Interest rate risk and purchasing power risk. Unsystematic risk** is related to a particular company or an industry. It arises due to firms in capabilities, technological changes, changes in consumer preference, labour problems *etc*. These problems are different from one industry to another and company to company. It can be further classified as **Business risk and Financial risk**. Business risk is related to the earning capability of the company. **Financial risk** is associated with the capital structure of the company.

(f) Asset Allocation

Portfolio is a combination of different kinds of financial assets. It is just like a **cocktail**. The taste of the cocktail depends upon the mixing of proportion of ingredients. Assets basically can be classified as **equity and debt**. Equity is the owner fund, Debt is a borrowed fund. Further the financial assets may be classified as **Money Market and Capital market instruments**. Money market assets are short-term nature of assets and has no risk. They are known as risk free assets. Hence it is better to keep **5-10 per cent** in cash, bank deposits and in money market instruments of the portfolio. The remaining will be filled with equity and debentures as per the objective of the client. The portfolio manager should design the investment strategy based on investors database. The design of portfolio depends upon investors strategy. Does he want a regular income? How? Regularly? Monthly or yearly? Does he want only capital appreciation or income oriented or both.

(g) Expected Return

Return is a reward to the investor. The investor should be paid a reasonable return for his invested amount in the firm. He lent his money for a expected return. The firm should pay the price for the utilisation of other's money. It may be either in the kind of dividend or interest. The return is available to the investor, based upon his level of risk acceptance. If the investor desires for more return he should be ready for accepting higher level of risk. If he does not take higher risk, no higher return is available him. Hence the degree of accepted level of risk provides proportionate return. Equities are more risky, Debentures are risky, money market instruments, cash, bank deposits are **risk free**. Hence the portfolio manager has to invest the majority of funds in equities with a Beta in order to get expected return of the investor.

(h) Borrowed Funds

Equities are more **risky**, debentures are risky and money market instruments, bank deposits and cash are **risk free assets**. Generally equities are related to long duration and have high betas. The range of beta and duration can be widened by borrowing for investment. **For example:** If the portfolio manager with Rs. **5 crore** borrows another **Rs. 5 crore** and invest Rs. **10 crore**, in equity portfolio, with a beta of **1.00**, his overall portfolio beta is actually **10**. It gives better returns expected and even after paying the interest on borrowed fund, he enjoys the leverage. Hence debt is not a dangerous element, but it should be utilised properly. Proper utilisation of borrowed fund can yield more revenue and enhances net worth of the borrower. The borrower should utilise and deploy the fund in a proper way. Then he will be able to enjoy the leverage on his investment. In addition to own fund, the borrowed money will definitely enhance the net worth of the investor. If it is properly deployed in the portfolio. If it is not utilised, it will become a costly error. The investor has to accept the responsibility for that borrowed fund.

Review Problems

1. From the following information calculate the average rate of return for each stock during the 2000-04 period. The return on two stocks M and N are as follows. These two scrips are held in **50:50** in a portfolio, what is the return of portfolio?

Year	*M Returns*	*N Returns*
2000	– 10.24	– 3.0
2001	21.67	17.55
2002	33.45	42.09
2003	3.82	1.00
2004	26.30	19.16

Solution

The average return of M scrip:

$$\bar{M} = \mathbf{85.24 - 10.24 = 75}$$

$$\bar{M} = \frac{75}{5} = 15$$

$$\bar{N} = 79.8 - 3.0 = 76.8$$

$$\bar{N} = \frac{76.8}{5} = 15.36$$

$$\sigma_M = \sqrt{\sum_1^n \frac{kt - k.Ave}{n-1}}$$

Year	*Duration*		*Deviation squared*		
2000	(–10.24–15)	=	$(-25.24)^2$	=	637.05
2001	(21.67–15)	=	$(6.67)^2$	=	44.68
2002	(33.45–15)	=	$(18.45)^2$	=	340.40
2003	(3.82–15)	=	$(-11.18)^2$	=	124.99
2004	(26.30–15)	=	$(11.30)^2$	=	127.69
					1274.61

$\sigma_M = \sqrt{318.65} = 17.88$ 1274.61/4 = 318.62

Calculation of σ_n

Year	*Duration*		*Deviation squared*		
2000	(–3.0–15.36)	=	$(-18.36)^2$	=	337.08
2001	(17.55–15.36)	=	$(2.19)^2$	=	4.79
2002	(42.09–15.36)	=	$(26.73)^2$	=	714.49
2003	(1.00–15.36)	=	$(-14.36)^2$	=	206.20
2004	(19.16–15.36)	=	$(3.8)^2$	=	14.44
					1277

$$\frac{1277}{4} = 319.25$$

$$\sigma_n = \sqrt{319.25} = 17.87$$

The stock M, and N is a combination in the ratio of **50:50**. Portfolio return equation is as follows:

(0.5 M) + (0.5 N)

=	(–10.24) **0.5** + (–3.0) (0.5)	= **– 6.62**
=	(21.67) **0.5** + (17.55) (0.5)	= **19.60**
=	(33.45) **0.5** + (42.09) (0.5)	= **37.76**
=	(3.82) **0.5** + (1.00) (0.5)	= **2.41**
=	(26.30) **0.5** + (19.16) (0.5)	= **22.73**
		75.88

$$\frac{75.88}{5} = 15.17$$

Portfolio risk = Standard deviation of portfolio:

$(-6.62-17.88)^2$	$= (24.5)^2$	= 600.25
$(19.60-17.88)^2$	$= (1.72)^2$	= 2.95
$(37.76-17.88)^2$	$= (19.88)^2$	= 395.21
$(2.41-17.88)^2$	$= (-15.47)^2$	= 239.32
$(22.73-17.88)^2$	$= (4.85)^2$	= 23.52
		1261.25

$$\frac{1261.25}{4} = 315.31$$

$$\sigma_n = \sqrt{315.31} = 17.78$$

D. Markowitz Theory

Markowitz Model is associated with the concept of risk measurement. It is based on study of **Risk and Return** relationship. Stock market is a game of risk and return. This theory is associated with he selection of portfolios. It is based on average investors desire. Markowitz published an article in the journal of finance in March 1952. After the publication of this article, numerous investment firms and portfolio managers developed **"Markowitz Algorthms."** It is a theoritical framework for analysis of risk and return and their inter relationship. It is fully utilised the statistical tools of measurement of risk. It is based on mathematical programming for selection of assets in a portfolio. It is emphasized about the quality of a portfolio.

Risk and Return are two important aspects of the investment. They are expected by assumptions. Risk is measured by the **variance and covariance.** Markowitz Model contributes about the qualification of risk and need for maximizing return. Portfolio is a combination of different financial assets. A portfolio is said to be efficient, if it is expected to yield the highest return possible for the lowest risk or a given level of risk. The theory of Markowitz is based on the following assumptions.

Assumptions

1. Investors desire is to minimise risk and maximise return.
2. Investors are rational behaviour.
3. There will be perfect markets exist in the economy.
4. Investors have free access to fair and correct information on the returns and risk.

The theory indicated the importance of correlation among different kinds of stock's return in the construction of a portfolio. He proved that one security in the portfolio dominants the other at a expected level of return: He focussed more on knowledge of the correlation between all securities in a portfolio.

Markowitz Diversification

Portfolio means, a group of financial assets with different levels of returns. A group of securities combined for the purpose of **desired return**. Return is reward to the portfolio owner. The group of assets may vary different characteristics and returns at the accepted level of risk. The financial assets may be stocks, debentures, bonds and money market instruments. Some times a vast number of different kinds of industries and companies scrips will be inserted in the portfolio. A large number of different kinds of Industries scrips are added to the portfolio, the **total risk** tends to decrease. The diversification can reduce the unsystematic risk in case of common stock portfolio. As per the experts and analyst guidelines, **15 stocks** are ideal portfolio to reduce the unsystematic risk at zero level. If the portfolio exceeds **15 stocks**, additional risk reduction cannot be gained. Diversification cannot reduce systematic risk. **In case of simple diversification**, securities are selected on random basis. There is no usage of statistical tools, mathematical and analytical tools in simple diversification. Hence simple diversification reduces the total risk. The total risk of the portfolio consists of **systematic and unsystematic risk**. Total risk is measured by the various rates of returns over a time period. The research studies shows that the **systematic risk** contains a quarter of total risk. The increase in portfolio size, the **total risk** will decline beyond that levels of limit, risk cannot be **reduced**. The vast diversification of portfolio is based on the following factors.

Vast Diversification

Diversification means, expansion of the existing portfolio. Portfolio can be described as a joint family. **For example:** A family consists of wife, husband and three sons. One of the son will add goodwill to his family by good behaviour, another son damaging the reputation of the family through his nature. Hence the goodwill of the family constructed by one member and dismantling by another. **Suppose** if the three sons show good behaviour, sincerity, honesty and maintains a good relation with society, the family will be with high reputation. If the three sons making malpractice's and showing worst performance, the family reputation will be declined automatically.

Vast diversification means expansion of the existing portfolio with wide areas of different kinds of industries. Spreading the investment base towards a wide variety of different industries is known as **vast diversification**. By expanding the existing portfolio, there will be some problems which are presented for thorough understanding of the intricacies of the stock market operations. The following problems arises in vast diversification:

(a) Wrong selection of scrips.
(b) Sources of information.
(c) Transaction cost.
(d) R&D.

(a) Wrong Selection of Scrips

Portfolio means a set of different kinds of financial assets. An ideal portfolio is a combination of **15** different kinds of financial assets. Of these, same scrips may add returns to the portfolio and the remaining provides **risk**. Hence the portfolio, is a game of chance of risk and return elements. Sometimes the investors may buy scrips which will not yield adequate returns. Therefore there will be a chance to increase the risk element in the portfolio. A wrong selection of scrip may dismantle the growth of the portfolio. The investor should always be cautious in selection of scrips.

(b) Information

The portfolio manager should observe the movements of the scrips which are in the portfolio combination. If the portfolio is very large and consisting of a number of different kinds of financial assets, it is very problematic situation to collect all the information regarding all securities.

The task of portfolio manager is not constructing the portfolio but also to observe the information regarding the performance of companies and industries. He has to collect the financial information, marketing information, production schedules and other information regarding the companies performance. Financial information provides an excellent sources of direction about the individual performance of the company. The portfolio manager should have to face many problems in collection of the information about the individual performance of the companies. The portfolio manager has to collect the financial information about all companies existing in the portfolio. **Financial information** like Gross profit, Net profit, profit before tax, profit after tax, provision of depreciation, provision of reserves, earning per share, pre-earning ratio, Dividend declaration, retention ratio, pay out ratio, *etc.*, will useful for analysing the company performance. **Marketing information** contains brand image, brand loyalty, product lifecycle, market share, market leader, market penetration consumers preference, consumer behaviour life style of consumers, purchasing capacity *etc.*, factors indicates about the future of the company. Hence the portfolio manager will face a lot of problems in acquiring all these information contents for all companies exist in the portfolio.

(c) Transaction Cost

Buying and selling of financial assets attracts brokerage charges. A frequent purchase of small quantities of shares leads to higher transaction cost. A large amount of bulk shares attracts less transaction cost for less frequent intervals. Mutual funds. Big financial institutions purchase different stocks at different levels of quantities. Hence individual investors has to pay more transaction cost than large institutions.

(d) Research and Development

Stock market is a game of risk and return. To play in stock market without knowledge is not safe. It is foolish, without entering sufficient knowledge, skills, talent and techniques of stock market. Research is the most important factor for acquiring knowledge. Knowledge is the powerful tool in the hands of individual investors. Knowledge about the companies performance, government policies, economic conditions current business affairs, consumers attitudes, demand and supply factors is necessary for making investment decisions especially in vast diversification. **Knowledge** is a store of valuable information. Information acquiring enhances the skills of the investors. Hence investment in stock market is not only simply handing over a cheque to broker, but also it requires more knowledge about the stock markets. Observation, concentration regarding stock market movements makes the investors to move in the market more confidently. The individual investors will not take care about all these things. But the mutual funds, Financial Institutions, foreign Institutional investors may appoint research staff and acquire knowledge and skills and they render scientific advises to buy, sell of hold the securities. Therefore, the establishment of **Research** wing involves high cost. But all firms may not be in a position to incur the expenditure.

The Markowitz Model

It is a fundamental belief in the stock market that, holding two stocks is less risky than holding one scrip. For instance holding stocks in Information, Communication and Technology is better than investing all the money in a textile company's stock. Hence the building of a good portfolio is a difficult task. But Markowitz provides a solution to it with the help of **Risk and Returns**. Already discussed that Risk and Return occupies a dominant role in getting success in the stock market. An intelligent investors escapes risk and capture the returns.

Assumptions

Markowitz model is based on the following assumptions:

(a) The investor estimates the risk on the basis of returns.
(b) Investors always prefer for higher returns at accepted level of risk.
(c) Investors would prefer to a given level of return, for lower risk than higher risk.

Theory

Markowitz theory is based on risk and return relationship in the market. He developed his theory and found that diversification can reduce the risk. A single stock portfolio will be good, if the investor expectations are perfect. But in the world of uncertainty it is not possible to stay with a single portfolio. Hence investors prefer Markowitz model, because a provision is made in the portfolio to reduce the risk through diversification. The aim of the diversification is not only to reduce **risk** of a security, but also to reduce the covariance or interactive risk of two or more securities in a portfolio. This theory gives more importance to standard deviation. The portfolio risk is more important factor in determination of diversification. The expected risk of the portfolio can be computed through the following formula:

$$\sigma p^2 = x_1^2\sigma_1^2 + x^2_2\sigma^2_2 + x^2_3\sigma^2_3 + 2x_1x_2r_{12}\sigma_1\sigma_2 + 2x_2x_3r_{23}\sigma_2\sigma_3 + 2x_1x_3 r_{13}\sigma_1\sigma_3$$

The following illustration will clearly explains the concept of portfolio risk:

Illustration

From the following information find out the expected risk of the portfolio:

	Name of the Security	*Expected Return*	*Proportion % invested*	*σ*
1.	ACC Ltd.	12	30	0.3
2.	Hindustan Lever Ltd.	17	30	0.3
3.	Reliance Industries Ltd.	22	40	0.4

Co-efficient of correlation is as follows:

$r_{12} = 0.6$
$r_{13} = 0.2$
$r_{23} = 0.3$

Solution

The portfolio risk can be computed by the following formula.

$$\sigma p^2 = x_1^2\sigma_1^2 + x^2_2\sigma^2_2 + x^2_3\sigma^2_3 + 2x_1x_2r_{12}\sigma_1\sigma_2 + 2x_2x_3r_{23}\sigma_2\sigma_3 + 2x_1x_3 r_{13}\sigma_1\sigma_3$$

$$x_1^2 - (0.30)^2\ \sigma_1^2 = (0.3)^2\ x_2^2 = (0.3)^2\ \sigma_2^2 = (0.3)^2\ x_2^3 = (0.4)^2\ \sigma_2^3 = (0.4)^2$$

$$\sigma p^2 = (0.30)^2(0.3)^2 + (0.30)^2 + (0.3)^2 + (0.40)^2(0.4)^2 + + 2(0.3)(0.3)(0.6)(.3)(0.3) + 2(0.3)(0.4)(-0.3)(0.3)(0.4) + 2(0.3)(0.4)(0.2)(0.3)(0.4)$$

$$\sigma p^2 = (0.09)(0.09) + (0.09) + (0.90) + (0.16)(0.16) + + 2(0.09)(0.18)(0.3) + 2(0.12)(-0.09)(0.4) + 2(0.12)(0.06)(0.4)$$

$$0.0081 + 0.09 + 0.90 + 0.0256$$
$$+ 0.00972$$
$$+ -0.00864$$
$$+ 0.00576$$
$$1.0237 + 0.00972 + -0.00864 + 0.00576$$
$$1.03342 + -0.00864 + 0.00576$$
$$\sigma p^2 = 1.03054$$
$$\sigma p = \sqrt{1.03054}$$
$$= \mathbf{1.01515}$$

Parameters in Diversification

Markowitz theory is based entirely upon diversification. Diversification means, expanding the existing portfolio with a wider asset base. According to this theory, diversification reduces risk. It set out guidelines for diversification on the pulse basis of the investors attitude towards risk and return. It also deals with quantification of risk. The financial assets will have different types of risk characteristics. It emphases on a proper number of securities, not too few or not too many which may have no correlation or negative correlation. For building up of efficient set of portfolio the following parameters are required:

(a) expected return.
(b) variability of returns.
(c) variance of one asset to another asset.

(a) **Expected Return**—Expected return on portfolio can be computed by the following formula:

$$ERp = WaE(Ra) + Wb\,E(Rb)$$

ERp = Expected return on portfolio.
Wa = proportion invested in "a" security.
Wb = proportion invested in "b" security.
Ra = Return from security a.
Rb= Return from security b.

(b) **Variability of Returns**—The variability in expected return of a scrip can be the lower in standard deviation or variance and lower is the correlation, the better will be security for investor choice.

$$\sigma P = \sqrt{\frac{\Sigma x^2}{n}}$$

σ^2 is square of standard deviation or called variance.

(c) **Variance of one asset to another asset**—The variance between two assets is called as **Dominance**. Dominance refers to superiority of one portfolio over the other asset. A set of one portfolio dominants the other portfolio. A particular portfolio always dominate others through higher return and lower risk. The following formula can be applied for minimising the portfolio risk by the equation:

$\sigma p = Wa\sigma_a^2 + W_b\sigma_b^2 + 2 (W_a, W_b, \sigma_a, \sigma_b, \sigma_{ab})$

σp = standard deviation of the portfolio.

W_a = proportion of the asset A.

W_b = proportion of the asset B.

σ_a = standard deviation of security A.

σ_b = standard deviation of security B.

$$\text{Covariance} = \frac{1}{N}\sum_{1}^{N}[Rx - \bar{R}x][Ry - \bar{R}y]$$

The theory indicates that two set of financial assets are better than one. Holding two assets may reduce the portfolio risk. The similarities between two stock price behaviour is known as **correlation**. Correlation is the most important measurement to study the behaviour of two assets. In correlation, covariance is not taken, but as an absolute value, standard deviation of the individual securities will be considered. Correlation shows that how much. A and B securities vary together as a proportion of their combined individual variations measured by standard deviations. The co efficient of correlation between two series can be found in the following ways:

(a) **– 1**

(b) **1**

(c) **0**

(a) **(–1)**—If the co efficient of correlation between two scrips is found as **–1**, It indicates there is a perfect negative correlation and the returns move in the **opposite direction**.

(b) **(1)**—The relation between two scrips is found **"1"**. It shows the **perfect positive** correlation exists between the two securities and they tend to move in the **same direction**.

(c) **(0)**—The relation between two securities is found "0". The independent returns are earned by them. There is no impact of returns on each other security. Therefore, the correlation between two securities depends upon the variance between two securities and standard deviation of each individual security. A change in portfolio proportions can change the portfolio risk. It requires a lot of skill for balancing the investment proportions in different securities. Hence the portfolio risk can be bought to Zero.

The combination of two securities in a particular proportion to be invested in each security can be known by the following formula.

$$X_1 = \sigma_1 \div (\sigma_1 + \sigma_2)$$

$$X_1 = \frac{\sigma_2^2 - (r_{12}\sigma_1\sigma_2)}{\sigma_1^2 + \sigma_2^2 - (2r_{12}\sigma_1\sigma_2)}$$

Review Problems

Illustration 1

From the following information, calculate average mean, standard deviation and compute **Total risk of the portfolio.** The market deviation is **10.4 per cent.**

Sl. No.	*Observations*
1.	**10 per cent**
2.	**– 5 per cent**
3.	**20 per cent**
4.	**35 per cent**
5.	**– 10 per cent**

Solution

(a) Calculation of arithmetic mean:

$$\bar{X} = \sum x/n$$

$$\sum x = +65 - \mathbf{15\%} = +\mathbf{50\%}$$

$$n = \text{number of items} = 05$$

$$X = 50/5 = \mathbf{10\%}$$

(b) Calculation of standard deviation:

$$\sigma = \sqrt{\frac{\Sigma dX^2}{n}}$$

deviation from the $\bar{X}$		X^2
10 – 10	= 0	0
–05 – 10	= **–15**	225

$20 - 10 = 10$	100
$35 - 10 = 25$	625
$-10 - 10 = -20$	400
	$\sum dx^2$ 1350

$$\sigma = \sqrt{\frac{\Sigma dx^2}{n}}$$

$$\sigma = \sqrt{\frac{1350}{5}}$$

$$\sigma = \sqrt{270}$$

$$\sigma = 16.43$$

$$\text{Total Risk} = \frac{\text{Standard Deviation}}{\text{Market Deviation}} = \frac{16.43}{10.40} = 1.57$$

Illustration 2

Mr. Ramesh Kumar Gajula hold the following portfolio. Stocks P, Q have yielded the following returns for the last two years.

	Return in Per cent	
Year	P	Q
2003	10	12
2004	16	10

(a) Calculate the expected return on portfolio with a combination of **60 per cent of P, 40 per cent of Q**.

(b) Calculate the standard deviation of P, and Q securities.

(c) Calculate the co-efficient of correlation between two stocks.

(d) Calculate the co-variance between two stocks P and Q.

(e) Calculate the portfolio risk, If the proportionate mix is **60 and 40 per cent** of P and Q securities respectively.

Solution

(a) Calculation of expected return on portfolio as follows:

$$\text{Expected rate of return} = \frac{\Sigma R}{n}$$

ER = Total of return

n = number of observations

$$\therefore \quad \text{Return of P stock} = \frac{10 + 16}{2} = \frac{26}{2} = 13$$

$$\text{Return of Q stock} = \frac{12+10}{2} = \frac{22}{2} = 11$$

Calculation of portfolio return with 60 per cent and 40 per cent proportion:

$$\text{Portfolio return} = \sum_{i=1}^{N} X_1 R_1$$

$$\text{Portfolio return} = \mathbf{(0.6 \times 13) + (0.4 \times 11)}$$
$$= 7.8 + 4.4$$
$$= 12.2 \text{ per cent}$$

(b) Calculation of standard deviation of stock "P":

$$\sigma = \sqrt{\frac{\Sigma(R_1 - \bar{R}_2)^2}{N}}$$

$$\sigma = \sqrt{\frac{\Sigma(10\text{-}13)^2 + (16\text{-}13)^2}{2}}$$

$$\sigma = \sqrt{\frac{\Sigma 9+9}{2}}$$

$$\sigma = \sqrt{\frac{18}{2}}$$

$$\sigma = \sqrt{9} \quad \sigma_p = 3$$

Calculation of standard deviation of Q:

$$\sigma_Q = \sqrt{\frac{\Sigma(R_1 - \bar{R}_1)^2}{N}}$$

$$\sigma_Q = \sqrt{(12-11)^2 + (10-11)^2}$$

$$\sigma_Q = \sqrt{1}$$

$$\sigma_Q = 1$$

(c) Calculation of co-efficient of correlation between P and Q stocks:

$$\text{Correlation} = r = \frac{\text{Covariance of PQ Stocks}}{\sigma_P \sigma_Q}$$

$$r = \frac{\text{Covariance}}{3 \times 1}$$

$$r = \frac{\text{Covariance}}{3} \quad r = \frac{-1}{3} = -0.33$$

(d) **Covariance can be computed as follows:**

$$\text{Covariance} = \frac{\Sigma(R_p - \bar{R}_p) + (R_Q - \bar{R}_Q)}{N}$$

$$\text{Covariance} = \frac{(10-13)+(12-11)}{2}$$

$= (-3) + (+1)$

$= -3 + 1 = -2/2 = -1$

(e) **Calculation of portfolio risk:**

$$\sigma_p = \sqrt{(x_1)^2(\sigma_1)^2 + (x_2)^2(\sigma_2)^2 + 2x_1x_2(r_{12}\sigma_1\sigma_2)}$$

$$R_p = \sqrt{\sigma_p^2}$$

$$\sigma_p = \sqrt{(0.6)^2(9) + (0.4)^2(1)^2 + 2 \times 0.6 \times 0.4\,(3 \times 3 \times 1)}$$

$= \sqrt{(0.36)(9) + (0.16)(1) + 0.48(9)}$

$= \sqrt{3.24 + 0.16 + 4.32}$

$= \sqrt{7.72}$

$= 2.79$

Illustration 3

Mr. Swarup Gajula holds the following stocks. As a portfolio manager, please suggest, is there any advantage of holding these combinations of securities.

Particulars	Associated Cements Ltd.	India Cements Ltd.
(a) Expected return	18	28
(b) Expected variance	14	23
(c) Co-variance	18	

Solution

The relation between these two companies can be calculated through co-efficient of correlation:

$$r = \frac{\text{Co-variable of the portfolio}}{\text{Standard deviation of the portfolio}}$$

$$r = \frac{18}{\text{Standard deviation of the portfolio}}$$

ACC $\sigma = \sqrt{14} = 3.75$ India Cement $\sigma = \sqrt{23} = 4.8$

$$r = \frac{18}{3.75 \times 4.80} = \frac{18}{13} + 1$$

The correlation between two scrips found positive. The risk cannot be reduced. Hence there is no advantage to hold these two securities as a portfolio.

Illustration 4

Mr. Koteswar Rao hold the following portfolio. As a portfolio manager, suggest him regarding management of the assets.

Probability Occurrence	*Return on Grasim Industries Ltd.*	*Return on Reliance Industries Ltd.*
0.10	–1.0	–2.0
0.15	8.0	5.0
0.45	11.0	10.0
0.15	14.0	13.0
0.15	**25.0**	**18.0**

(a) From the above information you are required to calculate expected rates of return for these two companies.

(b) A professional investors if invests in these scrips with **50:50** proportion, what would be return for the portfolio.

(c) If the investor changes the proportion of the portfolio with **75 per cent and 25 per cent** in Grasim and Reliance industries respectively.

(d) If the investor changes the proportion in **60 and 40** per cent in Grasim and Reliance industries respectively, what would be the expected rate of return.

(e) If the investor to construct the portfolio with **70 and 30 per cent** what would be the expected rates of return?

Solution

Calculation of expected rates of return for the:

(a) portfolio:

$$\bar{R} = \sum_{i=1}^{N} R_1 P_1$$

Return on = $\mathbf{R_1 (P_1) + R_2 (P_2) + R_3 (P_3) + R_4 (P_4) + R_5 (P_5)}$

Grasim Industries Ltd.

$\sum R_p = \mathbf{-1.0}\,(0.10) + 8\,(0.15) + 11\,(0.45) + 14\,(0.15) + 25\,(0.15)$

$\sum R_p = -0.10 + 1.2 + 4.95 + 2.1 + 3.75$

$\sum R_p = 12 \mathbf{-0.10} = 11.9$ per cent

Return on Reliance Industries

$\sum \mathbf{r_p} = \mathbf{-2.0}\,(0.10) + 5\,(0.15) + 10\,(0.45) + 13\,(0.15) + 18\,(0.15)$

$\sum r_p = \mathbf{-0.2} + 0.75 + 4.5 + 1.95 + 2.7$

$\sum r_p = 9.9 + -0.2 = 9.7$ per cent

(b) If investor invests 50 per cent: 50 per cent in both securities. Then calculation of return on portfolio as follows:

Return on portfolio = **0.5 × 11.9 per cent + 0.5 × 9.7 per cent**

= 5.95 + 4.85

= 10.8 per cent.

(c) The construction of portfolio with 75 per cent Grasim Industries and 25 per cent with Reliance Industries, then the expected rate of return can be calculated as follows:

$\sum r_p$ = **0.75 × 11.9 per cent + 0.25 × 9.7**

= 8.925 +2.425 = 11.35%.

(d) If the portfolio in **60% and 40%**

$\sum r_p$ = **0.60 × 11.9% + 0.40 × 9.7%**

7.14 + **3.88 = 11.02%.**

(e) The portfolio is in 70 per cent, 30 per cent. Then the expected return is as follows:

$\sum$ rp = 0.70 × 11.9% + 0.30 × 9.7%

= 8.33 + 2.91 = 11.24 per cent.

Illustration 5

Mr. Venkatesham Juluri holds thee following portfolio.

Probability of Occurrence	*Return on HLL*	*Return on Ponds India Ltd.*
0.10	– 3.0	– 4.0
0.25	10.0	7.0
0.40	13.0	12.0
0.10	16.0	15.0
0.15	27.0	20.0

(a) Calculate the expected rate of return for the given portfolio
(b) Calculate the expected rate of return for 50 per cent : 50 per cent proportion for HLL and Ponds Ltd.
(c) Calculate the expected rate of return in the following situations:

(i) HLL	10%	Ponds	90%
(ii) HLL	20%	Ponds	80%
(iii) HLL	30%	Ponds	70%
(iv) HLL	40%	Ponds	60%
(v) HLL	50%	Ponds	50%
(vi) HLL	60%	Ponds	40%
(vii) HLL	70%	Ponds	30%
(vii) HLL	80%	Ponds	20%
(viii) HLL	90%	Ponds	10%

(d) Calculate expected rate of return in the following situations:

(i) HLL	15%	Ponds	85%
(ii) HLL	25%	Ponds	75%
(iii) HLL	35%	Ponds	65%
(iv) HLL	45%	Ponds	55%

Solution

Calculation of expected rate of return on portfolio is as follows:

$$\bar{R} = \sum_{i=1}^{N} R_i P_i$$

Return on HLL: $R_1 (P_1) + R_2 (P_2) + R_3 (P_3) + R_4 (P_4) + R_5 (P_5)$

$\sum r_p = -3.0 (0.10) + 10 (0.25) + 13 (0.40) + 16 (0.10) + 27 (0.15)$
$= \mathbf{-0.3} + 2.5 + 5.2 + 1.6 + 4.05$
$= \mathbf{-0.3} + 13.35 = 13.05$ per cent.

Return on Ponds India Ltd.

$\sum r_p = R_1 (P_1) + R_2 (P_2) + R_3 (P_3) + R_4 (P_4) + R_5 (P_5)$
$\sum r_p = \mathbf{-4.0} (0.10) + 7 (0.25) + 12 (0.40) + 15 (0.10) + 20 (0.15)$
$\sum r_p = -0.40 + 1.75 + 4.8 + 1.5 + 3$
$\sum r_p = 11.05 + -0.40 = 10.65$ per cent.

(b) $\sum r_p$ at 50%, 50% proportion
$R_p = 0.50 \times 13.05 = 6.525$
$R_p = 0.50 \times 10.65 = 5.325$
$R_p = \mathbf{6.525 + 5.325 = 11.85}$ **per cent.**

(c) (i) $\sum$ rp at 10%, 90% proportion
$R_p = 0.10 \times 13.05 = 1.305$
$R_p = 0.90 \times 11.85 = 10.665$

$R_p = 1.305 + 10.665 = 11.97$ per cent

(ii) Σ rp at 20%, 80% proportion

$R_p = 0.20 \times 13.05 = 2.61$

$R_p = 0.80 \times 11.85 = 9.48$

$R_p = 2.61 + 9.48 = 12.09$ per cent

(iii) Σ rp at 30%, 70% proportion

$R_p = 0.30 \times 13.05 = 3.915$

$R_p = 0.70 \times 10.65 = 7.455$

$R_p = 3.915 + 7.455 = 11.37$ per cent

(iv) Σ rp at 40%, 60% proportion

$R_p = 0.40 \times 13.05 = 5.22$

$R_p = 0.60 \times 10.65 = 6.39$

$R_p = 6.39 + 5.22 = 11.61$ per cent

(v) Σ rp at 60%, 40% proportion

$R_p = 0.60 \times 13.05 = 7.83$

$R_p = 0.40 \times 10.65 = 4.26$

$R_p = 7.83 + 4.26 = 12.09$ per cent

(vi) Σ rp at 70%, 30% proportion

$R_p = 0.70 \times 13.05 = 9.135$

$R_p = 0.30 \times 10.65 = 3.195$

$R_p = 9.135 + 3.195 = 12.33$ per cent

(vii) Σ rp at 80%, 20% proportion

$R_p = 0.80 \times 13.05 = 10.44$

$R_p = 0.20 \times 10.65 = 2.13$

$R_p = 10.44 + 2.13 = 12.57$ per cent

(viii) Σ rp at 90%, 10% proportion

$R_p = 0.90 \times 13.05 = 11.74$

$R_p = 0.10 \times 10.65 = 1.06$

$R_p = 11.74 + 1.06 = 12.8$ per cent

(d) Σ rp at 15% and 85% proportion

(i) $R_p = 0.15 \times 13.05 = 1.957$

$R_p = 0.85 \times 10.65 = 9.052$

$R_p = 1.957 + 9.052 = 11.00$ per cent

(ii) Σ rp at 25% and 75% proportion

$R_p = 0.25 \times 13.05 = 3.26$

$R_p = 0.75 \times 10.65 = 7.98$

$R_p = 3.26 + 7.98 = 11.24$ per cent

(iii) Σ rp at 35% and 65% proportion

$R_p = 0.35 \times 13.05 = 4.567$

$R_p = 0.65 \times 10.65 = 6.922$

$R_p = 4.567 + 6.922 = 11.49$ per cent

(iv) Σ rp at 45% and 55% proportion

$R_p = 0.45 \times 13.05 = 5.87$

$R_p = 0.55 \times 10.65 = 5.85$

$R_p = 5.87 + 5.85 = 11.70$ per cent.

Illustration 6

Smt. Padma holds the following portfolio:

Probability of Occurrence		Rate of Returns	
		BPL	Videocon
(i)	0.15	20%	3%
(ii)	0.55	12%	13%
(iii)	0.30	-2%	23%

As a financial analyst:

(a) Determine the expected rate of return, variance and standard deviation.

(b) Is BPL scrip is riskless?

(c) Calculate the risk component if 50 per cent: 50 per cent proportion in these two securities.

Solution

Calculation of expected rate of return:

$$R_p BPL = \sum_{i=1}^{N} R_1 P_1$$

$= 20\times0.15+12\times0.55+-2\times0.30$

$= 3+6.66+-0.6$

$= 9.6 +-0.6 = 8.4$ per cent.

$\overline{R}_p$ Videocon $= 3\times 0.15+13\ (0.55) + 23\ (0.30)$

$= 0.45 + 7.15 + 6.9$

$= 14.5$ per cent.

$\sigma^2 BPL = (20-8.4)^2 \times 0.15 + (12-8.4)^2 \times 0.55 + (-2)-(8.4)^2 \times 0.30$

$= (11.6)^2 \times 0.15 + (3.6)^2 \times 0.55 + (-10.4)^2 \times 0.30$

$= 134.56 \times 0.15 + 12.96 \times 0.55 + 108.16 \times 0.30$

$= 20.18 + 7.128 + 32.44$

$= 59.74$

σ^2 Videocon $= (3\text{-}14.5)^2 \times 0.15 + (13\text{-}14.5)^2 \times 0.55 + (23\text{-}14.5)^2 \times 0.30$

$= (11.5)^2 \times 0.15 + (1.5)^2 \times 0.55 + (8.5)^2 \times 0.30$

$= 132.25 \times 0.15 + 2.25 \times 0.55 + 72.25 \times 0.30$

$= 19.83 + 1.237 + 21.67$

$= 42.74$

$\sigma_{BPL} \sqrt{\sigma^2} = \sqrt{59.74} = 7.69$

$\sigma_{Vediocon} \sqrt{\sigma^2} = \sqrt{42.74} = 6.50$

(b) **Yes BPL scrip** is comparatively risksless.

(c) $\sigma p^2 = x_1{}^2\sigma_1{}^2 + x_2{}^2\sigma_2{}^2 + x_1x_2\gamma_{12}\sigma_1\sigma_2$

$\sigma_p = \sqrt{\sigma_p{}^2}$

For the calculation of portfolio risk, correlation is required.

$$r_{BPL,\ Videocon} = \frac{\text{Covariance B,V}}{\sigma_B \sigma_V}$$

$$\text{Covariance} = \sum_{i=1}^{N} P_i (Y-\bar{Y})(Z-\bar{Z})$$

$=$ (20-8.4) (3–14.5) × 0.15 (12–8.4) (13-14.5) ×.55 + (–2–8.4) (14.5–23) × 0.30

$=$ (11.6) (–11.5) × 0.15 (3.6) (–1.5) × 0.55 (–1.04) (–8.5) ×.3– 13.34 × 0.54 (–)(.5) × 0.55 (–5.67)–7.736 × – 3.118 = 24.12

$$r = \frac{24.12}{7.69 \times 6.50}$$

$$= \frac{24.12}{49.98} = 0.48$$

(c) portfolio risk = **at 50%: 50%** proportion:

$\sigma p^2 = x_1{}^2\sigma_1{}^2 + x_2{}^2\,\sigma_2{}^2 + x_1x_2\,\gamma_{12}\,\sigma_1\,\sigma_2$

$\sigma p = \sqrt{\sigma_P^2}$

$= (0.5)^2 \times (59.74) + (0.5)^2 + (42.74) + (0.5)\,(0.48) \times 7.69 \times 6.5$

$= 0.25\,(59.74) + 0.25\,(42.74) + 0.12 \times 49.98$

$= 14.935 + 10.68 + 5.997$

$= 31.61$

$\sigma p = \sqrt{31.61} = 5.60$

Combination of these two securities reduces risk.

Illustration 7

Mr. Sumanth is considering to purchase securities from the stock market. The three securities provides the following returns.

	Situation of the Market	*Probability of Occurrence*	*Rates of*	*Return on*	*Securities*
(a)	**Recession**	**0.20**	12%	11%	16%
(b)	**Average**	**0.60**	16%	15%	14%
(c)	**Boom**	**0.20**	18%	20%	12%

(i) Calculate each stocks expected rate of return standard deviation and co-efficient of variation.
(ii) Calculate mean, variance to the investments.
(iii) If Mr. Sumanth invest one-third on each security what would be portfolio return.
(iv) Calculate the co-variance between securities.

Solution

Calculation of expected return:

(a) $\Sigma rp = \sum_{i=1}^{N} P_1 R_1$

$\Sigma rp_M = 0.20 \times 12 + 0.60 \times 16 + 0.20 \times 18 = \mathbf{15.6}$

$\Sigma rp_N = 0.20 \times 11 + 0.60 \times 15 + 0.20 \times 20 = \mathbf{15.2}$

$\Sigma rp_O = 0.20 \times 16 + 0.60 \times 14 + 0.20 \times 12 = \mathbf{14}$

(b) **Calculation of variance:**

$\sigma_M^2 \sum_{i=1}^{N} P_1 (R - \bar{R})^2$

For security M = $0.20\,(12\text{-}15.6)^2 + 0.60\,(16\text{-}15.6)^2 + 0.20\,(18\text{-}15.6)$

$= 0.20\,(-3.6)^2 + 0.60\,(0.4)^2 + 0.20\,(2.4)^2$

$= 0.20\,(12.96) + 0.60\,(0.16) + 0.20\,(5.76)$

$= 2.592 + 0.096 + 1.152 = \mathbf{3.84}$

For security N = $0.20\,(11–15.2)^2 + 0.60\,(15–15.2)^2 + 0.20\,(20–15.2)^2$

$= 0.20\,(-4.2)^2 + 0.60\,(-0.2)^2 + 0.20\,(4.8)^2$

$= 0.20\,(17.64) + 0.60\,(0.04) + 0.20\,(23.04)$

$= 3.528 + 0.024 + 4.608 = \mathbf{8.16}$

For security O = $0.20\,(16–14)^2 + 0.60\,(14\text{-}14) + 0.20\,(12–14)^2$

$= 0.20\,(2)^2 + 0.60\,(0) + 0.20\,(-2)^2$

$= 0.20 \times 4 + 0.60\,(0) + 0.20\,(4)$

$= 0.8 + 0 + 0.8 = \mathbf{1.6}$

(c) Portfolio return = Rp = $R_p = \sum_{i=1}^{N} X_1 R_1$
proportion 1/3, 1/3.
= 0.33 × 15.6 + 0.33 × 15.2 + 0.33 × 14
= 5.148 + 5.016 + 4.62
= 14.784

(d) **Calculation of co-variance:** $\sum_{i=1}^{N} P(R_1 - \bar{R}_1)(R_2 - \bar{R}_2)$
Covariance between M and N:
= (12–15.6) (11–15.2) 0.20 + (16–15.6) (15–15.2) 0.60 + (18–15.6) (20–15.2) (0.20)
= (–3.6) (–4.2) 0.20 + (0.4) (–0.2) 0.60 + (2.4) (4.8) (0.20)
= 15.12 (0.20) +-0.08 + 1.3824
= 3.024 + –1.3024
= 1.7216
Calculation of variance of M, O:
= (12–15.6) (16–14) 0.20 + (16–15.6) (14–14) 0.60 + (18–15.6) (12–14) 0.20
= (–3.6) (2) 0.20 + (0.40) (0) 0.60 + 2.4 (–2) 0.20
= (–1.44) + 0 + –0.96
= 2.40.

Calculation of Variance between N and O

Covariance between N and O:

= (11–15.2) (16–14) 0.20 + (15–15.2) (14–14) 0.60 + (20–15.2) (12–14) 0.20
= (–4.2) (2) 0.20 + (–0.2) (0) 0.60 + 4.8 (–2) 0.20
= – 1.68 + 0 + –1.92
= **– 3.60.**

Illustration 8

The NFCL and GFCL companies have the following expected risk and return for the year.

NFCL return 17 per cent σ^2 = 18 per cent r_{xy} = 0.65
GFCL return 20 per cent σ^2 = 27 per cent

The portfolio risk is 4.10 with a 50 per cent proportion. Determine the correlation co-efficient that will be necessary to reduce the level of portfolio risk by **75 per cent**. What is expected return of the equally weighted portfolio?

Solution

A 75 per cent reduction in risk is **(0.75) (4.10)** = 3.07 per cent. Hence, the new level of risk will be 4.10–3.07 = **1.03**. treated as 1:

$$\sigma_p = \sqrt{X_x^2\sigma_x^2 + x_y^2\sigma_y^2 + 2x_1x_2(rxy\sigma_x\sigma_y)}$$

$$1 = \sqrt{(0.5)^2 18 + (0.5)^2(27) + 2(0.5)(0.5)(r_{12})(4.256)(5.27)}$$

$$\sqrt{1} = \sqrt{4.5 + 6.75 + 0.5r22.42}$$

$$\sqrt{1} = 11.25 + 11.21r$$

$$\frac{-10.25}{11.21} = r$$

$$r = \frac{-10.25}{11.21} = -0.914$$

$$Rp: R_x x_1 + R_y X_z$$

$$Rp = 17 \times 0.5 + 20 \times 0.5$$

$$Rp = 8.5 + 1.0 = 9.5$$

Illustration 9

Mr. Akhil holds the following portfolio. Determine the risk portfolio on his stocks:

$R_M = 20$ $\quad$ $R_N = 18$

$\sigma_M = 13$ $\quad$ $\sigma_N = 16$

r_{mm}:-1

Solution

Calculation of risk portfolio of M scrip:

$$X_m = \frac{\sigma_n}{\sigma_m + \sigma_n} = \frac{16}{13+16} = \frac{16}{29} = 0.55$$

X_m = 55 per cent

X_m = 1– 0.55 = 0.45 or 45 per cent

Illustration 10

Mr. Sairam holds the portfolio. From the following information determine the minimum risk of the portfolio:

$R_a = 17$ per cent $\sigma_a = 32$ per cent
$R_b = 19$ per cent $\sigma_b = 27$ per cent $r_{ab} = 0.60.$

Solution

$$X_a = \frac{\sigma^2 b - r_{ab}\sigma_a\sigma_b}{\sigma^2{}_a + \sigma^2{}_b - 2r_{ab}\sigma_a\sigma_b}$$

$$X_a = \frac{(27)^2 - 0.60\times32\times27}{(32)^2 + (27)^2 - 2\times0.60\times32\times27}$$

$$X_a = \frac{729 - 518.40}{(1024) + (729) - 1036.80}$$

$$X_a = \frac{210.60}{1753 - 1036.80}$$

$$X_a = \frac{210.60}{716.20} = 0.29 \text{ per cent}$$

$X_a = 29$ per cent
$X_b = 1 - 0.29 = 0.71$
$X_b = 71$ per cent.

Illustration 11

Mr. Nag holds the following portfolio. Calculate the co-variance and co-efficient of correlation between stocks.

	Particulars	*Return*	*Expected Return*
(a)	Scrip x	9	11
	Scrip y	15	11
(b)	Scrip x	13	11
	Scrip y	07	11

Solution

$$\text{Calculation of co-variance} = \frac{1}{N}\sum_{t=1}^{N}(R_x - R\bar{x})\,(R_y - \bar{R}y)$$

	Particulars	*Return*	*Expected return*	*Variance*
(a)	Scrip x	9	11	-2
	Scrip y	15	11	+4
				– 2x + 4 = – 8

(b) Scrip x	13	11	+2
Scrip y	07	11	– 4
			+2x – 4 = – 8

Substituting the values in the equation.

$$N = 2$$

$$\text{Cov} = \frac{1}{2}\,[(9\text{-}11)\,(15\text{-}11) + (13\text{-}11)\,(7\text{-}11)]$$

$$= \frac{1}{2}\,[-8 + (+2)\,(-4)]$$

$$\frac{1}{2}\,[-8 + -8] = -\frac{-16}{2} = -8.$$

$$\text{Co-efficient of correlation} = \frac{\text{Covariance xy}}{(\sigma x)\,(\sigma y)}$$

$$r_{xy} = \frac{-8}{(2)(4)}$$

$$r_{xy} = \frac{-8}{8} = -1.0$$

The correlation is perfectly negative.

E. Capital Asset Pricing Method (CAPM)

Risk is **ginger** and return is **Jam** in the stock market. Stock market is a game of risk and return factors. Return is the outcome of dominating factor over risk. Escaping risk and capturing the **return** is the reflection of efficiency of the portfolio manager. Risk can be categorised as two components, *i.e.*, diversifiable risk and undiversifiable risk. **Diversifiable risk** can be eliminated through diversification. **Undiversifiable risk** cannot be eliminated. **Market risk** is uncontrollable by anyone. Therefore the investors would like to have assets with systematic risk. They would like to prefer the financial assets with **low beta co-efficients**, and if they provide high rates of earnings. The behaviour of the investors depends upon the acceptance level of **risk.** The **capital asset pricing theory** deals with the relationship between **Risk and Return factor.** It also reveals how the scrips are priced in the capital market. This theory was submitted by **Markowitz, William Sharpe, John Linter**. They provided the fundamental structure for the CAPM. It is based on a model of linear general equilibrium return. The rate of return of an asset is associated with assets **Beta value**. The capital asset pricing model is focussed on a more practical approach in stock valuation. It is based on the mean-variance approach to risk assessment. A risk assessment model was developed by **Markowitz**. The capital Asset pricing Model is based on the following assumptions.

Assumptions

1. There is no transaction cost.
2. There is no personal income tax.
3. The stock markets are perfect, no one can influence the price.
4. The investors can buy any quantity of shares.
5. All investors will have some expectations in the market.
6. Investment decision will depend upon the expected rate of returns.
7. There is no limit for short sales in the market.
8. The investors have access to riskless rate of interest assets.

Concept of CAPM

Now-a-days stock market has rapid changes in the assessment of future. The IT revolution has changed the affairs of the stock market operation. Technical sources have been established. Any small incident of corporate sector is known by stock markets within the fraction of minutes. Now, buying shares means a click of mouse with computer. **Online trading** has changed the entire stock market operations drastically. Information is readily available to the markets. The following factors will clearly explain the concept of **CAPM**:

(a) Access to riskless rate of interest assets.
(b) Composition of assets.
(c) Security Market Line.
(d) Capital Market Line.

(a) Access to Riskless Rate of Interest Assets

Capital market is a combination of different sources of flow of funds. The funds are available in the form of different kinds of financial assets. Money market is a combination of different kinds of financial assets. Some kind of sources of finance is available for cheap rate of interest rates. At the same time financial money instruments are available for investment at the **riskless rate of interest**. Hence, the investors could borrow or lend any amount of fund at **riskless rate of interest**. They can mix the blend of risk free assets with risky assets in order to reduce the risk level of the portfolio. The portfolio can be altered according to the needs and convenient of the investors. Portfolio is a mix of different kinds of financial assets. The expected return on the combination of risky and risk free assets can be computed through the following formula:

$$R_p = R_f x_f + R_m (1-x_f)$$

R_p = Return on portfolio

x_f = Ratio of funds invested in risky assets

R_f = Risk free rate of return

R_m = Return on risky assets

$1-x_f$ = Proportion of funds invested in risky assets:

Illustration 1

Mr. Kiran invests **50 per cent** in risk free assets and 50 per cent in risky assets. Calculate expected return on the portfolio, if he borrowed at **12.5 per cent** rate of interest. The risky assets generate the return **20 per cent**.

Solution

The expected rate of return can be computed by the following formula:

$$\begin{aligned} R_p &= R_f x_f + R_m (1-x_f) \\ &= 12.5 \times 0.5 + 20\,(1-0.5) \\ &= 6.25 + 10.00 \\ &= 16.25. \end{aligned}$$

Illustration 2

Mr. Ramu invests **60 per cent** in risk free assets and **40 per cent** in risky assets. He borrowed money at 9 per cent rate of interest. The risky assets generate return **16 per cent**. Calculate the expected rate of return on the portfolio:

(a) If the proportion is 70 per cent in risk free assets 30 per cent in risky assets. The risky asset generate return **14 per cent** calculate. Return on portfolio. He borrowed money at 6 per cent rate of interest.

(b) If he invests in 80 per cent risk free assets and 20 per cent in risky assets calculate the return on portfolio. The risky assets generate 18 per cent return. Funds are available to him at 8 per cent rate of interest.

Solution

$R_p = R_f x_f + R_m (1-x_f)$
$R_p = 9 \times 0.6 + 16 (1-0.6)$
$R_p = 5.4 + 6.4 = 11.80.$

(a) **Proportion: 70 per cent in Risk free assets:**
30 per cent in Risky assets
14 per cent Return from Risky assets
6 per cent Risk free rate of interest.
$R_p = R_f x_f + R_m (1-x_f)$
$R_p = 6 \times 0.7 + 14 (1-0.7)$
$R_p = 4.2 + 4.2 = 8.4$ per cent.

(b) **Proportion: 80 per cent in Risk free assets:**
20 per cent in Risky assets
18 per cent Return from Risky assets
8 per cent Risk free rate of interest.
$R_p = 8 \times 0.8 + 18 (1-0.8)$
$R_p = 6.4 + 3.6 = 10$ per cent.

Illustration 3

Smt. Veena invests 100 per cent risky assets. The return from the risky assets to be 15 per cent. She borrowed the fund at the rate of interest 6 per cent. Calculate return from the portfolio.

Solution

$R_p = R_f x_f + R_m (1-x_f)$
$R_p = 6 \times 100 + 15$ per cent $(1 - .1)$
$R_p = 600 + 15 \times 0$
$R_p = 600$ per cent.

The variance of the portfolio can be computed through the following formula:

$$\sigma p^2 = \sigma^2_f x^2_f + \sigma^2_m (1 - x_f)^2 + 2\,Cov_{fm} \times {}_f(1 - x_f)$$

(b) Composition of Assets

The combination of different kinds of financial assets are known as **"portfolio"**. The ratio of mixing blend of various kinds of stocks generates portfolio return. The portfolio either generate returns or incur losses.

Facing of loss is known as **"Risk"**. An intelligent investor always wants to escape the risk and capture return. Hence the stock market is a game of risk and returns. As per the CAPM approach all investors hold only the market portfolio and risk less securities. The market portfolio is a combination of all stocks existed in the stock market. The portfolio will be constructed with a different proportions of various financial assets in order to yield better returns to the investor. Each asset will occupy its proportion according to the market value of the scrip. The investors can combine riskless assets with risky assets in order to reduce the risk levels of the portfolio. The funds may be procured by him through cheaper sources of finance. The expected return can be computed through the following formula.

Expected Return = Price of time + (Price of risk × Amount of risk)

(c) Security Market Line

Stock market is a game of return and risk. The risk component has two factors *i.e.*, systematic and unsystematic risk. The risk and return relation can be studied through capital market line. The capital market line does not show the risk-return trade off for other portfolios and individual securities. Efficient portfolio of the risk and return relationship can be observed through capital market line. Inefficient portfolios cannot be observed through capital market line. It lies below the capital market line. The systematic and unsystematic risk consists of standard deviation. The portfolio contains the total risk component. But unsystematic risk can be diversified and eliminated from the portfolio. The systematic risk exit alone in portfolio. The alone risk component of the portfolio can be measured through **beta. The beta** is a powerful tool for analysis of risk component in portfolio whether efficient or inefficient. Generally all portfolios will be altered according to the desire of investors. Sometimes additional security will be added to the existing market portfolio. The addition of security enhences the risk levels also. Then the variance of a portfolio is equal to the weighted sum of the covariance's of the individual scrips in the portfolio. The addition of a security to the portfolio may also be stimulates the returns levels of earnings. Its marginal contribution to the variance of the market is the covariance between the individual scrip return and market portfolios return.

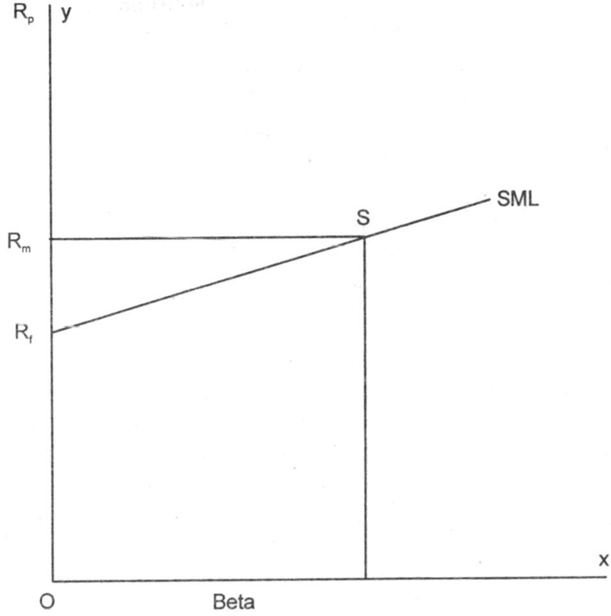

Fig. Security Market Line

Illustration 4

Mr. Venkat has the portfolio with four individual scrips A, B, C, D. The expected market risk premium is 10 per cent. The risk free rate of return to be 9 per cent. The beta values for these securities are as follows:

Security – A	$\beta = 1$
Security – B	$\beta = 1.15$
Security – C	$\beta = 1.25$
Security – D	$\beta = 0.90$

Calculate expected return for A, B, C and D securities?

Solution

The expected return on security can be computed as follows:

A: Security $\Sigma (R_i) = R_f + \beta_i [\Sigma (R_m) - R_f]$

$\Sigma (R_i) = 9 + 1 (10)$

$\Sigma (R_i) = 19$ per cent.

Calculation of expected return of B Security:

$\Sigma r_B = 9 + 1.15 (10)$

$$\Sigma r_B = 9+11.5$$
$$= 20.5 \text{ per cent.}$$

Calculation of expected return of C Security:

$$\Sigma r_C = 9+1.25\ (10)$$
$$= 9+12.5$$
$$= 21.5 \text{ per cent.}$$

Expected Return of D Security:

$$\Sigma rd = 9+0.90\ (10)$$
$$= 9+9$$
$$= 18 \text{ per cent.}$$

Evaluation of Securities

Portfolio means a mix of various assets for the purpose of gaining returns. Return is a reward to the investor. The investor should be rewarded with a reasonable amount of interest or dividend or in the form of capital appreciation. Buying and selling of securities at right price or reasonable or at intrinsic value is the most important factor. The security may be attracted by the investor for purchase or to introduce in the portfolio. The attractiveness of a security can be found out with the help of **"Security Market Line"**. Usually high return offer shares are involved with high risk. Stocks which provide low returns involve in **Low risk.** Hence the investor should know whether the stock provides return more or less proportional to its risk. The return is based on the level of accepted risk. The following diagram will clearly explain the relationship between **risk and return**:

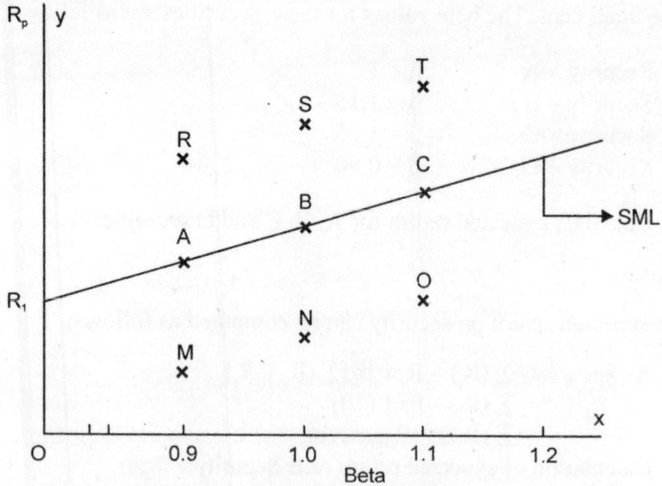

Fig.: Evaluation of Securities with Security Market Line.

The chart clearly indicates the performance of a given security. There are 9 points in the chart. A, B, C points lie on the **"security market line"**. The points R, S and T above the security market line and M, N and O below the **SML**. "ARM" have the same beta level of **0.9**. SBN 1.00, TCO 1.10. Hence the stock above the SML yield provides higher return for the same level of risk. The scrips are under priced to their value. Hence it is better to buy scrips immediately. The following formula can be applied for proving the under value price of an equity:

$$Ri = \frac{P_i - P_o + Div}{P_o}$$

Pi = Present price

Po = Purchase price

Div = Dividend.

Information

Information is the most powerful tool in the hands of the investors or portfolio managers. It provides a direction regarding share price movement. The information based decisions are mostly getting successful in the stock market affairs. It enables the investors to take a right and scientific decision in the portfolio management. A decision may be proved with wrong consequence due to lack of information available. Access to information may enhance the return levels of the portfolio. In perfection market may affect the value of securities. In a perfect market all securities should lie on the security market line. Markets are always perfect, because after the IT revolution in India, every small incident of the economic or business aspects will be exposed through media within a fraction of minutes. Markets knows everything, they discount all the affairs of the corporate sector.

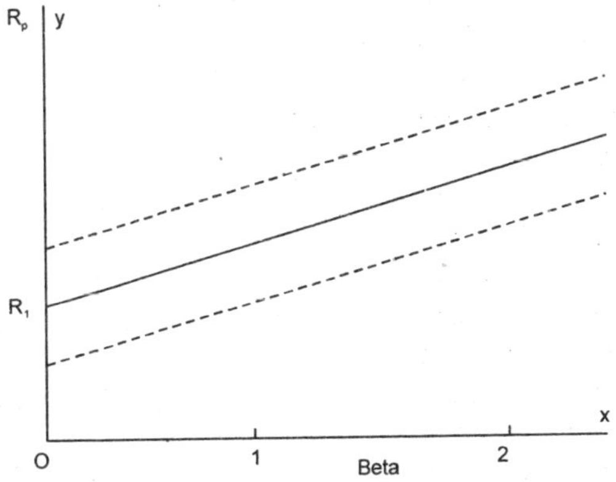

Fig.: Security Market Line in Imperfect Market.

Capital market imperfections would lead to a bond of SML rather than a **single line**. Imperfect situations affect the width of the SML to a bond. The width of the security market line depends upon market imperfection. Perfect markets will always represent the true value of financial asset.

Capital market consists a number of reflections of the economic and business environment. Portfolio is a combination of different assets and different levels of risk. All assets are not exposed equal risk. Some assets expose high risk but generates **large returns**. The risk is an unavoidable element in the portfolio. One can give assurance to return on asset, but one cannot give to risk element. The portfolio contains risk element. The total risk is consists of systematic and unsystematic. **Beta** is used to estimate the systematic risk of the security. It reflects the future volatility of the stock in relation to the market. The future price of a scrip can be estimated on the basis of past data. Past is always basis for future. Procuring the past data, with the help of regression and mathematical models provides the **Beta value**. The past betas are stable over a period of time, they would be good financial assets for expected return. The study about **Beta** is not a new one, but some social scientists have been tried to study depthly about the stability of the Beta. **Marshall E Blume, Robert and Levy** were associated with the study of the Beta. **Levy** particularly studied about the stability of the **beta** and his conclusions were presented for thorough understanding of the risk element:

(a) He calculated betas for individual securities and portfolios. He found that the betas of individual stocks are unstable. Hence the past **betas** are not useful for future decision-making. Therefore the validity of the beta have been questioned.

(b) The combination of **Ten or** more scrips are only selected indicates a stable betas. Therefore the past portfolios betas are good estimators of future.

(c) A lot of research have been made by the researchers to find out the validity of the portfolio model by calculating Beta and realised rate of return. The studied about risk free rate of interest financial assets. They used treasury bills as a ideal financial asset.

(d) The research study conducted several experiments to find out whether the line is **linear** and pas through the **beta 1** being required rate of return of the market.

(e) The researchers focussed on relative importance of the market and company risk. They found that these risks showed an impact on the price behaviour of the securities. According to CAPM theory, unsystematic is not desirable. But total risk influences the returns of a security. The portfolio risk can be reduced through a high portfolio returns. High returns are compensated for the reduction of total risk.

(f) **Richard Roll**, a well known researcher found that the ambiguity of the market portfolios leads the capital Asset pricing model untestable. He also found that **Indices** are not useful for using practice. It is surprising the different indices reveal different **Betas** for the single security. The ambiguity in the market will show different problems in the market.

(g) The research indicate that CAPM theory is not valid because it does not taken into all financial assets under consideration. Bonds are fully ignored and when analysis is made, the bonds do not fall on the **security market line**.

(d) Capital Market Line

Capital market line is associated with combination of riskless assets with risky assets. It reveals the importance of riskless rate of return financial assets. The money market instruments provide riskless assets. The riskless assets are the **oxygen** to the risky portfolio. The proportion of the riskless assets increases in the portfolio, the level of portfolio risk can be reduced and even sometimes fully eliminated. The treasury bills, short-term government bonds are best sources of riskless assets. They are issued for very short-term nature and assured by the Central Government. Hence investment in these securities are 100 per cent safe and provide reasonable rate of return. Therefore, the proportion of these instruments in the portfolio cannot be ignored and neglected. These assets are best weapons, when the risk levels reached beyond the level of expectation. The **capital market line** also deals with the combination of risky and riskless assets with a cheap sources of finance availability to the investor. In this theory, the borrowing and lending rate of interest occupies a dominant role in analysing the portfolio return. The following diagram will clearly explain the concept of capital market line:

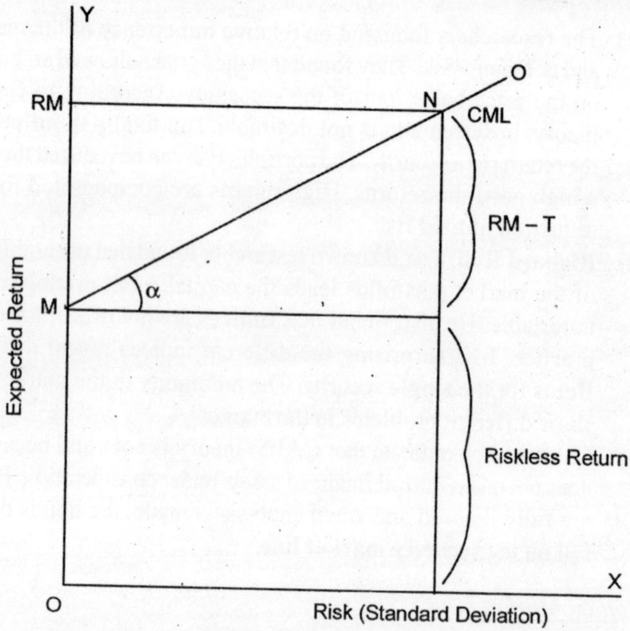

Fig. Capital Market Line

MNO = Capital Market Line

The chart shows the Capital Market Line with riskless rate of return. "M" is the riskless interest rate. The combination of a preferred investments along with borrowing and lending rate of interest is plotted on the **"MNO"** line. The slope of the MNO is the measure of the reward for risk taking. M is the risk free return, **RM-T** is the measure of the risk premium. Risk premium is a return for the **risk** taking. The riskless interest rate is "OM" and another reward is the return per unit of risk borne measured by the slope α of the "MNO" line.

The capital market line gives an importance to the borrowing and tending rate of interest in formation of a portfolio. If the investors have access to procure funds at cheap sources of finance, then the following diagram will explain about the portfolio return. It also deals with the lending rate of funds by the investor in fully risk free assets.

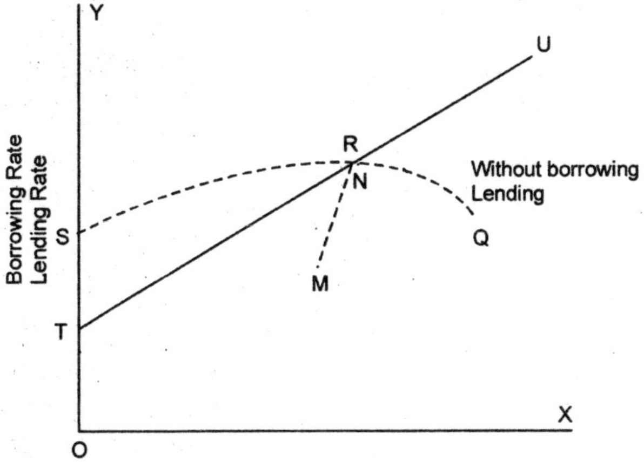

Fig. Capital Market Line (Lending and Borrowing)

The chart indicates the relationship about the borrowing and lending rate of interest in the portfolio. "OS" is the borrowing rate of interest and "OT" will be the lending rate as shown above chart. The efficient frontier line with differential borrowing and lending rates as shown above. "SRU" is the borrowing rate of "OS" and "TRU" is with the lending rate of OT and MNQ is the efficiency frontier line without borrowing and lending. The investors have choice of efficient portfolio somewhere along the line of capital market line. Those which are less efficient will be below the line "SRU" in the chart.

Limitations

The CAPM is useful to provide insights for investors but it has some limitations. They are:

(a) It is unrealistic for any professional investor or a portfolio manager, who believes the fundamental factors strongly.
(b) The researchers conducted many empirical tests of the model have not proved very useful.
(c) It is built on all investors have the same expectations about future. But the expectations of the future vary from one person to another.
(d) It is a nice theoretical concept, but in real life it is not useful to the common investors. The empirical tests have not given support to this theory.
(e) The calculation of Beta is not useful in prediction of future price of the scrip. The past betas may not reflect the future risk or return.

(f) The inputs cannot be estimated precisely, the expected return found is also subjected to criticism.

(g) Investors are concerned with company related risks. It focussed more attention about the market risk.

Review Problems

Illustration 1

Mr. Srikanth holds the following portfolio. Calculate the standard deviation and variance **Grasim Industries Ltd.**

Particulars (Return)	*Probability*	*Weighted Average Return*
10	0.10	1.10
11	0.15	1.70
12	0.25	2.90
13	0.30	2.10
14	0.20	1.70
		9.5%

Century Textiles Ltd.

Return	*Probability*	*Weighted Average*
11	0.35	2.60
12	0.45	3.90
13	0.20	3.20
		9.70%

Solution

The calculation of standard deviation is as follows:

$$\sigma = \sqrt{\frac{\Sigma dx^2}{n}}$$

Grasim Industries Ltd.

Return	*Arithmetic Mean*	*dx*	*dx²*
10	**9.5**	**0.5**	0.25
11	**9.5**	**1.5**	2.25
12	**9.5**	**2.5**	6.25
13	**9.5**	**3.5**	12.25
14	**9.5**	**4.5**	20.25
			41.25

$$\sigma = \sqrt{\frac{\Sigma dx^2}{n}}$$

$$\sigma = \sqrt{\frac{41.25}{5}}$$

$$\sigma = \sqrt{8.25}$$

$\sigma = 2.87.$ Variance = 8.25.

Century Textiles Ltd.

Return	*Arithmetic Mean*	*dx*	*dx²*
11	**9.70**	1.30	1.69
12	**9.70**	3.30	10.89
13	**9.70**	3.30	10.89
			17.87

$$\sigma = \sqrt{\frac{\Sigma dx^2}{n}}$$

$$\sigma = \sqrt{\frac{17.87}{3}}$$

$$\sigma = \sqrt{5.95}$$

$\sigma = 2.44.$

Risk on Century Textiles Ltd. is lower.

Illustration 2

Mr. Buchi Babu holds the following portfolio. Calculate the return on portfolio:

	Security	*Expected return*	*Proportion*
(a)	Bajaj Auto Ltd.	22%	30%
(b)	Lohia Machines Ltd.	27%	70%

Solution

The return on portfolio can be computed by the following formula:

$$R_p = W_1 R_1 + W_2 R_2$$

$$R_p = 0.30 \times 0.22 + 0.70 \times 0.27$$

$$R_p = 0.066 + 0.189$$
$$R_p = 0.255$$
$$R_p = 25.5 \text{ per cent.}$$

Illustration 3

Mr. Sujith holds the following portfolio. Calculate the expected rate of return on portfolio:

	Scrip	*Expected return*	*Proportion*
(a)	ACC Ltd.	12%	30%
(b)	NFC Ltd.	17%	30%
(c)	ABB Ltd.	22%	40%

Solution

The return on portfolio can be computed as follows:

$$R_p = W_1 R_1 + W_2 R_2 + W_3 R_3$$
$$W_1 = 0.30, R_1 = 12 \text{ per cent}$$
$$W_2 = 0.40, R_2 = 17 \text{ per cent}$$
$$W_3 = 0.30, R_3 = 22 \text{ per cent}$$
$$R_p = 12\times0.30+17\times0.40\times22\times0.30$$
$$R_p = 3.6+6.8+6.6$$
$$R_p = 17 \text{ per cent.}$$

Illustration 4

Mr. Sudhakar holds the following portfolio. Calculate the required measures of expected return:

	Name of the scrip	*Year*	*Return*	*Proportion*
(a)	Esab India Ltd.	2003	12%	
		2004	18%	45%
(b)	Advani Orlcon Ltd.	2003	14%	
		2004	20%	55%

Solution

Calculation of expected return on the portfolio:

$$= \frac{45}{100}\times\frac{12+18}{3}+\frac{55}{100}\times\frac{14+20}{2}$$

Esab India Ltd.

$= 0.45 \times 15 + 0.55 \times 17$

$= 6.75 + 9.35$

$= 16.1$ per cent.

Calculation of standard deviation:

$$\sigma = \sqrt{\frac{dx^2}{n}}$$

Esab India Ltd.			*Advani Orlkon Ltd.*		
Return	*dx*	*dx²*	*Return*	*dx*	*dx²*
12	-3	9	14	3	9
18	+3	9	20	+3	9
30		**18**	**34**		**18**

$$\bar{X} = \frac{\Sigma x}{n}$$

$$\bar{X} = \frac{30}{2} = 15$$

$$\bar{X} = \frac{\Sigma x}{n} = \frac{34}{2} = 17$$

$$\sigma = \sqrt{\frac{18}{2}} = \sqrt{9} \qquad \sigma = \sqrt{\frac{18}{2}} = \sqrt{9} = 3$$

$\sigma = 3$ Variance $= 9$ $\sigma = 3$

Calculation of Variance:

Esab $\sigma = 3$

Advani $\sigma = 3$

$$\text{Covariance} = \frac{1}{N}(Rx - R\bar{x})\,(Ry - R\bar{y})$$

	Name of the Scrip	*Return*	*Expected*	*dx*	*Product of devt.*
2003	Esab India Ltd.	12	16.1%	-4.1	–4.1×–2.1 = 8.61
	Advani Orlkond Ltd.	14	16.1%	-2.1	
2004	Esab India Ltd.	18	16.1%	+1.9	1.9×3.9 = 7.91
	Advani Orlkond Ltd.	20	16.1%	+3.9	

$$\text{Covariance} = \frac{1}{N}(Rx–R\bar{x}) + \frac{1}{N}(Ry–R\bar{y})$$

$$\text{Covariance} = \frac{1}{2}(12-16.1)+\frac{1}{N}(14-16.1)+\frac{1}{2}(18-16.1)\,(20-16.1)$$

$$= \frac{1}{2}(-4.1)\,(-2.1)+\frac{1}{2}\,(1.9)\,(3.9)$$

$$\frac{1}{2}\times 8.61+\frac{1}{2}\times 7.91$$

$$= 4.30 + 3.955 = \mathbf{8.255.}$$

$$\text{Co-efficient of correlation} = \frac{\text{Cov.}}{\sigma_x \sigma_y}$$

$$= \frac{8.255}{3\times 3}$$

$$= \frac{8.255}{9} = 0.917$$

The degree of risk in the portfolio is in high. Hence the portfolio is involved in high risk situation.

Illustration 5

Mr. Rathaiah holds a portfolio. The Market portfolio has an expected return of 16 per cent. The risk free rate of interest is 9 per cent. The standard deviation of the return is 27 per cent. What is the expected return of the portfolio having no unsystematic risk and 22 per cent standard deviation of return?

Solution

Expected return on Investment can be computed by the following formula.

$$R_i = R_f\left(\frac{R_m - R_f}{\sigma_m}\right)\sigma_i$$

$$R_i = 0.09 + \frac{(0.16-0.09)}{0.27}\times 0.22$$

$$R_i = 0.09 + \frac{(0.07)}{0.27}\times 0.22$$

$R_i = 0.09 + (0.259) \times 0.22$
$R_i = 0.09 + 0.056$
$R_i = 0.1469$
$R_i = 14.69$ per cent
The portfolio return is 14.69 per cent.

Illustration 6

Mr. Ramana holds the portfolio. He provides the following information for your consideration. As a portfolio manager give an analysis regarding whether they are under priced or over priced in terms of security market line.

	Name of the Scrip	*Expected Return*	β	σ
1.	M	0.31	1.75	0.52
2.	N	0.11	1.45	0.37
3.	O	0.24	1.15	0.42
4.	P	0.10	1.00	0.26
5.	Q	0.19	1.10	0.30
6.	R	0.12	0.75	0.20
7.	Sensex	0.11	1.05	0.22
8.	T-bills	0.07	0.00	0.00

Solution

The return on security market line can be estimated with the help of the following formula:

$$R_i = R_f + \beta_i (R_m - R_f)$$

Return on M Scrip:

$R_i = \mathbf{0.07} + 1.75\ (0.11–0.07)$
$R_i = 0.07 + 1.75\ (0.04)$
$R_i = 0.07 + 0.07$
$R_i = 0.14$ or 14 per cent.

Return on N Scrip:

$R_i = 0.07 + 1.45\ (0.11–0.07)$
$R_i = 0.07 + 1.45\ (0.04)$
$= 0.07 + 0.058$
$= 0.128$ or 12.8 per cent

Return on O Scrip:

$R_i = 0.07 + 1.15\ (0.11–0.07)$

$R_i = 0.07 + 1.15\ (0.04)$
$= 0.07 + 0.046$
$= 0.116$ or 11.6 per cent.

Return on P Securities:

$R_i = 0.07 + 1.00\ (0.11–0.07)$
$R_i = 0.07 + 1.00\ (0.04)$
$= 0.07 + 0.04$
$= 0.11$ or 11 per cent.

Return on Q Securities:

$R_i = 0.07 + 1.10\ (0.11–0.07)$
$R_i = 0.07 + 1.10\ (0.04)$
$= 0.07 + 0.044$
$= 0.114$ or 11.4 per cent.

Return on R Securities:

$R_i = 0.07 + 0.75\ (0.11–0.07)$
$R_i = 0.07 + 0.75\ (0.04)$
$= 0.07 + 0.03$
$= 0.1$ or 10 per cent.

Name of the Scrip	*Expected Return*	*Estimated Return*	*Result*
M	0.31	14%	Under priced
N	0.11	12.8%	Over priced
O	0.24	11.6%	Under priced
P	0.10	11.1%	Over priced
Q	0.19	11.4%	Under priced
R	0.12	10%	Under priced

Illustration 7

Arvind Mills stock is expected to sell at Rs. 140 a year. The company paid a dividend of Rs. 8 per share. The stocks correlation with portfolio is **–0.4**. The risk free rate of interest is 7 per cent. The standard deviation of the scrip is 38 per cent. Market standard deviation is 22 per cent. Calculate the expected rate of return on portfolio and also calculate the scrip's Beta.

Solution

Calculation of scrip's beta: $\beta x = \frac{\sigma_x}{\sigma_m} \times$ corelation:

$$\beta x = \frac{38}{22} \times -0.4$$

$$\beta x = 1.727 \times -0.4$$
$$= -0.69.$$

Calculation of expected return on portfolio:

$$\Sigma rp = Rf + \beta x\,(Rf)$$
$$\Sigma \mathbf{rp} = 7 + (-0.69)\,(7)$$
$$= 7 + -4.83$$
$$= 2.17 \text{ per cent.}$$

$$\text{Present selling price of the stock} = \frac{140 + 8}{1.0217}$$

$$= \frac{148}{1.0217} = 145$$

Illustration 8

Mr. Narayan holds the portfolio. He provide the following information:

The risk free rate of interest is 9 per cent.
Market risk premium 7 per cent.
Standard deviation of the market is 11 per cent.
Calculate the variance:

(a) Risk free Investments 30%. Risky Investment 70%.
(b) Risk free Investments 40%. Risky Investment 60%.
(c) Risk free Investments 50%. Risky Investment 50%.
(d) Diversified portfolio with β of 1.5.

Solution

(a) $\sigma_1 = W_1\, x_1 + W_2\, x_2$
$= 0.7\,(11\%) + 0.3\,(0)$
$= 7.7+0$
$= 7.7$ per cent.

(b) Risk free 40%. Risky 60%.
$\sigma = 0.60\,(11\%) + 0.3\,(0)$
$\sigma = 6.6+0$
$= 6.6$ per cent.

(c) Risk free 50%. Risky 50%.
$\sigma = 0.50\,(11\%) + 0.5\,(0)$
$\sigma = 5.5+0$
$\sigma = 5.5$ per cent.

Calculation of diversified portfolio:

$\sigma_2^2 = \beta_2^2 + \sigma m^2 + 0$
$\sigma_2^2 = (1.5)^2 (11)^2 + 0$
$\sigma_2^2 = 2.25 (121)$
$\sigma_2^2 = \sqrt{272.25}$
$\sigma^2 = 16.5$ per cent.

Illustration 9

Nagarjuna Constructions has a beta 1.30. The risk free rate of interest is 9 per cent. Expected return on market portfolio is 15 per cent. Company pay a dividend of Rs. 3 per share and expected growth in dividends is 15 per cent per annum:

(a) What is the expected rate of return.
(b) What is the stock's market price, assuming the required return.

Solution

(a) Return on portfolio = 9 + 1.30 (15 – 9)
= 9 + 1.30 (6)
= 9 + 7.8
= 16.8 per cent.

(b) Market price: Perpetual dividend growth model:

$$P_o = \frac{\text{Dividend in Growth}}{R_p - g}$$

$$P_o = \frac{3+0.30}{16.8-10}$$

$$P_o = \frac{3.30}{0.068} = 48.52.$$

Illustration 10

From the following information, calculate the stock equilibrium price:

Short-term government securities yield. 6 per cent
Stocks beta is 0.75
Growth rate is 3 per cent
Last dividend paid 1.50
Expected market return is 11 per cent.

Solution

$R_x = R_f + \beta_x (R_m - R_f)$
$R_x = Do + (1 + g) (R_x - g)$
R_x = Rate of return required on stock x
R_f = Risk free rate of interest
R_m = Return on market portfolio
β_x = Beta co-efficient of stock
g = growth rate of dividend
Do = Dividend per share.
$R_x = 6 + 0.75 (11 - 6)$
$R_x = 6 + 0.75 (5)$
$R_x = 6 + 3.75$
$R_x = 9.75$ per cent.

$$R_x = \frac{Do (1 + g)}{P_o} + g$$

$$R_x = \frac{1.50 (1 + 0.3)}{P_o} + 3$$

$$9.75 = \frac{1.50 (1 + 0.3)}{P_o} + 3$$

$$9.75 = \frac{1.95}{P_o} + 3$$

$$9.75 - 3 = \frac{1.95}{P_o}$$

$$6.75 = \frac{1.95}{P_o} \qquad P_o = \frac{1.95}{0.0675} = 28.88.$$

Illustration 11

The following information is related to a portfolio. The beta co-efficient of the scrip is **1.15**. The company is maintaining a 4 per cent rate of growth in earnings. The last dividend paid was Rs. 1.75 per share. The risk free rate of return is 9 per cent and return on market portfolio 14 per cent. The current market price of the company is Rs. 12. What is the equilibrium price per share of the company?

Solution

The expected rate of return = $R_f \beta (R_m - R_f)$
$\Sigma (R) = 9 + 1.15 (14 - 9)$

$\Sigma (R) = 9+1.15\ (5)$

$= 9+5.75 = 14.75$ per cent.

$$\Sigma (R) = \frac{D_1\ (1+g)}{P_o} + g$$

$$\Sigma (R) = \frac{1.75\ (1+.04)}{P_o} + 0.04$$

$$\Sigma (R) = \frac{1.75\ (1.04)}{P_o} + 0.04$$

$$0.1475 = \frac{1.82}{P_o} + 0.04$$

$$\frac{1.82}{P_o} = 0.1485\text{-}0.04 = 0.1075$$

$$P_o = \frac{1.82}{0.1075} = 16.93.$$

Illustration 12

From the following information, calculate β_1 and β_2. The data is related for five years. The risk free asset is treasury bills and provides a risk free rate of interest.

Year	*Return on Security "A"*	*Return on Security "B"*	R_m	R_f
2000	14	9	10	5
2001	–5	–1	–04	–04
2002	16	12	11	06
2003	17	8	10	05
2004	21	10	12	06

Solution

Calculation of systematic risk:

$$\beta_1 = \frac{N \times \Sigma xy - (\Sigma x)(\Sigma y)}{N\Sigma x^2 - (\Sigma x)^2 (R_b - R_f)}$$

$(R_a - R_f)\ (R_b - R_f)\ (R_m - R_f)$

Year	R_a	R_b	R_m	R_f	dy_1	dy^2_1	dy_2	dy^2_2	x	x^2	xy_1	xy_2
2000	14	9	10	5	9	81	04	16	5	25	45	20
2001	–05	–01	–04	–04	–09	81	–05	25	–08	64	72	40
2002	16	12	11	06	10	100	06	36	5	25	50	30
2003	17	08	10	05	12	144	04	16	5	25	60	20
2004	21	10	12	06	15	225	04	16	6	36	90	24
					37	631	13	109	13	175	317	134

$$\bar{Y}_1 = \frac{37}{5} = 7.4 \quad \Sigma dy^2_1 = 631 \quad \Sigma x^2 = 175 \quad \Sigma xy_2 = 134 \quad \Sigma x = 13$$

$$\bar{Y}_2 = \frac{13}{5} = 2.6 \quad \Sigma dy^2_2 = 109 \quad \Sigma xy_1 = 317 \quad \Sigma dy_2 = 13 \quad \Sigma y = 37$$

$$\beta_1 = \frac{5\times317-13\times37}{5\times175-(13)^2}$$

$$\beta_1 = \frac{1585-481}{875-169}$$

$$\beta_1 = \frac{1104}{706} = 1.56$$

$$\beta_2 = \frac{5\times134-13\times13}{5\times175-(13)^2}$$

$$\beta_2 = \frac{670-169}{706} = \frac{501}{706} = 0.70$$

Illustration 13

Merry Lynch, an investment company manages equity fund consisting of the five stocks.

	Stock	Market value	Betas
(a)	Reliance Ltd.	2,00,000	1.05
(b)	IPCL Ltd.	50,000	1.15
(c)	Borough Welcome	1,00,000	0.70
(d)	Castrol	2,50,000	0.55
(e)	MICO	3,30,000	1.25

The risk free rate of Interest = 6 per cent
Expected return on Market = 13 per cent
What is the expected return on portfolio?

Solution

Expected return on portfolio = $R_f + (R_m - R_f)\ \beta$

R_f = 6 per cent R_m = 13 per cent β = ?

β of the portfolio = $\Sigma W\beta$

Proportions of the portfolio

$$W_{Reliance} = \frac{2,00,000}{9,30,000} = 0.22$$

$$W_{IPCL} = \frac{50,000}{9,30,000} = 0.05$$

$$W_{Borrough\ welcome} = \frac{1,00,000}{9,30,000} = 0.110$$

$$W_{Castrol} = \frac{2,50,000}{9,30,000} = 0.27$$

$$W_{MICO} = \frac{3,30,000}{9,30,000} = 0.35$$

Total weight = 0.22 + 0.05 + 0.11 + 0.27 + 0.35 = 1.00

Beta of the portfolio = 0.22 (1.05) + 0.05 (1.15) + 0.11 (0.70) + 0.27 (0.55) + 0.35 (1.25)

= 0.231 + 0.0575 + 0.077 + 0.148 + 0.4375 = 0.951

Σrp = 6 + (13-6) 0.951.

= 6 + (7) 0.951

= 6 + 6.65 = 12.65 per cent.

Illustration 14

The following information is related to a portfolio:

(a) Risk free rate 6 per cent
(b) Market return 15 per cent
(c) Beta for the scrip 1.45
  (i) Determine the expected return for the security.
  (ii) Calculate expected return, if market return increases to 17 per cent assuming that other variables do not change.
  (iii) Calculate expected return if the beta falls to 1.30, 1.10, 1.05, 0.85, 0.75, 0.60

Solution

(i) Expected return on security = $R_f + (R_m - R_f)\ \beta$
$= 0.06 + (0.15 - 0.06)\ 1.45$
$= 0.06 + (0.09)\ 1.45$
$= 0.06 + 0.1305$
$= 19.05$ per cent.

(ii) $R_i = R_f + (R_m - R_f)\ \beta$
$= 0.06 + (0.17 - 0.06)\ 1.45$
$= 0.06 + (0.11)\ 1.45$
$= 0.06 + 0.1595$
$= 0.2195$
$= 21.95$ per cent.

(iii) $R_i = R_f + (R_m - R_f)\ \beta$
if Beta falls to 1.30
$= 0.06 + (.11)\ 1.30$
$= 0.06 + 0.143$
$= 0.203$
$= 20.03$ per cent.

If the Beta falls to 1.10
$R_i = R_f + (R_m - R_f)\ \beta$
$R_i = 0.06 + (0.17 - 0.06)\ 1.10$
$= 0.06 + (0.11)\ 1.10$
$= 0.06 + 0.121$
$= 0.181$
$= 18.1$ per cent.

If the Beta falls to 1.05
$R_i = R_f + (R_m - R_f)\ \beta$
$= 0.06 + (0.17 - 0.06)\ 1.05$
$= 0.06 + (0.11)\ 1.05$
$= 0.06 + 0.115$
$= 0.175$
$= 17.5$ per cent.

If the Beta falls to 0.85
$= 0.06 + (0.17 - 0.06)\ 0.85$
$= 0.06 + (0.11)\ 0.85$
$= 0.06 + (0.0935)$
$= 0.1535$
$= 15.35$ per cent.

If the Beta falls to 0.75
$= 0.06 + (0.17 - 0.06)\ 0.75$
$= 0.06 + (0.11)\ 0.75$

= 0.06 + 0.08
= 0.1425
= 14.25 per cent.

If the Beta falls to 0.60

= 0.06 + (0.17–0.06) 0.60
= 0.06 + (0.11) 0.60
= 0.06 + 0.066 = 12.6 per cent.

Illustration 15

The following information is provided:

(i) Risk free rate of interest 6 per cent
(ii) Market return 13 per cent
(iii) Return investment 17 per cent

(a) Calculate the Beta value for the stock.
(b) What is the stock's return if Beta increases to 1.85.

Solution

(a) $R_i = R_f + (R_m - R_f)\ \beta$
$17 = 6 + (13-06)\ \beta$
$17 = 6 + (07)\ \beta$
$7\beta = 17-06 = 11$
$7\beta = 11$
$\beta = 11/7 = 1.57.$

(b) $R_i = R_f + (R_m - R_f)\ \beta$
$= 6 + (13-06)\ 1.85$
$= 6 + (7)\ 1.85$
$= 6 + 12.95$
= 18.95 per cent.

Illustration 16

From the following information fill up the blanks. Calculate the required variance through CAPM equilibrium model with unlimited borrowing and lending at the risks rate of interest.

Name of the Scrip	*Expected Return*	σ	β	e^2_1
Andhra Petro Ltd.	0.13	-	1.80	0.07
T.N. Petro Ltd.	-	0.23	0.55	0.03
Andhra Sugars Ltd.	0.07	-	0.45	0.14

Solution

The expected return on investment = $R_i = R_f + \beta_1 R_m$

$$0.13 = R_f + 1.80\ R_m$$
$$0.07 = R_f + 0.14\ R_m$$
$$0.06 = +\ 1.66\ R_m$$
$$R_m = \frac{0.06}{1.66} = 0.3614.$$

Substituting it in equation 1:

$$0.13 = R_f + 1.80 \times 0.036$$
$$R_f = 0.13 – 0.0648$$
$$R_f = 0.0652.$$

Return T.N. Petro Ltd:

$$R_i = 0.06 + 0.55 \times 0.036$$
$$R_i = 0.06 + 0.0198$$
$$R_i = 0.0798.$$

σ^2 = given variance + residual variance

Given variance = $\beta^2 \times$ Variance of index

In case of T.N. Petro Ltd.

Given variance = Total variance – Residual variance

$$= (0.23)^2 – 0.03$$
$$= 0.0529 – 0.03$$
$$= 0.0229.$$

Given variance = β^2 + Variance of Index

$$0.0229 = (0.55)^2 + \sigma^2_m.$$
$$= 0.0229 = 0.3025 + \sigma^2_m$$
$$\sigma^2_m = \frac{0.229}{0.3025} = 0.75.$$

Standard Deviation for Andhra Petro Ltd.

$$\sigma = \sqrt{\text{Given variance} + \text{Residual Variance}}$$
$$\sigma = \sqrt{3.24 + 0.1}$$

β^2 = Given variance $1.80^2 = 3.24$

$$\sigma = \sqrt{3.24\ (0.036) + 0.1}$$
$$\sigma = \sqrt{0.1164 + 0.1}$$
$$\sigma = \sqrt{0.21664} = 0.46$$

Standard Deviation for Andhra Sugars Ltd.

$$= \sqrt{(0.20 \times 0.036) + 0.14}$$
$$= \sqrt{0.0072 + 0.14}$$
$$= \sqrt{0.1472}$$
$$= \mathbf{0.38.}$$

Table

	Name of the Scrip	*ΣR*	*σ*	*β*	σ^2_i
1.	Andhra Petro Ltd.	0.13	**0.46**	1.80	0.07
2.	T.N. Petro Ltd.	**0.07**	0.23	0.55	0.03
3.	Andhra Sugars Ltd.	0.07	**0.38**	0.45	0.14

Illustration 17

From the following information find out the return of the market portfolio and risk free rate of return. The assets are believed to be correctly priced on the security market line:

$R_1 = 8.40$ per cent $\qquad \beta_1 = 0.70$

$R_2 = 12.40$ per cent $\qquad \beta_2 = 1.20$

Solution

$$R_i = R_f + \beta\,(R_m - R_f)$$
$$R_i = 8.40,\ Rf_1 = ?,\ \beta_1 = 0.70,\ Rm_1 = ?$$
$$R_2 = 12.40,\ Rf_2 = ?,\ B_2 = 1.20,\ Rm_2 = ?$$
$$8.4\% = R_f + 0.70\,(R_m - R_f)$$
$$12.4\% = R_f + 1.20\,(R_m - R_f)$$
$$8.4 = 0.3R_f + 0.70\,R_m \qquad \ldots(1)$$
$$12.4 = -0.2R_f + 1.20\,R_m \qquad \ldots(2)$$

Multiplying with Ist equation with **0.67**

$$5.628 = 0.20\,R_f + 0.469\,R_m$$
$$12.4 = (-)\,0.20\,R_f + 1.20\,R_m$$

adding the both equations.

$$18.02 = 1.669\,R_m$$
$$R_m = \frac{18.02}{1.669} = 10.79$$

$\mathbf{R_m = 10.79}$ **per cent.**

Substituting R_m in any one of the equation.

$$8.4 = R_f + 0.70\,(R_f - 10.8\%)$$
$$8.4 = R_f + 7.56 - 0.7R_f$$
$$8.4 - 7.56 = R_f - 0.7R_f$$
$$0.84 = 0.3\,R_f$$
$$R_f = \frac{0.84}{0.3} = 2.8 \text{ per cent.}$$

$\mathbf{R_m = 10.79}$ **per cent**

$\mathbf{R_f = 2.8}$ **per cent.**

Illustration 18

Mr. Sanjay hold the scrip of Gas Authority of India Ltd. and analysed investment analysis. The results are as follows. The risk free rate of interest is **6 per cent:**

	α	b_i
(a) Market risk	**0.75**	**-1.60**
(b) Management risk	1.25	1.55
(c) Purchasing power risk	0.85	1.75
(d) Interest rate risk	0.85	0.85

The probability of getting return on GAIL is given below:

Return	*Probability*
18%	45%
23%	35%
13%	10%
11%	10%

is it the stock is worthable for purchase?

Solution

The expected return of the stock GAIL is as follows:

$$R_i = \alpha_0 + \alpha_1 b_{i1} + \alpha_2 b_{i2} + \alpha_3 b_{i3} + \alpha_4 b_{i4}$$
$$R_i = 6 + (0.85 \times 0.85) + (0.85 \times 1.75) + (1.25 \times 1.55) + (0.75 \times -1.60)$$

$$R_i = 6 + (0.7225) + (1.4875) + (1.9375) + (-1.2)$$
$$R_i = 6 + 2.9475$$
$$R_i = 8.9475 \text{ per cent.}$$

The probable return of the portfolio:

$$= (18 \times 0.45) + (23 \times 0.35) + (13 \times 0.10) + (11 \times 0.10)$$
$$= 8.1 + 8.05 + 1.3 + 1.0$$
$$= 18.55 \text{ per cent.}$$

As analysis of all the parameters, the stock **GAIL** can be purchased. The probable returns are higher than the return on investment according to the CAPM model.

Illustration 19

Mr. Sandeep is planning to buy a stock of NTPC. He expects the company will earn a return of 20 per cent in the forthcoming year. The scrip's beta is 1.7, the risk free rate of interest is 8 per cent and market return is 18 per cent. As a financial analyst, what advice you are going to provide Mr. Sandeep?

Solution

The equilibrium return according to the capital asset pricing model:

$$\Sigma R_p = R_f + \beta\,[\Sigma\,(R_m) - R_f]$$
$$= 8 + 1.17\,[18-8]$$
$$= 8 + 1.7\,(10)$$
$$= 8 + 17$$
$$= 25.$$

The actual return is less than equilibrium return, there it is overpriced and should not buy at present.

Illustration 20

TCS has a beta of 1.65. The risk free rate of interest is 8 per cent and the expected return on the market portfolio is 16 per cent. The company pays a dividend of Rs. 3 per share and investors expect a growth in dividend of 14 per cent per annum for years together. According to the CAPM, what is the required rate of return on the investment? What is the current market price of the share?

Solution

As per the security market line equation, we can calculate return on investment:

$$R_i = R_f + \beta_i (R_m - R_f)$$
$$R_i = 8 + 1.65 (16-8)$$
$$R_i = 8 + 1.65 (8)$$
$$= 8 + 13.2$$
$$= 21.2 \text{ per cent.}$$

The required rate of return of the scrip can be computed as follows:

$$P = \frac{D_o (1+g)}{k-g}$$

$$P = \frac{3 (1+.14)}{0.212 - .14}$$

$$P = \frac{3 (1.14)}{0.072}$$

$$P = \frac{3.42}{0.072} = 47.50.$$

The current Market price of the share in Rs. 47.50.

Illustration 21

From the following particulars, fill up the blanks. Mr. Santhosh holds the portfolio. The return on market portfolio is 13 per cent and the return on the zero beta portfolio is 8 per cent. The market standard deviation is 35 per cent.

	Name of the Scrip	ΣR	σ	β	Residual Variance
1.	Ranbaxy Ltd.	0.13	-	-	0.03
2.	Glaxo Ltd.	0.09	-	-	0.07

Solution

The problem required the following parameters σ, β of the two scrips.

Ranbaxy

The security market line equation is

$$R = \alpha + \beta (R_m)$$
$$\alpha = \text{zero return on beta portfolio.}$$

$$0.13 = 0.08 + \beta\,(0.13)$$

$$\beta = \frac{0.05}{0.13} = 0.38.$$

Glaxo

$$0.09 = 0.08 + \beta\,(0.09)$$

$$\beta = \frac{0.01}{0.09} = 0.11.$$

$$\text{Standard Deviation} = \sqrt{\beta^2 \times \text{Variance of index} + \sigma_1^2}$$

$$\textbf{Ranbaxy} = \sqrt{0.38^2 \times (0.35)^2 + 0.03}$$

$$= \sqrt{0.144 \times 0.122 + 0.03}$$

$$= \sqrt{0.01756 + 0.03}$$

$$= \sqrt{0.04} = 0.20$$

$$\textbf{Glaxo} = \sqrt{(0.11)^2 \times (0.35)^2 + 0.07}$$

$$= \sqrt{0.0121 \times 0.1225 + 0.07}$$

$$= \sqrt{0.001482 + 0.07}$$

$$= \sqrt{0.071} = 0.28$$

Illustration 22

Kothari Investment Company manages a portfolio consisting of 6 stocks with the following information:

Name of the Scrip	*Market Value*	*Beta*
Essar Steels Ltd.	4,00,000	1.20
Tata Steels Ltd.	3,00,000	1.24
SAIL Ltd.	3,00,000	0.90
Andhra Steels Ltd.	1,00,000	0.60
Mittal Steels Ltd.	2,00,000	0.75
Vishaka Steels Ltd.	2,00,000	0.80

Solution

The risk free rate of interest is 6 per cent and the market return is **13 per cent**. What is the portfolios expected return.

The total investment value of the portfolio:

$= 40,00,000 + 2,00,000 + 3,00,000 + 1,00,000 + 2,00,000 + 2,00,000$

$= 15,00,000.$

Proportion of the **Essar Steels Ltd.**

$$= \frac{4,00,000}{15,00,000} = 0.26$$

Tata Steels Ltd. $= \frac{3,00,000}{15,00,000} = 0.20$

SAIL $= \frac{3,00,000}{15,00,000} = 0.20$

Andhra Steels Ltd. $= \frac{1,00,000}{15,00,000} = 0.07$

Mittal Steels Ltd. $= \frac{2,00,000}{15,00,000} = 0.13$

Vishaka Steels Ltd. $= \frac{2,00,000}{15,00,000} = 0.13$

The proportion = 0.26 + 0.20 + 0.20 + 0.07 + 0.13 + 0.13 = 1.00

Calculation of expected return with security market line, the portfolio beta should be estimated:

$$\beta_p = \sum_{i=1}^{N} X_i \beta_i$$

$$\beta_p = (0.26 \times 1.20) + (0.20 \times 1.24) + (0.20 \times 0.90) + (0.07 \times 0.60) + (0.13 \times 0.75) + (0.13 \times 0.80)$$

$$\beta_p = (0.312) + (0.248) + (0.18) + (0.042) + (0.0975) + (0.104) = 0.98.$$

$$R_p = R_f + \beta_p (R_m - R_f)$$

$$R_p = 6 + 0.98\ (13\text{–}6)$$

$$R_p = 6 + 0.98\ (7)$$

$$= 6 + 6.86 = 12.86 \text{ per cent.}$$

Illustration 23

Mr. Shankar holds the Siemens India stock. He provide the following information:

Year	*Cash Flows*
2000	-10,000
2001	8,000
2002	10,000
2003	-4,000
2004	12,000

Expected return = 6+5b_{i1}; 8b_{i2} with beta value of b_{i1} = – 77 b_{i2} = 1.8. Determine the present value of the cash flows.

Solution

The required rate of return can be computed as follows:

$$\Sigma (R) = \alpha_o + \alpha_1 b_{i1} + \alpha_2 b_{i2}$$
$$\Sigma R = 6 + (5 \times -.77) + (8 \times 1.8)$$
$$\Sigma R = 6 + (-3.85) + 14.4$$
$$\mathbf{\Sigma R = 16.55 \text{ per cent.}}$$

Present value of cash flow is:

$$= \frac{-10000}{(1.1)^1} + \frac{8000}{(1.1)^2} + \frac{10000}{(1.1)^3} + \frac{-4000}{(1.1)^4} + \frac{12000}{(1.1)^5}$$
$$= -9091 + 6612 + 7513 + -2732 + 7453$$
$$= 21578 - 11823 = 9755.$$

Illustration 24

The information is related to an investments affairs of Mr. Chandar Rao. As a financial analyst you are required to give your professional advices on his portfolios.

Portfolio	*Beta*	*Correlation of the Return with Index Return*
X	1.45	1.00
Y	**–0.80**	**–0.90**
Z	1.25	0.85

Client requirements:

(i) A portfolio without unsystematic risk
(ii) He needs highest yielding return portfolio based on CAPM at normal market conditions.

Analysis

(i) Risk is a chance of future loss. It arises at any time. It may or may not be escaped. It consists of two kinds **systematic and unsystematic**. Systematic risk is related to market affair. Unsystematic risk is related to the company aspect. Systematic risk cannot be entirely avoided by the investors. It is unavoidable. Systematic risk will be arised in the form of **Market risk, Interest rate risk and Purchasing power risk.** Unsystematic risk arises due to managerial inefficiency, technological obsolence, availability of raw materials, labour problems, changes in consumers attitudes *etc*. The relationship of the portfolio with the market is given by the correlation co-efficient. The r^2 indicates the variation due to participation factor:

X portfolio = 1.00
Y portfolio = 0.81
Z portfolio = 0.72

In portfolio X, 100 per cent of the variation in returns arised by the market return. The unsystematic risk component is nil in the portfolio. Other portfolio Y, only 0.81 of the variation is accounted by the index return.19 is due to other factors. Hence the portfolio X has no unsystematic risk.

(ii) As per the clients requirement, the highest yielding of the portfolio through CAPM can be computed as follows:

$R_i = R_f + \beta_i (R_m - R_f)$
R_i = Average return, R_f = Risk free rate of interest
R_m = Market Return
$R_x = R_f + \beta (R_m - R_f)$ $\quad$ $R_z = R_f + 1.25 (R_m - R_f)$
$= R_f + 1.45 (R_m - R_f)$
$R_y = R_f + -0.8 (R_m - R_f)$
X portfolio has highest Beta and gives highest returns.

F. Share Portfolio Optimization

Portfolio means a combination of different kinds of stocks. An individual investor or a professional investor or a portfolio manager always desires to get highest return with lower risk from the existed portfolio. Stock market is a game of **Return and Risk**. The investor always dreams about better **Returns** and escapes **Risk**. For investor **Risk** is ginger and Return is like a **Jam**. Return word is the success mantra of the stock market. **Risk** can be described a speed braker on the Highway. **Return** is an accelerator and risk is speed braker. Hence the investor should manage these two factors efficiently and intelligently. Traditional analyst paid more attention to the **Return**. At present **Risk** has gained importance by the financial analyst. The analysts are making efforts to estimate the risk as well as return.

Markowitz Model had some certain limitations in management of a portfolio. This theory had faced rigorous problems for compiling the expected returns, standard deviation, variance, co-variance of all securities existed in the market. **Sharpe Model** has simplified all these compiling of variables and prepared a single market index. This theory has became popular as **"Sharpe Index Model"**. It reflects all well traded securities in the market. It reduced and simplified all the laborious work in compiling various parameters.

Sharpe has developed a simplified model to analyse the portfolio. According to sharpe approach, "The return of a security is linearly related to a single index like the Market Index." Market Index is a combination of all the securities traded on the stock exchange. Market index is not reflected in popular indexes such as **BSE sensex, BSE-100, NSE NIFTY** *etc*. Market index should consist of all securities trading on the exchange. All popular indices do not use all the scrips prices to construct indices. The movement of security price can be known as per the movement of Indices.

Single Index Model

Stock market is a combination of financial and psychological aspects. Generally the movement of indices reveal the price situation. A close observation of the share prices over a period of time indicates the movement of share prices with the market index. **For example: NIFTY** increases share prices also tend to increase. Therefore, we can assume that some underlying factors effect both market index and share prices. The relationship between **Market Index** and **share prices** is useful for estimation of the return on stocks. For this purpose, **"Single Index Model"** can be applied by the following formula:

$$R_i = \alpha_i + \beta_i R_m + e_i$$

R_i = Expected return on security i

α_1 = Alpha co-efficient or intercept of the straight line

β_i = Beta co-efficient or slope of straight line

R_m = Return on market index

e_i = Errors term.

According to Sharpe Index model, the return of a share depended upon two elements. The return has two influential factors such as (i) Individual security return, (ii) The return due to the market. Hence the equation shows the total return on security.

Return = Scrip individual return + Return due to market index.

Beta reveal the sensitiveness of the stock return to the changes in the market return.

Beta is an expression of the relation between the stock return and market return. **For example:** $\beta_{1.5}$ means, the stock return is expected in increase by **1.5 per cent** and the market index return increases by **one per cent β_i of 1** reveal that the market return and individual security return are tandem. α_i, β_i can be computed from the **regression analysis.** The single index model is based on the assumption that, stock prices are vary together. Share prices in market are fluctuating on various factors. Any change in fundamental factors, any change in political, economical aspects would lead to fluctuate the share prices. The movement of share prices are influenced by expected return standard deviation and co-variance of the variables. The average mean return is computed by the following formula:

$$R_i = \alpha_i + \beta_i R_m + e_i$$
$$\sigma^2 = \beta_i \sigma^2_m + \sigma^2_{ei}$$

Co-variance = $\sigma_{ij} = \beta_i \beta_j \sigma^2_m$

Variance = Market risk + Unsystematic risk.

Systematic or Market risk = β^2_i × Variance of market index

$= \beta^2_i \sigma^2_m$

Unsystematic risk = Total variance–Systematic risk.

$$e^2_1 = \sigma^2_i - \beta^2_i \sigma^2_m$$

Total risk = Systematic risk + Unsystematic risk = $\beta^2_i \sigma^2_m + e^2_i$

Portfolio variance can be computed as follows:

$$\sigma^2_p = \left[\left(\sum_{i=1}^{N} x_i \beta_i\right)^2 \sigma^2_m\right] + \left[\sum_{i=1}^{N} x^2_{i2} e_i^2\right]$$

σ^2_p = variance of the portfolio

σ^2 = expected variance of index

e^2_i = variation in securities return not related to the market index

x_i = proportion of stock i in the portfolio.

Return on the portfolio can be computed as follows

$$R_p = R_p = \sum_{i=1}^{N} x_i (\alpha_i + \beta_i R_m)$$

$$\sigma p = \sigma_p = \sum_{i=1}^{N} x_i \alpha_i$$

α_i = Value of alpha for the portfolio

x_i = Proportion of the investment on securities

α_1 = Value of alpha for security i

N = Number of securities in the portfolio.

$$\beta_p = \sum_{i=1}^{N} x_i \beta_i$$

β_p = Portfolio Beta
x_i = Proportion of the investment on security i
β_i = Beta value of security.

Illustration 1

Mr. Bachan hold the portfolio. He submits the information regarding stock prices and sensex for a period of one year. As a portfolio manager you are required to advise him regarding the management of the portfolio. Calculate the systematic and unsystematic risk for the given stocks. Calculate the portfolio risk in the following situations:

(a) A stock 50% B-stock 50%
(b) A stock 60% B-stock 40%
(c) A stock 70% B-stock 30%
(d) A stock 80% B-stock 20%
(e) A stock 90% B-stock 10%
(f) A stock 10% B-stock 90%
(g) A stock 20% B-stock 80%
(h) A stock 30% B-stock 70%
(i) A stock 40% B-stock 60%

	Particulars	*A Stock*	*B Stock*	*Sensex*
(i)	Average return	0.17	0.27	0.08
(ii)	Variance of return	6.35	5.91	2.30
(iii)	β	0.76	0.32	
(iv)	Correlation co-efficient	0.47		
(v)	r^2	0.23		

Solution

According to sharpe index model, the total risk may be computed as follows:

Total risk = Systematic + Unsystematic

Company A:

$$\begin{aligned}\text{Systematic risk} &= \beta^2 \times \text{variance of the market index}\\ &= (0.76)^2 \times 2.30\\ &= 0.577 \times 2.30\\ &= \mathbf{1.328.}\end{aligned}$$

Unsystematic risk = Total variance of security return–Systematic risk

$= e^2_i$

$= 6.35 - 1.328$

$= 5.022.$

Total risk $= 1.328 + 5.022$

$= \mathbf{6.35.}$

Company B:

Total risk = Systematic risk + Unsystematic

Systematic risk $= \beta^2 \times \sigma^2_m$

$= (0.32)^2 \times 2.30$

$= 0.1024 \times 2.30$

$= \mathbf{0.235.}$

Unsystematic risk = Total variance of the security return–**Systematic risk**

$= 5.91 - 0.235$

$= \mathbf{5.675}$

Total risk $= 0.235+5.675$

$= \mathbf{5.91.}$

Company A stock return, 23 per cent of variation is explained by the variation of the index and 77 per cent is not explained by the index.

Explained by the index = variance of security return × co-efficient of determination

$= 6.35 \times 0.23 = \mathbf{1.4605.}$

Not explained by the index = Variance of security return × $(1 - r^2)$

$= 6.35 \times 0.77 = \mathbf{4.88.}$

(a) Calculation of portfolio risk at 50 per cent of money proportionately allotted between two securities.

$$\sigma_p^2 = \left[\left(\sum_{i=1}^{N} x_i\beta_i\right)^2 \sigma_m^2\right] + \left[\sum_{i=1}^{N} x_i^2 e_i^2\right]$$

$= [(0.5 \times 0.76 + 0.5 \times 0.32)^2\, 2.30 + (0.5)^2 (4.88) + (0.5)^2 (5.675)]$

$= [(0.38 + 0.16^2)\, 2.30] + [1.22 + 1.41875]$

$= (0.670) + (2.6387)$

$= \mathbf{3.308.}$

(b) Calculation of portfolio risk at A-60 per cent, B-40 per cent:

$= (0.6 \times 0.76 + 0.6 \times 0.32)^2\ 2.30 + (0.4)^2\ (4.88) + (0.4)^2 (5.67)$

$= (0.456 + 0.036)\ 2.30 + (0.16)\ (4.88) + (0.16)\ (5.67)$

$= 1.1316 + 0.7808 + 0.9072$

$=$ **2.8196.**

(c) Calculation of portfolio risk **A-70 per cent, B-30 per cent:**

$\sigma^2_p = (0.7 \times 0.76 + 0.7 \times 0.32)^2\ 2.30 + (0.3)^2\ (4.88) + (0.3)^2\ (5.67)$

$= (0.532 + 0.244)^2\ 2.30 + 0.4392 + 0.5103$

$= 0.5715 \times 2.30 + 0.9495$

$= 1.3144 + 0.9495$

$=$ **2.2639**

(d) Calculation of portfolio risk **A-80 per cent, B-20 per cent:**

$(0.8 \times 0.76 + 0.8 \times 0.32)^2\ 2.30 + (0.2)^2\ (4.88) + (0.2)^2 (5.67)$

$= (0.608 + 0.256)^2\ 2.30 + 0.1952 + 0.2268$

$= 1.7169 + 0.1952 + 0.2268$

$=$ **2.1389.**

(e) Calculation of portfolio risk **A-90 per cent, B-10 per cent:**

$\sigma^2_p = (0.9 \times 0.76 + 0.90 \times 0.32)^2\ 2.30 + (0.10)^2\ (4.88) + (0.10)^2\ (5.67)$

$= (0.684 + 0.288)^2\ 2.30 + 0.01\ (4.88) + (0.01)\ (5.67)$

$= 0.94\ (2.30) + 0.0488 + 0.0567$

$= 2.162 + 0.1055$

$=$ **2.267.**

(f) Calculation of portfolio risk **A-10 per cent, B-90 per cent:**

$\sigma^2_p = (0.10 \times 0.76 + 0.10 \times 0.32)^2\ 2.30 + (0.90)^2\ (4.88) + (0.90)^2\ (5.67)$

$= (0.076 + 0.032)^2\ 2.30 + 3.9528 + 4.5927$

$= (0.011664)\ 2.30 + 8.5455$

$= 0.026 + 8.5455$

$=$ **8.572.**

(g) Calculation of portfolio risk **A-20 per cent, B-80 per cent:**

$\sigma^2_p = (0.20 \times 0.76 + 0.20 \times 0.32)^2\ 2.30 + (0.8)^2\ (4.88) + (0.8)^2\ (5.67)$

$= (0.152 + 0.064)^2\ 2.30 + 0.64\ (4.88) + 0.64\ (5.67)$

$= 0.1073 + 3.123 + 3.6288$

$=$ **6.859.**

(h) Calculation of portfolio risk **A-30 per cent, B-70 per cent:**

$\boldsymbol{\sigma^2 p} = (0.30 \times 0.76 + 0.30 \times 0.32)^2\ 2.30 + (0.7)^2\ (4.88) + (0.7)^2\ (5.67)$

$$= (0.228 + 0.096)^2\, 2.30 + 0.49\,(4.88) + 0.49\,(5.67)$$
$$= 0.1049\,(2.30) + 2.3912 + 2.7783$$
$$= \mathbf{5.4208.}$$

(i) Calculation of portfolio risk **A-40 per cent, B-60 per cent:**

$$\sigma^2_p = (0.40 \times 0.76 + 0.40 \times 0.32)^2\, 2.30 + (0.6)^2\,(4.88) + (0.6)^2\,(5.67)$$
$$= (0.304 + 0.128)^2\, 2.30 + 1.7568 + 2.0412$$
$$= 0.186 \times 2.30 + 3.798$$
$$= 0.4278 + 3.798$$
$$= \mathbf{4.225.}$$

Single Stock

Portfolio means a combination of different kinds of financial assets. The portfolio may be added or deleted by a scrip, it may generate a series of corner portfolio. In a portfolio a number of scrips may be added or deleted.

A stock is combined with another stock, the minimum attainable risk and the lowest return is known as corner portfolio. Portfolio means, a combination of various financial assets for maximising returns and minimising the risk.

Sharpe's Optimal Portfolio

Stock market is a game of return and risk factors. An intelligent investor always desires to reduce risk and maximising the return. The yield of the portfolio depends upon the quality of securities introduced in the portfolio. **Sharpe** had provided a model for the selection of appropriate quality of securities in a portfolio. The selection of appropriate securities in the portfolio is directly associated to its excess return beta ratio.

$$\text{Sharpe's optimal portfolio} = \frac{R_i - R_f}{\beta_i}$$

R_i = Expected return on stock i

R_f = Return on a riskless asset

β_i = The change in the rate of return on stock.

Usually, all portfolios are built for the purpose of achieving desired returns. Some portfolios may generate more yields than their expected return, that return is called as **"excess return"**. The excess return of a portfolio can be arrived by the following equation:

Excess return = Expected return on the stock–Riskless rate of Interest.

The riskless rate of interest is accrued from Government securities or from treasury bills. Generally portfolio managers would like to include in the portfolio, those stocks who have excess return to beta ratios. Stocks will be ranked as per the excess return to beta measure. The **high rank** securities will be included in the portfolio by portfolio managers. The **sharpe optimal portfolio** theory reveal that the high rank securities should be selected to include in the portfolio with a **cut-off rate** and stocks with lower ratios are left off. The **cut-off point** is indicated by **C**. The cut-off point is computed on the basis of the following formula:

$$C_i \frac{\sigma_m^2 \sum_{i=1}^{N} \frac{(R_i - R_f)\beta_i}{\sigma_{ei}^2}}{1+\sigma_m^2 \sum_{i=1}^{N} \frac{\beta_i^2}{\sigma_{ei}^2}}$$

σ^2_m = Variance of the market index.

σ^2_{ei} = Stocks systematic risk.

Illustration

Mr. Kirit Palakat hold the portfolio. From the available information findout the sharpe optimal portfolio.

Security	*Mean Return* (R_i)	*Excess Return* $(R_i - R_f)$	*Beta* β	$\sigma 2_{ei}$ *Unsystematic Risk*	$R_i - R_f/B_i$ *Excess Return to Beta*
A	21	16	1.5	22	10.66
B	25	20	2.0	32	10.00
C	13	08	1.0	12	8.00
D	27	22	2.5	42	8.80
E	15	10	1.5	22	6.66
F	11	06	1.0	52	6.00
G	16	11	2.0	32	5.50

The riskless rate of asset is **5%** and the market variance is 10. Determine the cut-off point.

Solution

The calculation of cut-off rate is based on the following table:

Security	$\frac{R_i - R_f}{\beta_i}$	$\frac{(R_i - R_f) \times \beta_i}{\sigma^2_{ei}}$	$\sum_{i=1}^{N} \frac{(R_i - R_f)\beta_i}{\sigma^2_{ei}}$	$\frac{\beta i^2}{\sigma^2_{ei}}$	$\sum_{i=1}^{N} \frac{\beta_i^2}{\sigma^2_{ei}}$	*(i)*
(1)	(2)	(3)	(4)	(5)	(6)	(7)
A	10.66	1.09	1.09	0.100	0.100	5.45
B	10.00	1.25	2.34	0.125	0.225	7.20
C	8.00	0.66	3.00	0.083	0.308	7.35
D	8.80	1.309	4.309	0.148	0.456	7.75
E	6.66	0.68	4.989	0.102	0.558	7.58
F	6.00	0.11	5.09	0.019	0.577	7.39
G	5.50	0.68	5.77	0.125	0.701	7.19

For calculation of 3rd column of the table:

$$A = \frac{(R_i - R_f) \times \beta_i}{\sigma^2_{ei}} = \frac{16\,(1.5)}{22} = \frac{24}{22} = \mathbf{1.09}$$

$$B = \frac{20\,(2)}{32} = \frac{40}{32} = \mathbf{1.25}$$

$$C = \frac{8\,(1)}{12} = \frac{8}{12} = \mathbf{0.66}$$

$$D = \frac{22 \times 2.5}{42} = \frac{55}{42} = \mathbf{1.30}$$

$$E = \frac{10 \times 1.5}{22} = \frac{15}{22} = \mathbf{0.68}$$

$$F = \frac{6 \times 1.0}{52} = \frac{6}{52} = \mathbf{0.11}$$

$$G = \frac{11 \times 2.0}{32} = \frac{22}{32} = \mathbf{0.68}$$

Calculation of 7th column of the table:

$$\text{For security A} = \frac{10 \times 1.09}{1 + (10 \times 0.100)} = \frac{10.9}{2} = \mathbf{5.45}$$

$$\text{For security B} = \frac{10 \times 2.34}{1 + (10 \times 0.225)} = \frac{23.4}{3.25} = \mathbf{7.2}$$

$$\text{For security C} = \frac{10 \times 3.00}{1 + (10 \times 0.308)} = \frac{30}{4.08} = \mathbf{7.35}$$

$$\text{For security D} = \frac{10\times4.309}{1+(10\times0.456)} = \frac{43.09}{5.56} = \mathbf{7.75}$$

$$\text{For security E} = \frac{10\times4.989}{1+(10\times0.558)} = \frac{49.89}{6.58} = \mathbf{7.58}$$

$$\text{For security F} = \frac{10\times5.09}{1+(10\times0.577)} = \frac{50.90}{6.77} = \mathbf{7.39}$$

$$\text{For security G} = \frac{10\times5.77}{1+(10\times0.702)} = \frac{57.7}{8.02} = \mathbf{7.19}$$

The highest C_i value is taken as the cut-off point. The cut-off rate is **7.75**. The selection of scrip is the most important factor in determining the portfolio. After the selection of appropriate securities for the portfolio, the portfolio manager has to decide the quantum of amount to be invested. The portfolio manager should findout how much amount to be invested in each security. He should calculate the percentage of funds to be invested in each security can be computed by the formula:

$$X_i = \frac{Z_i}{\sum_{i=1}^{N} Z_i}$$

$$Z_i = \frac{\beta_i}{\sigma_{ei}^2}\left(\frac{R_i - R_f}{\beta_i} - c\right)$$

The optimal portfolio can also be used with short sales. As per the approach, the following formula is useful for calculation of Z value:

$$Z_i = \frac{\beta_i}{\sigma_{ei}^2}\left(\frac{R_i - R_f}{\beta_i} - c\right)$$

$$Z_i = \frac{1.5}{22}\left(\frac{16-7.75}{1.5}\right)$$

$$Z_i = \frac{1.5}{22}(5.5) = \frac{8.25}{22} = \mathbf{0.375}$$

$$Z_i = \frac{2}{32}(20-7.75) = \frac{2}{32}\times12.25 = \mathbf{0.76}$$

$$Z_3 = \frac{1.0}{12}\ (8\text{–}7.75) = \frac{1}{12}\ (0.25) = \mathbf{0.02}$$

$$Z_4 = \frac{2.5}{42} = (22\text{–}7.75) = 0.05 \times 14.25 = \mathbf{0.71}$$

$$Z_5 = \frac{1.5}{22}\ (10–7.75) = 0.068 \times 2.25 = \mathbf{0.153}$$

$$Z_6 = \frac{1.0}{52}\ (6–7.75) = 0.019 \times -1.75 = \mathbf{-0.03}$$

$$Z_7 = \frac{2}{32}\ (11–7.75) = 0.06 \times 3.25 = \mathbf{0.19}$$

= negative value shares should be sold out.

Review Problems

Illustration 1

Mr. Viresh Palakot hold the portfolio. He provides the market information regarding his portfolio.

	Stock	α	β	e_i
1.	Wipro	**-0.06**	+1.75	0.05
2.	Ranbaxy	+0.09	**-0.4**	0.00
3.	Essar Steels	.01	+1.25	0.12

(a) Market index have a return of **0.25** and a variance of **0.30**. As a portfolio manager which single stock would be preferred to own from the risk and return point of dimension.

(b) Interpret the e^2_i value and the value of Ranbaxy.

Solution

(a) Calculation of scrip value on the basis of **return:**

(i) return $R_i = \alpha_i + \beta_i R_m$

Wipro = –0.06 + (1.75 × 0.25) = 0.375

Ranbaxy = +0.09 + (–0.4 × 0.25) =-0.08

Essar Steels = 0.01 + (1.25 × 0.25) = 0.322.

The above analysis indicate that Wipro shows higher return than other stocks, Wipro stock can be selected.

On the basis of risk:

Risk = Systematic + Unsystematic

Systematic risk = β^2 × Variance of Index.

Wipro = $(1.75)^2$ × 0.25 = 0.7656

Ranbaxy = $(-0.4)^2$ × 0.25 = 0.0400

Essar Steels = $(1.25)^2$ × 0.25 = 0.3906.

Total risk = Systematic risk + Unsystematic

Wipro = 0.7656 + 0.05 = 0.8156
Ranbaxy = 0.0400 + 0.00 = 0.0400
Essar Steel = 0.3906 + 0.12 = 0.5106
From the **risk** basis Ranbaxy, has the lowest risk. If the investor prefer risk, Wipro has the highest risk component.

(b) The zero value of e^2_i in Ranbaxy stock indicates that the unsystematic risk is nil. The stock return is 9 per cent.

Illustration 2

Mr. Venkatesh Palakot holds the following portfolio. His portfolio consists of four stocks. The market return is 14 per cent and variance of 7 per cent.

(a) Calculate the expected return for a portfolio consisting of equal portion of stocks.
(b) Calculate the expected return consisting of 40, 30, 20, 10 per cent of proportions respectively.
(c) Calculate the expected return consisting of **45, 35, 10, 10** percent of proportions respectively.
(d) Calculate the expected return consisting of 50, 25, 15, 10 per cent respectively.

The following table gives data on four stocks:

Scrip	*Alpha*	*Variance Systematic*	*Unsystematic*
W	**–.08**	7	6
X	0.13	4	8
Y	0.00	5	3
Z	**–.18**	5	4

Solution

The expected return on portfolio can be computed by the following formula:

$$R_i = \sum_{i=1}^{N} X_i(\alpha_1 + \beta_i R_m)$$

All of the variables are known but β values are not given. Beta value should be fiundout.

Systematic risk = $\beta^2 \times$ Variance of Index.

W security

$7 = \beta^2 \times 7$

$$\beta^2 = \frac{7}{7}$$

$$\beta = \sqrt{\frac{7}{7}} = \sqrt{1} = 1$$

X security

Systematic risk = $\beta^2 \times$ Variance of Index.

$4 = \beta^2 \times 7$

$$\beta^2 = \frac{4}{7}$$

$$\beta = \sqrt{\frac{4}{7}} = \sqrt{0.57} = 0.75$$

Y security

$5 = \beta^2 \times 7$

$$\beta^2 = \frac{5}{7}$$

$$\beta = \sqrt{\frac{5}{7}} = \sqrt{0.71} = 0.84$$

Z security

$5 = \beta^2 \times 7$

$$\beta^2 = \frac{5}{7}$$

$$\beta = \sqrt{\frac{5}{7}} = \sqrt{0.71} = 0.84$$

ΣR (W) $R_i = R_f + \beta_i (R_m)$

W = – **0.08 + 1 (14)** = 13.92 per cent

X = 0.13 + (0.75 × 14) = 10.63 per cent

Y = 0.00 + (0.84 × 14) = 11.76 per cent

Z = –.18 + (0.84 × 14) = 11.58 per cent

(a) Calculation of expected return in proportion of equal asset allocation:

$$R_p = \sum_{i=1}^{N} X_i (\alpha_i + \beta_i R_m)$$

Proportion is equal among four scrips:

W = 0.25, X = 0.25, Y = 0.25, Z = 0.25

$R_p = 0.25 \times 13.92 + 0.25 \times 10.63 + 0.25 \times 11.76 + 0.25 \times 11.58$

$= 3.48 + 2.65 + 2.94 + 2.89$
$=$ **11.96 per cent.**

(b) Proportion of asset allocation:
W = 40, X = 30, Y = 20, Z = 10
$R_p = 0.40 \times 13.92 + 0.30 \times 10.63 + 0.20 \times 11.76 + 0.10 \times 11.58$
$= 5.568 + 3.189 + 2.352 + 1.158$
$=$ **12.26 per cent.**

(c) Proportion of asset allocation:
W = 45, X = 35, Y = 10, Z = 10
$R_p = 0.45 \times 13.92 + 0.35 \times 10.63 + 0.10 \times 11.76 + 0.10 \times 11.58$
$= 6.264 + 3.720 + 1.176 + 1.158$
$=$ **12.318 per cent.**

(d) Proportion of asset allocation:
W = 50%, X = 25%, Y = 15%, Z = 10%
$R_p = 0.50 \times 13.92 + 0.25 \times 10.63 + 0.15 \times 11.76 + 0.10 \times 11.58$
$R_p = 6.96 + 2.657 + 1.764 + 1.158$
$=$ **12.53 per cent.**

Illustration 3

Mr. Dinesh wants to build a portfolio with four stocks. The market return is 13. Market return variance is 28. The investment is spread equally over the four stocks. Find out the portfolio return and portfolio variance.

Company	α	β	*Residual Variance*
Geetha	0.19	0.95	47.15
Seetha	2.50	1.39	134.15
Kavitha	1.49	1.75	198.28
Savitha	2.54	1.19	53.98

(a) Calculate the portfolio return, if the investment is allocated to four scrips as 30, 30, 20, 20 per cent.

(b) Calculate the portfolio return, if the investment is allocated to four scrips in the ratio of 20, 20, 30, 30 per cent.

(c) Calculate the portfolio return, if the combination is 40, 40, 10, 10 per cent.

Solution

Calculation of portfolio return:

$$R_p = \sum_{i=1}^{N} X_i(\alpha_i + \beta_i R_m)$$

Return on Geetha scrip = 0.19 + 0.95 (13) = 12.54 per cent
Return on Seetha scrip = 2.50 + 1.39 (13) = 20.57 per cent
Return on Kavitha scrip = 1.49 + 1.75 (13) = 24.24 per cent
Return on Savitha scrip = 2.54 + 1.19 (13) = 18.01 per cent.

$R_p = 12.54 \times 0.25 + 20.57 \times 0.25 + 24.24 \times 0.25 + 18.01 \times 0.25$
$= 3.135 + 5.142 + 6.06 + 4.502 = 18.83$ per cent.

Portfolio variance = σ^2_p = Variance of the index + Residual variance
variance of the index $\sigma^2_{m} =$

$$\left[\sum^{N}_{=1} (x_i\beta_i)^2 \sigma^2_m\right] + \left[\sum^{N}_{i=1} (x^2_i e^2_i)\right]$$

$(0.25 \times 0.95 + 0.25 \times 1.39 + 0.25 \times 1.75 + 0.25 \times 1.19)^2$
$= (0.2375 + 0.3475 + 0.4375 + 0.2975)^2$
$= (1.32)^2$
$= 1.7424$
$= 1.7424 \times$ Market return variance
$= 1.7424 \times 28 = 48.78$

Residual Variance

$$\sum^{N}_{i=1} X^2 ei^2$$

$=(0.25)^2 (47.15) + (0.25)^2 (134.15) + (0.25)^2 (198.28) + (0.25)^2 (53.28)$
$=2.94 + 8.38 + 12.39 + 3.33 = 27.04.$

$\sigma^2_p = 48.78 + 27.04 = 75.82$
$\sigma_p = \sqrt{75.82} = 8.70$

(a) **Calculation of portfolio return with asset allocation:** 30%, 30%, 20%, 20%

$R_p = 12.54 \times 0.30 + 20.57 \times 0.30 + 24.24 \times 0.20 + 18.01 \times 0.20$
$= 3.762 + 6.171 + 4.848 + 3.602$
$= 18.38$ per cent.

(b) **Calculation of portfolio return with asset allocation 20, 20, 30, 30 per cent:**

$R_p = 12.54 \times 0.20 + 20.57 \times 0.20 + 24.24 \times 0.30 + 18.01 \times 0.30$
$= 2.508 + 4.114 + 7.27 + 5.40$
$= 19.29$ per cent.

(c) **Calculation of portfolio return with asset allocation 40, 40, 10, 10 per cent:**

$R_p = 12.54 \times 0.40 + 20.57 \times 0.40 + 24.24 \times 0.10 + 18.01 \times 0.10$
$= 5.013 + 8.228 + 2.424 + 1.801 = 17.46$ per cent.

Illustration 4

Mr. Harish is constructing a optimum portfolio. He intends to consider five securities. The market return forecast reveals that it would be **15 per cent** for the next two years with the market variance of **12 per cent.** The riskless rate of return is 6 per cent.

	Company	α	β	σ^2_{ei}
1.	Charity	3.80	1.05	9.40
2.	Manish	0.68	1.32	5.97
3.	Arman	0.49	1.01	9.82
4.	Arif	**-0.30**	1.26	5.44
5.	Sarath	0.53	0.80	4.57

Solution

Calculation of expected return for individual security:

Ri $= \alpha + \beta R_m$

Charith $= 3.80 + 1.05\ (15) = 19.55$ per cent

Manish $= 0.68 + 1.32\ (15) = 20.48$ per cent

Arman $= 0.49 + 1.01\ (15) = 15.64$ per cent

Arif $= -\mathbf{0.30} + 1.26\ (15) = 18.60$ per cent

Sarath $= 0.53 + 0.80\ (15) = 12.53$ per cent.

Scrip	$\frac{R_i - R_f}{\beta}$	$\frac{(R_i - R_f)}{\sigma^2 ei}$	$\frac{\beta_i^2}{\sigma^2 ei}$	$\sum_{i=1}^{N} \frac{(R_i - R_f)\beta_i}{\sigma^2 ei}$	$\frac{\beta_i}{\sigma^2 ei}$	C_i
(1)	(2)	(3)	(4)	(5)	(6)	(7)
Charity	12.90	1.513	0.11	1.513	0.11	7.82
Manish	10.96	3.201	0.29	4.714	0.40	9.75
Arman	9.54	0.991	0.10	5.705	0.50	9.78
Arif	10.00	2.918	0.29	8.623	0.79	9.87
Sarath	8.16	1.143	0.14	9.766	0.93	9.63

$$\text{Calculation of C point} = C_i = \frac{\sigma_m^2 \sum_{i=1}^{N} \frac{(R_i - R_f)}{\sigma^2 ei} \times \beta_i}{1 + \sigma_m^2 \sum_{i=1}^{N} \frac{\beta_i^2}{\sigma^2 ei}}$$

$$C_1 = \frac{12 \times 1.513}{1 + 12 \times 0.11} = \frac{18.156}{2.32} = 7.82$$

$$C_2 = \frac{12 \times 4.714}{1 + 12 \times 0.40} = \frac{56.56}{5.80} = 9.75$$

$$C_3 = \frac{12 \times 5.705}{1+12\times0.50} = \frac{68.46}{7} = 9.78$$

$$C_4 = \frac{12 \times 8.623}{1+12\times0.79} = \frac{103.47}{10.48} = 9.87$$

$$C_5 = \frac{12 \times 9.766}{1+12\times0.93} = \frac{117.19}{12.16} = 9.63$$

The proportions of stocks in the optimal portfolios can be computed by the following formula:

$$X_i = \frac{Z_i}{N_i(\underset{i=1}{N})} \quad \text{scrip 1, 2, 3, 4 and 5}$$

$$Z_i = \frac{\beta_i}{\sigma^2 ei}\left(\frac{R_i - R_f}{\beta_i} - C\right)$$

$Z_1 = 0.11\ (12.90–9.87) =$ 0.3333	= 0.33/0.79	41%
$Z_2 = 0.29\ (10.96–9.87) =$ 0.3161	= 0.32/0.79	40%
$Z_3 = 0.10\ (9.54–9.87) =$ –0.33	= –0.33/0.79	–4%
$Z_4 = 0.29\ (10.00–9.87) =$ 0.420	= 0.420/0.79	53%
$Z_5 = 0.14\ (8.16–9.87) =$ –0.2394	= –0.24/0.79	–30%
0.797		

Illustration 5

Mr. Giri wants to built a portfolio. He received Rs. 15.00 lakhs from his pension fund. The risk free rate of interest is **6 per cent** and the market return variance is 12. Find out optimal portfolio?

Security	*Expected return*	*Beta*	σ^2_{ei}
M	17	1.25	35
N	14	1.75	25
O	13	2.25	45
P	10	1.05	15
Q	11	1.25	25
R	16	1.75	15

Solution

The securities should be arranged on the basis of highest return to beta to the lowest.

Security	R_i	β_i	R_i–R_f	R_i–R_i/β_i
M	17	1.25	11	8.80
N	14	1.75	8	4.57
O	13	2.25	7	3.11
P	10	1.05	4	3.80
Q	11	1.25	5	4.00
R	16	1.75	10	5.71

Ranked Table

Security	$\frac{R_i - R_f}{\beta}$	$\frac{(R_i - R_f)}{\sigma^2 ei}$	$\frac{\beta_1^2}{\sigma^2 ei}$	$\sum_{i=1}^{N} \frac{(R_i - R_f)\beta_i}{\sigma^2 ei}$	$\sum_{i=1}^{N} \frac{\beta_i^2}{\sigma^2 ei}$	C_i
M	8.80	0.39	0.044	0.39	0.044	3.06
R	5.71	1.16	0.204	1.55	0.248	4.67
N	4.57	0.56	0.122	2.11	0.370	4.65
Q	4.00	0.25	0.062	2.36	0.432	4.57
P	3.80	0.28	0.073	2.64	0.505	4.48
O	3.11	0.35	0.112	2.99	0.617	4.26

$$C_i = \frac{\sigma_m^2 \sum_{i=1}^{N} \left(\frac{R_i - R_f}{\sigma^2 ei} \right) \times \beta_i}{1 + \sigma_m^2 \sum_{i=1}^{N} \frac{\beta_i^2}{\sigma^2 ei}}$$

$$C_{iM} = \frac{12 \times 0.39}{1 + 12(0.44)} = \frac{4.68}{1.528} = 3.06$$

$$C_{iR} = \frac{12 \times 1.55}{1 + 12 \times 0.248} = \frac{18.6}{3.976} = 4.67$$

$$C_{iN} = \frac{12 \times 2.11}{1 + 12 \times 0.370} = \frac{25.32}{5.44} = 4.65$$

$$C_{iQ} = \frac{12 \times 2.36}{1 + 12 \times 0.432} = \frac{28.32}{6.184} = 4.57$$

$$C_{iP} = \frac{12 \times 2.64}{1 + 12 \times 0.505} = \frac{31.68}{7.06} = 4.48$$

$$C_{iO} = \frac{12 \times 2.99}{1 + 12 \times 0.617} = \frac{35.88}{8.404} = 4.26$$

Cut-off point is 4.67

The optimal portfolio consists of securities M and R. The proportion are:

$$X_1 = \frac{Z_i}{\sum_{i=1}^{N} Z_i}$$

$$Z_i = \frac{\beta_i}{\sigma ei}\left(\frac{R_i - R_f}{\beta_i} - c\right)$$

$Z_M = 0.044\ (8.80–4.67) = 0.181$
$Z_R = 0.204\ (5.71–4.67) = 0.212$

$$Z_M = \frac{0.181}{0.181 + 0.212}$$

$$= \frac{0.181}{0.393} = 0.4605 \text{ or } 46.05 \text{ per cent}$$

$$Z_R = \frac{0.212}{0.393} = 0.5394 \text{ or } 53.94 \text{ per cent}$$

The fund should be allocated on "M" security is **46.05 per cent** and on "N" security is **53.94 per cent.**

Illustration 6

Mr. Kaushik Palakot holds the different portfolios at his control. From the following information advise the investor as a portfolio manager to select best portfolio.

Portfolio	*Expected Return*	σ
1	12	6
2	14	9
3	15	7
4	18	14
5	22	16

(a) The risk free rate is **6 per cent** which portfolio is the best?
(b) Is it possible to earn 14 per cent return with σ of 5 per cent?
(c) If σ is 14 per cent what would be the expected return?

Solution

Calculation of return to risk ratio can be computed as follows:

Portfolio	$\Sigma R\text{-}R_f/\sigma$
1	12–6 = 6/6 = **1.00**
2	14–6 = 8/9 = **0.88**

3 $15–6 = 9/7 = \mathbf{1.28}$

4 $18–6 = 12/14 = \mathbf{0.85}$

5 $22–6 = 16/16 = \mathbf{1.00}$

(a) Among the portfolios, third portfolio yields highest portfolio return.

(b) If $\sigma = 5$, then the best portfolio will yield.

$\Sigma R_p = 6 + 5\ (1.28)$

$\Sigma r_p = 6 + 6.4 = 12.4$ per cent.

No, it may not possible to get 14 per cent return.

(c) If σ, is 14 per cent the expected return can be calculated as follows:

$\Sigma R = 6{+}14\ (1.28) = 6{+}17.92 = 23.92$ per cent.

G. Portfolio Selection—Diversification

Portfolio means a combination of different kinds of financial assets. Financial assets are available in the stock market. Construction of a portfolio is not a easy task for the portfolio manager. In the stock market, thousands of shares are available. Selection of a share from the pool of thousand shares is a difficult task. The selection from available shares means the picking up of unpolished diamond and gems. Some shares are unexposed, unpolished, undervalued, low profile, but with strong financial resources are available in the market, but picking up of such shares, gems, diamonds are not a easy task. Identification of growth oriented shares are possible by only a skilled, talented, knowledgeable persons. Generally in the stock exchanges, all listed shares are traded as normally, but all listed shares may not be easily sold at a time. Some companies are working silently with low profile, but they never advertise themselves and getting substantial profits. Such company shares are attracted by a skilled persons only. Hence these shares will become tomorrow's **blue-chip scrips**. Portfolio management is a specialized activity and it needs a lot of skill and talent. For efficient construction of portfolio is based on the following aspects:

(a) Selection of a portfolio.

(b) Diversification of portfolio.

(a) Selection of a Portfolio

Portfolio is a combination of different kinds of assets. The selection of different kinds of financial assets into portfolio, is based on many factors. In Bombay Stock Exchange, **4800** scrips are listed for trading, but it is very difficult to choose the best stocks. The professional investor or an experienced portfolio manager can only do this task more effectively, otherwise the investor may burnt his fingers in the stock market. Even sometimes, the experienced person may not expect the stock market events. The selection of assets depends upon the skills and talent of the investor. Identification of growth stock is the most important and crucial factor in selection of scrips. **90 per cent** of the risk will be escaped with the right selection of **appropriate growth stock**. The right stock should be selected at reasonable price. Buying price is another important factor in built up of the construction of the portfolio.

The selection of a portfolio depends upon the various objectives of the investor. The financial objectives of the common investors are presented below:

(i) Current Income.
(ii) Growth Income.

(i) **Current Income**—If the investor desires at present income from the portfolio, it should be built up with 60 per cent of the investment in **debt** and **40 per cent** in **equities.** The mix of two different kind of assets depends upon the discretion of the investor. If the portfolio is dominated by **Debt instruments,** it is called as **Debt portfolio.** If the portfolio is dominated by equity, it may be called as **equity** portfolio. Debt portfolio generates more present income through interest. Short-term debt instruments provides regular income in addition to the safety of the principal amount. Hence the investor prefers regular income along with the safety of the principal amount. **Capital appreciation** is not available for the short-term debt financial instruments.

(ii) **Growth Income**—A group of investors are interested to build up a good portfolio for not at current income aspect. They draw financial plans for their future. They give priority to the capital appreciation of the financial assets. Such investors will built the portfolio with **60 per cent to 100 per cent** equities and 10 per cent to 40 per cent debt instruments. The debt component of the portfolio provides tax exemptions to the investor. Capital appreciation is available another part of the portfolio. Hence the both of these combinations may stimulate the value of the portfolio. Investment in real estate is a good source of avenue for the long-term investors. Real estate provides a fast rate of capital appreciation but it lacks liquidity. Investment in shares occupies an important role in build up of a portfolio. Investors who prefer to invest for the long-term period is basically depends upon **"equity portfolio"**. The portfolio is built up with 100 per cent. Therefore, the risk is very high but returns are also more and useful for long-term nature. The aim of the investor is to get the substantial amount of money at desired long period of time.

(b) Diversification

Stock market is a reflection of various elements. It provides various kinds of financial instruments. Once the asset mix and ratio is determined the construction of portfolio will be commenced as per the vision of the investors choice. The next step is diversification of portfolio. Diversification is a technique of reducing risk element. It is a process of selection of assets of different kinds of instruments. Pool of all assets will create **Total risk**. Diversification reduces the **unsystematic risk** and promotes the returns for a given level of risk in portfolio. Unsystematic risk can be reduced through diversification into a number of companies and a number of various industries. Selection of a scrip from a industry is the main important aspect in the built up of a portfolio. The diversification can be done any of the following ways:

(a) Diversification in different kinds of assets. (Real estate, Gold, Government securities and corporate securities).
(b) Diversification on the basis of different kinds of financial **Instruments** (bonds, debentures, government securities and equity).
(c) Diversification on the basis of different Industries. (Pharmaceuticals, Information Technology, Chemicals, Engineering, Plastic, Cement, Steel, Heavy machinery).
(d) Diversification on the basis of companies. (New companies, growing companies).

Diversification means **"not putting all eggs in one basket"**. It is always better to invest in two companies/industries. A single company/ industry is more **risky** than two companies or industries. Proper diversification involves two companies or industries who fluctuate the prices sharply in different ways of each other or in the same direction. The diversification policy involves as many baskets as possible to reach the financial goals of the investors. It is better to have as many as companies and industries in one's portfolio. The diversification of portfolios can be studied in the following aspects:

(a) Random Diversification.
(b) Global diversification.

(a) Random Diversification

The fundamental aim of the diversification is to reduce the total risk of the portfolio. But it is not possible to reduce or manage or escape the **total risk.** Unsystematic risk can be reduced through diversification. The component of total risk can be shown as follows.

Total risk = Systematic risk + Unsystematic risk.

The return of the portfolio is always chased by the risk component. Unsystematic risk can be reduced by a proper diversification. In the modern technology, the markets are developing at a faster growth. The monitoring and evaluation of portfolio continuously requires a lot of skills about the stock market activities. It is a costly affairs to monitor and evaluation of portfolio. A proper random diversification is based on the following aspects:

(i) Once the asset mix and ratio is finalised, the next step is selection of proper financial asset. The selection of scrip should be done on the basis of **"Randomness"**.

(ii) The risk can be reduced with the adequate quantum of funds available. A limited amount of fund may not reduce the risk levels. If the higher amount of money is available, there will be diseconomies and difficulty of supervision monitoring and evaluation will increase risk again. Hence there should be optimum amount of fund available, in order to reduce the risk through diversification.

(iii) Diversification means, expansion of the existing portfolio or alteration of the portfolio without any flow of money in it. All traditional approaches stress on diversification. This involves as many industries and companies as possible to get the best results. A large number of scrips in wide areas of industries may not reduce risk at all times. But the selection of right kind of securities are important factor in diversification of portfolio.

(iv) There are so many approaches to reduce the risk levels of a given portfolio. **Markowitz** diversification suggest that, there should not be many or less shares. But there is a need for a right number of securities in the portfolio. He suggested a **10-16** companies may create a good portfolio. The aim of the portfolio is to maximise the return and minimise the risk to the investor.

(b) Global Diversification

Diversification of portfolio provides many benefits to the investors. The importance of diversification cannot be ignored by the portfolio managers. Diversification can be adopted by all developed countries in order to achieve their financial goals. As a globalisation process gaining more important on the worldwide basis, portfolio managers started investing in **Foreign bonds, securities and other instruments**. They apply diversification technique to the foreign assets containing the portfolio. In the **digital economy** global diversification is based on the following aspects:

(i) Globalisation policy created a good environment in the international market.

(ii) Information, communication and technology created a revolutionary waves in the global market. Distance between two nations have been reduced drastically. Trading in global market is based on "a click of mouse". Transfer of funds from one nation to another because very easy. Access to Internet is made easy for business transactions. The International Financial Markets have been expanded exponentially.

(iii) International financial markets are based on foreign exchange currencies. The returns on exchange is more than that of domestic markets. Returns in local currencies of some foreign countries are higher than in domestic markets.

(iv) International financial markets consists of economic trends, business conditions and profitability factors varies from one country to another country. The companies performance, financial aspects such as EPS, PE ratio, PBT, PBDAT, Net profit ratio plays an important and crucial role in the portfolio management.

(v) Global investment is a new business strategy to the **Foreign Institutional Investors**. Global markets provide lower risk component to the portfolio. The domestic market contains high risk component than global market. The degree of volatility, risks vary among the countries and in different degree and the possibility of high correlation will be low. Hence the global markets are more beneficial for the diversification of portfolio. The inclusion of foreign investment in portfolio may enhance the efficiency levels of the financial assets.

(vi) It is general practice that, many global portfolio managers prefer to invest in Indians market. The Indian portfolio managers can invest in International investment avenues.

Risk in Global Markets

Stock markets are functioning on the basis of Economic and political environment of the nation. Every country has its own economic and political policy of the government. The functioning of the corporate sector is influenced by the government policies. Hence different countries have different policies which will influence the International companies functioning. Hence the political and economic aspects may create uncertainties in the market. The global market transactions will be settled through **Foreign currency**. The foreign exchange always fluctuate in the international markets. The currency exchange risk is high in the global markets. The volatile in the foreign exchange market may pose danger to larger profits. The risk levels will be increased in the portfolio. The taxation of different countries may leads to **double taxation**. The **Information** is the most powerful element in the stock market. Information decides the return of the security. A capture of information in advance may lead to get substantial profits. Access to information of foreign countries is difficult and foreign accounting and reporting systems differ. All of the above risk factors reveal that international diversification as desirable with some little level of risk management for the portfolio. There will be differences in financial parameters such as **EPS, P/E ratio, Market capitalization. Inflation levels, Gross Domestic product** *etc.*

H. Capital Market Theory

Risk and Return is the game of stock market. The aim of the common investor is to get maximum return with **less risk**. All approaches in the stock market reveal about the risk and return management. Capital market theory is one of the traditional approach to study about the portfolio management. **Capital Market Theory** is an extension of **Markowitz** theory. It explains about the relationship between **risk and return**. It is focussed on build up of **efficient portfolio**. It is based on the following **assumptions**:

(a) All investors have same expectations with accepted level of risk.
(b) Personal tax is assumed as **zero**.

(c) Investors decisions are purely based on risk and return relationship.

(d) Market is based on perfect competition and no one can influence share price in the market.

(e) There are no transaction costs.

(f) Investors can borrow/lend at riskless rate of interest.

(g) Investors can buy and sell securities for any amount of shares without limit.

All of the above assumption are based for capital market theory. But some are un-realistic provide basis for built up of an efficient portfolio. Lending and borrowing at riskless rate of interest is helpful in construction of efficient portfolio. The riskless rate of interest fund may leverage the portfolio. Financial cost will be very low due to access to riskless rate of interest fund. The **Capital Market Theory** is based on the following formula:

$$R_p = XR_m + (1-x)\, R_f$$

R_p = Expected return on portfolio.

X = Per cent of funds invested in risky portfolio.

1 – x = Per cent of funds invested in riskless asset.

R_m = Expected return on risky portfolio.

R_f = Expected return on riskless asset.

Summary

Stock market is a highly volatile market. Portfolio is a combination of different kinds of financial assets. Risk plays an important role in the stock market. Strategy is a plan for achieving goal. The earning capacity of the financial asset can be measured through time factor. Diversification reduces risk. Risk can be classified as systematic and unsystematic risk. Beta is percent change in the scrip return divided by the percentage change in the market return. Portfolio management is a professional assignment. Speculation is the oxygen to the stock markets. Construction of portfolio can be done in traditional and modern approach. Traditional approach considers the needs of the client. Modern approach focuses an equity based portfolios. Arbitrage price theory is an equilibrium model of asset pricing. Modern portfolio theory gives top priority to select the best scrips in portfolio. Return is a reward to the investor. Markowitz model is associated with the concept of risk measurement. Markowitz theory is based on diversification. Capital asset pricing method deals with the relationship between risk and return factor. Sharpe has developed a simplified model to analyse the portfolio. Portfolio selection is an important factor in the selection of securities. The selection of a portfolio depends upon current income and growth income. Diversification of portfolios depends upon the aspects, Random diversification and Global diversification. Capital market theory is an extension of Markowitz theory. The capital market theory explains about relationship between risk and return factors.

Questions

1. What is portfolio? What are the basics of portfolio management?
2. What is budget? Explain the importance of finance act with regard to making investment decisions.
3. What are the recent trends in Banking and Capital Market sector?
4. Explain about the traditional approach of portfolio theory?
5. What is arbitrage portfolio theory?
6. Write about modern portfolio theory? Explain the importance of Beta factor in modern approach.
7. What is diversification of a portfolio? Explain the importance of Markowitz Theory.
8. What is capital asset pricing theory? What are the basic assumption CAPM?
9. Distinguish between CAPM and Arbitrage price theory?
10. Explain the Sharpe Index model. How can be arrive at the optimum portfolio?
11. What is portfolio selection? Explain the importance of diversification with reference to selection of a best portfolio.

UNIT - IV

- Portfolio Performance
  - (a) Portfolio Evaluation
  - (b) Treynor Performance Index
  - (c) Sharpe Performance Index
  - (d) Jensens Performance Index
  - (e) Portfolio Revision

INTRODUCTION

Portfolio means a blend of mix of different kinds of financial assets. A combination of different types of instruments will pool for the yield of maximum returns. Minimising **risk** and maximising the **return** is the aim of portfolio. The returns from the stock market one is based on various factors. Stock market is a game of risk and return factors. The portfolio performance is based on the quality of assets introduced in it. Portfolio manager will evaluate the performance and identifies the advantages and disadvantages. The evolution provides an excellent feed back about the performance to evolve better management strategy. Evolution of portfolio is a continous process the portfolio should be monitored continuously. Generally individual investors cannot get the experticism of portfolio managers. Mutual funds have the chance to appoint the **portfolio managers**. The managed portfolios are known as **mutual funds**. There are various mutual funds available in the capital market. Capital market is a reflection of various organs in the prevailing market. The following information gives an idea about the concept of mutual funds.

Mutual Funds

Mutual Fund is association of small investors. All investors will pool their savings in order to get desired financial goals. Mutual fund is an investment vehicle that collects money from the investors to build up a good portfolio. Mutual fund will pool the money to purchase stock, bonds or other securities. An investor can participate in mutual funds by purchasing desired units. An investor, who purchased the units from the mutual fund is known as **"unit holder"**. Each unit in the mutual fund is assured by a diversified pool of assets. The pool of all unit holders money will deploy in the stock market. The pool of money is known as **corpus fund**. The corpus fund will be managed efficiently in order to earn more returns from the stock market. The unit holders of the mutual fund always expect reasonable return from their investment. The pool of financial resources are managed by portfolio managers. The portfolio managers advice, expertiscm is only available to **Mutual funds, High Networth Individuals and corporates only**. It is not possible to get these services for individual investors. Hence the mutual funds are providing best skills and expertism of the portfolio managers to earn more returns. The units of the mutual fund will be listed in all stock exchanges in the country. They will be traded in the stock exchanges regularly on par with the equity shares. The units in the stock market will be traded on the basis of **"Net asset value"** of the fund. The **NAV** is more important in the mutual fund industry. The Net Asset Value is determined by the performance of portfolio. The pool of assets will generate revenues to the mutual fund. The mutual fund will pass the gain or loss to the investors after deducting the **administrative expenses and Investment consultancy fee**. The gains of the fund will be distributed to the unit holders in the form of **dividend** or reinvestment in the fund to generate further gains. The small investors will get high skilled best expertiscm and talents of the portfolio manager. The mutual fund will charge a commission or fee from the investors is known as **load factor**. The mutual fund may be with or without a load factor. Mutual fund industry continues to be a marginal player on the Indian stock market. The equity assets it manages are a just over **2 per cent** of the total market capitalisation. The equity assets under the management of Indian mutual funds added to over **Rs. 38,000 crore** at the end of **March 2005**, up sharply from over **Rs. 11,000 crore** at the end of **March 2003**. The meagre stake of the mutual fund industry is in keeping with the general trend of declining retail interest in equities. From nearly **15 per cent** in the early **1990s**, the share of equities in financial savings is down to less than **2 per cent** now. The investors burnt their fingers in many scams, continue to exit from equities at every opportunity.[1]

Indian stock markets have seen a record breaking rally that was largely fuelled by huge inflow of **dollars,** from overseas investors. Domestic institutions and banks have to emerge bigger and increase their stake in Indian companies to counter the dominance of **Foreign Institutional Investors**. The following table will reveal about the stock holding by different players in the market.

1. "An evershare", *The Economic Times*, 26-4-05, p. 7.

Free Float Stock Market Portfolio[1]

(Rs in crores)

P/s	Market Capitalisation	per cent
(a) Foreign Institutional Investors	2,14,835	29.99
(b) Indian public	1,93,887	27.07
(c) Banks, Financial Institutions & Insurance	1,01,800	14.21
(d) Private companies	53,429	7.46
(e) Mutual funds & UTI	49,094	6.85
(f) Others	67,471	9.42
(g) NRIs and OCBs.	35,788	5.00
Total free float market capitalisation	**7,16,305**	**100.00**

The performance of mutual funds an be observed through **"Net Asset Value"**. The **NAV** is the barometer to review the performance of the fund. The recent performance of the mutual fund has caught at the end of the interest rate cycle. Mutual funds can be categorised as **Debt and Income** funds. **Debt fund** build in better mechanisms to counter the volatility on account of changes in interest rates. Debt fund has turned in a piddly return of less than **one per cent** over the last one year. Debt specialty as a category has recorded a negligible gain over the year[2]. There are three types of funds that are better suited to a rising interest rate environment than an ordinary debt/Income fund. **(a) Fixed maturity plans, (b) Floating rate funds, (c) Dynamic debt funds**. Fixed maturity plans seek to lock in the investor till the maturity of the fund. FMPs invest in debt securities that themselves are maturing towards the end of the funds tenure. This enables the fund manager to reasonably estimate the return that he would be able to generate. **Floating rate funds** invest the money in floating rate instruments that carry fixed rates of interest. The advantage with this strategy in the current environment is that the interest rates on the securities held by the fund get revised after fixed intervals. This enables the funds portfolio to earn more as and when interest rates rise. Floating rate funds are essentially structured to earn from receipts of interest coupon rather than from change in the underlying price of security. Funds investing in floating rate instruments also tend to have a certain percentage of their portfolio in fixed rate instruments. **Dynamic debt funds**, also popularly known as **flexi funds,** allow themselves considerable play. Long-term debt securities are more

1. "Rupee rich", *The Economic Times, Investor's Guide,* 14-2-05, p. 1.
2. "Broaden your horizon". *The Economic Times*, 24-4-05, p. 10.

significantly impacted by interest rate changes than short-term debt securities. Such funds allow themselves to shift completely between to long-term or short- term depending upon the situation in the market. In a raising interest rate environment, the fund will typically cut down exposure to long-term paper and transfer money to the shortened. This prevents interest rate fluctuations from having a significant negative impact on the fund. The fund manager has to make the right calls at the right time.[1]

Financial Performance of Short-Term Debt Mutual Fund Schemes

Name of the Scheme	*Returns (%)* 1 Month	3 Month	6 Month	1 Year	Since launch
1. Prudential ICICI short-term	0.65	1.65	3.44	5.28	6.88
2. Alliance short-term fund-Growth plan	0.58	1.30	2.50	4.67	5.94
3. Templeton India short-term Income plan	0.56	1.63	2.73	4.28	6.45
4. Principal Inc short-term growth plan	0.54	1.49	2.80	4.80	6.29
5. Reliance short-term fund growth	0.53	1.62	3.13	5.17	.6.29
6. UTI Liquid short-term regular plan growth	0.49	1.56	2.80	4.55	4.92
7. ING vyshya Income short	0.48	1.48	2.58	4.76	6.12
8. JM short-term fund growth	0.47	1.36	2.62	4.56	6.44
9. Kotak Mahindra bond short-term plan-growth	0.47	1.35	2.65	4.42	6.18
10. Sundaram select debt short-term asset plan growth	0.46	1.21	2.32	4.73	5.97
11. Birla bond plus-Retail growth	0.45	1.50	2.84	4.57	6.42
12. HDFC short-term plan growth	0.45	1.39	5.47	3.72	5.98
13. HSBC Income short-term plan growth	0.45	1.39	2.45	3.99	5.15
14. Grindlays Super saver income fund short-term growth	0.43	1.36	2.35	3.63	6.76
15. Tata short-term bond fund growth	0.42	1.35	2.70	4.94	6.20
16. Deutsche short maturity fund growth	0.4	1.46	2.74	4.35	5.6
17. Can short-term plan growth	0.34	1.54	2.50	4.80	4.89
18. Chola freedom income short-term growth	0.31	0.91	1.77	3.49	5.96
19. Sahara short-term plan growth	0.28	1.03	2.02	4.42	6.17
20. Manglam NRI Investment short-term bond fund growth plan	0.16	0.56	1.22	2.48	2.5

Further mutual funds can also be classified as **open ended and close end schemes**. In the open end schemes, units are sold and bought continuously. These units are available at any time and will be repurchased

1. "Quick gains", *The Economic Times*, 24-4-05, p. 10.

by the fund management. The price of the units is based on its NAV. The NAV indicates the financial performance of the scheme. The net asset value is calculated on a daily or weekly basis. In the **close end fund,** the scheme is available for a specified period of time only. It is open for a limited period only. The investor has to contribute the money during the offer period only. It has a fixed number of units outstanding. These units are listed in the stock exchange like other securities. The units are available in the stock exchange either for sale or buy. The units will be traded on the flow of stock exchange. The unit prices will be allotted in the stock exchange. Mutual funds are becoming more popular in the investor's community. They provide the following advantages to the investors:

(a) Expert Advice
(b) Risk Reduction
(c) Liquidity
(d) Regulation
(e) Low Cost
(f) Flexibility

(a) Expert advice

Mutual fund is a vehicle to pool the small savings of the investors. The pool amount of resources is called as **corpus fund**. The fund is a combination and collection of small savings from the investors. The investors are scattered throughout the country and provide contribution by way of purchase of units. The pool of small savings will form a large amount of asset base. **For example:** Master gain-92, the scheme was managed by the UTI with an amount of **Rs. 4800 crores**. The huge amount of money collected by the mutual fund will be managed by efficient, highly talented, skilled managers with a professional out look. The appointed of skilled persons involves higher cost to the individual investors, but it is very convenient to the mutual fund. Hence the best advises, guidance, suggestions are available to the mutual fund. A highly skilled group of portfolio managers works for the achievement of the financial dreams of the millions of the investors. The mutual fund is a voluntary body established with non-profit motive to render the best services to the unit holders. The fund is managed by an excellent portfolio manager with backed by a strong research team. Mutual funds also appoint equity researchers to findout the unexplored scrips from the stock market. They always works for unpolished **diamonds, Jems** from the stock market. They scan the market information and built up a good portfolio. Portfolio is a combination of different kinds of financial assets. The management of a wide range of financial instruments requires a scientific research based decisions. A strong research approach is necessary for making investment decisions for the crores of the amount of the investors. Hence the individual investors will not get all these experts advice. He will enjoy all these advises, suggestions by purchasing units of the mutual fund.

(b) Risk reduction

Mutual funds collect a large amount of money from millions of investors. The pool of small savings leads to a higher capital base. The large amount of money collected from the investors will be deployed in the stock market. The funds will be distributed for construction of an ideal portfolio. Portfolio management minimise **risk** and maximise **return**. Stock market is a game of risk and return. **Risk** is a common phenomenon in the stock market and return is always chased by risk. Stock market is a play ground for the **risk and return elements. Return** is accelator and **risk is speed breaker**. Return is **Jam** and risk is **ginger.** The efficiency of the stock market is escape the **risk** and capture the **return**. Stock market is a reflection of risk and return aspects. Risk can be avoidable but not fully escapable. The large amount of capital base is always be useful for diversification. Diversification is the tool for the portfolio manager to reduce the risk levels of a portfolio. Generally mutual funds invest in a diverse range of securities and in many industries. All the eggs are not placed in one basket. It is the fundamental principle in the stock market. Hence the mutual funds can reduce the risk levels for a unit holder.

(c) Liquidity

Mutual fund is a voluntary organisation. It is established for the purpose of non-profit motive. It works for the rendering of services to the investors. All investors expects liquidity for their investment. Liquidity is one of the objective of investors, at any time, they require their money way back. The mutual funds will provide liquidity to their unit holders in two ways. The **open end scheme** unit holders will get back their investment by selling them at any time to the fund owners. The units will be repurchased at **NAV** related prices. In the **close end scheme fund**, the unit holders has option to sell the units through stock exchange. The close end scheme units are listed in the stock exchange and can be traded in the stock market **on par** with other securities. Hence the unit holders will get their amount of investment at any time as per the wishes. The units provide excellent liquidity position in the stock market. The ready market for sale of units provide higher liquidity to the investors.

(d) Regulation

The mutual funds are the custodians for others money. They are responsible for unit holders. Any misuse of funds will not be permitted by the government. The mutual funds should work as per the guidelines issued by the **Securities and Exchange Board of India**. SEBI is the most powerful organisation to regulate the mutual fund. It is the judiciary organ to monitor the activities of the mutual funds. Every mutual fund in India should get registration with the SEBI. It is the watchdog of the capital market. As per the registration of mutual fund with the SEBI, the fund is allowed to operate in the market. Mutual funds are established as a non-profit motive organisation. It is comprising with board of trustees. The fund will establish an **Asset Management Company**. All the operations, activities are operated by the **AMC**. The routine work of all the affairs are performed by the AMC on behalf of board. The policy matters are look after by the board of trustees. The board is governed by the group of trustees. All mutual funds in India in private sector or in public sector should get membership from the **Association of Mutual Funds**. It is a non-profit organisation rendering services for the benefit of mutual fund in India. It is an intermediary between government and any member of mutual fund in settlement of disputes if any arises. The government of India will control the activities through **SEBI, DCA, CLB and Stock exchanges**. Therefore the investors no need to worry about their investment.

(e) Low Cost

Mutual funds are pool the small savings in a large amount of financial resources. Mutual fund can be described as **reservoir** of funds. They handle the investments of large number of people. The large scale amount of shares or financial assets can be purchased at relatively low brokerage and other costs. The transaction costs and administrative costs are shared by millions of investors. Hence the operating cost, financial cost and other any incidental expenses will be marginally very flow. The mutual funds can take an advantage of cost factor.

(f) Flexibility

Mutual funds are working to the flexibility of the unit holders. The mutual funds offer regular investment plans, regular withdrawal plans and many other futures. They design the scheme to suit the needs of convenient of unit holders. Any mutual should work for the utmost satisfaction of the unit holders. They should work as representative of the unit holders. They should take any decision for the benefits of investors with in the accepted level of justice.

Portfolio Performance

Portfolio means a combination and blend of mix of different kinds of financial assets. The portfolio performance is based on abilities. The abilities are the reflection of capabilities. Capabilities will be acquired by knowledge, experience, observation and talent. **Knowledge** is the most powerful weapon in the hands of a skilled person. **Knowledge** is not a commodity to purchase with a price. Knowledge is more powerful than wealth. Knowledge can be acquired with the sources of **Information.** Capturing of information leads to gaining of scientific approach. Scientific approach never fail in the universe. Scientific observation creates zero per cent error free decision. The right decision in the stock market will stimulate the value of a portfolio. The performance of the portfolio can be studied through the following theories:

(a) Sharpe's Performance Index
(b) Treynor's Performance Index
(c) Jensen's Performance Index.

(a) Sharpe's Performance Index

Sharpe's performance index is associated with the performance ranking of various funds or portfolio. It compares with each portfolios, performance in getting the returns. The stock market is a game of risk and return elements. The management of risk and return factors can be measured through this index. It measures the risk premium of the portfolio relative to the total amount of risk in the portfolio. It is associated with the assessment of **risk premium**. The risk premium is the difference between the portfolios **average rate of return** and the risk free rate of interest. The portfolio risk can be measured through **standard deviation.** The index gives a single value to observe the performance of the portfolio. It assigns highest value to assets that have best risk adjusted rate of return. It measures the performance of the various funds or portfolios. It can be calculated through the following formula:

$$S_i = \frac{R_p - R_f}{\sigma_p}$$

S_i = Sharpe Index

R_p = Average return of the portfolio
R_f = Risk free rate of Interest
σ_p = Standard deviation of the portfolio return.

The index is based on the performance of the portfolio and not on the individual securities of the portfolio. The movement of individual securities cannot considered for the measurement of portfolio performance by the **Sharpe Index**. It only consider the movements of various portfolios. The risk adjusted average rate of return is the most important and influencial factor in determining the performance index. The larger value of performance index is placed in higher rank. The higher rank will be considered as best fund. The selection of best fund or portfolio is based on higher ranks. Higher rank portfolios can be considered as best. The following example will reveal the concept of Sharpe's performance index.

Portfolio	*Average Return*	σ	*Average Risk Free Rate of Interest*
M	18%	4%	8%
N	20%	6%	8%
O	22%	8%	8%
P	24%	10%	8%

By applying the formula, Sharpe performance index can be arrived:

$$S_i = \frac{R_p - R_f}{\sigma_p}$$

$$Si_m = \frac{0.18 - 0.08}{0.04}$$

$$M = \frac{0.10}{0.04} = 2.5 \text{ per cent.}$$

$$Si_N = \frac{0.20 - 0.08}{0.06} = 2.0 \text{ per cent}$$

$$Si_O = \frac{0.22 - 0.08}{0.08} = 1.75 \text{ per cent}$$

$$Si_P = \frac{0.24 - 0.08}{0.10} = 1.60 \text{ per cent}$$

The portfolio "M" is ranked highest 2.5 per cent more than the second "N". The second rank goes to N with 2 per cent. The third place occupied by "O" portfolio.

(b) Treynor's Performance Index

Treynor's performance index is associated with comparison of two funds or portfolios. The performance of the portfolio is based on the concept of characteristic line. The **characteristic line** is a relationship between market return and funds return or portfolio return. The fund or portfolio performance can be measured with reference to **market** performance. The total risk of the portfolio is replaced by **Market risk**. Market risk is measured by **Beta**. Beta cannot be diversifiable. The ideal portfolio return generally rises at a faster rate than the market return. If the market is moving upward or in the rising level of experiential growth, the ideal portfolio return would be higher. If the market is declining, the ideal portfolio return declines slowly than the market return. It is better to park the funds in the risk free assets while declining the market movement. The risk **free assets** generates positive return and reduces the risk level in declining market. The study of relationship between ideal portfolio rate of return and the market's rate of return is called as **"Treynor's Performance Index"**. The relationship between the market return and portfolio return is assumed to be **linear**. The linear relationship is revealed by the **characteristic line**. The characteristic line helps in measuring the Treynor performance index. The slope of the line is assessed by the following formula:

$$R_p = \alpha + \beta R_m + e_p$$

R_p = Portfolio return.

R_m = Market return.

α, β = Co-efficient to be estimated.

e_p = The residual or error term.

$$T_m = \frac{R_p - R_f}{\beta_p}$$

T_m = Treynor portfolio performance.

R_p = Portfolio average return.

R_f = Riskless rate of interest.

β_p = Beta co-efficient of portfolio.

Illustration

From the following information, select the best portfolio according to Treynor's performance index:

Portfolio	*Return*	β	R_f
M	26	0.75	8%
N	28	1.25	8%

$$\text{For portfolio } T_m = \frac{R_p - R_f}{\beta_p}$$

$$M = \frac{0.26 - 0.08}{0.75} = \frac{0.18}{0.75} = 0.24.$$

$$N = \frac{0.28 - 0.08}{1.25} = \frac{0.20}{1.25} = 0.16.$$

Portfolio M performance better than N.

(c) Jensen's Performance Index

Jensen's performance index is also associated with the study of risk element in portfolio management. It is one of the measures of the performance of portfolio. It is different from others. The other measures such as Sharpe, Treynor provides a measure of ranking the relative performance of various portfolios on a risk adjusted basis.

The Jensen's formula gives a measure of absolute performance of the portfolio on a risk adjusted basis. The absolute risk adjusted return measure was developed by **Michael Jensen**. It is popularly known as Jensen's performance index. It is associated with the measurement of absolute performance of the portfolio. It defines a **"standard set"** and the portfolio's performance will be monitored and measured. The framing of **standards** is based on the managers predictive abilities. Accurate prediction is the most important and influencing factor for measuring the portfolio performance. Portfolio Manager's predictive abilities will be based on professional experience, abilities, talent and stock markets skills. Portfolio Manager is a technician to handle all tests regarding stock market operations. A right prediction of security price would enable the portfolio to earn higher returns than common investors expectations. The risk is always chase the portfolio. Hence the prediction must be successful even risk awaiting in the stock market. The professional managers predictive abilities always expected to earn average portfolio return. If his predictive ability is superior, he should earn more than other portfolios at each level of risk. The Jensen's portfolio performance can be computed as follows:

$R_p = \alpha + \beta\,(R_m - R_f)$
R_p = Average return of portfolio
R_f = Risk free rate of interest
α = The intercept
β = A measure of systematic risk
R_m = Average market return.

The return of the portfolios varies in the same proportion of the Beta. Beta is a measure of systematic risk. The Jensen's performance of the portfolio shows the relationship between beta and portfolio return. The portfolio return can be determined by the following formula.

$R_p = \alpha_p + R_f + \beta\,(R_m - R_f)$
R_p = Portfolio return.
α_p = Predicting ability of the portfolio manager.
R_f = Risk free rate of interest.
β = Unsystematic risk.
R_m = Market return.

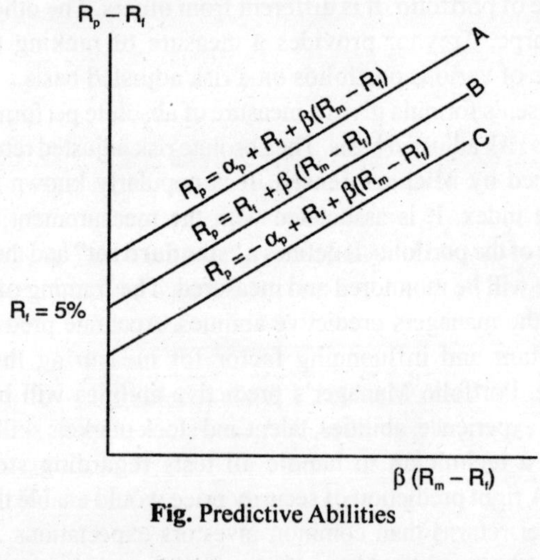

Fig. Predictive Abilities

The Jensen's evolution of portfolio performance involves two steps. (a) The expected return (b) Compare with actual and expected return. Afterwards the performance will be assigned with ranks. If the actual return is greater than expected return, then the portfolio will be considered as better.

CASE STUDY

Better corporate performance fuels present market rally. BSE sensex crossed on all time high **6400** mark on 15-12-2004. The market analysts have remained bullish that the present rally will continue. Equity analysts world over believe that the movement of stock prices are influenced more by future expectations of the investors than what they have received in the past.

May be the present rally in the Indian bourses too have been influenced by such expectations. But what is significant is that the rise in stock prices this time was backed by **strong fundamental** too. An Economic Times survey of **200** companies, ranked in terms of market capitalization on 12-15-04 finds that the magnitude of their stock prices has been strongly influenced by their earning capacity. Companies with higher **Earnings per share** in general, have fetched higher prices in the bourses and *vice versa*. Also, most of the companies which have witnessed increases in their EPS in **2004** over **2003** have recorded increases in their scrip prices too.

Statistically, the correlation co-efficient between stock prices and EPS of the sample companies was estimated at **0.8** as on December 15, 2004. It was estimated exactly at **0.7**, a year ago. That is not only there exists a significant correlation between stock prices and EPS, it has actually strengthened further over the year with rises in both stock prices and EPS.

In actual terms, about the 3/4th of the sample companies have witnessed an increase in their stock prices in 2004 over 2003 following increased in their EPS during the same period. Prices of 35 companies samples, at the other hand, have declined following a fall in EPS. There are of course, a few companies in the list whose scrip prices have moved up despite a fall in EPS. The price of **ONGC** scrip, for example has increased by **23.7 per cent** from **686** as on 15-12-2003 to **Rs. 848.65** on 15-12-2004, even as its EPS fell by 16.3 per cent during the same period.

Likewise, Ranbaxy Laboratories, Bharat Petroleum Corporation, Tata Power and Corporation Bank have recorded sharp rises in their scrip prices despite a fall in EPS. Ranbaxy's scrip value has increased by **17.4 per cent** during this period against a **35.6 per cent** decline in EPS.

The scrip price of corporation bank has risen by **50 per cent** despite a **22.3 per cent** fall in **EPS.**

Not surprising for, good track record of these companies must have influenced the investors to ignore the fall in **EPS** as a temporary phenomenon. Most of these companies, in fact, have continuously improved their bottom lines over the recent years.

But of cause, Indian investors this time were not influenced by higher EPS alone. They were equally influenced by the rise in intrinsic value of the scrip. The intrinsic value of a scrip as reflected in its book value and is defined as the sum of the equity capital and reserves less revaluation reserves divided by outstanding number of shares, has risen for **160** out of the **200** sample companies during this period. And its impact on share price movement can be seen in the high correlation that existed between book value per share and the scrip price. The correlation co-efficient between book value and share price was estimated at **0.8** on 15-12-2004 up from **0.7** on the same day a year ago.

Rise in Earning Per Share Led to a Rise in Share Price in 2004

Company	*BSE Closing Price (Rs.)*		*Change (%)*	*EPS (Rs.)*		*Change (%)*
	15/12/04	*15/12/03*		*15/12/04*	*15/12/03*	
ONGC	848.65	686.00	23.7	65.90	78.77	–16.3
Reliance Industries	495.00	499.10	–0.8	42.84	32.59	31.5
Infosys Technologies	2097.55	5143.95	–59.2	52.89	164.64	–67.9
Indian Oil Corpn.	504.40	405.40	24.4	59.63	49.04	21.6
Wipro	764.30	1668.50	–54.2	17.16	36.57	–53.0
Hindustan Lever	148.20	193.10	–23.3	6.17	7.98	–22.7
State Bank of India	604.40	485.50	24.5	74.71	64.86	15.2
ITC	1279.75	994.65	28.7	69.16	59.45	16.3
ICICI Bank	364.65	275.55	32.3	24.05	22.92	4.9
Ranbaxy Lab	1269.35	1080.85	17.4	31.03	48.19	–35.6
SAIL	56.95	44.35	28.4	10.60	2.23	375.3
GAIL	238.50	194.55	22.6	21.53	20.99	2.6
HDFC	794.95	629.40	26.3	37.83	30.89	22.5
Tata Steel	332.55	391.80	–15.1	49.71	38.42	29.4
Tata Motors	494.35	423.15	16.8	28.67	16.09	78.2
BHEL	723.95	443.90	63.1	29.71	19.40	53.1
HDFC Bank	747.15	353.40	34.2	20.15	15.50	30.0
Maruti Udyog	459.10	360.30	27.4	22.58	12.03	87.7
Satyam Computer	415.20	361.15	15.0	20.38	11.08	83.9
Bharat Petroleum	431.35	387.00	11.5	45.56	49.23	–7.5
Hindustan Petroleum	373.55	403.50	–7.4	54.35	46.15	17.8
Larsen and Toubro	947.75	441.95	114.4	64.70	19.75	227.6
Hindalco Industries	1295.25	1320.35	–1.9	93.40	66.25	41.0
National Aluminium	182.20	177.30	2.8	14.35	9.45	51.9

(*Contd.*)

Sources: *The Economic Times*, 27-12-2004, p. 13.

(Contd.)

Company	BSE Closing Price (Rs.) 15/12/04	15/12/03	Change (%)	EPS (Rs.) 15/12/04	15/12/03	Change (%)
Grasim Industries	1240.15	952.80	30.2	96.53	50.93	89.5
Neyveli Lignite Corpn.	65.25	62.80	3.9	6.31	8.03	–21.4
Bajaj Auto	1058.50	1040.95	1.7	71.09	63.88	11.3
HCL Technologies	353.95	286.30	23.6	10.99	11.12	–1.2
Hero Honda Motors	517.30	397.40	30.2	39.98	30.85	29.6
Mahanagar Telephone	157.60	117.15	34.5	19.49	14.09	38.3
Punjab National Bank	360.20	183.65	96.1	48.71	36.99	31.7
Reliance Energy	513.50	462.35	11.1	23.45	11.53	103.4
Sun Pharma	508.65	626.30	–18.8	16.93	27.04	–37.4
Cipla	291.00	1185.05	–75.4	11.74	41.71	–71.9
NMDC	650.00	430.75	50.9	46.91	23.63	98.5
Canara Bank	194.10	122.50	58.4	36.34	28.80	26.2
Zee Telefilms	178.05	143.40	24.2	4.04	2.37	70.5
Tata Power	363.20	278.50	30.4	24.36	28.88	–15.7
Guj. Ambuja Cements	382.45	299.10	27.9	22.98	14.29	60.8
Glaxo Smith Pharma	736.55	550.40	33.8	33.95	20.69	64.1
Bank of Baroda	217.40	184.05	18.1	33.05	32.62	1.3
VSNL	223.15	129.95	71.7	16.78	15.56	7.8
Dr. Reddy's Lab	821.75	1352.40	–39.2	16.22	57.72	–71.9
IDBI	96.15	57.30	67.8	4.75	6.51	–27.0
Oriental Bank of Commerce	320.25	241.25	32.7	40.32	28.37	42.1
Mahindra and Mahindra	525.85	351.85	49.5	39.64	16.80	136.0
Sterlite Industries	564.05	1208.35	–53.3	17.07	47.15	–63.8
Motor Industries	1861.00	13426.05	–86.1	114.12	695.57	–83.6
Nestle India	590.55	633.35	–6.8	22.97	26.48	–13.3
Associated Cement	313.35	228.05	37.4	16.15	8.81	83.3
Container Corpn.	785.00	616.25	27.4	63.26	43.19	46.5
Shipping Corpn.	180.00	163.70	10.0	32.55	15.60	108.7
Bharat Electronics	631.85	567.45	11.3	43.36	39.03	11.1
Hindustan Zinc	119.00	105.80	12.5	11.49	6.33	81.5
Nicholas Piramal	1298.10	691.40	87.7	56.39	36.22	55.7
Union Bank of India	103.85	47.55	118.4	17.55	14.59	20.3
Corporation Bank	329.70	219.85	50.0	25.49	32.80	–22.3
I-Flex Solutions	626.70	861.00	–27.2	20.34	23.61	–13.9
IPCL	177.40	217.20	–18.3	17.77	10.39	71.0
Siemens	1301.05	906.60	43.5	45.68	42.06	8.6
UTI Bank	174.55	115.05	51.7	11.99	9.89	21.2
Bharat Forge	988.40	717.05	37.8	35.67	28.41	25.6
ABB	918.50	611.00	50.3	31.34	27.35	14.6
Wockhardt	345.65	745.35	–53.6	16.79	30.12	–44.3
Bank of India	76.85	59.50	29.2	16.21	18.67	–13.2
Indian Overseas Bank	66.55	31.70	109.9	10.14	10.07	0.7
GE Shipping	181.60	145.50	24.8	29.65	16.67	77.9
Tata Chemicals	157.65	141.40	11.5	10.30	13.69	–24.8
Chennai Petroleum	223.55	89.60	149.5	41.41	22.27	85.9
Cadila Healthcare	529.10	385.95	37.1	24.23	15.68	54.5
Kotak Mahindra Bank	262.00	365.70	–28.4	6.77	10.17	–33.4
Asian Paints	325.15	330.00	–1.5	16.09	15.33	5.0
Kochi Refineries	224.05	171.65	30.5	46.85	39.91	17.4
Andhra Bank	76.45	47.10	62.3	11.68	12.72	–8.2
Matrix Lab	1999.15	1382.45	44.6	106.23	75.97	39.8

(Contd.)

(*Contd.*)

Company	*BSE Closing Price (Rs.) 15/12/04*	*15/12/03*	*Change (%)*	*EPS (Rs.) 15/12/04*	*15/12/03*	*Change (%)*
Lupin	705.80	728.70	–3.1	25.98	13.42	93.6
Nirma	355.95	388.35	–8.3	30.31	30.71	–1.3
Vijaya Bank	64.95	37.75	72.1	9.31	6.80	36.9
Castrol India	223.60	242.65	–7.9	11.10	11.75	–5.5
Moser Baer	239.90	301.10	–20.3	22.07	29.52	–25.2
Aventis Pharma	1141.85	650.70	75.5	60.05	36.99	62.3
HCL Infosystems	787.30	392.85	100.4	36.58	23.65	54.7
Tata Tea	461.05	321.30	43.5	19.55	13.83	41.4
Jindal Steel and Power	831.50	982.05	–15.3	143.51	119.02	20.6
Indian Hotels	565.30	419.10	34.9	18.20	9.76	86.5
Cummins India	123.80	115.20	7.5	5.78	5.95	–2.9
Dabur India	84.55	83.90	0.8	4.19	3.08	36.0
Colgate Palmolive	176.85	150.95	17.2	8.57	6.97	23.0
Glenmark Pharma	386.55	133.20	190.2	10.51	6.19	69.8
Syndicate Bank	48.30	32.85	47.0	8.87	8.84	0.3
Mpharis BFL	291.40	646.65	–54.9	7.45	25.33	–70.6
Allahabad Bank	63.40	25.15	152.1	17.96	7.08	153.7
Arvind Mills	112.15	61.30	83.0	4.23	6.54	–35.3
Novartis India	674.40	377.05	78.9	35.21	18.02	95.4
Britannia Industries	836.95	627.90	33.3	66.07	45.42	45.5
Gillette India	639.55	692.35	–7.6	16.96	12.47	36.0
Rashtriya Chemicals	37.35	36.90	1.2	2.68	2.83	–5.3
TVS Motor	83.00	1077.95	–92.3	5.51	60.34	–90.9
Engineers India	349.30	398.45	–12.3	15.69	14.42	8.8
Indian Rayon	327.05	244.25	33.9	16.98	21.32	–20.4
Jubilant organosys	823.40	700.80	17.5	43.22	36.42	18.7
Hughes Software	551.20	545.25	1.1	28.11	17.08	64.6
Bongaigon Refinery	93.45	82.90	12.7	20.31	15.33	32.5
Raymond	302.00	206.90	46.0	17.44	18.24	–4.4
National Fertilizers	37.05	45.85	–19.2	1.65	2.59	–36.3
Pfizer	607.85	554.70	9.6	14.54	9.55	52.3
Sesa Goa	876.95	554.85	58.1	91.70	11.96	666.7
P and G Huggiene	526.80	466.55	12.9	30.72	21.73	41.4
Nonsanto India	1967.45	1275.75	54.2	93.94	65.60	43.2
Reliance Capital	133.35	119.60	11.5	8.05	8.27	–2.7
Divis Lab	1313.55	1311.65	0.1	54.62	49.10	11.2
J and K Bank	346.15	284.85	21.5	64.54	80.26	–19.6
Aurobindo Pharma	329.55	418.45	–21.2	18.20	26.39	–31.0
Amtek Auto	173.25	456.50	–62.0	7.18	26.72	–73.1
EIH	314.35	284.50	10.5	4.79	2.25	112.9
LIC Housing Finance	192.40	211.30	–8.9	21.79	24.83	–12.2
Adani Exports	73.85	271.40	–72.8	5.84	35.22	–83.4
Nicro Inks	652.25	604.50	7.9	37.63	23.57	59.7
DSP Merrill Lynch	720.00	449.00	60.4	55.85	47.11	18.6
Polaris Software	162.45	212.20	–23.4	6.69	7.00	–4.4
Century Textiles	170.00	131.65	29.1	9.62	8.78	9.6
Indusind Bank	51.20	40.50	26.4	9.14	6.73	35.8
Glaxosmith Con Health	320.80	318.95	0.6	17.66	14.87	18.8
Godrej Con Prdts	250.05	161.20	55.1	12.70	9.56	32.8
Sterling Biotech	163.20	60.60	169.3	7.46	3.74	99.5

(*Contd.*)

(Contd.)

Company	*BSE Closing Price (Rs.)*		*Change (%)*	*EPS (Rs.)*		*Change (%)*
	15/12/04	*15/12/03*		*15/12/04*	*15/12/03*	
Crompton Greaves	264.95	147.05	80.2	16.78	5.67	195.9
Wexawase Techno	593.95	428.95	38.5	10.73	15.49	–30.7
Ballarpur Inds.	84.00	79.90	5.1	8.79	6.43	36.7
Alfa Laval	745.80	610.00	22.3	42.31	33.94	24.7
Mothesron Sumi	84.80	296.70	–71.4	3.65	12.83	–71.6
Syngerta India	413.90	208.10	98.9	24.50	11.76	108.3
Dredging Corpn.	463.90	439.45	5.6	52.90	60.05	–11.9
Vindal Iron and Steel	295.05	266.55	10.7	64.42	36.68	75.6
IBP	572.80	790.60	–27.5	28.56	54.70	–47.8
Thermax	525.65	368.20	42.8	20.73	25.20	–17.7
Sudarsan Clayton	653.20	527.80	23.8	28.64	23.85	20.1
Bharat Earthmovers	335.55	216.95	54.7	19.94	10.52	42.0
Sundram Fasteners	116.10	1001.80	–88.4	5.38	50.31	–89.3
Exide Industries	171.15	141.50	21.0	10.73	9.11	17.8
FDC	63.50	92.10	–31.1	3.21	5.40	–40.6
Punjab Tractors	194.65	243.05	–19.9	8.40	4.82	74.3
Wyeth	520.40	441.05	18.0	36.68	19.39	89.2
Hinduja TMT	281.50	363.60	–22.6	19.09	16.99	12.4
Birla Corporation	149.40	69.10	116.2	9.38	1.82	415.4
Asahi India Glass	143.80	146.05	–1.5	8.83	7.82	12.9
Pantaloon Retail	592.95	266.65	122.4	11.40	8.12	40.4
Torrent Pharma	533.05	401.50	32.8	32.72	29.57	10.7
IDBI Bank	51.90	39.05	32.9	6.84	4.79	42.8
Bayer Cropscience	280.05	248.15	12.9	12.66	8.90	42.2
Madras Cements	914.50	727.45	25.7	37.02	21.65	71.0
MRF	2571.90	2252.20	14.2	142.70	276.77	–48.4
Apollo Hospitals	260.55	172.70	50.9	10.70	7.92	35.1
CMC	711.45	582.30	22.2	40.88	26.75	52.8
Cruj Mineral Devp	333.35	199.00	67.5	32.25	22.37	44.2
SB of Bika and Jaipur	2079.85	1318.00	57.8	537.50	506.58	6.1
Abbott India	680.05	521.45	30.4	65.89	45.21	45.7
CESC	138.95	134.00	3.7	16.27	12.09	34.6
Alstoro Projects	152.70	118.85	28.5	13.08	8.87	47.5
Balrampur Chini	479.80	263.10	82.4	28.50	23.14	23.2
Marico Inds.	175.35	228.70	–23.3	10.81	19.08	–43.3
Ipca Lab	813.15	648.00	25.5	63.03	53.15	18.6
Lakshmi Machine	8124.00	4710.00	72.5	588.64	251.07	134.5
Goodlass Nerolac	390.05	427.40	–8.7	29.40	31.11	–5.5
Indo Rama Synth.	73.45	92.90	–20.9	11.92	7.45	60.0
Federal Bank	144.05	229.35	–37.2	16.06	59.27	–72.9
Apollo Tyres	247.05	256.35	–3.6	16.93	32.81	–48.4
Guj Narmada Valley	64.65	68.10	–5.1	8.67	7.43	16.7
Hotel Leela Venture	155.10	60.40	156.8	6.41	2.14	199.5
Jindal Stainless	92.65	459.15	–79.8	16.59	89.85	–81.5
Ambuja Cem Eastern	47.55	48.00	–0.9	2.67	6.29	–57.6
Bombay Dying	235.05	145.15	61.9	14.28	5.29	169.9
ICI	221.55	187.50	18.2	32.12	23.07	39.2
Tube Investment	244.20	204.25	19.6	21.30	28.33	–24.8
GTL	125.00	83.35	50.0	14.01	11.72	19.5
Pidilite Inds.	351.75	330.25	6.5	26.13	24.63	6.1
Orchid Chemicals	273.80	256.25	6.8	7.66	8.84	–13.3

(Contd.)

(Contd.)

Company	BSE Closing Price (Rs.) 15/12/04	BSE Closing Price (Rs.) 15/12/03	Change (%)	EPS (Rs.) 15/12/04	EPS (Rs.) 15/12/03	Change (%)
Saw Pipes	225.85	308.75	–26.9	14.43	19.52	–26.1
State Bank of Travan	1750.00	1206.00	45.1	494.50	455.06	8.7
Finolex Inds	70.05	60.75	15.3	9.67	3.92	146.7
Gammon India	600.30	460.25	30.4	24.06	18.38	30.9
Merek	514.75	435.90	18.1	42.94	28.93	48.4
Shree Cement	246.30	132.85	85.4	11.43	2.72	320.2
Ingersoll Rand	269.50	259.05	4.0	38.63	12.45	210.3
Bajaj Hindustan	96.40	235.55	–59.1	5.90	32.46	–81.8
Abon Loyd Chiles	1132.55	477.40	137.2	60.54	32.08	88.7
Gujarat Inds Power	75.30	66.40	13.4	4.25	2.13	428.2
Panacea Biotec	142.95	54.80	160.9	8.40	1.03	715.5
United Breweries	455.60	137.45	231.5	0.70	2.05	–65.9
Essel Propack	257.10	269.20	–4.5	13.98	11.18	25.0
Ahd Electricity	124.15	102.55	21.1	8.85	6.16	43.7
Alok Inds.	69.15	58.05	19.1	6.05	5.36	12.9
Gujarat Akalies	106.35	83.40	27.5	11.68	10.64	9.8
Atlas Copco	688.35	350.00	96.7	22.74	25.84	–12.0
Thomas Cook	530.55	429.95	23.4	18.28	14.83	23.3
Blue Dart Express	326.00	152.15	114.3	13.77	10.09	36.5
Maharashtra Seamless	262.95	244.70	7.5	25.84	21.87	18.2
Asian Hotels	327.35	141.60	90.8	7.05	0.381	1755.3
Trent	561.25	276.30	103.1	12.44	9.81	26.8
Titan Inds.	174.00	128.75	35.1	4.03	3.09	30.4
Hinatsingka Seicle	380.60	299.40	27.1	24.99	24.04	4.0

Source: Better Corporate Performance Fuels Present Market Rally, Tushar K. Mohanthi, *The Economic Times*, 27-12-2004, p. 13.

CASE STUDY

Predicting Abilities of a Common Investor

A Reaction and Forecasting with Reference to Finance Act, 2005.

Sources: *The Economic Times*, dt. 1-3-2005, p. 12.

ABB Higher Spend on Infrastructure will result in big orders for ABB

	Raw Material	% of Mfg Cost	Excise % Change	Custom % Change	Stock Movement (Rs.) 15 days	Today ↑	
	Components	80.90	–	–	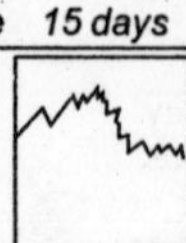	Prev.	1232
	Others	1.13	–	–		High	1299
Financial	Finished Goods	% of sale				Low	1230
Result	Switch gears	27.90	–	–		Close	1285
(Rs. Crore)	Project Items	34.67	–	–			

	Shareholding Per cent			
Sales 2310.77				
Net profit	Promoters	FIIs	FIS	Others
154.32	52.11	6.68	18.56	22.65
Equity 42.38				

ABB Government's huge outlay for infrastructure building will result in big orders for power sector players like ABB. On a specific note, the overseas cut in corporate tax is a positive.

Source: Corporate earnings, Union budget 2005, *The Economic Times*, 1-3-2005, p. 12.

ACC New SPV and infrastructure spend are positives

	Raw Material	*% of Mfg Cost*	*Excise % Change*	*Custom % Change*	*Stock Movement (Rs.) 15 days*	*Today* ↑	
	Gypson	12	–	–	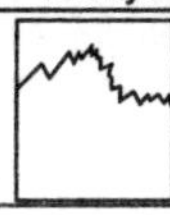	Prev	361
Financial	Power	70	–	–		High	368
Result	Finished Goods	% of sale				Low	360
(Rs. Crore)	Gray cement	83	–	–		Close	368

	Shareholding Per cent			
Sales 3888.3				
Net profit	Promoters	FIIs	FIS	Others
197.27		23.57	36.05	40.68
Equity 177.4				

ACC the creation of a Special Purpose Vehicle (SPV) with an allocation of Rs. 10,000 crore is likely to boost demand for cement for construction of new roads, ports and airports. Besides, the company should gain from allocation of Rs. 940 crore to north-eastern states for new roads and through outlay of Rs. 1400 crore for NHDP 111.

Bajaj Auto 8 per cent excise cut on tyres. Customs cut on aluminium.

	Raw Material	*% of Mfg Cost*	*Excise % Change*	*Custom % Change*	*Stock Movement (Rs.) 15 days*	*Today* ↑	
	Auto components	% of sale	—	—	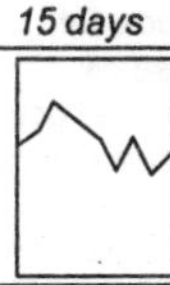	Prev	1020
	Tyres and Tubes	90.86	—	—		High	1039
Financial	Finished Goods	3.92	–8	—		Low	1010
Result	Motor Cycles	61.79	—	—		Close	1034
(Rs. Crore)	Three-wheelers	27.99	—	—			

	Shareholding Per cent			
Sales 5527.29				
Net profit	Promoters	FIIs	FIS	Others
738.39	29.80	17.26	7.47	45.47
Equity 101.18				

Bajaj Auto

Excise duty on two and three-wheelers has been left unchanged. However, the company will get some benefit as the excise rate on tyres and tubes has been reduced from 24 per cent to 16 per cent. Customs cut in Aluminium and Copper should help in reducing cost pressures. Mildly positive.

BHEL. Big order book position. Gainer on infrastructure expansion

	Raw Material	*% of Mfg Cost*	*Excise % Change*	*Service Tax % Change*	*Stock Movement (Rs.) 15 days*	*Today* ↑	
	Components	67.44	–	–		Prev	863
	Ferrous materials	2.45	–	–		High	865
	Finished Goods	% of sale				Low	843
Financial	Erection and	24.38	–	10		Close	855
Result	other services						
(Rs. Crore)	External erection	23.90	–	10			

	Shareholding Per cent			
Sales 9012.42				
Net profit 658.15				
Equity 244.76	Promoters 67.72	FIIs 23.04	FIS 7.33	Others 1.91

BHEL

Cut in corporate tax in a positive. The company could also gain from huge orders emanating from push in the infrastructure space. However, some of the activities of the company falling under Service tax, which could strain the bottom line.

BPCL. Oil sector will boom as demand rises and levies fall

	Raw Material	*% of Mfg Cost*	*Excise % Change*	*Custom % Change*	*Stock Movement (Rs.) 15 days*	*Today* ↑	
	Crude Oil	95.00	–			Prev	413
	Base oil	2.10	–			High	451
	Finished goods	% of sale				Low	431
Financial	Middle distillates	58.01				Close	427
Result		From 8% to Rs. 8% + Rs. 1.25/litre					
(Rs. Crore)	Light distillates	34.82 From 23% to 8% + Rs. 5/litre					

	Shareholding per cent			
Sales 53,884.75				
Net profit 1694.56				
Equity 300	Promoters 66.20	FIIs 13.99	FIS 16.19	Others 3.62

BPCL

The cut in customs duty on crude and base oil as well as cut in excise in light distillates are positives. BPCL will be a big gainer.

Bharti Tele. Increasing tele density is a big positive

	Raw Material	*% of Mfg Cost*	*Excise % Change*	*Custom % Change*	*Stock Movement (Rs.) 15 days*	*Today ↑*	
	Salaries	70.15	–	–		Prev	220
Financial						High	226
Result	Finished Goods	% of sale				Low	211
(Rs. Crore)	Telecom Services	47.25	–	–		Close	225

Sales 29.90				
Net profit 0.37	**Shareholding Per cent**			
Equity	Promoters	FIIs	FIS	Others
1853.37	46.62	14.18	2.92	36.28

Bharti Mobile telephone to be removed from the one in-six criteria for filing IT returns and extension of customs duty exemption on specified telecom network equipment are positives.

CIPLA. No package for anti-AIDS drugs a dampner

	Raw Material	*% of Mfg Cost*	*Excise % Change*	*Custom % Change*	*Stock Movement (Rs.) 15 days*	*Today ↑*	
	Purchased bulk dugs	37.32	–	–		Prev	259
	Others	31.70				High	263
	Fished goods	% of sale				Low	258
	Tablets & Capsules	52.85	–	–		Close	261
Financial Result (Rs. Crore)	Chemicals & malts	21.43	–	–			

Sales 2055.43				
Net profit 295.59	**Shareholding Per cent**			
Equity	Promotees	FIIs	FIS	Others
59.97	40.95	17.57	9.37	32.11

CIPLA

Positives for this R&D-based company are weighted deduction under Section 35(AB) on R&D extended to 2007, hike in R&D corpus of Rs. 150 crore, carry forward of MAT credit and cut is corporate tax rate. However government's silence on lowering of price of anti-AIDS drugs has come as a negative surprise.

Colgate-Palmolive. VAT and rising demand could save the day

	Raw Material	*% of Mfg Cost*	*Excise % Change*	*Custom % Change*	*Stock Movement (Rs.) 15 days*	*Today* ↑	
	Chemicals	34.6	–	–		Prev	183
	Oils	24.7	–	–		High	189
Financial	Finished goods	% of sale				Low	181
Result	Soap/toiletries	90.2	–	–		Close	188
(Rs. Crore)	Tooth brush	9.8	–	–			

		Shareholding Per cent		
Sales				
1042.08				
Net profit				
94.32				
Equity	Promoters	FIIs	FIS	Others
135.99	51	4.02	12.12	32.86

Colgate

The company is set to benefit from the implementation of VAT this year, which would remove the anomalies in taxes charged at this State level and bring them at a uniform level. The company should also gain from lowering of corporate has to 30 per cent.

Dabur.VAT a positive.No relief on ayurvedic products a dampness.

	Raw Material	*% of Mfg Cost*	*Excise % Change*	*Custom % Change*	*Stock Movement (Rs.) 15 days*	*Today* ↑	
	Sugar/molasses	10.2	–	–	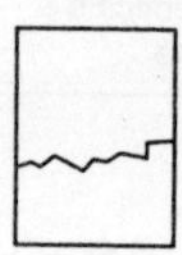	Prev	116.30
						High	117.60
	Finished goods	% of sale				Low	113.20
Financial	Ayurvedic products	25.41	–	–		Close	116.05
Result							
(Rs. Crore)	Hair oil	17.95	–	–			

		Shareholding Per cent		
Sales				
1151.87				
Net profit				
98.28				
Equity	Promoters	FIIs	FIS	Others
28.62	78.16	4.57	6.46	10.81

Dabur

The company would be able to get the benefit of VAT for any additional charges it may have to pay for molasses. These has been no change in indirect taxes for ayurveda/hair products, which is the main business of the company.

Dr. Reddy's. Gain on lower corporate tax and R&D Soaps

	Raw Material	*% of Mfg Cost*	*Excise % Change*	*Custom % Change*	*Stock Movement (Rs.) 15 days*	*Today* ↑	
	Fluro guinolonicacid	19.23	–	–		Prev	711
	Others	65.50	–	–		High	723
Financial	Finished goods	% of sale				Low	711
Result	Formulations	51.10	–	–		Close	722
(Rs. Crore)	Bulk drugs	42.60	–	–			

	Shareholding Per cent			
Sales 1839.09				
Net profit 263.2	Promoters	FIIs	FIS	Others
Equity 38.26	26.10	17.08	12.70	44.12

Dr. Redddy's

The company will could gain marginally from the exemptions granted to nine specified equipment in biotech and pharma sectors. Also, extending customs duty exemption to capital goods and raw materials used for R and D projects funded by CSIR being extended to ICNR, ICAR, etc and carry forward of NAT credit are positives.

GAIL. Major gainer as gas prices head towards decontrol

	Raw Material	*% of Mfg Cost*	*Excise % Change*	*Custom % Change*	*Stock Movement (Rs.) 15 days*	*Today* ↓	
	Gas	100	–	–5	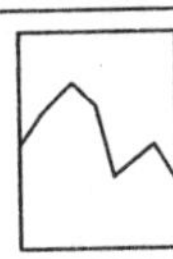	Prev	242
						High	243
Financial	Finished goods	% of sale				Low	235
Result	LPG	–36.36	–8	–		Close	241
(Rs. Crore)	Polymers	24.16	–	–			

	Shareholding Per cent			
Sales 12,422.38				
Net profit 1869.34	Promoters	FIIs	FIS	Others
Equity 845.65	67	14.38	7.11	11.51

GAIL

Gas prices increasingly being unstacked from government control as the prices of gas will eventually become a function of demand and supply. This will boost the fortunes of GAIL going forward as the company is constantly hiking its capacities.

Glaxo. Cut in corporate tax a face saver

	Raw Material	*% of Mfg Cost*	*Excise % Change*	*Custom % Change*	*Stock Movement (Rs.) 15 days*	*Today ↑*	
	Raw material	76.05	–	–		Prev	738
	Packing materiai	23.95	–	–		High	745
	Finished goods	% of sale				Low	724
Financial Result (Rs. Crore)	Tablets and capsules	50.65	–	–		Close	739
	Liquids: orals, parentals etc.	24.40	–	–			

Sales 1493.82 Net profit 333.09 Equity 87.32	Shareholding Per cent			
	Promoters	FIIs	FIS	Others
	49.15	10.52	17.66	22.67

Glaxo

No major effects, positive or negative for Glaxo except for cut in corporate tax.

Grasim. Major gainer on increased demand for cement

	Raw Material	*% of Mfg Cost*	*Excise % Change*	*Custom % Change*	*Stock Movement (Rs.) 15 days*	*Today ↑*	
	Dissolving pulp	34.25	–	–	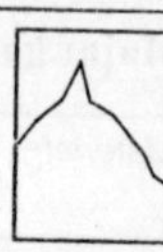	Prev	1318
	Limestone	8.4	–	–		High	1352
Financial Result (Rs. Crore)	Finished goods	% of sale				Low	1321
	Gray Cement	40.7	–	–		Close	1345
	Sponge iron	30.25	–	–			

Sales 6134.46 Net profit 728.67 Equity 91.69	Shareholding Per cent			
	Promoters	FIIs	FIS	Others
	21.94	23.69	20.68	33.69

Grasim

This is another company that should benefit due to the higher allocation to the infrastructure sector. The company's fortunes may remain unaffected due to the Rs. 100 per tonne excise hike in cement clinker. Since it sells gray cement and does not source clinker.

Gujarat Ambuja. Lower depreciation could hurt bottomline

	Raw Material	% of Mfg Cost	Excise % Change	Custom % Change	Stock Movement (Rs.) 15 days	Today ↑	
	Power	65.2	–	–	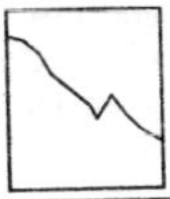	Prev	434
Financial						High	450
Result	Finished goods	% of sale				Low	435
(Rs. Crore)	Gray Cement	100	–	–		Close	449

Sales 2306.7	Net profit 289.46	Equity 179.45

Shareholding Per cent			
Promoters	FIIs	FIS	Others
23.66	28.7	19.2	28.44

Gujarat Ambuja

The company may not benefit from specific allocation to infrastructure for north-eastern states. Yet, it may end with higher volumes in other areas in light of the thrust to infrastructure sector.

HCL Tech. 4 per cent CVD exemption continued. Hardware costs

	Raw Material	% of Mfg Cost	Excise % Change	Custom % Change	Stock Movement (Rs.) 15 days	Today ↑	
	Personnel cost	43.06	–	–		Prev	330
	Others	50				High	340
Financial	Finished goods	% of sale				Low	324
Result	Software and	100	-4 (CVD)	–		Close	339
(Rs. Crore)	tech Services						

Sales 1127.98	Net profit 325.72	Equity 59.22

Shareholding Per cent			
Promoters	FIIs	FIS	Others
70.88	12.38	1.26	15.48

HCL Technology

The removal of customs duty on specified capital goods and all inputs required for the manufacture of information technology agreement found items will reduce hardware cost.

HDFC Bank. Cut in tax to boost profits. Access to foreign funds

	Raw Material	*% of Mfg Cost*	*Excise % Change*	*Custom % Change*	*Stock Movement (Rs.) 15 days*	*Today* ↑	
	Interest expenditure	55.18	–	–		Prev	570
	Personnel Cost	9.30				High	600
	Finished goods	% of sale					
Financial Result (Rs. Crore)	Investment/Div. Income	43.55	–	–		Low	571
						Close	586
	Interest earned	40.40	–	–			
Sales 3035.92 Net profit 509.50 Equity 284.79	**Shareholding Per cent**						
	Promoters 24.03	FIIs 28.99	FIS 5.16	Others 41.82			

HDFC Bank

Lower corporate tax will boost net profits. Banks are allowed to issue preference shares to help in meeting the Base II norms. They are also allowed to take foreign loans which will raise their liquidity position. Withdrawal of 80L, benefit, however, may hit deposit mobilisation somewhat in the coming months. The overall impact is positive.

Hero Honda. 8 per cent Excise cut on tyres Customs cut on aluminium

	Raw Material	*% of Mfg Cost*	*Excise % Change*	*Custom % Change*	*Stock Movement (Rs.) 15 days*	*Today* ↑	
	Auto components	98.77	–	–		Prev	519
	Steel sheets	1.23		–5		High	547
Financial Result (Rs. Crore)	Finished goods	% of sale				Low	520
	Motor cycles	95.22	–	–		Close	545
	Spares	4.76	–	–			
Sales 5839.55 Net profit 728.32 Equity 39.94	**Shareholding Per cent**						
	Promoters 54.96	FIIs 25.71	FIS 5.75	Others 13.58			

Hero Honda

No change in excise rate on two-wheelers. The company is however, expected to gain from the reduction in excise rate on tyres and tubes. Customs duty cut on aluminium and copper should help in reducing cost pressures. Mildly positive.

Hindalco. Competition will heat up as customs duties slashed

	Raw Material	*% of Mfg Cost*	*Excise % Change*	*Custom % Change*	*Stock Movement (Rs.) 15 days*	*Today ↑*
	Power	18.08	–	–		Prev
	Copper concentrate	53.85	–	–		High
Financial	Finished goods	% of sale				Low
Result	Aluminium ingots	22.9	–	–5		Close
(Rs. Crore)	Copper cathodes	34.8	–	–5		

	Shareholding Per cent			
Sales 6812.87				
Net profit 754.9				
Equity	Promoters	FIIs	FIS	Others
92.48	25.92	20.68	19.04	34.36

Hindalco

The company has lost out marginally. Customs duty on copper and primary aluminium inputs has been reduced to 10 per cent from 15 per cent earlier. This may put pressure on Hindalco's pricing power in the domestic market due to cheaper imports.

HILL Vat, exemption on excise front are positives

	Raw Material	*% of Mfg Cost*	*Excise % Change*	*Custom % Change*	*Stock Movement (Rs.) 15 days*	*Today ↑*	
	Chemicals/ perfumes	36.65	–	–		Prev	141
	Oils/Fats	15.05	–1 (Rs./kg.)	–		High	146
	Finished goods	% of sale				Low	140
Financial	Packet tea	21.3	–1 (Rs./kg.)	–		Close	145
Result	Personnel	20	–	–			
(Rs. Crore)	products						

	Shareholding Per cent			
Sales 11,222.16				
Net profit 1663.66				
Equity	Promoters	FIIs	FIS	Others
220.12	51.55	13.68	13.99	20.78

HILL

The company has received a major boost on several counts. The approval to the introduction of VAT would help the company fight off competition from local players. The company has been exempted from paying excise duty of Re. 1 per kg. on refined edible oils, Rs. 1.25 per kg. on vanaspati and additional excise of Re. 1 levied on tea, Sops have been announced for the tea sector.

HPCL. Integrated oil company to gain from lower levies

	Raw Material	*% of Mfg Cost*	*Excise % Change*	*Custom % Change*	*Stock Movement (Rs.) 15 days*	*Today* ↑	
	Crude oil processed	98.45	–	–5	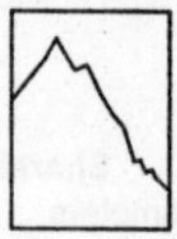	Prev	344
	Finished goods	% of sale				High	373
						Low	345
Financial	Lubricating oils	83.56	–10	–		Close	351
Result	Lubricating oil	11.87	–10	–			
(Rs. Crore)	base						

	Shareholding Per cent			
Sales 58,619.92				
Net profit 1903.94				
Equity 338.9	Promoters 51.01	FIIs 19.74	FIS 21.08	Others 8.17

HPCL

HPCL will be on overall gains because the decline in refining margins will be compensated by marketing margins. Also, cut in excise on 1 per cent will reduce the subsidy burden. Lower corporate tax rate will also be a positive.

HDFC Housing loan sops to continue cut in tax to boost profits

	Raw Material	*% of Mfg Cost*	*Excise % Change*	*Custom % Change*	*Stock Movement (Rs.) 15 days*	*Today* ↑	
	Finance charges	92.34	–	–		Prev	758
	Personnel cost	2.82	–	–		High	785
Financial	Finished goods	% of sale				Low	758
Result	Dividend	6.65	–	–		Close	782
(Rs. Crore)	Interest earned	83.70	–	–			

	Share Holding Per cent			
Sales 3068.98				
Net profit 851.78				
Equity 246.62	Promoters –	FIIs 63.17	FIS 5.45	Others 31.38

HDFC

Lower corporate tax will boost net profits. The income tax benefit on housing loan continues. The tax benefit on Interest payment on housing loan remains. This will give HDFC further boost in the coming months as higher budgetary allocation on infrastructure. Related projects will sense demand for residential houses.

ITC. Higher excise outflows. Lower corporate tax

	Raw Material	*% of Mfg Cost*	*Excise % Change*	*Custom % Change*	*Stock Movement (Rs.) 15 days*	*Today* ↑	
	Agri products	31.15	–	–		Prev	1288
	Raw tobacco	24.1	–	–		High	1305
Financial	Finished goods	% of sale				Low	1240
Result	Cigarettes	78.03	–	–		Close	1295
(Rs. Crore)	Agri products	8.07	–	–			

Sales
11,819.77
Net profit
1470.45

	Shareholding Per cent			
Equity	Promoters	FIIs	FIS	Others
247.68	32.42	16.18	33.59	17.81

ITC

Despite the benefit to its hotel division, ITC will have to pay higher taxes as excise surcharge on tobacco products like cigarettes, which is a major contributor to its revenue stream. The company could, however, gain from lower corporate tax rate. Mildly negative.

ICICI Bank. Cut in tax to boost profits. Access to foreign funds

	Raw Material	*% of Mfg Cost*	*Excise % Change*	*Custom % Change*	*Stock Movement (Rs.) 15 days*	*Today* ↑	
	Interest expended	73.30	–	–		Prev	368
	Personnel cost	5.46	–	–		High	383
	Finished goods	% of sale				Low	365
Financial	Interest earned	56.15	–	–		Close	383
Result	Investment/Div.	22.22	–	–			
(Rs. Crore)	Income						

Sales
11,509.26
Net profit
1637.11

	Shareholding Per cent			
Equity	Promoters	FIIs	FIS	Others
616.40	–	48.85	16.02	35.13

ICICI Bank

Lower corporate tax will boost net profits. RBI has been given more autonomy to decide SIR and CRR for banks. Banks are allowed to issue preference share to help in meeting the base II norms. Liquidity will rise as banks are now allowed to take foreign loans. Stamp duty on commercial paper to be rationalised. Withdrawal of 80L benefit may hit deposit mobilisation.

Indian Hotels. Vat and lower corporate tax are positives

	Raw Material	*% of Mfg Cost*	*Excise % Change*	*Custom % Change*	*Stock Movement (Rs.) 15 days*	*Today ↑*	
	Wages	30.5	–	–		Prev	590
Financial						High	606
Result	Finished goods	% of sale				Low	591
(Rs. Crore)	Services/rooms	96	–	–		Close	591
Sales							
683.02							
Net profit							
30.08	**Shareholding Per cent**						
Equity	Promoters	FIIs	FIS	Others			
45.12	34.79	5.91	19.47	39.83			

Indian Hotels

The proposed introduction of the much awaited VAT will bring good news for Indian Hotels as well as the entire hotel sector. With the introduction of VAT, the company will be able to avoid the agonies of facing double taxation at the input level and then the services side. Lower tax should help its bottom line.

CNX Indices: Figure Staking

	Weight in S&P CNX 500 as of Feb. 28, 05	*Index value as of July 8, 04 (Previous budget)*	*Pre-Budget closing Index value on Feb. 25, 05*	*Post-budget closing Index value on Feb. 28, 05*	*% charge between pre/post-budget*	*% charge from pre-budget*
Market Bench Marks						
S&P CNX Nifty		1518.15	2060.90	2103.25	2.05	35.54
S&P CNX 500		1247.35	1796.30	1827.38	1.73	46.50
CNX Midcap 200		1501.85	2730.50	2758.22	1.02	83.65
SCX Nifty Junior		2863.55	4305.75	4388.20	1.91	53.24
CNX FMCG		2186.18	2802.21	2834.95	1.17	29.68
CNX Service Sector		1829.61	2674.72	2749.69	2.80	50.29
CNX PSE		1278.86	1784.37	1803.98	1.10	41.06
CNX MNC		1344.70	1776.32	1796.17	1.12	33.57
CNX IT Sector		2054.50	2854.70	2919.05	2.25	42.08
S&P CNX industry Indices top Gainors						
Sugar	0.30	568.74	1524.79	1656.92	8.67	191.33
Tyres	0.22	506.47	889.82	953.61	7.17	88.28
Construction	0.70	476.99	1033.58	1074.30	3.94	125.23
Banks	11.46	2032.13	3328.53	3458.20	3.90	70.18
Solvent Extraction	0.13	1433.05	2839.83	2943.80	3.66	105.42
Steel & Steel products	4.31	524.63	1162.95	1201.32	3.30	128.99
Petro chemicals	0.46	1969.32	2415.59	2491.79	3.15	26.53
Tea & Coffee	0.26	1087.21	1662.92	1714.17	3.08	57.67
Leather & Products	0.05	117.44	268.83	276.53	2.86	135.47
Auto (2&3 wheelers)	1.57	3468.99	3807.22	3913.78	2.80	12.82
Air conditioners	0.08	1242.49	2261.31	2324.52	2.79	87.08
Metals	0.59	1778.82	4440.17	4563.28	2.77	156.53

(Contd.)

(Contd.)

	Weight in S&P CNX 500 as of Feb. 28, 05	*Index value as of July 8, 04 (Previous budget)*	*Pre-Budget closing Index value on Feb. 25, 05*	*Post-budget closing Index value on Feb. 28, 05*	*% charge between pre/post-budget*	*% charge from pre-budget*
Finance Housing	1.45	3342.16	4715.27	4833.77	2.51	44.63
Cement & Allied Products	2.56	1316.00	1991.79	2039.01	2.37	54.94
Textile Machinery	0.07	631.70	1022.30	1046.17	2.33	65.61
Computers Software	15.07	16234.21	23559.68	24107.92	2.33	65.61
Refineries	11.99	767.62	1024.41	1047.07	2.21	48.50
Mining	0.29	601.75	2236.06	2283.37	2.12	36.40
Financial Institutions	0.43	464.18	998.59	1018.13	1.96	279.45
Telecom Services	4.10	1066.26	1473.53	1501.23	1.88	119.34
Electrodes	0.09	827.39	1791.59	1824.63	1.84	120.53
Telecom Equipment	0.10	91.54	193.21	196.41	1.66	114.57
Plastic & Plastic Products	0.12	196.58	383.46	388.44	1.30	97.60
Compressors & Pumps	0.10	546.57	750.91	760.31	1.25	39.10
Oil Exploration	8.32	1265.07	1658.52	1678.61	1.21	32.69
Chemicals Organic	0.12	975.26	1510.37	1526.88	1.09	56.56
Auto Ancillaries	1.21	2152.38	3558.36	3597.03	1.06	67.12
Cables Telecom	0.05	228.27	379.38	382.98	0.95	67.78
Electrical Equipment	2.41	1838.90	3174.54	3198.61	0.76	73.94
Fasteners	0.08	2500.42	3314.00	3338.74	0.75	33.53
Consumer Durables	0.10	231.89	366.18	368.83	0.72	59.05
S&P CNX industry indices top losers						
Travel & Transport	0.43	63.13	101.03	97.29	-3.71	54.09
Textiles cotton	0.24	526.76	1166.55	1144.39	-1.90	117.25

(Contd.)

(Contd.)

	Weight in S&P CNX 500 as of Feb. 28, 05	*Index value as of July 8, 04 (Previous budget)*	*Pre-Budget closing Index value on Feb. 25, 05*	*Post-budget closing Index value on Feb. 28, 05*	*% charge between pre/post-budget*	*% charge from pre-budget*
Textiles Synthetic	0.48	240.29	430.99	422.83	-1.89	75.96
Paper & Paper Products	0.21	275.47	411.74	406.23	-1.34	47.47
Germs & Jewellery	0.07	329.86	709.93	700.63	-1.31	112.40
Fertilizers	0.61	407.11	597.19	589.39	-1.31	44.78
Abrasives	0.03	2072.45	4570.44	4521.67	-1.07	118.18
Packaging	0.14	373.23	634.90	628.27	-1.04	68.3362

Source: *The Economic Times*, 1-3-2005, p. 11.

Illustration

Miss Prasanna Kunchaparthy holds the following different portfolios. From the available information analyse portfolio return and market return. As per the approach of Jensen theory, which portfolio should be selected:

Portfolio	*Expected Return*	β	*Risk Free Rate*
M	17	1.5	7%
N	14	1.1	7%
O	17	1.8	7%
Market Index	14	1.3	7%

Solution

The return on portfolio can be computed as follows:

$$R_p = R_f + \beta\,(R_m - R_f)$$

Portfolio M = 7+1.5 (14–7) = 7+1.5 (7) = 17.5 per cent
Portfolio N = 7+1.1 (14–7) = 7+1.1 (7) = 14.7 per cent
Portfolio O = 7+1.8 (14–7) = 7+1.8 (7) = 19.6 per cent

Comparison of expected and actual return of the portfolios:

Portfolio M = 17–17.5 = **–0.5**
Portfolio N = 14–14.7 = **–0.7**
Portfolio O = 17-19.6 = **–2.6**

Among the risk adjusted performance of the three portfolio M is the best due to low level of risk exposure.

Illustration

Miss Saiprathyusha Kunchaparthy holds the three different mutual funds UTI, Sundaram Mutual Fund, and Kothari Pioneer Fund. The following information is available. She wants to sell the units of any one mutual fund. As a financial expert which fund should be sold by her? Give her a suitable suggestion:

	Funds	*Excess Average Return*	*Beta*
(a)	Unit Trust	8.0	1.32
(b)	Sundaram Mutual Fund	11.6	1.29
(c)	Kothari Mutual Fund	11.9	1.37
(d)	Market Index	8.1	1.30

Solution

The performance of the portfolios can be evaluated by arriving differential return:

$$R_p = \alpha_{p+} R_f + \beta (R_m - R_f)$$

Or

$$\alpha_p (R_p - R_f) - \beta_p (R_m - R_f)$$

Unit Trust = 8.00 – 1.32 × 8.1

$$\alpha_p = 8.00 - 10.692 = -2.69$$

Sundram Mutual Fund:

$$\alpha_p = 11.6 - 1.29 \times 8.1$$
$$= 11.6 - 10.44 = 1.16$$

Kothari Mutual Fund:

$$\alpha_p = 11.9 - 1.37 \times 8.1$$
$$= 11.9 - 11.09 = 0.81$$

From the above particulars UTI mutual fund provide negative returns. Hence she can sold the UTI mutual fund and keep the two other with her. Sundaram mutual fund provide higher return.

Review Problems

Illustration 1

Mr. Hari Boggarapu is holding two portfolios. The following information is related to his investments. Evaluate the portfolio performance as per the approaches Treynor and Sharpe Index methods.

Portfolio	*Return*	*σ*	*Riskless Rate*	*Beta*
R	8.00	16.24	4.0	1.10
S	5.30	5.92	4.0	2.95

Solution

As per Sharper's Index = $\dfrac{R_p - R_f}{\sigma_p}$

Return on **"R"** portfolio

$$= \frac{8-4}{16.24} = \frac{4}{16.24} = 0.24$$

Return on "S" portfolio

$$= \frac{5.30 - 4.00}{5.92} = \frac{1.30}{5.92} = 0.22$$

As per the Sharpe's measure of portfolio performance portfolio "R" is better than "S" portfolio.

As per Treynor measure of portfolio performance:

$$T_M = \frac{R_p - R_f}{\beta_p}$$

$$T_{MR} = \frac{0.08 - 0.04}{1.10} = \frac{0.04}{1.10} = 0.036$$

$$T_{MS} = \frac{0.053 - 0.04}{2.95} = \frac{0.013}{2.95} = 0.004$$

As per the Treynor portfolio performance "portfolio "S" shows higher performance.

Illustration 2

Miss Teju Boggarapu holds the three portfolios. The risk free rate of interest is 8 per cent. Market Beta is 1.25. The following information is related to her portfolio:

Portfolio	*Return*	*Portfolio Beta*
E	20%	1.50
F	17%	1.10
G	23%	1.80
Market Index	18%	1.30

Evaluate the portfolio performance as per the Jensen's approach.

Solution

Jensen's approach = $R_p = R_f + \beta_p (R_m - R_f)$

$Rp_E = 8{+}1.50\ (18{-}8)$

$= 8{+}1.50\ (10)$

$= 8{+}15 = 23$ per cent.

$Rp_F = 8{+}1.10\ (18{-}8)$

$= 8{+}1.10\ (10)$

$= 8{+}11 = 19$ per cent.

$Rp_G = 8+1.80\,(18-8)$
$= 8+1.80\,(10)$
$8+18 = 26$ per cent.

Actual–Expected returns:

Portfolio E = 20–23 = **–3 per cent.**
Portfolio F = 17–19 = **–2 per cent.**
Portfolio G = 23–26 = **–3 per cent.**

All portfolios shows negative impact.

Illustration 3

Smt. Bhagyalaxmi Juluri holds the following portfolios. Evaluate the portfolio performance as per the **Sharpe's Index**. Rank each portfolio and the risk free rate of interest is 8 per cent.

Portfolio	*Return*	*Risk (σ)*
G	13%	14%
H	11%	16%
I	10%	9%

Solution

$$Sp_G = \frac{R_p - R_f}{\sigma_p}$$

$$\text{Portfolio G} = \frac{13-8}{14} = \frac{5}{14} = 0.35 \quad \textbf{Rank I}$$

$$\text{Portfolio H} = \frac{11-8}{16} = \frac{3}{16} = 0.18 \quad \textbf{Rank III}$$

$$\text{Portfolio I} = \frac{10-8}{9} = \frac{2}{9} = 0.22 \quad \textbf{Rank II}$$

Illustration 4

Mr. Harish Gunda holds three investments. The risk free rate of interest is 8 per cent. Calculate the risk adjusted performance of each investment funds using the **Sharpe's approach**.

Year	X	Y	Z
2000	+7	+6.0	+8
2001	+2	+1.0	–3
2002	–7	–6.0	–12
2003	+10	+12	+20
2004	+7	+7	+9

Solution

$$\text{Sharper's Approach} = \frac{R_p - R_f}{\sigma_p}$$

Let us first calculate standard deviation of each fund:

X Return	*Y Return*	*Z Return*
+7	+6	+8
+2	+1	–3
–7	–6	–12
+10	+12	+20
+7	+07	+9
+26	+26	+37
–7	–06	–15
+19	+20	+22

$$\bar{X} = \frac{\Sigma x}{n} = \frac{19}{5} = 3.80$$

$$\bar{Y} = \frac{20}{5} = 4 \quad \bar{Z} = \frac{22}{5} = 4.5$$

$$\bar{X} = 3.8 \qquad \bar{Y} = 4 \qquad \bar{Z} = 4.5$$

x	*dx*	*dx*^{2}	*y*	*dy*	*dy*^{2}	*z*	*dz*	*dz*^{2}
+7	3.2	10.24	+6	02	04	+8	3.5	12.25
+2	–1.8	3.24	+1	–03	09	–3	–7.5	56.25
–7	–10.8	116.64	–6	–10	100	–12	–16.5	272.25
+10	6.2	38.44	+12	8	64	+20	+15.5	240.25
+7	3.2	10.24	+7	5	25	+9	+4.5	20.25
		178.80			202			601.25
	σp	13.37			14.20			24.5

$$Sp_x = \frac{R_p - R_f}{\sigma_p} = \frac{3.8 - 8}{13.37} = -0.31 \textbf{ Rank II}$$

$$Sp_y = \frac{4-8}{14.20} = -0.56 \textbf{ Rank III}$$

$$Sp_z = \frac{4.5-8}{24.5} = -0.14 \textbf{ Rank I}$$

All portfolio shows negative impact.

Illustration 5

Smt. Vani holds the following portfolios. Calculate the ranks as per the approaches of **Treynor performance index:**

Portfolios	Return	Risk	Beta	Risk Free Rate
A	17%	14%	1.25	5%
B	15%	16%	1.35	5%
C	14%	9%	1.00	5%

Solution

As per the Treynor approach the following ranks have been computed:

$$T_A = \frac{R_p - R_f}{\beta_p}$$

$$T_A = \frac{17-5}{1.25} = \frac{12}{1.25} = 9.6 \textbf{ Rank I}$$

$$T_B = \frac{15-5}{1.35} = \frac{10}{1.35} = 7.40 \textbf{ Rank III}$$

$$T_C = \frac{14-5}{1.00} = \frac{9}{1.00} = 9.00 \textbf{ Rank II}$$

Illustration 6

Miss Gowthami holds the following portfolios. Calculate the ranks as per sharpe's performance measure. The risk free rate of interest is 3 per cent:

Year	Fund "M"	Fund "N"	Fund "O"
2000	8	10	12
2001	3	5	7
2002	5	7	9
2003	7	9	11
2004	7	4	6

Solution

Let us first calculate Airthematic mean for the given funds, and after standard deviation is required:

Year	*Fund M*	*dx*	*dx²*	*Fund N*	*dx*	*dx²*	*Fund O*	*dx*	*dx²*
2000	8	02	4	10	+3	9	12	+3	9
2001	3	–03	9	05	–2	4	07	–2	4
2002	5	–01	1	07	0	0	09	0	0
2003	7	01	1	09	+2	4	11	+2	4
2004	7	01	1	04	–3	9	06	–3	9
	30	0	16	35	0	26	45	0	26

$$\bar{X} = \frac{\Sigma x}{n} = \frac{30}{5} = \mathbf{6} \qquad \bar{X} = \frac{35}{5} = 7 \qquad \bar{X} = \frac{45}{5} = 9$$

$\sigma^2_p =$ 16 26 26

$\sigma_p =$ **4** **5.10** **5.10**

$$\text{Sharpe's performance} = \frac{R_p - R_f}{\sigma_p}$$

$$M = \frac{6-3}{4} = \frac{3}{4} = 0.75 \textbf{ Rank III}$$

$$N = \frac{7-3}{5.10} = \frac{4}{5.10} = 0.78 \textbf{ Rank II}$$

$$O = \frac{9-3}{5.10} = \frac{6}{5.10} = 1.18 \textbf{ Rank I}$$

Illustration 7

Mr. Naresh holds the following portfolios. Calculate the ranks as per Jensen's performance index:

Stocks	*Alpha*	*Beta*
G	1.20	1.10
H	1.45	1.45
I	1.27	1.35
J	1.35	1.05

Solution

From the available data, Jensen's performance index can be computed by the following formula:

$$J_p = \frac{\text{Alpha}}{\text{Beta}}$$

Solution

$$Jp_G = \frac{\alpha}{\beta} = \frac{1.20}{1.10} = 1.09 \textbf{ Rank II}$$

$$Jp_H = \frac{\alpha}{\beta} = \frac{1.45}{1.45} = 1.00 \textbf{ Rank III}$$

$$Jp_I = \frac{1.27}{1.35} = 0.94 \textbf{ Rank IV}$$

$$Jp_J = \frac{1.35}{1.05} = 1.28 \textbf{ Rank I}$$

Illustration 8

From the following information, rank them in order of poor to the best portfolio as per **Sharpe's measure:**

Particulars	*Return*	σ	*Risk Free Rate*
A fund	14	12	4
B fund	17	17	4
C fund	15	19	4

Solution

$$\text{Sharpe portfolio performance} = \frac{R_p - R_f}{\sigma_p}$$

$$\text{A fund} = \frac{14-4}{12} = 0.83 \textbf{ III}$$

$$\text{B fund} = \frac{17-4}{17} = 0.76 \textbf{ II}$$

$$\text{C fund} = \frac{15-4}{19} = 0.57 \textbf{ I}$$

Illustration 9

From the following data, rank the three funds according to Treynor's performance measure:

Fund	Return	β	Risk Free Rate
R	19	1.10	4
S	17	0.80	4
T	10	0.50	4

Solution

$$\text{Treynor performance index} = \frac{R_p - R_f}{\beta_p}$$

$$\text{Fund R} = \frac{19-4}{1.10} = 13.36\% \text{ Rank II}$$

$$\text{Fund S} = \frac{17-4}{0.80} = 16.25\% \text{ Rank I}$$

$$\text{Fund T} = \frac{10-4}{0.50} = 12.00\% \text{ Rank III}$$

Illustration 10

From the following information calculate α and β Co-efficient for the five years:

Year	Ind Ratna	Nifty	Risk Free Rate
2000	17	14	6
2001	13	11	4
2002	15	12	5
2003	–07	–6	7
2004	09	07	3

Solution

α can be calculated through the following formula:

$$\alpha = \overline{y} - \beta\overline{x}$$

$$\beta = \frac{N\Sigma xy - \Sigma x \Sigma y}{N\Sigma x^2 - (\Sigma x)^2}$$

Let us first calculate $\overline{x}, \overline{y}$ for the given information:

$$\overline{X} = A + b\overline{x}$$

Year	Return	Market return	R_f	x	y	xy	x^2
(1)	(2)	(3)	(4)	3–4 = (5)	2–4 = (6)	(7)	(8)
2000	17	14	6	8	11	88	64
2001	13	11	4	7	09	63	49
2002	15	12	5	7	10	70	49
2003	–07	–06	7	–13	–14	182	169
2004	09	07	3	04	06	24	16
				+26	+36	427	347
				–13	–14		
				+13	+22		

$$\bar{X} = \frac{\Sigma x}{n} = \frac{13}{5} = \mathbf{2.6} \qquad \bar{Y} = \frac{22}{5} = \mathbf{4.4}$$

$$\beta = \frac{N\Sigma xy - \Sigma x \Sigma y}{N\Sigma x^2 - (\Sigma x)^2}$$

$$\beta = \frac{5 \times 427 - 13 \times 22}{5 \times 347 - (13)^2}$$

$$\beta = \frac{2135 - 286}{1735 - 169} = \frac{1849}{1566} = 1.18$$

$\alpha = \bar{y} - \beta\bar{x}$

$\alpha = 4.4 – 1.18\ (2.6)$

$\alpha = 4.4 – 3.068 = \mathbf{1.332}$

$\beta = \mathbf{1.18}$

Illustration 11

The financial performance of the various mutual funds is provided below. The risk free rate of interest is 6 per cent. Rank the funds according to **Sharpe and Treynor approaches**:

Name of the scheme	Return on portfolio	Standard deviation of the portfolio	Beta
(a) JM Mutual Fund	23.45	0.3	0.27
(b) Kothari Mutual Fund	22.95	8.98	0.54
(c) Merry Linch Fund	23.15	3.45	0.56

Solution

Ranking as per Sharpe's performance:

$$\text{Sharpe Index} = \frac{R_p - R_f}{\sigma}$$

$$\text{J.M. Mutual Fund} = \frac{23.45 - 6}{3} = \frac{17.45}{3} = 5.81 \textbf{ Rank I}$$

$$\text{Kothari} = \frac{22.95 - 6}{8.98} = \frac{16.95}{8.98} = 1.88 \textbf{ Rank III}$$

$$\text{Merry Linch} = \frac{23.15 - 6}{3.45} = \frac{17.15}{3.45} = 4.97 \textbf{ Rank II}$$

$$\text{As per Treynor Index approach} = \frac{R_p - R_f}{\beta}$$

$$\text{JM Fund} = \frac{23.45 - 6}{0.27} = 64.62 \textbf{ Rank I}$$

$$\text{Kothari} = \frac{22.95 - 6}{0.54} = 31.38 \textbf{ Rank II}$$

$$\text{Merry Linch} = \frac{23.15 - 6}{0.56} = 30.63 \textbf{ Rank III}$$

Illustration 12

The following information is related to the portfolios and you are required to analyse the performances of the schemes. The risk free rate of interest is 6. Use Sharpe and Treynor methods of ranking:

Portfolio	*Average Annual Return*	*σ*	*Correlation Co-efficient*
R	20	26	0.78
S	16	17	0.59
T	17	07	0.88
Market	15	11	–

Solution

$$\text{Sharpe approach} = \frac{R_p - R_f}{\sigma_p}$$

$$\text{Portfolio R} = \frac{20 - 6}{26} = 0.53 \textbf{ III}$$

$$\text{Portfolio S} = \frac{16-6}{17} = 0.58 \textbf{ II}$$

$$\text{Portfolio T} = \frac{17-6}{7} = 1.57 \textbf{ I}$$

$$\textbf{Treynor approach} = \frac{R_p - R_f}{\beta_p}$$

Beta value of the portfolios are not given. They can be computed by the following formula:

$$\beta = r\frac{\sigma_p}{\sigma_m} \qquad 0.78 \times \frac{26}{11} = \mathbf{1.84}$$

$$0.59 \times \frac{17}{11} = \mathbf{0.91}$$

$$0.88 \times \frac{7}{11} = \mathbf{0.55}$$

$$\text{Treynor for "R" portfolio} = \frac{R_p - R_f}{\beta_p}$$

$$= \frac{20-6}{1.84} = \frac{14}{1.84} = 7.60 \textbf{ III}$$

$$\text{Treynor for "S" portfolio} = \frac{16-6}{0.91} = \frac{10}{0.91} = 10.98 \textbf{ II}$$

$$\text{Treynor for "T" portfolio} = \frac{17-6}{0.55} = \frac{11}{0.55} = 20 \textbf{ I}$$

Illustration 13

Miss Agarwal Aarti is working as a financial analyst. The following data is related to various funds. She is assigned to predictive of the funds financial performance as per Jensen Index:

	Name of the scheme	R_p	σ_p	β
(a)	Merry Lynch	23.38	3.0	0.20
(b)	Canbank	34.28	4.9	0.49
(c)	Kothari Pioneer	43.56	2.3	0.60
(d)	S&P 500 CNX	34.74	1.7	0.97
(e)	Risk free rate of interest	6.00	–	–

Solution

$$\text{Jensen Index} = R_p - R_f = \alpha_p + \beta(R_m - R_f)$$

$$\textbf{Merrylynch} = 23.38 - 6.00 = \alpha_p + 0.20\,(34.74 - 6)$$

$$= 17.38 = \alpha_p + 5.748$$

$$\alpha_p = 17.38 - 5.748 = \mathbf{11.63}$$

$$\text{Jensen Index} = \frac{\text{Alpha}}{\text{Beta}}\ \frac{11.63}{0.20} = \mathbf{58.15\ I}$$

Canbank:

$$34.28 - 6 = \alpha_p + 0.49\,(34.74 - 6)$$

$$28.28 = \alpha_p + 0.49\,(28.74)$$

$$\alpha_p = 28.28 - 14.08$$

$$\alpha_p = \mathbf{14.2}$$

Jensen Index for Canbank mutual fund:

$$\frac{\text{Alpha}}{\text{Beta}} = \frac{14.2}{0.49} = 28.97\ \textbf{Rank III}$$

Kothari Pioneer

$$43.56 - 6 = \alpha_p + 0.60\,(34.74 - 6)$$

$$= 37.56 - \alpha_p + 17.24$$

$$\alpha_p = 37.56 - 17.24 = \mathbf{20.32}$$

$$\frac{\text{Alpha}}{\text{Beta}} = \frac{20.32}{0.60} = 33.86 = 33.86\ \textbf{Rank II}$$

Illustration 14

Alliance fund, Treasury Bills and Sensex have had the following returns over 2000-2004.

Year	*Fund Return*	*Treasury Bills*	*Sensex Returns*
2000	11	7	8
2001	–8	11	–7
2002	16	9	13
2003	14	8	12
2004	18	10	15

As a stock analyst, what is the predictive ability of the fund?

Solution

Alpha value can be determined by the following formula:

$$\alpha = \bar{y} - \beta\bar{x}$$

Beta can be computed by the following formula;

$$\beta = \frac{N\Sigma xy - (\Sigma x)(\Sigma y)}{N\Sigma x^2 - (\Sigma x)^2}$$

$$\beta = \frac{5\times438-(-4)(+6)}{5\times382-(-4)^2}$$

$$= \frac{2190-(-24)}{1910-16} = \frac{2214}{1894} = \mathbf{1.16}$$

Year	*Fund Return*	*Sensex Return*	R_f	(R_p-R_f) *y*	(R_m-R_f) *x*	x^2	*Xy*
2000	11	8	7	4	1	1	4
2001	–8	–7	11	–19	–18	324	342
2002	16	13	9	07	04	16	28
2003	14	12	8	06	04	16	24
2004	18	15	10	08	05	25	40
				+25	+14	382	438
				–19	–18		
				+6	–4		

$$\beta = 1.16 \qquad \bar{y} = \frac{\Sigma_y}{n} = \frac{6}{5} = \mathbf{1.20}$$

$$\alpha = \bar{y} - \beta\bar{x} \qquad \bar{x} = \frac{\Sigma x}{n} = \frac{-4}{5} = \mathbf{-0.8}$$

$$\alpha = 1.20 - 1.16\,(-0.8)$$
$$= 1.20 - (-0.928)$$
$$= \mathbf{2.128}$$

PORTFOLIO REVISION

Portfolio is a combination of blend of mix of different kind of financial assets. Generally portfolios consists of equity debt, bonds and risk free government securities. The majority of the portfolio consisted with equity, it is known as **Equity portfolio**. Debt is dominated in the portfolio, it is called as **"Debt portfolio"**. If the portfolio is dominated by the risk free assets, it is called **"Risk free portfolio"**. However portfolio should consist of all these kinds of financial instruments. The balance of ratio between these kinds of different assets must be maintained. Once the construction of portfolio has been completed, care should be taken to review and revision of the portfolio. The success in the market will depend upon a continuous monitoring, review and revision of the portfolio. A proper care should be taken by the portfolio manager according to the client needs and convenience. Success in the stock market is not a easy task. Fluctuations in the market cause substantial gain or loss to the investors. The investors or portfolio managers should have competence and skills in the revision of the portfolio according to the market fluctuations. It is a known fact that the average investor dislikes to sell in the bull market with the anticipation of future rise. In the same way he is not willing to buy in the bear market with the anticipation of further fall. But the fundamental principle in the stock market is **"enter in bear market and exit in bull market."** No investor can follow this principle rigidly. All portfolios need frequent changes in the composition of equity and debt instruments. The revision of portfolio should be done according to the investors policy. If the investors policy shifts from earnings to capital appreciation, the stocks should be revised accordingly. It is better to sell shares, if the prices reaches **historical levels**. If the shares does not fulfill the investor's expectations, it is better get rid of it. The investor or portfolio manager should consider important factors such as **risk, asset quality and available tax concessions.** If the holding stocks does not show better performance, investment should be shifted to other stock. Many investors in India find themselves in adequate knowledge, skills, abilities to trade and earn profit. In their view, stock market is a heaven which power money into their bank accounts. They invest blindly and depends upon the market rumours. They will not apply their brains. They always depends upon other's brain. In the stock market, many methods are available to adopt and earn better profits through proper timings. There are basically two approaches in the stock market:

(a) Index fund
(b) Forecasting method.

(a) Index Fund

It is one of the approach available in the stock market. It is also known as passive management. It is a process of holding a well diversified portfolio for a long term with buy and hold approach. It refers to construct a portfolio that resembles the overall market returns. The simplest form is holding the index fund. The index fund is designated to earn relatively good returns from the stock market. **For example: Sensex or Nifty fund.** The portfolio manager buys every stock in the index in exact proportion of the stock in that index. **For example:** If ACC stock constitute 10 per cent of the index, the portfolio manager also invest 10 per cent of money in ACC stock. Hence it is based on index fund. The portfolio will be constructed with the index funds scrips with same quantity of proportion. This approach is based for a long-term nature. The index fund has certain limitations and disadvantages:

(i) High transaction cost.
(ii) Holding a number of stocks.

(b) Forecasting Method

It is the second approach in the stock market to adopt a number of scrips in the portfolio. It is also known as **"Active Management"**. Active management means, holding securities based on the forecast about the future. Active management is based on professional skills of the portfolio manager. The portfolio managers will select the scrips based on **"beta"** parameter. The portfolio manager will vary cash position and decisions of the portfolios based on the market forecast. Forecasting is the most important skill and predicting ability of the portfolio manager. The portfolio manager may indulge in group rotation. The portfolio managers will make investment in different industries stocks depending upon the assessment of the future performance. In this method, the stock which provide more returns are given more weights in the portfolio and which gives less returns, are accommodated with lower proportion in the portfolio.

Stock market is a game of **risk and return**. The aim of the portfolio manager is minimise the risk and maximise return of the portfolio. There are mechanical methods are adopted to earn better returns through proper timing. The mechanical methods are:

(i) Formula Plans.
(ii) Swaps.

(i) Formula Plans

The purchase and sale of securities in the stock market are based on certain plans. In the first instance, the amount to be spent on securities to be fixed. The amount may be fixed either in constant or variable ratio. The ratio fixation is depends upon the risk perception of the investor. There are two kinds of portfolios **(a) Aggressive portfolio (b) Conservative portfolio**. The aggressive portfolio consists with ordinary shares with high return and high risk. This portfolios return is volatile because the share prices generally fluctuate. **Conservative portfolio** consists of more bonds. It can also be called as debt portfolio. Debt portfolio provide a fixed rate of returns. It provide a certain return and risk is less. There is no existence of capital appreciation value in the debt portfolio.

Assumptions

1. It is based on allocation in certain percentages of the portfolio.
2. There is no relation to scrip movement and market movement.
3. If the investor chooses this plan, he should not deviate it, in any circumstances.
4. The selection of scrip must be based on beta value, which should be around 1.0.

The formula plans will determine the purchased and sale of securities. The stock market is a game of **risk and return**. The formula plans can be further classified as:

(a) Rupee cost averaging
(b) Constant rupee value
(c) Constant ratio
(d) Variable ratio plans.

(a) Rupee Cost Averaging

This is one of the kind of formula plans. It is also termed as rupee averaging. It is the simplest type formula plan. It is based as purchase of securities at regular intervals with a fixed amount in selected securities. It does not take into consideration of the market conditions. Purchase price is the most important and influencing factor in profit booking from the stock markets. This system continuously buy securities without taking of purchase price fluctuations. The investor is able to buy more securities in declining market and less in bullish market. Hence, the investor is assured of a lower aggregate cost per share than the average of the market price. The following table will reveal the situation of the investor:

Market Price of Stock	Quarterly Investment	Shares Purchased	Cumulative Average Cost per Shares	Cumulative Average Market Price
200	2000	10.00	200.00	200
180	2000	11.11	189.48	190
160	2000	12.50	178.51	180
140	2000	14.30	166.97	170
120	2000	16.70	154.77	160
100	2000	20.00	141.82	150
120	2000	16.70	138.18	145.71
140	2000	14.30	138.39	145.00
160	2000	12.50	140.50	146.66
180	2000	11.10	143.66	149.99
200	2000	10.00	147.44	154.54

Advantages

(a) It facilitates to acquire securities at a low average price.
(b) It is very easy to purchase scrip as per schedule of the time plan.
(c) It is easy to provide funds at pre-determined dates and time.

Disadvantages

(a) It is based only on average cost per share factor.
(b) It ignores the trends of the market.
(c) Investment must be made on even **bad times**.
(d) Investment must be made a limited amount of money even the shares are available at lower prices.
(e) It does not indicate when to sell. It provides a strategy for buying of securities.
(f) There is no indication of appropriate interval time.
(g) Transaction costs are involved in frequent purchase of shares.

(b) Constant Rupee Plan

Constant rupee plan is plan for timing of buying and selling of securities. It force the investor to sell the shares at bullish market and purchases at bearish market. As per this approach, Forecast and other assumptions are not required to earn returns from the stock market. The consequences of the plan automatically help the investor to reap the benefits of the fluctuations in the stock markets. It consists of two portfolios. **(a) Aggressive portfolio, (b) Conservative portfolio.** The combination of two portfolios may facilitate the buying and selling of bonds. The plan enables the investor to shift his portfolio from bond to stock or stock to bond *etc.* It maintains a constant amount invested in stock portion of the portfolio. The plan commences with a fixed amount of money invested in selected bonds or stocks. When the stock prices increases, the investor sells stocks to return to the original amount of the investment in stocks. The investor will keep the aggressive portfolio constant, and the remaining amount invested in conservative portfolio. The portfolio manager or investor should always watch the market price movements. The portfolio manager is a professional, highly skilled talented person must choose **action points** in this system. The **action points** are the times at which the portfolio manager has to read just the values of the stocks in the portfolio. Share values in the market cannot be continuously the same. The values always fluctuate. Hence the investor should alter the portfolio according to the situation. The professional manager should fix the changes in prices in percentage form like **20 per cent, 15 per cent, 10 per cent, 5 per cent**. A small changes in prices does not yield better return and involves a lot of transaction cost. It would not be beneficial to the investor. If the action points are too large the investor may not be able to get advantage of the price fluctuations:

Constant Rupee Plan

Period	*Market price (Rs.)*	*No. of Shares*	*Value of Stock Portfolio*	*Value of Defesive Portfolio*	*Total*
1.	100	200	20,000	20,000	40,000
2.	88	200	17,600	20,000	37600
3.	80	200	16,000	20,000	36000
4.	80	250	20,000 Bought 50 shares	16,000	36000
5.	88	250	22,000	16;000	38,000
6.	100	250	25,000	16,000	41,000
7.	100	200	20,000 Sold 50 shares	21,000	41,000

The above table reveals that the investor has Rs. 40,000 and he allocates the money equally between stocks and bonds **50:50** that is Rs. 20,000: Rs. 20,000. The portfolio manager makes quarterly adjustment. If the stock portion falls or rises by 20 per cent. The movements and action points are shown in the table. The advantage of this plan is that **purchase and sales** are determined by automatically. In order to gain from this plan, stocks should not be at either high prices or at too low prices.

(c) Constant Ratio Plan

Constant ratio plan is another strategy to maintain the portfolios. Already we discussed that there are two kinds of portfolio *i.e.* **Aggressive and Conservative portfolios.** The constant ratio plan manages a constant ratio between these portfolios. The ratio between two portions must be fixed by the portfolio manager or investor. The risk perception of the investors attitude plays a major role in determining the ratios between two portfolios. The conservative portfolio contains major portion of bonds and the aggressive portfolio have more of stocks. Once the ratio between these two portfolios is fixed, it should be maintained as per the market movements up and down. The investor or portfolio manager should fix their action points and move accordingly. The action points may vary from investor to investor or portfolio manager to portfolio manager. However, the goal is minimise the risk and maximise the return. This plan offers a flexibility to shift from bonds to stocks or stocks to bonds. Hence, the stock market is a game of risk and return. Winning in the stock market is a chance rather than choice factor.

Constant Ratio Plan

Market Price (Rs.)	*No. of shares in stock portion*	*Value of stock Rs.*	*Value of defensive portfolio Rs.*	*Total portfolio Rs.*	*Ratio of stock portion to defensive portion*
100	100	10,000	10,000	20,000	1.00
96	100	9600	10,000	19,600	0.96
90	100	9000	10,000	19,000	0.90
Rs. 996 transferred from bond portion and 5.5 shares purchased.					
90	105.5	9496	9504	19000	1.00
81	105.5	8546	9504	18050	0.90
Bought 5.9 shares by transferring Rs. 478 from bond portion.					
81	111.4	9024	9022	18046	1.00
89.10	111.4	9914	9022	18936	1.10

5 shares are sold and invested in bonds to make the ratio equal 1:1.

(d) Variable Ratio Plan

Stock markets are highly volatile. They fluctuate the share prices frequently. Every change in the prices are discounted by the market.

Market knows everything and always it is perfect. The variable ratio plan discounts the market changes. According to this plan, if the market prices fluctuates, the proportions of the debt and equity instruments also changed. It is a situation based plan. Whenever the price of the stock increases, the stocks are sold, and new ratio will be adopted. The proportion of aggressive and defensive portfolios will be changed accordingly. This plan is based on predictive abilities. Forecasting of the market is essential and influential factor in the variable ratio plan. A wide fluctuations in the stock market is more useful for the plan. It is a long term based activity. The following table will reveal the activities of the **variable ratio plan.**

Variable Ratio Plan

Share price	*Value of stock proportions*	*Value of Defensive*	*Total portfolio value*	*Stock as % of portfolio*	*Portfolio Adjust*	*Shares in stock portion*
Rs.	*Rs.*	*Rs.*	*Rs.*	*Rs.*		*Rs.*
100	10,000	10,000	20,000	50.00	–	100
90	9000	10,000	19000	47.37	–	100
80	8000	10,000	18000	44.40	–	100
80	12640	5400	18040	70.60	Bought 58 shares	158
90	14420	5400	19620	72.48	–	158
100	15800	5400	21200	74.53	Sold 50 shares	158
100	10800	10800	21600	50.00	Sold 50 shares	108

According to this plan, the portfolio manager or investor has to adjust the portfolio for every 20 per cent change in the stock price. The fixation of percentage will vary from one investor to another or from one portfolio manager to another portfolio manger. However risk bearing capacity will occupy a dominant role in fixation of ratio in this plan. The total value of portfolio will consist of stock portfolio and bond portfolio. The portfolio is a combination of Rs. 10,000 each by equity and bond portfolio. **For example:** If the share prices declines then, the percentage of stock in the portfolio declines. **For example:** If the share price increases the investor sells the shares and the stock portion in the portfolio is reduced. Hence the investor has to move according to the action points. The investor has to more cautious about fluctuations in the stock market in alteration of the portfolio.

CASE STUDIES
MUTUAL FUNDS

Portfolio Management

The advantages are many

The equity mutual fund space is flooded with diversified funds. The advantage of these funds is that they give the fund manager the flexibility to invest in sectors and stocks that in his opinion are expected to do well in the future. Also, diversification helps in reducing risk. On the other hand, in a sector. Specific equity fund, the holdings are concentrated is one sector and if that sector doesn't do well, than the fund has no where else to park the money.

Principal mutual fund has launched yet another variation of an equity diversified fund called Principal Focussed Advantage Fund. This Fund is positioned between a diversified equity fund and a single sector fund in terms of the risk-return profile. The fund will focus on not more than six sectors at a time. This restriction on the number of sectors will help the fund select and invest is the best stocks from those sectors.

The strategy of the fund is that at any given point of time, it will not be invested in more than six sectors to avoid over diversification and not less than four sectors to present over concentration. The option to invest is the sixth sector will be used as a stand by which will be useful in building up quick positions when a sector starts to look attractive while not having to wait to exit one completely. According to the schemes fund manager Shyam Bhatt, "This fund is being positioned to take advantage of a few sectors from the perspective of relative growth and valuation."

The fund can be viewed as a concentrated diversified fund. Typically, a diversified fund has investments in about 12 to 13 sectors at any given time and the average weightage given to each sector is about 15-16 per cent. Principal Focussed Advantage Fund will have maximum exposure to only six sectors at any given time and the sector exposure will be capped at 25 per cent. On the other hand, the minimum exposure to each sector will have to be 15 per cent. This is the main differentiating factor of this fund from the regular diversified funds.

The fund will follow a two tiered portfolio construction with timely identification of select sectors combined with dynamic movement across sectors to give investment flexibility, as the top performing sectors will

Sources: *The Economic Times*, Big Bucks, 7-2-2005, p. 2.

rotate from time to time. In the end, this will be coupled with superior stock selection within the sectors.

The rationale behind introducing a fund with such on investment philosophy is that over different time periods, different sector have given higher returns than the indices and the fund manager believes that with the right selection of sectors, the fund will be able to outperform the index consistently. The fund house is also expecting a moderate year ahead for the equity markets. They believe that the market will not witness a broad-based rally as before. In such circumstances, sector selection will be very important.

We cant predict whether the equity markets will have another year of great growth or not, but we do agree that investments in the right sectors will help deliver good returns. And as investments in mutual funds are done with a long-term perspective it is important that the fund is able to outperform the market in both a bear and bull run as well as broad-based and sector-specific rallies.

Sector selection will depend on various qualitative and quantitative factors like the price earning of the sector vis-à-vis the market P/E; price earnings to growth of the sector versus that of the market *etc*. The effort will be to select sectors based on growth and valuation parameters. Within the selected sectors, there will be a strong focus on selecting companies with a consistent dividend track record, strong business fundamentals, good quality of management, strong balance sheets, reasonable operating profit margins and attractive valuations.

But on the flip side, while restricting the fund exposure to six sectors will being focus, there is a chance that the fund may lose out on turn around stories.that may not belong to the selected sectors. This fund has a focussed approach to investment and concentration on a few sectors means that the risk in the fund will be, more than the risk will be less than that of a sector specific fund. Investors have to evaluate their risk appetite and invest.

IPO Dates	January 31 to Feb. 22, 2005
Entry load	—For Applications below Rs. 3 crore-2.25 per cent. —For Applications of Rs. 3 crores and above-Nil.
Exit Load	Nil
Minimum Application Amount	Rs. 5,000
Options	Growth & Dividend.

No Indecent Exposure

JM Equity and Derivative Fund makes simultaneous transactions of long positions in cash and identical short positions in futures. The equity position is completely hedged to and no shorting in the cash market is allowed, points out Amrita Chauhan Sanyal.

Remember the good old days of badla finance? Those were the days when it was very easy to buy shares on credit and then carry forward the positions by paying interest. However, badla was not successful as it encouraged investors to take risky calls. It also led to an increase in speculation activities as badla ensured easy availability of credit.

To capitalise on this slot, JM Mutual Fund has launched the JM Equity and Derivative Fund. The fund aims to generate market-neutral returns, which can be generated without taking any directional exposures. The fund will make use of derivatives as these assets are not correlated with either equities or debt. This product is based on the simple concept of buying in the equity cash market and selling in the equity futures market and earn the cost of carry. Since this is the first time that such a product has been launched in India, comparisons are not available. Moreover, as it's a relatively new concept, selling the product will require extra effort. Its for this reason that JM Financial Mutual Fund has tied up with Dun and Brod street, the international training and financial information institution, to train retain as well as wholesale distributors. The fund house aims to complete 100 training seminars on the subject by the end of the product launch.

The fund aims to enter simultaneous transactions of long positions in cash and identical short positions in futures. A very important point here is that the equity position has to be completely hedged, no shorting in the cash market is allowed. When the futures contract reach expiry, the positions will either be reversed or rolled over. Nand Kumar Surti, Senior vice president-investments, said that rollover is an effective way of handling futures and added that nine out of twelve months they might be in the rollover mode.

If no arbitrage opportunity is available, then the fund has the option to invest in fixed income instruments, or fixed income derivatives. The assets will mostly be shifted to the money market and fixed income derivatives have been added as on enabler.

Sources: *The Economic Times*, Big Bucks, 14-2-2005, p. 2.

This fund is being offered as an alternate to an income fund and is aimed at all erstwhile income fund investors.

It is essentially aimed at all fixed income investors looking for steady returns over money market funds over a period of time. The Securities and Exchange Board of India (SEBI) has classified this fund as an income fund and not as an equity related fund. The returns are derived from the equity market but since all equity cash market positions will be fully hedged, there will be no open equity position and returns will be generated from the mis-pricing in the cash and futures market. Mr. Surti reiterated that the fund will be allowed to do only one activity and that is to buy stock cash and sell stock future. The fund cannot do any other activity like index, futures, options, revenue badla and so on.

The fund aims to give market neutral returns without taking any directional exposures to the underlying stocks and stores. Therefore, once a position is taken, the returns that will be generated are known and the fund will earn these returns irrespective of whichever way the market moves. The fund aims to generate returns similar to income funds or 2-3 per cent more than money market funds.

According to some calculations done by the fund house, in the last two years if the entire money was put in cash to futures, then the average return would have been 14-15 per cent. The JM Equity and Derivative fund is allowed to put only 50 per cent of the money into cash and hedge position and, therefore to that extent the returns may be slightly lower. According to the fund manager, money will only be put to utilize the arbitrage opportunity if the net returns (minus costs) are more than the money market returns.

Though there are a lot of advantages of this strategy as it capitalises on opportunities of mis-pricing, it is very safe as all positions are hedged and it aims to deliver higher returns that the other comparable investment avenues, few downsides also exist. For example, in a bearish market there will be fewer arbitrage opportunities and the market may become liquid and futures may quote at a discount and so on. In such a situation, the fund will be forced to invest in money market instruments and earn lower returns till better opportunities arise. There is also a rollover risk to be considered but that is not considerable.

This fund is trying to earn money through investing in a new asset class. The aim is to hedge the position and use arbitrage in different markets to earn returns. Investors should expect income fund like returns from this fund and use this fund to diversify their portfolio.

IPO Dates	4 Feb.-21 Feb. 05	
Minimum Application	Rs. 5000.	
Minimum Lock-in period	25 days	
Redemption Allowed	Only on the last Thursday of the month.	
Redemption on Any other Day.	Exit load	
	Above 5 lakhs	0.50%
	Below Rs. 25 lakhs	
	Upto 25 days	2%
	Upto 85 days	1.50%
	Upto 175 days	1%
Purchase of units	Open all days	

Don't Grin & Bear It, smile Instead

The markets may be in correction made but that's not deterring fund houses from announcing IPOs. The latest offering is from Sundaram Mutual Fund. On January 3, the fund house launched its Small and Medium Indian Leading Equities (S.M.I.L.E.) fund, which aims to invest predominantly in small and mid-cap companies. The IPO closes on January 24.

Sundaram has defined small and mid-cap companies as those that have a market-cap equal to or lower than that of the largest market cap company in the S&P CNX Midcap 200 index. Since the largest market cap in the specified index in December 2004 was Rs. 1950 crores, the fund will be looking at investing in companies that have a market cap of less than Rs. 1950 crores. The fund is bench-marked to the BSE 500.

The proposed asset allocation for the fund is a minimum 65 per cent and a maximum 100 per cent in small and mid-cap companies and a maximum 35 per cent in other equities, essentially large-cap companies. The does not intend to have more than 15 per cent in cash.

According to the fund manager there are certain internal guidelines to ensure risk management. These guidelines further bifurcate the asset allocation limits. The exposure to small-caps will be restricted to 30 per cent. Within this 30 per cent limit, not more than 5 per cent will be invested in companies with a market cap of less than Rs. 100 crores, 7-10 per cent in companies with a market cap of Rs. 150-200 crores.

Other risk control measures include limiting the exposure to a small-cap stock to not more than 2.5 per cent of the corpus and not buying more than 2 per cent of the free float in any stock. A care is being taken to

Sources: *The Economic Times,* Big Bucks, 10-1-2005, p. 2.

ensure that the exposure to small-cap stocks doesn't increase the risk profile of the fund or decrease liquidity. To ensure adequate liquidity the fund will invest a corresponding 35 per cent of the corpus in large-cap companies.

The fact that this fund has defined a clear-cut strategy to invest in small-caps is the differentiating factors. And, with the market flooded with mid-cap funds, having a strategy to invest in small-caps as well, will help in attracting investors who have a penchant for investing in small-caps along with other investments.

The fund manager will follow a bottom-up approach to investing by taking stock specific callswing criteria like Rot Plt and price-to-book basis. The fund manager is also not averse to the idea of a top down approach wherever applicable like in identifying themes. The individual stock limit will be restricted to 5 per cent while the industry limit will be restricted to 15 per cent. The emphasis will be on research based investing as well as field work such as plant and site visits.

The fund will seek to give regular dividends to its investors by booking profits on a regular basis. This strategy is expected to de-risk the portfolio a bit. The fund will assign pre-set weightage to every stock, which (weightage) will be in the form of a percentage bond. The minute any stock exceeds the upper limit of the bond, the fund will book profits. The fund will only exit a stock completely if there is a compelling investment opportunity elsewhere. The pre-set price bond will be based on three factors. Liquidity size in terms of mid-cap and industry outlook.

The fund will use derivatives for hedging purposes and not for active profit making. Derivatives will only be used if there are substantial gains relative to the cash market. The IPO period is from Jan 3-24, 2005. During the IPO period there will be no entry load. There will, however, be an exit load of 2.25 per cent for applications of less than Rs. 5 crore if redeemed within six months from the date of allotment.

In the Bag

Asset Allocation

Instruments *Equity*	*Minimum* *% of corpus*	*Maximum* *% of corpus*	*Risk*
(Small & Mid caps)	65	100	High
Other equities (incl. ADR & GDR)	0	35	High
Equity Futures, options	0	25	High
Money market instruments	0	15	Low

Outlook

Invest in this fund with a long-term perspective of at least 18 to 24 months. This fund is not suitable for investors who want to time the market frequently but for those who are looking for better portfolio return over the long term.

Investors should also not expect the funds NAV to rise as sharply as stock prices of money small-caps, as the fund will take time to be fully invested. Take a medium-term outlook and wait for the fund to deliver that extra return due to its small-cap exposure.

Uploaded

During IPO Jan 3 to 24, 2005

Entry load	• **Nil**
Exit load	• For applications < Rs. 5 Crores, 2.25% if redeemed within 6 months from the date of allotment.

Continuous Period

Entry load	• For applications ≤ Rs. 1 lakh: Nil • For applications > Rs. 1 lakh & ≤ Rs. 2 crore 2.25 per cent. • For applications > Rs. 2 crore. Nil.
Exit load	• For applications ≤ Rs. 1 lakh: 2.25 per cent if redeemed within 1 year. • For applications > Rs. lakh and ≤ Rs. 2 crore: Nil. • For applications > Rs. 2 crore: 2.25 per cent if redeemed within 6 months.

Master of the Game

Just like different categories of mutual funds have varied investment objectives, investors have too have varied reasons to invest in mutual funds. Some invest with the objective of making capital gains, others want regular dividends, and some invest for tax-saving purposes, etc. However, the final objectives is to earn above average returns over a long period of time.

Here we will stress on the need for investment with a long term perspective as capital markets can be volatile in the short term and investors may lose money if the investment horizon is short. Investor with a long term investment perspective have benefited from various schemes through means at capital appreciation as well as income distribution.

One such equity diversified scheme that is commited to rewarding its customers with regular payouts every fiscal is UTI Master Value Fund. This fund has declared a second consecutive dividend of 100 per cent, the record date for the same is February 7, 2005.

UTI Master value fund is an open-ended equity oriented value fund, which was launched in June 1998 as a closed ended fund. It went open ended from February 17, 2003. The investment objective of the scheme is to provide investors the benefits of capital appreciation and income distribution through investments in stocks that are relatively under valued to their expected long term earnings growth. The fund has a mandate of awarding investors with regular dividend payments. Keeping this philosophy in mind, the fund declared 140 per cent dividend in the last fiscal 2003-04. The break up of dividend payouts was 10 per cent in April 2003, 30 per cent in July 2004 and 100 per cent in December 2003. Continuing with the same trend, the fund has declared a 100 per cent dividend in the fiscal year 2004-05. The current dividend will result in a dividend yield of 34.94 per cent.

A value stock, according to the fund, is one that is currently being quoted at a substantial discount to its future expected earnings. There is a common misperception that value stocks are mid-caps. But in truth, value can be found in both small-cap as well as large-cap stocks. Therefore, this fund can be termed as a multi-cap fund, which has a mix of large, mid and small-cap value stocks. There is a mid-cap bias in this fund with around 65 per cent of the assets in such stocks, around 18 per cent in small-cap stocks and around 16 per cent in large-cap stocks.

UTI Master value fund uses in depth analysis and a bottom-up approach to identify stocks with attractive valuation, excellent management profile good visibility of future earnings, companies dominating niche segments, high dividend yield and turnaround potential. The investment criteria of the fund is invest at least 80 per cent of assets in stocks having one or more of the following four criteria: Low P/E ratio, attractive dividend yield, low price to book value, and companies with a positive EVA.

According to Vinay Kulkarni, fund manager, UTI Master Value Fund, "we believe that companies with high dividend yield are under valued

Sources: *The Economic Times*, 31-1-2005, p. 2.

compared to their intrinsic value and have higher potential to appreciate. Moreover, the companies with higher payout are confident of their future cash flow and hence, resort to generous payout." He added that a higher dividend yield provides protection to investors during market downtown.

The fund has some internal guidelines that help in stock selection. While identifying low P/E stocks, the requirement is that the P/E of the stock should be less than the market P/E or the sector P/E. Market P/E denotes the P/E of stocks in the Nifty and sector P/E denotes the P/E ratio of the sectoral index. Further, the dividend yield should be equal to or greater than the yield of the 364 day T-bill. EVA is the extant of shareholder value that a business has created in a given time period.

The fund follows a prudent asset allocation strategy both at a company as well as sector level within the prescribed SEBI limit. The fund also regularly keeps a tab on the risk undertaken for all the investment decisions and hence maintains a diversified portfolio. According to the fund manager, the fund would like to restrict the number of stocks to a maximum of 50 to maintain a manageable portfolio.

The fund has a good performance record. As on January 27, 2005, the fund has given 27.38 per cent returns since inception, 19.79 returns over the one year period and 55.92 per cent returns over the three year period.

The time horizon for value unlocking in the value stocks in not defined. It might take more time than envisaged. However, the returns fairly compensates the time period.

Dividend Payout (%)	*Record Date (03)*
10	April 21
30	July 18
100	December 26
100	February 7

Returns period	*Fund*	*Category*
Year to Date	–3.85	–4.84
1 month	–3.53	–3.19
3 month	16.98	14.74
1 year	19.79	18.94
3 year	55.92	41.52
5 year	14.6	9.58
Return since launch	27.38	–

As on January 27, 2005.

Steering the Mid-Cap Course

Like we have been writing in our previous editions, there is no death of IPOs from mutual funds, and mid-cap has been a persistent theme for many months now. There are many reasons why fund houses are looking to promote the mid-cap theme like valuations, out-sourcing, infrastructure spending and reforms. Its true that most existing equity diversified funds have a large-cap bias, and there was a need for funds that would look at the mid-cap category separately. But with so many mid-cap funds now in the picture, investors are having a tough time deciding which fund to invest in. There have been instances where investors have redeemed units from their investments in other existing schemes and invested that money in these IPOs. We would not recommend this strategy at all. This is because there is no difference in returns from an IPO scheme or an exiting scheme. Investors, somehow, have this impression that it is always better to invest in an IPO, be it mutual fund or stocks. While a lot of investors invest in IPOs of stocks with a view to make money from the short term listing gains, this strategy cannot be adopted for a mutual fund IPO. The fact that units are being offered at Rs. 10 during a mutual fund IPO doesn't mean that investors are benefiting in any way. The mindset that is after notice is that if the NAV of an existing scheme is at, say, Rs. 35 and there is an option of investing in an IPO where the investor will be offered the unit at Rs. 10, then the investor tends to prefer the IPO option. But this is not the right approach to investing in mutual funds.

This is because the returns that a mutual fund scheme gives will depend on the movement of the NAV, which is a direct reflection of the stock-picking, ability of the fund manager. In an existing scheme, the investor has the option of looking at the past performance of the scheme to judge whether the fund manager has done well in the past or not. In an IPO, there is no such comfort. There have been cases where the NAV of a new scheme (IPO) has listed at below Rs. 10. Therefore, don't be blinded by this IPO Craze invest after weighing all the pros and cros. We are not trying to say that investors should not invest in IPOs, we are only saying that investors should invest in IPOs if they like the investment theme, if the other schemes of the fund house have delivered good returns in the past, and if investors are looking to invest on additional sum in the scheme. If an existing scheme is giving good return, then the investor should not think of getting out of that scheme to invest in an IPO.

Source: *The Economic Times*, 2-5-2005, p. 2.

ING Vysya Mutual Fund has launched a new fund known as ING Vysya Mid-cap Fund. The IPO will remain open from 19 April 05 till 9 May 05. The fund will invest primarily in mid-cap stocks in the market capitalization range of Rs. 100 crore to Rs. 2000 crore. Just like other mid-cap funds, the level of risk in this fund will be higher than a fund focussed on large and liquid stocks, therefore the aim of the fund will be to generate higher returns than funds focussed on large and liquid stocks. The funds asset allocation will be 65-100 per cent in mid-cap stocks in the market cap range of Rs. 100 crore to Rs. 2000 croren and 0-35 per cent in stocks with a market cap of more than Rs. 2000 crore (large cap stocks) or less than Rs. 100 crore (small cap stocks). The fund also has a provision to invest 0.25 per cent in money market instruments. On the rationale of selecting the range of Rs. 100 crore to Rs. 2000 crore for the mid cap stocks, Ms. Kavita Hurry, Managing Director & CEO, ING Vysya Mutual Fund said, "The rate at which the companies will move from Rs. 100 crore to Rs. 2000 crore will be the strength behind the mid-cap sector, earnings stories and P/E re-ratings. This is what we would like to capture."

The fund aims to have a diversified portfolio comprising of about 35-40 stocks. The fund will follow a bottom-up stock specific approach. No one stock will have more than 5-6 per cent exposure to address the most critical aspect *i.e.* liquidity risk. The fund will not have any sector bias; the focus will be on stock picking. There will also be a cap on profit-taking on stocks, if a stock reaches a level set, then it will be sold fully or in part to book profits.

There are a lot of mid-cap funds in the market and some perform better than the others. In the end, it is the ability of the fund manager to pick stocks, manage risk and balance returns that makes the difference. A mid-cap story is not a sector specific story; it is based on the gains from India's structural changes, and investors should consider this as a long term structural play. Therefore, it is important that investors enter mid-cap funds with at least a one year horizon. If they wish to reap greater benefit then they should look at 2-3 years.

ING Vysya Mid-cap Fund

Asset Allocation

Equity Stocks with a Market Cap of Rs. 100 cr. to Rs. 2000 cr.	65-100%
Equity stocks with Market cap of More than	

Rs. 2000 cr. or less than Rs. 100 cr.	0-35%
Money Market Instruments	0-25%.

Fund Details

IPO Dates	19 April, 9 May 2005
Investment options	Growth, Bonus & Dividend (Payment or Reinvestment)
Benchmark	CNX Mid-cap 200.
Minimum investment	Rs. 2000.

Loads During IPO

Entry Load	Nil
Exit Load/CDSC	For investments Below 1 cr. Rs. 1 per cent if Redemption within 180 days. For investment of Rs. 1 cr. and Above: Nil.

Having Fund All-Year Round

Mid-cap funds seem to have monopolised the equity mutual fund space. This is very evident from the number of new mid-cap fund launchers in recent times. Though there are various reasons as to why mid-cap stocks are in favour, the fact is that investors seem to prefer investing in these mid-cap funds to traditional diversified equity funds. Mid-cap funds are also trying to break the myth of this being a great mid-cap rally and that investors should have make hay while the goings good. Hence, Kotak Mutual funds recently launched mid-cap fund has been positioned as on all reasons story.

The fund house defines mid-cap companies as those having survived the highest risk part of their life cycle and have now entered a period, of long-term growth. Kotak Mutual Fund believes that companies in the mid cap stage have the highest growth rate and will go on to become, the large-cap companies of tomorrow. Therefore by investing in companies which are going to give above average returns and out perform the large-caps, investors can be very well rewarded.

It has been noticed that mid-caps tend to generate higher growth than large-caps. In 2004, the CNX Mid-cap index gained 44 per cent against the BSE Sensexs 13 per cent over the same period.

The entire investment term at Kotak Mutual is extremely bullish on mid-caps. According to the AMC, with FII's stake in the top 50 stocks by market cap crossing 20 per cent in most cases. It leaves little scope for further investment. Thus, incremental investments will go into mid caps. And, since India is one of the three countries that are growing at a rate of more than 6 per cent per annum, FII money will continue to flow into the country. Also, till three years ago, about 5 per cent of the incremental investment was going into mid-caps, which has improved to 20 per cent today. This indicates the strong conviction in the mid-cap story.

The improved fundamentals of mid-caps have a lot to do with the growth in the Indian economy our economy is in a transition phase and when any economy grows, sectors across the board tend to do well. Structural changes like economic liberisation, level-playing field, access to cheap capital, increased focus on de-risking business across geographies, etc have all helped in giving a boost to companies across sectors. And, among such companies, mid-caps have benefited the most.

Asset Allocation

Kotak Mid-cap will have an asset allocation of 65-95 per cent in mid-caps, 0-30 per cent in other equities and 5-35 per cent in debt and money market instruments. The debt allocation is only on enables (at this is an equity fund) and will provide comfort in case certain debt assets are to offer more attractive returns. Most of the time this allocation will have cash as a component.

Strategy

The fund will maintain a well-diversified mid-cap portfolio and follow a bottom-up approach to investing. Top-down approach will be used on a macro basis to identify themes and broad sector trends.

The investment style will be to focus on companies in the early stage of their profit cycle and with strong balance sheets and excellent management quality. The companies should be in stable businesses, well positioned for long-term growth and should be priced reasonably by the market. The mid-cap market cap range will be Rs. 500 to Rs. 2000 crore and the fund will not have more than 35 stocks in its portfolio at any given time. Other such internal guidelines that the fund management has set for

Source: *The Economic Times*, 17-1-2005, p. 2.

this fund include 6-8 per cent individual stock limit and 25-30 per cent sector limit.

According to Rushabh Sheth, CIO, Equity, "The differentiating factor of this mid cap fund is the intensive research that happens before due take any investment decision." The investment team has been in touch with the management of many mid-cap companies for over 14 years now and therefore, has a very good understanding of these companies. In the end, it is the stock picking ability of the fund management that separates outperforming funds from others. The fund will lay special emphasis on the ownership of the company and make sure that the fund stays away from investing in momentum plays, he added.

A transitioning economy will provide successive waves of opportunity and an investor should stay invested for a reasonably long time to benefit from this growth. Investors should have a minimum two to three-year investment horizon before investing in Kotak Mid-cap Fund.

Kotak Mid-Cap Fund

Fund Features

Asset Allocation	→ 65-95 per cent in mid-caps. → 0-30 per cent in other equities. → 5-35 per cent in debt and money market instruments.
Minimum investment	Rs. 5000
Entry load	→ Switch-inform equity/balanced/FoF schemes, Switch-in ≥ Rs. 2 crores from other schemes. Purchase ≥ Rs. 2 crores: Nil → Else 2.25 per cent
Exit load	Redemption within 1 year from date of investment through SIP/STP: 2.25 per cent
IPO Dates	30 December 2004–28 Jan. 2005
Options	Growth, dividend payout and dividend reinvestment.

Summary

Portfolio means a blend of mix of different kinds of financial assets. Minimising the risk and maximising the return is the aim of the portfolio. Mutual fund is association of small investors. An investor can participate in mutual funds by purchasing the units. The performance of mutual funds can be observed through Net asset value. Mutual funds provide many advantages to the unit holders. Portfolio performance can be studied through 3 theories *i.e.*, **Sharpe, Treynor and Jensen's performance Index. Sharpe's performance index** is associated with performance ranking of various portfolios. **Treynor performance Index** is associated with comparison of two funds or portfolios. **Jensen's performance index** is associated with the study of risk element in portfolio management.

Questions

1. What is meant by portfolio?
2. What is mutual fund? What are the services rendered by it to the unitholders?
3. Explain different kinds of mutual funds.
4. What is portfolio performance?
5. Explain the theory of Sharpe index performance of a portfolio.
6. Explain the concept of Treynor index.
7. Narrate about Jensen's index performance of portfolio.
8. "Risk and Return" is the game of stock market do you agrees with this statement.
9. Do you agree "Risk is ginger, Return is Jam"?
10. **"Return is accelerator, Risk is speed braker"**. Comment it.

REFERENCES

1. "An even share". *The Economic Times*, 26-4-2005. p. 7.
2. "Rupees rich", *The Economics Times*, Investors guide, 14-2-2005, p. 1,
3. Broader your horizon", *The Economic Times*, 24-4-2005, p. 10.
4. "Quick gains", *The Economic Times*, 24-4-2005, p. 10.

Index